Frommer's®

500

adrenaline
adventures

1st Edition

By Lois Friedland,
Marc Lallanilla, Charlie O'Malley,
and Jennifer Swetzoff

WILEY

Wiley Publishing, Inc.

Contents

910.202
Fr
c.1

Published by:

Wiley Publishing, Inc.

111 River St.
Hoboken, NJ 07030-5774

ISBN 978-0-470-52803-7

Editor: Cate Latting with Jennifer Polland
Production Editor: Katie Robinson
Cartographer: Guy Ruggiero
Photo Editor: Alden Gewirtz
Interior book design: Melissa Auciello-Brogan
Production by Wiley Indianapolis Composition Services

Front cover photo: Ice climber climbing Ouray, Colorado © Brian Bailey / Getty Images
Back cover photos: Coney Island, Brooklyn, New York: Cyclone Roller Coaster © Michel Friang / Alamy Images; Monteverde Cloud Forest, Costa Rica: Young woman on a zip line © Alan Bailey / Rubberball / PhotoLibrary; White Water Rafting on New River in West Virginia © Marek Kasula / Alamy Images; Bungee jumping off Victoria Falls Bridge above Zambezi River between Zimbabwe and Zambia © Chad Ehlers / Alamy Images

About the Authors

Lois Friedland is a freelance Journalist and *About.com*'s Adventure Travel guide. She specializes in skiing, travel, and golf. Her work has appeared in regional and national magazines and newspapers. She has written special sections for *The New York Times, Travel + Leisure,* and *Texas Monthly.*

Marc Lallanilla is a New York–based freelance writer and editor. He has written extensively on health, science, the environment, design, architecture, business, lifestyle, and travel. His writing has appeared in the *Los Angeles Times, ABCNews.com, Weather.com, About.com,* and other print and online publications.

Charlie O'Malley lives in Mendoza, Argentina, in the foothills of the Andes. Though he's surrounded by some of the highest mountains in the world and some of the best rafting, he is mellowing with age and now gets his kicks from visiting wineries. Originally from Ireland, Charlie has contributed to Frommer's guidebooks about Argentina, Bolivia, Nicaragua, and El Salvador.

Jennifer Swetzoff is a New York–based writer and editor who focuses on travel and international affairs. She has worked for Frommer's, the Council on Foreign Relations, and Eurasia Group, and she freelances for various publications. When she's not in the office, she's exploring new parts of the world in search of her next adrenaline rush.

Acknowledgments

A big thank you to friends and family for their support. A special thank you to my editor, Cate Latting, for her encouragement and patience. My ultimate gratitude goes to my wife Ana for all her help and understanding.

—*Charlie O'Malley*

Words alone are insufficient to thank the friends and family members who helped me with this book—by sharing their favorite adventures, offering travel tips, reading first drafts, and giving me moral support when I was busy writing at night and on the weekends. I am eternally grateful to all of you. But my most heartfelt thanks go to Jeremy, my loving husband and favorite companion—both at home and on the road.

—*Jennifer Swetzoff*

Editors' Acknowledgements

Many people contributed to the ideas and entries in this book. We'd especially like to thank the entire Frommer's editorial staff, whose inspired suggestions are presented throughout this manuscript. Frommers.com readers were also a tremendous resource, and we thank them for pitching ideas to be included in this work. Derek Lock, contributor to whatsonwhen.com, also deserves our gratitude. Lastly, many thanks to Holly Hughes, Alexis Flippin, and Sylvie Murphy, whose generous contributions at the eleventh hour are especially appreciated.

—*Cate Latting*

An Invitation to the Reader

In researching this book, we discovered many wonderful places. We're sure you'll find others. Please tell us about them, so we can share the information with your fellow travelers in upcoming editions. If you were disappointed with a recommendation, we'd love to know that, too. Please write to:

Frommer's 500 Adrenaline Adventures, 1st Edition
Wiley Publishing, Inc. • 111 River St. • Hoboken, NJ 07030-5774

An Additional Note

Please be advised that travel information is subject to change at any time—and this is especially true of prices. We therefore suggest that you write or call ahead for confirmation when making your travel plans. The authors, editors, and publisher cannot be held responsible for the experiences of readers while traveling. Your safety is important to us, however, so we encourage you to stay alert and be aware of your surroundings.

Frommer's Icons

We use four feature icons to help you quickly find the information you're looking for. At the end of each review, look for:

 Where to get more information

✈ Nearest airport

 Nearest ferry

 Nearest train

🛏 Recommended accommodations

FROMMERS.COM

Frommer's travel resources don't end with this guide. Frommer's website, **www. frommers.com**, has travel information on more than 4,000 destinations. We update features regularly, giving you access to the most current trip-planning information and the best airfare, lodging, and car-rental bargains. You can also listen to podcasts, connect with other Frommers.com members through our active-reader forums, share your travel photos, read blogs from guidebook editors and fellow travelers, and much more.

About This Book

Why These 500 Places?

What is an adrenaline adventure? Ask 500 people and you'll likely get 500 different answers. Everyone has an opinion on how to get the adrenaline pumping. We cover a multitude of high-octane activities and daredevil sports in this guide—hang gliding, scuba diving, and mountain and ice climbing, to name a few. But not every adventurer is interested in jumping off a cliff, meeting a Great White shark face to face, or flying in a helicopter over a live volcano. That's why we've included a breadth of experiences to satisfy even the most esoteric adventure-seekers. Participating in an off-beat marathon, spending a week at cowgirl camp, attending the X-Games, or plunging downward in the front of a world-class rollercoaster can thrill some people as much as jumping out of an airplane. No matter how you define adrenaline, we've got an option for you.

We compiled this list through personal experience as well as discussions with and recommendations from fellow travel experts, friends, family, the frommers.com community, and countless other resources. We think it will serve as a fantastic jumping-off point (no pun intended) for many adventures to come.

We've grouped these experiences by theme rather than by destination. We figure animal enthusiasts will want to know all the best spots to convene with the wild things, that kayakers will want to know the top places to get on the water, and so on. (Consult the geographic index at the back of this book if you're interested in a specific part of the world.)

We know that you, our readers, have many ideas of your own about your favorite adrenaline adventures. We hope to hear your suggestions for the next edition of this guide, so feel free to send your ideas to us at Frommer's Travel Guides, 111 River St., Hoboken, NJ 07030. In the meantime, get out there, take a chance, and get that adrenaline racing!

A Note on Hotels

We've tried to recommend hotels across all budgets, but offerings will vary—some destinations cater to the backpacker, while others appeal to those who want a little more pampering. We've assigned price categories for recommended hotels using a system of $ (inexpensive), $$ (moderate), and $$$ (expensive). These price ranges are relative to the destination—meaning that a $$$ hotel in Nepal may be considerably less expensive than a $ or $$ hotel in Hawaii or Banff National Park. Keep in mind that for a number of the adventures in this guide, many of the recommended tour outfitters will arrange for your accommodation. For more extensive hotel descriptions and recommendations, as well as other useful travel advice, consult the relevant Frommer's guide to that destination, or search frommers.com. You can also use the contacts we've listed in the (i) section of each entry.

1 In the Air

MiGs over Moscow
A Top Gun Experience
Nizhny Novgorod, Russia

Almost anything seems possible in adventure tourism these days—if you have a dream and a big enough bank account. In post–Cold War Russia, even the sky has no limit. Anyone between the ages of 18 and 70 who's in relatively good health can mimic the world's best-trained fighter pilots and fly a Russian military jet high enough to see the earth's curve at 1½ times the speed of sound. Just be prepared to pay for this fantasy flight: A 5-day package costs around $20,000, not including international airfare. Aviation aficionados who have tried it say it's worth every penny.

Incredible Adventures began offering these Top Gun–inspired flights in 1993 after the company's founder, Kent Ertugrul, then a young American entrepreneur who traveled to Moscow in search of computer programmers for a software venture, took one ride on a MiG-29 and fell in love with the rush. He signed a deal to market similar flights worldwide, returned home to Florida, and ran an advertisement for them in the *Wall Street Journal*. An investment banker from New York was the first client to sign up, and since then more than 2,000 other daredevils have followed her lead. The company has offices in Sarasota, FL, and Moscow.

To climb aboard your own fighter jet, first you have to take a commercial jet to Russia's capital. After spending a couple of days exploring Moscow's historic monuments and lively city streets, you head to

Reach supersonic speeds in a Russian fighter jet.
Previous page: Ziplining at Cypress Valley Canopy Tours.

Nizhny Novgorod, home of the Sokol Aircraft Building Plant—which is where you lift off for the flight of your life. This place has been manufacturing top-of-the-line Russian fighter jets for more than 70 years and has an air museum that's worth a quick tour. Weather conditions permitting, you go through a final security clearance, safety briefing, and medical check. Then it's time to put on your helmet and flight suit, discuss the flight plan with your Russian co-pilot, and hop into the cockpit. Depending on which aircraft you're flying, you can reach heights of 21,336m (70,000 ft.), race at speeds of 3,862kmph (2,400 mph), roll over in airborne somersaults, and attempt other fancy tricks like a real military jet fighter. As your co-pilot gives directions and keeps an eye on things, you can take control of the aircraft and try some maneuvers yourself.

You have two jets to choose from: the legendary MiG-29 or the high-flying MiG-31. The MiG-29, known for its top gun capabilities, was developed in Russia during the 1970s to counter the U.S. F-16 Fighting Falcon and the F-18 Hornet. Today, the Russian Air Force and many other nations around the world continue to use this elite model. The MiG-31 is Russia's most advanced fighter, designed to fly high and fast but also perform well at lower levels. Whichever model you select, there's only one way to go—and that's up, at supersonic speeds. Mission accomplished. —*JS*

ⓘ **Incredible Adventures** (② **800/644-7382;** www.incredible-adventures.com).

WHEN TO GO: Spring, summer, or fall (flights are offered year-round, but the weather can be unpredictable and cause delays in the winter).

✈ Moscow Domodedova International Airport, with connection by train or plane to Nizhny Novgorod, where you take off from the Sokol Airbase.

🛏 $$$ **Metropol,** ¼ Teatralny proezd, Moscow (② **07/499-501-7800;** www.metropol-moscow.ru/en). $$ **Alexandrovsky Garden Hotel,** 3 Georgievsky Sjezd, Nizhny Novgorod (② **07/831-277-8141;** www.achotel.ru.eng).

② **Flying High**

Virgin Galactic
The World's First Spaceline
Outer Space

Okay, so your spaceship isn't quite ready for take-off yet—it's still in the development and testing stages—but if you want to be one of the first 500 people to get onboard, a future trip with Virgin Galactic, the world's first commercial spaceline, should be on your radar now. Since 2005, when the $200,000 pioneer tickets initially went on sale, nearly 300 have been sold.

The idea for Virgin Galactic, a company created by travel aficionado and entrepreneur Richard Branson, got off the ground a year earlier—along with the historic flight of SpaceShipOne. The world's first privately developed and funded manned spacecraft, designed and built by Burt Rutan and Scaled Composites, made three successful voyages into space in 2004, reaching altitudes higher than 100km (62 miles) and winning a $10-million prize for its accomplishment.

Branson quickly snatched up the exclusive rights to Rutan's innovative technology—including carbon composite materials, a hybrid rocket motor, and a wing feathering reentry system. Through Virgin Galactic, he plans to combine Rutan's advanced design measures with Virgin's aviation, adventure, and luxury experience to lead the way into space tourism. His goal is to launch non-astronauts into suborbit on a spacecraft known as SpaceShipTwo.

Once SpaceShipTwo is approved for lift-off, your Star Wars–like journey will go something like this: You begin with 3 days of preflight training at the spaceport, intended to introduce you to your crew and fellow passengers as you learn how to navigate a zero-gravity environment. After all preparations are complete, and the morning of your journey has arrived, your adrenaline is pumping as the pilot begins an official countdown . . . 3, 2, 1 . . . blast-off! Your spaceship catches a ride on its "mothership," a specially designed carrier aircraft, for about 15km/15,240m (10 miles/50,000 ft.) before an unimaginable burst of power pins you back into your seat as you accelerate to speeds of nearly 4,025kmph (2,500 mph) in mere seconds. Suddenly, you're traveling at more than three times the speed of sound, hurtling away from the earth's surface, watching the atmosphere transform from blue to black. Finally, the motor shuts off around 110km/109,728m (68 miles/360,000 ft.) and you're engulfed in silence. You realize you're floating, completely weightless.

Maybe you try a somersault. When you glance out the window again, your eyes open wider to take in the scene you've seen before only in NASA photographs: You're staring at the earth's curve.

Before you know it, gravity returns and it's time to head back toward home. Lying down, you feel a powerful drag as the atmosphere's force returns. But then the feathering system kicks in and you gracefully glide back to the earth's surface.

This new adventure will be a historic chance to explore virgin territory. Until the dream trip becomes a reality, keep your excitement level high with a visit to Space-ShipOne—now on display next to Charles Lindbergh's *Spirit of St. Louis* airplane at the Smithsonian Institute's Air and Space Museum in Washington, D.C. You can also check VirginGalactic.com for updates on SpaceShipTwo's progress. —JS

(i) **Virgin Galactic** (www.virgingalactic.com).

✈ Space flights initially depart from Mojave Air and Space Port in Mojave, California, but eventually take off from Spaceport America in Las Cruces, New Mexico.

Flying High 3

Thunder City Fighter Flights
Soaring into Space
Cape Town, South Africa

Picture yourself soaring 15,000m (50,000 ft.) above the earth in an **English Electric Lightning,** the fighter jet used to intercept the Russian "Bear" bombers during the Cold War. Ready to go supersonic and break the sound barrier?

Flash through the sky above Cape Town, South Africa, and over the Atlantic Ocean, climbing up to 150,000m (500,000 ft.). Take a look out the cockpit window and see the curvature of the earth. With your

adrenaline pumping and heart pounding, you come back down to earth with thrilling memories and a story to tell.

Thunder City operates the world's only twin-engine, two-seater (side-by-side) supersonic interceptor, and you can hitch a ride on this Lightning. (Lightning aircraft still hold a number of world climb-to-altitude records.) The day starts with a briefing session, which includes survival training, ejection seat training, and oxygen management.

The flight itself is only about 30 to 40 minutes due to the fuel consumption of up to 500 liters (132 gal.) per minute with the afterburners on.

If you want to fly high, but not touch space, Thunder City offers rides in other types of fighter jets. If you like roller coasters, try a 50- to 60-minute flight in the **Hawker Hunter,** an air-to-air combat jet that's agile and reacts extremely quickly to loops and rolls that create up to 4 g-forces. You can also fly as the navigator in the back of a **Buccaneer,** a nuclear strike attack bomber, assisting the pilot with the selection of transponder codes as you fly in sorties during a mock attack. During the 50- to 60-minute flight, you reach up to 5 g-forces for 5 to 10 seconds while going extremely fast—just subsonic—and low underneath the radar screen. Thunder City also has a **Strikemaster,** a subsonic jet pilot trainer. You get briefed on managing the cockpit and undergo training in the jet, which is great for aerobatics and famous for its spin maneuvers.

Aside from your sky-high adventures, there are plenty of activities and entertainment options in Cape Town. Take the cable car up to the top of **Table Mountain,** which dominates the city's skyline, for 360-degree views of the region (**377**). (See **194** for information on abseiling down Table Mountain.) The ferry to **Robben Island,** the prison-turned-museum, takes you where former South Africa president Nelson Mandela was imprisoned for 18 years. Oenophiles can spend a day sampling vintages at the many wineries in wine country, which is within a 2-hour drive of the city. Visit the tiny penguins that strut around nearby **Boulder Beach.** If you like sports, you can go surfing, sandboarding, hiking, or mountain biking. —*LF*

ⓘ **Thunder City** (✆ **27/21-934-8007;** www.thundercity.com).

WHEN TO GO: Year-round.

✈ Cape Town International Airport.

🛏 $$$ **Radisson Blue Hotel Waterfront Capetown,** Beach Rd., Granger Bay (✆ **800/333-3333** in the U.S. or 27/21-441-3000; www.radisson.com). $$$ **The Twelve Apostles,** Victoria Rd. (✆ **27/21-437-9000;** www.12apostleshotel.com). $$ **Winchester Mansions,** 221 Beach Rd. (✆ **27/21-434-2351;** www.winchester.co.za).

---

4 Flying High

Biplane SkyThrills!
Do Rolls & Hammerheads in a Biplane
Fullerton, California, U.S.A.

Picture yourself flying a biplane out over the Pacific Ocean, diving downward for speed, then heading nose up in a steep vertical ascent until the plane almost stops in mid-air. Next, you make a tight U-turn rolling to the left and plunge straight down toward the ocean. Congratulations! You've just performed a hammerhead aerobatic maneuver and made a flashy 180-degree turn. You've probably seen tricks like these performed at an airshow, and now you can try them out for yourself at SkyThrills!, a southern California biplane flight school that's been treating clients to thrilling sky adventures since 2000.

Don't worry. You won't be alone in the dual-control biplane as you perform these aerobatic maneuvers. SkyThrills! owner Mike Blackstone is at the other set of controls, coaching you through your aerobatic tricks. During the time you're in the air, you have hands-on lessons on rolling

Soaring skyward in a SkyThrills biplane.

Biplane, performs like a Formula I racing car with wings. Whichever plane you choose, you're sure to have a ball.

For the ultimate thrill, ask about the **Astronaut Adventure,** which includes hands-on high-speed dives followed by a 5-g pull-up toward vertical then a push across the top of an arc, which exposes you to weightlessness or zero gravity. You can hold a ball and watch it float out of your hands as you start arcing back down toward earth.

Every flight includes a briefing beforehand, when you learn about handling the plane. All flights are hands on and last between 30 minutes and 1 hour, depending on the program flown. Flights are followed by a debriefing, when you look at the video taken during the ride and see your reactions as you were doing loops and flying upside down.

These flights are an amazing introduction to the world of aerobatic stunt flying. You experience the sensation of flying a stunt plane in excess of 200 mph (322kmph) and feel the g-forces pushing you into the seat. Back on the ground, you leave with a DVD of your experience. The adrenaline rush is intense, and you definitely feel empowered as you fly the plane.

SkyThrills! planes fly out of Fullerton Municipal Airport in southern California. Disneyland, Knott's Berry Farm, Sea World, Universal Studios, and lots of other attractions are close by should you want to continue your thrill-seeking in the area. —LF

the plane, doing loops and hammerhead spins, and even flying inverted. First, you learn a roll—turning the plane 360 degrees like a corkscrew—then continue on your way. Next comes the vertical loop, where the smoke streams behind (so you can see exactly where you've just flown). If you're game for more, the hammerhead comes next, and then a spin. Your final maneuver is inverting the plane and flying upside down for about 30 seconds. If your heart hasn't skipped a beat yet, it will now! As for take-offs and landings, leave them to the expert. Blackstone will handle those.

SkyThrills! has two types of biplanes. Both are designed to perform the aerobatic maneuvers but the two have different personalities. The bright yellow Classic Biplane is really a 1996 replica of a 1935 Waco YMF-5 model, with room for two passengers in the front cockpit. It has a spruce frame covered with fabric, and purrs like a big kitten. The Pitts-S-2C, which Blackstone calls the Extreme

ⓘ**SkyThrills!** (ⓒ**866-4-SKYTHRILL;** www.skythrills.com).

WHEN TO GO: Anytime.

✈ Los Angeles International (34 miles/55km) or John Wayne Airport, Orange County (20 miles/32km).

🛏 $$ **Knott's Berry Farm Resort Hotel,** 7675 Crescent Ave., Buena Park, CA. (ⓒ **866/752-2444** or 714/995-1111; www.knottshotel.com). $$ **Anaheim Plaza Hotel & Suites,** 1700 S. Harbor Blvd., Anaheim, CA (ⓒ **800/631-4144** or 714/772-5900; www.anaheimplazahotel.com).

Heli-Cycling on High
No Mountain High Enough
Nepal

The magical kingdom of Nepal is, without a doubt, one of the most storied destinations in the world, and a mecca for adventure travelers of every stripe. What better way to see this exotic land than on a mountain bike? Well, actually, there *is* a better way—on a mountain bike that's transported by helicopter to a highland pass, allowing you to cruise downhill through some of the most spectacular terrain on earth. You can now ride through Nepal's magnificent scenery while avoiding the lung-busting uphill rides that would make the trip impossible for all but a handful of oxygen-carrying elite athletes.

Most trips to Nepal begin in Kathmandu, the country's capital and largest (and nois-iest) city. Heli-cycling programs organized by qualified tour operators who know the terrain are definitely the way to experience this activity; some operators have relatively short 1-day packages, while others offer longer excursions of several days. Thrill-seekers opting for longer tours are able to stop in remote teahouses for breaks, and stay overnight in lodges nestled in isolated villages.

If what you seek is adventure on the road less traveled, you'll find it here. Many of the spots visited by heli-cyclers are tiny hamlets, difficult to reach even by four-wheel-drive vehicles. The landscape is rich and varied: Icy, snow-capped mountain ranges give way to dense alpine forests,

Cycling through mountainous Nepal.

semi-arid steppes, surging rivers, lush farmland, and golden rice paddies. And for sheer death-defying thrills, try crossing a swinging suspension bridge on a windy day with a full pack and a mountain bike—not for the faint of heart.

It's not all hard work and sweat, however. Bikers make frequent stops to sample local foods and teas, including the region's apple ciders and brandies. In addition, there are hot spring pools along some routes that allow bone-weary riders a chance to soothe their aching bodies. And at the end of your journey, the sights and sounds of Kathmandu are yours to explore. —ML

TOURS: Black Tomato (© 877/815-1497; www.blacktomato.co.uk). **Himalayan Mountain Bike Adventures** (© 977/1/421-2860; www.hmbadventures.com).

WHEN TO GO: Oct–Nov.

✈ Kathmandu.

⊨ $$ **Kantipur Temple House,** Chusyabahal, Jyatha Tol, Thamel, Kathmandu (© 977/1/425-0129; www.kantipurtemplehouse.com). $$ **Hotel Courtyard,** 67/27, Z-St., Thamel, Kathmandu (© 977/1/470-0648; www.hotelcourtyard.com).

Flying High 6

Fly over Water & onto Ice
Helicopter Flight-Seeing in the Southern Alps
Milford Sound, New Zealand

Standing on an ancient glacier, thousands of meters above the earth's surface, is an exceptionally rare experience—typically reserved for expert mountaineers or intrepid heli-skiers. But adventurers up for the flight of their life can have the same thrill in New Zealand by riding high in a chopper as it gracefully slips between some of the earth's most remote and jagged peaks. When you finally land on a massive block of ice nearly touching the clouds, the mind-boggling views, not to mention the dizzying sensation that you're about to slide right off the mountaintop, is sure to get your adrenaline pumping. Flying over Milford Sound, once described by Rudyard Kipling as the eighth wonder of the world, before landing on a nearby beach isn't half bad either.

The Southern Alps in Fiordland, covering the southwestern corner of New Zealand's South Island, are just 35 minutes by plane or about 5 hours by car from Queenstown. There are more than 27 peaks reaching

over 2,743m (9,000 ft.) and about 60 glaciers in this mountain range, melting into rivers and lakes of dazzling blue-green hues. The entire Fiordland National Park, a UNESCO World Heritage Site, is full of nature's best: mountains, virgin forests, rivers, lakes, waterfalls, and, of course, fiords (long narrow estuaries with steep sides, carved by glacial activity). The main attraction is Milford Sound, which is actually a fiord, bordered by sheer granite mountaintops including the oft-photographed Mitre Peak. Its waters and the surrounding land have been relatively untouched, and feel almost primeval. Rain or shine, the area is magical. Perhaps that's why Peter Jackson filmed so much of *The Lord of the Rings* nearby.

While cruises and hiking are increasingly popular ways to explore the region, a helicopter ride offers the most exhilarating way to see more arduous sights. For one of the most thrilling overviews, try the **Milford and Fiordland Highlights** excursion with the locally owned company **Over the Top.** You swoosh past alpine lakes, rivers, forests, glacial valleys, and ice-capped mountains. After flying over the fjords, you land on a remote west coast beach and then a sparkling glacier. This trip takes about 2 hours, but the same company offers other journeys that range from 35 minutes to more than 5 hours. One of its other, and most unique, options is an active scientific expedition flight. On the **Glacier Recline** voyage, you work with a geologist, a mountain guide, and your fellow explorers to determine how New Zealand glaciers, their native flora, and local insect populations are responding to climate change.

Glacier Southern Lakes Helicopters is another reputable company that also takes you to areas that are inaccessible by other means. Upon departing Milford via the Harrison Valley, you swoop and zoom between rocky cliffs with staggering views of bright blue waters before gliding onto Mt. Tutoko's Ngapunatoru Plateau, an exclusive landing spot for this company that very few people have ever stood

upon. As you feel the ice crunch beneath your feet and gaze at the vast white fields, the seclusion makes you feel as if you and your fellow riders are the only people on the planet.

Up, up, and away! —*JS*

ⓘ **New Zealand Tourism Board,** Lakefront Drive, Te Anau (✆ **64/3-249-8900**; www.newzealand.com).

TOURS: Over the Top–The Helicopter Company (✆ **64/3-442-2233**; www.flynz. co.nz). **Glacier Southern Lakes Helicopters,** 2 Lucas Place, Queenstown Airport Base (✆ **64/3-444-3016**; www.glacier southernlakes.co.nz).

WHEN TO GO: Sept–May.

✈ Queenstown airport.

🛏 $$–$$$ **Hotel St. Moritz Queenstown,** 10–18 Brunswick St. (✆ **64/3-442-4990**; www.mgallery.com). $–$$ **Milford Sound Lodge,** 94 Milford Sound Hwy. (✆ **64/3-249-8071**; www.milfordlodge. com).

---

7 Flying High

Hawaii Volcanoes National Park
Flying over an Active Volcano
Big Island, Hawaii, U.S.A.

The roiling red lava spurts out of a pitch-black lava tongue that extends from the volcano and into the ocean. As the molten liquid oozes into the water, steam rises into the air. While the beat of the helicopter's rotors keep you from actually hearing any hissing sounds made as the lava quickly cools and hardens, you imagine that it sounds like some prehistoric animal spoiling for a fight. But this isn't a long-ago era. You're witnessing history in the making—literally new earth being formed. It's a powerful, breathtaking experience, one you'll never forget.

You're flying over **Kilauea,** the focal point in **Hawaii Volcanoes National Park.** Kilauea has erupted almost continuously from its east rift zone since 1983, and the lava flows that creep into the ocean have enlarged the Big Island by more than 500 acres (202 hectares). When the helicopter pivots, you're within sight of (but not too near) the ash-filled plume rising from a new crater within Halema'uma'u at Kilauea's summit. Flying over this area in a helicopter you can see old houses that were hastily abandoned when Madam Pele, the Hawaiian goddess of fire, lightning, volcanoes, and violence,

Lava flow in Hawaii Volcanoes National Park.

expressed her fury in the past. Through the years, the lava flows have covered 8¾ miles (14km) of highway on Kilauea's southern shore with lava as deep as 115 feet (35m).

By helicoptering over certain parts of the park's 333,086 acres (134,795 hectares), which rise from sea level to 13,677 feet (4,103m), you can see there are actually two volcanoes. The second is **Mauna Loa,** which last erupted in 1984. Today, there's an observatory near the top.

Volcanoes National Park has seven ecological zones where a variety of plant and animal communities—some endangered—thrive. Within the park are several archaeological sites and petroglyphs, reminders of the indigenous people who consider this region a sacred space. Seeing these ancient artifacts in person is a tremendous thrill. These are just a few of the reasons why Hawaii Volcanoes National Park is both a designated International Biosphere Reserve and a World Heritage Site.

Several companies offer helicopter rides over Kilauea. Depending on the package you choose, your plans can include a flight above the volcano, a stop on the volcano, or an extended excursion that takes you over black sand beaches, cascading waterfalls, and the lush rainforests of the **Hamakua Coast.** No matter which option you choose, you learn a lot about the history and the culture of the Hawaiian Islands. When booking, be sure to ask about the type of helicopter, the size of the windows, and how many people can sit near the windows. The tour routes and sights visited are always dependent upon where eruptions are occurring and the weather conditions. If you're staying on one of the other Hawaiian Islands, check at your lodge's front desk or with the concierge to see if there's a package that includes a flight to the Big Island and a helicopter tour.

The Hawaii Volcanoes National Park website has a section that describes where the eruptions are currently occurring. Stop at the visitor center for information about ranger programs, hike and bike trails, and areas it's safe to go the day you're visiting. —LF

(i) **Hawaii Volcanoes National Park** (www.nps.gov/havo).

TOURS: Blue Hawaiian Helicopters (© **800/786-2583** or 808/971-1107; www. bluehawaiian.com). **Paradise Helicopters** (© **866/876-7422** or 808/969-7392; www.paradisecopters.com).

WHEN TO GO: Year-round.

✈ Kona Airport (96 miles/155km).

⊨ $$ **The Inn at Volcano,** 19-4178 Wright Rd. (© **800/937-7786** or 808/ 967-7786; www.volcano-hawaii.com). $–$$ **Kilauea Lodge & Restaurant,** 1 block off Hwy. 11 on Old Volcano Rd. (© **808/967-7366;** www.kilauealodge. com).

8 **Flying High**

Mount Everest Helicopter Tours
Buzzing the Roof of the World
Everest & Annapurna Mountain Ranges, Nepal

"It's like seeing the world through 3-D glasses," is how one person described flying in the mountain range around Mount Everest in a helicopter. The speaker, on a helicopter excursion arranged by Cox & Kings, explained that right after touring the Buddhist monastery in Tengboche, which sits atop a hill in the Everest region, they took off and the ground dropped away. The valley floor was suddenly a thousand feet or so below and the jagged slopes of Mount Everest, and the other Himalayan mountains, loomed larger than life through the helicopter's windows. There's no comparison to the feeling you get seeing a sight like this. And there's only one way to do it.

Airplane flights through the region are available, but the fixed wing planes can fly only alongside the range. Helicopters can weave among the mountains, ensuring both panoramic and close-up views of the Himalayan ranges. **Cox & Kings,** which specializes in private travel arrangements to a wide range of places including Nepal, India, Asia, Africa, and Latin America, offers this 3-hour signature event, Mt. Everest: Roof of the World. The flight also includes a stop in Lukla, in the Khumbu region, the starting point for many visitors to the Himalayas near Mount Everest—a prime spot to photograph the surrounding mountains. A guide who knows these mountains well comes along to provide additional insight into the culture and geography of the region.

Himalayan Heliski Guides also offers sightseeing trips in the Everest and Annapurna regions of Nepal. Hikers should check into the company's heli-trekking trips, on which clients are flown to scenic spots in the Everest region where they can hike for a few hours before being picked up afterward. This company, which uses Russian and Nepalese pilots that have major flying time hours in the Himalayas, is also offering a "See all the Himalaya in a week" program, where guests will be flown to various regions to see all the 8,000m (26,240-ft.) peaks and other regions in Nepal. —*LF*

TOURS: Cox & Kings (© **800/999/1758;** www.coxandkingsusa.com). **Himalayan Heliski Guides** (© **33/9-71-39-03-59;** www.heliskinepal.com).

WHEN TO GO: Late fall to spring. Spring is climbing season.

✈ Kathmandu.

⊨ $$ **Kantipur Temple House,** Chusyabahal, Jyatha Tol, Thamel, Kathmandu (© **977/1/425-0129;** www.kantipurtemplehouse.com). $$ **Hotel Courtyard,** 67/27, Z-St., Thamel, Kathmandu (© **977/1/470-0648;** www.hotelcourtyard.com).

Zero-G Experience
Into the Wild Blue Yonder
Locations throughout U.S.A.

If the words, "T minus 30 seconds and counting . . . " make your heart race in anticipation, here's an adventure for you. Leave the gravitational pull of the earth behind and join other would-be astronauts in the same kind of zero-gravity environment that NASA trainers used to prepare Buzz Aldrin, Alan Shepard, and other space jockeys. There's nothing to compare to the feeling of weightlessness that adventurers can experience on a Zero-G flight—floating, flying, bouncing, and somersaulting through the air is guaranteed to thrill even the most jaded earthling.

The fun begins after check-in and orientation at one of Zero-G's training facilities located nationwide; past flights have started from Las Vegas, New York, Seattle, and Cape Canaveral, Florida. The 5-hour day includes a few warm-up periods where fliers experience Martian gravity (about one-third of earth's gravity), then lunar gravity (one-sixth of earth's gravity), and finally several periods of zero gravity, which resemble recess at the world's zaniest playground. Catching a floating blob of water in your mouth? No problem. Executing a perfect 360-degree somersault? Easy. Levitating in midair like a swami? Child's play.

The weightless environment is achieved in a specially designed Boeing 727 that conducts graceful up-and-down maneuvers called parabolic arcs. After climbing to 34,000 feet (10,200m), the plane slowly levels off, dips, then climbs again. These maneuvers are repeated 12 to 15 times, giving fliers several opportunities to practice their floating and flying skills.

Float with friends in a Zero-G experience.

Besides the most excitement you've had in years, the Zero-G Experience also includes your own flight suit (which looks like something straight out of *The Right Stuff*), other Zero-G merchandise, a Regravitation Celebration, a certificate of weightless completion, as well as photographs and a video of your weightless experience. And if you're thinking about a celebration or family reunion that guests will never forget, group flights can also be chartered. Though the price of the Zero-G flight may be sky-high (around $5,000 per person), those who would like to join in the fun but stay on the ground can pay less to participate in orientations and post-flight celebrations for a more reasonable fee (about $200 per person).

Folks like physicist Stephen Hawking and Martha Stewart have described Zero-G flights as "amazing" and "wonderful." Even former astronauts like Rick Searfoss and Buzz Aldrin, who called the flight "exhilarating," claim that they still have dreams of weightlessness. The flights have gained such popularity that a couple in 2009 decided to have their wedding in zero gravity—weightlessness, they decided, is a lot like falling in love. —*ML*

ⓘ **Zero-G Experience** (✆ **888/664-7284;** www.gozerog.com).

WHEN TO GO: Flights are scheduled throughout the year at various U.S. locations; charter flights are also available.

---

10 Leaping & Jumping

The Eiger Jump
A Leap of Faith
The Bernese Alps, Switzerland

There are a number of crazy ways to see the Eiger—you can climb it, jump directly off it with a parachute, or leap out of a helicopter that's flying over it. Of course, of these three death-defying feats, the only one you can even think about attempting without serious mountaineering or skydiving skills is the last option. To try it, you just have to be in relatively good shape and show up with a whole lot of nerve.

Set in the Bernese Alps, between Jungfrau and Grindewald, the Eiger—at 3,970m (13,025 ft.)—looms large, not just because of its natural stance but also thanks to its rich history. In 1858, an Irishman and two Swiss guides made the first successful ascent up its western side. In 1938, an Austrian-German group scaled its north face for the first time. Since then, adventurous climbers have found all kinds of new ways to Spiderman their way up the mountain and Superman back down it. In

2008, U.S. climber Dean Potts free soloed the northern face and then BASE jumped directly from the top with a special parachute. (The acronym "BASE" stands for the different stationary structures from which enthusiasts of this extreme sport catapult themselves: Buildings, Antenna towers, Spans, and Earth.) There are real dangers here, and at least 64 climbers have died trying both new and old feats on the Eiger. The increasing amount of rock fall and diminishing ice fields make it an extremely challenging climb, particularly in the summer—which, of course, is part of the thrill in conquering it.

With this in mind, you can now get even higher than the peak without even wearing out your hiking boots. From your perch in a tranquil helicopter, gliding right above the snow-covered peaks of the Alps, you can enjoy a panoramic look at this picturesque region—before jumping straight into it. In

10 Hot-Air Balloon Rides to Lift Your Spirits

Hot-air balloon rides aren't a cheap thrill, but the experience will undoubtedly knock you off your feet. When French brothers Joseph Michael and Jaques Etienne Montgolfier launched the first modern hot-air balloon in Paris in 1783, they used the smoke from a fire to blow hot air into a silk bag attached to a wicker basket. Today, the same basic engineering plan is used to carry adventure seekers high above the ground.—JS

⑪ Sacred Valley of the Incas, Peru: A version of a hot-air balloon may have been used 5,000 years ago in Peru's Nazca desert as a tool to draw the famous ground lines that are still visible there today. While there's little if any proof of this theory, the idea was enough to inspire the country's first official hot-air balloon company. Before flying, you make a traditional coca leaf offering to the mountain guides at dawn. Then your pilot will heat up your balloon and off you go from Maras over the Urubamba mountain range and high above its many small villages. *www.globosperu.com.*

⑫ The Alps, Switzerland: During the weeklong Festival International de Ballons that takes place in Chateau-d'Oex every January, competitors show off with daring stunts like parachute drops right out of their balloons. But for non-experts, simply climbing into a basket and floating over the snow-covered Alps is one of Europe's coolest things to do. After you take off in Chateau-d'Oex, you travel from Mont Blanc (see ㊽) to the Eiger (see ⑩), passing over the Grand Combin, the Cervin, the Jura, the Lemanique, and the Fribourgeouse region. *www.ballonchateaudoex.ch; www.hb-as.ch.*

⑬ Cappadocia, Turkey: Flying over this yellow and pink moonscape is surreal. Ever since Mt. Erciyes and Mt. Hasan erupted here more than three million years ago, the wind, rain, and other harsh weather conditions have molded their volcanic ash and soft rock into a strikingly phallic setting of jagged cliffs, oddly shaped peaks, tall pillars, conical formations, and caves—creating what is known today as the Goreme Valley. *www.goremeballoons.com.*

⑭ Serengeti National Park, Tanzania: For a bird's-eye view of east Africa's most acclaimed wildlife park, a hot-air balloon does just the trick. Depending on the time of year, you may see herds of wildebeest and zebra thunder across the savannah; a cheetah lurking in a tree, perhaps stalking its prey; a lion and lioness cuddling in the grasslands; or elephants splashing mud on themselves to keep cool. Serengeti Balloon Safaris donates a percentage of its revenue to conservation efforts in Tanzania's national parks and primarily employs locals. *www.balloonsafaris.com.*

⑮ Sedona, Arizona: There's only one way to fully appreciate the vastness of Sedona's vast crimson canvas. You have to rise above it. As you climb into a basket at dawn and float through the air as the sun rises overhead, the craggy red rock formations and deep grassy canyons come alive against an increasingly bright blue panorama. As you drift down, you see a wide variety of wildlife climbing over the jagged surfaces far below. Then you rise higher again, marveling at the rush you get from this slow and peaceful flight. *www.redrockballoons.com.*

16 Napa Valley, California: Like a great glass of wine, this region should be savored. As you leisurely float over vineyards, orchards, and fields in a hot-air balloon, your pilot will give you an overview of the area and point out landmarks. Long lines of grapes, apple trees, and mustard seeds blur into a patchwork quilt of bright greens, purples, browns, and yellows outlined by mountains. As you eventually move back toward earth and land in a meadow of wildflowers, the richness of this fertile area comes to life. *www.napavalleyballoons.com.*

17 Jackson Hole, Wyoming: It's easy to speed through this part of the Wild West, but from a balloon's perch more than 4,000 feet (1,220m) above the foothills, the natural beauty is profound. Watch as the sun rises over the Tetons. You drift over Jackson Hole, Teton Village, a working ranch bordered by Grand Teton National Park, the Bridger-Teton National Forest, the Snake River, and seven mountain ranges including the Yellowstone plateau. Keep a look out for elk and eagles. *www.wyomingballoon.com.*

18 Luxor, Egypt: Nearly a dozen balloons take off every morning from the west bank of Luxor and float above the Valley of the Kings—a sort of open-air museum—taking visitors high above the great pyramids, famous temples, and open fields that stretch toward the Nile River. You drift over the Ramesseum, a memorial temple for Pharaoh Ramesses II who ruled during Egypt's 19th dynasty, and perhaps land somewhere in the desert south of Hatshepsut's temple, built for one of Egypt's rare female pharaohs who ruled during the 18th dynasty. *Hod-Hod Soliman (© **20/95-370116**).*

19 Bagan, Myanmar (Burma): Architecture buffs, history lovers, and theologians will be astonished by this hot-air balloon voyage over Bagan's sacred sites. On the banks of the Ayerwaddy River, the ancient city of Bagan boasts the world's largest area of Buddhist temples, pagodas, stupas, and ruins—many dating to the 11th and 12th centuries. As you coast through the sky at dawn, mist swirls around the pagodas and monks line up for their daily procession. *www.easternsafaris.com/ balloons_over.html.*

Check out spectacular sights from on-high in Bagan.

20 Saga City, Japan: Experience the thrill of hot-air balloons in Saga City during the Saga International Balloon Fiesta. Every year in the beginning of November, more than 3,500 serious competitors gather here to fly nearly 650 colorful balloons along the Kase River. One of the most popular events during this competition is "La Mongtgolfier Nocturne," or the Night of Hot Air Balloons, when more than 50 inflated balloons tether to the ground after sunset and light their burners in a choreographed routine of illumination. Throughout the fall, more than 30 balloons take flight here every weekend. *www.sibf.info.*

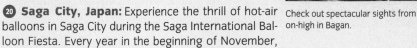

tandem with an experienced skydiver, you can leap straight out of your ride at 4,000m (13,123 ft.) and soar through the air over the Eiger. With one of the biggest adrenaline rushes you've ever experienced, you race toward the ground in a 1,500m (4,921-ft.) freefall for 30 seconds at 200kmph (124 mph) before your parachute launches and you gracefully float back to earth. —JS

(i) **Switzerland Tourism Board** (www.myswitzerland.com, www.grindelwald.com, and www.myjungfrau.ch/en). **Swiss Helicopter,** 3814 Gsteigwiler (© **41/033-828-9000;** www.swisshelicopter.ch/flights/passenger/special/show/10046).

TOUR: Skydive Interlaken (© **41/33-222-5848;** www.skydiveinterlaken.ch).

WHEN TO GO: Anytime, weather conditions permitting.

✈ Bern-Belt airport, Basel airport, or Zurich airport, followed by a train ride to Interlaken or Lauterbrunnen, or a drive to Grindelwald.

🛏 $$ **Hotel Belvedere Grindelwald,** CH-3818 Grindelwald (© **41/033-854-5757;** www.belvedere-grindelwald.ch). **Eiger Guest House,** CH-3825 Murrel (© **41/033-856-54-60;** www.eigerguesthouse.com).

Leaping & Jumping **21**

Shotover Canyon Swing
A Superman-Like Flight
Queenstown, New Zealand

When it comes to naming the Adventure Capital of the World, there's no contest: Queenstown is indisputably the heavyweight champion. (See **39**, **104**, and **139**, for more Queenstown adventures.) The list of fear-factor offerings in this city is too long to recount. But the scariest one, by far, is the Shotover Canyon Swing. As co-owner Hamish Emerson says, "The greater the initial terror—the feeling you're going to hit the dirt—the greater the resultant joy when you realize you're going to make it after all!"

The brainchild of two avid rock climbers, the Shotover Canyon Swing is the highest rope swing in the world—with its launch platform attached to a cliff's edge 109m (360 ft.) above the Shotover River. It was designed by innovative structural and mechanical engineers, carefully constructed over several years, repeatedly tested and modified, and finally opened to the public in December 2002. Today, you can swing in 1 of 10 positions (being suspended and then dropped by a pin-release system is the so-called easiest option, but you can avoid looking down if you go backward).

Whatever style you choose, remember to invoke your inner superman powers. The swing takes you straight down for 60m (200 ft.), a stomach-dropping freefall just meters away from the cliff's vertical face toward a deep canyon, during which you reach speeds of 150kmph (93 mph) and scream like you've never screamed before. As you finally glide into a 200m (656 ft.) arc, and then swing back and forth, you'll thank your lucky stars that you're still alive. Now it's time to simply let your pulse slow and appreciate the sensation of having land beneath your feet—unless, of course, you signed up for two jumps. In that case, get ready to sail through the air again.

The swing is a 15-minute drive from Queenstown, and the company will drive you there in one of its four-wheel-drive vehicles. After a short walk through the bush, you reach the launch area and are fitted into a seat and chest harness attached to ropes that are strong enough to lift four cars. All of the ropes, attachments, harnesses, and safety devices used here are regularly checked, maintained, and upgraded. But knowing that everything's secure won't be enough to quiet your nerves once you're about to swing. Some trepidation is the whole point here. Queenstown has a reputation to live up to, after all. —*JS*

ⓘ **Shotover Canyon Swing,** 37 Shotover St., Queenstown (✆ **64/03-442-6990;** www.canyonswing.co.nz).

WHEN TO GO: Anytime.

✈ Queenstown airport.

🛏 $$ **The Dairy Private Luxury Hotel,** on the corner of Brecon and Isle sts. (✆ **64/03-442-5164;** www.thedairy.co.nz). $$ **Heritage Hotel,** 91 Fernhill Rd. (✆ **64/03-442-4988;** www.heritagehotels. co.nz).

The Shotover Canyon Swing in Queenstown, New Zealand.

22 Leaping & Jumping

Flying over Florida
Skydiving in Orlando
Orlando, Florida, U.S.A.

The world looks different from 11,000 feet (3,353m) above the ground, especially when the airplane door opens and there's nothing between you and the ground below but 2 miles of thin air. And when you're about to make your first solo free-fall jump, the wind rushing past the airplane is drowned out only by the adrenaline rushing through your head.

For visitors to Florida, Orlando has established itself as ground zero for skydiving adventures, with several schools and centers near that entertainment capital. Those who've never tried skydiving may opt for a tandem flight, in which the diver is strapped to a professional instructor who controls the equipment and the descent—all the diver has to do is enjoy the scenery. (Some training centers dismiss those untrained dives as "an amusement park attraction.")

For real thrill jockeys, however, the fun that comes from a solo dive can't be beat. Some schools offer both kinds of dives, while others pride themselves on catering to those who want to take the classes needed to earn the right to an AFF, or accelerated freefall. It takes a little class time before you can jump out of an airplane, so expect to spend some time on the ground reviewing stability, forward movement, loops and turns, and radio-guided landings.

And if, by some chance, you're just not ready to leap out of an airplane, you can still capture the thrill of skydiving by trying indoor skydiving at SkyVenture. A collection of fans forces air at 100 mph (161kmph) through a wind tunnel, which lifts visitors above the ground, effectively mimicking the experience of skydiving for several blissful minutes. The experience requires a bit of training, and safety equipment like goggles, helmets, and jumpsuits are required, but it's

the closest you can get to skydiving without leaving terra firma. —*ML*

ⓘ **Skydiving Orlando** (✆ **800/691-5867;** www.skydivingorlando.com). **Florida Skydiving Center** (✆ **863-678-1003;** www.floridaskydiving.com). **Sky-Venture Orlando** (✆ **407/903-1150;** www.skyventureorlando.com).

WHEN TO GO: Year-round.

✈ Orlando.

🛏 $$ **Embassy Suites Hotel Orlando,** 8978 International Dr. (✆ **800/EMBASSY** [362-2779] or 407/352-1400; www.embassy suites.com). $$$ **Grand Bohemian Hotel,** 325 S. Orange Ave. (✆ **866/663-0024** or 407/313-9000; www.grandbohemian hotel.com).

Leaping & Jumping 23

Vegas Indoor Skydiving
Holding Your Own in a Wind Tunnel
Las Vegas, Nevada, U.S.A.

The anticipation is half the fun. As you nervously wait, dressed in a colorful flight suit, helmet, gloves, ear plugs, and protective eyewear, while lying on a trampoline-like wire mesh floor of a padded cell, your excitement almost gets the best of you. You're waiting for a giant fan to blow you skyward, a sensation like no other you've ever experienced. You're at Vegas Indoor Skydiving, where their giant DC-3 fan blows so hard (the wind speed reaches 120 mph [193kmph]) you fly high into a wind tunnel. It's as close as you can get to skydiving, without jumping out of a plane.

Before you get to the fun of floating, you begin your hour-long experience with a briefing session, which includes watching a short video, addressing safety concerns, learning proper body position and flight techniques as well as the necessary hand signals in the tunnel, and how to

tuck-and-roll properly in case you fly out of the main airstream and have to land on the padded rim. It seems like a lot to remember, but it's all in the name of safety.

Once in the wind tunnel, you get hands-on help from one of the staff members. As the wind speed picks up, the instructor helps steady you in the airstream. Look! You're flying—arms and legs spread out in a big X so you stay horizontal—and simulating the freefall aspect of sky diving. Just try to wipe the grin off your face.

The actual time spent in the wind tunnel will vary. It's based on 3 minutes per person: Up to five flyers at once are allowed, so grab four friends and you can stay in for 15 minutes. Keep in mind this is an athletic activity, so you might break a sweat as you're flying high. If you're going to get into skydiving, here's where you can learn the basics of body control techniques that would take far more time (and money) leaping from a plane. Skydivers who want more flight time for less money also come here to learn tricks, from spins and barrel rolls to front and back flips, before heading up in a plane for the full freefalling rush.

This is an activity for all ages, but there are weight and height restrictions. Minimum weight is 40 pounds, and the maximum weight allowed is linked to a person's height. This is important because guests who exceed the maximum may not generate enough lift to fly. Pricing is set so the second flight on the same day costs less than the first. Also available are five-flight packages, family block packages, and coaching packages that include five sessions and a video.

Skydiving in wind tunnels is offered in other cities, too. SkyVenture Colorado in a Denver suburb, Flyaway Indoors In Pigeon Forge, Tennessee, and iFLY Hollywood in Universal City, California, all offer indoor skydiving experiences. —LF

ⓘ **Vegas Indoor Skydiving,** 200 Convention Center Dr. (✆ **877/545-8093** or 702-731-4768 local; www.vegasindoorsky diving.com). **SkyVenture Colorado,** 9230 Park Meadows Dr., Littleton, CO (✆ **303/768-9000;** www.skyventurecolorado.com). **Flyaway Indoor Skydiving,** 3106 Parkway Dr., Pigeon Forge, TN (✆ **877/293-0639;** http://flyawayindoorskydiving.com/pf.html). **iFLY Hollywood,** Universal Studios City Walk, Hollywood Universal City, CA (✆ **818/985-4359;** www.iflyhollywood.com).

WHEN TO GO: Year-round.

✈ McCarran International.

🛏 $$ **Mandalay Bay,** 3950 Las Vegas Blvd. S. (✆ **877/632-7000** or 702/632-7000; www.madalaybay.com). **MGM Grand,** 3799 Las Vegas Blvd. (✆ **800/929-1111** or 702/891-7777; www.mgmgrand.com).

Bridge Day
Jump Together Now
Fayetteville, West Virginia, U.S.A.

For the past 30 years, hundreds of parachutists have been leaping off the New River Gorge Bridge during the world's only legally sanctioned BASE jumping event—Bridge Day. More than 450 BASE jumpers and up to 200,000 spectators attend this fall festival in Fayette County to celebrate and be entertained by the world's second-longest, single-arch bridge.

The acronym BASE stands for the different stationary structures from which enthusiasts of this extreme sport catapult themselves: buildings, antenna towers, spans, and earth. Most times, BASE jumpers run the risk of arrest because they must trespass to climb tall buildings. On Bridge Day, jumpers are safe from arrest,

but the other risks of this adrenaline rush, including death, are as great as ever.

While novices can safely attempt skydiving in tandem with experts because there's time for safety precautions and back-up measures like reserve chutes, BASE jumpers typically have just 2 to 4 seconds to deploy their parachutes because of the low altitudes from which they take off. BASE jumping is a seriously dangerous exploit reserved solely for practiced daredevils.

If you're one of them, you must pass strict requirements to qualify as a jumper off the 876-foot (267m) New River Gorge Bridge. You must have already completed at least 100 skydiving parachute jumps

10 Skydiving Adventures: Thrills on High

Skydiving has always attracted thrill-seekers and daredevils. Whether you're interested in overcoming a fear of heights or feeding an adrenaline-sports addiction, skydiving won't disappoint. Below are areas and outfitters who offer some of the best skydiving in the world. As usual, before you make the leap (er, fall) be sure to inquire about instructor experience and certification as well as about company safety records. —CL

25 Gruyere, Switzerland: Not only is the region in southwest Switzerland home to some of the world's most delicious cheeses, but it's also the launch-point for some of the world's most daring adrenaline junkies. It's hard to imagine more stunning scenery than the Swiss Alps. Good thing, because you'll be hurtling toward them after jumping out of a plane at 4,000m (12,800 ft.). **The Ecole de parachutisme de Château-d'Oex** keeps things interesting for its divers by moving around from location to location within the area on various weekends. ☏ *41/22-366-18-70; www.epco.aero.*

26 San Diego, California: Only 25 miles from downtown San Diego, **Skydive San Diego** offers a unique diving experience. Where else can you take off and land in the same spot? Because they're located at a dedicated skydiving airport, Skydive San Diego allows your friends, family, and others you want to impress to watch as you hurl yourself from sky high and float gracefully back to earth. Launch a tandem jump or an AFF Solo jump, depending on your level of experience (and nerves). The views are amazing. From 13,000 feet (3,900m) you can see downtown San Diego, Coronado Island, and the San Ysidro mountain range. ☏ *800/FREE-FALL [373-3325] in California or 619/216-8416; www.skydivesandiego.com.*

27 Oahu, Hawaii: Although it offers only tandem jumps (no soloing here), it's hard to beat the setting for skydiving over the island of Oahu. Known for its amazing surfing and the big city of Honolulu, the most urban of the Hawaiian isles is also spectacular from 14,000 feet (4,267m) in the air. From your sky-high vantage point, you can see the entire island, including Pearl Harbor, the North Shore, and all the way to Diamond Head. The experienced staff at **Pacific Skydiving Center** will outfit you and excite you for your amazing island adrenaline-inducing dive. ☏ *808-637-7472; www.pacific-skydiving.com.*

28 Motueka, New Zealand: Thrill-seeking newcomers can go for tandem jumps. Those with higher aspirations (no pun intended) can participate in a nine-stage AFF qualification course. And if that's not good enough for you, **Abel Tasman** offers AFF-qualified divers the opportunity to work toward their New Zealand Parachute Industry Association license, which allows divers to solo anywhere in the world. All jumps here afford divers brilliant views of New Zealand's Southern Alps, Abel Tasman and Kahurangi National Parks, and endless miles of beaches and ocean. ☏ *64/3-528-4091; www.skydive.co.nz.*

29 Interlaken, Switzerland: A city known for adventure opportunity, Interlaken also has arguably the most beautiful drop zone in Europe. Your jump will usually be from approximately 3,900 to 4,200m (13,000–14,000 ft.) and the trip up is almost as wonderful as the one down. From that height you can see multiple countries, including Switzerland, Austria, Italy, and France, and view some of the world's great mountains, such as the Jungfrau, Eiger (see the Eiger Jump ⑩), and the Matterhorn. *Skydive Interlaken* (ⓒ *41/33-222-5848; www.skydiveinterlaken.ch)*. *Skydive Switzerland* (ⓒ *41/33-821-00-11; www.skydiveswitzerland.com)*. —*LF*

㉚ **Gardiner, New York:** Though the skyscrapers of Manhattan offer some pretty impressive views, the vistas from 13,500 feet (4,050m) up in the air in upstate Gardner, New York, are amazing. Located next to the Shawangunk Mountains, **Blue Sky Ranch Skydiving** offers Tandem jumps and training for AFF dives. When the weather gets cold, Skydive The Ranch operates in cooperation with a sister company in Florida. ⓒ *845/255-4033; www.skydivetheranch.com.*

㉛ **Marion, Montana:** It's hard to beat the scenery in Montana when you're on the ground, so imagine the views from 9,000 feet (2,700m) nearby gorgeous McGregor Lake. Whether you're jumping tandem or solo, the rush you feel when freefalling is incomparable. **Skydive Lost Prairie** is an experienced outfitter in the area. Their highly qualified instructors are on hand every step of the way. ⓒ *888/833-5867* or *406/858-2493; www.skydivelostprairie.com.*

㉜ **Guam:** Anybody can travel halfway around the world to a Pacific isle and call herself an adventurer. But the adrenaline adventurer takes it a step further and checks out the stunning beauty of the West Pacific from 14,000 feet (4,200m) in the air. Priced on a graduated scale based on the altitude from which you're jumping, Skydive Guam offers "unparalleled views" of the island and surrounding blue waters. For a few extra bucks, they'll throw in photos and a DVD of your dive so you can earn your bragging rights back home. ⓒ *671/475-5555; www.skydiveguam.com.*

㉝ **Seville, Spain:** Home to world-class paella and gorgeous Moorish-architecture, the Andalucia region of Spain is hard to beat in terms of tourism bang for your buck. But why not be a tourist who takes in the sights from a different point of view? Say, from 4,500m (15,000 ft.)? Skydive Spain offers all manner of diving opportunities, from one-time tandem jumps (sometimes you just want to be able to say you've done something!) to AFF certification and solo parachuting. ⓒ *34/687-726-303; www.skydivespain.com.*

㉞ **Montalla, Oregon:** In Montalla, just south of Portland, Oregon, in the scenic northwest United States, **Skydive Oregon** takes flight from a dedicated private skydive airport. From up high you can jump tandem or solo (AFF certified divers only), as well as with a group. Imagine you and your friends (up to 23 can go at one time) careening toward earth from 13,000 feet (3,900m) with mile-wide smiles on your faces. For pals too chicken to join you, they can stay on the ground in a designated spectator area and photograph your antics for posterity. Group discounts are available. ⓒ *800/934-JUMP* [5867] or *503/829-3483; www.skydiveoregon.com.*

and attend an advanced training session called "Bridge Day First BASE Jump Course (FJC)" or be trained by an approved mentor. The Snake River BASE Academy (www.snakeriverbase.com) teaches training courses right before Bridge Day. To learn more about BASE jumping preparations, sign up for classes, or register for a jump pass; visit www.bridgeday.info.

If you're not ready to make your own BASE jump, coming to Bridge Day as a spectator is still a total rush. The first time you see a human body tumble off the bridge is enough to make your heart skip a beat and an involuntary "ohmygosh" to escape from your mouth. Watching hundreds of people soar off the bridge for 6 hours, deploying their colorful parachutes and sailing to graceful landings in less than 10 seconds each is mind blowing.

Of course, at this high-energy festival, even spectators don't stay on the sidelines.

A local outdoor adventure company, **Passages to Adventure** (www.passagesto adventure.com), sets up a special 1-day 600-foot (183m) zipline that drops 200 feet (60m) off the bridge, and anyone can try it. You can also rappel off the bridge or try rafting in the river below. —*JS*

(i) **Official Bridge Day Festival** (© 800/927-0263; www.officialbridgeday.com).

WHEN TO GO: The third Sat in Oct.

✈ Yeager airport in Charleston, West Virginia.

🛏 $$–$$$ **The Resort at Glade Springs,** 255 Resort Dr. (© **866/562-8054;** www.gladesprings.com). $ **Holiday Inn Oak Hill-New River Gorge,** U.S. 19 and Oyler Ave. (© **304/465-0571;** www.ichotelsgroup.com).

Leaping & Jumping 35

HALO Jumping
The Ultimate Skydiving Experience
Lumberton, Mississippi, U.S.A.

If you want to get high, *really* high, try HALO jumping out of a DHC-3 "super otter" airplane at more than 30,000 feet (9,000m) above the earth's surface. That's the cruising altitude for most commercial airlines, more than 1,000 feet (305m) higher than Mount Everest, and almost 6 miles (10km) from the ground.

HALO stands for a High Altitude, Low Opening parachute jump, which the U.S. military has been using for years as a way to insert Special Forces into enemy terrain. Using this maneuver, troops can drop stealthily because their aircraft is hidden by the clouds, invisible to ground-level observers, and looks like a commercial plane on radar screens. The technique

was first used in combat during the Vietnam War, though its development began during the Cold War. But it's a relatively new adventure for adrenaline-seeking civilians, and currently the world's highest parachuting experience available to them.

At this jumping altitude of 30,000 feet (9,000m), the temperature is somewhere between −25°F and −35°F (−32°C and −37°C). You only have about 30 seconds of useful consciousness before blacking out from the lack of oxygen and risk severe brain damage or death from hypoxia. Not to mention, of course, there's the obvious risk of death if your parachute malfunctions. You must be in excellent shape, go through a full afternoon of training, and

HALO Jumping over Lumberton, Mississippi.

wear a specially fitted oxygen mask for the duration of your entire journey—up and down. Even though you'll be taking a leap in tandem with an expert jumper, you need to learn some skydiving basics and practice pre-breathing techniques. (For instance, you need to breathe 100% pure oxygen on board the aircraft to prevent the sort of "bends" you can get while scuba diving if you're not careful.)

After you take off into the sky, try to ignore the waves of adrenaline crashing over you, and keep breathing calmly to get that adequate oxygen supply. When the jump master finally gives you a nod, get ready to exit. Depending on the weather conditions, you freefall for about 2 mind-boggling minutes before releasing your chute and settling into a floating mode. The earth appears in patterns and colors far before you can make out any detail of the landscape. But this jump isn't really about appreciating scenic views. It's just about jumping out of a plane as high as you can, and enjoying the outrageous experience of having a G.I. Joe fantasy come true. —JS

(i) **Incredible Adventures** ((C) **800/644-7382;** www.incredible-adventures.com).

WHEN TO GO: May–Nov.

✈ Gulfport-Biloxi International Airport or Louis Armstrong New Orleans International Airport.

🛏$$ **Hilton Garden Inn Hattiesburg,** 133 Plaza Dr. ((C) **601/261/3770;** www. hiltongardeninn.com).

Canyon Swing in Nepal
Swing Time
Bhote Kosi River, Nepal

If you have any fear of heights whatsoever, skip this adventure and just keep moving—there's nothing for you here. If, however, jumping off a bridge that's 150m (500 ft.) above a raging river and swinging back and forth across a rocky canyon at speeds approaching 161kmph (100 mph) sounds like a good idea, then have we got an adventure for you! Where the Bhote Kosi river comes surging down from the snow-capped mountains of Tibet, **The Last Resort** (a travel destination for daredevils and spa lovers alike) has built a 163m-long (544-ft.) steel suspension bridge over a

Taking a leap of faith over the Bhote Kosi River in Nepal.

gorge, then added a swing set that's definitely not for kids.

The Last Resort is located about 3 hours' drive from Kathmandu, and is perched above a lush river gorge near the Tibetan border. The site was chosen for its stunning natural beauty as well as for its potential as an action-sports center: Bungee jumping, canyoneering, whitewater rafting, kayaking, and mountain biking excursions are all available at the resort. There are also plenty of chances to unwind; massage therapists, sauna treatments, and other relaxing pursuits are available here.

This is the world's highest swing, and safety is an important goal. Those who dare are strapped into a full body harness and attached to a pair of ropes, each of which is capable of holding 2 tons of weight. Then, you simply walk out onto the jump platform, take one step forward, and let gravity do its stuff. After falling over 90 terror-inducing meters (300 ft.), the swing does something amazing—it smoothly lifts you up, so there's no jerking sensation. Instead, you're treated to a high-speed view of the canyon while suspended on a pendulum hundreds of feet above the river.

After several long, graceful swings, you will come to rest at a recovery rope near the bottom. All that's left to do now is pull yourself to the recovery platform, unstrap yourself from the harness, and sit quietly until the sound of your heart hammering gradually subsides.

For more bungee jumping thrills, turn to the box on p. 26. —*ML*

ⓘ **The Last Resort** (✆ **977/1/443-9501;** www.thelastresort.com.np).
WHEN TO GO: Sept–Dec.

Auckland SkyWalk
Use the Force, SkyWalker
Auckland, New Zealand

Maybe there's something in the water down in New Zealand, but Kiwis seem to have a perverse attraction to scary, adrenaline-rush-inducing sports and events. Among these is the SkyWalk, the latest "terrortraction" from the land that brought jumping off a bridge with a skinny elastic band to the rest of the world.

Auckland's iconic SkyTower—the tallest structure in the Southern Hemisphere at 328m (1,076 ft.) tall—is the home of this affair. Guests are taken out to an open-air platform where they're strapped into a safety harness that's attached to an overhead rail by two safety tethers. They are then invited to walk over to the edge of the thin metal grate that holds them up.

Through the openings in the grate are views of the pedestrians below who are blissfully ignorant of the petrified human suspended 192m (630 ft.) overhead. Guests can walk over to the edge of the grate, if they dare, and lean over the edge for an unobstructed view. Most decline the offer.

There are other skywalks around, notably in Macau and Sydney, but those have handrails and other boring safety features. Guests are advised to wear comfortable clothing and shoes—diapers are optional. No cameras or other loose items are allowed on the platform. Reservations are suggested, and guests should allow themselves 75 minutes to enjoy the sound of their heart jackhammering.

Views from the SkyTower in Aukland are breathtaking.

10 Bungee Jumps for Joy

The guaranteed adrenaline rush of bungee jumping for fun is a fairly new phenomenon—first attempted just 30 years ago—and not an activity for the faint of heart. Modern bungee jumping supposedly began in 1979, when members of the Oxford Dangerous Sports Club attached bungee cords to themselves and dived from the 75m (245 ft.) Clifton Bridge in Bristol, England. Today, the activity is offered around the world, and these are some of the top 10 spots to do it. —*JS*

38 Verzasca Dam, Switzerland: James Bond fans will recognize this place from the opening scene of *Goldeneye,* when 007 plummets 220m (728 ft.), daringly close to the solid concrete side of a dam. Now you can re-create Bond's experience and dive from the Verzasca Dam's edge, freefalling for just 7½ seconds at nearly 200kmph (125 mph). At that speed, you probably won't have time to fully appreciate the spectacular views here, so make sure to explore the area in this Italian-speaking region of Ticino. *www.trekking.ch/eng/007.asp.*

39 Kawarau Bridge, New Zealand: Home to the world's first commercial bungee jumping operation, the Kawarau Bridge—just outside of New Zealand's adventure capital Queenstown (see **21**, **104**, and **139**)—offers a 43m (141-ft.) drop. In 1988, when New Zealanders Henry van Asch and A.J. Hackett (Hackett still runs it today) started attaching rubber bands to jumpers' ankles, people called them crazy. Twenty years later, this jump is one of the area's most well known and popular. *www.bungy.co.nz/index.php/pi_pageid/17.*

40 Ottawa River, Canada: This jump starts at the top of the bungee tower in Morrison's Quarry, Wakefield, Quebec, more than 46m (150 ft.) above a deep aqua blue lagoon surrounded by limestone walls. This picturesque point is only 20 minutes from Ottowa, but it feels peacefully remote. After attaching your harness, leap head-first toward the water. This is the only jump in the Americas where you can submerge your head or your entire body 60m (200 ft.) into the river before a boat comes along to transport you back to dry land. *www.bungee.ca/packages.php.*

41 Bloukrans Bridge, South Africa: At 216m (709 ft.) high, the Bloukrans Bridge is the tallest bridge in Africa and the largest single span concrete arch bridge in the world. To reach the jumping-off point on the top of the arch, you can either walk along a unique 216m (709-ft.) roadway with breathtaking views or zip along a 200m (656-ft.) cable line called the Flying Fox. *www.faceadrenalin.com/bloukransbridge.asp.*

42 Victoria Falls, Zimbabwe: The Victoria Falls Bridge, which crosses the roaring Zambezi River, was originally built in 1905 to connect Zimbabwe and Zambia. Its more recent claim to fame is a small platform at its center, 111m (360 ft.) above the water, from which bungee jumpers freefall for nearly 5 seconds before rebounding. With the crashing Victoria Falls on one side of you and the turbulent Zambezi churning inside a gorge on the other, this may be the world's most spectacular setting for bungee jumping. *www.afrizim.com/activities/victoria_falls/Bungee.asp.*

43 Macau Tower, Macau: This 233m (764-ft.) plunge keeps jumpers screaming as they descend just a few meters away from the concrete side of Macau Tower. It has been deemed the highest commercial bungee jump in the world by the Guinness Book of World Records, and it is also the most technically advanced, with a special attachment and vertical wire cables running on either side of the jump platform. Jumpers fall at a speed of up to 200kmph (124 mph) for 5 seconds, before rebounding a few times approximately 30m (98 ft.) above the ground. A guided cable system allows a slow landing onto a specially designed airbag. *www.ajhackett.com/macau/bungy.html.*

44 Old Colorado River, Costa Rica: Just about an hour-long drive west from San Jose, this scenic spot is a haven for adventure seekers. From the Old Colorado River Bridge, gaze at lush jungle surroundings and powerful rapids rushing far below your feet—80m (265 ft.) below—before pushing off a platform and plunging toward them on a bungee cord. Tropical Bungee opened this picturesque jump site in 1991; today, it's the longest-running and highest bungee operation in Costa Rica. *www.bungee.co.cr.*

45 Viaduc de la Souleuvre, France: In picturesque Normandy, along the Channel coastline, this area was the landing site for the liberation of Europe from Nazi Germany during World War II. Although the original Souleuvre railway bridge, which was built between 1889 and 1893 by Gustave Eiffel, fell into disrepair and was ultimately removed in 1970, the 61m (200-ft.) stone columns that supported it still stand tall today. Around 1990, a suspension footbridge was constructed, providing access to a jump deck off the highest pillar and an official bungee operation opened for business. The site is open on the weekends from March through November, and every day from mid-June through mid-September. *www.ajhackett.fr/va/bungy.htm.*

46 Pacific Northwest Bridge, Washington State, U.S.A.: Just south of Mount St. Helen's in Washington state—about 2½ hours from Seattle and 1 hour from Portland—this private bridge in a forested canyon over a beautiful river offers the highest bungee jump in the United States (equivalent to about 20 stories). It's also the safest and most respected; Bungee Masters has been an industry leader since 1988, and its stunts have been featured on MTV's *The Real World, Road Rules Challenge,* and CBS's *Amazing Race,* among numerous other shows. Jumps from the bridge are offered all year on the weekends, and at other times by reservation. *www.bungee.com.*

47 Double Six Club, Bali: On the coast of Bali, Kuta beach is the only place in the world where you can party and bungee jump at the same time. The energy level really revs up when the sun goes down. Just off the white sands of the Double Six club, you can hop on an elevator and ride to the top of a 45m (150-ft.) tower, built by A.J. Hackett. As the music blasts and you gaze out into the darkness, you can dive toward a swimming pool, even dunking into it if you want to, before the rubber bands snap you back up. Night owls rejoice. *www.ajhackett.com/bali.*

The views from the SkyTower are breathtaking. Visitors can see the bridges and boats of Waitemata Harbor, Rangitoto Island, the skyscrapers of downtown Auckland, and depending on the weather, Mount Eden and the lush green slopes of the Waitakere Ranges in the distance.

Want more? No problem. There's also a gangplank made of glass—thin, transparent glass—that guests can walk out to for a real freak-out. What's that? More, you say? Fine. After your SkyWalk, if you have any adrenaline left, go upstairs and try the SkyJump, a type of bungee jump that drops you at 81kmph (50 mph) over the edge of the SkyTower. —ML

ⓘ **SkyWalk** (✆ **0800/759-925;** www.skywalk.co.nz).

WHEN TO GO: Nov–Apr.

✈ Auckland.

🛏 $$$ **Aachen House,** 39 Market Rd. (✆ **0800/222-436;** www.aachenhouse.co.nz). $$ **Duxton Hotel,** 100 Greys Ave. (✆ **0800/655-555;** www.duxton.com).

Gliding, Coasting & Floating · 48

Mont Blanc by Cable Car
Hanging Out over the Alps
Chamonix, France

Sure, you could hike up or ski down the French Alps—both adrenaline rushes in their own rights. (In fact, if you suffer from severe acrophobia, you really should keep your feet on land with one of those two options.) But if vertigo doesn't typically bother you, hop on the world's highest cable car for the ride of your life. As it ascends 3,842m (12,604 ft.) up to the Aiguille ("needle") du Midi, and then into Italy, you have the most astounding panoramic views of Mont Blanc, Western Europe's tallest peak, at 4,810m (15,780 ft.). At several points during this exhilarating full-day journey, your cable car is suspended 500m (1,640 ft.) above the ground.

The skyward route begins in the celebrated town of Chamonix, where skiing was allegedly invented and the world's first Winter Olympic Games took place in 1924. Not far from the meeting point of France, Italy, and Switzerland, this alpine valley framed by rows of towering snow-covered peaks is a near utopia for outdoor enthusiasts and nature lovers.

The cable car's steep ascent immediately displays the region's spectacular views. But this first part of your trip, a 9-minute run to the Plan des Aiguilles at 2,300m (7,546 ft.), is relatively relaxing compared to what comes next. During the ride's second segment, as you soar to the Aiguille du Midi station in about 10 minutes—your pulse will undoubtedly quicken and your stomach might drop as you climb such great altitudes so quickly. You traverse the Les Pelerins glacier and travel up the north face.

When you reach the top, you're on **Piton Nord,** where you find a cafeteria and one of the world's highest restaurants called "3842" (which is, of course, the altitude of the Aiguille du Midi in meters). Before or after getting a bite to eat, walk upstairs to the **Chamonix Terrace** for breathtaking views of the French, Swiss, and Italian Alps. When you've had your fill of the scenery here, walk across a perilous wooden footbridge covered with ice and snow to **Piton Central.** On this peak, you can take an elevator inside of the rock straight up to the **Summit Terrace,** about 100m (328 ft.) from Mont Blanc's peak—the closest you can get without climbing. On a clear day, you can see the Matterhorn, Monta Rosa, and the Grand Combin. There's just one more lookout point that you won't want to miss, **Mont Blanc Terrace,** where you're most likely to catch a glimpse of intrepid climbers scaling the summit.

Before heading back down to town, you can travel another 5km (3 miles) through the air on the panoramic Mont Blanc gondola over to Pointe Helbronner, Italy, at 3,462m (11,358 ft.). The three cable cars that run along this route provide a rare look at the high mountain landscape with its jagged snow-covered crests and valleys, and vast icy expanses sparkling in the sunlight. You might even see trekkers traversing the Valle Blanche glacier. You can disembark the cable car and explore the station's terraces without your passport, but remember to bring it along if you plan to spend more time in Italy. If you're planning to return to Chamonix, you can go back the way you came and make it in time for dinner. —*JS*

ⓘ **Compagnie du Mont-Blanc,** 35 Place de la Mer de Glace (✆ **04/50-53-3080;** www.compagniedumontblanc.fr).

WHEN TO GO: Mid-May to mid-Oct; that's the only time the route to Pointe Heilbronner operates.

✈ Geneva airport.

⇥ $$ **Les Chalets de Philippe,** 718 Route du Chapeau (✆ **33/06-07-23-1726;** www.chaletsphilippe.com). $$ **Le Morgane,** 145 Avenue de l'Aiguille du Midi (✆ **33/04-50-53-5715;** www.morgane-hotel-chamonix.com/en).

---

49 Gliding, Coasting & Floating

Kitty Hawk Kites Hang Gliding
Channeling Orville & Wilbur
Nags Head, North Carolina, U.S.A.

Dreams of flying are as old as mankind, and the same thrill Orville and Wilbur Wright felt over 100 years ago when they lifted into the heavens and made that dream come true can now be yours. The two brothers from Ohio had their pick of places to stage their first flight, but they chose Kitty Hawk, North Carolina, for its steady winds and miles of soft beach sand—because landings, back then, weren't always guaranteed to be smooth.

Kitty Hawk Kites offers hang gliding lessons from Jockey's Ridge State Park in North Carolina's Outer Banks, just a stone's throw from where the Wright brothers flew, and where steady breezes and soft sands can still be found in abundance. Beginner classes include 1 hour of ground school followed by 2 hours on the dunes with about five flights per student. Though in the past children under 85 pounds were restricted from going airborne (hang gliders need more weight to maneuver), Kitty Hawk Kites is able to offer kids' lessons by having instructors assist in the controls.

For those who want an unparalleled sky-high experience, tandem lessons take participants and an instructor up to 2,000 feet (610m) or more in a hang glider towed by an ultralight plane. Once unhooked from the tow plane, the flyers can practice dives and turns that were once experienced only by soaring birds. And if you find you've been bit by the flying bug, Kitty Hawk also offers a series of hang gliding camps lasting a full week, and special clinics can be arranged to perfect your launching, landing, and aero-towing skills.

If your body is still hungering for more adrenaline, Kitty Hawk Kites offers lessons and camps in kiteboarding, power kiting, surfing, wakeboarding, and parasailing. Had enough? Throw in some sailing,

Learning to hang glide at Kitty Hawk Kites.

jet-skiing, and aero-tours, and you've got a one-stop shop for all your adventure tour needs. —ML

(i) **Kitty Hawk Kites** (© **877/FLY-THIS;** www.kittyhawk.com).

WHEN TO GO: Classes offered year-round.

✈ Norfolk (80 miles/129km).

🛏 $$$ **The First Colony Inn,** 6720 S. Virginia Dare Trail (© **800/368-9390;** www. firstcolonyinn.com). $$ **Cypress House Inn,** 500 N. Virginia Dare Trail (© **800/554-2764;** www.cypresshouseinn.com).

Gliding, Coasting & Floating **50**

Rocky Mountain High
Hang Gliding in Colorado
Denver, Colorado, U.S.A.

Imagine flying like a hawk, gliding over the landscape as thermals lift you and move you along. And imagine that landscape is some of the most dazzling on earth—the Rocky Mountains, to be specific. This is how it feels when you're soaring for miles in a hang glider high above the mountains of Colorado, some of the most breathtaking in the Western hemisphere. It's just you and the earth, with only the sound of the wind for company. This is a singular and solitary thrill—an experience that will linger in your memory.

Airtime Above offers hang gliding experiences in Colorado. While the company is based near Denver, arrangements can be made to learn at several training sites along the Front Range and the Western Slope. When hang gliders are soaring off Lookout Mountain, you can see them from downtown Denver, about 20 minutes away. Other popular spots are on Kenosha Pass, where you can glide over the vast South Park, and on Williams Peak by Green Mountain Reservoir.

Hang gliders have a frame structure that holds the wings in a rigid configuration, so they won't collapse. The pilot is suspended below the frame in a harness. You can foot-launch hang gliders off a hilltop or mountainside, or get an aerotow by an ultralight plane. Once you're airborne you can glide or soar for up to 400 miles (644km) riding the ridge lifts and the thermal lifts.

If you're uneasy about hang gliding solo, sample the sport during a tandem ride. You and an instructor will share a hang glider. The two of you and your craft will be towed by an ultralight plane up to about 2,000 feet (966m), and then let

loose. As you soar through the skies, the instructor may let you handle the controls yourself. Meanwhile, enjoy the quiet and the views of the earth below you.

If you like the experience, start taking lessons. First you learn what's involved on flat ground, then progress to a small hill and finally to a hill with a 600- to 1,000-foot (180–300m) drop. It can take several months to be properly trained, but experienced hang glider pilots say there's nothing like the feeling when you take advantage of the wind—a gliding flight can become a soaring flight that can last for hours. —LF

ⓘ **Airtime Above** (✆ **303/674-2451;** www.airtimeabove.com).

✈ Denver.

🛏 $$$ **Brown Palace Hotel,** 321 17th St. (✆ **800/321-2599** or 303/297-3111; www.brownpalace.com). $$ **The Timbers Hotel,** 4411 Peoria St. (✆ **800/844-9404** or 303/373-1444; www.timbersdenver. com). $ **Innkeeper of the Rockies,** 1717 Race St. (✆ **303/861-7777;** www.innkeeper rockies.com).

51 Gliding, Coasting & Floating

Hang Gliding in the Alps
On a Wing & a Prayer
Interlaken, Switzerland

Interlaken is Europe's nerve center. The array of spine-tingling adventures available in this staggeringly pretty place makes it something of a mecca for adrenaline junkies. But before you get busy with the many ground-level activities here (hiking, biking, rafting, sailing, or canyoning, just to name a few), get a bird's-eye view of the greater Jungfrau region by hang gliding over it.

Set between two lakes (Thun and Brienz) in the Berner Oberland, Interlaken began as a summer resort more than 300 years ago. Since then, it's evolved into a hotspot for outdoor enthusiasts. Today, hang gliding in

tandem with an experienced pilot is actually one of the easier extreme sports to do here—if you can muster the courage to try it. A 10- to 20-minute flight provides a huge rush while displaying the most thrilling views of the sparkling white snow-covered peaks, bright turquoise water, and green grassy meadows.

After getting into a helmet and sturdy harness with multiple ropes and carabiners, you go through a pre-flight training with your pilot and then together are attached to a colorful wing. Side by side, the next step is just to run. As you jog down a hill for a few paces, suddenly your legs are spinning through thin air. And as the adrenaline gushes through your body, you realize you're flying. You can even reach your arms out and soar like an eagle as the pilot steers your flight and you just take in this amazing new perspective of the earth far below. But before you've had too much calm, your pilot can get your stomach flip-flopping again with tricks like stalls and spinners that take you on a roller coaster ride through the sky. You speed up and go higher, then drift back down, and then fly straight ahead, until finally, you make your way toward the ground and coast toward a grassy landing pad. With a few gentle bumps, the wildest ride of your life comes to a smooth end. —JS

ⓘ **Interlaken Tourism Office,** Hoheweg 37 (☎ **41/033-826-5300;** www.interlaken. ch) and **Bernese Oberland Tourism** (http://tourismus.berneroberland.ch).

TOUR: Hang Gliding Interlaken, Brunngasse 30 (☎ **41/079-770-0704;** www.hang glidinginterlaken.com).

WHEN TO GO: Mar–Oct.

✈ Zurich Airport or Geneva Airport, followed by a 2-hr. train ride to Interlaken.

🛏 $ **Hotel Rugenpark,** Rugenparkstrasse 19 (☎ **41/033-822-3661;** www. rugenpark.ch). $–$$ **Hotel Lotschberg,** General-Guisanstrasse 31 (☎ **41/033-822-2545;** www.lotschberg.ch).

Gliding, Coasting & Floating 52

Hang Gliding in Rio de Janeiro
Landing on Rio's Beaches
Rio de Janeiro, Brazil

One minute you're standing there like any normal person, both feet on the ground, and the next you're running off the side of a tall cliff—like any abnormal person. Then, without a word, you're suddenly floating, quietly, aloft like a bird hovering over the majestic cliffs and beaches of Rio de Janeiro. There's nothing between you and the lovely statue of Christ the Redeemer, the spires of Sugarloaf Mountain, and the sparkling sapphire Atlantic except a balmy tropical breeze. This, you realize, is the closest you'll ever come to realizing that age-old dream of mankind: flying.

There's a lot to see and do in Rio, so it's easy to forget that this is one of the preeminent places on the planet for hang gliding. The ocean breezes that lift up over the Sierra do Mar mountains create near-perfect conditions for liftoff. Most full-service hotels can put visitors in touch with a reputable hang-gliding operator, and in most cases, operators can provide hotel pickup and drop-off—just ask at the front desk of your accommodations for recommended tours or contact those listed below. It's also a good idea to check the weather before booking a flight, and wear athletic shoes—sandals and bare feet are not recommended.

Your flight will probably begin on a tall ridge in **Tijuca National Park,** one of the largest urban rainforest parks in the world, where toucans and monkeys are common sights. No experience is needed for many hang-gliding tours, because tandem flights allow the instructor to operate the control on the hang glider—all you need to do is, well, hang. Though there is usually a minimum age (around 7), there's no upper age limit. The flights can last up to 30 minutes, depending on weather conditions, after

Hang gliding in Rio offers views of the ocean, mountains, and city.

which time you touch down gently on one of Rio de Janeiro's soft, sandy beaches—which, when you think about it, is not a bad way to land. —ML

ⓘ**Riotur** (✆ **021/2217-7575**; www.riode-janeiro-turismo.com.br).

TOURS: Just Fly Rio (✆ **021/9985-7540**; www.justfly.com.br) **Hang Gliding Tour**

(✆ **5521/9343-3380**; www.hangliding tour.com.br).

WHEN TO GO: Apr–Nov.

✈ Rio de Janeiro.

🛏 $$$ **Pestana Rio Atlântica,** Av. Atlântica 2964 (✆ **021/2548-6332**; www. pestana.com). $$ **Copacabana Sol Hotel,** Rua Santa Clara 141 (✆ **0800/254-447**; www.copacabanasolhotel.com.br).

---

53 **Gliding, Coasting & Floating**

Canopy Walk
Up Among the Treetops
Kakum National Park, Ghana

Ghana is one of the most exhilarating places in West Africa—with vibrant cities, dense rainforests, picturesque coastlines, historic UNESCO sites, and heart-pounding traditional drum and dance performances.

At times, it can be a solemn place, given its tragic past as a major shipping point for Africans being sent to America as slaves. But mostly, it's lively and inspiring, renowned for its friendly people and

10 Ziplines to Make Tarzan Proud

Climbing trees and swinging from their branches is exciting, but zipping between them is even better. For centuries, miners used cable-and-pulley systems to transport supplies through inhospitable terrain. For decades, biologists and researchers in Central and South America used similar mechanisms to get themselves across low narrow river valleys and into the rainforest's high canopies. Finally, ecotourism companies got wind of the idea and developed a way for travelers to explore areas that were once impenetrable. Now, in places all around the world, you can hook on a harness, attach to some ropes, and embark on a flight made for speed lovers and tree huggers alike. —JS

54 Monteverde Cloud Forest, Costa Rica: Here's where it all started. In 1997, the Original Canopy Tour opened just below the peak of Monteverde. Though there are dozens of canopy tours offered in Costa Rica today, there's something special about the original course. After a short, guided hike through the cloud forest, you climb up to a platform attached to an enormous tree and fly through the sky. After a few zips, just when you're starting to relax, your heart begins pounding again as a steep cable takes you rushing down toward the forest floor. From there, it's back above the treetops before a final rappel from what the guides refer to as the "scary tree." *www.canopytour.com.*

55 Ziptrek Ecotours, Canada: The winter is the best time to take the 3-hour Ziptrek Eagle tour that takes you all the way from the wilderness back to Whistler Village at speeds up to 80kmph (50 mph). Soaring between the snow-covered Whistler and Blackcomb mountains—over the choppy waters of Fitzsimmons Creek in the valley below, surrounded by enormous Douglas fir trees and Western red cedars—is pure exhilaration in a winter-wonderland setting. *www.ziptrek.com.*

56 Flight of the Gibbons, Thailand: This zipline course is set in a 1,500-year-old rainforest just outside of Mae Kompong village, an hour from Chiang Mai, Thailand's largest northern city. From here, you spend about 3 hours crossing sky bridges, dangling from cables, and gliding between 18 platforms in the treetops, flying above the lush forest and swiftly moving streams far below. Along the way, your guides will fill you in on the story of this ancient ecosystem, which the company works to restore and maintain. *www.treetopasia.com.*

57 Flying Fox Neemrana, India: This is the world's first heritage zip tour and India's first zipline course. You fly above old forts, majestic palaces, and the rolling countryside while learning about the enchanted region of Rajasthan, once home to India's kings and queens. Flying Fox opened in 2009 at the Neemrana Fort Palace, originally built in 1464 and reopened in 1991 as a heritage hotel. Spend 2 hours whizzing across five long cable lines with spectacular views of the more than 2 billion-year-old, Acadia-covered Aravalli hills. *www.flyingfox.asia.*

58 Haleakala Skyline Adventure, Hawaii: The hottest thing to do on Maui is zip down the side of a massive volcano called Haleakala ("house of the sun" in Hawaiian). After hiking through the gorgeous upcountry for about a half-hour, you cross a long swaying footbridge, and finally sail across five super-fast ziplines far above sea level. This exhilarating journey showcases Maui's rocky nooks and crannies, abundant greenery, waterfalls, valleys, and rare vegetation. To help protect these rare natural wonders, this company donates 1% of sales to conservation efforts. *www.zipline.com.*

59 Scream Time Ziplines, North Carolina: In Boone, North Carolina, you'll find the only three-person-wide zipline course in the U.S.—and three times the rush. You meet at a pickup spot off U.S. 421 North, hop in the company's all-terrain vehicle, and take a bumpy ride across rolling hills at the outer edge of the Great Smoky Mountains. After a safety briefing on site, start off with a course of six ziplines—each running between 450 and 800 feet (137–244m) in length, about 150 feet (46m) above the ground— before embarking on the 2,000 feet (601m)—or about a half-mile—"super zip" line where you can reach speeds of more than 50 mph (80kmph). *www.screamtimezipline.com.*

60 Mokai Gravity Canyon, New Zealand: After a 15-minute climb up to your take-off point, don a required pair of goggles, strap into your harness next to two other passengers (three people can be attached on one zipline), and take a leap of faith. Before you know it, you'll be speeding along a 1km (0.6 mile) cable, 175m (574 ft.) above the Rangitikei River, at nearly 160kmph (99 mph). The velocity and views will render you speechless. *www.gravitycanyon.co.nz.*

61 ZipRider at Icy Straight Point, Alaska: This is North America's longest and highest zipline. At 1,330 feet (405m) above the ground, an innovative braking system maintains your speed at around 60 mph (95kmph) as you zoom along on one of six parallel cables for 5,330 feet (1.6km). You whoosh over a cliff, above woodlands and open spaces, with amazing views of Port Frederic and Icy Straight, for a full 90 seconds. *www.ziprider.com/rides/icy-strait-point*

62 Iguazu Forest Eco Aventura Canopy Tour, Argentina: After you spend time exploring the wondrous wet Iguazu Falls, you might want a break from being waterlogged. Dry off with a zipline tour in the nearby jungle along the Parana River coast, just 7km (4⅓ miles) from Puerto Iguazu and 15km (9⅓ miles) from the falls. The cables here run about 800m (2,625 ft.) long at heights between 15m (49 ft.) and 25m (82 ft.). This excursion will take you high above the trees, where you might see birds (such as the great dusky swift) and vibrant butterflies in this dense green forest. *www.iguazuforest.com.*

63 Cypress Valley Canopy Tours, Texas: At this private reserve outside of Austin, you can zip all the way home sweet home—straight into your own luxury treehouse for the night! After you soar over the gorgeous landscape, cross two swaying bridges constructed of narrow slats and cables, take a short hike, fly through the sky again on increasingly challenging lines, it's just one more zip into Lofthaven, your special sleeping quarters deep in the wilderness. *www.cypressvalleycanopytours.com/index.php.*

a government that's often cited as a model of democracy on the continent. After becoming the first sub-Saharan African nation to gain independence, it experienced some instability but then peacefully transitioned into a stable democracy during the 1990s.

While Ghana is politically calm, it doesn't lack excitement in other areas. For the biggest adrenaline rush, head to **Kakum National Park** in the Central Region, about an hour north of Cape Coast and Elmina. More than 200 species of birds and countless butterflies have been spotted in this pristine rainforest, and monkeys often swing from the tree branches. For your own bird's-eye view, venture across the long and wobbly **Kakum Canopy Walkway.** You might feel like a tightrope walker as you balance on this set of swaying bridges—suspended 40m (130 ft.) above the ground. It stretches for 330m (1,082 ft.) between seven trees with viewing platforms. As you step along the narrow wooden planks, attached to steel cables and netting, try to ignore your sweaty palms and shaking legs long enough to look around. Surrounded by lush, green plants and chirping birds, you'll be awed by the unforgettable perspective up here. Established in 1990 on 350 sq. km (135 sq. miles) of land, the Kakum National Park is protected by the **Ghana Heritage and Conservation Trust** (www.ghct.org.gh).

After you've survived your sky-high adventure, keep the energy level up by heading to Elmina for a Bakatue dance and drum performance. Every day, at 5pm, a small local troupe holds rehearsals in the west wing of **St. George's Castle.** Common instruments include a tall kaganu drum, a squat round kidi drum, and a cowbell-shaped gangkogui. Dances often include a call-and-response routine, and audience members are almost always invited to join in.

When the festive dancing isn't going on, St. George's Castle is a more somber place. This site, like **Cape Coast Castle,** was one of the major stops along the Atlantic slave trade route. Today, both structures have been extensively restored by the Ghanaian government and are recognized as UNESCO World Heritage Sites. These important remnants of a grave history are well worth visiting. But after you've seen them, head over to **Kotokuruba Market** for a brighter look at modern-day Ghana, where people enjoy lively commerce, rich cultural traditions, and, most importantly, freedom. —*JS*

ⓘ **Ghana Tourism,** P.O. Box GP 4386, Accra (✆ **233/21-222-153;** www.touring ghana.com) and **Kakum National Park,** Dunkwa Rd. (✆ **233/04-232-583;** www. ghana-net.com/kakumnationalpark.aspx).

TOUR: Expert Travel and Tours, P.O. Box 0823 Osu, Accra (✆ **233/21-775-498;** www.expertravel.com.gh).

WHEN TO GO: Year-round.

✈ Kotoka International Airport in Accra.

⊨ **$$ Coconut Grove Beach Resort,** Mmoframa Akyinim, Elmina (✆ **233/42-401-005;** www.coconutgrovehotels.com.gh).

2 On the Water

Snorkeling the Islands of Palawan
A Sea Lover's Sanctuary
The Philippines

Palawan's pristine nature beguiles even the most practiced snorkelers. Unspoiled beaches abut clear turquoise water teeming with schools of fish. The biodiversity—both on land and sea—is overwhelming. For adventure travelers willing to make a long and at times arduous journey, this remote area is pure paradise. (Make sure to bring a book to read while you're waiting for oft-delayed flights and boat rides.) Once you arrive in Palawan, you'll probably spend the bulk of your days in snorkeling gear (or scuba, if you're certified); that's how captivating you'll find this underwater world. But if you crave a momentary change of scenery, there are also ample opportunities to kayak and hike—just remember to leave some time for relaxing on the smooth white sand.

The islands of Palawan, a Philippine province that's often called "the last frontier," lie between the South China Sea and the Philippine Sea, stretching from Mindoro in the northeast to Borneo in the southwest. **Palawan Island** is the longest and narrowest, measuring 450km (280 miles) long and 50km (31 miles) wide. **El Nido** is one of the most popular destinations on Palawan. **Bacuit Bay** is home to more than 800 species of fish; 400 species of coral; endangered sea turtles; marine mammals, including the endangered dudong or sea cow; and marine invertebrates, including giant clams that can reach a meter in length.

While El Nido's beauty and biodiversity is gasp worthy, the area has become relatively developed as a tourism center. For more secluded waters, travel a bit farther to the northwest and explore the exquisite beaches, reefs, and mangrove forests of the **Calamianes Group of Islands**—comprising Busuanga Island, Culion Island, and Coron Island. The waters off **Coron** on Busuanga Island are renowned for the sunken World War II wrecks there. A few are even in shallow enough water for snorkelers to catch a glimpse. Toward the end of the war, a fleet of Japanese tankers and warships were found hiding in the sea near Busuanga. In response, the U.S. Army dispatched its entire aerial fleet to attack the Japanese, leaving an array of significant artifacts underwater. Floating around these pieces of history is a somber experience, but one juxtaposed with the wonder of seeing so many thriving marine species in the same place.

The other not-to-be-missed thrill comes from snorkeling through the reefs in **Coron Bay.** An exotic ecosystem lives in this complex of seven lakes surrounded by rugged limestone cliffs. If you're lucky enough to witness a feeding frenzy, you'll be overwhelmed by the vast numbers of fish swimming in circles around you. But at any time of day, your gracious marine hosts will undoubtedly show you a good time. —*JS*

(i) **Philippine Tourism Authority,** DOT Building, T.M. Kalaw St., Manila (✆ **0632/ 524-71-47;** www.wowphilippines.com.ph and www.tourism.gov.ph) and www. palawan.com.

TOUR: Wilderness Travel, Berkley CA (✆ **800/368-2794;** www.wildernesstravel. com).

WHEN TO GO: Nov–May.

✈ Busuanga (also called Coron) Airport, connecting through Ninoy Aquino International Airport in Manila.

Previous page: Whitewater rafting with Echo Canyon River Expeditions in Royal Gorge, Colorado.

$$–$$$ **El Nido Resorts Lagen Lodge,** Bacuit Bay, El Nido (✆ 632/750-7600; www.elnidoresorts.com). $$–$$$ **El Rio y Mar Island Resort,** San Jose, Coron (✆ 63/920-951-5009; www.elrioymar.com). $–$$ **Dive Link Resort,** Uson Island, Coron (✆ 632/376-2048; www.divelink.com.ph).

65 Diving & Snorkeling

Lady Elliot Island
Frolicking on the Great Barrier Reef
Great Barrier Reef Marine Park, Australia

I must apologize in advance to the Aussies who asked me not to tell folks back home about **Lady Elliot.** My favorite spot on the Great Barrier Reef is its southern-most coral cay, Lady Elliot Island, which is reached by small Seair Pacific planes from Bundaberg or Hervey Bay. A trip here is an experience you'll never forget. The atmosphere here is ultra laid back. Lodging ranges from permanent tents (Eco Huts) with wooden floors to small cabins. No spa. No gourmet food. No nightly entertainment. It's all about diving, snorkeling,

marine life, and the beach in this part of the Great Barrier Reef Marine Park. Lady Elliot is just one of more than 20 island resorts on the Great Barrier Reef. (Others are far more posh.) Visitors come here to keep things simple. What better way to commune with some of the most beautiful scenery and animals on the planet? Half the thrill of coming here is the knowledge that you're having a unique experience, the other half is the exhilaration you'll feel when encountering all that Lady Elliot has to offer.

Lady Elliott Island.

At Lady Elliot Island, you can walk off the shore to dive and snorkel, or take a boat to sites close by. Scratch the back of a green turtle, see giant clams and reef sharks parade around coral gardens, or put your head under water and hear the call of a humpback whale. Visit the site called Anchor Bommies and see giant manta rays swimming by colorful soft and hard coral. Here you can spend all day snorkeling and diving at numerous sites where you never go below 9m (30 ft.). And, unlike up north, you won't encounter stingers (jellyfish). Visit this island between November and January and you'll see nesting green and loggerhead turtles just feet from your door. Hatchlings emerge in February and March. The humpback whales migrate between June and October.

If you can swing it, get to the **Cod Hole** on the Great Barrier Reef in June and July. You can dive and see huge Potato Cod (they're quite comfortable around divers), and you'll have the opportunity to snorkel with the dwarf minke whales that frequent the area during those months. Ideally, yours would be a multi-day trip to this part of the reef. But if you can't swing that, there are plenty of places elsewhere on the reef to maximize whatever amount of time you have here. The Great Barrier Reef is without question one of the great dive and snorkeling locations in the world. It's also the largest, covering more than 344,470 sq. km (133,000 sq. miles) and stretching almost 2,500km (1,600 miles) along the Northeast coast of Australia. In the north there are numerous cities along the Queensland coast from which you can take a day trip to the reef. Northern tourism is centered in the Whitsunday Islands and Cairns, where there are hundreds of resorts and hotels and opportunities to make day trips. (See ⓙⓞⓩ for more on yachting in the Whitsunday Islands.) From Cairns, the Great Barrier Reef can be reached in approximately an hour by boat, and more than 300 boats depart from Cairns daily for various types of reef trips. Special dive locations, such as the Cod Hole and Ribbon reefs take longer and are better suited for multi-day trips on a live-aboard. —LF

ⓘ **Lady Elliott Island Eco Resort,** Runaway Bay (ⓒ **61/7/5536-3644;** www.lady elliot.com.au). **Cairns Tourism,** 27–29 Wharf St. (ⓒ **1300/554-636** within Australia or 617 4040 2111; www.cairns.aust. com). **Whitsunday Tourism** (ⓒ **1300-717-407;** www.whitsundaytourism.com).

TOURS: In Cairns: **Tusa Dive,** corner of Shield Street and the Esplanade (ⓒ **61/7/4047-9100;** www.tusadive.com). **Cairns Dive Centre,** 121 Abbott St. (ⓒ **61/7/4051-0294;** www.cairnsdive.com.au).

WHEN TO GO: Mar–Nov.

✈ Cairns Airport, Whitsunday Airport, Bundaberg Airport, and Hevery Bay Airport.

⊨ $$ **Lady Elliot Island Eco Resort,** Runaway Bay (ⓒ **61/7/5536-3644;** www. ladyelliot.com.au). Contact them far in advance as lodging and the number of visitors is limited. In Cairns: $–$$ **201 Lake Street Apartments** (ⓒ 61/7/5630-6637; www.201lakestreetapartments. com.au).

Ice Diving in the White Sea
The Coolest Scuba Experience on Earth
Karelia Republic, Russia

Submerged in the water below a frozen white sheet at the top of the earth on Russia's northwest coast is one of the world's most chilling dive experiences. Think sub-zero temperatures, icebergs, and only one way in or out.

Ice diving is popular in Antarctica, Newfoundland, and parts of Austria, but one of the best and most remote places to do it is in Russia's White Sea. Just getting here is an epic journey in itself, with a flight to Moscow, another flight and a long car ride, or a nearly 28-hour train ride followed by a few hours in a car and another few by snowmobile. But once you're jumping through a black triangle cut out of the ice and drifting beneath the frozen sea, the time it takes to get here is clearly worth it.

Floating around the underwater rocks and occasional wrecks are starfish, rainbow-colored jellyfish, sea urchins, spider crabs, large round anemones, countless shrimp, and a huge variety of gorgeous fish. Soft corals, sponges, algae, and kelp speckle the sea floor. Above it all is a vast ice cover, filtering sunlight into dazzling colors and shapes.

Marine life is particularly rich in the White Sea because the cold water holds more oxygen than warm water. In fact, temperatures can reach below freezing, which means you'll need your certification from the Professional Association of Diving Instructors (PADI), plenty of prior diving experience (or an intensive training program), and a whole lot of gear. Forget the typical wetsuit. For ice diving, you'll need a dry suit, made of neoprene to wick away sweat and keep you dry, along with

Thinsulate-insulated undergarments, at least one neoprene hood to protect your entire neck and face, warm gloves, rubber outer gloves, fins, a tank, weights, and a mouthpiece—among several other pieces of equipment. Your outfitter should supply all necessary equipment.

Diving in these cold conditions is dangerous. For one thing, valves can freeze, either shutting off or sending a diver up toward the solid ice above. As a safety precaution, each ice diver must be secured by rope to two other people: one in the water and one on the surface known as a tender. That way, if someone gets in trouble, the other person in the water can signal an emergency and the person on top can haul you to the surface. Of course, there's only way out, and that's through the same ice hole you used to get in. The risks are obvious, but so are the rewards. The exhilaration of slipping into the White Sea's icy underwater paradise is an out-of-this world, out-of-body experience. Afterward, warm up with a *banya*, the traditional Russian steam bath, and a good bottle of local vodka. —JS

ⓘ **The Arctic Circle Dive Center,** Building 1, 19A, Suvorovskaya St., Moscow (✆ **7/ 495-925-7799;** www.ice-diving.ru). The dive center also has a resort that provides accommodations and meals.

WHEN TO GO: Feb–Apr.

✈ Moscow International Airport, followed by a train ride to Chupa or a flight to Murmansk and a 6-hr. drive to the dive center.

Jean-Michel Cousteau Fiji Islands Resort
Floating in a Coral Garden
Vanua Levu, Fiji

Life is sweet at the Jean-Michel Cousteau Fiji Islands Resort, the multi-award wining resort where your (albeit hefty) tariff includes lodging, meals, and snorkeling, along with daily adventures, which range from hiking in a tropical rainforest to visiting a local market. (Scuba diving, deep sea fishing, and spa treatments are extra.) You could spend one morning sailing the resort's Hobie Cat or kayaking to nearby Split Rock or an uninhabited island. In the afternoon, you could relax on a beach, take a ride in the glass-bottom boat to snorkel on an outer reef, or play tennis. Whatever you choose, it'll be sure to satisfy the adventure traveler in you. But the real treat here is getting out on and in the water.

A typical diving trip could look like this: You're floating between two coral pinnacles and schools of orange and purple anthias, blue-fin trevallys. Butterfly fish are swirling around you. As you look at the yellow and purple soft coral, lion fish and stone fish swim by. Surfacing after the dive, you get into the boat for the 5-minute ride from the **Golden Nuggets** dive site back to the resort.

The resident marine biologist organizes daily snorkeling trips. The water is very clear here, and in many places spectacular coral formations rise close to the surface. In addition to the boat expeditions, the resort has self-guided snorkel trails minutes from the shoreline, not to mention excellent snorkeling at the end of its pier.

Watersports and relaxation are the main draw at Jean-Michel Cousteau Fiji Islands Resort.

The fun continues out of the water, too. Every day a different cultural or ecological tour or seminar is offered. One day, you might learn basic Fijian and test your language skills during a guided village tour and a ceremony with the Village Chief. Another, you might explore the reef with a marine biologist or learn how to weave Fijian fishing baskets and fans from coconut palm leaves.

Guests stay in luxurious Fijian-style *bures*, villas with air-conditioning and Internet access. The meals incorporate local fare: fresh fish and herbs and spices from the resort's garden. The eco-sensitive resort has created a clam farm, where some 40 giant clams thrive and data is collected to educate both guests and locals about sustainable resources. The goal is to help re-establish a food source for local villagers in future years.

Fiji has been called the "Soft Coral Capital of the World" for good reason. Some of the best diving is found in the Northern Group, where the resort is located. Boats take resort guests to spectacular dive spots, such as **Namena Island,** where barracuda, dog-tooth tuna, manta rays, and large sharks parade among the multicolored soft corals and coral gardens. At **Dreamhouse** in the Koro Sea, a sea mount is a wonderful feeding ground for small fish and the larger pelagic fish, such as barracuda and shark. —*LF*

ⓘ **Jean-Michel Cousteau Fiji Islands Resort** (ⓒ **800/246-3454** in the U.S. or Canada, or 415/788-5794; www.fijiresort.com).

WHEN TO GO: The water is warmest during Fiji's summer, Jan–Mar. A full wetsuit is recommended in winter, July–Aug.

✈ Savusavu Airport.

🛏 $$$$ **Jean-Michel Cousteau Fiji Islands Resort** (ⓒ **800/246-3454** in the U.S. or Canada, or 415/788-5794; www.fijiresort.com).

68 Diving & Snorkeling

A Submarine Tour
Embarking on a Covert Mission under the Sea
Tumon, Guam

Wish there was a thrill ride you could share with the kids? A submarine tour is the perfect family adventure. After all, it's never too early to start marveling at the earth's wonders, and the jaw-dropping underwater views off the coast of Guam are enough to get any 10-year-old's heart pumping. Teens will also get a kick out of the James Bond–like act of covertly slinking through the Pacific Ocean in a real submarine.

From the shores of Tumon, Guam, your tour begins with a 15-minute boat ride to a fully submersible 20m-long (65 ft.) submarine that can carry up to 45 passengers. Each dive lasts about 45 minutes, and the kids' faces will probably be pressed up against the custom-designed glass windows for most of it. Precise maneuvering allows the sub to get daringly close to coral reefs, teeming with tropical fish and other unique sea creatures. It's not quite as exciting as scuba diving, but you'll be able to go as deep as 45m (150 ft.) at times, and you don't have to squeeze into a wetsuit.

Even better, the fun isn't over once you get back on dry land. The far-flung tropical island of Guam, a U.S. territory in the Marina Islands of Micronesia, offers countless activities to keep the whole family amused for at least a week. To relax, you can hang out on the beach, or maybe sneak away for a round of golf at one of Guam's seven world-class courses. When you're ready to kick it back up a notch, choose from scuba diving (complete with underwater wrecks from World War II), snorkeling, jet-skiing, wind surfing, kayaking, parasailing, deep sea fishing, sky diving, eco tours, and hiking. Trekking through the undeveloped jungle and virgin beaches that cover a large part of this island is locally known as "boonie stomping," a popular but demanding pastime among visitors and residents. The Department of Parks and Recreation offers public boonie stomps every Saturday. For more information, visit **www.guam-online.com**.

Although the weather in Guam is uniformly warm and humid year-round, the island is located in a part of the Pacific Ocean that's ominously referred to as "typhoon alley." Typhoons are said to hit the island once every 8 years, usually in October or November, so you might want to avoid visiting during those months. The last typhoon occurred in 2002 with winds reaching 180kmph (112 mph). Guam is also home to a large U.S. military base, and the

U.S. plans to move another 8,000 marines plus 10,000 dependants here from the southern Japanese island of Okinawa by 2014. Because of its proximity to Japan, Guam is especially popular among Japanese tourists, and is sometimes called "America in Asia." If you don't plan to travel quite as far as Guam, but like the idea of taking your kids on a submarine, tours are also offered in Hawaii and the Caribbean. —*JS*

ⓘ **Guam Visitors Bureau,** 401 Pale San Vitores Rd., Tumon (℗ **671/646-5278;** www.visitguam.org).

TOUR: Atlantis Adventures, 319 Aqua World Marina Rd., Piti, Guam (℗ **671/649-5050;** www.atlantisadventures.com).

WHEN TO GO: Jan–Apr.

✈ A.B. Won Pat International Airport.

🛏 $$$ **Outrigger Guam Resort,** 1255 Pale San Vitores Rd., Tumon Bay (℗ **671/649-9000;** www.outrigger.com). $$ **The Westin Resort,** 105 Gun Beach Rd., Tumon (℗ **671/647-1020;** www.starwoodhotels.com).

Diving & Snorkeling **69**

Stuart Cove SUB Bahamas
See Coral Reefs in a Mini-Sub
Nassau, Bahamas

You don't have to be a scuba diver to experience the thrill of exploring the delicate coral reefs in the Bahamas. Using a bubble-headed mini-sub you can motor quietly among colorful parrotfish, red-and-white zebra striped lionfish, and other marine life swimming around coral reefs 4.5m (15 ft.) underwater. There is a powerful, magical mystery to the world floating by around you.

The personal SUBs (Scenic Underwater Bubbles) look like a futuristic underwater motor-scooter. (If you've ever seen the TV

series *Sea Quest,* the mini-subs are similar to the escape pods used by the crew to abandon the ships in an emergency.) You sit on the compact craft with your head inside a bubble, allowing for a clear view of the underwater world surrounding you. You breathe normally. The air you are breathing in the bubble comes from a SCUBA cylinder that uses a ScubaPro regulator to keep air flowing continually.

The 3-hour mini-sub adventure with **Stuart Cove's Dive Bahamas** starts with a brief orientation about using the SUB, then a short boat ride to one of the coral reefs near Nassau. Once in the water, you put your head in the bubble, slide your body onto the seat, and put your feet on floorboards. You're escorted underwater to about a 4.5m (15-ft.) depth, where you wait for the rest of your group. When the guide gives the go-ahead, simply turn on the SUB and steer it as you would a car. You motor along at a speedy 2 knots per hour among schools of fish and alongside the reef. (Be sure to bring along an underwater camera.) Everyone follows the guide, and there are also professional divers with the group, in case anyone needs assistance. The underwater adventure lasts about 30 minutes. The rest of the time you can swim or snorkel off the boat, or just laze in the sun.

Exploring the aquatic life in a personal SUB (Scenic Underwater Bubble).

Snorkel Bahamas, another Stuart Cove program, takes guests to three locations. With some fish food to spread around at the first stop on a shallow reef, you're sure to be surrounded by swarms of fish. At the second stop, you'll visit a shipwreck, perhaps one of the wrecks used to make the 007 film *Never Say Never Again.* It's your choice to get in the water or watch from the boat on the third stop, when a bait box is lowered in the water to attract sharks.

Stuart Cove's offers a full spectrum of diving experiences, too. The company has a 3-hour Learn to Dive program. Experienced divers can explore many of the reefs surrounding the island, and sign on for night dives. Scuba divers looking for thrills can choose the **Shark Adventure,** a two-tank dive that includes a "free swim" with Caribbean reef sharks. Take the **Wall Flying Adventure** and you'll hop on an underwater scooter to explore some of the walls formed by the 193km-long (120-mile) Tongue-of-the-Ocean trench. —LF

(i) **Stuart Cove's** (📞 800/879-9832; www.stuartcove.com).

WHEN TO GO: Year-round.

✈ Nassau International Airport.

🛏 $$$ **British Colonial Hilton,** 1 Bay St. (📞 800/HILTONS [445-8667] or 242/322-3301; www.hilton.com); $$ **Nassau Palm Resort,** W. Bay St. (📞 242/356-0000; www.nassau-hotels.com).

Diving & Snorkeling

70

World War II Wreck Diving
A Deep History Lesson
Papua, New Guinea

Papua New Guinea (PNG) is one of the world's most exotic diving destinations. It's far off the beaten path—hard to reach and even harder to get around. In fact, this tropical island nation in the Pacific Ocean is often referred to as "the land of the unexpected." Its mountainous interior blanketed in rainforest wasn't penetrated by Westerners until the 1930s, and today hundreds of different indigenous cultures and languages still exist within the country's borders.

For scuba divers, the best part of PNG lies in its surrounding waters, home to an abundance of rare marine life and significant relics from World War II. The many navy ships and various aircraft that remain beneath the sea are a somber reminder of hard-fought battles between the Allied troops and Japanese forces that took place here during the early 1940s. In the years since then, coral reefs have grown over these historic remnants, creating vibrant dive sights that merge old stories with new beginnings.

Depending on the strength of your sea legs, you can base yourself at a lodge in PNG and take day trips to dive, or embark on a "live-aboard" expedition, where you stay on a boat and dive from it as you travel around different islands. Barring any serious tendencies toward severe seasickness, the latter is the obvious choice for adrenaline junkies.

A good place to start diving is **Tufi,** just a short flight or boat ride from **Port Moresby.** This secluded jungle area with tropical plants, coconut trees, and damp earth near **Mount Trafalgar** offers a great dive resort and plenty of underwater adventures around large wrecks, majestic fjords, spectacular reefs, and countless fish. If you're lucky, you might even see a pygmy seahorse.

When you're ready for more adventures at sea, climb aboard the **Barbarian II** (www.niuginidiving.com). Its skipper, Rod Pearce, is credited with discovering the famous B17 bomber **Blackjack,** still intact beneath 50m (164 ft.) of water off **Milne Bay,** between the Solomon Sea and the Coral Sea. It's well worth a look.

Another special wreck awaits nearby. The **P38 Lightning,** a single-seat fighter ditched during World War II, resides 27m (90 ft.) underwater, with the guns in its nose pointing at a reef in front of the wreck. With many other wrecks to explore in the area, the serious diver will certainly not be bored. And while the wrecks themselves are the focus of this adventure, the added bonus is the unavoidable beauty of the area's fertile reefs swarming with fish and other sea creatures.

If you want to explore even more remote parts of PNG, head north to the waters off **Kimbe, Kavieng,** and **Rabaul** on the **MV Telita** (www.telitacruises. com). Diving highlights include **Der Yang,** deliberately sunken at 30m (100 ft.) to act

Underwater World War II relics abound in Papua, New Guinea.

as an artificial reef; an intact freighter; and a Japanese mini-submarine at 22m (72 ft.). Kavieng, in particular, is also known for pelagic fish action, when the change of tides produces strong currents and the number of fish is overwhelming.

Wreck diving is enough of a reason to visit PNG, but save time for a few worthwhile experiences on land while you're in the region. Visit a tribal village to learn about an indigenous culture. Stay at a local guesthouse and enjoy a traditional "singsing" performance. While in the jungle, you may even catch a glimpse of the Alexandra Birdwing, the world's largest butterfly.

Traveling anywhere in PNG, on land or under the sea, takes an intrepid spirit and a relaxed attitude. The infrastructure is poor, and things often take longer than expected. That's all part of the beauty.

Just dive in and you'll be amazed by what you find. —JS

ⓘ **Papua New Guinea Tourism Promotion Authority** (ⓒ **675/320-0211;** www. pngtourism.org.pg).

TOURS: Trans Niugini Tours, Mount Hagen (ⓒ **675/542-1438;** www.pngtours. com). **Telita Dive Adventures,** Port Mortesby (ⓒ **675/321-1860;** www.telita cruises.com).

WHEN TO GO: Apr–Dec.

✈ Jackson's International Airport.

🛏 $$ **Tufi Dive Resort,** Mount Trafalgar, 250km (155 miles) northeast of Port Moresby (ⓒ **675/323-3462;** www.tufi dive.com). $$ **Walindi Plantation Resort,** Kimbe Bay (ⓒ **675/983-5441;** www. walindi.com).

---

71 Diving & Snorkeling

Wreck Diving in the Western Pacific
Colorful Artificial Reefs
Micronesia

Simply the best shipwreck diving in the world. That's how the diving in parts of Micronesia is usually labeled by people who have been fortunate enough to go there. This underwater playground exists due to the United States Navy, which between February 17 and February 19, 1944, sunk more than 40 ships and destroyed hundreds of Japanese Imperial Navys airplanes in Truk (Chuuk) Lagoon. And, on March 30 and March 31, the Navy sank more than 60 ships and planes in and around Palau's lagoon. Attacks continued for months, destroying more ships and planes. Declared grave sites are legally protected from salvage and the artifacts have been removed from most of the wrecks, which are now artificial reefs covered with multicolored corals and serve as home to countless numbers of fish. The beauty encountered during the dive to

these historical relics itself will likely inspire awe. Coupled with thinking about the actions that led to these tremendous wrecks is even more heart-stopping.

While the waters of numerous islands in Micronesia contain wrecks, the best concentrations are around Truk and Palau. (The multi-island Federated States of Micronesia covers more than 2,500 sq. km/965 sq. miles in the Pacific Ocean nearly 5800km/3,600 miles from Hawaii.) Truk Lagoon, alone, is more than 64km (40 miles) long, so it's not possible to dive all of the wrecks in either Truk or Palau during one or two trips. Many divers get hooked into coming back year after year.

Truk Lagoon is likened to a huge lake. Water temperatures hover around 83°F (28°C) and visibility is between 9 and 30m (30–100 ft.) depending upon algae blooms and runoff. Thirty-five shipwrecks have been charted with 20 dived on a regular basis. The most popular are the *Frujikawa Maru,* the *Nippo Maru,* and the *Sankisan.* Some of the wrecks are deep while others, particularly a number of the warplanes, lie in shallower water. **Blue Lagoon Dive Shop** (www.truk-lagoon-dive.com), located at the Blue Lagoon Dive Resort (see below), and **Micronesia Aquatics** are well known Truk dive operations, taking divers to and from wrecks and instructing them on wreck-diving. Live-aboards at Truk include the *Truk Aggressor,* the *Big Blue Explorer,* and the SS *Thorfinn.*

Palau encompasses 343 islands over 161 sq. km of ocean. While most of the wrecks are in comparatively shallow water, Palau divers often come for the manta, shark, and wall dives rather than the wrecks. The *Iro Maru* is a large tanker sunk by torpedo with the main deck of the bow at 21m (70 ft.). It's a good penetration dive, with its holds containing oil drums and machinery, Plus, it's beautifully covered with marine life. The freighter *Chuyo* that was also torpedoed is a bit deeper with a stern gun at 24m (80 ft.) and considerable debris surrounding the ship. The shallowest part of the *Helmet* wreck is in only 7.5m (25 ft.) of water. The wreck, named for the Japanese helmets the boat carried (which

are now fused together) has many artifacts including ammunition, plane engines, and beer bottles. Dive operations in Palau include **Fish 'n Fins/Dive Palau** (www.fishfins.com) and **Sam's Dive Tours** (www.samstours). Live-aboards include the *Palau Aggressor* and the *Ocean Hunter II.*

At Palau, don't miss snorkeling in **Jellyfish Lake.** The lake has two different species of non-stinging jellyfish, which pulsate and reflect light with a unique eeriness. At Truk, be sure to visit the gun emplacements, caves, and fortifications during your gas-off day. —*LF*

ⓘ **Federated States of Micronesia** (ⓒ 691/320-5122; www.visit-fsm.org). **Diving Palau** (www.skin-diver.com/palaudest/sites.html). **Truk Lagoon.com** (www.truk-lagoon.com). **Rananim,** dive information on Palau and Truk Lagoon (www.rananim.com).

WHEN TO GO: Jan–Mar are the coolest months with the lowest humidity. Best time to visit Truk: Dec–Apr is the dry season.

✈ Chuuk International Airport and Palau International Airport.

🛏 **Truk Blue Lagoon Resort** (ⓒ 691/330-2727; www.bluelagoondiveresort.com). $$–$$$ **Pacific Resort in Palau** (ⓒ 680/488-2600; www.palauppr.com).

Diving & Snorkeling **72**

Wreck Diving in Bermuda
Uncovering History in the Wreckage
Bermuda

Ships have come to grief on Bermuda's reefs since a Spanish ship went down between 1500 and 1503. Depending on the person you ask, you'll hear there are between 300 and 400 documented wrecks on the reefs encircling the six major and 120 minor islands that comprise Bermuda. Exploring these wrecks connects you to the past in a way few other experiences

can. It's a thrill to see the wreckage up close. So take a dive into marine history and explore the amazing wrecks off the isles of Bermuda.

Unlike most wreck diving adventures, many of the wrecks in Bermuda are in water shallow enough to make diving up to three wrecks in a day possible. Wreckage can be found as shallow as 6m (20 ft.) and diving below 24m (80 ft.) isn't necessary, so divers can usually count on great visibility and adequate bottom time, allowing the flexibility for multiple dives in 1 day. This is a great trip for those who want to see as much as possible with limited time.

Around Bermuda there are actually 36 known diveable wreck sites, 12 of which are most frequently dived, 12 more occasionally dived, and 12 rarely visited. One of the premium sites is the **Cristobal Colon** which, weather permitting, is a must for divers—it's a spectacular site. The wreckage of the 150m (500-ft.), 1920's ocean liner covers acres of the sea bed more than an hour's boat ride from shore. She ran aground in 1936 and was used for bombing practice during World War II. Look for the huge boilers and deck equipment.

If you don't want to go so far out in the ocean, visit one of the wreck dives just off the coast. One of the oldest is the **Virginia Merchant,** which carried colonists from England. The ballast stones of the three-masted ship lie in 12m (40 ft.) of water. The **King,** a U.S. Navy Tugboat built in 1941 and sunk as an artificial reef in 1984, is intact and lies upright at nearly 20m (65 ft.). The 77m (255-ft.) **Mary Celestina** was a blockade-runner that now rests at 17m (55 ft.) underwater. One of her paddlewheel frames makes her readily identifiable. The **Hermes** was sunk as an artificial reef and sits on the bottom at 24m (80 ft.). It is upright and intact. So take your pick—you certainly won't be bored for lack of options.

There are numerous dive operators in Bermuda—we've listed a couple below.

All operations make dive-site selections based on the weather as well as diver experience and preferences.

Bermuda is vacation heaven on-shore as well, with many big resorts offering alternative adventure and sporty activity. The kid-friendly **Fairmont Southampton** has a tough 18-hole, par 3 golf course, and can make arrangements for sport fishing, diving, tennis, and cycling. **Cambridge Beaches** is adults only and has five private beaches and a spa. You can also rent a motor scooter and cruise around. —*LF*

ⓘ **Bermuda Tourism** (✆ **800/BERMUDA** [237-6832] in the U.S.; www.bermuda tourism.com). **Dive Guide International** (✆ **303/484-7575;** www.diveguide.com/ berm-scuba.htm).

TOURS: Blue Water Divers (✆ **441/234-1034;** www.divebermuda.com). **Fantasea Diving** (✆ **441/236-1300;** www.fantasea. bm).

WHEN TO GO: Apr–June are the colder months, but offer the best visibility. Sept–Oct are warmer with good visibility.

✈ L. F. Wade International Airport.

⌖ $$$ **Fairmont Southampton,** 101 South Rd. (✆ **800/257-7544** in the U.S. and Canada or 441/238-8000; www.fairmont. com/southampton). $$$ **Cambridge Beaches,** 30 Kings Point Rd. (✆ **800/468-7500** in the U.S. or 441/234-0331; www. cambridgebeaches.com). $ **Greene's Guest House,** 71 Middle Rd. (✆ **441/238-0834;** www.thegreenesguesthouse.com).

---

73 Diving & Snorkeling

Diving in East Africa
The Underwater Safari
Mombasa, Kenya

Kenya is a wildly popular safari destination, but most animal lovers only explore dry land. After cruising around the big-name game parks by jeep, they think they've seen it all. Don't make the same mistake. To spot some of the country's most spectacular wildlife, you have to dive in deeper; much of it lives underwater.

The most idyllic place to chill out and thrill out for a few days is on Mombasa's coastline. Besides sunshine and white sand, this area offers some of the Indian Ocean's best spots for scuba enthusiasts.

During the day, explore the area's most impressive upright wreck, MV *Dania*. In and around the artificial reef it created, you'll see a wide variety of diverse marine life including grouper, batfish, barracuda, and moray eels.

The biggest scuba rush, however, comes from diving at night off the northern part of the coast. The **Watamu Marine National Park,** 180km (90 miles) from Mombasa, is full of coral gardens in barrier-type reefs with gentle slopes ranging from 7 to 25m (23–82 ft.). In total, the marine park is home to approximately 600 species of fish, 110 species of coral, and countless invertebrates, crustaceans, and mollusks.

Diving here after dark gives you a unique chance to observe nocturnal creatures including lobsters, crabs, moray eels, and white tip reef sharks. You might also glimpse sleeping sea turtles. For information about volunteer opportunities to help protect the turtles, check out the **Local Ocean Trust** www.watamuturtles.com), which runs the Watamu Turtle Watch program.

Farther north, **Malindi Marine Reserve Park** is another exciting place to dive. It's home to more than 300 species of fish including angelfish, barracuda, butterfly fish, goatfish, grouper, jacks, parrotfish, sharks, snappers, and surgeon fish. And because there's very little fishing in the area, you might see some trophy-size fish gliding around the plentiful coral. In between your dives, you can enjoy the beaches at Nyali, Malindi, or Watamu.

If you've gotten into the beach-bum spirit by now, and you want to head somewhere more secluded for a few days, head farther off the beaten path to the serene island of **Lamu.** Settled by Swahili traders in the 14th century, the island's charming main square is often abuzz with traditional clattering carts and families running their daily errands. But just outside of town, you can soak in the sun on quiet sands before going for a long, lazy sail in a traditional dhow (wooden boat). After a few days of an exhilarating underwater safari, this laid-back paradise is the perfect place to recharge before your next adventure. —*JS*

ⓘ **Kenya Tourist Board,** Kenya-Re Towers, Regati Rd., Nairobi (✆ **254/20-271-1262;** www.magicalkenya.com).

TOURS: Blue Marine Diving, at the Serena Beach Hotel and Spa (✆ **20/233-4298;** www.bluemarinediving.com). **Buccaneer Diving,** at the Voyager Beach Resort on Nyali Beach (✆ **254/20-203-9463;** www. buccaneerdiving.com).

WHEN TO GO: Sept–May.

✈ Mombasa airport, also known as Moi International Airport.

⊨ $$$ **Mombasa Serena Beach Hotel & Spa,** Shanzu Beach (✆ **254/20-284-2333;** www.serenahotels.com).

Diving & Snorkeling **74**

Night Diving in the Caribbean
Night Moves
Bonaire

And you thought you couldn't jump when you were swimming 15m (50 ft.) under the surface! But, when the sea is black and an eel darts from behind a rock and grabs a parrotfish right in front of your face, you can. The dive master I was with claimed he'd never seen anything like it in all of his dives—and here it happened during my first night dive at Bonaire. Aside from being a once in a lifetime experience, it was also good for numerous free rounds of drinks later that night at a local bar.

I love night diving, especially because you can establish neutral buoyancy and turn out your light. It's a feeling like no other. Also, when you move your arms or legs you can watch the bioluminescence. It's a whole different world at night with coral opening and many creatures that sleep during the day coming to life in the dark. If you're lucky, you may find a large tarpon swimming with you. It's not there to keep you company, but has learned that your light might temporarily stun its next meal and make it easy pickings. That said, I've not seen anything to fear in the way of finned creatures while night diving around Bonaire.

Depending on which location you choose, you can dive from a marked site on the shore or enter at about 2.5m (8 ft.), swim a short way (at which point I like to anchor a small strobe), and then head down. It's an easy dive to drop to about 15m (50 ft.) on the way out and come back toward the shore at a depth of 9m (30 ft.). At these depths, there's plenty to see to keep your adrenaline pumping.

The dive from the **town pier** is renowned, and you'll hear about it all over the island. However, I found other dives to be more exciting. While there's good yellow-orange coral, lots of eels, fish, crabs, and even sea horses, along with old tires and other garbage, the dive is shallow, requires a dive master for each four divers, is limited to a scheduled 1 hour, and is crowded with other divers. A better night dive option might be the *Hilma Hooker* **wreck** or one from the beach off the Sand

Dollar Resort (see below). Discuss the options with your dive operator (for our recommendations, see below). They'll surely be able to recommend a dive site that will meet your needs.

Bonaire is one of the top dive sites in the world. The water is warm (75°–84°F/24°–29°C), visibility is generally in the 30m (100-ft.) range, coral and other marine life is abundant, rain is scarce, and hurricanes usually miss the island.

Bonaire's economy is tourism based and most of its visitors come to dive, snorkel, or just enjoy the water. The waters around the island are part of the **Bonaire National Marine Park.** There are numerous rules and regulations, such as the requirement for an orientation session before one can purchase ($25) the required tag for use of the park, so be sure to be accommodating. —*LF*

ⓘ **Info Bonaire** (www.infobonaire.com). **Bonaire Talk** (www.bonairetalk.com). **Bonaire National Marine Park** (☎ 599/717-8444; www.bmp.org).

TOUR: Bonaire Dive and Adventure, Kaya Gobernador N. Debrot 77A (☎ 599-717-2229; www.bonairediveand adventure.com).

WHEN TO GO: Year-round.

✈ Bonaire.

🛏 $$ **Sand Dollar Resort,** Kaya Gobernador N. Debrot 79 (☎ 599/717-8738; divesanddollar.com). $$$$ **Harbor Village Beach Club,** Kaya Gobernador N. Debrot No. 71 (☎ 800/424-0004 in the U.S. and Canada, 599/717-7500; www. harbourvillage.com). $$–$$$ **The Deep Blue View,** Kaya Diamanta No. 50 (☎ 599/717-8073; www.deepblueview.com).

Scuba Diving off Colombia
Swim with the Sharks
Malpelo, Colombia

From the sea, Malpelo looks like something out of a classic 007 movie—the remote Pacific hideout where the over-the-top villain plots some dastardly scheme from within a rocky fortress. The island's profile is so sinister it's almost campy: The "shoreline" consists of sheer cliffs, and the island's highest peak, **Cerro de la Mona,** looms 376m (1,234 ft.) above like a glowering overlord. The entire surface of Malpelo, a scant 350 hectares (865 acres), is harsh grey lavic rock, practically devoid of vegetation. And for 10km (6 miles) in every direction, the waters around Malpelo are a UNESCO sanctuary where some of the ocean's most menacing-looking creatures circle and feed. Yet it's thanks to this teeming and diverse population of sharks that Malpelo is one of the top scuba diving destinations in the world.

The miniscule above-water peak of an enormous undersea mountain that extends for 3.2km (2 miles) to the floor of the Eastern Pacific Ocean, Malpelo is located 506km (314 miles) off the western coast of Colombia. Because of its extreme isolation and the government permits required to visit Malpelo, most people travel there on organized

diving trips that include Costa Rica's Cocos Island, another fantastic dive site.

Massive, spectacular sea caves, where smaller fish seek harbor from rough mid-ocean conditions, are what make Malpelo and its offshore rock stacks such a consistently thrilling place to dive. These ecological conditions are a magnet for the shark species so frequently seen here, and at relatively shallow depths. Visibility underwater is generally excellent. There are more than 500 scalloped hammerheads swimming around Malpelo, as well as silky sharks, bull sharks, white-tip sharks, manta rays, barracuda, and an astounding number of moray eels. It's also one of few places in the world where the rare small-tooth sand tiger shark is commonly seen, off a rock wall known as "Monster Face." More friendly faced creatures in the vicinity include dolphins, sea turtles, and the occasional humpback whale on migratory routes. The prehistoric hammerheads, which measure up to 4.2m (14 ft.) in length and swim in formidable synchronized matrices—a dazzling sight for divers—may look monstrous, but neither they nor any of the other species off Malpelo are aggressive toward humans.

Unless you're an experienced and intrepid diver (there are strong currents to contend with in addition to the toothy sea life), there's no reason to visit Malpelo. The island's name is a corruption of the Latin nickname a sailor once gave this barren rock: *Malveolus,* or "inhospitable," which pretty well sums up the above-water aspect of the place. The island—"rock" is more like it—is uninhabited by humans except for a small Colombian navy garrison. Some other fauna, however, are perfectly suited to this seemingly hostile environment: A colony of

Divers come from all over the world to swim with the sharks in Malpelo.

some 25,000 Nazca, or masked boobies, thrives on tiny Malpelo, and there are a number of endemic species, including lizards and crabs, that live on the algae and lichens that grow on the crags. —SM

ⓘ http://whc.unesco.org/en/list/1216.

TOUR: Undersea Hunter, Puntarenas, Costa Rica (✆ **506/2228-6613;** www.underseahunter.com).

✈ San Jose International, Costa Rica. Diving trips depart from Puntarenas, Costa Rica.

Cenote & Cave Diving
A Sacred Underworld
Riviera Maya, Mexico

The many *cenotes* (canyons or sinkholes) running along the Riviera Maya have quite a history. Carved out of the Yucatan Peninsula's limestone surface, their pools of water sustained ancient cultures including the Mayans, who revered them as sacred places. It's easy to see why.

As you approach a cenote's cool cavernous opening, you'll see jagged edges caused by years of erosion, often overgrown with trees and other jungle vegetation. Bats hang overhead. Narrow streaks of light slip through the small hole above as you plunge into the crystal clear, calm

Cenote diving along Mexico's Riviera Maya.

Extreme Cliff Diving & Cliff Jumping

Cliff diving and jumping is said to have originated in 1770 when Hawaii's King Kajekili commanded his men to leap the island of Lanai's high cliffs and enter the water feet first without splashing in order to prove their courage and loyalty to him. Since then, cliff diving has morphed into a sport requiring not only courage, but skill. Cliff jumping is an experience adopted by many adventurous souls seeking extreme ways to enter water.

If you're considering trying cliff diving, keep in mind that even experienced cliff divers (including those who enter cliff diving competitions around the world) emphasize the necessary technical training, physical conditioning, focus, and experience in making dives at a variety of lower heights before leaping from more challenging high cliffs. Experience in platform diving is recommended. The depth of the water, weather, and waves are just some of the factors that must be taken into account when diving or jumping. Serious injury is always a possibility, so familiarize yourself with all the factors involved in your dive or jump before you, well, dive in. Contact the **World High Diving Federation** (www.whdf.com) or the **Cliff Jump Network** (www.cliffjumpingnetwork.com) to learn more about this risky sport. —LF

77 La Quebrada Cliffs, Mexico: Onlookers can sit on a restaurant terrace and watch divers soar off the spectacular 44m (148-ft.) cliff and into the water. Though it's a tourist attraction for laughing and dining visitors, cliff divers are totally focused on the rocks, wind, and other variables that will affect their respective dives. Proper timing is vital, because divers must land in the water when the ocean swells raise the water level where they land. *Acapulco, Mexico.*

78 Wolfgangsee, Austria: This lake in northwestern Austria is calm and clear, making it a popular spot for diving. There are several unofficial dive sites around the lake, but one of the best places for diving is the Falkenstein cliff wall in Frberg bay, where divers spring off a special high board, about 30m (100 ft.) above the water and do a tuck or somersault before landing in this beautiful lake. Boatloads of viewers cheer as divers resurface. This is also the site of the annual **Red Bull Cliff Diving** competition (www.redbull.com). There are other, lower places nearby where divers climb to the top of various ledges and jump into the water. *Wolfgangsee Tourist Association (www.wolfgangsee.at).*

79 Ponte Brolla, Switzerland: The European Cliff Diving Contest and the World High Diving Federation have held competitions at this lake, which is at the entry to the Valle Maggia. You can dive from several heights, ranging from roughly 7 to 20m (23–66 ft.). Before you take the plunge, check with the local divers because they monitor the water levels. Never dive when the river is running high. *www.whdf.com.*

80 Red Rocks Park, Vermont, U.S.A.: The locale, not far from South Burlington, is picturesque, but the cliff diving is dangerous. Scale the cliff and it's an 80-foot (24m) plunge into the icy water. In some places, the jumps are between narrow rock walls. Encompassing 100 acres (40 hectares), Red Rocks Park is mostly wooded and kept in natural condition. The park boasts 700 feet (213m) of public beach and several miles of trails for hiking, jogging, snow shoeing, and cross-country skiing. *South Burlington Recreation & Parks Department* (℃ *802/846-4108; www.sburlrecdept.com/redrocks.htm).*

⑧ Tar Creek Falls, California, U.S.A.: You must hike up a rock face about 70 feet (21m) before you can even reach a point to make a dive. The topography of the land makes this locale particularly dangerous. It's difficult to jump more than a few feet away from the side of the cliff and you don't want to slam into it on the way down. Tar Creek Falls is located near the Sespe Condor Sanctuary—where you may even see condors in the air—in Los Padres National Forest. You can enter the park near Fillmore, California. *Los Padres National Forest* (℃ *805/683-9711 or 805/968-6640; www.fs.fed.us/r5/lospadres).*

⑧ Waianapanapa Park, Maui, U.S.A.: If you want to reach one of Maui's most popular locations for cliff jumping, go to Ka'anapali Beach and walk to the end where you'll see Black Rock. Walk behind the spot where everyone is jumping, follow the coast around the point for about 2 minutes, and then you'll see the cliffs. Cliff to water is about 40 feet (12m), according to pro cliff jumper Jay Gural. *www.hawaiistateparks.org/parks/maui.*

⑧ Mount Hood Punch Bowl, Oregon, U.S.A.: This could be a good jump for rookies, according to Joe Sellers, a confirmed cliff jumper who runs AirAboveWater.com. The site has a sheer rock wall and you can climb up the inside of the bowl to dive from various heights up to a monster 70 feet (21m)! *www.portlandhikersfieldguide.org/wiki/Punchbowl_Falls.*

⑧ Lake Powell, Utah, U.S.A.: Head to Lake Canyon off the main channel to find colorful cliffs great for a jumping-off point. The leap is about 30 feet (9m) to the azure waters of Lake Powell below. *www.utah.com/lakepowell.*

⑧ Saguaro Lake, Arizona, U.S.A.: There are plenty of opportunities for cliff jumping into this Arizona lake, which is part of Tonto National Forest and is 41 miles from Phoenix. Jump heights range from roughly 6 feet (2m) to about 35 to 40 feet (11–12m). You need to make a running start for the higher jumps. Be sure to test the depth of the water first. *Tonto National Forest* (℃ *480/610-3300; www.fs.fed.us/r3/tonto).* **Go Arizona** *(www.go-arizona.com/Saguaro-Lake).*

⑧ "The Lake" at Saint Mary's Glacier, Colorado, U.S.A.: This small lake in Glacier National Park is simply called "the lake" by locals. Expect lots of hikers to watch you jump off the rocks into the glacier-fed lake below. Bonus: You might see snowboarders sliding down the glacier above you. A pretty cool combo. Get off at I-70 exit 238 and enjoy the winding 10-mile drive to the trailhead. The popular ¾-mile hike up to the tiny lake at the base of the glacier weaves through rock-strewn terrain. At the lake, scout out the safe areas for jumping, keeping in mind that the water level varies considerably throughout the year. *Glacier National Park (www.nps.gov/glac).* **St. Mary's Glacier** *(www.stmarysglacier.com).*

water. After your submerge, your eyes slowly adjust to the darkness (or you turn on your dive light), and countless bizarre stalactites—in the shape of columns, icicles, and chandeliers—come into view. Small fish glide between your legs. As you descend farther and explore this strange subterranean place, it's like entering another world.

Although it may be tempting to go even deeper, there are strict rules about who can dive where in this maze-like environment. Guidelines on standards and certifications differentiate a cenote from a cave. In the diving context, a cenote is defined as an area where there is visible light every 60m (200 ft.), while a cave extends beyond those dimensions. To explore a cenote as a certified open-water diver, you must go with a cave-certified guide. The only divers permitted to enter cave systems are certified cave divers, who have the skills and understand the safety procedures for this type of technical diving. If you're determined to go further than cenotes and dive in the caves, specialized certification courses are offered at the **Cenote Dive Center** (see below) in Tulum. This is also a good place to base yourself for other watersports, as well as remarkable ruins and hiking opportunities.

If you're not a scuba aficionado, you can swim and snorkel in some cenotes. And for most diving enthusiasts, these natural wonders offer more than enough adventure, so don't feel pressured to head for the caves. Cenotes are unique to this part of the world, and no two are exactly alike. The moon-shaped **Gran Cenote** is famous for its surreal mineral deposits and fantastic visibility. **Calvera** (Temple of Doom) includes three sinkholes filled with a mixture of fresh and saltwater called halocline. **Dos Ojos** (Two Eyes) is connected to the larger Nohoch Nah Chich cave system. **Caverna de Murcielagos** (Bat Cave) is a gallery of contrasts, with huge columns and smaller intricate rock formations. Whichever ones you delve into, you won't be disappointed. —JS

ⓘ **Mexico Tourism Board,** Calle 28 Mza. 4 Lote 1 Col. Ejidal, Playa del Carmen (ℂ **52/984-206-3150;** www.visitmexico. com and www.rivieramaya.com).

TOURS: Cenote Dive Center, Carretara Cancun-Tulum, across from the HSBC bank (ℂ **52/984-871-2232;** www.cenote dive.com). **Hidden Worlds,** Hwy. 307 (ℂ **52/984-877-8535;** www.hiddenworlds. com).

WHEN TO GO: Nov–Apr.

✈ Cancun airport.

🛏$$ **Ana y Jose Charming Hotel,** Carretera Cancun-Tulum Bocapaila Km 7, Tulum (ℂ **52/998-880-5629;** www.anay jose.com).

Boating **87**

Kayaking in the Sea of Cortez
Paradise Found
Baja California Sur, Mexico

The Baja peninsula is Mexico's hidden gem of solitude, biodiversity, and adventure. This finger of land jutting out into the Gulf of California, more commonly known as the Sea of Cortez, extends from the U.S. border south to Cabo San Lucas. Wild cactus-filled deserts and towering mountains meet one of the world's richest marine environments. The warm azure water is filled with whales, dolphins, sea lions, seals, manta rays, and tropical fish. Pelicans and seagulls soar through the skies and dive into the water. Hummingbirds hover from flower to flower.

Paddling through this intimate paradise is a must for intrepid travelers. There's plenty of heart-pumping activity on your kayak during the day, followed by peace and quiet as you settle into your sleeping bag on a remote beach beneath the starry sky at night. For nature lovers, it just doesn't get any better than the Sea of Cortez, home to one-third of the earth's marine mammals and hundreds of birds. Jacques Cousteau once called it the "world's aquarium." Plus, the relatively calm water makes it a great place for first-time sea kayakers to master the sport, or for experienced paddlers to embark on a long excursion.

Most kayak trips begin in **Loreto** and travel through the **Loreto Bay National Marine Park,** a UNESCO World Heritage Site. With more than 800 species of marine life and more than 600 kinds of plant species—many of them endangered—this delicate ecosystem is now protected. For more information about local conservation efforts, check out the **Nature Conservancy** (www.nature.org).

On a 5- to 10-day excursion, you'll probably stay in this part of the sea. You can circumvent **Isla Carmen** and **Isla Danzante,** tropical islands with stunning white-sand beaches, towering bluffs, and secluded caves. It's not hard to spot whales and sea lions. Each day, you'll explore different parts of the shoreline, kayaking through sheltered coves and past deserted beaches. There are plenty of chances to swim, snorkel, and take hikes through the island's spectacular canyons. If whale-watching gets your pulse going, spend a day in the federally protected **Magdalena Bay.**

If you're looking for more of a challenge and have at least 10 days, you can paddle the 105km (65-mile) stretch from Loreto to **La Paz,** past volcanic mountains rising out of the sea, red-hued desserts, sandy beaches, and plenty of wildlife. If you want to start in La Paz, you can explore the

The serene shores of the Sea of Cortez.

remote uninhabited islands of **Espiritu Santo, San Jose,** and **Catalana.** Few people have visited any of the desert islands speckling the southern part of the sea, and even fewer have seen them from the unique elbow-level perspective of a kayak. Whichever specific trip you choose, paddling yourself through any part of this open water with such mesmerizing views is an exhilarating and unforgettable adventure. —*JS*

(i) **Mexico Tourism Board,** Calle Juan Ruiz de Alarcon No. 1572 ((C) **664/682-3367;** www.visitmexico.com and www.discoverbajacalifornia.com).

TOURS: **Sea Kayak Adventures,** P.O. Box 3862, Coeur d'Alene, ID ((C) **800/616-1943;** www.seakayakadventures.com). **Baja Expeditions,** La Paz ((C) **800/843-6967;** www.bajaex.com).

WHEN TO GO: Nov–Apr.

✈ Loreto airport.

⊨ $$ **Posada de las Flores,** Av. Salvatierra y Fco y Madero s/n ((C) **52/613-135-1162;** www.posadadelasflores.com).

Kayaking to Cape Point
A Swell Time at Sea
Cape Town, South Africa

Kayaking off of Cape Point in South Africa.

Cape Town is South Africa's adventure capital. With a wide range of adventures—from abseiling off iconic Table Mountain (see ⑲④) to diving with sharks in the ocean (see ㉞④)—there's certainly no shortage of options to get your adrenaline pumping here. But if you're looking for one of the more physically challenging activities, there's nothing better than kayaking from Cape Town to Cape Point at the southern tip of Cape Peninsula.

During his intrepid voyage around the world in the 16th century, the English sea captain, Sir Francis Drake, wasn't exaggerating when he called this area "the fairest Cape we saw in the whole circumference of the earth." His words still ring true today. As the Indian and the Atlantic oceans meet, it creates prime conditions for sea kayaking and the views are breathtaking. Table Mountain rises up toward the sky and the bay sweeps into a seemingly endless coastline. Along the way, you'll also see Signal Hill, Lion's Head, and the 12 Apostles. The trip from Buffels Bay to Cape Point takes approximately 4 to 6 hours, with the option to transit around Cape Point, the Cape of Storms, and the Cape of

Good Hope. Seals and dolphins often swim alongside kayakers, and you might even see some whales in the winter. Shorter tours are also offered off the coast of Cape Town, often heading south past **Clifton Beach,** known for its white sand beaches and topaz blue water. There's abundant bird life on the rocks at Clifton, including cormorants, seagulls, and albatross.

Another incredible kayak trip departs from **Simon's Town,** a suburb of Cape Town on the peninsula's eastern side. After departing from the shores of sheltered False Bay, you'll paddle a few kilometers south to **Boulder's Beach,** where African penguins have lived since around 1985. Today, almost 2,500 of the tuxedoed birds call the beach home. On your way there, you'll go past Ark Rock, which is usually covered with sea birds. As you continue paddling through the waves toward Boulder's Beach, you'll probably hear the penguins long before you see them; their unique call carries across the water. Even though you know they're coming, your first sight of them is literally jaw dropping, as you see thousands of black-and-white birds waddling across a white sandy beach sheltered by giant granite rocks. This remarkable penguin colony is only one of two land-based colonies in South Africa; the other one is at **Betty's Bay.**

Kayaking around the southwesternmost part of Africa is sure to get your heart pounding, and not only because of the physical exertion. Paddling around the peninsula's rugged cliffs and private coves, among abundant marine life but few other people, you almost start to feel like an explorer yourself—one who would make Sir Francis Drake proud. *—JS*

ⓘ **Cape Town Tourism Information Center**, Shop 107 Clocktower, V&A Waterfront (✆ **021/405-4500**; www.tourism capetown.co.za).

TOURS: Real Cape Adventures, Cape Town (✆ **021/790-5611**; www.seakayak. co.za). **Paddler's Kayak Shop**, 62 St. Georges St., Simon's Town (✆ **021/786-262**; www.paddlers.co.za).

WHEN TO GO: Year-round, although you'll have the best chance of seeing whales from Aug–Oct; Nov–Mar brings warmer weather.

✈ Cape Town Airport.

⊨ $$ **The Cape Cadogan**, 5 Upper Union St., Cape Town (✆ **27/21-480-8080**; www.capecadogan.com).

---

89 Boating

Catamaran Sailing in Northern California
Flying Across the Golden Gate
San Francisco, California, U.S.A.

The spray is cold but I don't want to move. I'm in the front section of a two-hulled 55-foot (17m) catamaran flat on my stomach and mesmerized by the water rushing underneath me. The sun shines overhead as we fly across San Francisco Bay.

Passing Alcatraz, I sit up for a better look. "Watch your heads!" a voice calls. We all duck as the boom sweeps across the deck snapping the sails into a different position. Zigzagging from one side of the bay to the other, tacking to take advantage

Cruising across the San Francisco Bay in a catamaran is a thrill.

of the wind, the Adventure Cat sails toward the Golden Gate Bridge and the ocean beyond. Along the way, the catamaran screams past an occasional freighter, other sailboats, the Presidio, and Sausalito. When it's time to head home, the wind allows us to race back to the pier, at speeds maxing out above 13 knots. Lying back down on the bouncy trampoline that's strung between the two hulls, we all appreciate the quiet that comes with riding in a wind-powered boat.

Catamaran sailing is a simple pleasure, but it can also be exhilarating. Being a passenger on one is a great way for adventure seekers to get their thrills without having to take charge themselves, or risk their lives in the process.

Adventure Cat Sailing Charters offers two 1½-hour trips into the bay daily, plus a sunset cruise, several months out of the year. Cruises sail past the city skyline, Alcatraz, and under the Golden Gate Bridge, just touching the Pacific Ocean. (Keep an eye out for sea lions, popular in

this part of the country, though no less exciting to see because of their numbers.) The catamaran is moored near Pier 39 in San Francisco's famous Fisherman's Wharf area. While you're here, look beyond the many touristy shops to notice fisherman coiling nets on their boats tied to working piers, seagulls screeching in the sky, and the big ships passing by. —*LF*

ⓘ **San Francisco Convention & Visitors Bureau,** 900 Market St. (✆ **415/391-2000;** www.onlyinsanfrancisco.com).

TOUR: Adventure Cat Sailing Charters, Pier 39 (✆ **800/498-4228** or 415/777-1630; www.adventurecat.com).

WHEN TO GO: Early Mar through late Oct.

✈ San Francisco International.

🛏 $$$ **The Argonaut,** 495 Jefferson St. (✆ **866/415-0704** or 415/563-0800; www.argonauthotel.com). $$ **Larkspur Hotel,** 524 Sutter St. (✆ **800/919-9779** or 415/421-2865; www.larkspurhotelunionsquare.com).

Boating **90**

Kayaking Hoover Dam
Be Dammed
Boulder City, Nevada, U.S.A.

Hoover Dam has often been referred to as one of the engineering wonders of the world, and for good reason: Almost seven million tons of concrete rise 726 feet (218 m) from the bottom of Black Canyon, holding back the 247 square miles (398 sq. km) of water that make up Lake Mead. While tours of the dam are always exciting, those have been curtailed due to post-9/11 security concerns. However, it's still possible to enjoy the dam's monumental splendor from the surging water that spills over it by taking a kayak or canoeing tour of the Colorado River. Riding the water surrounding this manmade marvel

provides an awe-inspiring, adrenaline-inducing experience that will make your trip to Sin City a one-of-a-kind adventure.

Hoover Dam is just 30 miles (28km) southeast of Las Vegas, but it's a world away from the flashing lights and bing-bing-bing noise of the Strip's casinos. Most kayak tour operators will pick up guests right at their hotels. Kayaking tours depart from the bottom of Lower Portal Road at the landing just below the dam; it's a high-security area, so arrange with a licensed livery service if you're bringing your own watercraft to the landing, or simply sign on for an organized tour.

The Bureau of Reclamation (the government agency responsible for the dam) dug an exploratory cave before building Hoover Dam; that cave is now known as Sauna Cave for its warm mineral waters. In fact, numerous hot springs and hot waterfalls are located along this stretch of the Colorado River, so bring a swimsuit, as well as other action-ready gear like sunscreen, a hat, and appropriate footwear (some tour operators include water shoes in their package).

Other caves known as "rain caves" are right on the river's edge; some can be kayaked right into. And there are plenty of narrow slot canyons that make ideal hiking destinations. Whether in the water or on land, keep an eye peeled for the wildlife that frequents this area: bighorn sheep, falcons, bald eagles, and coyotes call this desert wonderland home. —ML

ⓘ **Bureau of Reclamation Lower Colorado Region** (ⓒ **702/494-2517;** www. usbr.gov/lc/hooverdam).

TOURS: Boulder City Outfitters (ⓒ **800/ 748-3702;** www.bouldercityoutfitters. com). **Desert Adventures** (ⓒ **702/293- 5026;** www.kayaklasvegas.com).

WHEN TO GO: Sept–Apr.

✈ Las Vegas (30 miles/48km).

🛏 $$ **Las Vegas Hilton,** 3000 Paradise Rd. (ⓒ **800/732-7117** or 702/732-5111; www.lvhilton.com). $$ **Luxor Las Vegas,** 3900 Las Vegas Blvd. S. (ⓒ **888/777-0188** or 702/262-4444, www.luxor.com).

---

91 Boating

Yacht Sailing in the Greek Isles
Exploring Offshore Greece
Greece

The yacht is cruising along at 10 to 15 knots. Your clothes billow with the brisk wind. The sun kisses your brow, but your steady pace keeps the sweat you're working up from lingering. You're having the time of your life. Your last name may not be Onassis, but you're still certain to revel in the special exhilaration that only sailing the Mediterranean can bring.

Sailing is a great way to visit Greece, with its 2,500 islands, wonderful people, beautiful sites and beaches, and of course, history and archaeology. By taking your hotel with you, you'll be able to avoid the crowds, especially in late summer, and find as much or as little sailing adventure as you desire.

The months of July and August provide the highest and steadiest winds along with the highest temperatures and busiest charter time, so we suggest going in early summer (May and June) for ideal sailing conditions. Sailing in the restless Aegean Sea around the Cyclades Islands and Dodecanese Islands can provide enough high-speed excitement for even the most experienced sailors. Take heed, though. The rough Aegean Sea and its winds, called the Meltemi, can sometimes be enough to drive chartered yachts to harbor and pose a significant danger to smaller bareboat (do it yourself) charters. The winds on the Ionian Sea are less dramatic winds and make for a safer location for bareboat sailing.

The multitude of yacht chartering options is almost overwhelming. You can charter a luxury yacht for a week costing more than most people pay to buy a house, or sign onto a smaller yacht for less than it would cost you for the flights within Greece and hotels—perhaps a more palatable option for those without deep pockets who are eager to spend time at sea.

Sailing also includes a ready swimming and snorkeling option.

The average size charter, which takes six to eight passengers, is approximately 15m (50 ft.) in length. Accommodations vary from berths to double cabins and a variety of meal options are available, from basic meal packages to gourmet cuisine. The incredible sunsets are thrown in for free. To maximize the number of islands you visit and to avoid tacking into the wind for days, consider a one-way charter.

Most charters provide the ability for novices to learn about sailing and for experts to brush up on their skills. Having a skipper provides you with an expert on the winds and currents, as well as an interpreter, a guide, a historian, and someone who knows the better restaurants and out of the way places.

Although they are two of the larger, more popular islands, **Santorini (Thira)** in the Cyclades and **Rhodes** in the Dodecanese still top the list of must-see islands. The west side of Santorini is a huge volcanic caldera which is so large that your yacht is little more than a speck when seen from the cliffs 300m (1,000 ft.) above. I particularly like the village of Oia on Santorini with its blue painted church domes and cave

houses. (Try to avoid visiting when the cruise ship hordes have descended on the island.) A trip to the caldera with a hike to the top is worthwhile. The Dodecanese Islands, which are a bit off the beaten path, can provide some exciting sailing mid-summer with steady winds of around 20 knots. The old city of Rhodes, where car traffic is forbidden, is surrounded by a high stone wall and provides you the opportunity to walk the same alleys the Knights Hospitallers (a religious military order) walked between 1309 and 1522. Hire one of the many private guides, such as **Rhodes Private Tours** (www.rhodesprivatetours. com) for a few hours to tour the restored castle and surrounding area. —LF

ⓘ www.sailingissues.com.

TOURS: Seascape Sailing (ⓒ **70/085-877-112;** www.seascape-sail.com/home). **Easy Sailing Ltd.**, 10 Poseidonos Ave. (ⓒ **30/210- 985936;** www.easysailing.gr).

WHEN TO GO: Mid-May through mid-June to avoid the heat and crowds.

✈ Athens International Airport; Corfu Airport; Heraklion Airport (Crete); or Rhodes International Airport.

Boating **92**

Kayaking Around Remote Islands
Paddling Spectacular Waters
Hebrides Islands, Scotland

You're quietly paddling along with your hand only a few inches from the water's surface in a craft designed by the Inuits thousands of years ago. To your left, on the crest of a small wave, a sea otter floats on its back enjoying lunch. There pops a seal's head less than 3m (10 ft.) away, almost startling you into tipping your sea kayak. Then, as you're heading toward land, you find yourself in the midst of a pod

of porpoises. You are sea kayaking in the magnificent Hebrides Islands of Scotland.

The Hebrides is a 241km-long (150-mile) chain of islands in the North Sea, approximately 81km (50 miles) off the west coast of Scotland. Sea kayaking in the Hebrides can take you to sand dune-fringed islands and islands with cliffs that explode straight up out of the water for hundreds of feet. The extraordinary sights are as varied as the numerous sea kayak operations that ply the Outer Hebrides waters.

One such operation is **Clearwater Paddling,** based on the island of Bara, which has a population of less than 1,500 Gaelic speaking Scots. Clearwater offers opportunities for beginners—who are taught bracing to keep the kayak upright and the Eskimo roll for unassisted righting—and more experienced paddlers. Clearwater will provide equipment or you can bring your own. All trips are guided.

Recreational paddlers can do day trips in the **Blue Lagoon,** paddle out to the ruins of **Kisimul Castle,** or head to the remote island of **Vatersay,** among numerous other trip options. More experienced paddlers can take a multi-day trip called the **Wild Hebridean Journey** to some of the more remote southern islands and see some great wildlife. One planned trip goes to the coast of Jura, known for its wildlife (especially deer); and another to Mull, one of the more touristed but mysterious islands.

If you go to Barra, be sure to check the schedule of the annual music festival and the annual games. —*LF*

ⓘ **Visit Hebrides** (www.visithebrides. com); **Isle of Barra** (www.fromscotland. com/barra/introduction.html).

TOURS: Clearwater Paddling (✆ 01871-810-443; www.clearwaterpaddling.com). **Adventure Hebrides** (✆ 44/1851-820 726; www.adventurehebrides.com). **Uist Outdoor Centre** (✆44/1876-500480; www.uistoutdoorcentre.co.uk).

WHEN TO GO: Spring, summer, and fall.

✈ Barra Airport. Flybe Airlines from Glasgow and Benbecula (✆ **0871 700 053;** www.flybe.com).

🛳 **Caledonian MacBrayne Ferries** (✆ **08000 665000;** www.calmac.co.uk) crosses from Oban to Barra.

🛏 $$ **Dunardlodge,** Castle Bay (✆ **01871-810-443;** www.dunardlodge. co.uk). $ **The Isle of Barra Beach Hotel,** Tangasdale (✆ **01871-810383;** www. isleofbarrahotel.co.uk). $ **Craigard Hotel,** Castlebay (✆ **01871-810200;** www. craigardhotel.co.uk).

93 Boating

Kayaking in the Andaman Sea
Paddling Through Mangroves
Krabi, Thailand

We were paddling slowly in our sea kayak alongside the limestone cliffs and through the mangroves of the Adaman Sea on the West Coast of the Southern Peninsula of Thailand. One of our guides spotted a monkey in the trees and a member of our group pulled a banana from her bag. The monkey jumped down, swam to the kayak—Will swim for food!—jumped aboard, and grabbed the banana. He grabbed her bag, too, and jumped back in the water. The bag sank as the monkey swam back to shore.

Except for that funny and unpredictable incident, gliding through the mangroves near Krabi is an extremely tranquil experience. And yet it's completely exhilarating. The current is gentle, the water is flat, and paddling is easy, but you never really know what you'll see around the next bend. This entire area is an ancient reef that's been weathered and eroded for eons by water and wind. The limestone islands with straight walled cliffs are filled with hidden lagoons, tunnels, and caves,

On the water in Thailand.

many of which have enthralling stalactites; others have ancient aboriginal drawings. Keep an eye out for wildlife, like birds of prey, monitor lizards, and possibly even monkeys. Each site is more interesting than the one before, leaving a lasting impression of this beautiful region. When (or if) you tire of just seeing the sights, take a more active approach. On our trip, the tide went out as we were paddling and sandbars became accessible. We beached the kayaks, had a great swim, and snorkeled before shoving off again.

Your best option is to do this trip with a guide (we've listed a couple of outfitters below), unless you know the region well and are an experienced kayaker. With a guide, even children and first-time kayakers will enjoy the trip.

Water-lovers will adore Krabi for more than just its kayaking. Less touristy than Phuket, the beaches are pristine with soft white sand. You can spend your days lounging, or take a cruise among the more than 150 mostly uninhabited islands. You can even hire a boat to take you to **Phang Nga Bay** and the island where the James Bond movie *The Man with the Golden Gun* was filmed. (The bay is stunning, but the island is now a tourist stop.)

The waters around Krabi are clear and ideal for snorkeling and diving. There are approximately 40 licensed dive operations around Krabi and they'll take you on dives to see gorgeous coral, leopard and whale sharks, moray eels, dolphins, and turtles. Rock climbing is also popular and available to novices and serious climbers. In the evening, don't miss going to one of the restaurants on the beach, where you can pick out your freshly caught fish and have it prepared for your dinner. —*LF*

ⓘ **Krabi Tourism** (www.krabi.com). **One Stop Krabi** (www.1stopkrabi.com).

TOURS: Sea Kayak Krabi (✆ **66/75-630-270;** www.krabidir.com/seakayakrabi). **Sea Canoe Thailand** (✆ **66/76-528-839-40;** www.seacanoe.net).

WHEN TO GO: Nov–Mar.

✈ Krabi Airport.

🏨 $$ **Red Ginger Chic Resort,** 168 Moo 3 T. Ao Nang (✆ **66/75-637-999;** www.redgingerkrabi.com). $$ **Sheraton Krabi Beach Resort,** 155 Moo 2, Nong Thale, Musang (✆ **66/75-628000;** www.sheratonhotels.com).

Bareboatin' in Tortola
Going Where the Wind Takes You
British Virgin Islands

In the opinion of many travelers, a "bareboat" vacation—in which you and your companions charter a sailboat for a week or so, load it with provisions, and head wherever the trade winds and your imagination take you—is the ultimate way to explore any island chain. And there's no better place to launch your own sailing adventure than in the bareboat capital of the world: Tortola, the largest (19×4.8km/12×3 miles) and most populous of the British Virgin Islands.

In terms of convenience, safety, affordability, and sheer number of attractive places to drop anchor, the 60-plus islands and cays of B.V.I. are tailor-made for the do-it-yourself island hopper. The capital of the British Virgin Islands, **Road Town,** nestled on Tortola's mountainous southern coast (the island's beaches are all on the northern, Atlantic side), is home to dozens of charter companies with well-maintained catamarans and single-hulled boats to choose from. (Powerboats and full-sized yachts with crew are also available.) Sail out of the town's well-protected natural harbor, and you'll find yourself a couple of hours away from **Norman, Peter,** and **Cooper islands,** all awaiting with white-sand beaches, reefs perfect for snorkeling, sheltered coves for anchoring overnight, and waterfront bars and restaurants that cater to the seaborne set. The larger islands of Virgin Gorda, to the northeast, and Jost Van Dyke, off Tortola's northern flank, are both less than a day's sail away. Scattered about are scores of uninhabited islets that are yours for the claiming.

The key to any successful bareboat vacation is advance planning. Charter companies all ask you to submit a "sailing resume" proving you have enough experience to handle their boats. The official B.V.I. tourist site, **www.bvitourism.com,** has a long list of reputable charter companies with links to their websites. While prices vary, bareboat vacations tend to be remarkably affordable, typically costing about as much as a cruise. If you're worried about rusty sailing skills, you can charter a boat with an extra sleeping space or two and pay for your own skipper and cook. In addition to knowing the best spots to drop anchor, the crews-for-hire in Tortola are also accustomed to blending in with new boat mates. For a little extra, you can even request a captain who's a certified sailing instructor.

Sailors aren't the only active travelers enjoying Tortola's sparkling seas. Divers and snorkelers have much to explore here, most notably the wreck of the **HMS Rhone,** a British Royal Mail steam packet ship that sank here in an October storm in 1867. The wreck lies in depths from 6 to 24m (20–79 ft.) just south of Tortola near Salt Island. Reserve a dive with **Blue Water Divers** (© **284/494-2847;** www.bluewaterdiversbvi.com) to the site of the Rhone and other gems of the deep.

For those who prefer to spend their time on solid ground, Tortola has its share of fine resorts and villas, all imbued with the relaxed, friendly, non–theme park atmosphere (no casinos here, thank you!) for which the B.V.I. are known. The beaches on Tortola are actually quite wonderful, from popular **Cane Garden Bay,** wrapped in soft green hills, to the secluded sands of **Long Bay,** where you can swim and snorkel in clear, gentle seas.

With half its income coming from tourism and the other half from the financial industry (the island is headquarters to many of the world's offshore companies), and a currency based on U.S. dollars, Tortola is an enchanting blend of old world and new. And when you're out in the archipelago, the wind filling your sails, it's all yours to discover. —AF

ⓘ www.bvitourism.com.

TOURS: Moorings, Wickham's Cay (ⓒ **888/ 952-8420** or 284/494-2331 in the B.V.I.; www.moorings.com).

✈ Tortola: Beef Island International Airport, connected to Tortola by the Queen Elizabeth Bridge.

🚢 Regular ferries from St. Thomas, U.S.V.I. (45 min.).

🛏 $ **Ole Works Inn,** Cane Garden Bay (ⓒ **284/495-4837;** www.quitorymer.com). $$$ **The Sugar Mill,** Apple Bay (ⓒ **800/ 462-8834** in the U.S., or 284/495-4355 in the B.V.I.; www.sugarmillhotel.com).

Boating 95

Sea Kayaking the Maine Coast
Paddling Among Lobster Pots
Maine, U.S.A.

The salty smell of the ocean tickles your nose. A harbor seal pops up out of the water and eyes the boat before ducking back under with a loud splash. The raucous screeching of gulls soaring overhead is a counterpoint to the chugging sound of lobster boats passing by. Eagles, osprey, loons, and cormorants decorate the sky. Lobster pots bobbing in the water, weather-beaten houses along the islands' shorelines, and pine-studded **Acadia National Park** (www.nps.gov/acad) in the distance all vie for attention as you kayak along Maine's coastline. The scenery is quintessentially Maine. And you're thrilled to be experiencing it all from your kayak.

This vantage point is peaceful, yet exhilarating. If you kayak when the water is smooth, you may feel as though you're flying through the harbor and around the many islands that lie just off the coast of Maine. But, when the wind kicks the waves up you stop thinking about the scenery

because your entire being is focused on paddling. The combination of exercise, stunning surroundings, and communion with nature is what makes kayaking here such an extraordinary experience.

Kayaking these parts is popular both with locals and tourists, so trips come in several styles. You can rent a kayak and take it out for a few hours, take an all-day guided kayak tour, do a sunset or a wildlife paddle, or a multi-day trip. If you've never been kayaking, guides will quickly give you basic instructions on how to paddle. Many of the tours are in two-person kayaks. Experienced kayakers may opt for a solo kayak. Many outfitters along the coast offer rentals, so seasoned kayakers can pick up a lunch, a kayak, and safety gear, and start exploring.

Coastal Kayaking Tours, based in Bar Harbor on **Mount Desert Island,** runs tours around the island, most often among the rugged Porcupine Islands of Frenchman

Kayaking in Acadia National Park.

Bay. This company offers half- and full-day tours, 5-hour solo tours, family half-day tours, sunset tours, and 3-day island camping expeditions. **Maine Kayak,** based in New Harbor, offers half- and full-day trips, sunset and wildlife trips, plus 2-day trips that include camping overnight on a remote island. Maine Kayak also offers 2- and 4-day "Inn-to-Inn" kayak trips, which include paddling along the coastline, exploring inlets and islands, and spending the nights in different B&Bs. Whichever tour you choose—or even if you just take a boat out for an afternoon paddle—you're sure to remember this breathtaking landscape for a long time to come. — *LF*

(i) **Hulls Cove Visitor Center,** Rte. 3 ((C) **207/288-3338;** www.nps.gov/acad).

TOURS: Coastal Kayak Tours, 48 Cottage St., Bar Harbor ((C) **800/526-8615** in the U.S. or Canada or 207/288-9605; www.acadiafun.com). **Maine Kayak,** 113 Huddle Rd., New Harbor ((C) **866/624-6352** in the U.S. or Canada or 207/948-5194; www.mainekayak.com).

WHEN TO GO: June–Aug.

✈ Portland, Maine or Trenton, just across the causeway from Mount Desert Island.

🛏 $ **Bar Harbor Campground,** 409 State Hwy. 3, Salisbury Cove ((C) **207/288-5185**). $$$ **Harborside Hotel & Marina,** 55 West St., Bar Harbor ((C) **800/328-5033** or 207/288-5033; www.theharborside hotel.com).

Night Kayaking in Mosquito Bay
Droplets of Water Sparkle Like Diamonds
Vieques, Puerto Rico, U.S.A.

It was a cloudy, moonless night. In the dark water below streaks of light flashed and disappeared. As our kayak glided slowly along a blue-green eerie glow surrounded us. We were at Mosquito Bay, on the south coast of Vieques, Puerto Rico, one of the most bioluminescent bodies of water in the world.

Most scuba divers who have gone night diving have witnessed bioluminescence. You turn off your lamps, wave an arm, and see a flashing of light. Mosquito Bay takes this to the extreme limits and the effects are gorgeous. Bioluminescence is caused by millions of microscopic, harmless creatures called dinoflagelates, which emit a small flash of light (think microscopic lightening bug) when disturbed. The trail of light under our boat was the result of a fish that swam by—not to mention all the commotion our kayak set off as it coasted through the water. When I lifted my paddle out of the waves, the droplets of water sparkled like tiny diamonds with light passing through them. Raindrops, too, can create this magical effect, but perhaps the most fun of all is swimming in the warm bay and having the water all around you glow as you move. This is an adventure kids will enjoy as much as adults. It's an experience they'll never forget.

A palm-lined white sand beach in Vieques.

The island of Vieques, which was once a pirate haven, is approximately 8 miles (13km) off the shore of Puerto Rico's mainland. After locals got the U.S. Navy to relinquish the 70% of the island that it was using as a military testing ground, tourists slowly started to find Vieques and its unique Mosquito Bay. Many visitors claim the best thing to do on the island is nothing, but with the water beckoning, it's hard to stay still for long. On dry land, a visit to the restored **El Fortin Condo de Mirasol,** the old Spanish fort built in the 1840s that is now a museum, is worthwhile. **El Faro Punta Mulas,** a restored lighthouse with a small museum, provides a great view of the area. Many tourists rent four-wheel drive vehicles and head to remote beaches. **Blue Beach** is excellent for snorkeling. If you need the casinos and shopping, you can always take the ferry to the mainland. —LF

(i) **Vieques Island** (www.viequestravel guide.com; www.enchanted-isle.com).

TOUR: Abe's Snorkeling and Bio Bay Tours ((C) 787/741-2134; www.abes snorkeling.com).

WHEN TO GO: Nov–Dec.

✈ Isla de Vieques Airport or San Juan Airport.

🚌 Isabel Segunda (1¼ hr. from Fajardo, P.R.).

🏨 $$ **The Crow's Nest,** Rte. 201, Barrio Florida ((C) 877/CROWS-NEST [276-9763] or 787/741-0033; www.crowsnestvieques. com). $$ **Trade Winds Guesthouse,** Calle Flamboyan 107, Esperanza ((C) 787/ 741-8666; www.enchanted-isle.com/ tradewinds). $$$ **W Retreat and Spa,** S R. 200 ((C) 787/741-4100; www.starwood hotels.com/whotels).

97 Boating

On the Water in Iceland
Paddling in Serene Fjords
Iceland

Paddling in the Hvalfjorour fjord, in western Iceland, you're surrounded by mountains that rise more than 960m (3,200 ft.) above the sea. The water is quiet and the scenery dramatic along the coastline. Sneaking in a few hours of sea kayaking, within an easy drive (approximately 24km/15 miles) from Reykjavik, will make your trip to Iceland all the more memorable. Getting out of the city and into the throes of nature is a sure fire way to excite the explorer in you.

Arctic Adventures, who run kayaking expeditions, also run an adventurous 5-day Fire Island Exploration trip throughout the summer, which includes river rafting, sea kayaking, snorkeling in the **Silfra Fissure,** as well as horseback riding, hiking, and visits to the **Golden Circle** and

the **Blue Lagoon.** A trip with them is anything but boring.

If you're interested in exploring Iceland from the water but don't want to do all the work yourself, call a yacht home base. Check into **Borea Adventures'** trip on the 18m (60-ft.) *Aurora*, which travels to the remote fjords and coves of the **Hornstrandir Nature Reserve** (www.ust.is) in the West Fjords of northwest Iceland, a perfect jumping-off point for sea kayaking tours. Here, you can paddle all day between anchorages or take the kayaks onboard and sail to different locations. The bird cliffs and lush valleys ensure vivid scenery. While kayaking or hiking along the coast or in the mountains, be sure to keep an eye out for arctic foxes, seals, whales, and porpoises. Your stops will

Steam rises from the Blue Lagoon in Iceland.

include Hornbjarg bird cliffs, Vigur Puffin Island, Leirufjörður with Drangajökull ice cap and glacier river, and Reykjanes hot springs. Even if your yacht outing does not offer a formal sea kayaking trip, there will likely be kayaks onboard. For travelers looking to be more self-reliant, Borea Adventures also offers kayak trips where guests camp in the fjords and bays of the Hornstrandir Nature Reserve. While previous paddling experience isn't vital, you need to be in good physical condition to take these trips.

During Iceland's summer, you can go hiking or biking among frozen lava flows, glaciers, and lakes. Take a whale-watching tour and look for minke, blue, and humpback whales, dolphins, and harbor porpoises. You can also go riding on sure-footed horses that will take you over grassy plains, up and down rocky slopes, through rivers, and over fields of rough lava. You can play golf under the midnight sun, go caving,

canoeing, diving, and trekking. Your outfitter will be determined by which activities you're looking for. **Visit Iceland** (see below) can recommend operators who specialize in the various sports and tours. Iceland has a reputation for being cold, but with all these adventurous options, you're sure to find something that warms your heart. —*LF*

ⓘ **Visit Iceland** (www.visiticeland.com).

TOURS: Arctic Adventures, Laugavegur 11, #101 (✆ **354/562-7000;** www.adventures.is/Iceland/Kayaking). **Borea Adventures,** Hildarvegur 38, 400 Isafjordur (✆ **354/869-7557;** www.boreaadventures.com).

WHEN TO GO: Summer.

✈ Reykjavik.

🛏 $$$ **Icelandia,** Tungata 34 (✆ **354/534-0444;** www.icelandia.com). $$$ **CenterHotel Klöpp,** Klapparstígur 26 (✆ **354/595-8520;** www.centerhotels.com).

98 Boating

Touring Musandam Peninsula by Dhow
Arabian Dreams at Sea
Khasab, Oman

The Musandam Peninsula at Oman's rugged northern tip is one of the Middle East's best-kept secrets. Just 2 or 3 hours by car from cosmopolitan Dubai, this secluded piece of land is ripe for adventure. For the most thrilling overview of the area, travel around for a few days on a dhow—a small wooden sailing vessel traditionally used for commercial journeys to transport goods such as dates, fish, and timber between the Persian Gulf and East Africa. Today, the small boats offer a unique way to visit places that would otherwise be unreachable.

Khasab—the peninsula's largest town and a picturesque one, set among date palms—is the launching point for any trip at sea. As you drive there from Dubai, a good place to stop along the way is the emirate of **Sharjah,** just north of Dubai. There are several interesting museums, shops, and traditional buildings to explore in Sharjah City, deemed a UNESCO World Heritage Site in 1998 for its commitment to preserving its Arab art, culture, and heritage. Continuing your ride along the Gulf's waters is a perfect tease for the epic sailing adventure that comes next.

After an overnight in Khasab, it's time to board your dhow. Plenty of tour operators offer short cruises, but adrenaline seekers will want to book a longer trip where you travel farther around the peninsula, sleeping beneath the stars on the dhow's deck or camping out on remote beaches for a couple of nights. (Typically, there aren't any cabins on board, but a basic toilet and shower are available.) Food and water are kept on the dhow, as well as provisions to make cups of customary mint tea.

During the day, eagles and falcons soar through the sky while dolphins and brightly colored fish glide through the azure waters.

You can even hop off the dhow at times to swim or snorkel along with them. You'll pass **Telegraph Island,** a rocky outcrop that was once home to British telegraph officers when the first telegraph message was supposedly sent through here in 1865. Today, however, the fiord is a military base that's off limits to visitors, and the best view of its mostly barren landscape is from your dhow.

On day two, you'll sail up the east coast to **Kumzar,** one of the most isolated communities on the peninsula; it can be reached only by boat or helicopter. A mixture of Arabic and Farsai is spoken, demonstrating the influence of nearby Iran. From here, the dhow will continue north past narrow inlets and sweeping bays to **Habliyan Beach.** After a good night's sleep, you'll head back south to a small bay and disembark the boat for a scenic mountain drive to Khasab. Spend the afternoon exploring, and don't miss the town's famous well-preserved fort, built by the Portuguese more than four centuries ago. —*JS*

ⓘ **Oman Ministry of Tourism,** Madinat Al-Sultan Qaboos, Muscat (✆ **968/24-588-700;** www.omantourism.gov.om).

TOURS: GAP Adventures, 19 Charlotte St., Toronto (✆ **800/708-7761;** www.gapadventures.com). **Khasab Travel & Tours,** P.O. Box 50, Khasab 811 (✆ **968/26-73-0464;** www.khasabtours.com).

WHEN TO GO: Oct–Mar.

✈ Dubai International Airport.

⊨ $$ **Golden Tulip Khasab Hotel Resort,** P.O. Box 434, Khasab (✆ **968/26-73-0777;** www.goldentulipkhasab.com).

Sailing from Argentina to Antarctica
The Cold Rush
Ushuaia, Argentina to Antarctica

The distant, icy, uninhabited expanse of Antarctica has tempted intrepid explorers since the 19th century. In the 1820s, two sealers first stepped foot on "the White Continent," but it wasn't until 1911 that anyone reached the South Pole. Roald Amundsen was the first to get there, although he and his team tragically froze to death on their return trip. They were discovered when Robert Falcon Scott and his team reached the same point 33 days later. In 1915, Ernest Shackleton deemed Antarctica "the last great journey left to man" and attempted to cross the continent. Ice ultimately trapped and sank his boat, but he and his team miraculously survived. His daring voyage highlighted the enormous danger of trying to reach the bottom of the earth, but also the area's alluring mystique. Less than 100 years later, this freezing cold continent has become one of the world's hottest adventure destinations. It's the purest stretch of wilderness in the world.

Of course, sailing to Antarctica isn't a typical cruise. It isn't cheap or easy, but that's part of the adventure. And it's sure to be one of the most incredible experiences of your life. This is not the time to pack light, though. You'll want to pile in the polar fleeces, thermal underwear, hand and feet warmers, a giant down-filled waterproof parka, anti–motion sickness medication, and sunblock. The sun typically shines for 18 to 24 hours each day.

Choose a relatively small vessel that takes no more than 100 passengers, and plan to book a trip that lasts at least 10 or 12 days. Also, try to find an active itinerary that includes options to get off the main boat, such as kayaking, camping, mountaineering, and cross-country skiing.

Almost all ships going to Antarctica depart from **Ushuaia,** the southernmost city on earth. But the routes they take from there differ, and smaller vessels can explore more off-the-beaten path areas. After your departure from Argentina, it takes about 2 days to cross the arduous **Drake Passage** (and another 2 days on the return). There's not much to do during this leg of the trip besides hang out, relax, and attend some educational lectures. Once you reach the **Antarctic Peninsula,** you'll have a chance to get out and start exploring the icy kingdom. Almost all tours stop at the **South Shetland Islands,** home to research base stations, colonies of elephant seals, and a variety of nesting penguins and sea birds. From here, you'll probably continue to the eastern side of the peninsula, pausing to gaze at wildlife like lounging seals and gasp at the giant icebergs floating by.

To get a closer look, you can hop in a kayak or a Zodiac (inflatable boat) and float right beside these jagged glacial sculptures. It's like entering another world. Snowy mountains sparkle beneath pink light and ice extends as far as the eye can see. You'll feel dwarfed by the endless white and blue panorama surrounding you.

After getting back on the main ship and traveling through the narrow, sheer-walled ice canals of **Lemaire Channel,** you might stop at **Paradise Bay,** where blue icebergs crash from the harbor's main glacier. The penguin havens on **Cuverville Islands** are well worth visiting with your camera. You'll ooh and aw at the penguins' endearing interactions with each other. Wherever you venture next, perhaps even into the **Polar Circle,** this pristine wonderland remains as powerful today as it must have been to its first explorers. —*JS*

ⓘ **International Association of Antarctica Tour Operators** (✆ **401/272-2152;** www.iaato.org).

TOURS: Quark Expeditions, Norwalk, CT (✆ **203/803-2888;** www.quarkexpeditions.com). **Geographic Expeditions,** San Francisco, CA (✆ **800/777-8183;** www.geoex.com).

WHEN TO GO: Nov–Mar.

✈ International Airport Malvinas Argentinas.

⊨ $$ **Los Acebos,** Av. Luis Fernando Martial 1911, Ushuaia (✆ **54/29-01-430-710;** www.losacebos.com.ar).

100 **Boating**

Hawaiian Sailing Canoe Adventures
Sailing into Hawaii's Heritage
Wailea, Maui, Hawaii, U.S.A.

Slicing through the waves in a "Hina," a Hawaiian outrigger sailing canoe, you realize how vast the ocean is and get a taste of how the original Hawaiians must have felt as they sailed 2,600 miles (4,000km) across open sea from islands in the South Pacific to reach what we now call Hawaii. When the wind dies, everyone in the canoe grabs paddles and pitches in with full-bodied strokes until the Hina reaches a mooring spot on a coral reef. From here, you can jump into the water and take in the tropical aquatic splendor surrounding you— the colorful coral, the green sea turtle on the ocean bottom, the red urchins and the multi-hued fish swimming past. Looking back at the island from which you set sail, **Haleakala,** the dormant volcano that

Whales surface close by a sailing canoe off Maui.

climbs up to 10,028 feet (3,008m) above sea level, towers over the white-sand beaches lined with hotels. Between the racing boat, the lush sea life all around you, and the dramatic view of the island, the excitement swells inside you.

Our pick for your outrigger sailing canoe experience is **Hawaiian Sailing Canoe Adventures,** run by a Hawaiian-grown husband and wife team who love the water. Sage Spalding took his first canoe ride when he was 10 years old and at 16 competed in his first sailing canoe race from Oahu to Kauai. Liz took up surfing as a teenager, before learning to sail. The two met at the California Maritime Academy. During the 2-hour sail with this duo, the two pass on to their guests their love of Hawaiian history, culture, and traditions. The Hawaiian outrigger canoes have a lot of "Kauna,"—hidden meaning—because it's a symbol of how the Hawaiians came here. Sage explains, "The Hawaiian word for the hull of the canoe is 'kino,' which translates to body. It reminds us to be 'pono,' which means righteous, and to 'malama,' or take good care of our bodies so that when we are hundreds of miles out to sea we can depend on our bodies to get us back to shore." By the time guests return to land—having seen breaching humpback whales and dolphins swimming by—they have a better understanding how the early seafarers must have experienced life in their 100-foot (30m) canoes.

Hawaiian Sailing Canoe Adventures earned the Hawaii Ecotourism Association's Ecotour Operator of the Year 2009 award. Every trip they run is a bit different, because the destination depends upon which way the wind is blowing. The Hina, which is now made of fiberglass instead of the traditional wood, holds up to six passengers plus the Spaldings. The trips leave from the beach in front of the Fairmont Kea Lani. Join them for an extraordinary sailing adventure, and go where the wind takes you. —*LF*

ⓘ **Hawaii Sailing Canoe Adventures** (✆ **808/281-9301;** www.mauisailing canoe.com).

WHEN TO GO: Year-round. Whale season is Nov–Apr.

✈ Kahului, Maui.

🛏 $$$ **Fairmont Kea Lani,** 4100 Wailea Analui Dr. (✆ **866/540-4456** or 808/875-4100; www.fairmont.com/kealani). $ **Dreams Come True on Maui,** 3259 Akala Dr., Kihei (✆ **808/879-7099;** www.dreamscometrueonmaui.com).

Boating **101**

Sampo Arctic Icebreaker
Swimming Among the Ice Floes
Bay of Bothnia, Finland

Try to remember the last time you dug windshield wipers out from under thick ice, or hacked hard frost from the sides of an old freezer, or even chipped apart a stubborn ice block for cocktails. Now imagine riding an Arctic icebreaker, designed to ram and bash its way through a sea-wide sheet of frozen brine. To call the experience pleasant would be a stretch, but the sheer power of the operation, the infernal crunch and splash of ice disintegrating, and the bitter cold on your face does get your heart pumping. And that's *before* you've dunked into the brutally frigid water below.

My Arctic adventure began in **Kemi,** a small Finnish town in the Lapland region on the Arctic Circle. In the middle of Kemi's deep-water harbor, the Bay of Bothnia, an icebreaker called the *Sampo* lay frozen in place. We rode snowmobiles over the ice to reach it. Once aboard, we stood by the rail and watched as the boat's massive engines revved and the *Sampo* slowly started churning through its frozen berth, cutting a path just wide enough to take us farther into the bay.

While the boat gouged its way through the ice, we toured the interior, checked out the massive engines that allow similar ships to keep Finnish trade moving during the winter, and learned how the *Sampo* works and how it came into the world. Built in 1920, it was used for nearly 30 years to keep shipping lanes free of ice in the northern Bay of Bothnia, at the northern reach of the Baltic Sea. Today, it conveys tourists from the middle of December through the end of April. A full-day adventure on the *Sampo* includes snowmobiling, the icebreaker cruise, and a reindeer sleigh ride. (You can walk away with a reindeer driver's license after a bit of training.)

A nourishing Finnish lunch in the warm onboard restaurant prepared us for the sensory overload to come. By now the ship had plowed through enough ice that we could swim among the smashed up chunks. The crew positioned steps down to the ice, and the most adventurous among us,

dressed in vibrant orange waterproof thermal suits, lowered into the 0° F (–32°C) water. At first we tried not to splash, but we soon gave up and got to experience the profound coldness on our faces. As we floated on our backs, laughing and splashing each other's suits, other passengers strolled around ship. A few took turns riding a reindeer sled.

When it was time to go, we clambered back onboard in ungainly motions before taking off the suits. As the ship surged upward then back down to the sound of cracking ice, almost everyone was glued to windows or standing on the deck watching the Northern Lights color the skyline. Finally, we hopped back on the snowmobiles to head back to land.

Kemi affords year-round adventure—skiing, snowmobiling, dog sledding, and reindeer safari in winter, or fishing, river rafting, kayaking, trekking, and boating in summer. But for sheer rush factor, nothing beats a dip in the brackish Arctic deep. —*LF*

ⓘ **Visit Finland** (www.visitfinland.com).

WHEN TO GO: Mid-Dec to late Apr.

✈ Kemi, a 1-hr. flight from Helsinki.

🛏 $$ **SnowHotel,** SnowCastle Kemi, Kauppakatu 16 (✆ **016/259-502;** www.snowcastle.net/en/snowhotel).

---

102 **Boating**

Sailing Tall Ships
Steering a World-Class Racing Yacht
Whitsunday Islands, Australia

I've just taken the helm of a refurbished former world-class racing yacht and I'm cruising around some of the 74 mostly uninhabited **Whitsunday Islands,** which lie along Australia's Queensland coast in the Coral Sea. The sails have been trimmed and there doesn't appear to be a breath of air, but we're still moving at almost 6 knots. This

is one of the many former racing yachts you can charter for 1, 2, or multi-day trips to the islands bordered by the Great Barrier Reef and providing miles of sheltered water for ideal sailing. With the wind in my hair, the sun on my brow, and the yacht at my command, I sail on—a thrilling experience for anyone who loves boating or the sea.

Sailing in the Whitsunday Islands.

You can ride the rails on mono-hulled Maxi Racers such as the *Matador, British Defender,* or *Spank Me. Matador* is a 26m (85-ft.) high-tech racer that was undefeated in more than 50 races. The *British Defender* is a 25m (83-ft.) high-tech yacht raced by the British Armed Services in an Around the World Race. *Spank Me* won the 1990 Sidney to Hobart Race in 1990. For those that prefer a boat that doesn't heal over, the 20m (67-ft.) trimaran, *Avatar,* is a screamer that rides flat.

For those excited and anxious to get hands-on sailing experience, most of these charters provide instruction and the opportunity to raise, lower, and trim the sails, take the helm, or just relax, enjoy the ride, and search for local dolphins or whales. Depending upon the charter you choose, you can snorkel or dive from the yacht, or arrange a rendezvous with a dive boat and dive the Great Barrier Reef. When you contact an operator make certain that you specify the type of trip you want, ask what you should bring aboard. Many of the boats provide drinking water, but soft drinks and alcohol are BYO. Food is provided. Also check out the sleeping and bathroom accommodations. Don't expect a private cabin or bath. For those who don't want to overnight, day trips are available with several operators.

For those that wish another sailing experience, century old, wood-deck tall ships such as the *Solway Lass* are available for charter. Get up in the rigging and reef the sails. For experienced sailors there are numerous bareboat (sail it yourself) charters. Most of the boats are in the 9 to 12m (30–40-ft.) range, with numerous Catalinas and Bavarias available. Crews can be arranged for some of the larger boats.

The Whitsunday Islands are the closest point between Queensland and the Great Barrier Reef. Diving and snorkeling opportunities are abundant in the area and trips to the Reef for diving can be arranged. Big game fishing, ATV trips, and golf are also available. —LF

(i) **Whitsunday Tourism** (℗ **1300-717-407;** www.whitsundaytourism.com).

TOURS: Blue Paradise Sailing (www.blueparadisesailing.com.au). **Southern Cross Sailing Adventures** (℗ **61/7/4946 4999;** www.soxsail.com.au).

WHEN TO GO: Apr–Nov; best whale-watching is July–Sept.

✈ Whitsunday Coast Airport, Proserpine, and Hamilton Island Airport.

🛏 $$ **Long Island Resort,** Whitsunday Passage (℗ **61/7/3391-2890;** www.long islandresort.com.au). $–$$ **Summit Apartments Airlie Beach,** 15 Flame Tree Court (℗ **61/7/4946- 3400;** www.summit airliebeach.com.au).

Jet Boating on Swan River
A Wet & Wild Ride
Perth, Australia

Perth is one of the most isolated cities in the world. Set on the westernmost coast of Australia, it's more than 3,220km (2,000 miles) from any other major city in the world and separated from Sydney by a vast continental desert. But its setting makes it one of Australia's best cities for outdoor enthusiasts—and water lovers in particular. A Mediterranean climate, an abundance of parkland, and a vast public waterfront along Swan River and the Indian Ocean create a natural oasis in an urban environment. Scuba diving and surfing are popular pursuits on the sea. Sailing, water-skiing, and boating are constant activities on the river.

Of the many ways to get wet when you visit Perth, the most exhilarating is a jet boat ride. As you speed through Swan River for 25 minutes, with an upbeat soundtrack blasting from the speakers, you'll experience a mixture of 360-degree spins, wild fish tails, and amazing power brake stops. At full power, a 9m (30 ft.) vessel that seats 14 passengers can reach nearly 80kmph (50 mph). Hold on tight and keep your eyes peeled to catch a glimpse of the city's famous **Kings Park and Botanic Garden** (www.bgpa.wa.gov.au) and **Old Swan Brewery** (www.oldswan brewery.com.au) as you race past.

If this rousing tour sparked your curiosity about the history of the area's waterways, you can learn more at the **Western Australia Maritime Museum** (www. museum.wa.gov.au/maritime) on Victoria Quay in Fremantle. Or, if you'd rather stay close to the river, take a long walk or bike ride on the path running along its shore.

When you've had enough fun in the city, take a side trip into the countryside. The **Swan Valley vineyards** are just about 20 minutes away from downtown. For a slightly farther-flung excursion, take a 3-hour drive to explore wineries in the gorgeous **Margaret River** area. Whatever you do in Western Australia, you'll be wowed by this nature-lover's paradise down under. —*JS*

(i) **Western Australia Tourism and Visitor Center,** at the corner of Forest Place and Wellington St., Perth (© **800/ 812-808**; www.westernaustralia.com and www.wavisitorcentre.com).

TOUR: Swan Jet, Perth Sightseeing Centre, Shop 1, Old Perth Port, Barrack Square (© **61/89-225-4166**; www.swanjet.com).

WHEN TO GO: Sept–May.

✈ Perth Airport.

⊨ $$ **Medina Executive Barrack Plaza,** 138 Barrack St. (© **61/89-267-0000**; www.medina.com.au). $$$ **The Outram Perth,** 32 Outram St. (© **61/89-322-4888**; www.wyndhamvacation resorts.com.au).

Boating **104**

Jet Boat Rides in the Shotover Gorge
Doing 360s in Queenstown
Queenstown, New Zealand

A ride through the Shotover River Canyons meshes strain-your-neck views of the towering walls and up-close encounters with the massive boulders that have tumbled into the river at the narrowest spots. As the driver hits the accelerator, you're pushed back into your seat and the water sprays alongside (and into) the boat. The boats—nicknamed *Big Red* because of their color—are so maneuverable that the trip's high comes when the drivers whips the boat around in a 360-degree turn, making you dizzy as the rocks seem to loom closer and closer to the boat. Drivers for the Shotover Jet company have taken more than two million passengers through these canyons, so they know just when to turn to avoid the rocky outcroppings and when to slow down so you can view the **Edith Cavell Bridge** overhead or catch your breath while enjoying the scenery. So sit back and relax—you're in good hands. That said, get ready for the ride of your life!

The Shotover Jetboat rides are just part of the fun in and around Queensland, one of New Zealand's South Island's friendliest cities. Where do you want to go bungee jumping? Your options are plentiful, including **Kawarau Suspension Bridge,** the first commercial bungee jump site in the world (see **39**). Or you could take a four-wheel drive out to the **Ledge Bungy and Sky Swing,** where you are harnessed in and swing out before you fall downward.

In the summer, spring, and fall, there is tramping (hiking). Several multi-day hikes start from here, including routes on the **Routebourne Track,** the **Rees-Dart Track,** and the **Greenstone Caples Track.** If you choose skydiving, you'll have a spectacular view of Queenstown and the surrounding mountains. You can go horseback riding on trails into river gorges, visit old mining towns, or ride on paths with sensational views of the surrounding mountains. You can go river rafting, take four-wheel drive vehicles up to waterfalls, or even go to **Mt. Aspiring National Park,** where parts of the Middle Earth portion of *The Lord of the Rings* trilogy was filmed.

In the winter, **Coronet Peak Skifield** beckons skiers with views of the Wakatipu basin. There are also the three bowls of the Remarkables. The skiing is fun, but don't expect the on-slope grooming and comforts of a Colorado or Utah resort. (And, don't be surprised if you have to stop the car and wait while a flock of sheep cross the road on your way there.) Heli-skiing is another option. You can even arrange, weather permitting, to ski down the **Tasman Glacier** (see **174**), stopping on your way down to investigate ice caves. —*LF*

A jet boat careens through the Shotover Gorge.

ⓘ ✆ **64/3-442-8570** or 0800-SHOTOVER only in New Zealand; www.shotoverjet.com.

WHEN TO GO: Year-round (weather and river conditions permitting). Closed Christmas.

✈ Queenstown.

⌂ **Queenstown House,** 69 Hallenstein St. (✆ **64/3-442-9043;** www.queenstownhouse.co.nz). **Hotel Sofitel Queenstown,** 8 Duke St. (✆ **03/450-0045** or 0800/444-422 in New Zealand; www.sofitel.com).

105 Boating

The Na Pali Coast by Zodiac
A Raft Ride on Steroids
Kauai, Hawaii, U.S.A.

Flying along the Na Pali Coast of Kauai in a Zodiac is like riding a river raft on steroids. The rigid inflatable rafts, originally used by the military, are powered by large outboard motors. They bounce through the surf like a demented bronco when the sea is choppy and like a raft through Class IV rapids when it's calm. Depending upon which craft you end up on, you will either be sitting on an inflatable seat or sitting on a pontoon holding onto strategically placed ropes. The options of ways see the island's famed Na Pali Coast cliffs—with spectacular faces rising over 1,000 feet (300m)—are limited. The only year-round options are by helicopter ride or boat: There are no roads that tour this part of Kauai. In the summer months, you can also kayak or charter a sailboat around the northwest coast of the island. Seeing these cliffs from the waters below is an unparalleled sight—a breathtaking view that will have your heart pounding.

Depending upon the weather and seas, your captain may take you on a hair-raising ride through sea caves, stop at beaches for swimming and snorkeling (the aquatic life is fantastic), or to visit the 800-year-old fishing village, Nu`alolo Kai. During the ride you may encounter dolphins swimming alongside your craft or whales breeching during the months of December through April. You're so close to the water it gives you a special connection when you do come face to face with these incredible creatures. Because of the trade winds, early morning rides are preferable because they provide the best opportunity to see dolphins and visit the caves.

Kauai is my favorite of the Hawaiian Islands. Though seeing if from the sea-level viewpoint has its advantages, the hiking opportunities are also exceptional. Hiking along the **Na Pali Coast Trail** and seeing this landscape from a different point of view is an adrenaline charge all its own. The trail is fairly difficult, with significant elevation changes and potentially slippery conditions. But the payoff is worth it. The scenery—especially the waterfalls and Kalalau Beach—is spectacular.

Scuba diving in Kauai is also a thrill, though not along the Na Pali Coast. There are frequent, dangerous rip tides there. **Makau Beach** is a better choice. The reefs are full of creatures including reef and nurse sharks, eels, dolphins, and sea turtles, not to mention a huge variety of fish. It's periodically possible to see a Monk seal. And of course, being Hawaii, beaches for relaxing and surfing for every level are everywhere. —*LF*

ⓘ **Captain Andy's Sailing Adventures** (✆ **800/535-0830** or 808/335-6833; www.napali.com/kauai_rafting). **Napali Riders** (✆ **808/742-6331;** www.napaliriders.com). **Kauai Explorer** (www.kauaiexplorer.com).

WHEN TO GO: Dec–Apr.

✈ Lihue Airport, Kauai.

⛵ $$ **Hanalei Colony Resort,** 5-7130 Kuhio Hwy. (ⓒ **808/826-6235;** www.hcr.

com). $$$ **St. Regis Princeville Resort,** 5520 Ka Haku Rd. (ⓒ **808/826-9644;** www. stregisprinceville.com).

Boating **106**

Cruising Among Calving Glaciers
The Most Dramatic Ice Falls
Prince William Sound, Alaska, U.S.A.

An estimated 90% of glaciers are receding in Alaska. Climate change isn't entirely to blame, but it does appear to be accelerating the normal process of glacier calving. "Calving" is what happens when large pieces of ice—sometimes as big as a home or office building—fracture and separate from a tidewater glacier, crashing into the sea. The trend is clearly visible in **Prince William Sound,** an otherwise blissfully serene place. In fact, it's hard to believe that the Exxon Valdez crashed here just over 20 years ago. The disaster spilled 11 million gallons of crude oil, damaging 1,300 miles (2,000km) of shoreline and polluting one of the country's most plentiful fishing areas. But since then, at least $2 billion has been spent on cleanup and recovery efforts, and the area remains one of Alaska's most popular tourist destinations. Cruising around, it's easy to see why.

The sound covers nearly 15,000 sq. miles (39,000 sq. km) and is home to at least 150 glaciers, secluded bays, and diverse wildlife. For the best adventure in this icy wonderland, steer clear of the large ships and instead opt for a small boat that offers a multiday "live-aboard" experience. **Discovery Voyages** (see below) will take you on a six-cabin, 65-foot (20m) motor yacht with frequent opportunities to kayak on the sound and hike along the coast. These up-close-and-personal encounters give you a unique perspective on glacier calving.

Although kayaking through Alaska's icy blue water can be cold, the strong sun—not to mention your adrenaline—helps ward off a major chill. You'll be wowed by the spectacular **Harriman Fjord** and, depending on the weather, you might even be able to paddle farther off the beaten path toward **Chenega Glacier,** one of the largest tidewater glaciers in Prince William Sound. Wherever you go, you'll be awestruck by the landscape. Skyscraping mountains and massive ice formations surround you, as you cruise past adorable harbor seals, sea lions, and sea otters resting on floating chunks of ice. Salmon and halibut swim underwater, and a whale spouts in the distance. Then, just when you're completely relaxed, enjoying the pristine setting, a giant piece of a glacier plummets into the sound. Your heart pounds so hard and fast you think it's going to jump out of your chest. This awesome sight and thunderous sound is truly mind blowing.

When you're ready to rest your paddling arms, there are ample opportunities to stretch your legs on dry land. The surrounding **Chugach National Forest** is home to brown and black bears, deer, and a variety of birds including bald eagles. But the main event is on the water. As Dean Rand, the captain of Discovery Voyages, says, "When people first witness [glacier calving], they almost always say, 'Wow, I didn't know it would be like this!' There's nothing else in the world to compare it to." —*JS*

ⓘ **Travel Alaska,** 524 W 4th Ave., Anchorage (ℰ **800/478-1255;** www.travelalaska.com). **Chugach National Forest** (www.fs.fed.us/r10/chugach).

TOUR: Discovery Voyages, P.O. Box 688, Whittier (ℰ **800/324-7602;** www.discovery voyages.com).

WHEN TO GO: May–Sept.

✈ Ted Stevens Anchorage Airport.

107 Boating

Niagara Falls
The Big Spill
New York, U.S.A. & Ontario, Canada

Everyone's seen a Kodachrome photo of **Niagara Falls,** that stupendous curve of cascading water that lies between the United States and Canada. It's one of those sites, however, to which postcards will never do justice: To stand on a viewing platform and see, really see, how big it is, to hear the thunder of falling water, to feel the mist spritzing your face and the earth shaking under your feet, is another thing altogether. You don't understand how amazing it is until you're actually there.

There are actually two waterfalls here, both of them doozies: the **American Falls** and **Horseshoe Falls.** Both are around 175 feet high (53m), although Horseshoe Falls, at 2,500 feet (762m) wide, is more than twice as wide as its sibling. The Canadian

Be prepared to get wet on a Whirlpool Jet Boat Tour at Niagara Falls.

shore has the real panoramic view; both falls can be seen from the American side, but not together (Prospect Point for the American Falls, Terrapin Point for Horseshoe Falls). The Canadian side tends to have better hotels and more attractions, as well. No matter where you stay, you can easily visit both, by crossing the **Rainbow Bridge,** preferably on foot—it's only the length of a couple city blocks. Bring a passport (or other secure, accepted documents, which may include a driver's license and original birth certificate; you'll need birth certificates for the kids as well).

On the U.S. shore, head for **Niagara Falls State Park** (© **716/278-1796;** www.niagarafallsstatepark.com) to explore the falls: An **Observation Tower** overlooks the river, and the **Cave of the Winds tour** (Apr–Oct; © **716/278-1730**) takes you by elevator down onto boardwalks, where you can walk around the base of the American Falls. Canada's 236m (775-ft.-high) **Skylon Tower,** 5200 Robinson St. (© **905/ 356-2651;** www.skylon.com), has a revolving restaurant on top, and the **Journey Behind the Falls** (© **905/354-1551;** www.niagaraparks.com) allows you to descend via elevator to tunnels punctuated with portholes that look out through the blur of water right behind Horseshoe Falls. The coolest way to see the falls, of course, is the classic *Maid of the Mist* boat ride (Apr–Oct; © **716/284-8897;** www.maidofthemist.com), which plays no favorites; it departs from either shore.

You'll chug upriver toward the American and Horseshoe Falls, sailing right up the base of both (don't worry; blue slickers are provided to keep you dry).

Want more of an adrenaline rush? Book a 10-minute helicopter ride over the cascades with **Niagara Helicopters** (© **905/ 357-5672;** www.niagarahelicopters.com) or **Rainbow Air** (© **716/284-2800;** www. rainbowairinc.com), or crash through the white waters of the Niagara gorge with **Whirlpool Jet Boat Tours** (Apr–Oct; © **888/438-4444** in the U.S., or 905/468-4800 in Canada; www.whirlpooljet.com). This being a major tourist destination, there's a ton of other attractions around, from historic old forts and botanical gardens to aquariums and amusement parks. But overdeveloped as it may be, the spectacular Falls are still there. —*HH*

ⓘ U.S. (© **877/FALLSUS** [325-5787] or 716/282-8992; www.niagara-usa.com). Canada (© **800/563-2557;** www.niagara fallstourism.com).

WHEN TO GO: May–Oct.

✈ Buffalo Niagara International Airport, 34km (21 miles).

⌷ $$ **Courtyard by Marriott,** 5950 Victoria Ave., Niagara Falls, Ontario, Canada (© **800/771-1123** or 905/358-3083; www.nfcourtyard.com). $$$ **Red Coach Inn,** 2 Buffalo Ave., Niagara Falls, NY, USA (© **866/719-2070** or 716/282-1459; www. redcoach.com).

Boating **108**

Kayaking in the Port Wine Region
The Sweetest Sort of Paddling
Porto to Pocinho, Portugal

There are relatively few regions in Europe that remain off the beaten path, but northern Portugal is one of them. Full of old-world charm, this part of the country is home to rolling hills, picturesque medieval towns, romantic Baroque-style *quintas* (farm estates), several UNESCO World Heritage Sites, hearty local cooking, and plenty of wine.

The Douro River, often known as the "River of Gold," curves through the region, traversing deep canyons blanketed with grapevines. This river valley has been producing authentic port—the famous dessert wine fortified by adding grape brandy—for more than 2,000 years. Its microclimate of brutally hot, dry summers and extremely cold winters creates intensely flavorful grapes. In the past, flat-bottomed boats called *barcos rabelos* would carry the wine from vineyards along the Douro River to storage cellars in Porto on the Atlantic coast. Today, tanker trucks are used instead, but you can still follow the boats' ancient river route in a modern kayak.

Begin in **Porto,** Portugal's second-largest city, famous for the eponymous beverage and a historic downtown with spectacular architectural sites. After exploring the city for a day, take the train to **Pocinho,** and settle in for a night at a local farm to get a real taste of the area. A traditional feast and local wines will fortify you for the next several days of kayaking. The next morning, drive a bit farther inland to the river's mouth. Once you start paddling through the Douro's upper gorge, you'll be overwhelmed by the striking views of mountain ranges, bountiful olive and almond orchards, terraced grapevines, and the lush countryside. When you're ready to rest your tired arms, stop at the quaint village of **Nossa Senhora da Ribeira.**

Refreshed, you can take off the next morning to kayak past more vineyards. You might stop to chat with workers harvesting grapes or see the wine being prepared for transport. On the following day, paddle through the dramatic **Valeira Gorge,** once the river's scariest passageway. Still a narrow, granite gorge, it's more accessible today because the accompanying rapids were dynamited in the 18th century and a dam was built. Making your way along the water, you'll see countless birds, particularly kingfishers, before stopping for lunch in the village of **Tua.**

As you journey down the river for another couple of days, you might begin to think you've traveled back in time. Although some large conglomerates now make wine

Kayakers take a break on the rocks in Portugal's port wine region.

in this area, many of the smaller independent vineyards still use artisanal techniques. Grapes are hand picked, loaded into rustic baskets, and even stomped by foot to the tune of guitar strumming, joyful singing, and lots of drinking. If you're lucky enough to witness one of these events, there's only one thing to say, which sums up the entire experience of traveling along the Douro: *Saúde* (which means "cheers" in Portuguese)! —*JS*

(i) **Portugal Tourism Board,** Rua Ivone Silva, Lote 6 ((C) **351/211-140-200;** www. visitportugal.com).

TOUR: Mountain Travel Sobek, 1266 66th St., Emeryville, CA ((C) **888/831-7526;** www.mtsobek.com).

WHEN TO GO: Early fall for harvest season.

✈ Oporto (Porto) airport.

🛏 Tour company provides lodging, but in Porto: $-$$ **Pestana Porto,** 1 Praça da Ribeira, Ribeira ((C) **351/223-402-300;** www.pestana.com).

Whitewater River Rafting

Fun comes in degrees with whitewater rafting. You can choose a calm ride, where your river guide does the rowing and you relax and take pictures, or you can choose a trip where you'll assist the guide by paddling frantically while he or she shouts "four forward," or "five backward," so you won't high-side the raft on the huge rocks right in front of you. Here are 10 memorable and adrenaline-inducing rafting trips. —LF

109 Grand Canyon, Arizona, U.S.A.: Observe eons of colorful history, etched into the steep walls of the Grand Canyon gorge, when you raft the Colorado River through the Grand Canyon. On a rafting trip here, you'll alternately float downstream or plunge through massive rapids. After a day on the water, you'll sleep on a sandy beach under a star-bright sky. *Rafting the Grand Canyon & Utah* (℡ *800/222-6966 or 702/655-6060; www. raftingthegrandcanyon.com).* *Western River Expeditions* (℡ *866/904-1160 or 801/942-6669; www. westernriver.com).*

110 Apurímac River, Peru: On Peru's Apurímac River, you can raft beneath steep canyon walls until you reach pastoral valleys and a tropical rainforest. Expect lots of Class III and IV rapids, and an occasional Class V. These trips usually last about 4 days. If you can escape for 12 days, raft on the Tambopata River, which runs through the Tambopata-Candamo National Park. *www.andreantravelweb.com/peru.*

111 White Nile, Uganda: This river flows from vast Lake Victoria, and has both wild and mild stretches. Float past untouched woodlands or rock and roll in rapids reaching Class V. Here, you'll find some of the most outstanding technical rafting through sustained rapids in the world. Don't be surprised if you flip, race over waterfalls, or high-side on huge rocks. You'll lunch on islands in the middle of the river, and camp where there is African music and dancing. A trip down this part of the Nile should only be part of a trip to Uganda. *Nile River Explorers* (℡ *256/772-ADRIFT [237438]; www. raftafrica.com).* *Adrift* (℡ *256/312-237-438; www.adrift.ug).*

112 Rafting in Croatia: The rivers near Croatia's coast are lined with lush vegetation and karstic canyons. Much of the rafting is on rivers with Class II and II rapids, and the occasional IV rapid. The season on the dam-controlled Dobra River is May to November. On the Cetina river you'll pass by caves and waterfalls while rafting by verdant shores. A raft trip on the Neretva starts right below one of the highest waterfalls in Europe. *Hidden Croatia* (℡ *44/207-594-0600; www.hiddencroatia.com).* *Dalmatia Rafting* (℡ *385/21-321-698; www.dalmatiarafting.com).*

113 Jackson Hole, Wyoming, U.S.A.: The first part of the 8-mile (13km) trip through the Grand Canyon of the Snake River is a good warm-up for the big waves on the second half of the ride. On the 16-mile (26km) Upper Canyon Continuous Combo, you float down the river through eagle-nesting habitat for half the trip, then paddle through the Grand Canyon of the Snake for the final 8-mile (13km) stretch of rapids. *Dave Hansen Whitewater and Scenic River Trips* (℡ *800/732-6295 or 307/733-6295; www.davehansenwhitewater.com).*

⑭ Gauley River and New River, West Virginia, U.S.A.: The snowmelt from the Appalachian Mountains fills the Gauley River and the New River, making this an exciting rafting spot. The 26-mile (42km) stretch of river drops 650 feet (195m), so you'll be rafting through big holes and waves that will drench you. Consider the drops and big waves on the Lower Gauley stretch a warm-up. The upper Gauley, where the rapids drop 15 to 35 feet (4.5–11m) in less than a ¼ mile (.4km), is technically demanding. Some of the rapids are rated V+. Rides on the Gauley begin the first weekend after Labor Day and continue for five 4-day weekends and a 2-day weekend. *New & Gauley River Adventures* (✆ *800-SKY-RAFT [759-7238]; www.gauley.com).*

⑮ Royal Gorge, Colorado, U.S.A.: On this stretch of the Arkansas River, you raft through rapids with names like Sledgehammer and the Narrows, which can reach Class IV and V when the water is high. The river flows through sheer 1,100-foot-high (330m) cliffs during this stretch. If you want to do lots of paddling, ask about the adrenaline rafts that only hold four people. Families might enjoy the raft and ride trip, which includes a ride on a passenger train with dome and dining cars that runs along the top of the gorge. *Echo Canyon River Expeditions* (✆ *800/755-3246; www.royalgorgerafting.com).*

⑯ Tuolumne River, California, U.S.A.: The 27 miles (43km) you can raft on the Tuolumne River, which originates in Yosemite National Park, blends a wilderness experience with the excitement of challenging Class IV and V rapids. On one trip, you can start with big jolts, as you go over rapids with names like Nemesis and Rock Garden, then hone your paddling skills as you descend over drops, through chutes and maneuver around boulders. You're getting ready for a swift ride through Clavey Falls, a series of three staircase drops. Occasionally, there will be calmer water, where you can catch your breath. Peace comes at night while camping alongside the river. *Outdoor Adventure River Specialists* (✆ *800/346-6277 or 209/736-4677; www.oars.com).*

⑰ Pacuare River, Costa Rica: The Pacuare River winds through pristine rainforest in the Cabecar Indian Reservation. The Upper Upper, the Upper, and the Lower— the three sections of the river that are rafted most often—vary in degree of difficulty. The 26km (16-mile) long stretch called the Upper Upper has Class II to IV rapids, while the more technical Upper, a 16km (10-mile) stretch of whitewater with waterfalls, portages, and Class IV and V rapids, is more commonly run in kayaks. On the Lower, with its Class III and IV rapids, rafters see waterfalls flowing into the river. Trips range from 1 to 4 days and can include stays at a remote eco-lodge, where guests can go ziplining and hiking with a nature guide. *Rios Tropicales* (✆ *866/722-8273; www.riostropicales.com).*

⑱ Zambezi River, Zimbabwe/Zambia: The Zambezi River is considered one of the top-10 rivers in the world for whitewater rafting enthusiasts. Below the thundering Victoria Falls, rafters encounter long stretches of technically difficult rapids, big drops, and massive holes as the Zambezi flows through the narrow Batoka Gorge. *Safari Par Excellence* (✆ *44/845-2930512; www.whitewater.safpar.com). Bio Bio Expeditions Worldwide* (✆ *800/246-7238 or 530/582-6865; www.bbxrafting.com).*

Waveskiing on the Atlantic Ocean
Sitting Down When the Surf's Up
Cornwall, England

Waveskiing is like a dream come true for aspiring surfers. Instead of trying to balance while standing upright on a board, the basic premise of waveskiing is to sit down and surf. This relatively new extreme sport involves sitting on top of a sort of kayak-surfboard crossbreed, putting your legs straight ahead of you, buckling up for a bumpy ride, and using your paddles as rudders to navigate the waves. The learning curve tends to be more moderate than surfing, but the adrenaline rush can be just as high when you paddle into some major swells.

One of the best places to get your bum wet on a waveski is in Cornwall, England's most southwesterly county. Jutting out into the Atlantic Ocean with nearly 485km (300 miles) of rocky coastline warmed by the Gulf Stream and a mild climate, Cornwall boasts some of the U.K.'s best beaches, and perhaps some of the most popular surf in Europe. This historic seaside region is home to small ports, old inns, and sweeping bays, but most remnants of the old mining and fishing industries are gone. Today, tourism is clearly the biggest business and the town of **Newquay,** in

The glorious beaches in Newquay in Cornwall are a hot spot for waveskiing.

particular, is a virtual paradise for beach bums. Just north of Newquay, **Watergate Bay** is one of the hot spots for waveskiing and other watersports. **The Extreme Academy** (see below) rents equipment, and offers lessons for both novices and experienced surfers. As the academy's sports manager and former world waveski champion Carl Coombes says, "Waveskiing at Watergate Bay is amazing. Throughout the year, the sand banks at the beach move around, adding to the variety and quality of the waves."

An introductory lesson at the Extreme Academy includes a safety briefing on all the equipment you'll use to waveski and an overview about general surf etiquette. You'll watch a practical demonstration on the beach, go through a dry run on the sand, warm up, stretch, and hit the water. Your instructor will then offer personal coaching tips throughout the rest of your lesson.

If you can bear to dry off for a few hours, you won't be disappointed by Cornwall's other offerings. Check out the **Tate Gallery** (www.tate.org.uk/stives) outpost in St. Ives; **Tintagel Castle,** the legendary birthplace of King Arthur in Tintagel; the **Eden Project** (www.edenproject.com) in St. Austell, which boasts the world's largest greenhouse; and the popular cycling path known as the **Camel Trail,** which runs from Padstow to Poley's Bridge. After dark, top-notch restaurants and a vibrant nightlife keep visitors fully entertained. But the real thrill comes at dawn when it's time to ride the waves again. In Cornwall, despite the many tempting distractions, almost no one stays out of the water for very long. —*JS*

ⓘ **Newquay Tourist Information Centre,** Marcus Hill, Newquay (✆ **44/0-1637-854-020;** www.visitnewquay.org and www.cornwalltouristboard.co.uk).

WHEN TO GO: May–Sept.

✈ Newquay Cornwall Airport, a 4-hr. drive from Heathrow Airport or Gatwick Airport in London, or a 6½-hr. train ride from Paddington Station in London.

🛏 $$ **Watergate Bay: The Hotel and the Extreme Academy,** Watergate Bay, Cornwall (✆ **44/0-1637-860-543;** www.watergatebay.co.uk).

---

120 Watersports

Parasailing on the Red Sea
High Adventure in the Promised Land
Eilat, Israel

Israel is most often visited for its notable religious and historic sites, but it has plenty to offer adventure travelers. In addition to seeing archaeological wonders and sacred places, which are sure to jump-start your adventure, add some other escapades to make your trip even more memorable. In a week, you can go from the Western Wall in Jerusalem to hiking at Masada (see ⑯) to sleeping under the stars in the Negev Desert to floating in the Dead Sea to parasailing in Eilat, Israel's southernmost city.

Ever since the days of King Solomon, Eilat's location has made it a strategic port. Today, it's Israel's most popular resort town and a mecca for watersports. It boasts a warm climate, a tropical sea, and a backdrop of mountains.

To get an overview of the area, start out by parasailing. You'll put on a seat-like harness with a parachute and climb aboard a small motorboat. After you're attached to the boat by a tow rope, just sit back and try to relax as the boat speeds through the water and air fills your parachute, lifting

Parasailing in Eilat allows for a one-of-a-kind view of sea and mountains.

then speed up, raising you higher. After a few rounds, you're slowly reeled back onto the boat.

Now that you've had a bird's-eye view of southern Israel and its neighboring nations, you might want to take a closer look at Eilat. The **Coral Beach Nature Reserve,** an underwater marine reserve filled with brightly colored tropical fish, is a popular spot to scuba dive and snorkel. Nearby, another reef is home to a school of dolphins. If you explore the beaches, you'll find plenty of tour operators offering canoe, paddleboat, and motorboat rentals. You can also try water skiing or go for a banana boat ride. One thing's for sure: Israel isn't all history and religion—it's adventure activity and excitement, too! —JS

you up into the sky. The breeze tickles your arms and legs, your heart pounds, and your stomach drops. Once you're suspended in the air, feeling weightless, you might notice an Egyptian flag in the distance, or a Jordanian one on the other side of the gulf. After about 5 minutes, just when you're getting used to your new vantage point and starting to breathe normally again, your guides might try to get your adrenaline pumping again. They'll lower you down to skim the water and

ⓘ **Israel Ministry of Tourism,** 800 Second Ave., New York (ⓒ **212/499-5660;** www.goisrael.com).

TOUR: Red Sea Sports Club, Bridge House, North Beach (ⓒ **972/86-38-2240;** www.redseasports.co.il).

WHEN TO GO: Sept–May.

✈ Eilat Airport, also known as J. Hozman Airport, or Tel Aviv International Airport followed by a 5-hr. drive.

🛏 $$–$$$ **Dan Eilat Hotel,** Hotel Area, North Beach (ⓒ **972-8-636-2222;** www.danhotels.com).

Watersports 121

Parasailing & More on the Indian Ocean
The Thrills of Paradise
The Maldives

Paradise doesn't come cheap—at least not in the Maldives. But if you can pony up the cash, this off-the-beaten-path archipelago in southern Asia delivers a strong dose of adrenaline. Far from any other landmass and the rest of civilization, its 1,190 coral islands in the Indian Ocean are grouped into 26 coral atolls. The luxury resorts

sprinkled on only about 80 islands offer the quintessential beach getaway, complete with crystal clear blue water, secluded soft white sands, lush green jungles, and abundant underwater life. You won't struggle to find a private stretch of beach, and many resorts even promote a "no shoes" policy to reinforce the haute-bohemian vibe.

When you've had your fill of rest and relaxation, you can explore the island's more deserted areas and even attempt a few daredevil stunts on the water.

Getting to and around the Maldives is an adventure in itself. Outside of the capital city, Malé, seaplanes (often called air taxis), boats (also used like taxis), and private yachts are the main modes of transportation. Cars are rarely used. The two main air taxi operators are **Maldivian Air Taxi** and **Trans Maldivian Airways;** both fly DHC-6 Twin Otter seaplanes that seat about 10 passengers.

Once you arrive at your resort and settle in, the best way to appreciate this near utopia is to get above it all. After putting on a seat-like harness with a parachute, you'll climb aboard a motorboat and stay attached to it by a tow rope. As the boat speeds through the water, air fills your parachute, lifting you up into the sky. The wind rushes past you and the ocean spray mists your skin. Your stomach drops as you rise higher, your arms and legs dangle freely in the air. Before you know it, you're serenely floating over the ocean in silence, interrupted only be the sound of own pounding heartbeat.

When you're ready for a closer look, dive in deeper. The Maldives offer scuba divers some of the world's best visibility and most diverse marine life. The plentiful coral reefs attract manta rays, whale sharks, sea turtles, countless colorful fish, and even a few wrecks. If you ever tire of these underwater wonders, or just want a change of scenery, head back up to the ocean's surface. You can try snorkeling, swimming, water-skiing, wakeboarding, surfing, kayaking, sailing, tubing, and deep sea fishing. Whether you're lying in the sun or playing in the waves, excitement is easy to find in the Maldives. —*JS*

ⓘ **Maldives Government Tourist Information Office,** Aschaffenburger St. (✆ **49/6182-9-934-857;** www.visitmaldives.de).

WHEN TO GO: Nov–Apr.

✈ Malé International Airport.

🛏 $$$ **Four Seasons Kuda Huras,** North Malé Atoll (✆ **960/664-4888;** www.fourseasons.com/maldiveskh) and **Four Seasons Landa Giraavaru,** Baa Atoll (✆ **960/660-0888;** www.fourseasons.com/maldiveslg). $$$ **One&Only Reethi Rah,** North Malé Atoll (✆ **960/664-8800;** www.oneandonlyresorts.com). $$$ **Shangri-La Villingili Resort and Spa,** Villingili Island, Addu Atoll (✆ **960/689-7888;** www.shangri-la.com).

122 **Watersports**

Coasteering with TYF Adventures
When You Can't Scramble Anymore, Jump!
Pembrokeshire Coast, Wales

Coasteering is adrenaline-fueled entertainment. Don a wetsuit, helmet, and life jacket, then begin scrambling up the rocky walls that make up the Pembrokeshire coastline. Keep climbing or traversing along the rugged shore until you can't go any higher. Then jump! You crash into the ocean, then bob up again (thanks to the life jacket) and get washed around in the whitewater until you get your bearings and swim back to shore. Each time you try it you get a bit more aggressive and climb a bit higher.

Coasteering has been informally practiced for decades, but **TFY Adventure** claims to be the first commercial coasteering operation, opening in 1986. Since then it's become a fast-growing adventure sport. Today, TFY takes people on many different routes, each specifically chosen to reflect the adrenaline surge desires of the participants. Each day, the routes are chosen based on the group, the swell, and the tide. There are routes that require endurance for adrenaline junkies, and easier choices for families and people who just want to see the Welsh coastline from a different angle. Each adventure, which lasts about a half-day, includes a combination of scrambling, climbing, cliff jumping, and swimming.

Pembrokeshire Coast National Park (© **44/845-345-7275;** www.pcnpa.org.uk), on Wales's southwestern shore, is the United Kingdom's only truly coastal park. It encompasses the jagged, often cliff-fringed coastline backed by green, cultivated fields. Look offshore and you'll see kayakers paddling in sheltered coves. Onshore, walkers are hiking along parts of the **Pembrokeshire Coast Path National Trail,** which twists and turns for 300km (186 miles), mostly in the park, passing the cliffs, open beaches, and winding estuaries.

Within Wales, the best places for coasteering are the Pembrokeshire coast, the North Wales coast, and the Gower Peninsula. This is an increasingly popular sport, and you may find it in other coastal cities from France and Spain to Croatia and South Africa.

TYF Adventure, which is based in historic St. David's and Freshwater East, offers other adrenaline activities such as rock climbing, surfing, and kayaking. In this region of Wales,

Coasteering encompasses an array of adrenaline-inducing activities including hiking, rock climbing, cliff jumping, and swimming.

you can also go jet-boating to explore the coves and beaches along this wild coastline, or head out to sea for a day of whale and dolphin watching. Wales has an extensive system of mountain biking trails, a mix of single track, fire roads, and natural trails along mountainsides. Throughout Wales, there are some 4,000 geocaches that geocaching fans can try to find. —*LF*

ⓘ **TYF Coasteering** (© **44/1437-721633;** www.coasteering.com). **Visit Wales** (© **44/ 8701-211851;** www.godo.visitwales.com). ✈ Cardiff.

🛏 $$ **Laphey Court Hotel,** Laphey, near Tenby (© **44/01646-672273;** www. lapheycourt.co.uk). $$ **Coach House Hotel,** 116 Main St. (© **44/01646-684602**).

Watersports **123**

SwimTreks
In the Swim of Things
Locations Worldwide

Imagine a long swim surrounded by scenery that takes your breath away. You're getting lots of exercise and visiting a new pocket of the globe, too. It's a tropical island vacation, it's a great workout, and it's culturally rewarding. Impossible? Not on a "swimcation," which takes you to exotic locations and gets you in touch with the natural splendor of each by getting you into the water. Led by SwimTrek, a British tour operator, these holidays take avid swimmers out of the pool and into the open waters of the Caribbean, the Mediterranean, and other regions to swim from one shore to the next, or in some cases from island to island, while accompanied by a support boat.

Swimmers should be in good enough shape to handle the activity levels specified for their trip; some trips are longer and more rigorous than others, but each assigns swimmers to a group based on their swim speed. Almost all swimmers can expect to swim 2 to 3 hours a day total. The group offers suggested training distances to help athletes prepare for each trip, and swimmers are videotaped during the trips for coaching tips on improving their stroke, speed, and swim technique. The guides who accompany travelers are experienced swim coaches hailing from all corners of the globe.

SwimTrek takes travelers to some of the most historic and alluring bodies of water in the world. The Hellespont, the legendary strait near the Black Sea that separates Europe from Asia, is among their travel offerings. Swimmers can also visit the Egyptian Red Sea, the British Virgin Islands, the Greek Cyclades, Alcatraz Island in San Francisco Bay. Not all their tours are saltwater: The lakes of Finland and the River Thames are among their offerings. —ML

ⓘ **SwimTrek** (𝄢 **44-0/1273-739-713;** www.swimtrek.com).

WHEN TO GO: Year-round.

---

124 **Watersports**

Manhattan Island Foundation
Swim Around Manhattan
New York City, New York, U.S.A.

If you thrive on open-water swims in novel settings, head for New York City. No, I'm not kidding. Stretch out one arm then the other, kicking all the way. Only a few more miles to go before finishing the 28.5-mile (46km) **Manhattan Island Marathon Swim,** which circles the entire island of Manhattan. During this ultra-marathon swim, which organizers carefully time so participants can take advantage of the tides, swimmers begin by Battery Park and follow the tide on the East River. They continue via the Harlem River to the Hudson River, before coming back to Manhattan's southern tip.

Each swimmer is escorted by a power boat and a kayaker who works with the swimmer's crew to supply food and drink to the swimmer. They also guide the swimmer around hazards, watch for signs of hypothermia, and make sure everyone plays fair.

If you want to dip your toe into an open-swim adventure but aren't ready for the big-time, try another one of the events organized by NYC Swim such as the **Governors Island Swim** or the **Aquathlon,** a combination swim and run event. Newcomers to open water swims might try the **Park to Park swim,** which is about two miles.

"Is the water safe to swim in?" is a question often asked by prospective swimmers and anyone hearing about these events. The answer is yes, under supervised conditions. The exception is after significant rain when contaminants may enter the water. (At that point, swimmers are advised of the conditions and make their own decision about entering the event.) Swimmers, however, do relate tales of dodging some debris and the occasional dead fish. Water temperatures range from about 60°F (16°C) to the low 70s, depending upon the time or year.

Certain qualifications are required, including proof of a pool swim or previous open-water competition of a specific length, before one is accepted to enter an event. Landlubbers can watch marathon swimmers pass by all along the Manhattan shore, including Battery Park, the East River between 18th and 34th streets, along the Harlem River, and the 70th Street Pier in Riverside Park.

NYC Swim's mission is to support and expand Learn to Swim programs, particularly those that serve at-risk youth; and to raise public awareness of the waters that surround New York City by supporting efforts to clean and protect them. Since 1993, NYC Swim has organized more than 110 openwater swimming events in the waters around Manhattan that have attracted more than 10,000 participants. —LF

ⓘ **NYC Swim** (✆ **888/692-7946;** www.nycswim.org).

✈ JFK International (15 miles/24km), LaGuardia (8 miles/13km), or Newark Liberty International (16 miles/26km).

🛏 $$ **Excelsior Hotel,** 45 W. 81st St. (✆ **800/368-4575** or 212/362-9200; www.excelsiorhotelny.com). $$$ **Le Parker Meridien,** 118 W. 57th St. (✆ **800/543-4300** or 212-245-5000; www.parkermeridien.com).

Watersports 125

Skimboarding
Skimming the Waves
Laguna Beach, California, U.S.A.

Check out the guy doing a Shove It. He just got the board to spin 180° and jumped as it turned, so he's now riding the board backwards. This is typical of a hot-shot skimboarder. But even if you're not an experienced skimboarder, you can still get your heart pumping hopping on a board and riding waves out from the shore. You may get an old-fashioned strawberry or two on your knees as you tumble from your board onto the sand, but that will just add to your glory and the tales of your found sport you tell to friends back on dry land.

You can do lots of cool tricks on a skimboard, which is typically smaller and thinner than a surfboard. Skimboarding is similar to surfing, but skimboarders start on the sand. When they see the right wave, they run toward the ocean and drop their boards on the thin layer of water receding from the wave. Think hydroplaning. Skimboarding uses momentum from running and speed to slide along the surface of the water as the tide withdraws from the shore and out to the breaking waves. At this point, the boarder can shift his or her weight and direction and ride back to shore similar to a surfer. Skilled skimboarders can even ride down the line like a surfer, or launch off the wave and do aerial tricks, such as a Wrap, a Superman or a Coffin (lying on one's back on the skimboard with feet facing straight out).

Old photographs of Laguna Beach lifeguards skimming across the sand on large plywood boards indicate this sport dates back to the 1920s. Today, the skimboards are made of much more sophisticated materials than they were back then: fiberglass or carbon fiber wrapped around high density foam. The sport now thrives in Laguna Beach, where many pro skimboarders live, and elsewhere in the world including on inland lakes.

Laguna Beach is still considered the center of the skimboarding universe. Some companies who make skimboards, such as Victoria Skimboards, are located here, and it's the site of the annual **Victoria Skimboards World Championships,** an invitational event for qualified amateurs and pro riders. Watching this event can induce a little adrenaline of its own.

For all things skimboard related, check out **Skimonline.com,** a website maintained by pro skimboarder Aaron Peluso. Here, too, you'll find a list of Skimspots suggested by the webmaster and other skimboarders around the globe. World-class skimboarders have made **Tenth Street** in Laguna Beach, with its side-washes, home. **Ninth Street** is usually a straight wave. It's also known for its powerful shore break. —LF

ⓘ www.skimonline.com.

✈ John Wayne Airport, Orange County (15 miles/24km).

🛏 $$$ **Montage Resort & Spa,** 30801 South Coast Hwy. (ⓒ **866/271-6953** or 949/715-6000; www.montagelagunabeach.com). $$ **Casa Laguna Inn & Spa,** 2510 South Coast Hwy. (ⓒ **800/233-0449** or 949/494-2996; www.casalaguna.com).

126 Watersports

Windsurfing Cape Town
Top Freestylers & Beginners Play Here
South Africa

With so many beach-lined shores on the Indian and the Pacific oceans, inland lakes, and rivers, you won't have to go far in South Africa to find good wind and currents. Windsurfing is a popular sport in this country, so if you head here it won't be necessary to bring your own board and sail. You can easily book a tour, with lodging, rentals and more at several locations. The point is to get out on the water and take advantage of the fantastic windsurfing conditions off the coast of remarkable Cape Town.

If you stay in Cape Town, you'll have your choice of top windsurfing spots nearby. The **Langebaan Lagoon,** about a 1-hour drive from Cape Town, is a hot spot for boardsailing and other watersports. Although the surf may crash against some of the rocks near the shore, the lagoon located within the **West Coast National Park** is sheltered so you won't find big waves. The lagoon is ideal for beginners because of the flat water, but some of world's top freestyle windsurfers come here to train.

The folks at **Cape Sports Center,** which is a large retail shop in town that also offers lessons and monitors the wind forecast, say the Southeaster is a reliable wind. On a normal day, It starts blowing around 10am and builds—at times In a gusty fashion—until peaking around 3pm before it begins to die down.

Langebaan Lagoon is equally popular with kitesurfers and other watersports enthusiasts. In summer, thousands of migratory birds gather on an island in the middle of the lagoon. You can sail or paddle nearby and watch the gulls squabble with the cormorants and gannets, although it's a bird sanctuary so setting foot on the island is prohibited.

The town of Langebaan is a popular getaway spot for South Africans, and many guesthouses cater to the windsurfers and kitesurfers who flock here. This region is packed with activities for vacationers, from visiting **Cape Town** and taking the ferry ride to **Robben Island,** where Nelson Mandela was incarcerated for many years, to watching the tiny penguins strut around at the **Boulders.** You can hike up to the lighthouse at the **Cape Point** and stand at the **Cape of Good Hope,** which is the southwestern most point of the African continent—a thrill in and of itself. —*LF*

(i) **Cape Sports Center** ((C) **27/22-772-1114;** www.capesport.co.za).

WHEN TO GO: Oct–May.

✈ Cape Town, South Africa.

⊨ $ **The Farmhouse in Langebaan,** 5 Egret St. ((C) **27/22-772-2062;** www.the farmhouselangebaan.co.za). $$$ **Radisson Blu Hotel Waterfront Capetown,** Beach Rd., Granger Bay ((C) **800/395-7046** in the U.S. or 27/21-441-3000; www. radissonblu.com/hotel-capetown).

Watersports **127**

Windsurfing the Columbia River Gorge
High-Speed Turns & Aerials
Columbia River Gorge, Oregon & Washington, U.S.A.

The colorful sails of windsurfers dot the water in the Columbia Gorge, which is landlocked by cliffs that climb up to 4,000 feet (1,200m) above the Columbia River causing the wind to whip through. The Columbia River slices through the Cascade mountain range here as it flows westward to the Pacific Ocean, but summer winds usually sweep against the river's current so you get rolling swells. Locals will tell you with a grin: When the swells get big, smooth, and are widely spaced, there's lots of room to make high speed carving turns and sneak in a forward or backward loop. You can ride the waves like a surfer on the ocean but without a breaking lip. This smooth ride brings a gratifying rush.

The winds average between 20 and 25 mph (32–40kmph) but can rush along even faster at times, which is when you'll get a show from skilled windsurfers doing aerials. If you have a car, you can follow the wind from one prime launch spot to the next. However, windsurfing/lodging packages are available (see below) and outfitters will likely know the best spots to hit.

Columbia River Gorge National Scenic Area encompasses an 80-mile (129km) stretch of river that is the border between Oregon and Washington. Although dozens of launching sites for windsurfers and kitesurfers crop up along the river, the heart of this watery sport is in the town of Hood River. Here, you'll find lodging, restaurants, and sport shops, from whom you can rent or buy windsurfers and take lessons. Beginners are welcome, as are experienced windsurfers who want to learn aerials. The town of **Hood River,** located at the base of **Mount Hood** and about 60 miles (97km) from Portland, is a good base for a variety of outdoor activities. You can go whitewater rafting on the White Salmon or the Deschutes rivers, fly fishing in nearby streams, mountain climbing, and hiking. It's also a big mountain biking region, with trails starting just minutes from downtown.

The **Columbia Gorge Windsurfing Association,** a non-profit group, is dedicated to enhancing windsurfing on the gorge. Their website offers information about river access, popular sailing spots, and links to live gorge cameras. **Big Winds Hood River,** one of the region's largest shops and run by experienced windsurfers and kitesurfers, has a large lesson and rental center in the gorge. —*LF*

(i) **Columbia Gorge Windsurfing Association** (© 541/386-9225; www.cgwa. net). **Big Winds Hood River** (© 888/509-4210; www.bigwinds.com).

WHEN TO GO: June–Sept.

✈ Portland.

🛏 $ **Gorge View B&B** (run by boardsailors), 1009 Columbia St. (© 541/386-5770; www.gorgeview.com). $$ **Hood River Hotel,** 102 Oak Ave. (© 800/386-1859 in the U.S. or 541/386-1900; www.hoodriver hotel.com).

Riverboarding in Colorado
Face-First Adrenaline Rushes
Aspen & Steamboat Springs, Colorado, U.S.A.

If extreme whitewater rafting or kayaking don't give you enough thrills, try knifing through rapids face-first. Picture yourself lying on a riverboard and racing along as the rushing water blasts through churning rapids. On this tough plastic board, which is similar to a boogie board but molded to fit arms and upper body and covers your hips, you hang onto the handle grips to help control how you slide through the water. You are armored in a helmet, wetsuit, gloves, booties, fins, and knee or shin guards (and, we hope, a life jacket), as you dodge the rocks that create the rapids.

Riverboarding has long been popular in parts of New Zealand, where it's called "sledging" (see 139). Several years ago some Kiwis brought the sport to Colorado, a state where extreme sports thrive. It was the perfect marriage of sport and place. The hot spots in Colorado are around Steamboat and Aspen.

Aspen Seals, based in Aspen, runs riverboarding trips on the Roaring Fork and Arkansas rivers. Where the trips go depends upon the river flow at the time of your trip, but can range from Class II and III water, where you'll have time to enjoy scenic stretches, to Class V water, where you'll be totally focused on maneuvering through the rapids. **Boarddom Bound** in Steamboat gives riverboarding lessons in the spring and early summer. When you take lessons, equipment is usually provided. You need to be physically fit and adventurous for this

sport. Age minimums may vary according to the difficulty of the trip.

Both Aspen and Steamboat offer a lot more than riverboarding and are both excellent homebases for adrenaline-inducing experiences of all kinds. Aspen has it all, from mountain biking, hiking, and paragliding off the surrounding mountainsides to the summer-long Aspen Music Festival performances by world renowned musicians. The ambiance in Steamboat is more laid back, but all of the mountain sports, including skiing, snowboarding, hiking, biking, and more, are there. —LF

(i) **Aspen Chamber,** 420 Rio Grande Place (© 970/925-1940; www.aspenchamber. org). **Steamboat Chamber,** 125 Anglers Dr. (© 877-754-2269 or 970/879-0880; www.steamboatchamber.com). **Facelevel Industries** (www.facelevel.com).

TOURS: Aspen Seals, Aspen. (© 970/618-4569; www.aspenseals.com). **Boardom Bound,** 1205 Hilltop Parkways, Steamboat Springs (© 970/846-5926; www.boardom bound.com).

WHEN TO GO: Spring or summer.

✈ Aspen, Steamboat.

🛏 $$ **Sky Hotel,** 709 E. Durant Ave., Aspen (© 800/882-2582 or 970/925-6760; www.theskyhotel.com). $$ **Hotel Bristol,** 917 Lincoln Ave., Steamboat Springs (© 800/851-0872 or 970/879-3083; www. steamboathotelbristol.com).

10 Places to Go Fly a Kite . . . on the Water

Kiteboarding started picking up speed in the late 1990s, and it's now one of the fastest-growing twists on surfing. The basic idea is to balance on a relatively small and lightweight board while controlling a powerful kite, attached to a seat-like harness that wraps around your waist and thighs. In the right wind conditions, this equipment allows you to accelerate across the water and perform some awesome flips, turns, and other tricks. Even if the sea is fairly calm, a skilled kiteboarder can catch 30 or 40 feet (9 or 12m) of air. This extreme sport takes at least few days to learn and much longer to master, but the intense adrenaline rush it instantly creates will encourage you to keep at it, especially in these 10 spots. —JS

129 Tarifa, Spain: This southernmost European spot on the Andalusian coast is widely considered to be the mecca for kiteboarding because of its mighty wind and relaxed vibe. The Moorish town, just 13km (8 miles) north of Africa, is situated at the meeting place of the Mediterranean Sea and the Atlantic Ocean, where there's an ideal collision of offshore levanter and onshore poinente winds. A major pro event usually takes place here each year in early July. www.hotelhurricane.com.

130 Cabarete, Dominican Republican: Life in Cabarete—on the Dominican Republican's north coast—pretty much revolves around three things: kiteboarding, partying, and resting up to hit the water again. The best time to visit is between December and April or June and August, when the wind regularly reaches speeds of around 25 to 30kmph (15–20 mph). Frequent sporting events, such as the Kiteboarding World Cup and the Red Bull Masters of the Ocean event, continue to draw pros as well as spectators to the world-renowned area. The main beaches for kiteboarding are **Bozo Beach** and, farther west, **Kite Beach.** www.laureleastman.com.

131 Ceará, Brazil: From mid-July to mid-January, there's almost constant wind and big white-crested swells off the pristine coastline between Fortaleza and Jericoacoara in northeastern Brazil. This area has become the South American hot spot for kiteboarders. As warm air from the Amazon in the south hits trade winds from the north, Ceará gets steady and strong gusts. **Cumbuco,** just 32km (20 miles) away from the Fortaleza International Airport, is the best place to begin your kiteboarding adventure. **Paracuru** and **Prea** are also popular destinations along the coast. www.kiteadventures.com.

132 Mui Ne, Vietnam: This unassuming fishing village and resort town in Vietnam's quiet Binh Thuan Province, about a 5-hour drive from the chaos of Ho Chi Min City, is one of the most popular kiteboarding destinations in Asia. The allure is the consistent crosswinds from December to May that encourage long glides over and above the South China Sea. Lessons in this area tend to be fairly cheap. www.stormkiteboarding.com.

133 Viuex Fort, St Lucia: This tropical paradise gets strong prevailing winds that average between 18 and 20 knots in the winter and 14 and 16 knots during off-peak season, though the best weather usually comes between December and August. Upping the adrenaline ante, a high-tech kiteboarding school opened in fall 2009 at the

Coconut Bay Resort and Spa. It offers state-of-the-art equipment including walkie-talkie–like radios on all the helmets and video coaching, so that instructors can review and help improve performances while you're on the water. *www.2elements.co.uk.*

134 Maui, Hawaii, U.S.A.: Kiteboarding isn't just a sport in Maui; it's an obsession—especially at Ka'a Point, on the western end of Kahana Beach (also known as Kite Beach). Set in a valley between the West Maui Mountains and Haleakala, wind funnels across Kite Beach, creating a thrilling mix of conditions. Fairly predictable trade winds are common from May to October, while more diverse onshore winds typically blow through in the winter. *www.ksmaui.com.*

135 Traverse City, Michigan, U.S.A.: From June to September, consistent onshore winds and clear water create optimal conditions for kiteboarding along the almost 180 miles (290km) of shoreline in Traverse City. You can choose from stretches with flat water, perfect for learning new tricks, or other locations with big freshwater waves. Close to Chicago, Detroit, and Cincinnati, this area of northern Michigan is the Midwestern hub of kiteboarding. *www.broneah.com.*

136 Hood River, Oregon, U.S.A.: If you drive about an hour east of Portland between June and August, you'll see a rainbow of kites soaring over the Hood River along the Colombia River Gorge, where steady wind gusts can reach between 20 to 40 mph (32–64kmph). As kiters take off from the popular launching spot on Kite Beach, known as "the Spit," they speed across the rippling waves created by the warm air blowing upstream from the Pacific Ocean that passes through the drier region east of the Cascade Mountains. *www.brianswindsurfing.com.*

137 Outer Banks, North Carolina, U.S.A.: Each summer, the sand-dune-speckled islands of the Outer Banks attract kiteboard enthusiasts from all over the world. Pamlico Sound, off of Cape Hatteras, is one of the area's most renowned spots because of its steady robust winds and smooth shallow water. If you're just starting out, one of the best places to learn is at the Kitty Hawk Kiteboarding Resort in Rodanthe on Hatteras Island. *www.kittyhawkkites.com.*

138 The Best Odyssey, various locations: The *Discovery* is a Lagoon 570 catamaran that sails around the world, offering 10-day adventures to some of the earth's most remote waters and rarely visited islands. To get on board, you have to purchase a yacht share for around $20,000, which gets you one trip per year with a cabin that sleeps two people. Most cabins include flat-screen TVs, DVD players, and air-conditioning. The boat's got piles of kites and kiteboards, surfboards, scuba gear, and paragliding equipment—among plenty of other toys for water lovers. In 2010, the *Discovery* itinerary includes trips to the Andaman Islands, the Maldives, Chagos, Madagascar, and Mozambique. In 2011, it will sail to Tanzania, Kenya, the Seychelles, or the Red Sea. *www.offshoreodysseys.com.*

White Water Sledging
Riding the River Face Down
New Zealand

Racing through Roaring Meg's rapids or the infamous Chinese Dogleg sections of New Zealand's Kawarau River, you'll want to use those flippers on your feet to steer. Face down, you're river sledging through turbulent whitewater. The tour operators claim previous experience isn't required, so you put on the padded wetsuit, the helmet, booties, life jacket, and fins, not quite sure what to expect.

Before hitting the big-time rapids, you'll probably be introduced to maneuvering the sledge in quieter backwater eddies. First you rest your chest on the sledge, which looks a bit like a modified boogie board, and put your arms in groves on each side for a good grip and control. Using your flippers you start moving with the flowing water, gradually working up to steering through rougher whitewater. Each time you successfully steer around rocks and jockey among eddies and whirlpools, you get a thrill. Maybe it's the sense of control, maybe it's the scene of the water roaring all around you. Or maybe it's just the fun of bouncing up and down, soaking wet, one on one with Mother Nature.

River sledging (or river boarding as it's called in the U.S., and hydrospeeding in Europe) is popular on the more turbulent sections of the rivers near Queenstown and Wanaka on New Zealand's South Island. A number of companies run 3- to 5-hour excursions on the Kawarau and Clutha rivers. You could take a trip through Roaring Meg, which provides a mix of fast-flowing rapids, whirlpools, and boils, with a quieter section at the end. For a bigger adrenaline rush, choose an all-day trip through the Gorge, with its Class IV rapids, and Roaring Meg. Frogz Whitewater Sledging and Mad Dog River Boarding are based in the Queenstown area. If you're staying in Queenstown and need a little time out of the water, lots of other activities including bungee jumping, four-wheeling, horseback riding, and hiking are all close-by.

On the North Island, you can river sledge on the Kaituna River in Rotorua, a region famous for its Maori culture, and its geothermal geysers and mud pools. Kaitiaki Adventures offers excursions on the Kaituna River and a heli-sledge excursion to the Okere River, which includes a jet boat ride. You can also go sledging down the Waingongoro River then "dam dropping" over a high water weir, under the shadow of Mount Taranaki. —LF

ⓘ **Waingongoro Sledging** (✆ 64/274/706899; www.damdrop.com). **Frogz Whitewater Sledging,** Queensland (✆ **800/4-FROGZ** or 03 441 2318; www.frogz.co.nz). **Kaitiaki Adventures** (✆ **800/338-736** in New Zealand or 0064/7/357-2236 outside New Zealand; www.kaitiaki.co.nz). **Rotorura Tourism** (www.rotoruanz.com). **New Zealand Tourism** (www.newzealand.com).

WHEN TO GO: Dec–Feb (New Zealand summer).

✈ Queenstown or Rotorua.

⌂ In Queenstown: $$$ **Queenstown House,** 69 Hallenstein St. (✆ **64/3-442-9043;** www.queenstownhouse.co.nz). $$$ **Hotel Sofitel Queenstown,** 8 Duke St. (✆ **03/450-0045** or 0800/444-422 in New Zealand; www.sofitel.com). In Rotorua: $$$ **Peppers on the Point,** 214 Kawaha Point Rd., Rotorua (✆ **64/7/348-4868;** www.peppers.co.nz). $$ **Rydges Rotorua,** 272 Fenton St., Rotorua (✆ **800/446-187** in New Zealand, 1300/857-922 in Australia, or 61/2/9261-4929; www.rydges.com).

140 Watersports

Tsitsikamma Coastal National Park
Ocean Reefs to Treetop Adventures
Eastern Cape, South Africa

Adrenaline junkies will love South Africa's Tsitsikamma Coastal National Park because there are so many ways you can get high or low. You can take a 10-zipline adventure, leap off the highest commercial bungee jump in the world, go scuba diving, tubing, or hiking. Located in the Eastern Cape Province, Tsitsikamma stretches from the Indian Ocean, where rolling waves crash into rocks and spew spray 6m (20 ft.) in the air, to the 27m (90-ft.) high pines in temperate forests.

Tsitsikamma means "the place of much water," and racing in a jet boat on the **Storms River** between narrow canyon walls you can see high-water marks where water rushes downstream after a heavy storm in the forest beyond. When the water is calm check out the Lilliputian-sized people walking across the suspension bridge hung from one canyon side to the other at the mouth of the river.

It's also possible to **scuba dive** and **snorkel** on the Storms River and the Indian Ocean, though you'll have to rely on calm waters. Trips usually depart from Storms River Mouth. You will have opportunities for seeing vibrant reefs and colorful fish. Shark and dolphin sightings are also common.

If your plans in Tsitsikamma involve staying dry, there are plenty of distractions above water, too. Snug in a harness, you'll become hooked to your first **zipline.** Looks and sounds easy, until it's time to take, literally, a leap of faith. Jump into the air and you're halfway across the line to the next platform before you start breathing again. Just nine more ziplines to go. The lines are strung from one tree to another, at times stretching almost 270m (900 ft.). At each platform, guides offer tidbits about the park's history and the forest you're zipping through.

If you like to leap off bridges, the Bloukrans Bridge has the highest commercial **bungee jumping** operation in the world (see **41**). You'll don a full body harness, then walk out on a special catwalk to the top of the arch (212m/708 ft. above the river), count down, and jump off. If you don't want to take the catwalk, the Flying Fox, a 197m (656 ft.) cable slide is the fast route to the bridge's archway. If you don't want to do the bungee jump, or even just the Flying Fox for the thrill, you can still take a tour of the bridge on the catwalk.

Tsitsikamma Coastal National Park is a comfortable day trip from Port Elizabeth, although you won't be able to experience all of the adventures in 1 day. If you're staying in Cape Town, plan on an overnight trip. At Storms River Mouth Rest Camp, there is comfortable lodging perched on the rocks above the coastline offering spectacular views of the Indian Ocean. —LF

ⓘ **South Africa National Parks** (☏ **27/42/281-1607;** www.sanparks.org/parks/tsitsikamma). **South Africa Nature Reserves** (☏ **27/21/424-1037;** www.nature-reserve.co.za/tsitsikamma-coastal-national-park.html).

WHEN TO GO: Year-round.

✈ Cape Town International (483km/300 miles).

⊨ $$ **The Cape Cadogan,** 5 Upper Union St., Cape Town (☏ **27/21-480-8080;** www.capecadogan.com). **Storms River Mouth Rest Camp,** in the National Park (see above).

Deep Sea Fishing
In Line with Hemingway's Hooks
Jardines de la Reina, Cuba

Fishing almost becomes its own character in many of Earnest Hemmingway's novels, probably because he was so intensely passionate about it. He particularly loved getting out on the water when he lived in Cuba. For good reason: This Caribbean country offers secluded waters with an abundance of bonefish, tarpon, permit, and many other coveted species of fish.

During the 1930s and 1940s, Hemingway was one of the first explorers to set sail off the shores of **Cayo Guillermo** on Cuba's northeastern coast, searching for marlin and swordfish in the Atlantic Ocean. Connected to **Cayo Coco** by a 15km (9-mile) *pedraplén* (a walkway that bridges the distance btw. the mainland and the cays), this area boasts clear turquoise water and spectacular beaches including Playa El Paso, Playa del Medio, and Playa Larga. There's even a deep sea fishing competition here named in honor of Hemingway that's been going on since the 1950s.

Cayo Guillermo is a good place to start your fishing adventure in Cuba. Relax at an all-inclusive resort and book a short fishing excursion with **Marlin Marina** (© **33/30-1737-1323**) to catch some marlin of your own. After you've chilled out for a few days, you'll want to venture a bit farther for the real excitement.

From Cayo Coco, it's about an hour and a half drive southeast to **Jucaro,** the main port in **Jardines de la Reina,** or Gardens of the Queen. This is the departure point for most multi-day fishing trips in Jardins de la Reina. The 160km-long (100-mile) chain of uninhabited cayes (keys) is protected by the third-longest barrier reef in the world. In Jucaro, you can either board a "live-aboard" yacht (*Halcon, La Reina,* or *Caballones*) or a transport boat to take you to **La Tortuga,** the double-decker floating houseboat hotel that's permanently secured in a small protected channel about 3 hours from Jucaro. Whichever you choose, you'll spend your days at sea—with a small group of other anglers and without cellphone or e-mail access—just trying to reel in some big 'ol bonefish, tarpon, and permit. The saltwater fly-fishing grand slam would be to catch all three on the same day, but that's nearly impossible. Permits are particularly difficult to get a hold of; they're elusive, skittish, and smart. There are plenty of other fish here too, including snapper, a variety of jacks, and grouper.

Trying to wrestle any 30-pound fish out of the water is no small feat, and any experienced angler knows it. As you maneuver your fishing rod, trying to hold on, the thrill of the fight—and eventually the catch—pulses through your whole body. As Hemingway once said during a 1965 interview in *The Atlantic Monthly,* "It's wonderful to get out on the water. It's the last free place there is, the sea." *—JS*

(i) **Cuba Tourist Board in Canada,** 1200 Bay St., Ste. 305, Toronto (© **866/404-2822;** www.gocuba.ca). **Cuban Portal of Tourism** (www.cubatravel.cu).

TOUR: Avalon Cuban Fishing Centers (© **011/39-335-814-9111;** www.cuban fishingcenters.com).

WHEN TO GO: Oct–Aug.

✈ Aeropuerto Internacional Jardines del Rey.

142

Sportfishing off Cabo
Gone Fishin'
Cabo San Lucas, Mexico

Cabo San Lucas is sometimes called "the town that marlin built," and it comes by that reputation honestly. Landing a marlin that's well over 100 pounds or larger is a regular occurrence here, and with yellowfin tuna, wahoo, dorado, yellowtail, and sailfish in plentiful supply, there's no wonder this once-sleepy town on the southern tip of Baja California has been drawing anglers from around the world for decades. But if there's one prized catch that keeps them coming back, it's the billfish, those stunning beautiful sailfish, swordfish, and marlins that put up a titanic fight at the end of a line, even to the point of occasionally injuring the fisherman lucky enough to land one. Wrestling one of these beasts of the sea is a jolt of an experience—the kind from which legends are born.

Cabo San Lucas and its sister resort town, San Jose del Cabo, are easily reached from Los Cabos International Airport. From either town, or just about anywhere on the tip of Baja, it's a simple affair to arrange a fishing trip. Strolling onto a marina with that "I want to fish" look in your eyes will net you several options for taking a trip out on a panga, the small, speedy boats that are a favorite with the local *pescadores* (fishermen). Those who prefer a more cushy experience should make reservations with one of the larger cruisers that offer an all-inclusive experience combining lunch, drinks, fishing license, beer, bait, gratuity to the crew and the filleting and freezing of your catch.

The tip of Baja isn't all about fishing, either. When the fish aren't biting, ATV trips out of town, glass-bottom boat cruises, horseback riding, snorkeling, scuba diving, and surfing—as well as plentiful golf and tennis opportunities—can help anglers pass the time.

Marlin and their fellow billfish are fast, aggressive, powerful predators that make for a fantastic man-vs.-nature struggle. They're also increasingly in danger of being overfished, so most reputable captains and pescaderos insist on catch-and-release fishing, to ensure that stocks of these magnificent creatures remain ample for generations, and that the balance of all fish species in the region's waters is maintained. As one lifelong fishing aficionado stated, "If you love something, set it free." But you won't walk away empty-handed; anglers usually get a certificate that the fish they caught was tagged and released humanely back into its deep blue home. —*ML*

(ⓘ) **Los Cabos Tourism Office,** Plaza San José, Locales 3 and 4 (© **624/146-9628**).

TOURS: Pisces Fleet (© **624/143-1288;** www.piscessportfishing.com). **Minerva's** (© **624/143-1282;** www.minervas.com).

WHEN TO GO: Apr–Nov.

⊨ $ **Cabo Inn,** 20 de Noviembre and Leona Vicario (© **624/143-0819;** www. caboinnhotel.com). $$ **Casa Bella B&B,** Hidalgo 10 (© **624/143-6400;** www.los cabosguide.com/hotels/casa-bella-hotel. htm.com).

Spearfishing in Baja
Catching More than Rays in Mexico
La Paz, Mexico

Spearfishing is one of the most primal ways to put meat on the table, and you can't find many places better suited for an undersea hunt than Baja California. With its gin-clear water and plentiful sea life, Baja is a sport-fishing paradise. Several world-record catches have been landed here, and the variety of blue water species such as wahoo, amberjack, yellow-fin tuna, dorado, and billfish, and reef dwellers such as pargo and cabrilla, keep spearfishers coming back to Baja year after year to partake in the spirited, often hair-raising contest between man and fish.

La Paz enjoys a well-earned reputation as a sportsman's paradise, and is a prime spot for beginning a seafaring adventure. It can be reached by air from a number of North American cities or, for hard-core adventurers with time on their hands, it's a few days drive south of the U.S. and Mexico border through the ruggedly beautiful Baja California peninsula. (Some folks fly into San Jose del Cabo, then charter a flight or drive the 2–3 hr. trek to La Paz.) Visitors can choose from a number of good hotels in La Paz, or arrange for a live-aboard experience, where your entire stay takes place on a boat. With a live-aboard, you can travel to more distant fishing spots and choose whether to spend the day fishing, kayaking, diving, or simply relaxing on the beach.

One of the many advantages to this kind of adventure travel is, of course, dining on the day's catch. Add to that the knowledge that spearfishing is an environmentally sustainable means of fishing that doesn't contribute to the depletion of fisheries, and you've got a meal you can feel good about.

Don't be dismayed if the fishing—or your aim—isn't good. La Paz has plenty of active pursuits to keep adventurers happy. Sea kayaking, whale-watching, and hiking are popular options, and a large colony of sea lions on Los Isolotes just north of La Paz will be happy to keep you entertained. —*ML*

ⓘ **La Paz Tourism Board** (ℂ **612/122-5939;** www.vivalapaz.com).

TOURS: Desea Adventures (ℂ **310/691-8040;** www.deseabaja.com). **Tailhunter International** (ℂ **626/638-3383;** www. tailhunter-international.com).

WHEN TO GO: Apr–Nov.

✈ La Paz.

🛏 $$$ **Posada Las Flores,** Alvaro Obregón 440 (ℂ **877/245-2860;** www. posadalasflores.com). $$ **La Concha Beach Resort,** Carretera Pichilingue Km 5 (ℂ **612/121-6161;** www.laconcha.com).

Riding the Riptide
Let It Rip!
Rangiroa, French Polynesia

There are a handful of places in the world where, due to some fluke of geography, the incoming tides are unusually large and strong. Most of those tidal surges seem occur in cold, rocky, forbidding regions (northern Canada, anyone?), but then there's the tropical atoll of Rangiroa, the jewel of French Polynesia. This immense volcanic landform stretches like a coral necklace for some 110 miles, all surrounding a sapphire blue lagoon about as big as the entire city of Los Angeles. Despite its size, there are only two narrow passes through which the rising or falling tide can flow, and when the rip tide begins, a spectacular show ensues. Bottlenose dolphins frolic in the 12-foot-high, surging waves, while a marine menagerie flows past. Manta rays, several species of sharks, hawksbill turtles, barracudas, even humpback whales all call Rangiroa home, and they're happy to welcome snorkelers and divers to their playground.

Most flights to this off-the-beaten track destination arrive from Papeete, French Polynesia. Visitors expecting wild nightlife or deluxe shopping may be disappointed to learn that the two towns of Avatoru and Tiputa really don't offer much more than an incredibly relaxing tropical paradise and world-class watersports. There are exceptions, however; Avatoru is home to Boutique Ikimasho, which specializes in exquisite black pearl jewelry, and other shops turn out charming handicrafts.

But it's the water that draws people and other creatures to this Eden of the South Seas. Riding the riptide through the pass at Tiputa is a great rush, and makes "Rangi" one of the world's premiere diving and snorkeling destinations. Rubber Zodiac boats drop thrill-seekers in the drink outside Tiputa Pass right before the tide is scheduled to change. When the tide surges, fish, dolphins, and humans alike are swept into the lagoon on the underwater ride of their lives.

The surge lasts several minutes, and if that's not exciting enough for you, some tour operators will let you swim with the sharks. No, not in a protective steel cage—that's for sissies—but next to a chum line where dozens of sharks, including those known to attack humans like hammerheads, tiger sharks, lemon sharks, and black-tips are engaging in a feeding frenzy just a few feet away from your unprotected flesh. If you still need more adrenaline after that, get an injection. —ML

TOURS: Caradonna Dive Adventures (✆ **800/328-2288;** www.caradonna.com). **TOPdive** (✆ **689/96-05-60;** www.topdive. com). **Dive Tahiti Blue** (✆ **310/507-0211;** www.divetahitiblue.com).

WHEN TO GO: Year-round.

🛏 $$$ **Hotel Kia Ora Sauvage,** P.O. Box 198-98775, Avatoru (✆ **689/96-04-93;** www.hotelkiaora.com). $$ **Novotel Rangiroa Lagoon Resort,** P.O. Box 17-98775, Avatoru (✆ **689/96-02-00;** www.novotel. com).

10 Places to Ride the Curl: Surfing Around the World

Ask 10 avid surfers about their favorite surf spots and you'll get 10 different answers. But, no matter where you decide to surf, always check with the locals and lifeguards before entering the water for advice on where to find the best waves for your skill level and where the danger zones are. For more great surf spots and reports on daily swells visit www.surfline.com and www.wannasurf.com. —LF

145 Oahu, Hawaii, U.S.A.: Some surfers make the case that the **North Shore** of Oahu is the best surfing location on the globe. In the winter, thunderous waves have been known to reach 30 to 40 feet (9–12m), especially around **Ehukai Beach,** often called The Pipeline. The massive tubes formed by curling waves are only for the very

experienced. Closer to Waikiki and Honolulu, the **South Shore** has numerous breaks where beginners can learn the sport, and experienced surfers will have fun. **Waimea Beach** is the site of the annual Quicksilver Eddie Aikau Invitational, held when the wave height is 20 feet (6m) or higher. This beach attracts the "big wave" surfers in the winter. While in Oahu, be sure to stop by the **Honolulu Surfing Museum** in Jimmy Buffett's at the Beachcomber in Waikiki. *www.visit-oahu.com.*

Oahu is a surfing mecca.

146 Santa Cruz, California, U.S.A.: Steamer Lane in Santa Cruz is one of the most popular surf spots in California, so expect an audience when you paddle out from shore. Because of its location, the big waves from the west and the northwest even out here as they slide into Monterey Bay. Locals say that **Cowells,** nearby, is a better choice for the less experienced surfer. *www.ci-santa-cruz.ca.us.*

147 Jeffreys Bay, South Africa: The waves roll onto the shore with a rhythmic intensity at Jeffreys Bay, one of the most popular surfing spots among the many favored in South Africa. An increasingly popular place for weekend and summer homes set amidst some of South Africa's wildest coastline, J-Bay on the Indian Ocean is an easy drive from Port Elizabeth. The best time for waves here is the end of May through August. In July, a Billabong Pro stop is held at **Supertubes** beach, where the waves continually roll in perfectly formed for championship surfing. *www.infojeffreysbay.com.*

148 San Diego, California, U.S.A.: Take your pick from a number of great surfing hot spots in the San Diego area: La Jolla Shores, Pacific Beach, Ocean Beach, and in the North County, Oceanside and Carlsbad State Beach. Strong riptides are prevalent along this coast, where waters are cold nearly year-round (you'll likely need a wetsuit no matter what season), so be sure to check with locals before making assumptions about conditions. *www.sandiego.org.* **La Jolla Surf Systems** (© 858/456-2777; *www.lajollasurf systems.com*). **Ocean Beach Surf & Skate** (© 619/225-0674; *www.oceanexperience.com*). **Kahuna Bob's Surf School** (© 760/721-7700; *www.kahunabob.com*).

149 Donegal Bay, Ireland: Isolated and rugged, the Northwest Ireland coastline has lately been luring both professional and amateur surfers. You'll have to prepare for the cold weather and waters, but those same challenges keep away large crowds. Pair that advantage with the friendly Irish locals and other nearby wild and scenic destinations such as **Glenveagh National Park** (www.glenveaghnational park.ie), and you'll understand why surfing this destination offers a unique and exhilarating experience. Bundoran makes a good home base. (© *353/71-9841968; www. bundoransurfco.com.*

150 Tamarindo, Costa Rica: The surfing flick *Endless Summer 2* put these waves on many a surfer's radar. You'll find big waves and great weather at breaks such as **Little Hawaii** and **Witches Rock.** There are waves for both short and long boards here. *www.visittamarindo.com.*

151 Hanalei Bay, Kauai, Hawaii, U.S.A.: Because the 2-mile long, crescent moon-shaped bay on Kauai's North Shore is home break for some world champion surfers, the water here has become a hot spot for surfers. Locals may advise you to hang around the **Hanalei pier** to find out where the waves are gentle. Those looking for a bit more excitement should head to **Pine Tree** to watch the pro surfers rip daily in the winter. *www.kauaiexplorer.com/kauai_beaches/hanalei_bay.php.*

152 Tavarua Island, Fiji: Cloudbreak is touted as one of the gnarliest reefs on the planet, but you'll have to stay at the private Tavarua Island surf camp to surf here. This break is in the middle of the ocean, a short ponga ride from the resort. Both **Cloudbreak,** a reef break, and **Restaurants,** which wraps around part of the island, are for experienced surfers, but there are more gentle spots for beginners. Plan on booking in advance—there's room for only 36 guests at the resort. On changeover days, non-guests may be allowed to surf here. *Tavarua Island Resort (© 805/686-4551; www.tavarua.com).*

153 Taghazout, Morocco: The excellent break and lack of crowds draw surf aficionados to this small surf town on the coast of Morocco. In addition to Taghazout, advantageous breaks can be found all the way from north of Rabat **(Mehdiya Plage)** to south of Agadir **(Sidi Ifni).** The lagoon at Oualidia is a great place for beginners. **Imessouane** and **Anchor Point** are also prime destinations. *Rapture (© 43/720-70-17-52 [Austria]; www. rapturecamps.com). Pure Blue Surf Adventures (© 44/1326 316363; www.purebluewater.com).*

154 Bells Beach, Australia: Bells Beach, a point break where waves can range from 2 to 15 feet (4.5m), is the most famous of the dozens of breaks along the Great Ocean Road in Victoria, Australia. Located about 100km (62 miles) from Melbourne, this is the spot for the **Rip Curl Pro Surf & Music Festival,** the world's longest-running surfing competition, held every Easter. The area is only for experienced surfers and swimmers, but other large ocean swells land on cliff-sided sandy beaches elsewhere along the road. *www.bellsbeachaustralia.com.*

Nicaraguan Surf Camp
Surf's Up, Amigo!
Nicaragua's Pacific Coast

In a land once famous for death squads, drug trafficking, and CIA-backed revolutionaries, a new breed of fanatic has found a home: the surfer dude. Nicaragua was, until recently, not even a blip on the international surfing radar screen. But when Costa Rica's once-isolated beaches became congested with tourists, surfers cast their eyes toward the undiscovered country to the north. World-class waves, desolate beaches, and ridiculously cheap food and lodging—not to mention the balmy climate—turned this tropical country into surfing's new hot spot.

Most of the best surfing spots are found on the country's southern Pacific coast, about 3 hours' drive from the capital city of Managua, home to the country's largest airport. Unlike more developed countries, surf lodges here are fewer in number and most are simple affairs with friendly staff but few amenities. It's not unheard of, for example, to find a lizard in your bedroom, or discover that the camp's lounge is a thatched hut with a dirt floor and a cooler full of beer. (In other words, if you're looking for a four-star luxury vacation, keep looking.) Travelers should also be aware

A surfer learns to ride the waves in Nicaragua.

that some places calling themselves "surf camps" don't offer lessons; call or check your destination's website to confirm that lessons are available.

Fortunately for newbies, surfing is one of the few sports where you can have a blasting good time on your first day out, and most surf instructors tend to be relaxed folks who are happy to spend time getting you up on your board. No surfboard to call your own? No worries—surfboard rentals are available at just about every surf camp.

Nicaragua has earned its newfound reputation as a primo surf destination. A steady offshore wind keeps the waves high, and there is a variety of reef and beach breaks to keep beginners and pros happy. For non-surfers, Nicaragua has a number of other attractions like kayaking, snorkeling, horseback riding, deep-sea fishing, and touring coffee plantations. And if the waves start to get a little too crowded for your "taste," just think like the adventurous surf god you now are and cast your eyes to the next destination up the shore—in this case, El Salvador. —*ML*

TOURS: Monty's Jiquilillo Surf Camp (© **505/8884-4461;** www.nicaraguasurf beach.com). **Chica Brava All-Girls Surf Camp** (© **832/519-0253** or 505/8894-2842; www.chicabrava.com). **The Surf Sanctuary** (© **505/8894-6260;** www.the surfsanctuary.com). **Tours Nicaragua** (© **505/2252-4035;** www.toursnicaragua. com).

WHEN TO GO: The biggest surf is usually found from Apr–Sept, and smaller swells (perfect for beginners) can be found from Dec–Feb.

✈ Managua.

3 Mountains & Canyons

156 Hiking

Hiking Perito Moreno Glacier
Ice, Ice, Baby
Santa Cruz, Argentina

At over 29km (18 miles) long and 5km (3 miles) wide, Perito Moreno glacier is often described as one of the greatest natural wonders of the world. Glistening castles of ice tower 45m (150 ft.) over the surface of Lake Argentino, where ice calves the size of apartment buildings go crashing into the lake every few hours. The entire glacier is an enormous shifting mass of creaking, groaning ice that can move and crack without notice; hikers are strongly advised to seek out an experienced guide before trekking across this beautiful but dangerous icescape.

The town of El Calafate (a 3-hr. flight from Buenos Aires) is most visitors' first stop before taking the 2-hour bus journey into **Los Glaciares National Park** (www.losglaciares.com), a 607,028-hectare (1.5 million-acre) wonderland of mountains, forests, glaciers, and lakes that was declared a UNESCO World Heritage Site in 1981. Tours of the glacier can take up to five hours on a full tour, which often includes a surprise break of chocolates and whiskey chilled by—what else?—fresh-chipped glacial ice. There's also a shorter "mini-trek" that takes roughly 90 minutes. Hikers on either tour can expect to wear crampons, or metal spikes that attach to their hiking boots, when traversing the ice. There are also boat tours that glide across Lake Argentino, giving visitors close-up views of calving icebergs and the lofty clifflike face of the glacier.

Every few years, the glacier advances far enough to form a natural dam across part of the lake; as a result, one side of the lake rises up to 30m (100 ft.) above the other. When this happens, pressure builds up in the higher part of the lake until the ice barrier explodes in a spectacular eruption. It's impossible to predict when this will occur, but those lucky enough to witness it are treated to an event they'll never forget. Los Glaciares National Park is also home to several other impressive glaciers, including **Upsala** and **Spegazzini** glaciers; adventurous hikers may also want to take in **Mount Fitz Roy** and **Cerro Torre,** a massive spike of granite that's among the world's most challenging climbs. —*ML*

TOURS: Interlagos (✆ **02902/491179;** interlagos@cotecal.com.ar). **SurTurismo** (✆ **02902/491266;** www.surturismo.com.ar).

WHEN TO GO: Nov–Apr.

✈ El Calafate (48km/30 miles).

🛏 $$$$ **Los Notros,** Parque Nacional Los Glaciares (✆ **11/4814-3934;** www.losnotros.com). $$ **Miyazato Inn,** Egidio Feruglio 150, El Calafate (✆ **02902/491953;** mIyazatoInn@cotecal.com.ar).

Previous page: Heli-hiking in Banff.

Mount Fuji
Scaling the Symbol of Japan
Fuji-Hakone-Izu National Park, Japan

The Japanese call it "Fuji-san," as if it were a dear old friend. It's not only the tallest mountain in Japan—an almost perfect cone 3,776m (12,388 ft.) high, its majestic peak usually swathed in clouds—it symbolizes the very spirit of their country. Today, about 600,000 people climb Fuji-san every year, mostly on July and August weekends. It's not like climbing Everest, a challenge for the expert mountaineer; you'll see everyone from grandmothers to children wending their way up those level slopes. It's the quintessential Japanese experience.

You don't need climbing experience to ascend Mount Fuji, just stamina and a good pair of walking shoes. Six well-established trails lead to the summit; another six lead

Mount Fuji.

back down. Each is divided into 10 stages, with the actual climb beginning around the fifth stage. From Tokyo, which is only about 100km (62 miles) from Fuji, **Kawaguchiko Trail** is the least steep and easiest to get to. Take a shortcut directly to Kawaguchiko's Fifth Stage by **bus** from Tokyo's Shinjuku Station (be sure to book in advance); the trip takes about 2½ hours. From this starting point, it's about a 6-hour climb to the summit, with another 3 hours to make the descent; at the top, a 1-hour hiking trail circles the crater.

The highlight of the classic Fuji climb is to watch the sunrise from the peak, which in summer means being there by 4:30am. There are three ways to accomplish this: Take a morning bus, start climbing in early afternoon, spend the night near the summit in a mountain hut, and get up in time to arrive at the peak at sunrise; or alternatively, take in the sunrise from your hut—that still counts, honest!—and then climb to the top. Then there are the night climbers, who get off the bus at the Fifth Stage late in the evening and climb through the night using flashlights, timing it to hit the summit at sunrise. The mountain huts have futons for as many as 500 hikers each and serve simple Japanese meals (dried fish, rice, soup) if you aren't carrying your own grub; they're open July to August only and you must book early. One of the most popular with foreigners is the **Fujisan Hotel 2** (*(C)* **81/555/22-0237**) at stage 8.

It may be disconcerting to get off the bus at the Fifth Stage and see a crush of souvenir shops, blaring loudspeakers, and tour bus hordes—hardly the atmosphere for a purifying ritual. But don't worry; most of those tourists aren't here for the climb. You'll soon find yourself on a steep rocky path, surrounded only by scrub brush and a few intent hikers below and above you. Settle into your stride, and after a couple of hours you'll find yourself above the roily clouds—as if you are on an island, barren and rocky, in the middle of an ocean. Ah, there's your spiritual high. —*HH*

ⓘ **Fujiyoshida City Tourist Office** (✆ **81/555/24-1236**; www.city.fujiyoshida. yamanashi.jp).

TOUR: Mt. Fuji Mountaineering School GoRiki (✆ **81/555/24-1032;** www.fuji tozan.jp/english).

WHEN TO GO: July–Aug.

✈ Narita International (48km/30 miles). Shizuoka Airport (81km/50 miles).

🛏 For help with booking huts, call the **Japanese Inn Union of Mount Fuji** (✆ **81/555/22-1944**).

158 Hiking

Trekking to Mt. Everest Base Camp
Walking Among the World's Tallest Mountains
Nepal

Imagine making 19 trips to the 8,711m (29,035-ft.) summit of Mt. Everest. That's the record set recently by the Sherpa Appa. If you've always wanted to see Mount Everest up close, but you don't have the technical climbing skills and a burning passion to summit the tallest mountain in the world, there is an option. Numerous tour companies lead treks to the Everest Base Camp at 5,276m (17,585 ft.). From here, you can watch climbers set off on their dream to reach the peak of the world. But just because they're ascending all the way to the peak, doesn't mean that you can't get your thrills a little farther down the hill. The Base Camp trek can be an exhilarating trip in its own right, and the challenge of tackling this gargantuan mountain at any altitude will be an unforgettable experience.

Most of the treks to the Everest Base Camp follow a similar itinerary. Upon leaving Kathmandu, you will fly approximately 40 minutes to Lukla, where the Sherpas divide up the gear and load pack animals. Then, you will hike to Phakding, along the way seeing a monastery in Ghat with colorful prayer wheels and shrines. The next day your trek takes you over suspension bridges and into Sagamatha National Park. After checking in and showing your

trekking pass (the company you book with should provide this), it's on to Namche Bazaar at 3,386m (11,286 ft.). Near Namche Bazaar is a rhododendron forest, which is gorgeous when in bloom, and wonderful waterfalls. All along the way the views are almost as breathtaking as the altitude. At Feriche, sited at approximately 4,200m (14,000 ft.), you'll pass by the only medical facility in the area and the staff will likely give a lecture on altitude sickness.

Once you reach a destination village, such as Dingboche at approximately 4,350m (14,500 ft.), you will spend a leisurely day acclimatizing to the thin air. From there it's a 2- or 3-day trek to the

Trekking to base camp is an alternative to conquering Mt. Everest.

Everest Base Camp. At Loboche you will trek along the moraine of the Khumbu Glacier and pass stone memorials to climbers who have lost their lives on Everest. (More than 150 climbers have died on the peak.) Several tour companies include a hike up Kala Pattar (5,535m/18,450 ft.), to give you some of the most spectacular views of Everest. Some treks spend just a few hours at the Everest Base Camp, while others arrange for trekkers to spend a night in one of the tents. Normally, you'll have an opportunity to interact with the climbers who plan to keep going and watch them prepare for their assent. Don't expect to see just a few climbers here. Especially in May and prime climbing season, there may be over a hundred people at Base Camp.

The tour packages that take you to this dizzying height usually start out in Kathmandu, Nepal, and generally last between 16 and 20 days. Most days you will walk between 5 and 6 hours and carry a daypack. With the exception of an overnight stay at Base Camp—should your trip include a night there (ask, don't assume)—you will sleep in tents, primitive hotels, lodges, or possibly a monastery. Along the trail are very primitive outhouses.

If you make this trip, you will see views that you'll never forget and that relatively few people have seen. But realistically there's another side. The tour brochures make this sound like a walk in the park. It isn't. You must be in very good shape physically. And even if you are, the altitude will make breathing difficult. For some trekkers altitude sickness is totally debilitating. Sleeping at altitude can also be difficult with frequent awakenings to take a deep breath There is no way to predict who will be seriously affected by the altitude and you may have to turn back. Trip insurance with repatriation is recommended. Weather is not always as pristine as the brochures portray. There could be snow at night and an 80°F (27°C) temperature during the day. That said, if you can handle it, you will have a once in a lifetime experience. —LF

ⓘ www.welcomenepal.com.

TOURS: Peak Freaks Expeditions (www. peakfreaks.com). **i Explore** (ⓒ **800/iEXPLORE** [439-7563] or 312/492-9443; www. iexplore.com). **Berg Adventures** (ⓒ **866/ 609-4148** or 403/609-4148; www.berg adventures.com). **Crystal Mountain Treks** (ⓒ **977/4416813;** www.crystal mountaintreks.com).

WHEN TO GO: May and Oct.

✈ Kathmandu.

Hiking 159

Hiking Waimea Canyon
The Grand Canyon of the Pacific
Kauai, Hawaii, U.S.A.

It's claimed that Mark Twain dubbed Waimea Canyon "The Grand Canyon of the Pacific." Although much smaller in size, you'll think it's big enough as you walk along part of the 10-mile-long (16km) and 1-mile-wide (1.6km) Waimea Canyon, which is more than 3,000 feet (900m) deep. Here, you will find many of the colorful crested buttes, deep gorges, and rugged crags similar to those one sees in the Grand Canyon in Arizona. Plus, there are those emerald-green slopes with the lush vegetation that helped give Kauai its nickname as the Garden Isle. A hike through this dramatic terrain is unforgettable. And with all the beauty that surrounds you, you'll hardly notice your own physical exertion.

Waimea Canyon was carved by rivers and floods that flowed from Mount Waialeale's

Waimea Canyon in Kauai is called the "Grand Canyon of the Pacific."

summit eons ago. As you stand on many of the lookout points, you'll be able to see the lines in the canyon walls that depict different volcanic eruptions and lava flows that occurred over the years.

Forty-five miles (72km) of trails wind throughout the canyon, which is protected by the Koke'e State Park, and the nearby Alakai Swamp. You'll find trails for all types of hikers here. Many of the routes intersect, but they range considerably in difficulty. Before starting out, pick up hiking maps of the area at the Ranger's Station located at the Koke'e Museum.

The **Iliau Nature Loop** is a short easy nature walk, with views of the canyon. The **Kukui Trail,** which begins off the Iliau Loop, is a difficult hike down a steep trail that drops 2,000 feet (600m) into the canyon. At the bottom, you can cool off in a swimming hole. The **Cliff Trail** leads to an overlook, where wild goats may be standing on cliffside ledges. The moderate **Canyon Trail,** which spurs off the Cliff Trail and follows the North Rim, is also popular. All of these hikes are day trips and you can do them without a guide as long as you are

properly prepared for hiking and have a good map.

If you're going to hike, bring plenty of water to prevent dehydration. Also keep in mind that the air at this elevation is 10° to 15°F (–12° to –9°C) cooler than in the valley and many spots are often shrouded in clouds by mid-afternoon. You'll be smart to bring an extra layer of clothing such as a fleece or light jacket.

All of Kauai is a playground for outdoor and water lovers. In addition to hiking in the canyon, there are plenty of opportunities to hike Kauai's rainforest. Beaches encompass the island, but check that you can swim off the shore near where you plan to book lodging. Some waters are more treacherous than others. The most popular way to see the steep cliffs plunging into the water off the Na Pali coast is by way of a Zodiac boat trip (see **105**). And when your adrenaline is tapped, but you've still got some energy, there's ample opportunity to hit the links. The golf courses on Kauai range from expensive, tough resort courses, including the Prince Course (at the St. Regis Princeville Resort; see lodging below), to the 9-hole **Kukuiolono** (854 Puu Rd., Kalaheao; ℂ **808/332-9151**), close to the South Shore. —*LF*

ⓘ **Go Hawaii** (ℂ **800/GO-HAWAII** [464-2924; www.gohawaii.com). **Kauai Visitors Bureau**, 4334 Rice St. (ℂ **800/262-1400** or 808/245-3971; www.kauaidiscovery.com).

WHEN TO GO: Year-round.

✈ Lihue, Kauai.

⊨ $$$ **Grand Hyatt Kauai Resort and Spa,** 1571 Poipu Rd. (ℂ **800/233-1234** or 808/742-1234; www.kauai.hyatt.com). $$$ **St. Regis Resort Princeville,** 5520 Ka Haku Rd. (ℂ **800/826-4400** or 808/826-9644; www.princevillehotelhawaii.com).

Hiking 160

Hiking in Southwestern Utah
Eyeing Hoodoos
Bryce Canyon National Park, Utah, U.S.A.

We didn't see a person for the first hour we were on the Tropic Trail, but we did see horse droppings. We felt completely isolated, but knew we were not completely alone. At the suggestion of a local, we took one of the back trails leading up to Bryce Canyon's horseshoe-shaped amphitheaters populated by the fantastically shaped hoodoo spires. Walking through the ponderosas and fir pines was easy at first, but breathing became harder as the trail got steeper and we found ourselves walking among the rocks. Before us rose sheer canyon walls with tints stretching from pale pink and red to orange and white. We finally understood why this small national park in southwestern Utah is such a popular hiking area. The raw and vivid landscape is awe-inspiring. To spend time and hike here is to experience nature at its mysterious best.

Although called Bryce Canyon, the park isn't a canyon. It holds more than a dozen amphitheaters, and every one is carved at least 1,000 feet (300m) into the limestone of the Colorado Plateau, formed millions of years ago. The chromatic walls and the fantastical spires, called hoodoos, were formed both by constant freezing and thawing, and the rain wearing away the limestone in the Claron Formation, which was created 60 million years ago by sedimentary deposits in a large prehistoric lake. The pink limestone, which has both iron and manganese oxide, creates the chromatic rock.

When we linked to the more popular **Navajo Loop** and the **Queens Garden** trails, the sense of isolation disappeared. Walking on well-worn paths that took us through a maze of weird and fragile-looking hoodoos, we started meeting chattering

Bryce Canyon National Park is famous for its dramatic rock formations.

tourists who began their walks at **Sunrise Point.**

Bryce Canyon has many marked hiking trails—some easy, some moderate, and some strenuous. In addition to the trails, hikers can also venture into the park's backcountry, considered a primitive area, with the appropriate permit. If you're after views but don't want a strenuous hike, try the easier portion of the **Rim Trail** between Sunrise and Sunset points, which provides minimal elevation changes but wonderful views of the main amphitheater. **Swamp Canyon,** rated as a moderate hike, takes you past hoodoos to an overlook with views into amphitheaters, from which you can descend and connect with other trails. One of the more strenuous routes, the **Fairyland Loop Trail,** takes you among amazing hoodoos, delivers spectacular views from the rim, and takes you into amphitheaters.

If you head into the more primitive areas, you'll walk among high meadows and forests of pines and see interesting geological sites. Backcountry permits are required for all overnight hikes and must be obtained in person at the Visitor Center at least 1 hour before closing. In-person reservations may be made up to 48 hours in advance.

Park rangers suggest wearing hiking boots with good lug traction and ankle support. Also carry plenty of water (at least a quart per 2–3 hr. of hiking per person).

Keep in mind the park tops out more than 9,000 feet (2,700m) above sea level. You're changing elevations when walking at the bottom of the amphitheaters, so watch out for altitude sickness.

Heading back down to the park entrance, we again descended into a quiet zone, turning around occasionally for a last glimpse of the amphitheaters. At the end of the trail, we met up with a group of horseback riders who were unsaddling their mounts and raving about the experience of riding among the hoodoos. We had similar feelings about walking among the 60-million-year-old spires.

Zion National Park (www.nps.gov/zion) and other colorful Utah parks such as **Cedar Breaks National Monument** (www.nps.gov/cebr) and **Pipe Spring National Monument** (www.nps.gov/pisp) are within easy driving distance. —*LF*

ⓘ **Bryce Canyon National Park** (✆ 435/834-5322; www.nps.gov/brca).

WHEN TO GO: Spring, summer, and fall.

✈ Bryce Canyon Airport.

⊨ $$ **Bryce Canyon Lodge,** 1 Bryce Canyon Lodge (✆ 435/834-5361; www.brycecanyonlodge.com). $ **Bryce Country Cabins,** 320 N. Utah 12 (✆ 888/679-8643 or 435-679-8643; www.brycecountrycabins.com).

161 Hiking

Hiking on a Live Volcano
Watch the Steam Vents
Mount Rainier, Washington, U.S.A.

Hiking on a live volcano. Sound dumb? Not really. Thousands of people hike Mount Rainier annually. In fact, the Native Americans, who call the mountain Tahoma, frequented the mountain hundreds of years before it was "discovered" by the white man. Steam vents at the top attest to the subsurface volcanic activity of the mountain, which last spewed small amounts of ash in the 19th century. The threat of an eruption while you're on the mountain is next to nonexistent. But the mere knowledge that you're traipsing across an active giant will give you an extra charge in your already exhilarating hike.

Mount Rainier National Park.

Mount Rainier, in **Mount Rainier National Park,** is located approximately 2 hours by car from Seattle, Washington. (The area was designated a national park in 1899 by President McKinley.) At over 14,400 feet (4,380m) above sea level (9,000 feet /2,743m base to summit), Rainier is the most prominent and glaciered mountain in the Cascade Range. The mountain is available for great public outdoor activity including fishing, horseback riding, mountaineering, and hiking, along with a host of winter sports such as skiing, snowboarding, and snowshoeing.

With almost 40 designated trails, the variety of hikes is almost limitless and ranges from short, easy walks to difficult hikes and multi-day or multi-week trips. The **Nisqually Vista Trail** is a short, easy trail that covers about 1¼ miles (2km), from which you can see the Nisqually Glacier and the beginning of the Nisqually River. A relatively easy 4- to 5-hour hike along the **Skookum Flats Trail** takes you to the base to

Skookum Falls, a waterfall with a 250-foot (76m) drop.

A more difficult hike follows the **Rampart Ridge Trail** to Indian Henry's Hunting Ground. Henry was a Cowlitz Indian, who hunted goats in the area more than 100 years ago. In season, the meadows are full of wildflowers and incredibly beautiful.

The most difficult hike is the 93-mile-long (150km) **Wonderland Trail,** which circumvents Mount Rainier and should be undertaken only by experienced hikers in very good physical condition. Stretches of the trail go from fairly easy to very difficult with significant elevation changes. Water periodically destroys parts of the trail and can make passage difficult. The views encountered along the way are never–to-be-forgotten spectacular. If you want to see the famous view of Mount Rainier from **Mirror Lake,** the lake is just north of the junction of the Wonderland Trail and the Kautz Creek Trail. Campsites are small and not always available, so it's a good idea to reserve sites well in advance. To make the long hike a bit easier, it is possible to cache food at some of the ranger stations to lighten your load.

A few words about weather: Heavy rain and wash can affect the condition of the trails and turn easy treks into difficult and even dangerous ones, so check trail conditions before you start out. And, mountains tend to make their own weather. Conditions can change quite quickly, so be prepared. —LF

ⓘ **Visit Rainier** (✆ **877/270-7155;** www.visitrainier.com). **Mount Rainier Visitor Association** (✆ **877-617-9951;** www.mt-rainier.com). **Mount Rainier National Park** (✆ **360/569-2211;** www.nps.gov/mora).

TOUR: American Alpine Institute, 1515 Twelfth St., Bellingham, WA (✆ **800/424-2249;** www.aai.cc).

WHEN TO GO: Mid-June to Oct.

✈ Seattle-Tacoma International Airport.

🛏 $–$$ **Mount Rainier Cabins,** 30005 S.R. 706 E (✆ **360/569-2682;** www.rainiercabins.com).

Hiking Samaria Gorge
A Stony Route to the Sea
Samaria Gorge, Crete

The Greek island of Crete is riven with gorges, but the most thrilling is Samaria, one of Europe's longest—a 16km (10-mile) gash in the Avlimanakou and Volakias mountains, descending from a height of 1,250m (4,100 ft.) down to the turquoise deeps of the Libyan Sea. Part fun house, with shapeshifting walls that rise as high as 500m (1,640 ft.) in places and narrow to 3.5m (11 ft.) in others, and part kaleidoscope, framing an ever-changing range of scenery, the gorge rarely ceases to surprise its visitors.

The path starts at **Xyloskalo,** which means "wooden staircase" or "ladder." The gorge is fairly wide at this point, as it will be for the first couple of kilometers or so (1 mile) of your trip, but the incline is intensely steep. Hikers quickly learn to tread carefully over the worn-down stones and hold onto the wooden parapet erected to aid their balance. The pitch eventually lessens, and the walking becomes easier, but you will still be criss-crossing a dry river bed and leaping from rock to rock over a water-filled tributary (travelers with knee problems would do well to skip this adventure).

A popular midway stop is the ruined village of **Samaria.** Around the village edges, stay on the lookout for *kris-kris,* goats found only on the island of Kris Kris and here. Eventually, you reach a pebbly riverbed at the bottom of the gorge. As you walk across the stones, the cliffs on each side of you undulate in intriguing patterns, stretching upward to seemingly touch the sky at their highest reaches. The highlight of the last stretch is the photogenic "Gates," where you'll walk single file as the walls close in on you.

The tiny village of Agia Roumell is a welcoming depot at the end of your hike. As you enter the town, resting hikers seated on the porch of a local bar will cheer and congratulate you for finishing the trek and reaching town in time to catch the last afternoon ferry—the only way back to the parking lot to fetch your car or meet your tour bus. Don't miss it!

Unfortunately, the gorge is mobbed by tourists and locals on day outings—as many as 3,000 people a day in summer. It's stupendous enough to be sufficiently distracting, but go early or late in the season if you want to avoid the madding hordes. It's open from early May to October, subject to closures due to torrential rains, when falling rocks and swift-flowing streams may be hazardous. May is particularly spectacular, when wildflowers abound.

I recommend booking your hike through a tour group, as getting to and from your accommodations to the gorge itself can be tricky, requiring transportation by bus and ferry. You'll be independent while hiking—these tours are simply a way to get from your lodging to the gorge entrance, and a ride home after the ferry lands. Once on the path, people walk at their own pace, and groups don't meet up again until the end of the hike, at a pre-arranged time in Agia Roumell. Most tour buses are air-conditioned and the guide gives you a sense of what to expect during the hike. Hikers leaving a car at Omalos near the park entrance must get a ride by bus or taxi after getting off the ferry.

Otherwise, be sure to wear sturdy walking shoes, a hat, and sunscreen; drink plenty of water and make sure the batteries in your camera are fresh. —*LF*

ⓘ www.west-crete.com; www.explore crete.com.

TOUR: Dikytnna Travel, 6 Archotaki St. (© **28210/43-930;** www.diktynna-travel.gr).

WHEN TO GO: Spring.

✈ Chania.

🛏 $$$ **Creta Paradise Beach Resort Hotel,** Gerani Beach, Chania (© **28210-61-315;** www.cretaparadise.gr). $–$$ **Hotel Porto Veneziano,** Akti Enosseos, Chania (© **28210/27-100;** www.porto venezian.gr).

Hiking **163**

Mount St. Helens
Climbing a Slope of Pumice & Ash
Mount St. Helens National Monument, Oregon, U.S.A.

You may start to question your decision to make this climb, as you hone your focus and carefully navigate the last 1,000 feet (300m) of your ascent to the rim of the crater. It's a slippery slope composed of the pumice and ash. But once you're at the rim, 8,364 feet (2,509m) above sea level, and can peer into the crater, with its lava dome and volcanic debris, you're thrilled you had the stamina to take the hike. The payoff comes in the way of the 360-degree views of three other volcanoes: Mount Rainier, Mount Adams, and Mount Hood in the distance, as well as a glimpse of the ravaged blast area on the volcano's north side and Spirit Lake far below.

In early 1980, after years of dormancy, minor earthquakes started shaking Mount St. Helens, and ash and steam began spewing from the volcano's top in fits and starts. In May of that year came the big eruption that literally tore away the north side of the mountain and blew an ash cloud 80,000 feet (24,000m) in the air. Today, Mount St. Helens has quieted down and hiking it has become a favorite quest of locals and tourists alike.

The route you choose depends upon your stamina, and hiking or climbing experience. There are two major courses you can take: the **Worm Flows** route, used in the winter, and the more popular summer route, **Monitor Ridge.** The Monitor Ridge Climbing Route is challenging, leading climbers up and over volcanic boulder fields. Although it does not usually require special equipment or previous mountain climbing experience, climbers should be prepared for variations in terrain and weather. It's the most direct route to the summit and takes you past some of the older lava flows. From near Climbers Bivouac, follow the Ptarmigan Trail # 216A to the timberline. Blue markers on the trees will help you locate the trail as it weaves through the forest. From the timberline, wooden route-marking posts help guide climbers on Monitor Ridge, a 400-year-old lava flow, to the crater rim. Once you've arrived, don't expect to see inside the crater and Mount Rainier in the distance until you navigate that last 1,000 feet (300m). Climbers should be in good condition for this route because it's approximately 9½ miles round trip and will take 7 to 10 hours to ascend 4,600 feet (1,380m) to the crater's rim and then go back down.

If you want to get a real sense of the power of the 1980 blast, walk through the blown down forest, especially during wildflower season, on the popular 13-mile **Boundary Trail #1** from the Norway Pass trailhead to Mount Margaret. The trail starts at about 3,800 feet (1,140m) above sea level and ascends to the highest point on the ridge, at 5,858 feet (1,757m). When you reach the junction at Independence Pass trail, you'll have a spectacular view of

Spirit Lake and Mount St. Helens. From this point on there are continuous views of Mount Hood, the lava dome, the blast area, and peek-a-boo views of Mount Rainier.

No matter which trail you take, plan enough time to visit **Lava Canyon #184** and **Ape Cave.** A steep narrow trail leads to a suspension bridge over Lava Canyon and gorgeous waterfalls below. Ape Cave offers a darker adventure in a basalt lava tube. This 2-hour rock scramble brings you through the upper cave and out into the light. Here, you begin your hike back over the forest that has grown over the lava tube to return to the parking area.

During the winter, skiers and snowboarders love to hike up the south side of the volcano and ski or ride down. One Portlander reports that it's easy, intermediate skiing on un-groomed terrain. Make your own decision depending upon your skill level.

Climbing permits can only be purchased online through **Mount St. Helens Institute** (see below) and they are required for

each day above 4,800 feet (1,463m) elevation on the volcano's slopes between April 1 and October 31. Only 100 climbers per day are permitted from May 15 through October 31. November 1 through March 31, free climbing permits are self-register. E-mail confirmations must be exchanged for permits at the climbing register at the Lone Fir Resort, where climbers must sign in before and sign out after their respective climbs. —*LF*

ⓘ **Mount St. Helens information** (http://mountsthelens.com). **Mount St. Helens Institute** (ⓒ **360/891-5107** for registration or 360/449-7861 for climbing conditions; www.mshinstitute.org).

WHEN TO GO: Late June to mid-Sept, if you don't want to climb on snow.

✈ Portland, OR (71 miles/114km).

🛏 $$$ **Blue Heron Inn Bed & Breakfast,** 2846 Spirit Lake Hwy. (ⓒ **800/959-4049** or 360/274-9595; blueheroninn.com).

164 Hiking

Sunrise at Masada
Following Martyrs' Footsteps
Masada National Park, Israel

The race to climb up the Roman Path and reach the cliff top in time to see the sunrise keeps the adrenaline pumping through your body. When you finally arrive, you're sitting atop this rocky rise in the desert called Masada and it's still dark. Before the sky begins to brighten, there's just enough time to sense how isolated this refuge must have felt for the Jewish rebels who died here rather than be enslaved or killed by the Romans. Suddenly, streaks of gold and orange pierce the darkness, spreading light until the surrounding desert and the harsh blue of the Dead Sea slowly materialize as the sun tops the horizon. Once daylight breaks, it's time to begin exploring.

Masada, which rises some 390m (1,300 ft.) above the desolate Judean Desert, about 48km (30 miles) from Jerusalem, was built as a walled palace fortress by Herod the Great in the First Century B.C. After the Romans conquered Jerusalem and the Jewish Temple was destroyed in A.D. 70, some 1,000 Jewish resistors and their families fled to remote Masada. Led by Eleazar ben Jair, the zealots withstood a 2-year siege by the Romans. In A.D. 73, the Roman Tenth Legion encircled the base of Masada with eight camps and constructed an earth and stone ramp leading up to the top of the cliff. In spring of the following year, the Romans carried a

Masada, a former palace fortress, is a World Heritage Site.

battering ram up this ramp and breached the fortress wall. Looking on, all but seven of the zealots chose to die by their own hands—they committed mass suicide—rather than surrender to the enemy.

Today a World Heritage Site, Masada is visited by members of all religions. Some hike up via the **Roman Path** or the steep zigzagging **Snake Path,** while others ride up in a **cable car.** At the top, there's a vast complex of ruins to explore, ranging from **Herod's Northern Palace** and the enormous storehouses to the cisterns and remains of the oldest synagogue in the world.

In 2007, a unique museum opened, which gives visitors a guided tour of the Story of Masada through a combination of archaeological artifacts set in a theatrical atmosphere, accompanied by radio play and audio explanations. Twice a week, a dramatic sound and light show tells the history of Masada by way of a performance at the Masada amphitheater.

Many visitors combine a visit to Masada with a float in the Dead Sea and a spa treatment featuring the mineral-rich Dead Sea black mud. Hiking in **Ein Gedi Nature Preserve,** where four springs create a haven in the desert for flora and fauna, is another popular stop after a visit to Masada. —*LF*

ⓘ **Masada National Park,** Dead Sea Hwy. (Rte. 90), 18km (11 miles) south of Ein Gedi (ⓒ **972/7/658-4207;** www.parks.org.il).

WHEN TO GO: Year-round. In the summer morning is best because of the desert heat.

✈ Jerusalem, 112km (70 miles).

⊨ $$$ **Golden Tulip Dead Sea,** Ein Bokek (ⓒ **972/8/662-9444;** www.golden tulipclubdeadsea.com). $ **Masada Youth Hostel,** Masada National Park (ⓒ **972/8/ 995-3222;** www.hihostels.com).

165 Hiking

Mount Kilimanjaro
Africa's Great White Mountain
Kilimanjaro National Park, Tanzania

It's an unforgettable sight—the snowy plateau of Mount Kilimanjaro, rising above the Tanzanian plains, just south of Kenya. Named Oldoinyo Oibor, or "white mountain," by the Masai tribesmen and Kilima Njaro, or "shining mountain," in Swahili, it's Africa's highest mountain and one of the world's largest free-standing peaks, a triple volcano thrusting out of equatorial jungle and moorland. As world-class peaks go, it's a relatively easy climb—the lower slopes are downright gentle—but you don't need to go all the way to the summit to get the Hemmingway-esque thrill of exploring Kilimanjaro.

Ascending, you pass through four radically different climate zones. First comes the lush, steamy Kilimanjaro Forest Reserve surrounding the base; then the grassy moorlands of the shouldering slopes; above 3,962m (13,000 ft.), the mountain suddenly becomes steeper and more barren, with rocky scree underfoot. Last of all, you hit glacial ice fields, dazzling in the reflected African sun. It's not a technical climb, but it's a strenuous steep hike, and the extreme altitude makes it physically challenging if your body hasn't acclimated properly.

Enter at the **Marangu Park Gate**—you should already have obtained park permits and hut reservations (available through a licensed tour operator or local hotels in Moshi), but at the park gate you'll hire a guide, and possibly a porter (you won't be allowed on the mountain without a guide). Park fees are substantial, but they include hut accommodations on the

mountain; guides and porters ask ridiculously low wages, hoping for generous tips on top. If you book with a tour operator (which I recommend), most of this, along with a cook to prepare all meals en route, will be included in your package.

It takes 5 to 7 days round-trip to reach the summit, staying in mountain huts all the way. If you've brought kids along or aren't up to the full climb, you may be content to abbreviate this trek, going only partway up the well-traveled **Marangu Trail.** You'll spend your first night on the mountain in the wooden A-frame huts at Mandara, a 3- to 4-hour 12km (7½-mile) walk from the gate through misty, mossy rainforest. On your second day, hike across grassland to the gardenlike Maundi Crater; scramble up to the rim for panoramic views of the barren highlands towering above you. If you're not gung-ho mountaineers, head back down from here, or go on to Hotombo Hut that night and Kibo Hut the third night before turning around. —HH

ⓘ **Kilimanjaro National Park** (www.tanzaniaparks.com/kili.html).

TOUR: Destination Africa Tours, Pretoria, South Africa (📞 **27/12/333-7110;** www.climbingkilimanjaro.com); **Roy Safaris,** Arusha, Tanzania (📞 **255/27/250-2115;** www.roysafaris.com); and **Tanzania Adventure,** Arusha, Tanzania (📞 **255/73/297-5210;** www.tanzania adventure.com).

✈ Kilimanjaro International, 56km (35 miles).

The Inca Trail
Treading Ancient Inca Pathways
Machu Picchu, Peru

Travelers can reach Machu Picchu by an air-conditioned train but the more adventurous route is hiking along the Inca Trail. The route passes by crumbling temple ruins and tiny towns, where women still carry babies wrapped in shawls on their backs while leading a donkey down the road. While trekking, you'll snake through lush sub-tropical jungles, and keep catching your breath as you climb over mountain passes. The sea of peaks surrounding you is breathtaking. During portions of the trek, hikers actually walk along paths the Incas trod when traveling from Cuzco, the Inca's imperial capitol, to the sacred city of Machu Picchu.

The classic trail, the shorter Inca Trail, and the Salkantay trek are the most well-known routes, but a growing number of trekking companies are finding other, less crowded routes. These, too, meander through desolate valleys, past isolated shacks with thatched roofs and men herding scraggly cows, and up and down mountainsides. Most treks end at the narrow flight of hand-hewn stone steps that leads to Intipunko, the Sun Gate entrance to Machu Picchu. Groups usually arrive here at dawn, so they can watch the sun climb above a mountain peak and foot by foot slowly reveal the remains of temples and structures that once housed the Inca elite.

The classic route, most often a 4-day trek, usually begins at kilometer 82, the farthest point reachable by bus, or kilometer 88, reachable by train. The short route, which starts farther along the Vilcanota River Valley, is an easier trek, which can be done in 1 day. Both treks are partly on a trail in the **Machu Picchu Historical Sanctuary,** a national park. The Salkantay trek, called the alternative route, is the choice for many travelers who want a less touristy experience. This route, often a 7-day trek, is the toughest. Trekkers may spend 6 to 8 hours hiking and will be going over passes that top out around 4,500m (15,000 ft.) above sea level.

Travelers must hike the Inca Trail with an accredited trekking company, but choose the company you trek with carefully. Before booking a trip, confirm that the company has the requisite number of permits to handle hikers, guides, and porters on the dates you will be there. Because the Inca Trail began to resemble pedestrian highway,

Machu Picchu.

government authorities now limit the number of trek permits to 500 per day—and that includes visitors, guides, porters, and cooks—for the classic trail, the shorter Inca Trail, and the Salkantay trek.

Although some brochures suggest that any reasonably fit person can handle the trek, hikers should be in good shape and have hiking boots that have been broken in well before the trip. Altitudes during the classic trek range from 2,790m (9,300 ft.) above sea level in the Urubamba Valley to 4,080m (13,600 ft.) above sea level while going over mountain passes. Hikers living at sea level should consider arriving in Cuzco a few days before the trek starts, to start acclimating to the altitude. —LF

(i) **Machu Picchu Tourist Information** (www.machu-picchu.info). **GO2Peru** (© **305/728-4717** in the U.S. or 511/627-4331 in Peru; www.go2peru.com). **iPerú,** Av. Pachacútec, cdra. 1 s/n (© **084/211-104**).

TOUR: Mountain Travel Sobek (© **888/831-7521;** http://mtsobek.com).

WHEN TO GO: Best in Peru's dry season Apr–Nov. Most popular time to trek is June–Sept.

✈ Cuzco, 111km (69 miles).

🛏 Stay in tents during 4-day trip. $$ **Gringo Bill's Hostal,** Calle Colla Raymi 104, Aguas Calientes (© **51/1/84/211-406;** www.gringobills.com). $$$ **Inkaterra Machu Picchu,** next to the ruins (© **800/442-5042** in the U.S., 0800/458/7506 in the U.K., or 51/1/610-0400; www.inkaterra.com).

167 Hiking

Isla Navarino
The Bottom of the World
Chile

It is a certain kind of traveler who seeks out a place like Isla Navarino. Remote and sparsely populated, it has plenty to recommend it: dramatic landscapes, thrilling sea passages, and, in **Puerto Williams,** a self declared southernmost town in the world (that title is under dispute with Ushuaia in Tierra del Fuego). Isla Navarino lies at the tail end of Chilean Patagonia. It's just north of Cape Horn, the southernmost point of South America and the place where the Atlantic and Pacific meet, spectacularly. Next stop: Antarctica.

Isla Navarino is not an easy island escape. It takes a lot of effort to get here, and once you do, don't expect to be pampered. Tourism is in its raw early stages. The towns have a deserted, tucked-in feel, with wooden bungalows topped with corrugated iron roofs. The weather can be wildly unpredictable—sun out one minute, snowing the next (even in summer), winds

blowing crazily—so that even a leisurely hike can turn into extreme sport. A trip to Isla Navarino is usually a mix of serious outdoor adventure and sedate explorations of the little island towns. What won't let you down is the stunning scenery: from unspoiled forests to glaciers and Chilean fjords framed by towering granite needles called the "Teeth of Navarino."

To hikers, Isla Navarino is one of trekking's holy grails. The island rises in the center, around which are coiled hiking trails of low and high intensity through a landscape of almost grave purity. The 5-day hiking circuit around the peaks of Navarino is known as the **Dientes de Navarino,** or "The Dientes Circuit." Hikers camp around pristine lakes and streams that trickle down the mountains. The landscape is little changed since Charles Darwin hiked these hills in 1832 on an expedition aboard the British survey ship the HMS *Beagle*.

123

You can get here by air—Puerto Williams has a small airport—or by ferry from Punta Arenas, some 346km (215 miles) away (you first fly to Punta Arenas from Santiago); the scenic ferry ride gets you there in a day and a half. The Patagonian airline **Aerovias DAP** (*C* **56/61-616100;** www.aeroviasdap. cl) has daily 1-hour flights from Punta Arenas into Puerto Williams. You can also take a little boat from Ushuaia, Argentina. But perhaps the best way to see the island and its amazing surrounds is by small cruise ship. **Victory Adventure Expeditions** (www. victory-cruises.com) has two full-service 100-passenger cruise ships, MV *Mare Australis* and MV *Via Australis,* that have regular itineraries including Cape Horn and Tierra del Fuego.

Puerto Williams is a town of about 2,400 people, many of them members of the Chilean navy. It is within shouting distance of the stunning Tierra del Fuego in Argentina, separated from the Chilean town by the narrow Beagle Channel. Magellan discovered Tierra del Fuego and its snowy peaks on his expedition to find a route to the East. The Magellan Strait, which rounds the imposing rocky promontory known as Cape Horn, opened up trade between East and West.

Cape Horn marks the southernmost point of South America and extends into Drake Passage, the Antarctic strait connecting the south Atlantic and south Pacific oceans. This is one of the most dangerous sea passages on the planet—winds swirl, currents collide, and icebergs lurk beneath the water. Rounding "the Horn" is one of the world's last great ocean adventures.

As Darwin wrote of the Horn in 1832: "On our weather-bow this notorious promontory in its proper form—veiled in a mist, and its dim outline surrounded by a storm of wind and water. Great black clouds were rolling across the heavens, and squalls of rain, with hail, swept by us. . . ."

Whether you've chanced the perilous Cape Horn or hiked the needles of Navarino, a night in Puerto Williams is not complete without a drink around the wood fire at the town's "yacht club," a cozy lounge inside the pilothouse of a junky old Swiss freighter (the *Micalvi*) listing dockside in a sheltered inlet. At the **Club de Yates Micalvi** (*C* **56/61/621020**), you may be hobnobbing with ship captains and crew on refueling stops, yachties preparing to round the Horn, off-duty Chilean naval personnel, and intrepid travelers from around the world—it's a warm, lively escape from the cold, lit with the *frisson* of being with fellow adventurers at a real crossroads of the world. —*AF*

(i) www.visit-chile.org

TOUR: Victory Adventure Expeditions (see above).

✈ Punta Arenas (346km/215 miles).

🚢 **Turismo Comapa** (www.comapa. com) or **Victory Adventure Expeditions** (www.victory-cruises.com).

🛏 $ **Bella Vista Hostal,** Puerto Williams (http://cape-horn.net/bella_vista_hostal. html). $ **Lodge Lakutaia,** Puerto Williams (*C* **56/61/621721;** www.lakutaia.cl).

Hiking **168**

Night Hiking
Going Bump in the Night
Costa Rica

There's a whole new world out there, and it's all around you—all you have to do is wait until dark. After the sun sets and darkness descends, thousands of creatures great and small end their daytime naps and come out to hunt, to search for mates, to feed, and to send shivers up and down your spine with their nocturnal screeching and scurrying. Think you're brave enough to wander through the wilderness armed only with a flashlight and some night goggles? Then come to one of the world's greatest animal sanctuaries, Costa Rica, for a night hike.

There are a number of national parks around Costa Rica where one can take in a nocturnal hike. After flying into San Jose, the nation's capital and largest city, consider hightailing it to the areas around **Manuel Antonio** (www.manualantoniopark.com), **Monte Verde** (www.monteverdeinfo. com), or **Corcovado** (www.costarica-nationalparks.com/corcovadonationalpark. html) national parks. Each of these areas (and dozens of others) offers unparalleled opportunities to see an immense and colorful menagerie unlike any on Earth.

Many of the largest and most iconic animals in Costa Rica are most active at night. The jaguar, for example, and other native cats like the ocelot, the caucel, and the tigrillo are notoriously elusive and are best seen—or only seen—after dark. Leatherback sea turtles, endangered throughout most of their habitat, emerge at night to lay their eggs on sandy beaches. On an evening kayak trip through the lush mangrove forests along the coast, paddlers can expect to come face-to-face with sloths, crocodiles, and squirrel monkeys.

Beyond night hikes, Costa Rica enjoys a well-deserved reputation as an eco-tourist's dream destination. With miles of tropical beaches, active volcanoes, mountain cloud forests, and plunging waterfalls, opportunities are limitless to explore the natural history of this country—even during the day. But why see only half of this gem of a country, when the other side is waiting for you after dark? —ML

(i) **Costa Rican Tourist Board** ((c) **866/ COSTA RICA** [267-8274]; www.visit costarica.com).

TOURS: Desafio Adventure Company ((c) **506/2-645-5874;** www.monteverde tours.com). **Wilderness Inquiry** ((c) **800/ 728-0719** or 612/676-9400; www.wilder nessInquiry.org). **i-to-i** ((c) **800/985-4852;** www.i-to-i.com).

WHEN TO GO: June–Feb.

✈ San Jose.

---

(169) Hiking

Heli-Hiking to a Via Ferrata
Reaching New Heights
Banff, Canada

The first time you're waiting for your ride—a 14-seat, Bell 212 helicopter—you're crouched down, heart racing, in a quiet parking lot south of Golden, British Columbia. When you finally see the chopper, making its way through the vast blue sky, you can't help but be stunned by its power and grace. After it lands, with its propellers loudly whirling, you creep forward and climb aboard—on your way to hike along the new, helicopter-accessible-only via ferrata (which means "iron road" in Italian) opened by **Canadian Mountain Holidays** in 2008. As your pilot glides over grassy meadows and weaves between snow-capped mountain peaks, you're quickly rendered speechless. But this breathtaking journey is just the first of many to come over the next few days as you embark on your "heli-hiking" adventure.

Heli-hiking is basically the summer version of heli-skiing. Instead of skiing down

Rappelling is only part of the fun when you heli-hike on a via ferrata with Canadian Mountain Holidays.

immaculate powder-covered slopes, you hike on pristine glaciers, across boulder fields, through flower-dotted fields, and up mountains—all so remote they're reachable only by helicopter.

On Day 1, your first stop is at the helicopter-accessible-only **Bobbie Burns Lodge.** After settling into your rustic but luxurious digs and enjoying a hearty lunch, you'll take off again for an introductory heli-hike in the afternoon. But Day 2 is when the fun really begins. In the morning, your chopper takes you high up into the

surrounding mountain range, maybe even landing on a glacier. Following a short walk, it's time to conquer **Mount Nimbus,** deep in the Purcell Mountains.

Thanks to the via ferrata recently built here, special skills or prior experience aren't required to climb this mountain. You'll use vertical pathways that feature permanently fixed cables for safety and metal rung ladders to aid your movements. But the ascent is still mentally and physically challenging. One of the biggest obstacles is a long, swinging bridge made of wooden planks and cables that stretches between two cliffs. Although it's perfectly safe, it can be awfully scary to walk across. If your heart wasn't pounding yet, it will be now. For the super adventurous, a very high ropes course was added to the route in 2009.

As Sarah Pearson from Canadian Mountain Holidays says, "The via ferrata takes you to places you would never reach in any other way. It gives you a chance to feel like you're a serious mountaineer, even though you've never done anything like that before. It isn't physically easy, but it isn't impossible. And at the end of the day, you're completely excited by what you've accomplished."

As difficult as this heli-hike can get, there's good news at the end. Your helicopter will always be waiting to pick you up and whisk you back to your lodge for a hot shower, a massage if you want one, and a well-deserved dinner. —*JS*

ⓘ **Canadian Mountain Holidays,** 217 Bear St. (© **800/661-0252;** www.canadian mountainholidays.com).

WHEN TO GO: July–Sept.

✈ Banff or Calgary Airport.

Hiking & Backpacking in Oregon
Exploring the Beaver State
Oregon, U.S.A.

Whether you are a white-knuckle scrambler in fighting trim or an avid, observant stroller who won't leave home without binoculars, spectacular views awaits you in Oregon, home to hundreds of trails with dozens of hiking books dedicated to them. In the span of one trip, you can follow cliff tops overlooking the Pacific Ocean and then descend through forests to the sand beach below; calculate every footfall on mountainsides in the Cascade Range; scramble hand-over-foot on wild trails up steep slopes and over running water in the Columbia River Gorge; or just meander along a wooded urban trail long enough to make way for a calorific first-class meal, rich with fresh ingredients from the Willamette Valley.

The **Columbia River Gorge**'s Rock of Ages Loop is a rewarding place to start if you're willing to bushwhack a little and sweat for thrilling views that may include volcanic activity from the gorge's disruptive neighbor, Mt. St. Helens. The hike starts at the **Horsetail Falls**, a popular tourist spot, but from there the 10-mile (16km) loop gets much more challenging, on overgrown trails shooting 900 feet (270m) uphill within the course of a mile; across a creek on slippery rocks; and through a tangled network of poison oak. Carrying a backpack makes it all the more difficult. Notable landmarks include the manmade-looking **Rock of Ages Arch**, accessible via a steep spur trail from the main path (snap a photo on your

The magnificent Oregon landscape makes for memorable hiking.

cellphone, so you can send an "I was here" photo to your friends). The apex of this trail—the ridge known as the **Devil's Back-bone**—affords spectacular views down into the Gorge. On a clear day you might even spot the notorious cone of Mt. St. Helens.

The **Central Cascade Range** near Bend is home to many more moderate hikes along the **Corral Swamp Trail.** You can hike trips of varied length, including a nice easy walk of approximately 4 miles (6.5km) through old growth, with an elevation gain of less than 500 feet (150m). It's not heavily traveled by humans, though wildlife is common along the path. You will traverse the **Three Sisters Wilderness Area** on this trail, but a permit is required, available for purchase from the Forest Service in Bend, Oregon. (I prefer to make this hike in the fall. The mosquito may be the "state bird" of Alaska, but it has lots of cousins here early in the season.)

In the **Oregon Dunes National Recreation area,** marching lines of waves crash against the shore, and dunes, sculpted by wind and water, rise almost 500 feet (150m) above the Pacific Ocean. In this amazing landscape, more than a dozen designated hiking trails encompass ever-green forests, open dunes, wetlands, and ocean beach, providing an entertaining variety and good photo opportunities. Many of the trails are designated moderate to difficult.

Oregon Peak Adventures offers half-day hikes in Portland's Forest Park to full-day trips to the Central Oregon Coast, the Columbia River Gorge, and other locations. Trips include door-to-door transportation and experienced guides. The company also offers several yearly backpacking trips.

Portland makes a good base for day hikers who want to retreat to the city after all that nature. Stroll through Portland's Arboretum, or the Japanese and Rose gardens. Browse the art galleries and the boutiques in the thriving Pearl District. Wander through the arts and crafts section in the Saturday market in the Old Town historic district. And replenish all those calories you burned in one of Portland's many inventive restaurants, stocked with food and wine from the bounty of the Willamette Valley about 45 miles (73km) away. —*LF*

ⓘ **Travel Oregon** for general tourism info and hikes (www.traveloregon.com). **Oregon State Welcome Center,** Portland (℡ **800/424-3002**).

WHEN TO GO: Spring–Fall.

✈ Portland International.

Hiking **171**

Exploring the White Mountains
An All-weather Playground
White Mountains, New Hampshire, U.S.A.

I still remember the hike that triggered my exploration of the White Mountains—in part because I had trouble walking for the next 3 days. We went up the **Beaver Brook Trail,** which climbs 3,100 feet (930m) in less than four miles, with some sections exceptionally steep. But all the scrambling we did was worth it—the areas along the cascades are incredibly beautiful as are the mountain flowers and the views. At the bottom of the trail, on the way out, I saw a sign that read, "This trail is difficult and should only be undertaken by experienced hikers in excellent physical condition." No wonder I was so sore.

Since then I have explored other parts of the White Mountains on foot, including portions of the Appalachian Trail. The hiking

The White Mountains of New Hampshire.

routes are endless and the lush woods and mountain top views are fantastic. Some hikes are tougher than others, while some can be done in flip-flops (though I don't recommend this). In particular, I like **Mount Washington**, which at almost 6,300 feet (1,890m), is the highest peak in the northeast. Hiking should be limited on this mountain to summer months. Though there are plenty of modern day amenities and perks—cog railway, an Appalachian Mountain Club mountain hut, the Mt. Washington Auto Road, and a visitor center—people have died on this mountain, often in sudden storms.

Summer in New Hampshire opens up opportunities to explore the region by raft and kayak, too. The Pemigewasset River in the Lincoln area has some heart-stopping stretches, but the sections around Woodstock are much easier to navigate. Stretches on the Ammonoosuc River near Berlin fall somewhere in the middle. Kayak rentals are available from **Outback Kayaks** in Lincoln (© **603/745-2002;** www.outbackkayak. org).

In the winter, heading out on snowshoes and cross-country skis is a wonderful way to explore the region. **Franconia Notch State Park** (www.nhstateparks. org) is particularly beautiful; one of the nicest snowshoeing trips is a bit more than three miles around Lonesome Lake. The **Falling Water Trail** at Mittersill, at 5½ miles (nearly 9km) round-trip, takes you to a picture postcard view of a frozen cascade approximately 75 feet (23m) high. Excellent snowshoeing and cross country skiing can be done in an around Bartlett, Lincoln, North Conway, among other White Mountain towns.

There is so much to do in the White Mountains that you can't do it all in a lifetime. There are eight **ski areas,** including Loon Mountain, Cannon Mountain, and Waterville Valley. (Learn to ski these when the slopes are "hard" and you can ski at any ski area in the world.) There are now several great **ziplines,** including the one at Wildcat Ski Area. You can go **rock climbing** in the Mt. Washington Valley, mountain bike throughout the White Mountain National Forest, and for the less outdoorsy adventure-inclined, shopping and antiquing are popular pastimes throughout the region. And, if you've never seen the fall foliage in the White Mountains, put it on your bucket list. Just remember not to go without hotel reservations if you plan to be there several days and don't want to sleep in a tent or your car. —LF

ⓘ **New Hampshire Tourism** (ⓒ **800/ FUN-IN-NH** [386-4664]; www.visitnh.gov). **New Hampshire.com** (www.newhamp shire.com/explore-nh/white-mountain. aspx).

WHEN TO GO: Anytime.

✈ Manchester.

🛏 $$ **Mount Washington Resort Hotel,** Rte. 302, Bretton Woods (ⓒ **800/ 314-1752** or 603/278-1000; www.mount washingtonresort.com).

Auyuittuq National Park
Endless Winter
Baffin Island, Canada

That sniffing sound outside your tent—could that be a hungry polar bear? Way up here above the Arctic Circle, it could very well be. Auyuittuq National Park, one of North America's most isolated and pristine reserves, is home to polar bears, caribou, rabbits, arctic fox, lemmings—and not much else. The name "Auyuittuq" means "the land that never melts," and the dearth of vegetation here makes life rough for

animals, including humans. Nobody comes here looking for lush forests or a fantastic menagerie of exotic animals. It's all about the splendid isolation of this land, and the spectacular beauty of the immense fjords, ragged, icy peaks, and massive glaciers that define this lonely peninsula of Baffin Island.

And yet they come, hundreds of them each year, to trek across this brutal landscape. Getting here is a bit of an ordeal itself, as air service to the settlement of Pangnirtung is infrequent. Visitors who enter the park at Pangnirtung or Qikiqtarjuaq must register at the park offices there, pay a fee, and attend a rather intense orientation that's designed to ensure they don't risk their lives in the wilderness.

For lives have been lost in this park, most notably by those who dare to challenge **Mount Thor.** This awe-inspiring pinnacle is famous among rock-climbers and nature photographers alike for its fantastic 105-degree overhanging mountain face, considered the biggest unobstructed vertical drop in the world—over 1,230m (4,100 ft.) of sheer granite. More climbing routes are established each year, including some on **Mount Asgard**'s 780m (2,600-ft.) face,

Auyuittuq National Park.

but none can rival Thor for its imposing grandeur. Outdoor adventurers who prefer to keep their feet on terra firma hike the **Akshayuk Pass,** a 97km (60-mile) trek that follows the Owl and Weasel Rivers, connecting the east and west coasts of Baffin Island.

Only seasoned, extreme-weather backpackers attempt to trek this wilderness without guides. Mere mortals should consider contacting an experienced tour group (see below) for their introduction to this amazing land where the summer sun never sets. —*ML*

(i) **Parks Canada Auyuittuq National Park** (© **867/473-2500;** www.parks canada.gc.ca).

TOURS: Black Feather (© **888/849-7668** or 705/746-1372; www.blackfeather.com). **Equinox Expeditions** (© **604/222-1219;** www.equinoxexpeditions.com).

WHEN TO GO: June–Aug.

$$ **Auyuittuq Lodge,** Pangnirtung (© **867/473-8955;** www.innsnorth.com). $$ **Capital Suites,** Building 807, Iqaluit (© **867/975-4000;** www.capitalsuites.ca).

---

173 **Winter Sports**

Park City Mountain Resort
Skiing Backcountry Lite
Park City, Utah, U.S.A.

I'll never forget my first time on **Jupiter Peak.** You could have hidden a Volkswagen in some of the moguls on the trail I chose that day. Everything started out fine, but when I slid off the side of one and tumbled, I did a complete somersault before stopping—the terrain was that steep. Since then, I've explored more of the landscape off the top of the Jupiter lift and it's arguably some of the most interesting, ungroomed "backcountry lite," terrain in the Rockies.

Backcountry lite is an informal name some ski resorts give to extreme inbounds terrain that is steep and never groomed, but is avalanche-controlled. You can get similar thrills to skiing or snowboarding backcountry terrain, where snow sliders should only go if they have the proper equipment and knowledge about weather and snow conditions. If everything falls in line, a backcountry ski experience can be one of the most fun, adrenaline-inducing times of your life.

If you have the skills and technique to handle the steep slopes, glades, and chutes on Jupiter Peak, it's a wonderful

playground. (If you don't, many resorts offer clinics to teach adventurous skiers and snowboarders ways to handle ungroomed terrain.) Resort ski patrollers warn:

Steep slopes and deep powder are the calling cards of Park City's backcountry ski areas.

"There's no easy way down" the runs on this double-black-rated terrain.

Take your pick from the slopes atop the Jupiter lift: the open slopes on **Main Bowl** right under the chair, traversing over to the wide-open **West Face,** or entering **Silver Cliffs, Six Bells,** or one of the other super-steep tree chutes. Ready for a short hike to even steeper terrain on the **"Peak,"** as ski patrollers call the East Face of Jupiter Peak? Here, you may see local expert skiers in some of the resort's narrowest and steepest chutes, with names such as 50-51 (the degree of the slopes), or raising rooster tails at they slide through the deep powder in **Puma Bowl.**

If challenging inbounds backcountry-style extreme terrain doesn't appeal to you, there are plenty of other runs at **Park City Mountain Resort,** which has 3,300 acres (1,335 hectares) of terrain spread over seven peaks and nine bowls. Intermediates and novices will find more terrain than they can explore in a week.

The resort rises above Park City, Utah, where the storefronts on Main Street retain a Wild West look, but are filled with trendy boutiques, galleries, and restaurants. Many of the skiing and snowboarding events during the 2002 Winter Olympics were held here. You can take a bobsled ride or try a ski jump at Utah Olympic Park (see ❿). —*LF*

ⓘ **Park City Mountain Resort** (🕐 **800/ 222-PARK;** www.parkcitymountainresort. com). **Park City Chamber,** 1862 Olympic Pkwy. (🕐 **435/658-9616**) or 333 Main St. (🕐 **435/615-9559;** www.parkcityinfo.com).

WHEN TO GO: Winter.

✈ Salt Lake City.

🛏 $$$ **Hotel Park City,** 2001 Park Ave. (🕐 **888/999-0098** or 435/200-2000; www. hotelparkcity.com). $$ **Park City Marriott,** 1895 Sidewinder Dr. (🕐 **800/754-3279;** www.parkcitymarriott.com).

Winter Sports
174

Ski the Tasman Glacier
Sliding Down a Ribbon of Ice
New Zealand's Southern Alps

Somewhere in Japan, there's a photograph of me on skis, towering over four tiny Japanese women shivering in high heels and dresses on New Zealand's longest glacier. They had plunked down by plane for a photo-op where I'd spent the day on skis, exploring the Tasman Glacier, bracing against the cold and shielding my eyes against the sun's glare on the snow as I glided across its surface. I was too busy fending off the elements to take pictures, but I'll settle for the indelible memory of wiggling into the Tasman's frozen caves and staring into deep recesses of blue ice.

The Tasman Glacier dates back to the Pleistocene ice ages, some 2 million years ago. In the Anoki/Mount Cook National Park,

in the South Island's Southern Alps, this vast iceberg has advanced and retreated several times, leaving great moraines and carving out what is now Lake Pukaki, with its distinctive blue color created by glacial flour, finely ground rock particles from the weight of ice sliding downhill.

On **Alpine Guides'** "Ski the Tasman" day trips, small groups of skiers follow a guide across open snowfields then deep into snow bowls, with dips between the seracs in the icefalls. For the most part, the terrain is moderate, which is a blessing amid such distracting views. After the first run, a ski plane whisks participants to another side of the ice pack for a second run there, affording 360-degree views of the landscape along the way. Runs may go from 8 to 10km (5–6 miles), ending when the ice thins out into a tiny ribbon surrounded by stones and dirt. At the end of the day, the ski plane picks you up again and returns you to the Mount Cook airport. (Air transfers to and from Queenstown are available.)

Skiers should be of at least comfortable intermediate skill level and able to handle a variety of snow conditions, which might range from powder and corn snow to teeth-rattling hardpack. Snowboarders aren't allowed because there are some long traverses. Maximum group size is seven skiers, but a minimum of three skiers is required. Trips take place daily from July through September. Ski the Tasman actually operates about 60% of the time because trips are cancelled due to inclement weather. If you're visiting Queenstown or other places in the region, plan a flexible schedule in case you can't go on the day you originally booked. In case of cancellation

due to bad weather, skiers can request the option of carrying the reservation to the following day.

Skiers staying in Queenstown can partake of a wide range of adrenaline-charged activities, including bungee jumping off a high bridge, jet-boating in the Shotover River Canyon, and skiing at the lift-served Remarkables, Treble Cone, Cardrona, and Coronet Peak. —*LF*

ⓘ ☎ **64/3-435-1834;** www.skithetasman.co.nz.

WHEN TO GO: Powder is predominant July and Aug; spring snow conditions from early Sept.

✈ Queenstown Airport.

🛏 $$–$$$ **Queenstown House,** 69 Hallenstein St., Queenstown (☎ **64/3/442-9043;** www.queenstownhouse.co.nz). $$$ **Hotel Sofitel Queenstown,** 8 Duke St. (☎ **0800/444-422** in New Zealand or 64/3/450-0045 international; www.sofitel.com).

---

175 Winter Sports

Les Glissades de la Terrasse
Zooming Downhill on a Toboggan
Quebec City, Canada

The sound of the wind buffeting your ears and face doesn't dull your howls of joy as you zoom downhill in a toboggan that reaches up to 97kmph (60 mph). The thrill of the slide stays with you even after you've finished your quick ride. Once your heart stops pounding, it's time do it over again—starting with the walk up to the top of the ramp, stopping occasionally to take in the squealing delights of the others racing downhill on Les Glissades de la Terrasse in Quebec City.

The ride itself may have taken your breath away, but the scenery surrounding you could also do the trick. On one side of Les Glissades de la Terrasse, ferries traverse the broad **St. Lawrence River.** At

the base of this manmade toboggan run looms **Le Chateau Frontenac,** the historic Fairmont hotel with its rounded turrets and massive wings reminiscent of ancient castle, built in the late 1800s to house railway passengers and encourage tourism.

Les Glissades de la Terace, located on Dufferin Terrace, is open only from mid-December through late March, so make time to take advantage of it if you're in town in winter. A maximum of four persons to a toboggan are allowed, but there's no minimum age, height, or weight, so it's great family entertainment. The low cost ($2 for one) also keeps it family-friendly. You must rent toboggans on site that are specifically designed to fit this run. Be sure to stop by the miniature sugar shack at the base of the run to purchase little cake cones filled with maple syrup.

When you're not coursing downhill at top speed, there's plenty else to keep you busy. Travelers who love winter sports and festivals will enjoy Quebec City in the cold season. For 2 weeks every winter, **Carnaval de Quebec** (the largest winter carnival in the world) turns the city into a cold-weather version of Mardi Gras. Parades, the canoe race on the St. Lawrence (where participants paddle in open areas, then push their canoe across the ice to the next open area), and dog sled races are great spectator events. You can keep warm by staying active with snowtubing, snowrafting, and even riding a zipline across the **Plains of Abraham** in the heart of the city. Quebec City also attracts skiers and snowboarders who want an urban setting after a day on the slopes. Skiing at nearby Mont-Sainte-Anne, with its 56 trails, is a great day

outing before returning to Quebec for the vibrant nightlife.

If you're interested in indoor entertainment, visit the **Musée de la Civilisation** and in particular the "Memoires" exhibit (85 rue Dalhousie; ✆ **418/643-2158;** www.mcq.org) that depicts the city's multi-faceted heritage. Also be sure to indulge in the city's excellent cuisine—an adrenaline rush in its own right. Don't miss the locals' favorite, Poutine: French fries topped with cheese curds and brown gravy. —*LF*

ⓘ **Quebec City Tourism,** 399 Saint-Joseph Est (✆ **877/783-1608** or 418/641-6654; www.quebecregion.com).

WHEN TO GO: Mid-winter.

✈ Quebec City.

🛏 $$$ **Le Chateau Frontenac,** 1 rue des Carrières (✆ **800/257-7544** or 418/692-3861; www.fairmont.com/frontenac).

Winter Sports **176**

Skeleton & Bobsled Runs
Sliding Downhill, Face Inches from Ice
Lake Placid, New York, U.S.A.

A skeleton sled ride at the race track that hosted the 2009 International Luge Federation World Championships and the International Bobsleigh and Skeleton Federation World Championships is a heart-stopping, hair-raising experience. Your face is just inches from the ice as you careen downhill reaching speeds of up to 30 to 35 mph (48–56kmph) on an ice-sheathed track that twists, turns, and terrifies during its course of eight curves. You're wearing a helmet, to be sure, but that's little consolation as you scream your way along this adrenaline-inducing track.

Too aggressive for you? Try the bobsled ride instead. On this you sit between a pilot who does the steering and a brakeman. The skeleton rides are offered only in

the winter when the track is icy, but bobsled rides can be enjoyed year-round. A winter bobsled ride feels something akin to the sensation of riding a roller coaster—you zoom around the track's corners at speeds of 45 to 52mph (72–84kmph). Winter rides start about halfway up the aboveground track. (It was built in 2000 and now is used for national championships.) In the summer, the bobsleds are on wheels—you'll reach speeds of about 50 mph (81kmph)—and you're racing down the lower part of the original track used during the 1980 Winter Olympic Games.

In addition to the skeletoning and bobsledding, the Lake Placid Olympic Sports Complex offers plenty of other activities. In the winter, there's a Be a Biathlete clinic, where you'll get a cross country skiing lesson and instruction on the shooting range with a 22-caliber rifle. You can also go downhill skiing or snowboarding on Whiteface Mountain, skating on the oval used during the 1980 Olympics, or cross-country skiing.

In the summer, the Be a Biathlete clinic includes an aerobic exercise to get the sense of cross-country skiing and instruction on the shooting range. The Gold Medal Adventure includes learning how to steer a luge on wheels, and how to start a bobsled by pushing it, then jumping into it. If all this careening and curving has you a little dizzy, there are other sporty options as well. You can go mountain biking on the cross country trails at the Olympic Sports Complex. And hiking trails are abundant

on the high Adirondack peaks surrounding Lake Placid. —*LF*

ⓘ **Lake Placid Olympic Region** (✆ **518/ 523-4436**; www.whitefacelakeplacid.com). **Lake Placid** (✆ **800/447-5224**; www.lake placid.com).

WHEN TO GO: Winter or summer, depending upon the sports you prefer.

✈ Burlington, Vermont (50 miles/81km) or Albany, New York (135 miles/217km).

🛏 $$ **Hilton Lake Placid Resort,** 1 Mirror Lake Dr. (✆ **800/755-5598** or 518/523-4411; www.lphilton.com). $$$ **Lake Placid Lodge,** Whiteface Inn Rd. (✆ **877/523-2700** or 518/523-2700; www.lakeplacid lodge.com).

---

177 Winter Sports

Appalachian Mountain Club
Cross-Country Skiing to Mountain Huts
White Mountains, New Hampshire, U.S.A.

It doesn't matter how skilled a cross-country skier you are—the inherent rewards are there for the taking. Whether you huff and puff on the more gentle spots along the trail, or skillfully traverse through the birches, the exhilaration is the same. Simply being outdoors in New Hampshire's White Mountains on a trail leading to one of the **Appalachian Mountain Club**'s (AMC) huts creates its own high. You'll start among maples and birch forests and climb to higher altitudes where the spruce and fir reign, all the while keeping an eye out for moose and deer. A sighting completes the experience.

AMC keeps several mountain huts open in the winter for people who enjoy skiing or snowshoeing through the wilderness. The easiest way to the **Zealand Falls Hut,** recommended for intermediate backcountry skiers, is a gentle but long 6-mile (nearly 10km) route. Stay on the unplowed road for the first 3½ miles (5.6km), then glide onto

the Zealand Trail, an old logging railroad grade, for the rest of the trip. The hut is in a wonderful setting, near waterfalls, with a spectacular view of the eastern edge of the Pemigewasset Wilderness. The even longer, more challenging route to the hut is on the Spruce Goose trail, which resembles a gentle roller coaster with its dips, before meeting up with the Zealand Trail and the hut beyond.

Near the hut, adrenaline junkies have the chance to go backcountry skiing in the birch glades, where less-skilled skiers dare not go. (Because of changing snow conditions, the folks at AMC suggest you take snowshoes along for ski tours near and beyond the hut.) You'll need to bring skins along if you want to take the steep trail that ascends nearby Mt. Hale, where the views of the surrounding wilderness are brilliant. You can also experience difficult skiing in a remote area down the back side of Mt. Hale.

An Appalachian Mountain Club hut in the White Mountains of New Hampshire.

The Lonesome Lake trail to the **Lonesome Lake Hut** is a popular but shorter 1.6 mile-long (2.6km) trail that intermediate and advanced skiers may enjoy. More adventuresome skiers can go to the hut via the Cascade Brook trail, a 3-mile-long (4.8km) route that's more difficult, but has less traffic. The hut, nestled against the flank of Cannon Mountain, has a wonderful view of the Franconia Range across a glacial tarn.

In the winter, the huts are self-service, so plan on bringing your own cold-weather sleeping bag and food. The huts do have a kitchen with a stove, oven, and utensils,

but, you'll have to hand-pump your water from an outside well. Hut reservations can be made on AMC's website (see below) and it's wise to make them up to 4 months in advance for the best availability on weekend nights, especially Saturdays. Mid-week is quieter and you might even get a hut to yourself. If planning in advance isn't your strong suit, keep checking the website for last-minute availability.

AMC offers a few ski trips to the three huts each winter, although most of the skiers visiting the huts are touring independently. Keep in mind that it's backcountry skiing, so the conditions may vary greatly, from powder to icy terrain. Appropriate winter gear is necessary; visit the AMC website for a recommend list of gear. In addition the winter ski trips, AMC offers a wide variety of trips and activities year-round in the mountains, rivers, and trails of the Northeast and Mid-Atlantic regions. —LF

ⓘ **Appalachian Mountain Club** (ℂ 603/ 466-2727; www.outdoors.org).
WHEN TO GO: Feb–Mar.
✈ Manchester, New Hampshire.
🛏 The huts.

Winter Sports **178**

Skiing the Steeps
Learning Backcountry Skiing Skills In-bounds
Crested Butte Mountain Resort, Colorado, U.S.A.

Peering over the edge of the bowl, all you see is a patchwork of rocks and ungroomed snow. "Take it carefully and remember what we discussed," says your guide. Sliding into the first turn, you carve carefully around a rock and onto a big plot of snow. "I can do this," you think. And you can. It's late morning and you've spent the last hour on the North Face working with a trained Crested Butte Mountain Guide to learn backcountry ski skills.

The **Adventure Guide Program** at Crested Butte Mountain Resort's Ski and Ride School educates adventurous skiers and snowboarders about skiing in the backcountry during guided in-bounds and out-of-bounds programs. In groups of four to eight people (or in private lessons), a guide starts with a few ski-off runs on single black-diamond trails, and on the crud snow alongside a trail. Once the students' skiing or riding abilities have been assessed and deemed competent, the guide will move the group over to the North Face, with its un-groomed, double-black diamond terrain. (This is where the U.S. Free Skiing Championships are held.) The choice of runs available on this section of extreme terrain at Crested Butte depends upon the snow conditions and weather on a particular day, but could include serious steeps on the North Face Bowl, or even Third Bowl, if the students are good enough. A guide might take very skilled skiers or riders into Sock-It-To-Me Ridge or Staircase, both technical rocky chutes.

The Adventure Guide Program is offered as a half-day or full-day experience. Per the director of the Ski and Ride School, skiers and snowboarders should be at least advanced intermediate or more skilled. When calling the ski school to make reservations for the program, discuss your skill level and comfort level in un-groomed terrain to see if this is the right program for you. The program is a joint partnership between the Ski and Ride School and Crested Butte Mountain Guides. If you really want to immerse yourself in backcountry skiing, take the CB Backcountry Guide 2-Day Program. Day 1 is spent on the mountain learning backcountry skills, safety procedures, and how to use backcountry equipment, including skins and avalanche transceivers. Day 2 is spent exploring the backcountry with your guide.

Crested Butte, in southwestern Colorado, is a historical mining town turned resort community, with many good restaurants and lively bars. The slopes on Crested Butte Mountain Resort are a few miles up the road. Here you'll find plenty of slopes for beginner and intermediate skiers. Snowshoeing and cross-country skiing are also popular in this area. There's plenty of lodging at the base of the slopes and down in town. Everything is connected via shuttles. —LF

(i) **Crested Butte Mountain Resort** (℡ 800/810-7669; www.skicb.com). **Ski School** (℡ 970/349-2252). **Crested Butte Chamber** (℡ 970/349-6438; www.cb-chamber.com).

WHEN TO GO: Dec (if there's enough snow to open the North Face) through mid-Apr.

✈ Gunnison, Colorado (28 miles/45km)

⊨ $$–$$$ **Crested Butte Mountain Resort** (℡ 800/810-7679; www.skicb.com). $–$$ **Elk Mountain Lodge,** 129 Gothic Ave. (℡ 800/374-6521 or 970/349-7533; www.elkmountainlodge.net).

---

179 Winter Sports

Snowkiting
Sailing with the Wind
Sun Valley, Idaho, U.S.A.

When you're sailing through the air, it feels as though there's a giant rope tow in your backpack that is lifting you off the ground. The feeling lasts for only 5 to 10 seconds, until you softly land back on the ground and keep skiing. But then it happens again and keeps on happening over and over again. This is how snowkiting works. This lift, both literal and figurative, brings with it a rush of adrenaline, and anyone with any experience snowkiting knows what invigorating business this sport can be.

Snowkiting attaches skiers and snowboarders to a kite that billows out like a parachute and allows them to ride across and above the snow propelled by wind power. Nature is the guide, and though you help navigate, you're really just along for the ride.

Heli-Skiing Hot Spots

Avid skiers and snowboarders live for a chance to fly to unpopulated mountaintops in a helicopter and have abundant downhills all to themselves. Deep powder, unparalleled views, and a dearth of people make this a sport hard to resist. All this privilege and privacy doesn't come cheap, though. Be prepared to shell out for heli-skiing adventures. Contact individual outfitters for exact pricing. —LF & CL

180 Canadian Rockies in British Columbia, Canada: The Bugaboo, Moonashee, Purcell, and Selkirk ranges are excellent areas for first-rate heli-skiing. **Canadian Mountain Holidays** (© 800/661-0252; www.canadianmountainholidays) flies skiers on a variety of trips, ranging from Powder Intro, for first-time heli-skiers, to Powder Max, for fit, strong, experienced skiers. **Mike Wiegele Heli-Resort** (© 800/661-9170; www.wiegele.com), in Blue River, on the shore of Eleanor Lake, flies snowcats skiers and snowboarders daily to extraordinary ski sites. First-timers and women's trips are available. Both outfitters have lodge accommodations with first-class dining and international clientele.

181 Ruby Mountains, Nevada, U.S.A.: The rugged mountains and grand landscapes here make the Ruby Mountains a heli-skiing haven. The powdery peak conditions for heli-skiing in this narrow, 60-mile-long (97km) range are usually in February and March. Our choice for outfitters is the **Ruby Mountain Heli-Experience** (© 775/773-6857; www.helicopterskiing.com), which offers packages that include 3 nights lodging and daily heli-skiing with snowcat skiing back-up, if weather prevents the helicopters from taking off on a particular day. Four heli-skiers or snowboarders venture out with a guide to explore a mix of open bowls and glades.

182 New Zealand: Heli-skiing in New Zealand is growing in popularity, especially in the Liebig and Malte Brun ranges as well as on the Tasman Glacier (see **174**). To ski the mountains, contact **Wilderness Heliskiing** (© 64/3/435-1834; www.wildernessheli.co.nz) or **Ski the Tasman** (© 64/3/435-1834; www.skithetasman.co.nz). Their packages offer an array of accommodations, ranging from an upscale hotel to a youth hostel in Cook Mountain Village. If you prefer to ski the Arrowsmith and Ragged ranges, contact **Methven Heliskiing** (© 64/3/302 8108; www.methvenheli.co.nz). Methven lands its operations at the highest elevations of all the South Island heli-skiing outfitters, ensuring long runs.

183 Himalayas, Nepal: You may not have the desire or wherewithal to climb Mt. Everest, but why should that mean you can't take on the Himalayas in another fantastic fashion—heli-skiing? A trip with **Himalayan Heliski Guides** (© 33/97/39-0359; www.heliskinepal.com) starts in Kathmandu, then flies you to the world's highest mountains—in the Everest and Annapurna regions of Nepal. There, you'll ride and ski for several days with experienced and licensed Russian and Nepalese pilots and guides.

184 Chugach Mountains, Alaska, U.S.A.: The southern Alaskan mountains see more snowfall than almost anywhere else in the world, ensuring pristine powder for heli-skiing expeditions for all stripes. **Chugach Powder Guides** (© 907/783-HELI

[4354]; www.chugachpowderguides.com) is a popular choice for skiers who want a single day of heli-skiing followed by a stay at a luxury lodge. **Valdez Heli-Camps** (© **907/783-3243;** www.valdezhelicamps.com) hosts skiers who want a more intense experience. **Valdez Heli-Ski Guides** (© **907/835-4528;** www.valdezheliskiguides.com) caters exclusively to advanced and expert skiers and offers an array of packages.

185 Telluride, Colorado, U.S.A.: Helitrax (© **970/728-8377;** www.helitrax.com) is the company to go with for heli-skiing in Colorado. The operation ferries skiers to slopes in the stunning San Juan Mountains, with altitudes up to 13,000 feet (3,900m). Pickup is in the Mountain Village, in the heart of Telluride's lift-served slopes, and the runs range from 1,000 to 2,500 feet (300–750m). Day and multi-day trips are available for adventurous intermediate, advanced, and expert skiers. Snowboarders are welcome but must be comfortable with long traverses.

186 Wasatch Range, Utah, U.S.A.: Be whisked away to the Wasatch and heli-ski to your heart's delight. With the help of a chopper, among these peaks found just outside of Salt Lake City, skiers will find hidden wide-open powder bowls and some of the best chutes in the country. **Wasatch Powderbird** (© **800/974-4354;** www.powderbird.com) has scheduled and charter heli-skiing adventures available. With a guide-to-guest ratio of 1:4, you're sure to get all the attention you desire and require.

187 Greenland: And you thought all there was to do in Greenland was go dog-sledding (see **125**)? Why not take your exploration of this population-sparse, snow-heavy land to a different elevation? West Greenland provides an abundance of unspoiled terrain on which to drop and go, with Maniitsoq being one of the most inviting destinations. **Powderbird** (© **800/974-4354;** www.powderbird.com), the same operation who flies in the Wasatch Range in Utah (see **186**), also runs game here.

188 Sweden: Because of its chilling temperatures and near 24-hour daylight in the months of March through June, heli-skiing in the Scandinavian country is ideal for those who want to hit the powder almost year-round. Though the peaks in the region aren't particularly high (around 1,800m/5,900 ft.), you can get a surprising amount of distance on the way down (1,000 vertical meters/nearly 3,300 ft.). A number of reputable companies run heli-skiing adventures here. Among them are **Elemental Adventures** (© **44/207-836-3547;** www.eaheliskiing.com) and **Arctic Elements** (© **46/70-341-50-35;** www.arcticelements.com).

189 Yellowstone National Park, U.S.A.: Yellowstone National Park takes on an entirely new dimension when you approach it from the sky. On your way to undisturbed slopes of powder, you'll pass jagged peaks, lakes, and geysers as well as wildlife. You'll have the opportunity to ski in three states: Wyoming, Montana, and Idaho, depending on which heli-skiing adventure you choose. Trips usually depart from either Bozeman, Montana, or Jackson Hole, Wyoming. For local operators, check out www.yellowstonewinterguide.com/skiing/heli_skiing.php.

Snowkiting in Sun Valley, Idaho.

niques and safety to backcountry-guided service. During the 1½-hour basic training course you learn about wind theory, the power zone, the wind window, launching, landing, and safety all before you fly a trainer kite. During your first mission, you learn about setting up and handling your kite, controlling your speed, how to climb hills, and maneuver through obstacles. By the end you'll be kiting through the powder. During the advanced course, experienced riders start to jump, ski, or board up mountains, tack upwind, and ride in deep snow—all a thrill.

Snowkite Soldier's instructors take beginners to a scenic area near Sun Valley, centrally located in Idaho, not far from the Sawtooth National Recreation area. More advanced snowkiters are taken to an area near Fairfield, Idaho, to the southwest of Sun Valley, to a large, open section of backcountry, where one can snowkite for many miles. The company also offers all-inclusive 4-day/3-night adventure camps.

Sun Valley has been a popular resort with the rich and famous since the 1930, but community—rife with galleries, restaurants, and shops in addition to the incredible surrounding wilderness—has enough riches of its own that there's plenty for visitors of all walks of life. —LF

You can ski in the powder for miles, explains Andrew Monty Goldman, who runs Sun Valley–based **Snowkite Soldier** (see below). Snowkiting is an exciting eco-friendly alternative to skiing and snow-boarding on lift-served mountains because while others are hitching a ride up the mountain on a ski-lift, skilled kiters can be swept by the wind along backcountry terrain at speeds up to 50 mph (81kmph), sail up 40 to 50 feet (12–15m) in the air on flat ground or up to 100 feet (30m) in the air while ascending a hill or mountain.

This crossover sport, which was born from kite surfing (p. 146), is growing in popularity. Anyone who is an intermediate skier or snowboarder should be able to go snowkiting. (You must be at least 8 years old.) Snowkite Soldier offers a variety of programs ranging from basic kiting tech-

ⓘ **Snowkite Soldier** (© **208/484-1620;** www.snowkitesoldier.com). **Sun Valley/ Ketchum Chamber & Visitors Bureau** (© **866/305-0408;** www.visitsunvalley. com).

WHEN TO GO: Winter.

✈ Sun Valley or Hailey, Idaho.

🛏 $$–$$$ **Sun Valley Resort,** 1 Sun Valley Rd. (© **800/786-8259** or 208/622-2001; www.sunvalley.com).

Free-Sledding Lincoln Gap Road
Extreme Sledding, You Add the Brakes
Lincoln Gap, Vermont, U.S.A.

Adrenaline rushes come easily as you steer a sled down the narrow, snake-like road that descends from the top of Lincoln Gap, a pass in Vermont's Green Mountains. The rushes escalate if you're skilled enough to sled through gaps in the trees in the woods that line this road, so narrow that two cars can barely navigate past one another when it's open in the summer. But in wintertime, this road between Warren and Lincoln isn't plowed, so it has become a favorite spot for free-sledding.

Part of the thrill of sledding is that compared to skiing or snowboarding, it's a very intimate experience with the mountain. Rather than standing as you make your way down, with sledding you're right down on ground level, getting a close-up of every bump and curve. Every weekend, hardcore sledders mix with first-timers and the less-experienced to take on Lincoln Gap Road. Some zip downhill at speeds up to 40 mph (65kmph), navigating the road just like one might see in a rally car race. Others creep along at only 10 mph (16kmph) around the road's many twists and turns. Many of the more skilled sledders take to the woods alongside the road, grabbing at trees to steer around them.

Sledders can drive their cars only so far up the road, at which point they must park. From there, they must hike up with their sleds to the peak of the road, about ¾ of a mile, before turning around and sliding downhill. Some hikers are fortunate enough to hitch a ride on a passing snowmobile, a bonus thrill on your way to the sledding. While many Lincoln Gap Road sledders own their own sleds, you can rent them in the local towns nearby. **Clearwater Sports** (www.clearwatersports.com) in Waitsfield has rental sleds, as does **Umiak** (www.umiak.com) in Stowe. Clearwater

Sports and Umiak offer the Mad River Rocket sled—basically a kneeboard in the snow. It has a negative keel on the bottom that picks in snow and you steer by leaning or directing yourself with your hands on the snow. The Hammerheads, offered at Umiak, have an aluminum frame and are ergonomically shaped, so you can lie on the sled. They have a steering mechanism and skis. (Picture a high-tech version of that sled you played on as a kid.) The Hammerheads are designed to be used on snow-packed areas, or with "powder" skis in snow up to about 6 inches. The Madriver Rocket sleds work wonderfully in deeper snow and unpacked trails, and skilled riders say a ride through the wood dodging trees gives the same thrill as kayaking in rushing water or snowboarding through glades.

If you want to test extreme sledding before buying your own equipment, rent a sled. Clearwater Sports in Waitsfield has a Rocket-Snowshoeing Adventure, which includes snowshoeing up Lincoln Gap and sledding back down. Umiak in Stowe rents sleds and it's close to Smugglers Notch, another road closed in the winter that's popular with free-sledders. —*LF*

ⓘ **Green Mountains National Forest,** 231 North Main St., Rutland, VT (✆ **802/747-6700**).

WHEN TO GO: Check with locals or the sled companies to see when the snow is good.

✈ Burlington, Vermont (40 miles/64km).

⌫ $$$$ **Pitcher Inn,** 275 Main St., Warren (✆ **802/496-6350;** www.pitcherinn.com). $$ **West Hill House,** 496 West Hill, Warren (✆ **800/898-1427** or 802/496-7162; www.westhillbb.com).

Comet Bobsled Rides
One Minute of Terror
Park City, Utah, U.S.A.

The "Comet" bobsled ride is not for the faint of heart. During the minute it takes a trained bobsled driver to steer you and two other passengers through 15 curves, almost 5 Gs of force smack you around as your sled descents the ice-covered track. You'll be jolted back and forth, as the sled reaches up to 80 mph (nearly 130kmph) and careens around the curves.

Billed as the most intense minute of your life, this ride will give you a good idea of what Olympic bobsled athletes experience day in and day out. The track you'll ride on is the same one that Olympians raced on during the 2002 Winter Olympic Games in Utah. While the winter ride is the most intense experience, summer ride are

also offered on the same track in a bobsled on wheels. During the warm weather rides, you'll only experience about 4 g-forces while sliding downhill. That's still enough to get your spine tingling.

Before the ride, you go through an orientation session to learn safety procedures and what to expect. Rides are offered daily in the winter, and 5 days a week during the summer. Reserve a space well in advance of your trip because these rides, though expensive ($200 in winter; $65 in summer), are popular. Passengers must be at least 14 years old and in good health.

The Utah Olympic Park, a few miles from the historic heart of Park City, offers other adrenaline rushes in the summertime. When it's warm outside, you can fly along the **Xtreme Zipline,** which takes you right over the K-120 ski jump hill, or the **Ulta Zipline.** A ride down the **Quicksilver Alpine Slide** keeps the summer heat at bay for a few minutes.

Outside the Olympic Park, Park City is a good base for active summer adventures. There are miles of trails for mountain biking and hiking in the surrounding mountains. Peddle on trails that start near the city line, or hook a bike on a ski lift and ride trails from the top down. Rent a bike at **Jans Mountain Outfitters (© 800/745-1020;** www.jans.com). Hikers often take the lifts at one of the resorts and choose trails that lead along ridges with spectacular views of the Wasatch Mountains. You can go rock climbing in Parley's Canyon, or along the walls of some of the other canyons that spread out like fingers from the palm of Salt Lake City.

Park City, in a canyon about a half-hour drive from downtown Salt Lake City, is a

A ride on the Comet bobsled is fast and intense.

year-round playground. During the winter, visitors have a choice of three ski resorts: Park City Mountain Resort, Deer Valley Resort, and The Canyon. Between the three, there's spectacular terrain for skiing and snowboarding on open slopes, glades, steep bowls, and chutes. Home to the Sundance Film Festival every January, Park City has lodging for budget-minded as well as fat-wallet visitors, and lots of good restaurants. —*LF*

ⓘ **Utah Olympic Park** (ⓒ **435/658-4200;** www.olyparks.com). Park City info (www.parkcity.org).

WHEN TO GO: Summer or winter.

✈ Salt Lake City (33 miles/53km).

🛏 $$$$ **Stein Eriksen Lodge,** 7700 Stein Way, Deer Valley (ⓒ **800/453-1302** or 435/649-3700; www.steinlodge.com). $$$ **Washington School Inn,** 543 Park Ave., Park City (ⓒ **800/824-1672** or 435/649-3800; www.washingtonschoolinn.com).

192 Winter Sports

Snowtubing
Totally Tubular
Western North Carolina, U.S.A.

It started off as a fun, safe way to hit the slopes—even the kiddies could get into the fun by swooshing down a snowy hillside on an inner tube. Then some adrenaline junkies got into the act, built up a couple of steep moguls, and pretty soon people were catching air for 30 feet (9m) or more. Snowtubing has gone from backyard fun to big business as more and more ski resorts are getting into the act by constructing specially groomed courses just for snowtubers.

Though it can get wild, snowtubing is an adrenaline adventure that both adults and kids will love.

Western North Carolina has emerged as a hot spot (cold spot?) for this wintertime thrill, and a number of resorts on the slopes of the Blue Ridge Mountains offer snowtubing lessons and runs. Even when conditions for skiing and snowboarding aren't ideal, snowtubing offers resort visitors a good wintertime rush. There isn't much skill involved, so folks can tube the slopes without much in the way of training.

While any fully inflated inner tube will suffice, actual snowtubes are a much better ride—instead of a "donut hole" in the center, the snowtube is more of a disk that's dimpled in the middle, providing a seat for the rider that reduces drag and increases speed. Speaking of speed, riders can hit some surprising velocities on their downhill run because the snowtube has so little resistance on snow or ice. That fact, plus the near-total lack of steering control, have led to some fairly impressive accidents and injuries. Newcomers—and people who value their teeth and bones—might want to obey the signs that instruct them to snowtube *only* on slopes that are specifically groomed for the tubes.

Safety precautions aside, this is great family fun that can be enjoyed by young kids as well as old-timers—especially when the snowtubes are lashed together and everyone goes down together. And if that's not enough of a thrill for you, some folks have even taken to towing snowtubes behind snowmobiles—much to the delight of cosmetic dentists everywhere. —*ML*

ⓘ **Hawksnest Resort,** 2058 Skyline Dr., Seven Devils, NC (✆ **800/822-4295** or 828/963-6561; www.hawksnest-resort.com). **Moonshine Mountain,** 5865 Willow Mountain Rd., Hendersonville, NC (✆ **828/696-0333;** www.moonshine mountain.com).

WHEN TO GO: Jan–Mar.

✈ Asheville Regional Airport (75 miles/121km).

🛏 $$ **Hidden Valley Motel,** 8725 NC Hwy. 105 S., Boone, NC (✆ **828/963-4372;** www.hiddenvalleymotel.com). $$ **High Country Inn,** 1785 Hwy. 105, Boone, NC (✆ **800/334-5605** or 828/264-1000; www.highcountryinn.com).

Winter Sports **193**

Extreme Ski Touring
Sweat Your Way to the South Pole
Antarctica

South Pole ski expeditions are for serious adventurers only. If you think it will be fun (as well as an extreme challenge) to ski 6 to 10 hours a day over the top of a 3km-thick (2-mile) ice pack day after day, all the while pushing against relentless winds, perhaps this trip is for you. You'll have to train for months ahead of time because you'll need terrific endurance and stamina to spend so many days hauling a heavy sled across the Polar Plateau. And when it's time to camp, you must have enough

energy left over from the day's trek to set up tents, make dinner, and heat snow for water. People who have made this trek say there's nothing to match the extreme beauty and isolation of the Polar Plateau. The collective experience of knowing you may be the only people within hundreds of miles gives you a sense of the ultimate challenges faced by the original teams who explored this region. And reaching the geographical South Pole by your own efforts will change you forever.

Polar Explorers, which has been ranked as one of the Best Outfitters on Earth by *National Geographic* magazine, offers trips to the Geographic South Pole, the most southerly point on earth. You could take the South Pole One Degree Ski Expedition or the longer South Pole Two Degree Ski Expedition, the two shortest trips. They run simultaneously, once a year around New Year's, when the sun never sets in this part of the world. (Polar Explorers also offers a two-month ski touring expedition across the White Continent.)

Both Polar Explorers South Pole Expeditions start at Patriot Hills base camp in the Antarctica. Weather permitting, after a few days to acclimate to the cold and prepare for the expedition, you'll fly to either 88° or 89° south (depending upon the trip you choose) to start your expedition. Six to 19 days (again, depending which trip you choose) of ski touring across the Polar Plateau later, the South Pole will be in sight. After popping the cork and celebrating your arrival, you'll camp and await the return flight to Patriot Hills. If time permits, you may tour the Amundsen-Scott South Pole Research Center.

Another outfitter also conducts South Pole expeditions. Each year, **Adventures Network International (ANI)** offers several options for Ski South Pole All The Way expeditions. The first is a 1,175km (730-mile), 2-month trek from Hercules Inlet on the Antarctic coast to the South Pole. The shorter 40- to 45-day version, a *mere* 934km (580 miles), begins where Reinhold Messner began his famous Transantarctic crossing. Skiers are picked up by aircraft for the return trip. Other start points are possible but all require a resume of previous expedition experience. Minimum numbers are required for these guided expeditions but ANI will support self-guided ones. —*LF*

TOURS: Polar Explorers (✆ **800/732-7328** or 847/256-4409; www.polar explorers.com). **Adventure Network International** (✆ **801/266-4876;** www. adventure-network.com).

WHEN TO GO: Mid-winter.

✈ Carlos Ibañez del Campo International Airport, Punta Arenas, Chile.

194   **Climbing & Rappelling**

Abseiling off Table Mountain
A Real Cliff Hanger
Cape Town, South Africa

Let's start at the top of Table Mountain. The real reason to make your way up this sandstone monstrosity is to go down it, and there's only one respectable way to do that: backwards, off a cliff, attached to a single sturdy rope.

Table Mountain in Cape Town, on the southernmost peninsula of South Africa, is home to the world's highest commercial abseiling experience. Abseiling (or rappelling, as it's more commonly known in the U.S.) is the controlled descent from

a mountain by rope. Expert climbers use the technique to safely navigate steep or otherwise dangerous terrain. For the rest of us, it offers a stupefying (though relatively safe) ride down a jagged, vertical rock face. With professional guides in charge, all you have to do is get through your safety briefing, wear the proper equipment, attach to a rope-and-anchor system, and step off a cliff's edge straight into thin air.

Snowboarding Extreme Terrain

Major to moderate steeps, perhaps a chute or three, and glades where good carvers can slide between the trees—these are the types of terrain where you're liable to find expert snowboarders who are looking to ride in ungroomed territory. Here's a list of resorts filled with areas to entice riders seeking extreme terrain. Boarders who like to cruise and carve down groomed and manicured slopes will find plenty of choices, too. —*LF*

⑲⑤ Big Sky, Montana, U.S.A.: While riding up the Lone Peak Tram at Big Sky, much of the extreme terrain is within view. You're at the peak of the resort and the only way down is via steep routes, such as the Gullies. If you and a buddy have the proper avalanche gear and experience, you can check out with ski patrol to challenge Big Couloir, with its 53-degree pitch near the top. Boarders' favorite runs include the natural half-pipe located off the Swift Current high-speed quad chair next to Lower Morning Star and Shedhorn, which they call Shredhorn. Boarders who want to carve head up the high-speed quads on Andesite Mountain for fast runs down. ✆ *800/548-4486; www.bigskyresort.com.*

⑲⑥ Kirkwood, California, U.S.A.: This small resort is tucked away from the main hubbub of South Lake Tahoe, but it's worth the drive over Carson Pass to frolic on the high-altitude open bowls, chutes, and steep runs that fall off of a horseshoe-shaped ridgeline. Many of the slopes are north-facing, so they hold snow well into the spring. Add on an average annual snowfall of 40 feet (12m) and you have the making of an extreme place to rip up the mountain. ✆ *800/967-7500* or *209/258-6000 for lodging, 877/KIRKWOOD [547-5966] for conditions; www.kirkwood.com.*

⑲⑦ Mammoth, California, U.S.A.: The sheer number of slopes and the length of the resort's season—often late October into June—make this a popular place for snowboarders. Freestyle riders can be found jibbing on the rails in the terrain parks, which are designed for different levels, from the Disco Park where groms and other beginners tackle small bumps to the Unbound Main Park where freestylers perform radical maneuvers such as 720s. Riders catch big air in the 22-foot-tall (6.6m) Super Duper Pipe. ✆ *800-MAMMOTH [626-6684]* or *760/934-2571; www.mammothmountain.com.*

⑲⑧ Jackson Hole, Wyoming, U.S.A.: Here, there are lots of lines for snowboarders. Newbies can learn on the lower half of Apres Vous Mountain. Casper Bowl has a mix of terrain for intermediate to advanced boarders. The North Hobacks and the Headwall are popular spots for skilled boarders. Grand is an amazing cruiser for carvers who enjoy groomed runs. Jackson Hole offers clinics for advanced snowboarders and skiers who want to learn to enjoy the off-piste terrain that surrounds the resort. ✆ *888/Deep-SNO [333-7766]* or *307/733-2292; www.jacksonhole.com.*

⑲⑨ Crested Butte, Colorado, U.S.A.: The steeps, bumps on trails, couloirs, chutes, and overall terrain on Crested Butte's North Face attracts extreme snowboarders and skiers. Names like Headwall, with its steep, rock-strewn face, and Banana Funnel, with its ultra steep tree runs, are mouthed reverently by the excess of excellent boarders who play on the slopes here. Crested Butte holds the U.S. Extreme Ski and Snowboard Championships every year. ✆ *800/810-7669; www.skicb.com.*

⑳ Livigno, Italy: Snowboarders congregate at Livigno because the prices are low and party quotient is high. This duty-free, high-altitude resort is in northern Italy near the Swiss border. Most of the slopes are wide open, and with the Alta Vatellina lift pass, boarders can explore the slopes around Bormio and Santa Caterina, too. Some of the toughest terrain at Livigno is off the Mottolino gondola. The terrain park there has a half pipe, jumps, rails, and a bordercross course. ✆ *39/342-05-22-00; www.livigno.eu/en.*

㉑ Mayrhofen, Austria: This ski town in the Zillertal Valley is an easy train ride from Innsbruck. You can board in the popular Gerent area, or buy the Zillertal Super Skipass, which opens up 502km (312 miles) of trails and 160 lifts. With the pass, you can ride on trails moving from one lift to another. If you end up in another town simply take a bus back. The Hintertux glacier isn't far from here. The Vans Penken Park in Mayrhofen is lauded as one of the best snow parks in Europe, with terrain for big tricks in the Pro line, and gentler rails and kickers in the Public line. ✆ *43/528/567-60; www.mayrhofen.at.*

㉒ Avoriaz, France: One of the first European resorts to embrace snowboarding, Avoriaz has four terrain parks and a half pipe. Avoriaz boasts The Stash, an ecological snow park designed by snowboarding guru Jake Burton. The Biotop has a long jib-monster. Arare is filled with advanced kickers, corner jumps and rails, and a super-pipe. La Chapelle is for newbie freestylers still perfecting their skills. Avoriaz is linked to Les Portes du Soleil, a group of resorts straddling the French/Swiss border, where there are off-piste areas for shredding. ✆ *33/450/74-02-11; www.avoriaz.com/ski-holidays.*

㉓ Niseko, Japan: According to *Forbes Magazine,* Niseko is the second snowiest ski resort in the world, receiving an average of 1,511cm (595 in.) of snow annually. You can snowboard at night at the Niseko Hirafu area, because a large portion of the mountain is illuminated until 9pm. Take the gondola up and you can board on groomed terrain or in and out of the trees. The Niseko terrain park and half pipe, also lit in the evening, has large tabletops, rails, and kickers. Wonderland Park has spines, waves, hits, and rails for various skill levels. *www.niseko.ne.jp/en.*

㉔ Portillo, Chile: One of the biggest advantages to snowboarding south of the equator is that resorts there are just getting their season started while those in the northern hemisphere are closing up shop. Come to Portillo, the oldest ski area in South America, located in the Andes mountains near Lagune del Inca (Inca of the Lake). With 14 lifts and a relatively small crowd, snowboarders can go all day without having to fight the masses. Portillo's amazing mountain views, international ski- and snow-school instructors (many of whom are past Olympic medalists), and friendly South American locals offer a refreshing change of atmosphere from many of the U.S. and European snowboarding destinations. ✆ *56/2/2630606; www.skiportillo.com.*

Abseiling off Table Mountain.

Hands down, Cape Town is South Africa's most exhilarating city. It offers top-notch hotels, dining, arts, culture, and shopping, plus a celebrated **wine region** (www.southafrica.net/sat/content/en/us/wine) less than an hour's drive away. There's also a broad range of outdoor pursuits available in and around **Table Mountain National Park** (www.san parks.org/parks/table_mountain). The star of the show is the ubiquitous Table Mountain, reaching more than 1,000m (3,500 ft.) above sea level and dominating the area's landscape. The flat-topped massif is sandwiched between two other mountains called Devil's Peak and Lion's Head, as well as a small hill called Signal Hill, that together cradle the city until it juts out into the Atlantic Ocean.

Standing atop its vast horizontal plateau, reaching more than 3km (2 miles) across, you'll be wowed by the unparalleled views of a vast national park, deep blue sea, and bustling cosmopolitan life far below. Just be sure to check the weather before heading up; a cloudy "tablecloth" draped over the mountain can prevent good sightseeing-and sometimes even halt abseiling trips.

Assuming the sky looks clear enough, you can ascend Table Mountain by hiking or riding the popular **Table Mountain Aerial Cableway** (www.tablemountain. net), which runs every 10 minutes or so. If you want to travel on your own, check out *Frommer's South Africa* travel guide for details on the best paths to take; there are more than 300 trails to choose from and frequent rain can quickly create hazardous conditions in some areas. To reach the mountain's highest point, you'll want to continue past Platteklip Gorge—a direct route to the summit that takes about 2½ hours—for another 19m (62 ft.) to Maclear's Beacon. After that, take some time to catch your breath and get your bearings—not to mention your balance. You'll need it for what comes next.

As you peer over the staggeringly high 112m (367 ft.) drop, your heart pounds so hard and fast that you think it might break through your chest. Your instincts scream at you to turn around and make a run for the cable car. But don't do it—even if your harness, gloves, and helmet do little to calm your nerves. When you finally step off the mountain and rappel into sheer space, feet bouncing off the rocky vertical wall in front of you, the rush is head-to-toe intoxicating. As you slowly realize you're secure and an overwhelming silence fills your ears, the mountaintop begins sliding from view and you experience a weightless sensation unlike any other. You start to feel surprisingly comfortable dangling on a rope, breathing the fresh mountain air, far above the crowded city streets. Finally, it sinks in: You're on top of the world—or Cape Town's part of it anyway.

To extend your high, add *kloofing* to your itinerary. This combo of cliff jumping and scrambling down river gorges culminates with another rappel down a shorter waterfall. By the end of it, you'll be an abseiling pro, not to mention a cooler, more refreshed one. —JS

ⓘ **Cape Town Tourism,** 107 Clocktower, V&A Waterfront (ℂ **27/21-405-4500;** www.tourismcapetown.co.za).

TOUR: Abseil Africa, Long St. (ℂ **27/21-424-4760;** www.abseilafrica.co.za).

WHEN TO GO: Oct–May.

✈ Cape Town Airport.

🛏 $$ **Derwent House**, 14 Derwent Rd. (ℂ **27/21-422-2763;** www.derwenthouse.co.za). $–$$ **Hotel Protea Fire and Ice,** New Church and Victoria sts. (ℂ **27/21-488-2555;** www.proteahotels.com/protea-hotel-fire-and-ice.html).

205 **Climbing & Rappelling**

Climbing Mount Elbrus
Where Eagles Dare
Azau, Russia

When Zeus sought to punish Prometheus for giving humans the secret of fire, he chained him to the top of the highest mountain in the ancient world, where his body was picked apart by an eagle. That mythical mountain is still around, the volcano named Mount Elbrus. At 5,553m (18,510 ft.) above sea level, Elbrus is the highest point in Europe and is one of the so-called Seven Summits, the highest points on each of the seven continents. If you're like most people, climbs up the likes of Mount Everest may be just beyond your reach, but Elbrus can be conquered by relatively inexperienced trekkers who are willing to endure the hardships of high-altitude climbing.

This long-dormant volcano is in Russia, just north of its border with Georgia. Most visitors fly from Moscow to Mineralnye Vody, then take a 4-hour bus ride to Azau, a remote outpost in the shadow of Elbrus. Because of the numerous bureaucratic and security issues involved (including visas, permits, and registrations), most climbers are better off working with an outfitter who can handle the details.

When choosing an outfitter, remember that about 20 people die each year trying to reach the summit of Mount Elbus,

Altitude and weather are serious concerns when hiking Mount Elbrus.

usually due to poorly organized and equipped groups trekking beyond their means. Though little technical mountaineering experience is needed here, some training is required because there are real risks involved—the weather at these altitudes is unstable, temperatures even in summer can be extremely cold, and low oxygen can cause serious health problems. Be sure to ask your outfitter about their safety record.

There are several routes to the top, and the one known as "the normal route" is supported by a cable car and chairlift system, which can shorten the trip to a few hours. It can also get a little crowded in summer, with dozens of peak-baggers making quick ascents. When it comes time to descend, some adventurers break out their touring skis and take a downhill run

that's as unforgettable as it is demanding. Elsewhere in the area, **Terskol**—known to some as the Chamonix of the Caucasus—boasts a couple of lift systems and plenty of hotels catering to skiers. —*ML*

ⓘ **Elbrus Info Site** (✆ www.elbrus.org).

TOURS: Geographic Bureau, P.O. Box 375, St. Petersburg, Russia (✆ **7/812/230-5794;** www.geographicbureau.com). **Alpine Ascents International,** 121 Mercer St., Seattle, WA 98109 (✆ **206/378-1927;** www.alpineascents.com).

WHEN TO GO: May–Sept.

🛏 $$$ **Hotel Ozon-Cheget,** Cheget Glade (✆ **7/866/387-1453;** www.hotelozon.ru). $$ **Hotel Balkaria,** Azau Glade (✆ **7/866/387-1257**).

Climbing & Rappelling **206**

Moaning Caverns
Rappelling into Darkness
Vallecito, California, U.S.A.

The Statue of Liberty would fit comfortably inside the depths of **Moaning Cavern,** one of California's largest caves, about 100 miles (161km) southeast of Sacramento in the town of Vallecito. From the opening to the cave floor, it's 165 feet (50m) down—a drop that seems to double if you're dangling from a rope above the abyss. Some visitors take the 234 scrap metal steps to the cave floor, but rappelling is a vastly more thrilling way down.

The first half-dozen feet are easy, down a rock shelf, but then the bottom falls out, and nothing comes between you and the cave floor but your gear and thin air. The cavern is lit, so there's no mistaking the distance. As you and several others work your way down simultaneously, hand over hand, limestone formations come into view, as well as the stairs, one

by one underscoring how far you are from solid ground. It's most nerve-wracking if a rappeller below you slows or stops or gets hung up; all you can do is hang there until he gets moving.

Once you reach the bottom, you're unharnessed and have the opportunity to learn about the cave. You'll see bones of prehistoric locals who lacked rappelling gear. The Miwok Indians reportedly used the cavern as a convenient burial ground years ago, and the bones of humans and animals have been found here. An optional 2-hour spelunking tour takes you through unlit, meandering caverns. You'll crawl or slide along the wet, muddy floors and squeeze through narrow openings to see some wonderful stalactites and stalagmites.

You'll need tied shoes to rappel down the sheer face—flip-flops don't make it.

You'll also have to sign a release form and watch an instructional video before you start down. A member of the Sierra Nevada Recreation staff fits you with a hard hat, gloves, coveralls, kneepads, and lights. Then you move over to the "pit," where they check your gear, give you a few last words of instruction, strap you into your harness, and send you on your way.

Outside the cavern is a new 1,500-foot (450m) zipline, and horseback riding for an above-the-ground adventure. The nearby **Calaveras Big Trees State Park** (www. parks.ca.gov), with its Giant Sequoia trees, is worth a visit. So are the numerous old mining towns, small local museums, and additional caverns and mines. Golfing

opportunities are available in nearby Angels Camp, which also has its share of antiques shops, galleries, and wineries. —*LF*

ⓘ **Cave & Mine Adventures** (✆ 866/762-2837; www.caverntours.com/MoCav Rt.htm).

WHEN TO GO: Fall.

✈ Sacramento International Airport.

⊨ $ **Best Western Cedar Inn & Suites,** 444 South Main St., Angels Camp (✆ 209/736-4000; www.bestwestern angelscamp.com). $$$ **WorldMark at Angels Camp,** 123 Selkirk Ranch Rd. (✆ 209/736-9549; www.worldmarkthe club.com).

207 Climbing & Rappelling

Ice Climbing in Little Switzerland
The World's Best Ice Climbers Gather Here
Ouray, Colorado, U.S.A.

On any given winter day along the edge of Colorado's Uncompahgre Gorge, you're nearly guaranteed to spy at least one daredevil dangling from a rope below you, clinging to an icy cliffside by crampons and the buried edge of an ice-axe. These rocky walls, amid the towering peaks of the San Juan mountain range, make up part of the world's only ice park, steps from the small Victorian town of Ouray. Designed by expert climbers to challenge extremely skilled practitioners are 160 routes with names like "Evil has no Boundaries," "Verminator," and "Dizzy with the Vision." Even the way down to the base of these routes, along a rough trail with only a rope for support, can test the steeliest nerves.

Faucets line the canyon's rim and, in December, when it's cold enough for water to freeze on a one-mile stretch of rocky walls, park officials turn on the spigots. Water trickles down the rock outcroppings and sleek walls that fall downward

to the Uncompahgre River below. Gradually a sheath of frozen water covers the canyon sides, and it's time to start ice-climbing.

During the 3-day **Ouray Ice Festival** every January, a huge crowd shows up to watch some of the world's best climbers tackle challenges laid out on the 2-mile (3km) stretch of canyon primed for climbing. Three thousand visitors come to town for the event, and some 90% are ice climbers, so the routes can get crowded. During the remainder of the ice-climbing season (mid-Dec through Apr), it's much calmer.

Interactive ice clinics take place during the festival and throughout the ice-climbing season. High-profile climbers teach basics such as setting anchors as well as advanced leading and other maneuvers. Local youngsters learn to climb early here on the Kids Wall.

Ouray is a special spot for people who want to explore the outdoors in a remote

Ice climbing in Ouray, Colorado.

swimming, a water slide, a shallow area for youngsters, and a game section popular for water volleyball. In the winter, cross-country and backcountry skiing are close to town. Summertime offers jeep trips up to Yankee Basin, ATV rides, and hiking and mountain biking trails that start from town. —LF

ⓘ **Ouray Ice Park** (✆ **970/325-4288;** www.ourayicepark.com). **Chicks with Picks** (offers women-only ice-climbing classes in Jan; ✆ **970-626-4424;** www. chickswithpicks.com). **Ouray Visitors Center** (✆ **800/228-1876;** www.ouray colorado.com).

WHEN TO GO: Mid-Dec to Mar or early Apr.

✈ **Montrose Regional Airport,** Colorado (36 miles/58km).

🛏 $ **Ouray Chalet Inn,** 510 Main St. (✆ **800-924-2538** or 970/325-4331; www. ouraychaletinn.com). $–$$ **Box Canyon Lodge,** 45 Third Ave. (✆ **800/327-5080** or 970/325-4981; www.boxcanyonouray. com). $$–$$$ **Beaumont Hotel,** 505 Main St. (✆ **888/447-3255** or 970/325-7000; www.beaumonthotel.com).

location and then relax in natural hot springs at the end of the day. The town has a pool complex with sections for

Climbing & Rappelling **208**

Via Ferrate
A Mountain Playground of Ropes & Ladders
The Dolomites, Italy

Imagine scaling up rock faces and crossing narrow passages high up in the mountains like an expert, but without any actual climbing skills or practice. That's the kind of experience that via ferrate (Italian for "iron roads") make possible. Think of it as vertical trekking. Wearing a helmet and a harness, you're clipped onto cables and metal apparatuses that could supposedly carry the weight of a car, which should be comforting. But it doesn't make the feeling of scrambling up cliffs at insane heights any less harrowing.

This alpine playground—an extensive network of cables, rungs, ladders, and bridges built directly into the mountainside—delights outdoor enthusiasts who want to combine the scenic beauty and fresh air of typical treks with a big adrenaline rush. Italians built the first via ferrate during World War I in the Dolomites to help soldiers navigate the steep, uneven terrain as they fought against the Austrians. Since then, many of the original ladders and rungs (often constructed from wood) have been restored with stronger metal, and old cables have been replaced with ropes. But the basic system remains the same, and it has grown so popular among adventurers that mountain regions around the world have replicated the idea. There are now versions of the via ferrata in Canada, the U.S., and other parts of Europe. Inching your way along these steep mountain obstacle courses far above the ground is a thrill anywhere, but there's something special about exploring these routes in the place where they were invented.

Tinted in shades of rose, yellow, and gray, the chiseled pillars and dramatic rock walls of the Dolomites are majestic. As you explore their peaks and valleys, you'll come upon pastoral meadows speckled with wildflowers, fairytale villages, and glistening lakes.

To get started, you'll need your own harness, a helmet, some rope, and a few carabineers. Although it's perfectly permissible to set out on your own, a guide is recommended. He or she can map out the best routes; show you basic climbing techniques; captivate you with great tales about the region's history, wildlife, and flora and fauna; and coordinate overnight stays in unique *rifugios,* or mountain huts, along the way. If you're heading out on your own, you can try to make arrangements for similar accommodations through the **Italian Alpine Club** (www. cai.it). If, on the other hand, you'd rather stay in one place and make day trips, **Corvara** (a charming and less expensive choice than the swankier **Cortina d'Amprezzo**) makes a good base.

No matter how you choose to travel through the region, a few via ferrate really shouldn't be missed. One of the most historic and best sightseeing routes is **Via Delle Trincee,** which follows the dramatic Porta Vescova ridge on the southern edge of Arabba. Much of your climb will be on volcanic rock, but you'll also come upon bridges, tunnels, trenches, and other remnants of World War I. You'll have spectacular views of the Sella massif to the north and the Marmolada glacier to the south, looming over Lake Fedaia. A shorter but just as sweet option is **Piz da Lec,** a more moderate route above Corvara. It's accessible by cable car, but has a nerve-wracking finale with two steep ladders that offer staggering views if you can overcome the vertigo. Reward yourself for conquering the majestic mountain with a cold beer at **Rifugio Kostner** (www.rifugiokostner.it) on your way back down. —*JS*

ⓘ **Trentino Tourism,** Via Romagnosi (✆ **39/0461-219-300;** www.trentino.to).

TOURS: Guide Alpine Star Mountain, Via Gallesio 27/29 (✆ **39/019-681-6206;** www.guidestarmountain.com). **Collett's Mountain Holidays** (✆ **01/763-289-660;** www.colletts.co.uk).

WHEN TO GO: May–Oct.

✈ Venice airport.

🛏 $ **Garni Delta,** Via Ronn 11 (✆ **39/ 0471-836-350;** www.garnidelta.com).

209 Climbing & Rappelling

Ice Climbing Maligne Canyon
Climbing the (Frozen) Walls
Jasper National Park, Alberta, Canada

During the winter you can walk on water in Jasper National Park's Maligne Canyon. It's frozen, so you're treading on ice as you stroll on the Maligne River, guarded by high limestone walls. Along the way, you'll see ice climbers challenging the cascades of ice that are waterfalls in the summertime. This frosty cold playground is a haven for winter ice climbers.

If you're an avid rock climber in warm weather, try ice climbing. It's a wintertime extreme sport that will have you inching up ice-sheathed cliffs, rock slabs, and frozen waterfalls using ropes, belays, and other climbing gear. Ice climbing isn't for the timid. It requires training and endurance.

On your climb, you may find yourself straddling the flows on the **Queens Curtain,** which sprawls out in multi-tiered layers cascading downward from the canyon's rim. The neighboring **Queen** is instantly recognizable because the bottom portion is a free-standing column with a very thick base. Because it's one of the most popular ice climbs, top-roping (a practice in which fellow climbers leaves ropes anchored for other climbers to use) is common on the weekends. The **Last Wall** is a large sheet of ice downstream from the Queen that often has enough room for two people to climb at the same time.

Throughout Jasper National Park a wide variety of ice-climbing routes from long alpine ice routes to short bolted mix and dry tooling routes are available. Connect with **Parks Canada** (www.pc.gc.ca) and local ice climbers, such as the folks at Gravity Gear (see below), about local conditions and guide service if you are going to climb Maligne Canyon or any of the many other ice-climbing routes in the park or along the Icefields Parkway. You'll want advice on the best way to reach the routes in Maligne Canyon. The trail many climbers follow along the rim of the canyon is very slick and there have been instances of climbers sliding over the edge and falling 25 meters into the canyon. (Some climbers have been killed.)

If you're going to ice climb, be aware of the dangers. Avalanches can be common, so be sure to use good judgment (or better yet, an expert's experience) before picking a climb site. Follow the link below or call the Jasper National Park office for more specifics and suggestions about ice climbing here. Parks Canada lists *Waterfall Ice* by Joe Josephson, Published by Rocky Mountain Books, as a comprehensive reference. Local guides are available, too. Whether you go with or without a guide, always let someone know where you intend to climb.

In addition to the amazing ice climbs available, Jasper National Park has many offerings that appeal to cold weather sports enthusiasts. Once you get away from the small Jasper townsite, there's a large wilderness to explore on cross-country skis or snowshoes. Check in with **Edge Control Ski Shop** (626 Connaught Dr., Jasper; ✆ **888/242-3343** or 780/852-4945; www.explorejasper.com/edgecontrol) for equipment rental. Downhill skiers spend the days at **Marmot Basin.** Bring a camera if you're going wildlife viewing because you'll probably see moose, elk, deer, and maybe foxes or even a cougar. —*LF*

ⓘ **Jasper National Park of Canada** (✆ **780/852-6176;** www.pc.gc.ca). **Gravity Gear** (✆ **888/852-3155** or 780/852-3155; www.gravitygearjasper.com).

WHEN TO GO: Many of the waterfall ice-climbing routes start to form in Nov. Many of the avalanche-prone climbs can be climbed most safely in earlier months of the winter before the snow has accumulated in the alpine. Ice routes are generally in their best condition from Dec–Mar.

✈ Edmonton (362km/225 miles).

🛏 $$$ **Fairmont Jasper Park Lodge,** Old Lodge Rd. (✆ **800/441-1414** or 780/852-3301; www.fairmont.com). $$ **Sawridge Inn,** 82 Connaught Dr. (✆ **888/ 729-7343** or 780/852-6590; www. sawridge.com).

210 Climbing & Rappelling

Ice Climbing in the Alps
Scaling Frozen Falls
Chamonix, France

It's hard to beat the French Alps when it comes to spectacular scenery, winter sports, and European feel. So why not believe the hype and come to Chamonix, the small French resort town framed by Mont Blanc, to partake of the wintertime fun? Ice climbers claim there are more than 200 routes where you can use your crampons and ice axes in and around Chamonix. The Chamonix Valley is almost at the junction where France, Italy, and Switzerland meet, so ice climbers staying here can challenge ice routes in the neighboring countries as well. That's a lot of icy opportunity.

In Chamonix, the routes range from frozen waterfalls and north-facing gullies to snow ridges. Access to many of the ice routes is within 15 minutes to 1 hour of town. Beginners head to **La Cremerie,** in Argentiere, where some easier routes can be found. Other ice-climbing spots are located on both sides of the Argentiere Glacier, the **Col des Montets** and **Le Tour.** According to **Alps Adventures** (see below), a guiding service that offers ice-climbing courses and takes ice-climbers on multi-pitch routes in the Chamonix Valley and the Cogne Valley in Italy, some of the ice falls have belays and most have abseil descents. The ice falls at the higher altitudes usually begin forming in December, followed by the falls at lower altitudes in January. The best climbing months are January and February.

Ice climbing is inherently dangerous and many safety factors must be taken into consideration while deciding when and where to climb. Unless you are very experienced and know this region extremely well (and even then), it's highly advisable to climb with a certified mountain guide.

The Chamonix tourist office has a list of qualified mountain guides. In town, Alps Adventures offers ice-climbing courses for beginner and intermediates. Ice-climbing equipment can be purchased or rented at **Snell Sports** (104 Rue Du Docteur Paccard; © **33/450530217;** www.cham3s.com).

Chamonix is a wonderful home base for all variety of cold-weather adrenaline adventures. It has long been considered one of the most popular European villages for alpine skiing. Around the valley there are five main resorts, with lifts and cable cars (see ❹❽) coming down to the town's edge. Skiers throughout the world have heard of the famous **Vallee Blanche,** a 19km (12-mile) ski that is one of the most challenging in Europe.

Chamonix, which sprawls in a narrow strip along both banks of the Arve River, is a stopping point for travelers who have gone through the Mont Blanc tunnel from Italy. In the summertime, the town fills with hikers eager to get on the trails in the surrounding mountains, and mountain climbers who want to challenge Mont Blanc, Western Europe's highest peak. —*LF*

ⓘ **Chamonix Valley** (© **33/450/53-00-24;** www.chamonix.com).

TOUR: Alps Adventures (© **33/670/069 143;** www.alps-adventure.com).

WHEN TO GO: Jan–Feb.

✈ Geneva (81km/50 miles).

🛏 $ **Chalet Chantel,** 391 Route de Pêcles (© **33/450-530-669;** www.ski ambiance.co.uk). $ **Hotel de l'Arve,** 60 Impasses des Anémones (© **33/450/53-02-31;** www.hotelarve-chamonix.com).

Ice Climbing in Canmore
Scaling Frozen Waterfalls
Canadian Rockies Around Canmore, Canada

So many waterfalls and ice floes cling to the mountainsides in the stretch of the Canadian Rockies between Canmore and Jasper, the biggest decision you'll have to make is where to climb. The beauty of this region is that so many of the frozen waterfalls are easily reached. There's no need to trek for long distances, and that may be one of the reasons climbers from all over the globe show up here.

Canmore, a small town about 100km (62 miles) north of Calgary, is where the hardcore climbers gather. Within a 100km (62-mile) radius, there are plenty of places to climb. Climbing guides at **Yamnuska** (see below), a local mountaineering shop, offer the following ice climbs.

The shop's guides take beginning climbers who want lessons to nearby **Junkyards,** one big ice flow frozen at a moderately steep angle. Another popular spot, where the ice climbs tend to be grade 4 and higher, is the mountainside around the town of **Field,** just west of Lake Louise. The narrow Johnston Canyon has a mix of beginner to advanced ice climbs along one wall. If you want to drive along the scenic **Icefields Parkway,** which links Lake Louise and Jasper, there are several popular climbs including **Polar Circus** and **The Weeping Wall,** which has several different lines. *Waterfall Ice* by Joe Josephson, published by Rocky Mountain Books, is a comprehensive reference to ice climbing in this region.

Ice climbing is a popular sport in the Canadian Rockies.

No matter where you climb, it is vital to check current avalanche conditions and the avalanche forecast before heading out. Park Canada says, "Ice climbing is an inherently dangerous sport. Poor protection and the varied quality of ice require a great degree of experience and judgment to be managed safely. Avalanches are common in the drainage features where ice climbs often occur." In addition, always let someone know where you are going to climb.

Conditions for ice climbing are fairly consistent from year to year. It may be possible to go ice climbing at higher elevations in November and in shady locations into April. Again, always familiarize yourself with the weather conditions and check in with local experts about climbing conditions.

This region is a favorite with people who enjoy cold-weather sports. Cross-country trails thread the region, including more than 60 kilometers (37 miles) out of the **Canmore Nordic Center** (www.canmorenordic.com), which was developed for the 1988 Winter Olympic Games. Several ski areas are within an hour's drive

of here, including **Nakiska** (www.skinakiska.com) and the larger resorts of **Sunshine Village** (www.skibanff.com) and **Lake Louise** (www.skilouise.com). You can also race along trails through the woods on a dog sled. **Banff** (www.banff.ca), a popular tourist destination with hot springs in the heart of **Banff National Park** (pc.gc.ca), is about a half-hour away. —LF

ⓘ **Tourism Canmore** (✆ 866/CAN-MORE [226-6673]; www.tourismcanmore.com). **Yamnuska Mountain Adventures,** 200–50 Lincoln Park (✆ 866/678-4164 or 403/678-4164; www.yamnuska.com). **Canada Guide Association** (www.acmg.ca).

WHEN TO GO: Dec–Feb.

✈ Calgary.

🛏 $$–$$$ **Delta Lodge,** 1 Centennial Dr., Kananaskis Village (✆ 888/890-3222 or 403/591-7711; www.deltahotels.com). $$$ **Fairmont Banff Springs,** 405 Spray Ave. (✆ 866/540-4406 or 403/762-2211; www.fairmont.com/banffsprings).

212 Climbing & Rappelling

Climbing 14ers
Peak Bagging in Colorado
Colorado, U.S.A.

How many mountain names have you checked off on your T-shirt listing Colorado's 14ers? None? Maybe it's time to start hiking! Upon peaking some of these great mountains you'll be standing atop the Continental Divide. Eastward, there's nothing higher than you are the entire way to the Atlantic Ocean. Westward, it's all downhill to California.

Colorado boasts 53 or 55 mountains that top out at 14,000 feet (4,200m) or more above sea level. (The exact number is argued constantly by peak baggers, quoting a variety of ways the peaks are

measured, including the official numbers posted by the U.S. Geological Survey.) Hiking as many as one can, until you can brag about climbing all of them (or wear a fully checked T-shirt, a common site), is a popular activity in this state. Even if you don't want to climb every one, walking or scrambling up and down one or two during a vacation is a must for many visitors to Colorado.

The peaks are centered in several mountain ranges, including the Sawatch, the Sangre de Cristo, the Front, the Tenmile-Mosquito, the San Juan, and the Elk

Range. Each of the ranges has a special character, and if you're just starting to climb 14ers you should get local advice on which ones are appropriate for your skill level. A good online resource is **14ers. com**, where you can learn more about these mountains, whether you live in Colorado or you're planning a visit and want to connect with dedicated peak baggers. The site lists the 14ers, has routes, trip reports, and a forum where you can connect with other hikers and climbers.

Mount Elbert is the highest peak at 14,433 feet (4,330m), and Sunshine Peak just makes the list at 14,001 feet (4.200m). But choosing which peak to climb and what route to follow should be based on your experience and physical condition. Many of the peaks are walk-up hikes; others require scrambling or climbing skills. Among the 14ers with less difficult routes are Mt. Elbert, Mt. Bierstadt, and Quandry Peak. Some of the most difficult routes are on Mt. Wilson, Capitol Peak, and Crestone Peak. One popular way to "claim" two peaks in 1 day is to climb one peak and traverse along the ridgeline to another. Climbing Evans and traversing to Bierstadt, or the reverse, is popular. Other choices for claiming two in a day include Grays and Torreys, and Maroon and North Maroon.

Bagging 14ers has become so popular that on weekends, some of the routes get very crowded. Some of the trails on the busiest routes have also become worn down. Because these routes go above treeline, there are points where hikers must scramble up loose rock and follow cairns set along the way, which at times are hard to find.

Don't start climbing any mountain in Colorado without proper preparations. You need to wear or bring layers and waterproof gear, because it can rain or snow even in the summer. Bring enough water, energy bars, and other snacks to keep yourself from becoming dehydrated or weak. If you experience altitude sickness, which may happen if you live at sea level, head back down right away. Everyone should bring a route map and a compass; many climbers bring a GPS. Afternoon thunderstorms with lightning are common in the summer, so locals climb early in the day and plan to be off the ridges and mountaintops (where you could be the target of lightning) before storm clouds gather. *—LF*

ⓘ www.14ers.com.

WHEN TO GO: Summer or early fall.

✈ Denver International Airport.

Climbing & Rappelling

Rock Climbing the Gunks
On Belay!
New Paltz, New York, U.S.A.

Outdoor enthusiasts accustomed to the dramatic scenery of the American West tend to look at landscapes in the eastern U.S. and smirk, "You call *that* a mountain?" While most of the Appalachians lack the grandeur of, say, the Canadian Rockies, there are nonetheless places back East that can hold their own anywhere, and New York's Shawangunk Ridge and the sur-

rounding cliffs is one such place. Widely recognized as the rock-climbing capital of the east, "the Gunks" is the most popular climbing destination in all of North America, with about 50,000 climbers scaling its heights each year. One of these climbing routes, "High Exposure," is frequently cited as the single best route in the world for the technical challenges it presents.

Located roughly 90 miles (145km) north of New York City, the area around the Gunks is a patchwork of private land, state parks, and private land preserves, most notably Mohonk Preserve, which manages almost 7,000 acres of wilderness. The Gunks' most popular climbing cliff, the Trapps, is located within Mohonk Preserve, as are several other climbing sites. Most of the documented climbing routes in the Gunks are from 150 to 300 feet in height, and are vertical or near-vertical rock faces, so inexperienced climbers may want to visit one of the several local outfits that sponsor rock climbing instruction in the Gunks. These offer a range of classes from beginner to advanced, as well as group outings that are a popular way to meet fellow climbers.

Besides climbing, the Gunks are known for a number of outdoor activities. There's swimming in nearby Lake Minnewaska, hiking around the historic Mohonk Mountain House hotel, blueberry picking in summer, and bird-watching for the local population of peregrine falcons. To cool off, try visiting one of the area's famed ice caves, where deep fissures in the rock create microclimates that preserve ice and snow through the summer. With all these options and some of the best scenery in the Northeast, it's no wonder the Nature Conservancy listed the Gunks as one of its "75 Last Great Places on Earth." —ML

The Gunks are widely recognized as the rock climbing capital of the American east coast.

ⓘ **Mohonk Preserve** (𝄢 845/255-0919; www.mohonkpreserve.org).

TOURS: Alpine Endeavors (𝄢 877/ **GUNKS-NY** [486-5769] or 845/658-3094, www.alpineendeavors.com). **Eastern Mountain Sports** (𝄢 800/310-4504 or 845/255-3280; www.emsclimb.com).

WHEN TO GO: Apr–Nov.

🛏 $$$ **Mohonk Mountain House,** 1000 Mountain Rest Rd. (𝄢 800/772-6646 or 845/255-1000; www.mohonk.com). $ **New Paltz Hostel,** 145 Main St. (𝄢 845/255-6676;** www.newpaltzhostel.com).

---

214   Climbing & Rappelling

Rock Climbing in Joshua Tree
Climb On!
Joshua Tree, California, U.S.A.

Few outdoor destinations can compete with Joshua Tree National Park. Spectacular weather year-round, awe-inspiring scenery, and dozens of activity options make this a prime destination for adventure-seekers from around the world.

Rock climbers of all experience levels can find challenges at Joshua Tree National Park.

Perhaps more than any other sport, rock-climbing is what put this park on the map, and for good reason. The granite boulders that erupt from the desert floor, surrounded by rocky hills and mountains, make this a playground for climbers of every experience level.

The park is situated about 98 miles (158km) east of Los Angeles, 40 miles (64km) north of Palm Springs, and encompasses parts of both the Colorado Desert and the cooler, higher-altitude Mojave Desert. The nearly 795,000 acres of this desert wonderland are home to several primitive campgrounds set among massive boulders that glow red and gold in the setting California sun. There are also motels and other services available in the nearby towns of Joshua Tree and Twenty-nine Palms, but for climbers who like to get an early start, it's hard to beat waking up beneath the very rocks you'll be climbing after breakfast. Some say the Hidden Valley campsite is the climber's preferred place to pitch a tent, because it's close to

many great climbs and rangers sometimes show up to offer a friendly "Climber's Coffee" at 8am and to discuss access issues and answer questions. But a number of other campsites are just as accessible and may be quieter than the active social scene at Hidden Valley.

Though the park was initially a place for rock-climbers to practice during winter months when Yosemite and other parts of the Sierra Nevada were snowed in, the rough granite and lack of vegetation made it popular in its own right. Though most of the boulders are little more than 200 feet (60m) high, they're easily accessible, which makes it possible to climb several in 1 day. When you've had your share of conquering boulders, take in some of the area's world-class bird-watching (the park is part of the Pacific Flyway migratory route), mountain biking, bouldering, and mountain climbing. —ML

ⓘ **Joshua Tree National Park** (ⓒ **760/ 367-5500;** www.nps.gov/jotr).

TOURS: Uprising Adventure Guides (✆ **888/254-6266;** www.uprising.com). **Sierra Rock Climbing School** (✆ **877/686-7625** or 760/937-6762; www.sierrarockclimbingschool.com). **WHEN TO GO:** Sept–May.

✈ Palm Springs (40 miles/64km).

🛏 $$ **29 Palms Inn,** 73950 Inn Ave. (✆ **760/367-3505;** www.29palmsinn.com). $$ **Holiday Inn Express Hotel and Suites,** 71809 Twentynine Palms Hwy. (✆ **760/361-4009;** www.hiexpress.com).

215 Climbing & Rappelling

Rock Climbing in Cuba
Climbing Libre
Viñales, Cuba

"The Revolution," said Fidel, "was the work of climbers and cavers." Señor Castro was referring to the mountain strongholds from which guerrilla fighters in the late 1950s staged attacks that eventually led to an overthrow of the government. Climbers have always had a rebellious streak, so what better place to indulge it than in the land that still celebrates "La Revolucion"? Though it has yet to gain the international prominence of climbing destinations like Yosemite or the Alps, the Viñales Valley in western Cuba nonetheless offers world-class climbing to adventurers willing to try new routes with a revolutionary flavor.

Traveling to Cuba brings its own set of rewards as well as challenges—though restrictions have eased tremendously in recent years, Americans are still technically unable to visit the Island except under certain conditions mandated by the U.S. Department of State. Nonetheless, every year thousands of American adventurers join *turistas* from Europe, Canada, and throughout Latin America to explore this tropical Eden. The trip from Havana to the town of Viñales is relatively easy; two different bus lines serve the area, and taxis also offer to make the ride for slightly more. It's about a 3-hour ride, depending on road and weather conditions.

Climbing in Cuba brings its own challenges as well: Because this destination is the new kid on the international climbing scene, many of the mountainsides in this lush agricultural valley are virgin rock. Not all routes are well established or well known, maps aren't readily available, and there aren't retail establishments set up to accommodate climbers who need to buy equipment.

Those limitations shouldn't deter travelers looking for a great adventure, however. The Viñales Valley is a dramatic geological anomaly, a karst topography with massive limestone mountains that look like giant blocks left behind by a playful child-god. The whole valley, a UNESCO World Heritage Site, is dotted with palm trees, small farms, and pleasant little homes, and visitors compare it to a trip through a long-lost agricultural past. There's also an extensive network of caves to explore, local beaches for relaxing, and the inimitable hospitality of the Cuban people. —*ML*

ⓘ **Cuba Climbing** (info@cubaclimbing.com; www.cubaclimbing.com).

WHEN TO GO: Nov–Apr.

✈ Havana (193km/120 miles).

🛏 $$ **Horizontes La Ermita,** Carretera de La Ermita (✆ **548/796-250;** reserva ermita@vinales.hor.tur.cu). $$ **Horizontes Los Jazmines,** Carretera A Viñales (✆ **538/796-411;** reserva@vinales.hor.tur.cu).

Canyoneering Grand Staircase/Escalante National Monument

Slickrock & Roll

Southern Utah, U.S.A.

Death Hollow. Hell's Backbone. The Devil's Garden. With names like these, you know that a visit to Grand Staircase/Escalante National Monument won't be just another picnic in the national park. And canyoneering—a silver-dollar word that describes hiking, scrambling, swimming, crawling, and scraping your way through a narrow canyon—may be the best way to explore this little-known and utterly breathtaking park.

Located in south-central Utah, Grand Staircase/Escalante takes up 1.9 million acres (760,000 hectacres) of some of

Canyoneering at Grand Staircase/Escalante National Monument.

America's most remote backcountry. It's not easy to get here: The nearest airports are hundreds of miles away in Salt Lake City or Las Vegas, and few roads traverse this region. But this isolation gives visitors the chance to explore a wilderness area virtually unchanged since the Anasazi natives abandoned it hundreds of years ago, leaving behind relics such as petroglyphs, building ruins, and even dried and preserved corn cobs.

Don't come here expecting a sprawling visitors center with gurgling fountains and lavish exhibits. The national monument wasn't established until 1996, and park amenities are few and far between: a handful of primitive campsites, a sign-in logbook nailed to a post, a pile of rocks denoting a trail head, and that's about it. You might see another hiker or two, but most of your companions will be lizards, eagles, jackrabbits, and the indescribable beauty and silence of this rugged, colorful land.

The staircase that gives this national monument its name is a series of sedimentary rock layers that have been sliced open by wind and water to reveal over 600 million years of our planet's history. The canyons that form the pages of this natural history book are as narrow as eight inches in some places, and glow with an almost psychedelic palette: pink, orange, blood red, chocolate and gold, all exposed under a mantle of perfect blue sky. Canyoneering here involves wading through ice-cold pools, scrambling over smooth slickrock, and squeezing your frame through narrow slot canyons. A good topographic map, a keen sense of direction, and an adventurous spirit will all come in handy here—as well as an appreciation for the beauty of this rare and magical landscape. —*ML*

ⓘ **Escalante Chamber of Commerce** (✆ **435/826-4810;** www.escalante-cc.com).

WHEN TO GO: Year-round.

🛏 $$ **Zion Ponderosa Ranch Resort,** North Fork Rd., Mt. Carmel, UT (✆ **800/293-5444;** www.zionponderosa.com). $$ **Grand Staircase Inn,** 105 North Kodachrome Dr., Cannonville, UT (✆ **435/679-8400;** www.grandstaircaseinn.com).

Canyoning & Caving

Canyoning Through Costa Rica
Me Tarzan; You Jane
Costa Rica

Sure, it's nice to look at a lovely waterfall, but standing on the edge of a steep cliff and looking over the edge down a 150-foot (45-meter) plunge is another matter entirely. Canyoning is the closest you can get to actually going *down* a waterfall without taking a barrel over Niagara Falls.

And there's probably no better place to try this than on a canyoning expedition through Costa Rica. Also known as abseiling, the art of canyoning is not unlike rappelling, but here there's an obvious difference: You get really, really wet, which feels great when the water is cascading

Channel your inner Tarzan or Jane while canyoning down a waterfall in Costa Rica.

down a tropical mountainside on a hot afternoon.

Several tour operators offer canyoning adventures in the majestic mountains of Costa Rica. Most are located in the area around Arenal Volcano or in the mountains northeast of the capital city, San Jose. Call ahead to check availability and dates, as some canyoning tour operators work only with groups of a minimum size or larger.

Expect to spend your day taking a four-wheel-drive vehicle deep into the Costa Rican rainforest, where you'll begin your hike—most involve a zipline tour of some distance and trekking across rope or cable suspension bridges, adrenaline rushes in their own right. The real fun begins when you meet your first waterfall, at which point you'll don your safety equipment and start swinging, hopping, and rappelling your way like Tarzan down the face of the falls, across slick rocks and over steep ledges. Some drops are well over 100 feet (30m), and there are usually several falls to

conquer before you find yourself at journey's end.

Besides experiencing the magic of Costa Rica's lush vegetation and exotic wildlife, expect to be served lunch at the base camp; operators usually throw in some snacks and other amenities on these tours, which last from 4 to 6 hours. Most folks in reasonably good shape can handle this adventure, since the ropes, harnesses, carabiners, and other equipment do most of the work. Most tours will accept beginners, and children of a certain age will usually be welcomed. Of course, you'll want to wear your water-friendly clothes and shoes, and perhaps bring a change of dry clothes for afterwards. —ML

TOURS: Pure Trek Canyoning (© 866/569-5723 in the U.S. or 506/2479-1313 in Costa Rica; www.puretrekcostarica.com). **Costa Rica Canyoning** (© 506/556-4032; www.costaricacanyoning.com).

WHEN TO GO: Year-round.

Canyoning & Caving **218**

Canyoning in the Blue Mountains
Between a Rock & a Wet Place
Katoomba, Australia

Australia's Blue Mountains, a UNESCO World Heritage Site, are just 2 hours north of Sydney, but they feel like they're a world away. Cast in an eerie omnipresent glow, the area was given its name because of its many eucalyptus trees that emit a haze as light hits the oil evaporating off their leaves. While "blue" is a fairly apt description, "mountains" may be a bit of an exaggeration for what are mostly bush-covered hills and golden sandstone plateaus. But the area's vast national park is full of jagged cliffs, deep gorges, waterfalls, dense rainforests, and ancient trees—the perfect geography for canyoning (or canyoneering).

This extreme adventure, which began as a commercial operation in Utah, takes you below the mountains' surface and into their most interesting nooks and crannies. The basic idea is literally to explore cool, dark, and wet canyons.

To start, you'll put on a wetsuit, a helmet, sturdy shoes, a climbing harness, ropes, carabineers, and a waterproof backpack. Then you'll follow your guide on a fairly easy hike, descending into a canyon, and begin scrambling over slippery wet rocks through tunnels and caves, jumping off ledges, plunging into ice cold pools, swimming through pitch black waters filled with who-knows-what (though crayfish are usually among the creatures in there), and abseiling down vertical waterfall-covered rock faces.

If the idea of crawling over slimy rocks puts a knot in your stomach, not to mention feeling your way in the dark to avoid tripping over crevices because you can't see what comes next, just wait until you actually try it. Your adrenaline will be surging for the entire 2-hour excursion, and maybe even for a while once you're back on dry land.

Of course, there are some serious risks when canyoning. You don't want to be stranded in a cave if heavy rains cause a flash flood. And, when you're already soaking wet, you can become chilled pretty quickly if temperatures drop. But going with an experienced guide who knows the area well mitigates most of these hazards, making the thrill relatively safe and immensely fun.

To calm down after your spine-tingling experience in the canyons, take a leisurely hike to see the area's most famous site—a rocky monument called the **Three Sisters.** These spires (Meehni, Wimlah, and Gunnedoo), carved from millions of years of erosion, tower more than 900m (2,953 ft.) over Jamison Valley, reaching toward the sky. After paying your respects to the ladies, walk around the villages of

Katoomba or **Blackheath,** where you can grab some dinner.

The next day, consider booking another activity with **Tread Lightly Eco Tours** (www.treadlightly.com.au) if the fear-factor stunt of canyoning whet your appetite for more adventure. This company offers guided hikes, four-wheel-drive excursions, and night tours during which you can view the area's amazing astronomy and nocturnal wildlife, including some fellow crawlers such as glow worms. —JS

ⓘ **The Blue Mountains Visitor Information Center,** Echo Point (✆ **1300/653-408;** www.visitbluemountains.com.au). **Australia Tourism Board,** 201 Sussex St., Sydney (✆ **61/2-9360-1111;** www.tourism.australia.com and www.environment.nsw.gov.au/nationalparks).

TOUR: Blue Mountains Adventure Company, 84a Bathurst Rd., Katoomba (✆ **02/4782-1271;** www.bmac.com.au).

WHEN TO GO: Oct–Apr.

✈ Sydney airport.

🚌 $$ **Jemby-Rinjah Eco Lodge,** 336 Evans Lookout Rd., Blackheath (✆ **02/4787-7622;** www.jembyrinjahlodge.com.au).

219 Canyoning & Caving

Caving in the Mayan Underworld
A Spooky Trip to Find Spectacular Artifacts
Cayo District, Belize

Besides archaeologists, few people typically get the chance to spend more than 3 hours investigating a well-preserved cave filled with precious artifacts. Western Belize offers a rare opportunity: If you can muster the courage to enter some slightly claustrophobic spaces, swim through cold water, and climb over rocks, you'll be rewarded with a spine-tingling peek at

extraordinary remnants from the Mayan underworld.

The most awe-inspiring cave in Belize, and perhaps all of Central America, is **Actun Tunichil Muknal.** After a 40-minute hike through the lush subtropical forest in Tapir Mountain Reserve, during which you'll cross three shallow rivers, you'll come to the special cave. It isn't easy to navigate—mentally or physically—but that's all part of the adventure. Just channel your inner Indiana Jones. A sort of haunted house, this cave was the stage for 14 human sacrifices, six of them babies, during Mayan times. The Maya probably made most of the sacrifices in the hope of conjuring rain. Today, the cave entrance is filled with water that's about 3.8m (12 ft.) deep, which means you'll start your tour with an invigorating swim. Once you reach shallower water, you'll hike through it, surrounded by striking stalactites and stalagmites. At different times, the water may reach your ankles, knees, or chest. You'll also need to use your arms and legs to clamber over and between boulders.

When you finally reach the cave's dry chamber, it's like walking into an old cathedral. In fact, your guide will ask you to remove your shoes in this sacred area, so remember to wear or bring socks. (To preserve the cave, it's important to prevent the body's oils, acids, and bacteria from touching any of its surfaces.) As you tread across the soft limestone floor, you'll be amazed by the extraordinary assortment of Mayan pots and vessels here. Many of them are thousands of years old. The real adrenaline rush comes when your headlamp first illuminates some skeletal remains. There's even a fully intact skeleton called the "crystal lady," which you can view by climbing up a narrow 3m (10 ft.) ladder. History buffs and adventure junkies will be equally sated by this unique 3½-hour tour.

For a slightly more relaxing and kid-friendly version of caving, try floating through the underworld. To explore **Caves Branch,** you'll start with a relatively easy walk along a dirt road followed by a 45-minute hike through valleys and farmland. Then it's time to get wet—so dress accordingly—but this tour is much less strenuous that the previous one. After strapping on a battery-powered headlamp, you'll hop on an inflated inner tube and head into a network of caves. As you drift through limestone tunnels, you'll learn about the cave's geology and see some surreal stalactites as a few bats hang overhead. Your guide will point out Mayan artifacts, including clay pots, and you might even glimpse some bones. As the current speeds up, you'll get a thrilling ride over small rapids before coming to a small natural pool where you can hop out and take a quick swim. Whichever way you journey through the Mayan underworld, you'll be astounded by the sacred wonders hidden beneath the earth's surface. —*JS*

ⓘ **Belize Tourism Board,** 64 Regent St., Belize City (✆ **501/227-2420;** www.travel belize.org).

TOUR: Mayawalk Tours, 19 Burns Ave., San Ignacio (✆ **501/824-3070;** www.mayawalk.com).

WHEN TO GO: Nov–Apr.

✈ Phillip S.W. Goldson International Airport.

⊨ $$–$$$ **Chaa Creek Lodge,** San Ignacio (✆ **501/824-2037;** www.chaacreek.com). $–$$ **Black Rock Lodge,** San Ignacio (✆ **501/820-4049;** www.blackrocklodge.com).

Canyoning & Caving **220**

Mammoth Cave Wild Cave Tour
A Visit to the Underworld
Mammoth Cave, Kentucky, U.S.A.

There are cave tours where hundreds of people are herded along walkways that any old granny can navigate, and then there is the Wild Cave Tour at Mammoth Cave. This ain't your granny's tour, but a physically demanding, rough-and-tumble day of knee-scraping, bone-jarring, clothes-ripping spelunking that will reward you with some awe-inspiring caves views that will take your breath away—if you have any breath left.

Mammoth Cave is located in the verdant hills of central Kentucky about 90 minutes' drive from both Louisville, Kentucky, and Nashville, Tennessee. If you're planning to take this particular tour, make reservations ahead of time, because the tour is limited to just 14 spelunkers max. They're also strict about preparations for the tour: Visitors must be over the age of 16, wear high-top, lace-up hiking boots with a serious tread (no low-cut or athletic shoes), and have hip or chest measurements of 42 inches max due to some very claustrophobic 9-inch squeezes on this journey. Getting stuck or injured can be a serious problem, and emergency rescue teams can take several hours to help those who get stranded. And don't wear your designer duds; you'll end this tour covered head-to-toe in mud and grit.

Even seasoned athletes have reported scheduling a recovery day after this exhausting cave tour, but they also tell of seeing some amazing sights that nobody can even get close to on Mammoth Cave's regular tours. Cathedral Dome towers hundreds of feet above an enormous canyon formed by an underground stream. Frozen Niagara is an immense, colorful curtain of flowstone that plunges downward for 75 feet (23m). Towering stalagmites and sparkling white gypsum crystals decorate this home to eyeless fish, blind beetles, and white spiders.

While most visitors to Mammoth Cave focus on the spectacle underground, the national park is also a great site for aboveground activities: The birding is unrivaled, old-growth forests dot the hillsides, and the Green River is ideal for canoeing and fishing. —ML

ⓘ **Mammoth Cave National Park** (ℂ **270/758-2180;** www.nps.gov/maca).

WHEN TO GO: Year-round.

🛏 $ **Mammoth Cave Hotel** (ℂ 270/758-2225; www.mammothcavehotel.com). $ **Best Western Kentucky Inn,** 1009 Doyle Ave., Cave City, KY (ℂ 270/773-3161; www.bestwestern.com).

221 Canyoning & Caving

Frio Bat Cave
Quick—To the Bat Cave!
Concan, Texas, U.S.A.

As the sun sinks quietly in the west Texas sky, there's electricity in the air. Something is about to happen—something big (this is Texas, after all). The crowd gathers, waiting, watching. At first, there's nothing. Then a flutter. And another. And in an instant, millions and millions of bats are pouring out of the cave entrance, like an immense pillar of dark smoke, in one of the most thrilling spectacles in the animal kingdom. The noise and the flurry of this mass movement of mammals are an amazing sight that holds people in awe year after year.

The Frio bat cave is located about 80 miles (129km) west of San Antonio, deep in the heart of the Texas Hill Country. The cave is tucked away on a private ranch, but it's open to the public by taking an inexpensive scheduled tour. The tours operate on a weather-permitting schedule; call ahead for details. There are several other caves in the area that also host millions of bats, but they're closed to the public.

This nightly ritual, when the Mexican free-tail bats come out to feed, involves so

Bats head out of the Frio Bat Cave into the Texas sunset.

many bats that they show up on weather radar as rain clouds. And like rain clouds, they're a welcome sight to Texas farmers—the bats eat roughly 2 *million* pounds of insects each night, including those that destroy local crops.

While waiting for the bats to emerge, you'll be treated to a tale of the cave's history. From the Civil War through World War I, it was mined for bat guano, which was used to make gunpowder; the guano drying kilns are still standing near the cave's entrance. A much stranger part of military history comes from World War II, when bats from the cave were trapped to take part in top-secret Project X-Ray; it was believed that thousands of bats

carrying small incendiary devices could be released over Japan, setting off thousands of fires—the plan was scuttled in favor of the atomic bomb, and the bats returned to civilian life. —*ML*

TOUR: Hill Country Adventures (✆ 830/966-2320; www.hillcountryadventures.com).

WHEN TO GO: Apr–Nov.

✈ San Antonio (83 miles/134km).

🛏 $$ **Neal's Lodges,** Concan (✆ 830/232-6118; www.nealslodges.com). $$ **River Haven Cabins,** Ranch Rd. 1120, Leakey (✆ 866/232-5400; www.river havencabins.com).

Caving, Spanish Style
Enveloped in Darkness
Mallorca (Majorca), Spain

Bring up Mallorca, the island off the southeast coast of Spain, and people usually think of cultured pearls and beaches. But this limestone island is honeycombed with more than 200 caves and home to many caving adventure opportunities. The caves range in category from those appropriate for the casual tourist who wants simply to visit a cave to more recreational caving opportunities to those caves appropriate only for those with experience in the more technical and challenging aspects of caving. No matter which category you fit into, there's a caving adventure awaiting you in Mallorca.

The casual tourist who wants to go caving on Mallorca might be sent to the well known **Cuevas del Drach** (Dragon Caves) outside of Porto Cristo for a 2km (1¼-mile), 1-hour tour. You'll walk to and can even ride to the underground lake. The chamber is roomy enough for approximately 1,000 visitors who are provided with a short classical music concert. Then you're hustled out. Commercial kitsch? Yes. But it's an opportunity to see some great formations. Try to take the first or last tour to minimize the crowd experience. The **Cuevas dels Hams**, also near Porto Cristo, are popular, too. The **Cueva de Arta,** located approximately 5km (3 miles) from Arta, on the east coast, with its large entrance and huge 7m-high (24-ft.) stalagmite, is the one of the highest caves in Europe. Arta also has some great sightseeing, including the **Sanctuary of Saint Salvador** and the **Church of the Transfiguracio.**

Those searching for a more active and recreational caving experience often opt for less-trodden caves. Some caves have been outfitted with lights and walkways among other manmade amenities so commercial companies can take tours into them. Going into a non-commercial cave is quite an exciting experience. Turn off your lights and the darkness envelopes you. There is little to compare to this sensation. (Be aware of your limits, however; some people experience bouts of claustrophobia.) In many places along this expedition you're inching along on your back or belly and the ceiling is only inches over your head. The reward is seeing the great stalactites, stalagmites, and columns Mother Nature created over thousands of years.

Technical level caves should be left to skilled and experienced spelunkers. Caves such as the **Cave of la Gleda,** which is nearly 10km (more than 6 miles) under the seabed of the Mediterranean, requires rebreathers or scuba gear to explore. There are no guides for the Cave of La Gleda. Diving in this cave requires many years of specialized cave diving experience, plus equipment costing thousands of dollars. Most people exploring the cave go with a team of highly experienced divers. Though this is a high-adrenaline dive, those who undertake it must recognize that errors can result in death.

In addition to caving in Mallorca, there's good diving, snorkeling, swimming, kayaking, and boat charters, along with trekking and rock climbing. You can play golf in Arta, go ballooning, or horseback riding. If you enjoy local markets, make your way to the town square in Sineu on Wednesday for the weekly market, which started around A.D. 1306. —*LF*

ⓘ **See Mallorca** (www.seemallorca.com).
TOURS: Skualo Mallorc Diving (✆ 34/971-81-50-94; www.skualo-mallorca diving.com). **Rocksport Mallorca** (✆ 34/629/948-404; www.rocksportmallorca. com/caving).

WHEN TO GO: Oct is best. Avoid the Apr–Sept high season.

✈ Palma de Mallorca Airport.

🛏 $$ **Hotel Can Moragues,** C/Pou Nou No. 12 E, Arta (✆ **34/971/829-509;** www. canmoragues.com). $ **Hotel Playa Esperanza,** Avda. S'Albufera No. 4, Platja de Muro (✆ **34/971/890-568;** www.playa esperanzamallorca.com). $$$ **Insotel Club Cala Mandia,** Puerto Christo (✆ **34/902/112-345;** www.insotelhotel group.com).

Canyoning & Caving **223**

Exploring Natural Tennessee
Overnights in a Cave
Chattanooga, Tennessee, U.S.A.

The term "pitch black" takes on new meaning deep inside an unlit cave, where you can't see your own fingers wiggle in front of your face. Not everyone can brave that sort of darkness for even an hour, let alone spend the night there. Yet the expert spelunkers at Raccoon Cavern promise you'll sleep like a rock if you can overcome your flight response and bed down beneath their stalactites.

With the right gear, sleeping in a cave is actually quite comfortable. Humidity is high, at 95%, so warm layers are essential, but the temperature remains about 60°F (16°C). Yes, you will share space with the few creepy critters that can hack the cool, damp darkness—mostly salamanders, millipedes, and crayfish—but, preferring low temperatures, they won't get near warm human bodies. What about the bats you'll see if you tour the cave by day? Don't worry—they fly the coop at night in search of food.

Before bedtime you'll have plenty of time to adjust to the atmosphere and the dark. Raccoon Cavern's 4-hour overnight tour leads you through 2½ miles (4km) of mapped passageways past stalactites,

stalagmites, limestone draperies, and vast "rooms" with waterfalls and 75-ft. (23m) ceilings. You'll traverse some passages on your hands and knees and slide on your belly through others. A few tight "squeezes" are optional, but 75% of participants try them and manage to break on through to the other side. Raccoon Cave provides helmets, lights, gloves, and knee pads for the tour. Guests bring their own sleeping bags and camping pads, and most fall asleep quickly after dining and setting up camp.

Reservations for overnight tours must be made at least 2 weeks in advance. If you're satisfied with seeing the caves by day, you can just show up for the Crystal Palace walking tour or, if you don't mind getting muddy, a Wild Caves Expedition to little-explored sections of the system.

The **Ruby Falls Lantern Tour,** deep within nearby Lookout Mountain, is another unique underground experience. Tours start in an elevator that descends 260 feet (78m) inside the mountain. The guide and a few designated members of the group carry small hand-held electric lanterns, which make shadows dance on the walls as you walk toward the falls. Your guide tells tales of unexplained phenomena and the history of the Ruby Falls Caves, and then a rainbow of colored lights illuminates the waterfall.

This region of Tennessee is teeming with natural wonders and opportunities for hiking, camping, mountain biking, climbing, and skydiving (see www. outdoorchattanooga.com for details).

Raccoon Mountain is also just 10 minutes from historical downtown Chattanooga, the Chattanooga Choo-Choo, and the Tennessee Aquarium. And, thanks to Raccoon Caverns' onsite bath house, you don't have to head into town looking like a troglodyte just because you slept in a cave. —LF

ⓘ **Raccoon Mountain Caverns** (✆ **800/ 823-2267;** www.raccoonmountain.com). **Ruby Falls** (✆ **423/821-2544;** www.ruby falls.com). **Outdoor Chattanooga** (www. outdoorchattanooga.com).

WHEN TO GO: Year-round.

✈ Chattanooga Metropolitan Airport.

🛏 $$ **Chattanooga Choo Choo Holiday Inn** (✆ **800/TRACK29** or 423/266-5000; www.choochoo.com). $$ **Bluff View Inn** (✆ **800/725-8338;** www. bluffview.com).

Caving Raccoon Cavern in Chattanooga, Tennessee.

4 Staying Grounded

Bicycling on "Death Road"
It's All Downhill from Here
La Paz to Coroico, Bolivia

In the thin mountain air 5km (3 miles) above sea level, dense fog and clouds are common—probably a good thing, because if you could actually *see* the precipitous cliffs plunging down the side of Bolivia's Death Road, you might be tempted to huddle in the back of your support vehicle for a safe drive home. But as your newfound bike buddies suit up for the steep ride downhill, you just ignore the fact that the only things separating you from certain death are your thin rubber bicycle tires. Instead, you take part in a generations-old safety ritual—just pour a little beer onto the dirt as a sacrifice to the ancient Incan earth goddess Pachamama that she may hold onto you as you plunge downhill at breakneck speeds over a muddy road that has no guardrails. Feel safe now?

The 5-hour ride goes down one of the most thrilling—and most deadly—stretches of roadway on Earth. Covering the 64km (40 miles) from La Paz to Coroico, the route is a favorite of thrill seekers worldwide. Since the 1990s, over 30,000 mountain bikers have completed the trip (though, ominously, a few have not). From La Paz, a handful of tour operators are available to pick up bikers, and after driving them to the top of La Cumbre mountain pass, there's a safety demonstration, the ritual beer pour, and from that point on your life is literally in your hands: While the downhill jaunt from 4,800 to 1,500m (16,000–5,000 ft.) above sea level isn't too taxing on the legs, hands get a ferocious workout by keeping a white-knuckle grip on brake levers for the entire trip.

Bolivia's Death Road comes by its name honestly. Since opening in the 1930s, thousands of travelers have been killed on its tortuous, twisting route, and about a

dozen of these have been daredevil bicyclists. The reputation of this stretch of highway is so notorious that in 1995 the Inter-American Development Bank christened it the deadliest road in the world, ironically attracting the attention of extreme mountain bikers everywhere. Even calling this a "road" is really an exaggeration—in many areas the dirt pathway is just a few feet wide and strewn with large rocks, slathered with muck from rain and waterfalls, and dotted with crosses that mark the places where unlucky travelers have met their doom.

Travelers should choose their tour operator wisely; some are reportedly less rigorous about safety than others. It's wise

Bolivia's "Death Road" is rife with precipitous cliffs and hairpin turns.

Previous page: Mountain biking in Yosemite National Park.

to pack goggles, sunscreen, insect repellant, layers of waterproof clothing that can be shed as the ride progresses, and a fresh change of clothes for the end of your day. And all bikers should prepare for dense clouds of dust from passing vehicles, thick fog, heavy rain, lack of oxygen, bitter cold, intense heat—and, just in case, make sure your last will and testament is completed. —ML

TOURS: **Vertigo Biking** (© **591-2/279-9605;** www.vertigobiking.com). **Gravity**

Assisted Mountain Biking (© **591-2/231-3849;** gravitybolivia.com).

WHEN TO GO: Many travelers prefer the dry season, from Apr–Oct.

✈ La Paz.

🛏 $ **Hotel Rosario,** Av. Illampu 704 (© **010-2/245-1658;** www. hotelrosario. com). $$$ **Hotel Europa,** Calle Tiwanaku 64 (© **010-2/231-5656;** www.summit hotels.com).

Cycling 225

L'Etape du Tour de France
The Wheels on the Bike Go Round & Round
France

Your legs feel like someone poured gasoline on them and lit a match. Each breath you take gives you half the oxygen you need, and your heart is pounding in your throat. No, you're not in the emergency room—not yet, anyway. You volunteered and paid good money to ride in L'Etape du Tour (one stage of the famous Tour de France bicycle race), and like so many others around you, you're now wondering if you don't have some kind of a masochistic edge, if not an all-out death wish. Up ahead you see a fellow rider bloodied and broken like roadkill on the side of the highway, surrounded by medics with worried looks on their faces. But for the grace of God . . .

Each year, organizers of L'Etape du Tour pick one stage of the actual Tour de France and make a one-day race of it—one long, hellish day of heaving up the mountain passes of the Pyrenees or the French Alps, where grueling climbs of more than 2,100m (nearly 7,000 ft.) are commonplace. Downhills, while a welcome respite, aren't exactly risk free either; groups of riders ripping around curves at high speeds have almost no margin for error, and one slip-up can wipe out 20 cyclists or more.

Signing up for L'Etape should be done months in advance, and of course training should begin at least a year before the actual event. The well-organized ride has plenty of van support and medical teams to assist fallen riders. Expect plenty of company on the ride; each year over 8,000 riders enter this event. The course changes each year, but is generally about 161km (100 miles) long more or less, and some courses can have a total of 3,000m (10,000 ft.) of climbing. Though the weather in July can be pleasant, freezing weather and mountaintop hailstorms can destroy the resolve of even the hardiest bikers. But the hundreds of onlookers cheering riders to the finish can restore the adrenaline of beleaguered bicyclists, and at the end of the ride—assuming you make it—there's plenty of free wine and cold beer. *Bon courage!* —ML

ⓘ **L'Etape du Tour** (© **33/1/41-331-468;** www.letapedutour.com). **WHEN TO GO:** July.

226 **Cycling**

Maah Daah Hey Trail
Going Maah Way?
Medora, North Dakota, U.S.A.

One hundred miles of spectacular Badlands scenery, endless skies, frequent wildlife sightings, and some of the best and most challenging mountain biking terrain anywhere (yes, including even Moab, Utah [see 231])—yet amazingly, even some avid bikers have never even heard of the Maah Daah Hey Trail in North Dakota. That's changing fast, however, now that the ride has been granted Epic status by the International Mountain Biking Association.

The Maah Daah Hey Trail is cobbled together from a number of different landowners, including the Little Missouri National Grasslands, Theodore Roosevelt National Park, state-owned land, and private property. The trail head is found in Sully Creek State Recreation Area near Medora; from there, the narrow single-track trail travels northward to the U.S. Forest Service's CCC Campground near Watford City. Most tour operators leave from Bismark or from the Dakota Cyclery (www.dakotacyclery.com) in Medora, which is also an ideal place to pick up maps and check current trail conditions.

It's not called the Badlands for nothing, and bikers should be prepared for extreme conditions. Water is scarce, so bring extra and use water filters to make safe what little water is available on the trail. Rainy weather turns the trail to mud—the thick, heavy kind that sticks to shoes and tires. And with plenty of cactus around, there's no shortage of sharp needles to puncture tires, so consider investing in a good-quality patch kit as well as extra inner tubes. One extra note of caution: There are cattle all along this trail, so watch out for cow chips.

Though the trail is long, one need not conquer its entire length to experience the rugged beauty of this region—though you may be tempted to go the distance, given the dramatic landscape and the frequent encounters with wildlife such as bison, golden eagles, mule deer, and coyotes. Bikers who do opt for a longer journey will find primitive campgrounds along the route. More adventurous souls may want to investigate the ice caves that are a short detour off the main trail; ask locally for directions. —ML

A biker rides along the Maah Daah Hey Trail.

TOURS: Escape Adventures (📞 **800/ 596-2953;** www.escapeadventures.com). **Western Spirit Cycling Adventures** (📞 **800/845-2453;** www.westernspirit. com).

WHEN TO GO: May–Sept.

✈ Bismarck, ND (130 miles/209km).

🛏 $$ **Best Western Doublewood Inn,** 1400 E. Interchange Ave., Bismarck (📞 **701/ 258-7000;** www.bestwesternnorthdakota. com). $$ **Eagle Ridge Lodge,** 3653 W. River Rd., Medora (📞 **866/863-2453** or 701/ 623-2216; www.eagleridgelodge.com).

Cycling **227**

Bike Hawaii
Dirt Biking in Movie Set Paradise
Oahu, Hawaii, U.S.A.

Don't feel bad huffing and puffing as you climb the Green Monster; your **Bike Hawaii** guide did warn that it's a cardio workout. This steep grassy slope is just one of the ascents awaiting you when you dirt bike at **Kualoa Ranch** in Kaaawa Valley on Oahu. Along the way, too, you'll peddle fast on dirt roads dodging cow patties and the cows they came from. And from time to time, you just have to stop and look down the steep cliffsides at the kayakers paddling through the azure ocean toward China-man's Hat, the pointy spit of island nearby. On your trip you'll also enter a World War II bunker that was converted in a movie museum. And dotted along the terrain you're exploring are sites where parts of the movies *Jurassic Park, Godzilla, Pearl Harbor, 50 First Dates,* and the television show *Lost,* were filmed.

Dirt-bike riding choices vary on this scenic 4,000-acre (1,619-hectare) ranch. While wimpier friends or family members might stay on dirt roads, you can charge up single-track trails toward hilltops, or thread among trees on a zigzagging path. You may encounter swollen river streams, so get ready to jump, but be prepared for the muddy bank on the far side. Ride along the rutted ground covered with tree roots that's interspersed with rocky terrain and you'll reach the site where some of the *Windtalkers* war scenes were filmed. Who knows? If you're lucky, you might even

stop for a rest and get to watch a monster movie being filmed.

Bike Hawaii, based in Honolulu, offers 2- to 3-hour dirt biking excursions twice a week. The company will pick you up at your lodging and bring you to the ranch. Bike rental is included, and a Kona full-suspension upgrade is available. After an intro session, the groups go out with a few guides, so the more skilled and stronger riders can take the single track over rugged, jagged terrain and

Amazing scenery and challenging trails await bikers at Kualoa Ranch on Oahu.

hillsides, while the less adventurous take tamer trails. While the mileage listed on the website is approximately 6 miles (10km), don't be fooled. Bicyclists and runners training for the XTERRA and Mountainman competitions train here. Though the courses might be relatively short, they can be challenging.

Bike Hawaii has several other adventures including an Oahu Hike, Kayak, and Snorkel Adventure, and a Bike, Hike, and Snorkel Adventure. The family-owned Kualoa Ranch, a working cattle ranch, has its own offerings for tourists. On the ranch you can go horseback riding or drive an ATV tour on rough trails around the ranch. —*LF*

ⓘ **Bike Hawaii** (ⓒ **877/682-7433** or 808/734-4212; www.bikehawaii.com). **Kualoa Ranch,** 49–560 Kamehameha Hwy. (ⓒ **808/237-7321;** www.kualoa.com).

WHEN TO GO: Year-round.

✈ Honolulu (18 miles/29km).

228 Cycling

Biking the Golden Gate Bridge
Open Your Golden Gate
San Francisco, California, U.S.A.

There are bridges, and there are bridges . . . and then there is the Golden Gate Bridge. Beloved by millions, the majestic span that connects San Francisco with the headlands of Marin County not only *is* a breathtaking view—it also gives travelers spectacular vistas of the Pacific Ocean, Alcatraz Island, the hills and towns of the East Bay, and the cool, gray city of love herself, San Francisco. And though it's possible to walk or drive across the bridge, the most exciting way to experience this engineering marvel is by biking across. Having crossed the bridge by bike countless times as a resident of San Francisco, I can attest to this being one attraction that nobody ever gets tired of—it really is a thrilling ride.

There are several ways to approach the 1¾-mile-long (nearly 3km) bridge with your bike. Most folks from the city go through the Presidio, a forested former military base located at the northwest tip of the city, now part of Golden Gate National Recreation Area, or along the waterfront at Chrissy Field, a mecca for hikers, windsurfers, and bird-watchers. Weekends might be the best time to go, when the west side of the bridge (facing the Pacific) is open to bike traffic only. Some say the views are better on the east side, which faces San Francisco Bay, but don't get so enamored of the scenery that you slam into a pedestrian—as a huge tourist attraction, the bridge's walkways can get crowded, even on foggy weekdays.

Once you cross the bridge, the verdant hills of the Marin Headlands—also part of the Golden Gate National Recreation Area—await your exploration. There are some challenging climbs here, particularly Conzelman Road, which hugs the cliffs overlooking the Pacific. If you can make it to the top, keep going and you'll be rewarded with a white-knuckle plunge down a terrifyingly steep road with nothing between you and the rocks below but a breeze and a prayer. The south-facing coves at Black Sand beach are a favorite sunning spot—families favor the east-side beaches, while the clothing-optional beaches are farther west and require a bit of scrambling over rocks to get there. A visit to the Headlands Center for the Arts, the Point Bonita Lighthouse, and the Nike Missile Site are always rewarding.

Too whipped for a bike ride back the same way you came? No worries—just

Biking across the Golden Gate Bridge.

point your bike toward the ferry landing in charming Sausalito, hop a ride on the bike-friendly ferry, and enjoy the sunset as you churn across the bay back toward the San Francisco waterfront. —ML

ⓘ **Golden Gate National Recreation Area** (✆ **415/331-1540;** www.nps.gov/goga).

TOURS: Blazing Saddles Bike Rentals & Tours (✆ **415/202-8888;** www.blazingsaddles.com). **Bike and Roll** (✆ **866/736-8224;** www.bikeandroll.com).

WHEN TO GO: May–Oct.

✈ San Francisco International.

🛏 $$$ **Hotel Adagio,** 550 Geary St. (✆ **800/228-8830** or 415-775-5000; www.thehoteladagio.com). $$ **Hotel del Sol,** 3100 Webster St. (✆ **877/433-5765** or 415/921-5520; www.thehoteldelsol.com).

Cycling 229

Biking Sichuan Province
Chinese, to Go
Sichuan, China

For sheer epic grandeur, it's impossible to beat a bike tour of western Sichuan Province. Feudal towers crumbling into dust, bubbling hot springs, serene Buddhist temples, and lush, bamboo-covered panda reserves are among the hundreds of sights that greet travelers to this out-of-the-way region, one of China's most mountainous and most gorgeous. The roads here tend to be well-maintained (with some jarring exceptions), the traffic light, and the vistas sweeping; if it's an unforgettable, long-distance adventure you seek that will get your legs and buns into Olympic shape, look no further.

Most bicyclists begin their tour in Chengdu, a 2½-hour flight from Beijing. (If your trip takes you into Tibet, check local conditions to ensure there will be no administrative problems with travel to the area.) From Chengdu, it's a steady uphill climb into the foothills of the Himalayas and the western reaches of Sichuan. Vehicle support is usually available on organized bike tours, making visits to the most remote hamlets and farming villages possible without lugging too many supplies in bike panniers.

The Wolong Nature Reserve is a must for panda-lovers; at 2,785m (8,950 ft.), it's a cool, humid sanctuary for these lovable beasts. Most routes take bicyclists to the base of magnificent, snow-peaked Four Sisters Mountain. The city of Danba beckons with its 500-year-old lamasery; the hillsides around this ancient town are dotted with Tibetan defensive towers. Bamei is another favorite stop, where road-weary bikers can soak their bones in the local hot springs—a welcome relief after grinding over a 3,790m

(12,630-ft.) mountain pass. And throughout the entire region, breathtaking glacial valleys with rivers sparkling like silver ribbons in the distance mesmerize travelers to this magical land. It's a journey of about a thousand miles, and it's worth every one of them. —ML

TOURS: China Roads (☎ **86/136/1888-7507;** www.china-roads.com). **Bike China**

(☎ **800/818-1778** in the U.S. For direct dials from other countries consult the website; www.bikechina.com).

WHEN TO GO: Mar–June and Sept–Nov.

✈ Shuangliu Airport (18km/11 miles).

⊨ $ **Traffic Hotel,** Linjiang Zhong Lu 6, Chengdu (☎ **028/8545-1017;** www.traffic hotel.com). $$$ **Shangri-La Chengdu,** Binjiang Dong Lu 9, Chengdu (☎ **028/8888-9999;** www.shangri-la.com).

230 Cycling

Biking & More in El Salvador
One Thing After Another
El Salvador

Yesterday you were learning to surf in the postcard-perfect waves off white-sand, tropical beaches, but today you're trying your hand at wakeboarding in a warm lagoon under the shadow of an immense volcano. Tomorrow you'll be straddling a mountain bike that's crashing down a dirt path through a lush rainforest. For thrill jockeys with a touch of Attention Deficit Disorder, Access Trips comes to the rescue with a multisport, adventure-instruction package that's guaranteed to hold your attention for at least a week.

Your adventures begin shortly after you arrive in San Salvador, the capital of this Central American nation once torn by strife, but now poised to become the next eco-tourism mecca to rival nearby Costa Rica. You'll be picked up from Comalapa Airport and taken to your seaside hotel. There's time to relax or, if you're rarin' to go, indulge in a little sunset surfing. The next three days are chock-full of instruction in surfing and wakeboarding, all in small groups where the instructor-to-guest ratio is an admirable 1:5. Beginners are welcome, and veterans are given ample opportunities to hone their skills.

Once you've got those watersports activities down, you'll head up into the mountains to the charmingly named **El Imposible National Park.** The edge of the park is lined with little-used singletrack paths that are perfect for practicing your mountain biking techniques. You'll bike through jungles, on volcanoes, and by other resplendent natural wonders. While there, you'll stay in a family-owned villa on the edge of a coffee plantation and, if time permits, take in a local falconry.

The instructors on this trip, as well as the co-founder of Access Trips, Alain Chuard, are former World Cup champions at snowboarding, surfing, and mountain biking. Their goal is to combine world-class instruction from seasoned professionals with unique travel destinations and fun activities. Other multisport offerings from Access include kayak/bike/hike tours of New Zealand and whitewater kayaking/biking in Costa Rica. —ML

TOUR: Access Trips, Scotts Ferry, RD1 Bulls, New Zealand (☎ **650/492-4778;** www.accesstrips.com).

WHEN TO GO: Year-round; check website for schedule.

Mountain Biking Around the World

There's little to compare with the rush of shredding down a steep hill at breakneck speeds on a mountain bike. As a way of getting close to nature, exploring out-of-the-way villages, and trekking through isolated canyons, it really can't be beat. It's also one of most economical and eco-friendly ways to see the world while burning calories (instead of gasoline) and getting into great shape. The following destinations stand out as some of the most exotic and thrilling rides on the planet. —*ML*

231 **Slickrock in Moab, Utah, U.S.A.:** Many trails here take riders past red and gold cliffs that were once home to the Anasazi people—their cliff dwellings can be toured at nearby **Canyonlands** (www.nps.gov/cany) and **Mesa Verde** (www.nps.gov/meve) National Parks. You can choose from rides that feature spectacular vistas of the Colorado River, preserved dinosaur tracks, woodlands of piñon pine and juniper, or just spend the day soaking up the mellow culture of downtown Moab. *www.discovermoab.com.*

232 **Volcanic Trails on La Palma, Canary Islands:** Spain's Canary Islands are a paradise year-round. La Palma, the northernmost island, is known for its incredible natural scenery. Towering Roque de los Muchachos, a volcano that lords over the island at almost 2,400m (8,000 ft.), also gives the island some outstanding bike trails. Expect to see enormous calderas, indigenous plants like the Canarian pine, plunging ravines, and from every vantage point, the sapphire blue Atlantic. *www.spain.info.*

233 **Wildlife Reserves on the Galápagos Islands:** This string of volcanic islands is home to some of the rarest and most amazing wildlife on earth. Most of the animals are utterly unafraid of humans, making it like a petting zoo for adults. The volcanic craters that dot these islands, such as El Junco, where the local frigate birds flock to find fresh water, are ideal destinations. Historic towns and plantations round out your mountain biking tour. *www.galapagospark.org.*

234 **Mountain Villages in the Piemonte, Italy:** This ancient land offers some of the best mountain biking on the continent. If you like to take it easy and drink in the culture (and the phenomenal wines), a number of tours concentrate on ancient hill towns and the rich farms and forests of the Po Valley. When you're ready for more adventure, head uphill toward the Italian Alps, where historic forts loom atop steep hills, and tall bridges span vast canyons. *www.italiantourism.com.*

235 **Off-Road in Cappadocia, Turkey:** There are few mountain biking destinations more exotic and beautiful than this region of Turkey, home of the annual Cappadocia Mountain Biking Festival. The area is known for its abundance of off-road trails that wind through an otherworldly landscape. Bizarre rock formations like "fairy chimneys" dot the plains and hillsides, and isolated villages with frescoed churches, ancient Roman ruins, and vineyards are yours to explore. Look out for the hotels, homes, and villages that are carved entirely out of rock. *www.cappadocia.travel.*

㉖ Pearl Pass in Colorado, U.S.A.: This ride is legendary among mountain bikers, who first attempted the nearly 40-mile (64km) crossing in 1976, riding only jury-rigged cruisers with fat tires. Starting in Crested Butte and finishing in Aspen, the ride took those intrepid adventurers a couple of days of huffing and puffing their way on unpaved jeep roads over this 12,705-foot (3,800m) pass. Their initial feat has become an annual event, usually taking place in late summer. This ride is rugged, steep, and has unpredictable weather, but riders are rewarded with spectacular scenery. *www.visitcrestedbutte.com.*

㉗ Singletrack in Wales: What they might lack in vowels (Cwm Carn, Clywyds, Gwydyr Forest), the mountain biking trails of Wales more than make up for in epic single-track adventures. In recent years, Wales' lush forests and open, rolling hillsides have been developed as mountain bike trail centers, many of which have bike rental shops and other amenities. Some of the most popular and challenging singletracks are Coed Y Brenin, Afan Forest Park, Coed Llandegla, and Nant yr Arian. *www.mbwales.com.*

㉘ Dodging Cow Pies in the Texas Hill Country, U.S.A.: The rocky, semi-arid terrain and sunny climate of the Texas Hill Country makes for perfect mountain biking—just watch out for the cow pies, as some of the best rides are on working cattle ranches. Hill Country State Natural Area is 5,370 sq. miles (13,908 sq. km) of cow-free biking bliss, offering overnight camping, fishing, and swimming. Mountain bikes shred their way through oak woodlands, canyons, spring-fed creeks, and rocky, rolling hills—and it's all on shared equestrian trails (a whole different flavor of trail pie). *www.tpwd.state.tx.us.*

㉙ The Dalat Highlands, Vietnam: The cool pine forests around Dalat are the perfect place to breathe fresh mountain air, kayak through clear lakes, and trek past the mountain villas built by French colonists back when the region was still known as Indochine francaise. The mountain biking is world-class, with climbs ranging from mellow, afternoon hill rides to multi-day journeys deep into the heart of the highlands, down to the coast, or to national parks in the area. Try to visit during the dry season from November through April. *www. phattireventures.com.*

A bike ride through a Vietnam pine forest.

㉚ Willow Creek Trail, Bass Lake, California, U.S.A.: This is not a starter trail—if your quads are solid meat, your lungs are bulletproof, and you hunger for white-knuckle shreds down a technical, complex trail, then *maybe* you're ready for this advanced black diamond plunge. Bikes with less than five inches of play in the front suspension will reward riders with a long, bone-jarring ride through hell, so come prepared with your best equipment. Expect the unexpected here: hairpin turns and switchbacks, wet, slimy rocks in clear, dry weather, loose slides of granite gravel, and drop-dead gorgeous views of the region's mountains. *www.yosemitebicycle.com.*

The Coal Mines of Arigna
Mining the Black Gold of Ireland
Arigna, County Roscommon, Ireland

Beneath the emerald hills of County Roscommon, a darker and more sinister world has existed for centuries. The coal mines of Arigna, renowned for having some of the narrowest and most difficult mining conditions in the world, were Ireland's only source of coal beginning in the 1700s. To chip away at the black bituminous rock found here, miners were forced to work by lying on their backs or sides in tunnels as narrow as 51cm (20 in.)—and you thought your cubicle was small. The mines have been closed since 1990, but the **Mining Experience Centre**—winner of a Rural Tourism Award—gives adventurous visitors a taste of the life of a working miner.

The **Arigna Mines** are nestled within the lush Arigna Valley, and can be reached by traveling the Arigna Scenic Drive, a 60km (37-mile) loop that begins and ends in nearby Boyle. Look for the brown signposts with the word *Sli*, meaning route, indicating the course of travel. The narrow road leads visitors past verdant hills, blue loughs (lakes), and lush river valleys until it reaches the Arigna Mines and its Mining Experience Centre, a modern architectural stunner that resembles a large, angular block of coal.

The 45-minute mine tour begins at the mine's rocky entrance, crowned by a statue of the Virgin Mary—often the last thing the miners saw before descending into the dark, stony depths. Tours into the mineshafts are led by former miners, who are able to provide an authentic, first-hand insight into the daily life of a coal miner. Lights and recorded noises replicate the conditions of an operating mine, as do the hardhats visitors must wear when underground. Sturdy, comfortable walking shoes are also recommended.

Mining has been an important part of this region's history for over 500 years, due in part to the discovery of local iron ore deposits—nearby Slieve Anierin, in fact, translates to "Iron Mountain." Coal was used as an energy source in local iron foundries after nearby forests were clearcut. Though the iron industry didn't last in this area, coal continued to be an important source of fuel with the advent of the Industrial Revolution. The Arigna coal mines stayed open and active until 1990, when the local power station—the coal mine's main customer—closed down.

Energy continues to play a part in the local economy, though from a more environmentally sustainable source; nearby hills are dotted with wind turbines that feed electricity into the nation's energy grid. If you can't get enough of underground adventures, you may also want to visit other caves in west-central Ireland, including **Aillwee and Doolin Caves** (www.aillweecave. ie, www.doolincave.ie) in County Clare and the **Glengowla Mines** in County Galway (glengowla.goegi.com). The region is also home to Ireland's only tree canopy walk, located in **Lough Key Forest Park** (www. loughkey.ie). —*ML*

(i) **Arigna Mining Experience** (© 353/ 7196/46466; www.arignamining experience.ie).

WHEN TO GO: Apr–Oct; prices higher July–Aug. Tour open year-round.

✈ Shannon (135km/84 miles).

🛏 $$$ **The Landmark Hotel,** Carrick-on-Shannon, Leitrim (© **7196/22222;** www.thelandmarkhotel.com). $$ **Ramada Lough Allen Hotel,** Drumshanbo (© **7196/ 40100;** www.ramadahotelleitrim.com).

Easter Island Archaeological Expedition
Someone to Watch Over Me
Rapa Nui (Easter Island), Chile

The sun has been blazing down on you all day, sweat is beading on your forehead, and you're covered with dust from the rock pit you've been working in since sunrise. You decide it's time for a break, but wait—there, right at your feet, you discover a prehistoric spear point that hasn't seen the light of day for centuries. As the brooding heads of Easter Island tower above you, you holler out to your teammates, "I found one!" Easter Island is one of the great mysteries of the ancient world, and you've just taken another step to helping researchers uncover the secrets of this now-extinct island culture.

To be a part of such important work is a once-in-a-lifetime experience.

Easter Island, a territory of Chile, is a remote volcanic island in the South Pacific. Located about 3,700km (2,300 miles) west of Chile, the island (also known as Rapa Nui or Isla de Pascua to the Spanish-speaking natives) can best be reached by airplane from Santiago. Several institutions support archaeological programs here for students and researchers, but **Earthwatch Institute,** an environmental research and exploration group, sponsors archaeological trips to Easter Island that are open to volunteers from the general public. These and other visitors find lodging and other essentials in Hanga Roa, the only town on the island.

Adventure seekers could hardly choose a more fascinating location to visit or work. An isolated island with three extinct volcanoes looming over its 163 sq. km (63-sq.-mile) landmass, Easter Island's past is shrouded in mystery. Once heavily forested, it's believed that the Polynesian settlers of the island cut down the forests, which in part led to the natives' decline; disease and warfare further reduced the population to a low of about 100 people by the end of the 19th century. As a result, little knowledge of the culture that created Easter Island's iconic stone heads remained.

Also known as *moai,* the heads of Easter Island are its best-known archaeological feature, but the island is rich in other cultural remains that are just as puzzling. Dozens of caves show signs of human use. Petroglyphs featuring birdmen, fish, and other creatures, have been discovered at over 1,000 sites. Stone houses have been discovered with human remains inside. The island even has its own ancient form of writing known as rongorongo; though

Some of Easter Island's 600 *moais.*

it's been seen since the 1800s, the writing has never been deciphered, further adding to the sense of mystery and wonder that this UNESCO World Heritage Site evokes. —*ML*

ⓘ **Earthwatch Institute,** 3 Clock Tower Place, Ste. 100, Maynard, MA 01754 (𝒞 **800/ 776-0188** or 978/461-0081; www.earth watch.org).

WHEN TO GO: Oct–Apr.

✈ Santiago, Chile, then flights to Easter Island.

🛏 $$ **Tauraa Hotel,** Atamu Tekena S/N, Hanga Roa (𝒞 **56/32/210-0463;** www. tauraahotel.cl). $$$ **Hotel Explora Rapa Nui** (𝒞 **56/2/395-2700;** www.explora. com/rapa-nui).

Exploring & Admiring 243

Mammoth Site
My, What a Big Tusk You Have
Hot Springs, South Dakota, U.S.A.

He's 14 feet tall, weighs 10 tons, eats 700 pounds a day—and he's staring you in the face. Fortunately for you, he eats only vegetation, and he's been dead for about 30 thousand years. Still, there's a rush of excitement because you're the first person to uncover this animal since he was trapped in a prehistoric sinkhole and buried under sediment. Amateur archaeologist Dan Hanson had just such a thrill when in 1974 he literally stubbed his toe on an exposed mammoth tooth. Archaeological digs to the **Mammoth Site** at Hot Springs in South Dakota have yielded a treasure trove of Ice Age finds, including the fossilized remains of two kinds of mammoths (Columbian and wooly), as well as camels, llamas, giant short-faced bears, and wolves.

The site where the 60-foot-deep (18m) sinkhole once formed a prehistoric graveyard is now a world-class research facility and museum dedicated to the investigation of Ice Age ecology. Located in a remote corner of southwestern South Dakota, the Mammoth Site hosts amateur archaeologists through two organizations, the Earthwatch Institute and Elderhostel. Both programs include accommodations in nearby motels and fresh-cooked, family-style meals. Unusual for an archaeological dig, the site is inside a climate-controlled building; visitors to the museum can view ongoing excavations first-hand. And for young visitors during the summer, the

Remains at the Mammoth Site in South Dakota.

museum provides an area where children can practice their digging technique in a simulated excavation; replicas of mammoth fossils are buried beneath the sand.

The Hot Springs area is also a hotbed of historic and natural attractions. **Mount Rushmore National Monument** (www.nps.gov/moru), **Crazy Horse Memorial** (www.crazyhorsememorial.org), **Jewel Cave National Park** (www.nps.gov/jeca), and other wonders are located nearby. And if you've tired of fossilized animals, you can see thousands of free-roaming bison in **Wind Cave National Park** (www.nps.gov/wica), which has the largest herd of these once-endangered animals in the United States. —ML

ⓘ **The Mammoth Site,** 1800 Hwy. 18 Truck Rte. (© **605/745-6017;** www.mammothsite.com). **Earthwatch Institute** (© **800/776-0188** or 978/461-0081; www.earthwatch.org). **Elderhostel** (© **877/426-8056;** www.elderhostel.org).

WHEN TO GO: Year-round.

✈ Rapid City, SD (57 miles/92km).

244 **Exploring & Admiring**

Molokai Mule Ride
The Narrow Path to Enlightenment
Kalaupapa, Molokai, Hawaii, U.S.A.

Evidence doesn't suggest that St. Matthew ever made it to Hawaii. But it's easy to think he was talking about the mule ride to **Kalaupapa National Historic Park** (www.nps.gov/kala) when he said "the way is narrow that leads to life." The harrowing mule route, thin as a sidewalk, twisting from the world's highest sea cliff to the Pacific Ocean beach 1,700 feet (510m) below, may instill the fear of God in even the most secular visitor. Indeed it helped make a saint out of local legend Father Damien, who was canonized in 2009 for his work in the 19th century with a former leper colony on the beach below.

The **Molokai Mule Ride** (http://muleride.com) starts with a brief tutorial on handling these beasts of burden trained specially for steep descents. Then, after mounting your mule, you'll travel a very short stretch on an open path before reaching the first of 26 hair-raising switchbacks on the 3-mile (4.7km) trail to the beach that leads to Kalaupapa. Dazzling views and precipitous drops compete to make your heart pound and blood surge as you steadily plod downhill and around hairpin turns for an hour before reaching the beach for your journey into the world of Hawaii's courageous patron saint.

A Belgium-born missionary priest, Saint Damien took his life in his hands when he came here in 1873 to care for lepers who were cast off other islands, shipped here, and forced to swim the last few yards to shore. Now called Hansen's Disease, which is treatable with sulfone antibiotics, leprosy claimed St. Damien too in 1889—but not before he organized schools, turned shacks into painted houses, provided medical and spiritual care, and guaranteed basic civil rights for his flock of outcasts.

During the fascinating tour you'll learn about the banished community's struggle to create a colony from a narrow strip of land surrounded by ocean and steep cliffs; visit various buildings and the church where Father Damien preached; and then eat lunch with a view of the seaside cliffs on the central northern coast of Molokai. By mid-afternoon, you'll remount the mules to negotiate the steep ascent, switchbacks and all. By this time you'll

Mules and riders descend a narrow trail on Molokai.

probably feel heavy in the saddle, but just as likely you'll feel enlightened by the resplendent views and glimpse into the life of a brightly shining human being. —LF

ⓘ **Visit Molokai** (www.visitmolokai.com). **TOUR: Molokai Mule Ride,** 100 Kalae Hwy. (Ⓒ **800/567-7550** or 808/567-6088; www.muleride.com).

WHEN TO GO: Year-round.

✈ Molokai Airport.

🛏 $$ **Dunbar Beachfront Cottages,** Kamehameha V Hwy., past mile marker 18 (Ⓒ **800/673-0520** or 808/558-8153; www. molokai-beachfront-cottages.com). $$ **Hotel Molokai, Kamehameha V Hwy.** (Ⓒ **808/553-5347;** www.hotelmolokai. com).

Exploring & Admiring 245

Cliffs of Moher
Hang Your Head Over the Cliff's Edge
Cliffs of Moher, County Clare, Ireland

At Ireland's Cliffs of Moher it's common to see people stretched out on the ground with just their heads peering over the cliffs' edges to look straight down at the pounding waves, some 210m (700 ft.) below. The view of the sea and the miles of cliffs to both sides from this high point in western Ireland is awesome, especially if you go on a clear day.

The cliffs, which stretch 8km (5 miles) along the coast of the Atlantic Ocean, are formed of layers of siltstone, shale, and sandstone. The layers are a geological history dating back to the end of the Lower Carboniferous period, a time of glaciation some 290 to 360 million years ago. In 1835 Sir Cornelius O'Brian, recognizing the tourist potential of these cliffs in County Clare,

The breathtaking view atop the Cliffs of Moher.

built a round observation tower that is still open to the public. From its observation platform, visitors can view the cliffs and surrounding area. On a clear day visitors can see the Aran Islands in Galway Bay, the mountains of Kerry, and the Loop Head at the southern tip of Claire. The nooks and crannies of the cliffs are home to thousands of birds in the spring, summer, and fall. In mid-April, it's even possible to see the Atlantic Puffin.

The Cliffs of Moher, about 1½ hours by car from Galway, are one of the most visited tourist sites in Ireland, attracting as many as one million visitors each year. (You can also reach the cliffs by bus or rail.) The road to the top is paved and today there is a large, modern, tasteful visitor center built into the cliffs and covered with grass where one can take an interpretive tour, view the exhibits, and enjoy something to eat. Stop at the visitor center for information about the 600m (1,950 ft.) of walkways along the cliff tops and viewing platforms. Rangers are stationed throughout the complex to answer visitors' questions.

There are numerous tours from town, but they usually last only an hour. We recommend taking more time in order to really absorb the experience. Consider hiking

from O'Brian's Tower along the cliffs to Hag's Point (approx. 8km/5 miles). While there are few places to view the cliffs from the trail, it's a good trek and the route passes the remains of an old watchtower at the point. *A few words of caution:* Do the trek in good weather. Avoid rainy or very windy days, and take a rainproof jacket just in case. Stay on the landward side of any barriers. (There are no protective barriers at the cliff's edge. Several deaths are reported yearly, so be careful.) Be especially watchful of children; better yet, don't go with young children. If you're afraid of heights or get vertigo, skip the trek.

An alternative to viewing the cliffs from the top is taking a ride on the ferry or cruise boats that can be boarded in the nearby town of Doolin and sailing around the base of the cliffs. While you're in the area, a great day trip includes a ferry ride to Inishmore in the Aran Islands, followed by a ride in a horse drawn cart to Dun Aengus, an iron-age fort with nearly 4m-thick (12-ft.) walls. Other worthy explorations nearby include visiting Aillwee Cave, Doolin Cave, and the restored Bunratty Castle. —*LF*

ⓘ **Cliffs of Moher** (www.cliffsofmoher.ie). **Doolin Tourism** (www.doolin-tourism.com).

WHEN TO GO: Spring and fall. Winter weather can be nasty, though the crowds will be smaller. The summer crowds are huge.

✈ Shannon.

✉ $$ **Ballinalacken Castle Hotel,** Doolin (✆ 353/65/707-4025; www.ballinalacken castle.com). $$–$$$ **Gregans Castle Hotel,** Ballyvaughn (✆ 353/65/707-7005; www.gregans.ie).

Exploring & Admiring

246

Aurora Borealis
Dancing Lights Fill the Sky
Northwest Territories, Canada

The blue-green and yellow-green bands of light swirl and dance from one horizon to the other, illuminating the snow-covered landscape. It's a cloudless, dark night and your eyes are locked skyward watching the Aurora Borealis, often called the Northern Lights, from one of the best vantage points on earth, Yellowknife in Canada's Northwest Territories. The Aurora Borealis is a natural phenomenon of colorful lights displayed in the sky created by interactions between charged solar particles and atmospheric gases in the enormous magnetic fields circling the North Magnetic Pole. Because Yellowknife is located at 62°, right under the Auroral arc, the lights are often the brightest here.

The Aurora Borealis viewing season extends from mid-August through mid-April—basically when the sky is dark enough so you can see the lights. But, the most favorable conditions are when it's the darkest, January through March, and the skies are clear.

Yellowknife is snow adventure central during the winter. You could go dog sledding by day or night, when you can combine the adventure with Aurora viewing. You decide if you want to ride behind a musher controlling the sled, or learn to mush your own team. During the day, you can go cross-country skiing, snowshoeing, or trophy pike fishing on the Great Slave

Lake. Outfitters offer snowmobiling tours that can include Aurora viewing. Other adrenaline-inducing activities include ice-road tours and winter fly-ins for caribou viewing. Take advantage of your daylight hours to experience all that this area has to offer, but save your nights for the extravaganza in the sky.

Packages are available which include Aurora viewing, lodging, and other activities. You can stay in Yellowknife, choose a wilderness, lodge, or even stay in a teepee. —LF

ⓘ **Northwest Territories** (✆ **800/661-0788** in Canada or 867/873-7200 international; www.spectacularnwt.com).

TOURS: Yellowknife Outdoor Adventures (✆ 867/444-8320; www.spectacular nwt.com/node/878). **Beck's Kennels Aurora Viewing and Dog Sled Tours** (✆ 867/873-5603; www.beckskennels. com).

WHEN TO GO: Aug–Apr; very best time Jan–Mar.

✈ Yellowknife.

✉ $$ **Enodah Wilderness Travel & Trout Rock Lodge** (✆ 867/873-4334; www.enodah.com). $ **Aurora Village** (mostly teepees; ✆ 867/669-0006; www. auroravillage.com).

247

Marfa Lights
The Lights at Night, Are Big & Bright
Marfa, Texas, U.S.A.

Some say the lights are nothing more than static electricity. The native Apache believed they were stars fallen to Earth. Other folks say they're the result of swamp gas, ball lightning, UFOs, secret military weapons, St. Elmo's fire, or distant headlights reflecting off layers of warm air. The mystery may never be solved, but everyone who sees the famous Marfa lights swears that a view of these enigmatic glowing orbs, floating in the night above the desert floor, is a once-in-a-lifetime experience that's sure to raise the hair on the back of your neck. People have come from all over the world to see and study this luminous phenomenon, and nobody has yet developed a universally accepted explanation.

The Marfa lights are seen in an isolated, rural area of west Texas near the intersection of U.S. Highways 67 and 90. Similar lights have been reported throughout the region, but the greatest numbers of reported sightings occur here, between the towns of Marfa, Alpine, and Presidio. There is an "official" viewing platform on U.S. Highway 90, just east of the Highway 67 junction. Though the lights seem to occur in any kind of weather and regardless of the season, they have been witnessed only at night. Visitors to the area should be aware that temperatures can drop precipitously in the desert at night, even after a hot day; jackets or coats are recommended year-round.

First reported in 1883 by a settler named Robert Ellison, the lights are usually described as white, red, yellow, or orange globes, roughly the size of a basketball, that float about 5 or 6 feet (1.5–1.8m) above the ground. Though they have never been seen close-up, they are said to appear in pairs or groups, floating, merging, disappearing, then reappearing in a mysterious nighttime dance. The otherworldly lights, which seem to appear unpredictably throughout the year, may last from just a second or two to several hours, according to reports.

If you happen to see the lights one night, head into the town of Marfa (www.marfacc.com) to share your story with the residents of this quirky town. Once a ranching center on the Texas and New Orleans Railroad, in recent years the area has become a major player in the International arts scene, with Donald Judd and other renowned artists setting up studios here. Adventure seekers will note that the region is close to 800,000 acres (32,375 hectares) of wilderness at **Big Bend National Park,** including the Rio Grande River (www.nps.gov/bibe), and **glider lessons** that take advantage of the region's warm desert air thermals are available at the Marfa Municipal Airport (www.flygliders.com). —*ML*

(i) **Marfa, TX Chamber of Commerce,** 207 N. Highland Ave. ((C) **800/650-9696** or 432/729-4942; www.marfacc.com).

WHEN TO GO: The lights can be seen year-round; the Marfa Lights Festival occurs each Sept.

✈ El Paso (194 miles/312km).

🛏 $$ **Hotel Paisano,** 207 N. Highland ((C) **866/729-3669** or 432/729-3669; www.hotelpaisano.com). $$ **The Thunderbird Hotel,** 601 W. San Antonio ((C) **432/729-1984;** www.thunderbirdmarfa.com).

Baja Off-Road Adventures
The Road Less Traveled
Baja California, Mexico

Most of the SUVs you'll see at the mall have just one off-road experience: the garage. If you want to experience the real thrill of off-roading, you have to go to a place where there are no malls, no luxury SUVs—and no roads. For you, Baja California beckons. With its sun-baked deserts, rugged mountains, and sapphire blue waters, this 1,000 mile-long (1,609km) peninsula has been a playground for adventure-hungry gringos, and a few companies have developed tours to let folks who want to take a vehicle to places that their air-conditioned mall-mobile could never touch.

Tours usually begin in a city near the border such as San Diego, California, or Ensenada, in Mexico; another option is to fly to Cabo San Lucas and begin your tour there. Most tour operators offer a variety of trips, from an afternoon tearing around on a 3-mile (nearly 5km) course outside Cabo to a full week trekking from one end of the Baja Peninsula to the other. Once your adventure begins, you'll stay in local hotels, dine on fresh-caught seafood, and sip tangy margaritas.

Travelers are matched with a professionally maintained vehicle that has all the features a road rat could want: massive all-terrain tires, powerful engines, and racing shocks that make small boulders feel like dust bunnies. The vehicles are also outfitted with a five-point racing harness and a two-way radio system that lets vehicles stay in contact with one another. Don't expect posh appointments: These babies are built with dirt in mind, and most are open-air monsters replete with steel roll bars and dozens of garish racing decals.

Once you've tapped into your inner Mad Max, and you think you've got the chops, why not enter a rented off-road vehicle in a race like the **Wide Open Baja Challenge?** With ready-made race cars, a big support staff, pre-race training, and great accommodations, it's the best in good, not-so-clean fun. —ML

ⓘ **Baja California Tourism** (✆ **664/682-3367;** www.discoverbajacalifornia.com).

TOURS: Baja Racing Adventures (✆ **602/619-2277;** www.bajaracingadventures.com). **Wide Open Adventures** (✆ **949/635-2292;** www.wideopenbaja.com).

WHEN TO GO: Oct–May.

AcroYoga
Defying Gravity
Classes Worldwide

Yoga might be the last thing you think of when someone says "extreme sports," but here's a twist on an old routine: yoga combined with acrobatics in an intense, partnered skill called AcroYoga. Think of it as extreme yoga, or yoga as a contact sport. This non-traditional pursuit features poses that even experienced yogis have never seen, like one partner lying on his back and, with just one foot in the air, supporting another partner who is balanced in a flying posture. It's a gravity-defying, graceful form of yoga that—through physical contact with a partner—also offers the benefits of acupressure and reflexology.

AcroYoga was started several years ago by Jason Nemer and Jenny Sauer-Klein, two experienced San Francisco yogis who also have backgrounds in gymnastics and circus arts. As this discipline grows in popularity, classes, workshops, and retreats have become available in cities throughout North America, Asia, Australia, Europe, and South America. While most classes are up to 90 minutes long, workshops last 2 to 3 hours each, and

focus on conditioning, stretching, and—perhaps most important of all—learning to trust and support your partner, who will soon be lifting you into the air.

Those with serious injuries or high blood pressure are advised to stay away from this rigorous practice; even though it's not quite as rigid as some forms of yoga, AcroYoga does require a certain focus and a willingness to adapt your practice to a partner's needs and limitations. But the benefits can be tremendous, say the founders, who claim AcroYoga releases tension from the spine as well as enhancing concentration, focus, and flexibility. And how many other extreme sports have participants who hug after working out together? —ML

(i) **AcroYoga** (www.acroyoga.org).

Colorado Cattle Company
Yippie Tie-Yie-Tah!
New Raymer, Colorado, U.S.A.

The sun's barely up and you've already groomed and saddled your horse, gathered and sorted a few dozen cattle, and started the fire for branding the calves later in the morning. After lunch, you'll ride out north to check on the fences, make sure there's enough water in the stock tank, and check for strays. And last week, you were just another desk jockey sitting in a cubicle.

Located in a remote corner of northern Colorado, the **Colorado Cattle Company** offers city slickers the chance to spend a week in the old West. A shuttle service is available from Denver's Stapleton airport. Once they arrive, guests are shown to their accommodations at the bunkhouse, a 19th-century structure—and one of the original buildings at the ranch—that's been updated with modern conveniences like wireless Internet service and air-conditioning.

Life at the Colorado Cattle Company isn't your typical high-end silver-plated dude ranch—this is a 5,000-acre (2,023 hectare) working cattle ranch that allows only a few guests at a time, so folks who show up are given the full cowboy treatment—riding, roping, and rodeos are on the schedule just about every day. You'll be expected to put in some time in the saddle, so you should come prepared to do so: Pack cowboy boots, boot socks, a long-sleeved shirt or two, plenty of sunscreen, and a cowboy hat with a stampede string in case you need to do some hard, fast riding. Some folks also recommend padded bike shorts to prevent saddle sores.

Tough as it is, life as a cowhand at the Colorado Cattle Company isn't all work and no play. The folks there are happy to help greenhorns who want to practice the

Help work the cattle at the Colorado Cattle Company.

fine arts of barrel racing, roping, and auctioneering. There's also a well-stocked fishing pond, an indoor swimming pool, and a sauna for relieving aching muscles. The cooks can accommodate special requests like vegetarian meals, and after a long day in the saddle, what could be better than bellying up to the ranch's bar for a nice cold beer? —*ML*

(i) **Colorado Cattle Co. & Guest Ranch**
(c) **970/437-5345;** www.coloradodude ranch.com).
WHEN TO GO: Apr–Nov.
✈ Denver (67 miles/108 miles).

Unconventional Undertakings **251**

Space Shuttle Lift-Off
T-Minus 10 & Counting . . .
Kennedy Space Center, Florida, U.S.A.

One of the most dramatic events in the course of human civilization was the space race of the 1960s, beginning with the successful launch of the Sputnik satellite by the Soviet Union. The whole world watched in awe as the U.S. and its former Cold War adversary competed to be the first to the moon and back. The best way

to relive the excitement of that era is to witness the launch of a space shuttle from the Kennedy Space Center. The blaze of white-hot light, the thundering noise, and the sight of a manned shuttle tearing across the skies is sure to reignite the thrill of space exploration.

Space shuttles generally take off from Launch Pad 39A of Kennedy Space Center, located on a barrier island off Florida's Atlantic coast near Titusville, about 52 miles (84km) east of Orlando. If you're in Orlando, there are tour buses available, or you may wish to rent a car. Either way, it pays to plan ahead to see a shuttle launch. The best public viewing is from the NASA Causeway just south of the launch pad, but the area is accessible only with pre-purchased tickets. The next-best places to watch the lift-off are either Spaceview Park in Titusville (just south of the 406 bridge, east of Rte. 1) or the Kennedy Space Center Visitors Complex. The Visitors Complex lacks a clear view of the launch pad, but it's close enough that the explosive sound is terrific and the shuttle usually flies right overhead once it has lifted off.

Visitors can sign up for NASA Causeway e-mail ticket alerts; tickets can be purchased online once they are available for sale, but act fast because these events have been known to sell out in a matter of minutes. Remember too that launches are sometimes scrubbed due to bad weather or other conditions.

Besides the thrill of watching the shuttle lift-off, there are dozens of space-related attractions at the Visitors Complex, including IMAX films, astronaut encounters hosted by real astronauts, and the Shuttle Launch Experience, an interactive simulation hosted by shuttle personnel that comes complete with videos, sound, and lighting that mimics the experience of an actual shuttle launch. —*ML*

(i) **Kennedy Space Center** (© 321/449-4400; www.kennedyspacecenter.com).

The space shuttle blasts off from Kennedy Space Center.

TOURS: Gray Line Orlando Launch (© **800/537-0917;** www.grayline.com). **All Orlando Tours** (© **702/233-1627;** www.allorlandotours.com).

WHEN TO GO: Open year-round; check website for launch schedule.

⊨ $$$ **The Inn at Cocoa Beach,** 4300 Ocean Blvd. (© **800/343-5307** or 321/799-3460; www.theinnatcocoabeach.com). $$ **Riverview Hotel,** 103 Flagler Ave. (© **800/945-7416** or 386/423-8927; www.riverviewhotel.com).

Grass-Skiing
Please Stay on the Grass
Basye, Virginia, U.S.A.

If those lazy, hazy days of summer are driving your inner ski bum crazy, take heart; you can still hit a ski resort and get the same heart-pounding rush you got last winter on the slopes. No, NASA scientists haven't developed some magic non-melting snow; it's grass-skiing, an adrenaline craze imported from Germany for your warm-weather fun.

Bryce Resort is one of the few areas worldwide to offer this thrill ride (most ski resorts have slopes that are too sandy, rocky, or rough to accommodate grass skiing). Located in the lovely Shenandoah Valley of Virginia, just west of Washington, D.C., Bryce Resort is home to a number of outdoor adventure activities, including mountain-boarding, a zipline tour and a bungee ride.

Grass-skiing uses ski boots just like snow skiing, but the boots are attached to shorter skis roughly 3-feet long; the skis have rolling belt treads on them similar to those found on a tank. (Other designs use small wheels and work like inline skates.) You'll also need ski poles and a complement of safety equipment—without a soft layer of snow, falls while grass skiing often result in plenty of bruises, bumps, and scrapes. Consider a helmet and pads for your knees and elbows.

You should also consider taking a lesson; even experienced snow skiers report having some difficulty mastering the intricacies of grass-skiing their first time on a grass-ski run. But if you decide to bail out, Bryce Resort offers a consolation; access to their mountain-tubing slide, where participants whoosh down a 340-feet (102m) waterless slide. —*ML*

ⓘ **Bryce Resort Grass Skiing** (✆ **800/ 821-1444** or 540/856-2121; www.bryce resort.com).

WHEN TO GO: May–Oct.

✈ Shenandoah Valley Regional Airport (62 miles/100km).

🛏 $$ **Wayside Inn,** 7783 Main St., Middletown (✆ **877/869-1797** or 540/ 869-1797; www.alongthewayside.com). $ **Frederick House,** 28 N. New St., Staunton (✆ **800/334-5575** or 540/885-4220; www.frederickhouse.com).

Mountainboarding
Son of Snowboard
Centers Worldwide

If a snowboard and an SUV got married and had a baby, it would probably look like a mountainboard: a big flat board with foot straps, curved upward at each end, with solid truck-like suspension and four fat, all-terrain tires. It would get its breakneck

Throughout the U.S., Ireland, Australia, and the U.K., there are now dozens of mountainboarding centers that cater to fans of this fast, fun thrill ride. The best of them offer lessons and rental equipment, including boards, helmets, knee and elbow pads, and gloves. Though lessons can certainly help the newcomer, the spot you choose to learn this fast-growing adrenaline sport is perhaps more important. Some places offer several other outdoor sports as well as mountainboarding; at these, you'll compete for slope space with other sports and often end up on gravelly tracks that are no fun to wipe out on. If only to save your skin, look instead for a mountainboarding center that has grassy, groomed hillsides dedicated to mountainboarding.

The All-Terrain Board Association, an organization based in Cardiff, Wales, U.K., gives instructor accreditation, but some aficionados claim that with a sport that most folks can pick up in an hour or two, one simple lesson should suffice. Within a single afternoon, even neophytes can be turning, carving, and—most importantly for a sport where speeds up to 64kmph (40 mph) are common—coming to a controlled stop. —*ML*

Mountainboarding scratches the itch for snowboarders looking for an off-season adrenaline rush.

attitude from its snowboard dad, and its mucky, dirty appeal from its mud-splattered mom. Mountainboarding is, in fact, the spawn of frustrated snowboarders; standing atop English hills, draped in greenery most of the year, they decided to stop waiting for the next Ice Age and took matters into their own hands. By the mid-1990s, the United Kingdom was home base for a new adrenaline sport that has since captured the hearts—and a few skinned elbows and knees—of millions worldwide.

ⓘ **Ivyleaf Mountainboarding,** Bude, Cornwall, U.K. (📞 **44/0-777-306-9716;** www.ivyleafmountainboarding.co.uk). **Surfin' Dirt Mountain Boarding,** Tullyree Rd., County Down, Northern Ireland (📞 **077/ 3-921-0119;** www.surfindirt.co.uk). **Another World Mountainboarding Centre,** Keighley Rd., Ogden, Halifax, U.K. (📞 **01-422/245-196;** www.mountain boarding.co.uk).

Volcano Surfing in Nicaragua
The Crater Crashers
Cerro Negro, Léon, Nicaragua

The ominous black slope of Cerro Negro in Nicaragua drops dramatically below the feet of some brave backpackers. It appears like a giant coal mound with a frightening drop to the dusty fields of this volcanic wonderland in the north west of this Central American country. This steep incline has become the latest place for the latest craze in exotic adventure sports—volcano surfing. Brave volunteers don bright orange jump suits and goggles before mounting a plywood sled and shuffle toward the edge. Suddenly they are off, heltering down the charcoal slope in an aftermath of hot dust and stones. The scraping noise is deafening as the board rocks and bounces, reaching speeds of 81kmph (50 mph). Some riders get scared and try to break—a big mistake as the speedy flow is suddenly interrupted and the riders tumble and somersault in the dust, the board skittering on ahead of them. Savvy riders go with the flow and bound down the 720m (2,400-ft.) mountain, reaching the bottom in a matter of minutes. It is actually wise to be in a rush. This volcano is live.

Cerro Negro is the youngest and most active volcano in the Americas. It first sputtered to life in 1850, creating an ever growing mound that has erupted 20 times since, the last in 1999. It is part of a chain of volcanoes known as the Maribios that stretch all along Nicaragua's northern coast like smouldering sentinels. This particular smoking mound is located 24km (15 miles) northeast of the university city of León, a rambling town of revolutionary murals, majestic churches, and charming colonial architecture. León was the center of operations for the Sandinista movement that toppled Nicaragua's dictatorship in 1979. It's now a flowering city with some excellent hotels and lively nightlife.

Revolutionaries are now few and far between and the only thing fiery about this part of the country is the sulphur emitting craters that top each volcano. Cerro Negro has several craters, new ones submerging the old in beds of rock and ash.

Several hostels and hotels in the city ferry people up every day to the base of the volcano. It is then a 45-minute hike over rock and shale to the crater edge where there is a marvelous view of the countryside. Then it's onto the board for the white-knuckle ride down the 40-degree slope. Riders want to scream but they can't open their mouths for all the dust and rock. Below a reception party measures their speed with a radar gun and survivors stand around clapping and cheering and somewhat relieved, their faces as black as coal miners. —*CO'M & ML*

ⓘ **Bigfoot Youth Hostel** (organized volcano trips; ✆ **505/8917-8832;** www.bigfootnicaragua.com).

WHEN TO GO: June–Jan.

✈ Managua.

🛏 $$ **La Perla,** 1 Av NO, León (✆ **505/311-3125;** www.laperlaleon.com). $ **Big Foot Hostel,** ½ block Servicio Guardian, León (✆ **505/8917-8832;** www.bigfootnicaragua.com).

255

Mountain Tubing
Tubing, or Not Tubing?
Kauai, Hawaii, U.S.A.

On hot, humid afternoons back in the early days of Hawaii's sugar cane plantations, the local kids knew how to cool off and have fun: Just grab an inner tube and, making sure the guards didn't see you, jump into the wide network of irrigation canals that watered the fields. Kids of all ages can now enjoy this thrill as Kauai Backcountry Adventures (see below) takes tubers through the dark, watery tunnels and inclined flumes that were built by hand in the 1800s—a true engineering marvel—to channel the cool, clear water running off Mt. Waialeale.

The adventure begins at Kauai Backcountry's offices, just a few minutes from Lihue Airport on Highway 56. From there, visitors are taken by four-wheel-drive vehicle to Lihue Plantation's headwaters. Tubing tours last about 3 hours and, because there is a limit to the number of tubers on each tour, reservations are strongly suggested. The cost of $100 per tuber may seem prohibitive, but that figure includes your inner tube, headlamps (for seeing in the tunnels), protective gloves, and a picnic lunch at tour's end. Tubers should bring water-friendly shoes with a strap (no flip-flops), towels, sunscreen, and a dry change of clothes.

You might also want to bring a waterproof camera, because the mountain scenery from this 17,000-acre (6,880-hectare) plantation is stunning, and the fern-lined canals are a lovely sight. You'll have a chance at an overlook stop to peer into the immense volcanic crater of Mount Waialeale. Headlamps flickering in the long, dark tunnels—one of which is almost a mile (1.6km) long—are an eerie thrill. The canal route takes tubers through the lush fields and forests of this 19th-century plantation, most of which are off limits to visitors. And if that's not enough, Kauai Backcountry also has a zipline tour through their property for some aboveground fun. —ML

ⓘ **Kauai Backcountry Adventures** (ⓒ **888/270-0555** or 808/245-2506; www.kauaibackcountry.com).

WHEN TO GO: Year-round.

✈ Lihue, Kauai.

⌖ $$$ **Kiahuna Plantation Resort,** 2253 Poipu Rd. (ⓒ **800/OUTRIGGER** [688-7444] or 808/742-6411; www.outrigger.com). $$ **Hanalei Surf Board House,** 5459 Weke Rd. (ⓒ **808/826-9825;** www.hanaleisurfboardhouse.com).

Bobsledding through the Rainforest
A Winter Sport Reinvented in the Caribbean
Ocho Rios, Jamaica

To practice for the 1988 Winter Olympics in Calgary, the Jamaican bobsled team raced down the island's Blue Mountains in a modified pushcart. Famously spoofed in the 1993 film, *Cool Runnings*, the idea of bobsledding without any snow or ice got plenty of well-deserved laughs. It was admittedly funny, but it also looked like a lot of fun.

Now you can re-create the experience with **Rainforest Bobsled Jamaica** at **Mystic Mountain,** a new eco-themed park, opened in 2008 by Rainforest Arial Tram, which also has attractions in Costa Rica, St. Lucia, and Dominica. In Ocho Rios, on Jamaica's northeast coast, film buffs, thrill-seekers, aspiring Olympic athletes, and even adventurous families can hop in custom-designed, high-tech bobsleds and speed down a 1,000m-long (3,200-ft.) track of rails that, at one point, drops 122m (400 ft.) at about 48kmph (30 mph).

The departure point is located at the top of Mystic Mountain. To get there, you have to ride one of the park's other attractions, the Sky Lift Explorer, a chairlift that takes you more than 210m (700 ft.) up, high above the treetops. From here, you bobsled down a winding route that carves through a dense tropical forest. If you're craving another escapade after this stomach-dropping rush, check out the park's zipline called the Tranopy Ride.

The resort town of Ocho Rios also offers active pursuits for adrenaline junkies, in addition to its revered sunshine and sandy beaches. One of the most popular exploits is clambering up a limestone-tiered 285m (940 ft.) waterfall called **Dunn's River Falls** (www.dunnsriverfallsja.com). Just try to avoid going when cruise ship passengers are in the port; it can quickly get overcrowded. A more off-the-beaten-path option is a 3-hour horseback ride and swim with **Chukka Caribbean Adventures** (www.chukkacaribbean.com). You'll ride through historic St. Ann, two of the island's oldest sugar estates, and along the coastline of Chukka Coves' private beach. This company also offers kayaking trips on the **White River** and tours of **Nine Miles,** Bob Marley's birthplace and burial site. Feel free to adopt the reggae spirit and chill out for a while. When you're ready for more excitement, you'll find it. After all, the country that figured out how to bobsled without snow clearly knows a few things about adventure. —*JS*

ⓘ **Jamaica Tourist Board,** 18 Queens Dr., Montego Bay (✆ **876/952-4425;** www.visitjamaica.com).

TOUR: Rainforest Bobsled Jamaica, Mystic Mountain (✆ **876/974-3990;** www.rainforestbobsledjamaica.com).

WHEN TO GO: Dec–Apr.

✈ Sir Donald Sangster International Airport in Montego Bay.

🛏 $$$ **Jamaica Inn,** P.O. Box 1, Main St. (✆ **800/837-4608;** www.jamaicainn.com). $$ **Riu Ocho Rios,** Mammee Bay (✆ **876/972-2200;** www.clubhotelriuochorios.com).

Sandboarding the Dune of Pyla
Le Surf C'est Arrive
Pyla-sur-Mer, France

When the surf goes flat at France's renowned Silver Coast (Cote d'Argent), and there's no snow in the French Alps, there is still a thrill ride that awaits diehard adrenaline junkies: sandboarding down the largest sand dune in Europe, the dune of Pyla. At 110m (360 ft.) high, there are few waves that can really compare to that height, and the fine-grained sand that makes up the dune acts like snow—sandboarders can reach dizzying speeds comparable to those attained by snowboarders. All it takes to conquer the dune is a boogie board or a snowboard, and a whole lot of *joie de vivre*.

Sometimes spelled as Pilat, the great dune is located about 64km (40 miles) from the beautiful old city of Bordeaux, capital of one of France's great wine-producing regions. The 258km long (160 mile) Silver Coast, which stretches from the Spanish border north to the English Channel, has become famous for its pristine beaches, surf culture, and reliable surfing waves that are surprisingly uncrowded.

The hike from the beach to the top of the dune takes a few minutes, so you might want to pack some water. And because you'll be shredding sand and not water, some experienced boarders recommend bringing goggles or some other kind of eye protection. Once you reach the top, you'll be rewarded with a spectacular view of the ocean, Archachon Bay, and the dense forest of the Landes, planted in the 18th century by Napoleon to halt the progression of the sand dunes. Once you're done drinking in the view, take the plunge over the forest side of the dune on your board, and enjoy the ride!

If all that sandboarding doesn't leave you whipped, there are more thrills to be had in the area. Besides world-class surfing, the charming seaside resort of Arcachon enjoys the steady ocean breezes that make it a favorite windsurfing destination. And **Arcachon Aqualand** (www.aqualand.fr) is a local water park with waterslides, toboggans, and a wave pool. —*ML*

ⓘ **Dune of Pyla** (www.dune-pyla.com/english).

WHEN TO GO: Year-round.

✈ Bordeaux (64km/40 miles).

⊨ $ **Tulip Inn Bordeaux Le Bayonne Etche-Ona,** 15 cours de l'Intendance, Bordeaux (ⓒ **33/5-56-48-00-88;** www.bordeaux-hotel.com). $$ **Mercure Château Chartrons,** 81 cours St-Louis, Bordeaux (ⓒ **33/5-56-43-15-00;** www.mercure.com).

Dyke Jumping
First, Wooden Shoes, Now This
The Netherlands

While some adrenaline adventures are deadly serious business, dyke jumping will no doubt go down in history as one of mankind's sillier pastimes. It works like this: First, find a creek or a water-filled ditch (known as dykes in northern Europe). Run toward it, fully clothed, carrying nothing but a long stick or pole. Use the pole to vault over the dyke—or, if you fail to make it to the other side, get sopping wet and endure the ridicule of your dry dyke-jumping friends until your next turn.

According to legend, dyke jumping began less as amusement and more as a means of survival. Wandering vagrants would jump over the dykes that surrounded farmers' land, steal eggs and other foods, then jump back over before getting caught. The sport originated in Friesland, a province in the northern Netherlands that remains the capital of dyke jumping. Shortly after World War II, the sport evolved—though not much—into a competitive activity known as "fierljeppen" that some folks take very seriously. Belgium, the U.K., and even Japan have mounted teams to compete in the world dyke jumping championships. If you decide to give dyke jumping a go, you may want to wrap the rubber inner tube from a bicycle tire around your ankles and/or feet—not for the fashion appeal, but to help you grip the pole as you vault over the dyke. As you dig the pole into the muck, remember to shimmy up the pole while it's vertical to gain the necessary inch or two needed to make it across the dyke. Hopefully, your comrades in dyke jumping have prepared a soft landing spot on the other side made of sand or other material. You might not break the world record (currently set at an amazing 19m/64 ft.), but if you stay dry, consider yourself a winner. —*ML*

✈ Amsterdam.

🛏 $$$ **Bilderberg Garden Hotel,** Dijsselhofplantsoen 7 (✆ **31/20/570-5600;** www.gardenhotel.nl). $$ **Canal House,** Keizersgracht 148 (✆ **31/20/622-5182;** www.canalhouse.nl).

Zorb Globe Riding
Having a Ball
Rotorua, New Zealand

If you've ever wondered what it's like to be stuck inside a giant washing machine, here's your chance to find out: Zorbing, the newest adrenaline adventure that involves absolutely no skill whatsoever, puts you in the center of a gigantic bubble made of clear plastic and then sends that bubble—with you inside it—rolling down a steep hill. You can do this adventure without adding water (to find out what it's like inside a giant dryer, I suppose), but why not go the distance and add water for an extra splash of fun?

Rotorua, located in the center of New Zealand's North Island on the western shores of sulphur-smelling Lake Rotorua, is the premier place to experience Zorb—this is the original Zorb site and has been in operation for over 14 years. Just follow the signs to the Agrodome in Ngongotaha, and you're there. This sport originated in New Zealand, home of bungee jumping and other "stupid things to do on vacation," as the company's website proudly declares.

The Zorb globe looks like a huge cell from high school biology class. You'll enter the Zorb head-first through its "mouth" after taking off your shoes and jewelry. There's actually a smaller sphere inside the outer sphere, and the air space in between the two spheres helps to absorb the shocks you'll feel when you hit bumps at 32kmph (20 mph). After getting strapped in, you may want to invite a friend to join you in the Zorb—it can hold up to three adults. And because you'll be spinning upside down uncontrollably for a few minutes, it's best not to Zorb on a full stomach or while intoxicated, for reasons that should be obvious.

Some folks have reported that the plastic on older Zorbs has aged and become cloudy, which significantly reduces the visibility and the fun factor—call ahead to make sure you can get a clear Zorb. And afterwards, stick around the Rotorua area for more fun: the **Riverjet Thermal Safari** (www.riverjet.co.nz), the **White Island Volcano** (www.wi.co.nz), **Kaituna Cascades Raft & Kayak Expeditions** (www.kaitunacascades.co.nz), and **Waimangu Volcanic Valley** (www.waimangu.co.nz) are all top adventure destinations. —ML

ⓘ **Zorb Globe Riding** (✆ **64-7/357-5100;** www.zorb.com).

WHEN TO GO: Sept–Apr.

✈ Auckland (225km/140 miles).

🛏 $$ **The Springs,** 16 Devon St. (✆ **07/348-9922;** www.thesprings.co.nz). $$ **Duxton Hotel Rotorua,** 366 St. Hwy. 33 (✆ **0800/655-555;** www.duxton.com).

260 Unconventional Undertakings

Oregon Dunes National Recreation Area
Mr. Sandman, Bring Me a Dune
Reedsport, Oregon, U.S.A.

Some folks like driving the wide-open road, but if you'd rather drive where there's no road at all, you're going to love **Oregon Dunes National Recreation Area.** The area has more than 32,000 acres (12,950 hectares) of stunning wilderness right on the Pacific coast, stretching for 40 miles (64km) from one end to the other, and much of that is open for off-road adventures. Whether you choose to bring your own all-terrain vehicle (ATV), rent one from a local shop, or take a tour on a dune buggy, there's nothing like the thrill of the wind whipping through your hair as you fly across miles and miles of the largest expanse of coastal sand dunes in all of North America.

The Oregon Dunes National Recreation Area is part of Siuslaw National Forest (www.fs.fed.us/r6/siuslaw) and is contiguous to Honeyman State Park (www.oregonstateparks.org/park_134.php). Visitors can find up-to-date information on off-road access and other news at the Visitors Center in Reedsport, or through a number of local stores catering to the ATV crowd.

Be aware that there are decibel limits on vehicles (currently set at 93 db), and not all quarters of the dunes are open to off-road vehicles. The three main areas for off-roading are the Florence area between South Jetty and the Siltcoos River, the dunes between Spinreel and Horsfall, and the big, dramatic dunes in the Umpqua riding area.

These spectacular sand dunes are as high as 500 feet (150m) in some places, and there are some wildly steep drops and sharply angled dune crests for catching some serious air. Most tour operators and rental shops will emphasize the importance of safety—a number of recent crashes have filled up local hospital emergency rooms, which are not the place you want to end your vacation (or your life).

If, after sailing over dunes at breakneck speeds, you're looking for a slower or quieter pastime, the region has plenty to offer. An extensive trail network takes hikers through dense forests of Douglas fir and Sitka spruce, and dozens of lakes and ponds beckon water-skiers, canoeists, sailors, and fishermen. Horseback riding, beachcombing, and camping round out the activities available in this adventure-lovers mecca. —*ML*

ⓘ **Oregon Dunes National Recreation Area,** 855 Highway Ave., Reedsport (✆ **541/271-3611;** www.fs.fed.us/r6/siuslaw).

TOURS: Sand Dunes Frontier (✆ **541/997-5363;** www.sanddunesfrontier.com). **Sandland Adventures** (✆ **541/997-8087;** www.sandland.com).

WHEN TO GO: Apr–Oct.

✈ Eugene, OR (82 miles/132km).

▸ $ **Winchester Bay Inn,** 390 Broadway Ave., Winchester Bay (✆ **541/271-4871;** www.winbayinn.com). $$ **Salmon Harbor Landing,** 265 8th St., Winchester Bay (✆ **541/271-3742;** www.salmon harborlanding.com).

Unconventional Undertakings **261**

Desert Sailing
Parting the Dunes
Marsa Alam, Egypt

The Red Sea is not actually red. Its turquoise waters hold a myriad of colors, mostly Technicolor coral reefs and exotic marine life that has made it a major magnet for divers and sailors, especially along the Egyptian coast that has been christened the New Riviera. This ancient waterway is bordered by countries as diverse as Israel and Somalia and has an ancient heritage that involves pyramid-obsessed pharaohs and water-parting slaves. One of its newer, untold stories is the fact that it makes an excellent location for rattling along the golden sands on a three-wheel buggy and sail while onlookers sip tea in flapping tents.

The desert around Marsa Alam is hot, blazing, and silent, its emptiness belying a history as deep as a cave full of Red Sea Scrolls. This Egyptian fishing village on the southeast coast has so far avoided the hordes of sea divers that are thronging to the faux Moor domed resorts that have popped up around the northern shores of this long sea inlet that stretches nearly 2,300km (1,400 miles) south to the Indian Ocean. Cairo is 644km (400 miles) to the north of Marsa Alam, but it could be an eternity away as you stand in this flat, eerie land surrounded by pastel mountains colored pink, green, and yellow. Such serenity rudely evaporates as you mount the modern buggy with pneumatic wheels and race across the scrabble terrain. The tall, sleek sails harness brisk winds that propel screaming racers toward the gentle dunes at 48kmph (30 mph). It certainly makes a nice break from ogling hammerhead sharks in the shimmering bays.

Desert sailing is organized by an outfit called Red Sea Adventures, based in burgeoning Marsa Alam. It's a 2-hour excursion into the Hamata desert that makes up part of the vast Arabian desert, an inhospitable plain that runs south into nearby Sudan. A jeep takes you out into the desolate dunes where a patch of plain with strong winds proves an ideal spot for sailing without currents or buoys. The only waves are the rippled mountains of sand in the distance. After some brief instruction and donning some protective gear such as a helmet and goggles, you lie feet first and prostrate as the buggy gathers alarming speed and carries you with ease. It is certainly more exciting than a local camel ride and induces more of a rush than a visit to the nearby emerald mines. The day ends with a tiny cup of tea brewed by the local Bedouin tribe known as Ababda. You look across the ancient landscape and think of how Caesar and Napoleon may have conquered this land but they cannot claim to have done it on a sail buggy.

Marsa Alam is itself a tropical town of palm trees and mangroves divided between an ancient market town and an ambitious modern expansion of new resorts and stores besieged by the relentless desert. Goats scamper amidst the dusty streets while dolphins leap in the glistening waters. —CO'M

(i) **Red Sea Adventures** ((C) **20/123-993860;** www.redseadesertadventures.corn).

WHEN TO GO: Year round.

✈ Marsa Alam.

🛏 $$ **Iberotel Coraya Beach Resort,** Madinat Coraya, Marsa Alam, Egypt ((C) **20/65/375-0000;** www.iberotelegypy.com). $$ **Crowne Plaza Sahara Sands Resort,** Port Ghalib, P.O. Box 23, Marsa Alam, Egypt ((C) **20/65/336-0000;** www.ichotelsgroup.com).

262 Unconventional Undertakings

Schiermonnikoog
Wadlopen: A Walk on the Sea
The Netherlands

Low-lying Schiermonnikoog is like the pearl in a necklace of islands known as the West Frisian Islands on the Netherlands' northern shore. At 16km (10 miles) long and 4km (2½ miles) wide, Schier, as it's known to the locals, is the smallest of the inhabited islands in the Wadden Sea, and possibly the prettiest. But at low tide, something magical happens: The shallow sea actually disappears and you can walk all the way to the next island.

Mud flat hiking—*wadlopen*—is a wildly popular summer pastime around these parts. Hiking on these soggy surfaces lets you see up close and personal just how alive the mud flats can be, with worms, shrimp, crabs, and fish providing sustenance for a wide range of fauna. You can actually mudwalk from the village of Kloosterburen to Schiermonnikoog (8km/5 miles). If you're game for a *wadlopen*, however, don't even think about doing it alone—Dutch law prohibits self-guided mud-walking. Always go with a tour operator or outfitter (see below) and be sure to reserve a spot well in advance—fools sure do love company.

Since 1989, the whole island of Schiermonnikoog has been protected as a national park, a remarkable collection of habitats that range from birch forests to broad, white-sand beaches along the North Sea coast. In its salt marshes and wetlands you'll find thousands of migratory seabirds, with plenty of gulls, terns, and spoonbills. Ducks, herons, and reed birds gather around the freshwater Westerplas pond; seals sun themselves on sandbanks off the northwest coast. Rare plants like tiny orchids and Parnassus grass can be found around the moss- and lichen-covered dunes. Most vacationers visit between spring and fall; only a hardy few brave the winter gales. —*AF*

ⓘ **Visitor center,** Torenstreek 20 (✆ **31/ 519/531-641;** www.nationaalpark.nl/ schiermonnikoog). **Tourist office,** Reeweg 5 (✆ **31/519/531-233;** www. vvvschiermonnikoog.nl).

TOUR: Stichting (✆ **31/59/552-8300;** www.wadlopen.com).

✈ Amsterdam (2 hr. to Lauwersoog).

🚢 45 min. from Lauwersoog.

🛏 $ **Hotel van der Werff,** Reeweg 2 (✆ **31/519/531-203;** www.hotelvanderwerff.nl). $ **Pension Westerburen,** Middenstreek 32 (✆ **31/65/221-2287;** www. westerburen.nl).

Texas Grape Stomp
The Lone Stomp State
Locations throughout Texas, U.S.A.

Your feet are purple, your clothes are ruined, and there's a grin as big as Texas on your face. You must be at a grape stomp, one of the Lone Star State's newest adventures. Though better known for beer and barbecue, Texas has a wine industry that's been gaining attention among oenophiles nationwide, and what better way to celebrate the state's newfound status as a wine-producing region than with a good, old-fashioned grape stomp?

A handful of wineries located throughout central and west Texas sponsor grape stomps on a monthly or annual basis. Some of these events are competitive— *very* competitive—and individuals or teams stomp ferociously to see who can squeeze out the most juice from a barrel of grapes, with proceeds going to local charities or youth groups. Grape stomping may seem easy, but it's a real workout; 10 minutes of stomping grapes can exhaust most weekend warriors.

After a long afternoon of stomping grapes, slake your thirst by sampling some fruit of the vine—most wineries that sponsor grape stomps also offer wine tastings. At many events, you can also expect to find live music concerts, food-and-wine pairings, grape picking, and wine classes. And be sure to bring the kids along, because most festivals also sponsor a kid's grape stomp, as well as other family-friendly fun. —*ML*

ⓘ **Great Grape Stomp Championship,** 8484 Hwy. 46, New Braunfels, TX 78132 (✆ **800/303-6780;** www.grapestomp. com). **Caprock Winery,** 408 E. Woodrow Rd., Lubbock, TX 79423 (✆ **806/863-2704;** www. caprockwinery.com). **Pleasant Hill Winery,** 1441 Salem Rd.,

Grape stomping in Texas.

Brenham, TX 77833 (℡ **979/830-VINE;** www.pleasanthillwinery.com). **Bernhardt Winery,** 9043 C.R. 204, Plantersville, TX 77363 (℡ **936/894-9829;** www.bernhardt winery.com). **Messina Hof Winery,** 4545 Old Reliance Rd., Bryan, TX 77808 (℡ **979/778-9829;** www.messinahof. com).

WHEN TO GO: Summer and autumn; check local listings for festivals and dates.

5 Great Journeys

Jbel Toubkal
Northern Africa's Tallest Peak
High Atlas Mountains, Morocco

Morocco is magical—and climbing Jbel Toubkal, the highest mountain in Northern Africa, is one of its most spellbinding experiences. But it's no small feat; it takes will, determination, and a spirit of adventure—not to mention a sturdy pair of hiking shoes and strong legs. The best time to go is during the late spring and summer, when you can ascend without special climbing skills or equipment.

Just 64km (40 miles) south of Marrakesh, the eco-friendly **Kashbah du Toubkal**—a secluded mountain retreat run by the local Berber community—makes a perfect starting point for your trek and feels much farther than it is from the bustling city. Unless you recognize it from Martin Scorsese's film *Kundun*, arriving at this "Berber hospitality center" feels like uncovering a hidden palace. For the

90-minute ride from Marrakesh, you can take a bus or hire a car and driver. Toward the end of the journey, you'll wind along a steep mountain road until you reach the village of Imil, where it's time to start using your legs.

Along with a guide and a couple of mules to carry your luggage, your adventure begins. You'll walk for 15 minutes or so along a gravel path, up some stairs, into a grassy garden, and finally through the kasbah's heavy wooden doors. On the terrace, as you sip a small glass of sweet mint tea, you'll see the snow-capped peak of Jbel Toubkal in the distance. It takes about 2 days from here to reach the summit at 4,167m (13,665 ft.).

The journey begins with a fairly steep zigzag route to an easier roadway that takes you through a small gorge, past the

The Kashbah du Toubkal.

village of Aremd. After crossing into a valley of fields and orchards, you'll continue trekking for about 2 hours, along the mountain paths with only sparse vegetation, sheep, and goats until you reach Sidi Chamharouch (2,320m/7,612 ft.). There are several small shops and cafes at this settlement, as well as a white-roofed mosque and water that is supposed to have healing powers. About 2 hours later, you'll approach Neltner Hut. If you'd rather not sleep in the tented encampment here, which is quite nice by camping standards, you can arrange accommodations in a local Berber family's home or at the Toubkal Lodge.

The next day, hiking begins again after crossing a small river gorge and walking up a steep slope for about 2 hours until you reach Tizi-n-Toubkal (3,940m/12,927 ft.). The altitude here can make you dizzy and nauseous, so remember to walk slowly and drink plenty of water as you follow the mountain ridge for another 3 to 4 hours until you reach the summit.

At the summit are a large, iron, pyramidal structure and excellent views—haze and weather permitting. Look toward the south, where you can see the Saharan plateau broken by the extinct volcano Siroua. After you descend, plan to spend another night at the kasbah and relax your tired muscles with a long scrub in the beautiful *hammam* (Morocan bath). —*JS*

(i) **Moroccan Tourist Office** (C **212/537-67-4013** or 212/537-3918; www.visit morocco.com).

TOUR: Mountain Voyage Morocco (C **212/524-42-1996;** www.mountain-voyage.com).

WHEN TO GO: Apr–Oct.

✈ Marrakesh-Menara Airport.

⊨ $$–$$$ **Kasbah du Toubkal,** Imil (C **33/052-905-0135;** www.kasbahdu toubkal.com).

Expeditions **265**

Valle de la Luna
An Out-of-This-World Adventure
Atacama Desert, Chile

If you've ever wanted to take a walk on the moon, this is the place for you. Set in the Cordillera de la Sal (or Salt Mountains), west of San Pedro de Atacama (about a 2-hr. flight from Santiago) and south of the new highway, the Valley de la Luna (or Valley of the Moon) has an otherworldly feel. The unique formations of reddish-brown stone, petrified salt, and sand have been molded by floods and winds over thousands of years. Virtually no rain has fallen here to alter the landscape or help things grow; the Atacama Desert is the driest place on earth.

The best way to explore this surreal terrain is to climb the massive sand dunes, and the prime time to do it is in the late afternoon. As dusk falls, the light casts long shadows on the vast expanses. The

wind whisks grains of sand back and forth, creating a sort of moving mountain beneath your feet as you make your way across the flat peaks of massive dunes. Walking across the narrow top of a sand dune at such a high altitude is a bit dizzying, but mostly you feel like the "King (or Queen) of the Mountain." Once you get your balance and some confidence, walk faster or run. Just make sure you've reached a good spot to witness one of the world's most magnificent sunsets.

The temperature drops quickly after the sun falls, so roll down the dunes and head back to the tiny town of San Pedro for dinner. Afterward (or the following night if you're too tired), dress warmly and head out into the darkness to gaze at the countless stars twinkling in the sky. Because of the desert's high altitude, nearly non-existent cloud cover, and lack of light pollution or radio interference, it's one of the best places in the world to conduct astronomical observations. You can see this for yourself on an astronomical tour—led by French astronomer Alain Maury and his wife—called **SPACE Agency,** Caracole St. 166 (✆ **565/585-1935** or 569/817-8354; www.spaceobs.com). You'll take a van to the couple's home, where you'll view constellations and nebulae through brilliant telescopes in their backyard, followed by an indoor slideshow and hot chocolate. Don't miss this eye-opening experience.

If you're staying in the area for 4 or 5 days, you'll find plenty to do. San Pedro itself is well worth exploring. In fact, when you first arrive, walk around the town for a day before embarking on any hikes or potentially exerting activities. You'll need to adjust to the altitude, and set up your tours for the things you want to do (like Valle de La Luna). Other area highlights include the El Tatio Geysers, Lagunas Altiplanicas, and Salar de Atacama. After your many adventures, relax by bathing in the volcanic hot springs at Termas de Puritama. —*JS*

ⓘ www.sanpedroatacama.com.

TOUR: Choose from one of the many tour operators along the main street in San Pedro de Atacama.

WHEN TO GO: Apr–Nov, late afternoon before sunset.

✈ Calama, Chile.

🛏 $$–$$$ **Hotal Aliplanico Atacama** (✆ **56-55/851-212;** www.rapanui.cl).

Horseback Riding in Argentina
Drink Up & Giddy Up Like the Gauchos
Mendoza, Argentina

A bottle of Malbec and a steak dinner is obviously the best way to get a taste of sun-kissed Mendoza, Argentina's most beloved wine region. But the area isn't revered only for its wineries; it's also home to one of the country's best and most accessible outdoor playgrounds. To work up your appetite and a thirst, spend some time giddying up into the wilderness.

Just 3 hours from Buenos Aires, Mendoza makes the perfect getaway for adrenaline seekers too short on time to reach Patagonia. Outside of the small but lively center city, the countryside's vineyards, desert landscape, rolling hills, rushing river, charming villages, and ski resorts are framed by the Central Andes, best known for the Western Hemisphere's highest peak—Mt. Aconcagua—at 6,962m (22,840 ft.). November to March is climbing season, when you can attempt to reach its summit or take one of the many other challenging hikes through this vast mountain range. Bikes are readily available for exploring wineries. And the Mendoza River is a popular place for white water rafting. But the most exceptional thrill in this part of the world comes from galloping into the rugged landscape on horseback with an Argentine *gaucho* (cowboy).

Depending on your skill set and interest level, local tour companies and *estancias* (ranches) can arrange horseback rides that last a few hours or a few days. The best place to ride a hardy Argentine Criollo, the favored breed among gauchos and an equestrian symbol across Latin America, is at **La Guatana** (www.criolloslaguatana.com.ar). Ask for Cesar.

As your horse picks his way through the bush, up and down steep terrain, between the rows of orderly vineyards, through

209

streams, and straight across open plains, the environment's diversity is startling.

Around noon when the sun is really beating down, it's time for a break. If you're lucky, you'll be rewarded with a traditional *asado*, the Argentine barbeque cooked on a *parilla* (grill). Starting with *morcillas* (blood sausage), followed by *mollejas* (sweetbreads), the meal slowly progresses toward finer cuts of meat such as ribs and flank steak. The customary carafe of red wine is a perfect complement to this midday feast. —*JS*

ⓘ **Argentina Tourism Board** (ℰ **0800-555-0016;** www.turismo.gov.ar/eng).

TOUR: Malbec Experience (ℰ **54/0261-454-8981;** www.malbecexperience.com).

WHEN TO GO: Year-round, but especially Oct–May.

✈ Mendoza airport.

⊨ $$ **Finca Adalgisa,** Chacras de Coria (ℰ **54/0261-496-0713;** www.fincaadalgisa.com.ar). **Estancia el Puesto,** Alto Valle de Uco (ℰ **54/261-439-3533;** www.estanciaelpuesto.com.ar/English).

Expeditions 267

Trekking Bhutan
The Himalayas' Most Captivating Kingdom
Paro, Thimphu, Punahka & Gangtey, Bhutan

Ever since tourists were first allowed into Bhutan in 1974, the government has continued to limit the number of people granted access, inherently casting an aura of mystique over this intensely spiritual Buddhist kingdom in the beautiful Himalayas. Independent travel is strictly forbidden, so even if tour groups make your skin crawl, you'll have to get used to the idea if you want to get a foot in the door here.

Bhutan isn't a cheap or easy destination, but it's a real utopia for adventure lovers who love trekking through the world's most remote mountains and lush valleys, learning about ancient cultures, and meeting friendly locals. After touring the top sights in **Paro, Thimphu,** and **Punahka**—including a hike to Tiger's Nest Monastery, a stroll through weekend markets, and visits to important temples—a 2-day hike through **Gangtey** is a must. This gorgeous region of snow-capped peaks; primeval forests carpeted with bamboo, magnolia, and rhododendrons; and secluded monasteries is the essence of Bhutan. The valley is home to the country's largest monastery for Nyingmapa Buddhists, and legends about it abound in

the monks' storytelling of its history. If time allows, you can also arrange to do more trekking, try fly-fishing, visit local farmhouses, or even meet with local monks and politicians.

For a longer trek, don't miss the 7-day hike to **Chomolhari,** Bhutan's most sacred peak, rising 7,308m (23,977 ft.) along its border with Tibet. If you come here in the spring, you'll walk through tiny remote villages, valleys with pear and apple trees, and forests covered in blooming azaleas and wildflowers. In the fall, you'll see yak herders bringing their animals down from summer pastures, and ice paddies ripening to a golden brown.

If your feet are itching for more movement, take the 10-day trek to the world's highest unclimbed mountain, **Gangkhar Puensum,** reaching 7,540m (24,735 ft.). The Bhutanese have declared its peak off limits out of respect to its holy character, but you're permitted to hike to the base. On your way, you'll pass through dense evergreen forests, up a green and gold tundra valley, across Thole La, and along the Chamkar River to the mountain's icy beginnings. This is the only place in the

The Tiger's Nest Monastery in Bhutan.

vowed to maintain Bhutan's distinctive Gross National Happiness measure, which gauges the country's progress by placing a high value on spiritual development.

Even here, though, things are beginning to modernize. The country held its first parliamentary elections in March 2008, making it the world's youngest democracy. And, as modern technology, such as cellphones and the Internet, continue seeping in—along with higher-end hotels like the Aman Resorts chain that now operates here—Bhutan is likely to undergo more palpable changes. Don't wait too long to wander through this captivating kingdom for yourself. —JS

ⓘ **Tourism Council of Bhutan,** Thimphu (ⓒ **975/2-323-251;** www.tourism.gov.bt).

TOUR: Geographic Expeditions, 1008 General Kennedy Ave., San Francisco, CA (ⓒ **800/777-8183;** www.geoex.com). **Artisans of Leisure,** 18 East 16th St., New York, NY (ⓒ **800/214-8144;** www. artisansofleisure.com). **Mt. Travel Sobek,** 1266 66th St., Emeryville, CA (ⓒ **510/ 594-6000;** www.mtsobek.com).

WHEN TO GO: Spring and fall.

✈ Paro Airport.

⛴ Work with your tour operator to make arrangements for hotels, guesthouses, or camping.

world where snow leopards and Bengal tigers cohabitate.

The small kingdom of Bhutan, which was never colonized by Western powers, remains an independent and peaceful haven in Asia. The government's travel restrictions have helped protect much of the country's natural environment and traditional culture, making it one of the planet's most entrancing destinations. The newest king, Jigme Khesar Namgyel Wangchuck, recently

---

268 Expeditions

Trekking in the Dogon Country
Traveling Back in Time
Kani Kombole to Sangha Villages, Mali

One of West Africa's few remaining animist communities, the Dogon people still live in longstanding villages sprinkled throughout Mali's central plateau region. While nearly 500,000 people carry on the traditional ways of life here and speak more than 50 distinct versions of the original Dogon dialect, things are beginning to

change as trekking the "Dogon country" becomes one of Mali's more beaten paths.

Despite the area's recent popularity and the ensuing touts who are overly eager (though often unqualified) to show you around, getting here and around isn't easy—it's an extremely long and arduous journey that mainly appeals to adventure travelers who don't mind roughing it. If that sounds like you, go soon and make the trip in September or October to avoid the crowds; that's the end of the rainy season but just before the tourist season begins. If you don't mind being around lots of other backpackers, you'll have fine weather through February.

The Dogon country is bisected by the Bandiagara Escarpment, a sandstone cliff that reaches nearly 500m (1,640 ft.) high and about 150km (100 miles) across. Its walls allegedly provided some defense when the Dogon refused to convert to Islam almost a thousand years ago. The choice of this location was probably also based on its proximity to the Niger River.

Today, the Dogon are best known for their unique mask dances, wooden sculptures, and architecture. They perform moving, time-honored mask dances at the end of mourning periods to encourage a loved one's spirit to depart the village and join his or her ancestors. Sculptures revolve around religious ideals, and often portray figures with raised arms, bending from the waist, or covering their faces; women with children, grinding grains, or carrying vessels on their heads; and animals such as horses, dogs, and donkeys. They are not intended for public viewing, and are often kept inside houses and sanctuaries. Dogon villages are composed of

beautifully intricate mud buildings, many with pointed roofs and multiple levels.

To visit, you'll need a visa, proof of your yellow fever vaccination, and anti-malarial pills. With those in hand, you'll take a long flight to Bamako, followed by a 9-hour bus ride to Sevare. After an overnight there, and perhaps a side trip to Djenne (home to the world's largest mud mosque), you'll take another (albeit shorter) bus ride to the Dogon country where the much-anticipated trekking portion of your trip begins. As you travel between small villages, you'll hike between 10km (6.2 miles) and 20km (12.4 miles) each day, eat what's put in front of you (and don't expect it to be vegetarian), and sleep in a no-frills tent on the ground.

The Dogon country remains an exciting destination for anyone fascinated by different kinds of culture, art, and religion. The money generated by tourism is also an important revenue source for the local community. —JS

ⓘ **The U.S. Embassy of Mali** (ℂ **202/ 332-2249;** http://maliembassy.us).

TOUR: Saga Tours, Magnambougou rural, Secteur 2 (ℂ **223/2020-2708;** www. sagatours.com).

WHEN TO GO: Sept–Feb.

✈ Bamako Senou International Airport, followed by a bus ride to Dogon country.

Trekking the Taman Negara Rainforest
Exploring the Land of the Lost
Taman Negara National Park, Malaysia

Most forest hikes will take you back into nature, but some treks can take you back in time. Taman Negara is the ideal place for such an experience; some 130 million years old, the forests that make up this immense park are relatively untouched by human hands, making it one of the rarest and most beautiful nature reserves in the world. The million-plus acres of this park

are home to rare orchids and other exotic plants, as well as endangered animals such as the Malayan peacock-pheasant, leopards, the Sumatran rhinoceros, the Indochinese tiger, leaf monkeys, monitor lizards, and the Asian elephant. A glimpse of these creatures in their spectacular home is a breathtaking experience.

Located near the center of the Malay Peninsula, the park is easily accessible by bus from Kuala Lumpur, and traveling by boat to your resort destination only adds to the mystery and allure of this tropical rainforest. There are several resort operators who, in addition to providing meals and arranging treks and other activities, will provide a coach transfer to and from Kuala Lumpur.

There's no shortage of things to do once you're settled into your accommodations. **Gunung Tahan,** the tallest mountain in peninsular Malaysia at 2,150m (7,175 ft.) above sea level, can be reached by climbers departing from Merapoh or Kuala Tahan. The park's canopy walkway, which takes hikers through the treetops of the rainforest, is the longest in the world and is over 24m (80 ft.) off the ground, affording spectacular views to those without vertigo. **Gua Telinga,** or Ear Cave, named for a rock formation that's shaped like a human ear, is one of several cave systems in the

area; it's home to several species of rare bats, frogs, and other fauna. And **river tours** are available for those who love to fish or swim in the area's pristine rivers. Whether you choose a short day hike, a night trek, or a longer, more strenuous multi-day adventure, you'll come to appreciate why the Malaysian people are justly proud of this jewel in the crown of their park system. —ML

TOURS: Tahan Holidays (✆ **603/5636-1898;** www.tahan.com.my). **Han Travel** (✆ **03/2031-0899;** www.taman-negara. com).

WHEN TO GO: Apr–Sept.

✈ Kuala Lumpur.

🛏 $$$ **Mutiara Taman Negara Resort,** Kuala Tahan, Jerantut, 27000 Pahang (✆ **609/266-3500;** www.mutiarahotels. com). $ **Agoh Chalet,** Kuala Tahan (✆ **609/ 266-9570;** www.agoh.com.my).

---

270 Expeditions

Exploring the Land of Fire & Ice
An Adventurer's Dreamland
Reykjavik to Landmannalaugar, Iceland

Iceland hasn't had it easy for the past few years. One of the first countries to crumble under the weight of the global financial crisis, it is just now slowly moving toward economic recovery—thanks to multilateral assistance and domestic policy measures—but forecasts predict that growth is still a ways off. In the meantime, this young European country could really use your tourism dollars, and you'll get a huge bang for your buck. If you like peculiar, often isolated, places with wildly odd geological formations, you'll find a lot to get excited about in Iceland.

Don't let its name fool you. Although nearly 11% of the country is covered in ice and it's home to Europe's largest glacier, the other 89% of its terrain varies from green fertile valleys and farmlands; to

fjords, waterfalls, and hot springs; to sandy beaches; to volcanoes, lava rocks, and mountains. In other words, you'll have countless opportunities for adventures— including hiking, ice climbing, abseiling, biking, horseback riding, motorcycle riding, kayaking, white water rafting, fishing, and caving. During the summer solstice, the country is bathed in everlasting sunlight, a thrilling experience in itself.

One of the best ways to explore Iceland is by driving around its coastline on the roughly 1,335km (830 miles) **Ring Road,** more formally known as Highway 1. After arriving, make **Blue Lagoon** your first stop. Tucked into lava rock, this large manmade bathtub filled with hot blue-green saltwater and sulfurous steam clouds is the perfect place to unwind after your

Rafting in Iceland is a great way to see some of the unusual geological formations that dot the country.

flight. Temporarily refreshed, spend a night in **Reykjavik,** a charming city with cobblestone streets that offers some pretty rambunctious nightlife—particularly when it stays light outside well after midnight. When you've had enough late-night fun in the sun, get some sleep and then hit the road to see some of nature's most astounding creations.

As you start off in the coastal countryside, plan to spend a couple of nights on a **farm** for a chance to see how locals really live, and even lend a hand with some of the crops or animals. **Icelandic Farm Holidays** (© 354/570-2700; www.farmholidays.is) can help you set up your stay. From here, drive northeast toward **Lake Myvatn,** where you'll find a vast body of water among volcanic craters and lava

that creates a sort of eerie moonscape. The village of **Vogar** has a fine guesthouse, and there are plenty of interesting sites nearby. If you've got a four-wheel-drive vehicle, head inland next, crossing the central highlands to **Asjka.** This stark, desolate volcanic caldera is allegedly where U.S. astronauts first trained before going to the moon. Once you make it back to the coastal highway, continue south until you reach the town of **Vik.** From here, drive to **Landmannalaugar,** a geothermal hotbed that boasts colorful dreamlike hills and lava outcroppings. One of Iceland's most popular and exhilarating experiences is the **Laugavegurinn,** a 4-day trek to **Thorsmork,** an alpine oasis. If you're short on time, skip the Ring Road and catch a bus from Reykjavik to get here. You can make arrangements with **The Icelandic Touring Association** (© 354/568-2533; www.fi.is) to stay in mountain huts along the way. Whatever fascinating elements of fire and ice you discover in Iceland, you won't be disappointed. In fact, you might even start conjuring up your next trip back here on your plane ride home. —*JS*

ⓘ **Iceland Tourist Board** (© 800/245-6555; www.icelandtouristboard.com).

TOURS: Arctic Adventures, Laugavegur 11 (© 354/562-7000; www.adventures.is). **Nonni Travel,** Brekkugata 5 (© 354/461-1841; www.nonnitravel.is).

WHEN TO GO: May–Sept; Dec–Jan to see the Northern Lights.

✈ Keflavik International Airport.

🛏 $–$$ **Alfholl Guesthouse,** Ranargata 8, Reykjavik (© 354/898-1838; www.islandia.is/alf). $$ **Hilton Reykjavik Nordica,** Sudurlandsbraut 2, Reykjavik (© 354/444-5000; www1.hilton.com).

271 Expeditions

River Boating Along the Amazon
Where the Wild Things Are
From Iquitos, Peru

The Amazon has tempted explorers since the 16th century when an intrepid European first encountered it. In 1912, after losing the election for a third term as president, Teddy Roosevelt set off into the deepest depths of the Brazilian jungle and ventured toward one of its then uncharted tributaries known as the River of Doubt. Today, the world's largest river by volume and second longest (after the Nile) is much easier to navigate, but just as alluring.

Most boat rides into the Upper Amazon begin in Iquitos—the most populous city in the world that's unreachable by road, and an adventure destination in its own right. This urban oasis is a good spot to settle in for a few days before immersing yourself in the rainforest. Don't miss the open-air **Belen Market,** where you'll get a taste of local life.

From Iquitos, you'll travel about 80km (50 miles) down the Amazon. Traveling along the dark waters, far into the depths of the wild, your senses become increasingly acute and your heart pounds, unsure of what might be lurking around the next bend. The Amazon is home to a vast biodiversity: more than 2,000 species of fish; 4,000 different

kinds of birds; 60 reptiles, including anaconda, the world's largest non-poisonous snake; and mammals ranging from anteaters and pumas to dolphins and crocodiles. Scientists are still working to classify it all, and environmentalists are still striving to preserve this wondrous part of earth.

When you reach the **Yanamono Stream,** you'll check into the secluded **Explorama Lodge.** Using this as your base for a day or two, you'll hike through the lowland rainforest or take short boat excursions if the water's too high to walk through. You may even spot a freshwater dolphin.

Next, head farther into the Amazon until you reach the **Napo River,** where there's a field station for research and another solitary lodge nearby, this one a bit more rustic than the last. Here, you can walk across a swaying canopy walkway, suspended high up in the treetops, that spans 500m (⅓ mile) and reaches more than 35m (115 ft.) above the forest floor. You can take other boating excursions, hike into the forest to learn about medicinal plants with a shaman, visit with local river people, and even take a jungle walk at night. When it's finally time to retire to your lodge or camp out beneath the pitch black sky, you may or may not actually glimpse the nocturnal animals lurking around, but just knowing they're somewhere out there is enough to keep your heart racing and eyes open for part of the night. —*JS*

ⓘ **Peru Tourism Bureau** (www.visit peru.com).

TOUR: Amazon Explorama Lodges (✆ **51/65-25-2530;** www.explorama.com).

WHEN TO GO: Dec–May for the highest waters and most boat excursions; July–Oct for more trekking.

✈ Iquitos airport.

A canopy walkway suspended above the great river.

Make a Difference

Taking a trip that includes volunteering in a local community or helping after a natural disaster can be an extremely gratifying experience. Combine that altruistic agenda with an opportunity for an adrenaline rush, and you have the experience of a lifetime. We've listed some of our top choices below for ways to make a difference, while still having an awfully good time. —LF

272 Roadmonkey Adventure Philanthropy: Roadmonkey's trips are designed for travelers who want to combine rugged adventures and hands-on volunteer work. Each of the participants on a trip must raise $500 in tax-deductible contributions through their own social networks. The donations fund the group's volunteer projects. In Tanzania, for example, along with climbing Kilimanjaro (see **165**), the team helps a local community build a clean-water system and build and paint several school classrooms in Mbagala. ✆ *917/319-8070; www.roadmonkey.net.*

273 U.S.A. Ranch Volunteers: Not many people get the opportunity to spend 3 weeks on a working ranch in Wyoming, horse wrangling, gathering cattle, and helping brand cows. In addition to long hours riding the range during cattle drives, you may also have a chance to help veterinarians during their weekly visits and vaccination days. You'll get a chance to rest those saddle-sore muscles, if you take a half-day or occasional full day off to explore the surrounding region. If you have a car, **Yellowstone** (www.nps.gov/yell) and **Grand Teton National Parks** (www.nps.gov/grte) are both an easy drive. *Real Gap Experience* ✆ *866/939-9088; www.realgap.com).*

274 Crocodile Conservation Center, Chennai, India: After immediate hands-on training during your month-long assignment with the Crocodile Conservation Center, you act as a visitor's guide, supervising guests as they handle baby crocodiles and pythons. Of course, you have to spend time feeding animals, too, as well as cleaning out pens that hold Mugger, Gharial, and Saltwater crocs. The center, which cares for about 2,400 crocodiles, is set on eight acres of coastal land south of Chennai. *Twin Work and Volunteer Abroad* ✆ *800/80-483-80; www.workandvolunteer.com).*

275 Tropical Wildlife Conservation & Adventure Project, Cambodia: Based in a remote field camp in Cambodia's **Botum Sakor National Park,** participants on this trip trek through the jungle and forests to survey mammals, record botanic and soil findings, and seek tracks and signs of the elusive sun-bear and fishing cat. Along the way, you may visit small villages where, with the aid of an interpreter, you'll assess how reliant the communities are on the forest and jungle resources around them. Expect to live in tents you help construct, sleep in hammocks, and bathe in the river. Trips run from 3 to 20 weeks. *Frontier-Cambodia* ✆ *44/20-7613-2344; www.frontier.ac.uk).*

276 i-to-i: If you'd like to save sea turtles in **Costa Rica,** work with children and see the country's endangered Mountain Gorillas in **Uganda,** or coach soccer in **Argentina,** i-to-i can help you make the connections. This adventure volunteer organization matches you with local groups, so you can do volunteer work and experience the country and culture while you are there. © *800/985-4852; www.i-to-i.com.*

277 Earthwatch: Every year some 4,000 volunteers with Earthwatch collect field data in such areas as rainforest ecology, wildlife conservation, marine science, and archaeology. On one trip, you're based at the **Cheetah Conservation Fund**'s working farm in Namibia, where you get to feed and care for captive cheetahs on-site and participate in wildlife surveys. Alternatively, you could take an **Amazon boat trip** to help with the conservation of monkeys, sea otters, and birds as well as track puma, jaguarundi, and other cats in Argentina's pampas grass. © *800/776-0188 or 44/1865-318 838; www.earthwatch.org.*

Those on a trip organized by Earthwatch help release a cheetah in Namibia.

278 Sierra Club Outings: This arm of the Sierra Club offers hands-on volunteer vacations in the U.S. aimed at getting participants involved in adventurous and rewarding volunteer work. The dozens of volunteer trips run the gamut from rugged backcountry challenges and base-camp trips to a lodge-based volunteer travel experience. You could work on Santa Cruz Island in the **Channel Islands National Marine Sanctuary,** where sightings of endangered blue, humpback, and sei whales are common during seasonal migrations. On the island, you'd be removing invasive plants, including eucalyptus and periwinkle. © *415/977-5522; www.sierraclub.org/outings.*

279 Projects Abroad: This company offers so many volunteer-based trips that it's hard to focus on just one. For example, a trip to the **Romanian countryside** allows you to work with the **History Museum of Brasov** to investigate ancient Dacia and the medieval environs of Transylvania. You'll be in and around archaeological sites in the Carpathian Mountains that have already yielded some remarkable information about the time of the infamous Vlad the Impaler, the supposed inspiration for Dracula. Volunteers may work on digs during the summer or assist with restoration work during the winter. © *888/839-3535 in the U.S., 877/921-9666 in Canada; www.projects-abroad.org.*

280 GlobeAware: GlobeAware offers lots of short-term (1 week) adventures in service that focus on cultural-awareness and sustainability. For example, you could spend a week helping with community projects in a tiny village that borders Costa Rica's **Carara Rainforest.** The villagers here want to create sustainable community-based tourism. The specific project you'll work on will be determined based on the community's needs at the time you are there. Previous projects have included building pedestrian bridges, a recycling center, and a first-aid center. Other countries with adventure trips available include Mexico, Brazil, Nepal, and Laos. © *877/LUV-GLOBE* (588-4562); *www.globeaware.org.*

Wildebeest Migration
The Last Mass Herd Migration on Earth
Masai Mara National Reserve, Kenya

No doubt about it, nature reigns in Kenya, and the annual wildebeest migration is its most spectacular show. Every year in June, more than a million wildebeest form a single herd and move from Tanzania's Serengeti National Park toward Kenya's Masai Mara National Reserve in search of greener pastures. By August or September, most of the animals have arrived and spread out to graze in the Mara. They fertilize the plains before making their way south in late October. This awe-inspiring event, Earth's last remaining mass herd migration, lures countless adventure seekers and nature lovers who come to witness masses of animals moving to their own soundtrack of pounding hoofs and guttural grunts.

It's seductive. As you wait for it, watching, your heart beats faster, your eyes open wider, and your ears hear more clearly. Your body tingles with anticipation. You pass a lone baobab tree. White morning glories dot the earth's green canvas. And then suddenly you witness it—pure natural wonder. Throngs of wildebeest gallop past, followed by zebras and gazelles. Elephants wave their trunks up and down, rhythmically splashing themselves with red mud (a natural sunblock and bug repellent). A lion and lioness cuddle in open grassland. Hippos pop their heads in and out of water. Warthogs mate. Florescent birds gloat above the earth. Buffaloes graze. A predator attacks a weaker creature, pointed teeth pulling apart flesh, before a hyena comes by for leftover scraps.

To get the best overview of the animal kingdom, fly into Nairobi and out the next day. Spend as much time as possible outdoors in Masai Mara (Kenya's most well known and popular game park), but also consider spending a few days exploring Amboseli National Park and Tsavo West National Park.

During most times of the year in Kenya, it's hard to plan or promise things—largely because no one can control what animals you'll see on your safari. The country's poor roads and oft-delayed flights also tend to discourage precise timetables. But during the wildebeest migration, you're pretty much guaranteed to spot wildebeests, zebras, and gazelles in the Mara. In fact, you'll probably see most of the Big Five—elephant, lion, black rhino, and leopard—or even the Big Nine, which includes hippopotamus, zebra, giraffe, and cheetah, plus hundreds of birds.

The best kinds of accommodations for a safari in Kenya are tent camps on conservancies. Hearing hyenas howl at night, with just thick canvas separating you from them, is thrilling. Tents set on private land, often leased directly from local Masai communities, also have fewer restrictions than ones directly in the national parks, which means that you might be able to try a walking or nighttime safari.

After an adrenaline-packed afternoon of discovering animals in the wild, there's no better way to unwind than with a sundowner. You'll head to a picturesque spot, maybe with Mount Kilimanjaro in the distance to enjoy a gin and tonic, Tusker beer, or glass of wine while reminiscing about the breathtaking phenomenon that nature has just shared with you. —*JS*

ⓘ **Kenya Tourism Board,** Kenya-Re Towers, Ragati Rd. (✆ **866/44-KENYA;** www.magicalkenya.com).

TOUR: Gamewatchers Safaris (✆ **800/ 998-6634;** www.porini.com). **&Beyond** (✆ **27/11-809-4314;** www.andbeyond. com).

WHEN TO GO: Aug–Oct for the wildebeest migration, but May–July and mid-Dec to Feb are good times for other safaris.

✈ Nairobi International Airport (also known as Jomo Kenyatta International Airport).

🛏 $$$ **Mara Porini Camp,** Ol Kinyei, and **Porini Lion Camp,** Olare Orok Conservancy (📞 **254/20-712-3129** or 254/20-712-2504; www.porini.com). $$$–$$$$ **Kichwa Tembo,** Oloololo Escarpment (📞 **27/11-809-4314;** www.kichwatembo.com).

282 **Animal Treks**

Reindeer Migration
Following Rudolph in the Arctic
Lapland, Sweden

Beyond the Arctic Circle, in the far north of Sweden, the nomadic Sami people have been herding reindeer for centuries. But few people from other parts of the world have explored this unspoiled and enchanting place.

With its stunning rugged landscape of mountains, lakes, forests, and tundras, Lapland is one of the most unique places on Earth to enjoy nature. Just 3½ hours by plane from London's Heathrow airport, the town of Gällivare is where you'll meet your Sami guides before embarking on a journey into the wilderness to witness the spectacular reindeer migration.

Each spring, more than 200,000 reindeer migrate more than 200km (124 miles) from the woodlands to the mountains in Laponia, a UNESCO World Heritage Site. Brace yourself for the cold (the temperature is often –6 to 1°C/ 20–30°F this time of year), and be prepared to carry a light pack of your personal belongings, while you follow a reindeer herd and help the local Sami herders with their work. In groups no larger than 10 people, you'll travel on skis and snowmobiles for about a week, learning about the Sami's traditional way of life. Reindeer have been central to the Samis throughout history—they eat their meat, and use them to carry heavy loads (including most of your camping gear and the heavier equipment necessary for your trip). There are about 20,000

Sami Sweden, and while most now live urban lives, about 2,500 Sami families still carry on the reindeer herding tradition. The Sami are Europe's only indigenous people.

As you travel through the remote Arctic highlands, you'll sleep in a time-honored Sami "kata" or "lavvu" (similar to a teepee tent) with a stove burning in the center for warmth, or in a herder's cabin. You'll work together to set up camp, chop firewood or help with cooking, feed the reindeer, and build corrals to protect the animals from predators such as wolves, wolverines, and lynx. On some days, you can try ice fishing for Arctic char or track birds and rabbits. At night, the Northern Lights provide breathtaking displays across the sky.

After your week outdoors, reward yourself with a Swedish sauna and another night or two in Jukkasjarvi at the very cool (both literally and figuratively) **Ice Hotel** in Jukkasjarvi (📞 **46/0-980-66-800;** www.icehotel.com), the world's largest hotel constructed from ice and snow. Even the bed is made of ice, but don't worry: The mattress is covered by—what else—a thick reindeer skin, plus a down-filled sleeping bag and a fur hat will keep you surprisingly warm. —*JS*

ⓘ **Swedish Tourist Board** (📞 **212/885-9700;** www.visitsweden.com).

TOURS: **Crossing Latitudes** (© 800/572-8747; www.crossinglatitudes.com). **Pathfinder Lapland** (© 46/070-688-1577; www.pathfinderlapland.se).

WHEN TO GO: Mar–Apr.

✈ Kiruna airport, Lapland (connection from Heathrow in London).

Animal Treks **283**

Camel Trekking in the Sahara
Arabian Nights & Sun-Drenched Days
Douz to Ksar Ghilane, Tunisia

For a real Arabian adventure, forget magic carpet rides and think camel humps. Swaying some 2.3m (7½ ft.) above the ground on an undulating Arabic dromedary is the best way to get a real feel for the Sahara's shifting sands. This mode of transport is admittedly much slower and more awkward than Aladdin's quick and graceful lift, but that's part of the fun. (Of course, if you really have your heart set on a taking a flight here, booking a hot-air balloon ride early one morning should suffice.)

The Sahara, widely considered the world's greatest desert, deserves some time and patience. After all, stretching from the Red Sea to the Atlantic Ocean, covering huge parts of Algeria, Chad, Egypt, Libya, Mali, Mauritania, Morocco, Niger, Western Sahara, Sudan, and Tunisia, it's almost as large as the United States. The expanse of orangey-red dunes with very little vegetation and strikingly few people evokes both biblical times and an otherworldly vision of Mars.

A good place to begin your camel trek is in the small, sunny market town of Douz, Tunisia's unofficial gateway to the "sand sea," more formally known as the Grand Erg Oriental. The Tunisian Sahara reached wide public acclaim during its appearances in *Star Wars* and *The English Patient,* both of which were filmed in this area.

Before taking off to explore it yourself, try to spend a Thursday in Douz, when you'll see the market at its busiest as nomads come to trade their camels and sell crafts including silver Berber jewelry,

woven blankets, carpets, and adorned saddles. You might also want to check out Chott el Jerid, a nearby salt lake.

If you haven't set up an excursion in advance, you can arrange overnight or multiple-day camel and camping treks into the Sahara through your hotel or with a professional guide at the official tourist office in Douz. Another option is to hire a four-wheel-drive vehicle and go directly from Douz, heading southeast for about 60km (37 miles), or 4 hours, to **Pansea Ksar Ghilane,** one of the world's most unique places to stay, with 60 air-conditioned tents set near a pool in the heart of the desert. You can embark on daily camel excursions from here, but come back at night to sleep in relatively comfortable accommodations.

Whichever option you choose, once you're on a camel, try to get comfortable in the rigid saddle. You'll be here for a while. As you hold onto that hump and bounce across shifting sands, just breathe in the pure desert air and listen to the complete silence of this barely populated land as you slowly rock across the desert.

You'll spend about 3 hours exploring the sun-drenched Sahara before taking a break around noon for some lunch and sugary mint tea. You'll then ride another 3 or 4 hours in the afternoon before the sun falls, a chill sets in, and you get the chance to witness some of the planet's most serious stargazing. —*JS*

ⓘ **Tunisian tourism office,** 1 Ave. Mohamed V, Tunis (Ⓒ **216/71-341-077;** www.tourismtunisia.com).

TOUR: Find an official tour operator in Douz, or ask your hotel to arrange an excursion. If you want to plan ahead, try designing a custom itinerary with **TunisUSA** (Ⓒ **888/474-5502;** www.tunisusa.com).

WHEN TO GO: Apr–June and Oct–Nov.

✈ Tozeur airport or Djerba airport.

⊨ $ **Hotel 20 Mars,** Rue 20 mars (hotel 20mars@planet.tn). $$-$$$ **Pansea Ksar Ghilane,** 4 Rue El Andalous (Ⓒ **216/75-759-330;** www.pansea.com).

284 Animal Treks

Safari by Horseback
Giddy Up for the Ride of Your Life
Okavango Delta, Botswana

Forget the idea of touring Africa by jeep. Imagine, instead, galloping on a horse alongside herds of wildebeest and zebras, cantering beside a cluster of giraffe, or trotting toward a group of buffalo or elephants. As the wind rustles through the long green and yellow blades of grass, the only other sounds you'll hear are the animals' hooves pounding against the ground amid a symphony of birdcalls. On a safari by horseback in Botswana, you'll do more than just see the animal kingdom—you'll become a part of it.

The famed **Okavango Delta,** the largest inland delta in the world, covers more than 15,000 sq. km (5,800 sq. miles) of flood plains in the northwestern part of Botswana. This oasis of waterways, islands, and forests—surrounded by a sea of desert—attracts the most coveted game, including the Big Five: lions, elephants, buffalo, leopards, and rhinoceros. As these mighty creatures wander freely through the wilderness here, you'll roam along with them.

Okavango Horse Safaris, based on the banks of the Xudum River, takes no more than eight experienced riders at a time into the western Delta and a private area bordering the Moremi Game Reserve. You must be able to trot for at least 10 minutes at a time, and know how to gallop out of trouble if the need arises. You

should also be prepared to spend 4 to 6 hours in the saddle per day. As you're riding, you might get lucky and come upon a pride of lions, relaxing after their feast, or a leopard enjoying his recent kill. But if one of these powerful beasts seems hungry, you'll need to get out of its way—and quickly. In addition to the Big Five, other creatures commonly spotted include giraffes, zebras, wildebeests, kudus, impalas, antelopes, duikers, foxes, jackals, wildcats, monkeys, badgers, hyenas, warthogs, tortoises, ostriches, hippos, and crocodiles. Countless birds fly above and around you, and your guides are well versed in the various species.

Itineraries last between 5 and 10 days, and include stays at the **Kujwana Camp** (with spacious, permanent tents that include en-suite bathrooms), the **Moklowane Camp** (which offers tree houses with private bathrooms), and the **Qwaapo Camp** (a "fly camp" with traditional safari tents and camping beds that can be easily moved, bucket showers, and bush toilets). The best time to ride is in the early morning or late afternoon, away from the hot midday sun. When you're ready for a break, don't miss taking a trip in a traditional *mokoro,* a narrow, canoe-like boat that allows you to quietly explore the delta's shallow waterways.

After a full day, as the dark red sun sinks beneath the horizon, you can sit by a campfire, reminiscing about your adventurous ride. Perhaps you'll hear a hyena's laugh interrupt the other animals' rhythmic chorus. As you sip a gin and tonic, waiting for dinner, you'll easily feel right at home. —JS

ⓘ **Botswana Tourism Board,** Plot 50676, Fairgrounds Office Park, Gaborone (ⓒ **888/675-7660;** www.botswanatourism. co.bw).

TOUR: Okavango Horse Safaris, Okavango Delta (ⓒ **267/686-1671;** www. okavangohorse.com).

WHEN TO GO: Apr–Oct.

✈ Maun Airport.

Animal Treks **285**

Birding in Panama
Catching a Glimpse of the Quetzal
Panama City to the Chiriqui Highlands, Panama

The euphoria of spotting a rare bird in its own habitat can become mildly addictive. For self-proclaimed birders—nature enthusiasts who often chronicle the species they've seen on long lists or in detailed notebooks—the challenge of trying to glimpse some of the world's most beautiful but elusive creatures has a hugely rewarding payoff. Even for non-birders, it's easy to get caught up in the birds' game of hide and go seek. As Hernan Arauz, one of Panama's most reputable birding guides, said, "Once you see, through a good scope or binocular, a crimson-backed tanager, a blue cotinga, or for that matter, a resplendent quetzal . . . in good light, in its own habitat, feeding, flirting, or just perching, your brain will experience a sensation that not even the finest glossy *National Geographic* photo can accomplish. You will know that it's *alive* . . . in real time. The iridescence of its plumage will dazzle your perception, enrich your memory, and trigger the desire to see more."

You can begin marveling at Panama's vast bird population less than an hour outside of Panama City, at the **Canopy Tower,** an eco-lodge in Soberania National Park. More than 280 different species of birds have been spotted in this vicinity, and you can admire some of them right from your room's observation deck. Of course, you'll also want to spend some time on the ground. It's a short ride from here to the nearby **Pipeline Road,** a popular hiking trail due to its accessibility and the immense number of bird species found along it—you might see mot mots, trogons, toucans, antbirds, colorful tanagers, or flycatchers. For the past several years, this trail has set the world record for 24-hour bird counts, according to the Audubon Society.

While you're still in the city limits, you'll also want to spend some time in the protected rainforest at the **Metropolitan National Park,** where you could see a mixed flock of nearly 25 birds at once. There are more than 260 bird species in this park, including lance-tailed manakins, rosy-thrush tanagers, orange-billed sparrows, rufous, green honeycreepers, and white wrens. But to spot a famed resplendent quetzal, you'll need to travel a bit farther into western Panama.

The Aztecs and the Mayans revered the resplendent quetzal; Panama's royalty and priests even wore its feathers during special ceremonies. Today, many birders consider it be the most beautiful bird in the Americas. The iridescent male quetzal boasts dense plumage and a long, green tail that can reach almost a meter (3 ft.) during mating season. Although the females don't have such long tails and tend to be somewhat less vibrant than males, they share the brilliant blue, green, and red coloring of their mates.

Most of these birds live in the mountainous, tropical forest regions of Central America. The best place to see a vibrant quetzal in Panama is in the cloud forests of the Chiriqui highlands, particularly by hiking the Sendero Los Quetzales (the Quetzales Trail) on the north side of the **Volcan Baru National Park** and at Finca Lerida above Boquete. For an overview of Panama's amazing bird wonderland, check out **Ancon Expedition's Highlights of Avian Panama** tour. If you have time for a bit more, consider the **Birds of Panama** trip, which also includes a visit to the acclaimed bird Eden in **Darien National Park** and the **Cana field station.**

By the time you've spent a week traveling through this bird-lover's paradise, you'll probably have your own notebook full of excitedly scribbled lists. Happily, the birding addiction appears to have no harmful side effects. —*JS*

ⓘ **Panama Authority of Tourism** (www.visitpanama.com).

TOUR: Ancon Expeditions of Panama, Calle Elvira Mendez, Eldif. El Dorado 3 (ⓒ 507/269-9415; www.anconexpeditions. com). Ask for Hernan Arauz, the company's master naturalist and birding guide.

WHEN TO GO: Dec–May.

✈ Tocumen International Airport, followed by 1-hr. flight or approx. 5-hr. drive to Boquete.

🛏 $$ **Canopy Tower,** Apartado 0832-2701 WTC (ⓒ **800/930-3397;** www.canopy tower.com). $ **Finca Lerida Ecolodge,** Boquete, Chiriqui (ⓒ **507/720-2285;** www.fincalerida.com). $–$$ **Los Quetzales,** Guadalupe (ⓒ **507/771-2291;** www. losquetzales.com).

---

286 Animal Treks

Birding & Deep-Sea Fishing
Island in the Middle of Nowhere
Mykines, Faroe Islands

Do you want to visit an island so remote that most people don't know it exists? Mykines is the westernmost of the Faroe Islands, just dots in the North Atlantic Ocean northwest of Scotland and midway between Iceland and Norway. Vikings settled the Faroe Islands more than a thousand years ago and their descendants live here today in the island's small village. Only 11 people live here year-round. Like all of the Faroe Islands, Mykines slants sharply upward and ends in steep cliffs on one side, a pattern created by blasts from giant volcanoes 60 million years ago. This dramatic landscape has proved to be an ideal home for several species of birds, and an exhilarating place to observe them.

It's believed, at least locally, that Mykines is the mysterious "paradise of birds" that St. Brendan, the seafaring Irish monk, wrote about in the middle of the sixth century. Thousands of migratory birds fly around or perch on the steep cliffsides, which are composed of layers of volcanic basalt. Colonies of puffins live on the ledges and the swaths of green atop the cliffs. Have your camera ready, so when the puffins pose with fish in their brightly colored beaks, you can snap a picture. As you watch the birds, the cacophony of notes from guillemots, storm petrels, and fulmars surrounds you.

To see the striking white gannets, you'll head to the tiny piece of land reachable only by crossing a footbridge spanning a 35m-deep (115-ft.) gorge. You'll pass by a lighthouse to reach the headland, where you can see the gannets and their young perched atop two sea stacks (rock out-croppings close to the coastline), the only nesting spot for the species in the Faroe Islands. There are no organized birding tours to speak of on the island. For more information, contact the tourist board (information below).

While Mykines is tiny, there are a few hikes. Visit the "stone" forest in Korkada-lur, actually a long line of basalt columns, or walk to the top of Knukur, for a view of the nearby islands. Fishing is the main way families are supported in the Faroe Islands, and there are boats waiting to take you deep-sea fishing. You can also sail around the Faroe Islands either in a private boat, in the restored schooner, *Norðlýsið,* which sails from Tórshavn, or the restored sailing ship **Dragin** (© **298/456939;** www.dragin.fo/?id=37237), which sets out from Klaksví. For a scenic tour on the waters, or

a day of fishing, contact **Norðlýsið** (www.nordlysid.com).

The locals speak a derivative of the ancient Norse language, but English is also spoken by some. Ferries come to Mykines and there is helicopter service a few days a week.

The gulfstream encircles the Faroe Islands, tempering the climate. The mari-time weather here causes quick changes, from misty fog to light showers to blazing sunshine within the hour, so bring raingear. —LF

ⓘ **Faroe Islands** (© **298/30-6900;** www.faroeislands.com). **Visit Faroe Islands** (www.visit-faroeislands.com).

TOURS: Faroe Saga Travel (© **866/423-7242;** www.faroesagatravel.com). **Five Stars of Scandinavia** (© **800/722-4126;** www.5stars-of-scandinavia.com).

WHEN TO GO: Summer.

✈ Vagar.

🛏 $ **Kristianshus Mykines** (© **298-31-29-85**).

Hitting the Road 287

The Great Ocean Road
Australia's Most Dizzying Drive
Torquay to Warrnambool, Victoria, Australia

There's always something liberating about a road trip, but this one along Australia's wild coastline will make your heart race. Navigating hairpin turns on the edges of cliffs high above the sea is nothing short of exhilarating. Until 1932, when the Great Ocean Road was completed (built by returning World War I veterans), this stretch of Earth was one of the most iso-lated in the world. Besides the fisherman who lived in nearby villages that were accessible only by boat, few humans had laid eyes on the juxtaposition of land and sea here. Set between Torquay and Warrnambool, the Great Ocean Road is an

awe-inspiring feat of construction, and a tribute to Australia's rugged landscape.

To really hug the curves and get the most out of this thrill-inducing ride, rent a convertible or a motorcycle. Actually, any kind of small car will do, but don't even think about getting on a bus with a tour operator. Even though the nearly 240km (150 miles) drive takes just 3½ hours—maybe even less depending on how fast you drive—allow at least 3 days for the journey. You'll want to stop and experi-ence some off-the-road adventures too.

The most eastern portion of the drive, starting in Torquay, is called the Surf Coast

Along Australia's Great Ocean Road.

and is home to the world-famous Bells Beach (see ⑮), featured in *Point Break*. If you brought your surfboard, stop your wheels and ride some waves. Even if you don't surf, plan to spend an hour or so watching other enthusiasts. Each April, the world's best surfers come here to compete in the Rip Curl Pro Surf and Music Festival.

To spend some more time surfing or to try your hand at fishing, chill out in the cool town of Lorne before continuing on to Apollo Bay—the drive is especially harrowing as the pavement narrows and twists along a cliff edge. In Aireys Inlet, take a horseback ride on the beach or in **Anga-hook-Lorne State Park** with **Blazing Saddles** (℡ **03/5289 7332;** www.greatocean road.com.au/blazing_saddles). If you'd rather stretch your legs, the state park also has a number of good hiking trails through the rainforest. For a quick 30-minute stroll just past Apollo Bay, walk along the **Maits Rest Rainforest Boardwalk.**

The road then cuts inland past the Otway Lighthouse, built by convicts in 1848. This area is a great place to see some wildlife at the **Cape Otway Centre for Conservation Ecology** and perhaps spend the night. You'll want to be alert for the next part of the drive, as it spectacularly

winds along 61m (200-ft.) sea cliffs. Be sure to stop and see the **Twelve Apostles,** a world-renowned series of wave-chiseled rock formations; the **London Bridge,** which looked like the real thing until the middle portion crashed into the ocean in 1990; and the **Loch Ard Gorge.** Before you hit Port Fairy, stop in the Aboriginal run **Tower Hill Nature Preserve** (℡ **03/5561-5315;** www.worngundidj.org.au).

The Great Ocean Road officially ends in Warrnambool. If you want to try the curves going the other direction, turn around and head back toward Melbourne. But even adventure junkies need a break sometimes. If you've had enough adrenaline for one trip, take the easier inland route back and head an hour north into the rural **Southern Grampians Ranges.** You can stay next to a fully operating sheep station at the Royal Mail Hotel's **Mt. Sturgeon Cottages** (℡ **03/5577-2241;** www.royal mail.com.au). —*JS*

ⓘ **Great Ocean Road Visitors Centre** (℡ **03/5275-5797;** www.greatoceanrd. org.au).

WHEN TO GO: Anytime, but particularly in the summer and fall (Nov–May).

✈ Melbourne Airport, approx. an hour-long drive from the eastern start of the Great Ocean Road.

🛏 $$–$$$ **Great Ocean Eco-Lodge,** Cape Otway (ⓒ **03/5237-9297;** www.capeotwaycentre.com.au). $$ **Sea Foam Villas,** Port Campbell (ⓒ **03/5598-6413;** www.seafoamvillas.com).

Hitting the Road ⬤**288**

The Amalfi Drive

Hugging the Curves on Italy's Raciest Road

Sorrento to Salerno, Italy

Most Italians don't just drive; they race. They tailgate, pass other cars with inches to spare between them, and lean on the horn—all of which makes getting behind the wheel on Italian roads challenging at best and terrifying at worst. But their recklessness won't stop you from taking the most adrenaline-inducing road trip in

The Amalfi Drive.

Europe. Just remember to drive carefully. Very carefully.

The hairpin curves on the Amalfi Drive (Rte. 163), running from Sorrento to Salerno, are racetrack worthy. This feat of engineering and construction takes you twisting and turning high above the spectacular Mediterranean coastline, so close to the edge that you might get a few twinges of vertigo. Don't think about getting on a tour bus here; adventure junkies will want to be in control here, experiencing the tight turns, even if it takes a white-knuckled grip. (It does, however, help to have a trusted copilot with you, so you can take an occasional break and soak in the dramatic scenery along the way.)

Starting in **Sorrento,** the Amalfi Drive takes you up to Sant'Agata Sui Due Golfi along the Sorrentine peninsula, offering views of the Bay of Naples and the Bay of Salerno. As you follow along pavement that clings to the rock face, with few roadside railings to give any illusion of safety, you'll gasp at the striking azure water and sandy alcoves far below, before being wowed by the quaint pastel-hued villages cascading down steep mountainsides. When you arrive in **Positano,** stop over for a night or consider returning after you see more of the coast. The cafes and boutiques are admittedly overpriced here, but this village is the quintessential Amalfi Coast of postcard fame. Exploring the town by foot is a worthy side trip. You'll pass olive and lemon groves as you hike upward, past donkeys and perhaps a pick-up soccer game. Make sure to enjoy a leisurely lunch at the unnamed restaurant in the hamlet of Nocelle.

From Positano, it's about a 30-minute drive to **Amalfi,** a historically important trading port, a UNESCO World Heritage Site, and a chic beach resort area. Check out the breathtaking Duamo di San't Andrea, and climb the steps to see its bronze door that was cast during the 11th century. It's also worth taking some time to explore the town's narrow side streets with their unique Moorish-influenced whitewashed houses.

Back in the car, heading east, you'll have to negotiate a dramatic stretch of road that curves through the Valley of the Dragon for about 6km (3¾ miles) before coming upon **Ravello,** a town with a serious medieval history and views that inspired writers ranging from D.H. Lawrence to Gore Vidal. It's probably best known for its gardens at Villa Cimbrone and Villa Rufolo, which are both open to the public year-round. From here, you can complete the drive by continuing on to the port city of **Salerno.**

If you still haven't had enough of the treacherous roadway, head back the way you came and spend some more time along the coast. For a faster and more direct route, opt for the tamer A3 highway, which cuts back toward Naples. Whichever way you choose, settle into a hotel for at least 1 night and as your heartbeat slows, reward yourself for surviving the Amalfi obstacle course with a well-deserved glass of wine and a heaping plate of linguini topped with fresh seafood. *—JS*

ⓘ **Italian Government Tourist Board** (www.enit.it) and the **Sorrento tourist office,** Via Luigi de Maio 35, Sorrento (ⓒ **081/807-4033;** www.sorrentotourism. com).

WHEN TO GO: Anytime, weather permitting.

✈ Naples airport.

🛏 $$ **Casa Albertina,** Via Travolozza, 3 (ⓒ **39/089-811-540;** www.casalbertina. it). $$$ **Le Sirenuse,** Via C. Colombo, 30 (ⓒ **39/089-875-066;** www.sirenuse.it).

---

289 **Hitting the Road**

MacKenzie River Ice Road
Driving on Frozen Water
Northwest Territories, Canada

Hold the wheel gently but firmly and be prepared to deal with a skid where it's slick as glass. Expect a bumpy ride where the road's surface looks like frozen waves. They may actually be frozen waves, created by the undulating surface of the Beaufort Sea underneath the temporary ice road that connects Inuvik and Tuktoyaktuk, in the Northwest Territories, in the winter. The roughly 250 km-long (155-mile) ice road is a plowed road-width swath on the surface of frozen MacKenzie River that extends for a short stint on the

Beaufort Sea. This public road, maintained by the Territorial Department of Transportation, is the wintertime earth-bound link between two towns north of the Arctic Circle. (During the summer, you'll have to fly or take a boat from one town to the other.) To traverse it in winter is as exciting as it is dangerous.

Truckers who use this road in the winter to deliver supplies have described it as one of the most desolate, barren roads they've ever driven because you can drive for so many miles without seeing anything other than a frozen landscape. Their discussions about the experience and challenges of driving this road, and the images shown during the television series *Ice Road Truckers* attracted the attention of travelers who now want to drive this road, too. The road usually opens in late December or January, when the ice is deemed thick enough. But, because it's a road built on water that is constantly moving underneath, especially along the portion that goes over the sea, the depth and state of the ice are constantly monitored. Pay attention to the speed limits. They are chosen for drivers' safety, because holes can open in the road if cross current are created in the water under the ice by speeding traffic.

The town of Inuvik, built on permafrost, is two degrees above the Arctic Circle alongside the MacKenzie Delta, Canada's largest freshwater delta close to the Arctic Ocean. Large town buildings are erected on piles driven into the ice and, because the climate can't sustain outdoor vegetable or flower growth, a big communal greenhouse is housed in a Quonset-style hockey rink. The two main tourist sites in town are the Lady of Victory Roman Catholic Church, which looks like a huge igloo, and the Ingamo Friendship Centre, the largest log structure north of the Arctic Circle. If you're seeking adventure in remote locales, start here then take the ice road to Tuktoyaktuk, a tiny Inuvialuit community. Adventurous tourists can go dog sledding, watch the Northern Lights, and go cross-country skiing around both towns. You could plan a drive to experience Inuvik's annual Muskrat Jamboree winter festival, the first weekend in April. —*LF*

ⓘ **Spectacular Northwest Territories** (☏ **800-661-0778**; www.spectacularnwt. com). Request a map of the province and *The Explorers Guide,* which lists lodging and outfitters. **Inuvik** (☏ **867/777-8600;** www.inuvik.ca)

WHEN TO GO: Jan–Apr, ice permitting.

✈ Inuvik.

▙ $$ **Arctic Chalet,** 25 Carn St., Inuvik (☏ **800/685-9417** or 867/777-3535; www. arcticchalet.com). $$$ **Mackenzie Hotel,** 185 Mackenzie Rd., Inuvik (☏ **867/777-2861;** www.mackenziedeltahotel.com).

Hitting the Road **290**

Motorcycle Adventures
Riding with the Wind
Western and Southwestern United States and Mexico

You're astride a Honda XR250, tucked in, heart in your mouth as you go flat out across a dried lakebed in the Baja—then one of the other riders zips past you! No, you're not riding in the Baja 500 or 1000. You're on a motorcycle adventure trip that takes you from town streets over sand, down dry washes, up mountains, across deserts, and across dry lake bottoms. When you're on the all-inclusive Baja Adventure tour with **Chris Haines Motorcycle Adventure Company,** speeds range from slow in the more technical areas to as fast as you want to push your machine.

The trip originates in San Diego, California. You'll go by van to Ensenada, Mexico, and spend 3 days riding off-road bikes approximately 500 miles (805km) through Baja, Mexico, partly on the Baja 1000 course. Longer trips are also available, which can provide the opportunity to see the Sierra de San Francisco rock art. The equipment, meals along the way, and scenery are all first-rate.

Haines, your guide, won the Baja 1000 more than a dozen times, but you don't have to be a racer to enjoy this trip. Groups are made up of novices, intermediates, and expert riders. Outriders from the company help beginners through tricky areas and ensure the headcount is correct at the end of the day. Support vehicles carry gear, spare parts, and equipment.

Another company, **Elite Motorcycle Adventures,** runs day trips and point-to-point trips through some of the most beautiful country in the western United States. Trips leaving from Moab, Utah, take you through canyons past natural arches and old homestead cabins, along rivers, and through the red sandstone country. The company's Barlett Slickrock Tour takes you over age-hardened sandstone and provides a unique opportunity to test the limits of your riding skills. The Dubinky Desert Trail ride will leave you awestruck by the beauty of parts of Utah that relatively few have seen. Elite will take novice and expert racers on their tours, providing separate guides based upon rider ability. For touring trips there are numerous companies. **Rocky Mountain Motorcycle Holidays** in North Vancouver, British Columbia, Canada, provides guided tours through western Canada and the western United States. **Ayres Adventure Travel,** based in Plano, Texas, offers tours in the United States, Alaska, Africa, Canada, Europe, South American and New Zealand. —*LF*

ⓘ **Chris Haines Motorcycle Adventure Company** (✆ 866/262-8635; www. bajaoffroadtours.com). **Elite Motorcycle Adventures** (✆ 435/259-7621; www.elite motorcycletours.com). **Ayres Adventures** (✆ 877/275-8238; www.ayres adventures.com). **Rocky Mountain Motorcycle Holidays** (✆ 888/299-5534; http://rockymtnmoto.com).

WHEN TO GO: Sept–May for Baja; Mar–Nov for Utah.

✈ San Diego International Airport, Canyon Lands Field.

🛏 In general, tour companies make lodging arrangements.

291 Hitting the Road

Touring Route 40
Dear Motorcycle Diary
Argentina

Spectacular glaciers glowing blue in the moonlight of the Andes. Vast sun-drenched plains, home to some of the best wineries in the world. Prehistoric cave paintings in isolated canyons where condors swirl overhead. If you're ready for hundreds of adventures like these on the trip of a lifetime, try motorcycling down Route 40 through Argentina. Passing through 20 national parks, 27 Andean mountain passes, and over 18 major rivers, this is journey not easily forgotten.

Tours along this fabled roadway (made famous by Che Guevara's *The Motorcycle Diaries*) usually begin in Salta, in the northern part of the country. From there, it's about 3 to 4 weeks of riding until you reach your journey's end 6,900km (4,300 miles) south in Ushuaia, the southernmost city in the world, located deep in Tierra del Fuego. Air transportation is usually arranged between these two cities and the capital city, Buenos Aires.

This is not an entry-level motorcycle trip. Besides the length of the journey and the time involved, you'll pass through several climate zones, from the searing heat of the Patagonian desert to the sub-zero alpine conditions in the Andes. Nor is Route 40—locally known at Ruta 40 or "La Cuarenta"—a smooth lane of blacktop: Expect hours of bone-rattling washboard road conditions, vast clouds of dust, and mud that will stick to your bike, your clothes, and your skin long after your ride is over. Distances between towns can be vast, and riders should be expected to endure the occasional hardship with the adventure traveler's secret weapon: a sense of humor.

But those who can weather the hazards of this journey are rewarded with unforgettable thrills. Packs of wild guanacos (cousins of the llama) crossing the roadway are a familiar sight. The towering spires of Fitz Roy, Cerro Torre, and other snow-capped Andean mountains loom overhead, because much of Route 40 follows the eastern spine of the Andes. The pristine beauty of the Perito Moreno glacier makes a visit to Los Glaciares National Park a must (see ⓚ). And the legendary hospitality of Argentine estancias (ranches), with sublime regional wines, and world-class food, await weary riders at each stop along the way. —ML

TOURS: Overland Patagonia (© 02944/ **438654;** www.overlandpatagonia.com). **Adventure Motorcycle Tours** (© 760/ **249-1105;** www.admo-tours.com). **Lef Expeditions** (info@lefexpeditions.com; www.lefexpeditions.com).

WHEN TO GO: Nov–Apr.

Hitting the Road **292**

Vietnam by Motorbike
Next Stop Is Vietnam
Vietnam

If you're ready for a truly epic adventure, visiting an ancient land steeped in history, beauty, and bloodshed, it would be hard to beat a motorbike tour through Vietnam. Traveling by motorbike can take you to places cars and buses can't visit, and gives visitors to this magical land a taste of local life that few Westerners will ever experience. From the frenzied blur of Hanoi and Ho Chi Minh City (formerly Saigon) to the serene beauty of remote mountain temples, the journey of a lifetime awaits those willing to trade the comfort of a resort spa for a mud-splattered motorcycle helmet.

Most tours of Vietnam begin in Hanoi or Ho Chi Minh, and concentrate on the northern reaches of the country, where the more mountainous terrain yields spectacular vistas and unexpected treasures in villages once considered inaccessible. Depending on your itinerary and your spirit of adventure, you could also consider a trip across the border into Laos and/or Cambodia; some motorbike tours offer this as an option, and most will custom-design a tour depending on the group's interests.

What, you might ask, is there to see in this formerly war-torn region? Pristine tropical beaches, lush pine forests, towering limestone mountains, and thundering waterfalls are all part of the natural scenery. Crowded markets where vendors hawk exotic jewelry, embroidery, and local delicacies like grilled snake kabob are a regular sight. Picturesque stilt houses, rice paddies, and lumbering water buffalo dot the countryside.

Of course, you can expect to get a little dirty on any real motorcycle trip, and with roads that range from spanking-new expressways to mud paths, Vietnam has plenty of dirt to throw in your face. Add to that the grime you'll get on your hands from trying to fix the 1950s-era engine on your Russian-made Minsk rental motorbike, and you'll have tales that will last much longer than the grit in your teeth. —*ML*

ⓘ **Vietnam Motorbike Tours** (ⓒ **84/58-282092;** www.vietnammotorbiketours. websyte.com.au). **Offroad Vietnam** (ⓒ **844/3904-5049;** www.offroadvietnam.com).

WHEN TO GO: Sept–Dec.

✈ Hanoi or Ho Chi Minh City, depending on which tour you choose.

🛏 $$$ **Grand Hotel,** 8–24 Dong Khoi St., Ho Chi Minh City (ⓒ **08/823-0163;** www.grandhotel.com.vn). $$ **Army Hotel,** 33C Pham Ngu Lao St., Hanoi (ⓒ **04/825-2896;** armyhotel@fpt.vn).

293 Hitting the Road

Four-Wheel Drives in Colorado
Riding on the Edge in Telluride
Telluride, Colorado, U.S.A.

As you slowly make your way up the narrow, crumbling Tomboy Road outside of Telluride, Colorado, don't make the mistake of looking down. Your truck's wheels may be less than a foot from the edge of the road and the oblivion below. The road, which was originally a Ute Indian Trail, winds its way from the Town of Telluride up to Imogene Pass at 13,100 feet (3,900m). Up until around 1925 it was the primary route to the gold and silver mines high on the mountainside, and was traversed by periodic stagecoach runs and lots of mule-pulled wagons hauling supplies and ore. Today, although officially a county road, it's a narrow, moderately difficult four-wheel-drive road that is not well maintained. Traversing it, though dangerous, is a real thrill.

Vehicles bounce over large and often sharp rocks—this is not the road for a Cadillac or a BMW sedan—around blind corners, and along continuous twists and turns. It really gets interesting when two vehicles meet (the vehicle heading uphill always has the right of way). Though the tour companies have specialized vehicles with heavy-duty tires and suspensions, on any given day you may see Jeeps and Range Rovers inching up the road. Most of the vehicles have to stop at times, so hikers and mountain bikers can safely squeeze by. This rough road is not a recommended trip for novice off-roaders.

Atop the road is the ghost town that housed the miners working in the Tomboy Mine, which is not far from the summit. Along the road you'll pass through the "Social Tunnel," a favorite location for the miners to meet with the prostitutes who made the trip up from town. You'll also see the cables that were strung between rocks to stop the mules and their wagons from taking their last one-way trip down. The ghost town still has many deteriorating buildings, the pilings from the miners dormitory, old cable, broken bottles, timbers, and other remnants of a day when "environmentally friendly" was not a part of the lexicon.

You might consider going on a tour and learning the history associated with the mines and how they operated. For example, while mine owners made millions, the hard rock miners were paid $3 per day and, as might be imagined, there was considerable labor strife and union busting. When the Ames power plant was built, the mines in this area became the first commercial users of alternating current. Of particular interest were the huge cable car-like pieces of equipment in which they would load the ore and let gravity take it to the mill in the valley below. The weight of the ore heading down brought the empty, or supply and miner laden, buckets back up the mountain.

In addition to the trip to the Tomboy, there are jeep tours to Ophir Pass and the Alta ghost town, Black Bear Pass, with its fields of summer flowers, and Bridal Veil Falls, Colorado's highest.

Telluride became a ski town in 1972 and has grown to a full functioning resort community. In town are excellent lodging and dining possibilities. A relatively new village on the mountain can be reached from town by gondola, eliminating the need for a vehicle in town. There are festivals almost every week in the summer, and such activities as golf, river rafting, hiking, and mountain biking will keep you as busy as you wish. —LF

ⓘ **Telluride Tourism Board** (℃ **888/ 605-2578;** www.visittelluride.com).

TOURS: Telluride Outside, 121 W. Colorado Ave. (℃ **800/831-6230** or 970/728-3895; www.tellurideoutside.com). **Telluride Sports Adventure Desk,** 150 W. Colorado Ave. (℃ **800/828-7547** or 970/728-4477; www.telluridesports.com).

WHEN TO GO: Summer for 4x4 touring.

✈ Telluride Regional Airport or Montrose.

🛏 $$ **New Sheridan Hotel,** 231 W. Colorado Ave. (℃ **800/200-1891** or 970/728-5024; www.newsheridan.com). $$$ **Capella Telluride,** 568 Mountain Village Blvd. (℃ **970/369-0880;** www. capellatelluride.com).

Hitting the Road **294**

Snowmobiling & Mountain Sledding the U.P.
Ride with Yooupers
Upper Peninsula of Michigan, U.S.A.

The spray of snow flying over your windshield while mountain sledding (snowmobiling off-road) is a rush akin to that a skier experiences going through deep powder. But even if you prefer to stay on snowmobile trails, instead of powering through the woods, you'll still get your kicks. Imagine your surprise as you come around a corner and a moose is blocking your way!

Yooupers, residents of the Upper Peninsula of Michigan, which is commonly referred to as the U.P., know they live in some of the best snowmobiling country in the nation. In many parts of the U.P., which covers almost 16,500-square-miles, snowfall exceeds 20 feet during a winter. This makes for excellent snowmobiling and mountain sledding conditions.

With fewer than 350,000 people in the U.P., most of the communities are small and in the winter the economies are heavily dependent on snowmobiling. Locals have built and maintain thousands of miles of snowmobile trails throughout the U.P. More adventurous types are eager to explore off-road, so mountain sledding in the powder has also become a popular pastime and tourist interest. More physically demanding than trail riding, there are dangers associated with mountain sledding and it should be done in groups only after safety training.

Newberry, Michigan, designated the official Moose Capital of Michigan and located in the eastern third of the U.P., has hundreds of miles of groomed, marked snowmobile trails and it's surrounded by state and national forests. It's a great place to go for a ride. If you go snowmobiling around Newberry, take a ride to the **Tahquamenon Falls.** Whether the falls are frozen or running, when there's snow on the trees and ground both the upper and lower falls are gorgeous and a photographer's dream. A ride through the Tahquamenon Falls State Park could result in sighting moose, black bear, deer, otter, mink, and beaver. Early in the morning or in the evening you might even see eagles fishing at the lower falls when they're not frozen. It was along the shores of the Tahquamenon River that Longfellow's Hiawatha built his canoe.

From Newberry, you can also go snowmobiling at the gorgeous **Pictured Rocks National Lakeshore,** with its sandstone walls and formations. In the winter, unplowed roads are often open to snowmobiles, including the roads to the famous **Miner's Castle formation.** The frozen waters of Lake Superior and Grand Sable Lake are also open to snowmobiles—ice conditions permitting—and the wide-open terrain can provide for a thrilling time. If you want to take a break from snowmobiling, there are numerous opportunities for snowshoeing, cross-country skiing, and dog sledding. —LF

ⓘ **Upper Peninsula Snowmobiling** (http://upsnowmobiling.com). **Newberry, Michigan** (www.newberrymichigan.net). **Tahquamenon Falls State Park** (www. exploringthenorth.com/tahqua/tahqua). **Pictured Rocks National Lakeshore** (✆ **906/387-4025;** www.nps.gov/piro).

TOUR: U.P. Rental, Newberry (✆ **906/ 293-5515;** www.uprental.com).

WHEN TO GO: Dec–Mar.

✈ Chippewa County International Airport (68 miles/110km). Sault Ste. Marie (67 miles/108km).

🛏 $ **Sno-Shu Inn,** P.O. Box 67, Hulbert (✆ **906/876-2324;** www.exploringthenorth. com/snoshu/sno).

295 Hitting the Road

Snowmobiling & Bicycling
The Paul Bunyan Trail
Brainerd, Minnesota, U.S.A.

The story about Paul Bunyan, the giant mid-Western lumberjack, is a tall tale, but the promise that you'll enjoy exploring the 100-mile-long Paul Bunyan Trail is real. In winter, snowmobilers and cross-country skiers travel along this snowy freeway that stretches from Brainerd to Bemidji, Minnesota, passing through several logging towns. In summer, the converted railroad bed is a popular bicycling and hiking trail. No matter what time of year you decide to go, you won't be let down. This stretch of trail offers year-round excitement to anyone who ventures to this mid-west hotbed of outdoor fun.

You don't have to cover the entire length of the trail during a vacation, because there are 14 towns along the way where you can stop for lunch, explore local sites, or spend the night. Summer or winter, many people choose one of the towns as "home base," a make day trips from there.

If you want to travel the entire trail in the winter, start in Brainerd and plan on 3 to 4 days for the snowmobile ride to Bemidji. You'll want to stop in some of the small towns along the way. In these towns you'll find local craft shops—where you can pick up hand-knitted mittens and a scarf (you'll

Snowmobiling in the Brainerd Lakes area, Minnesota.

towns along the Paul Bunyan Trail, shorter snowmobile routes branch off into forests and across ice-capped lakes. For a slower-paced, but equally exciting brand of winter fun, head to the annual **Ice Fishing Competition** on Gull Lake sponsored by the Brainerd Jaycees. Contestants brave the bitter cold to be the first to catch a fish (and hopefully a sizeable one) in the frozen-over lake. The competition attracts thousands and the prizes equal $150,000.

If you want a break, park your snowmobile at the **Grand View Lodge** on Gull Lake and sample other kinds of winter sports. The friendly staff at the lodge can arrange dog sledding, cross-country skiing, snow tubing, or downhill skiing outings. Then have sore muscles soothed at the resort's **Glacial Waters Spa.** In warmer weather, an array of watersports awaits visitors at Grand View Lodge.

In the summer, many hikers and bikers like to overnight in one of the towns along the Paul Bunyan Trail and make day trips. With a car, it's easy to take your bike to other points on the trail. In this area there are lots of lakes where you can enjoy boating, swimming, and other water sports. —*LF*

need them for Minnesota's cold winters)—museums and restaurants run by friendly locals. When the snow falls, trail conditions are posted weekly. Snowmobile rentals are available in several towns.

Along the way you might be tempted to explore some of the 1,200 miles (1,900km) of networked trails in the Brainerd Lakes Area, go downhill skiing at Ski Gull, or try the cross-country and snowshoe trails at the Northland Arboretum. In many of the

ⓘ **Paul Bunyan Trail** (www.paulbunyan trail.com). **Minnesota Tourism** (ⓒ **800/ 657-3700** or 651/296-5029; www.explore minnesota.com).

WHEN TO GO: Year-round.

✈ Brainerd Lakes Regional Airport.

⊨ $$–$$$ **Grand View Lodge,** 23521 Nokomis Ave. (ⓒ **866/801-2951** or 218/ 963-2234; www.grandviewlodge.com).

6 Camps & Schools

296

Alligator Wrestling Lessons
Gator Bait
Monte Vista, Colorado, U.S.A.

What's 9 feet long, weighs 600 pounds, has 80 razor-sharp teeth, and wants to kill you? Why, the alligator that you're holding in your arms, of course. Few adventures can match the thrill of grappling with a prehistoric beast to see who comes out on top, and who will give up a pound of flesh. Not all who try to wrestle a gator walk away unscathed—most folks who've tangled with alligators for a while have the scars to prove it, and possibly a missing finger or two.

Think you're ready to wrestle with one of nature's most successful meat eaters? Then head to Monte Vista, Colorado, where alligator wrestling lessons and other thrills are available at **Colorado Gators,** described as the home of the biggest gators in the West. While there are still plenty of places in the swampy South to watch alligators and the men and women who wrestle them, none can provide you the up-close-and-personal intimacy of grabbing your very own carnivorous reptile that Colorado Gators offers every weekend (Fri–Sun). Be sure to sign up at least a week in advance, and wear clothes that you won't mind getting muddy—or bloody. You'll start the 4-hour course handling smaller alligators, gradually working your way up to the big 9-foot (12m) beasts.

Heated by geothermal waters, the attraction was originally founded as a tilapia fish farm, and alligators were brought in to act as "garbage disposals." (The site is still an active fish farm, providing fish to Denver-area restaurants.) Gators have now been joined by emus, tortoises, pythons, and other exotic animals that were either abandoned by their owners or retired from Hollywood careers—one gator named Morris has starred in several movies and television programs.

If you'd rather leave the gator wrangling to others, you can still get your hands on a number of other reptiles (including baby alligators) in a 3-hour reptile handling program. Other species thrive here, too—because the site is home to a geothermal wetland, it acts as a kind of bird-watcher's paradise for a number of rarely seen bird species. —*ML*

(i) **Gator Farm Alligator Wrestling** (℃ **719/378-2612;** www.gatorfarm.com).

WHEN TO GO: Year-round.

✈ Denver (250 miles/40km).

🛏 $ **Best Western Movie Manor,** 2830 U.S. Hwy. 160 W. (℃ **719/852-5921;** www.bestwesterncolorado.com). $ **Monte Villa Inn,** 925 First Ave. (℃ **719/852-5166;** www.montevillainnbudgethost.com).

Previous page: Roping cattle at Cowgirl Camp.

297

Covert Ops Training Camp
Unleash Your Inner James Bond
Undisclosed Location Outside Tucson, Arizona, U.S.A.

You're sitting in your chair listening to the conference speaker drone on when WHAM! The door to the room is kicked open and six rifle-toting men in black ski masks march in. Amid the spray of gunfire, everyone hits the floor except one of your group—he is attacked and dragged from the room as a hostage. Panic situation? For weaker men and women, perhaps, but your nerves are steady as a rock, because you're in your third day of covert ops training, and have been prepped in how to keep your cool during hostage taking, terrorist activity, hand-to-weapon combat, and other Rambo-esque skills. You know that now's the time to implement your hostage-recovery strategy. Let's roll!

The adventure begins as soon as you arrive at Tucson International Airport, where you're instructed to meet a beautiful blonde at the airport lounge. Using coded language, she will transmit to you the instructions for meeting your transport to the former CIA training facility in the desert. Your 2- or 3-day package is no luxury spa: Rooms are comfortable but spartan, meals are filling but not gourmet, and your day begins at dawn whether you're ready or not. Attendees (no more than 20 are admitted per session) can expect a full slate of training in the activities that would come in handy in a terrorist attack or military coup: gunning a fast-attack vehicle down a dirt road, close-quarter handgun training, martial arts, and high-speed evasive driving.

The highlight of your training comes in the aforementioned hostage-taking situation. You have just a few hours to determine the terrorists' hideout location, arm yourself with paintball weapons, develop a tactical strategy, and move in for hostage rescue operation without getting "killed" or losing the hostage.

If this is all sounding a little like Bond, James Bond, it's no accident. The men behind Covert Ops sport resumes with years of real-world experience in international "situations" such as espionage with the Green Berets in Southeast Asia, African mercenary operations, seventh-degree black belt karate training, and Navy SEAL experience. It might seem intimidating, but if some *mano-a-mano* action is what you need to inspire your business colleagues or to make it through another weekend with your family, consider one of their group packages. —ML

ⓘ **Covert Ops** (✆ **800-644-7382;** www incredible-adventures.com/covert1.html).

WHEN TO GO: Whenever the international situation becomes dangerously unstable.

✈ Tucson International Airport.

298

Cowgirl Camp
The Wild Women's West
Gila, New Mexico, U.S.A.

Ridin', ropin', and round-ups are time-honored traditions of cowboy culture, but women have often been excluded from these aspects of life in the American West. Now's your chance to settle that old score, ladies. In the spectacular mountains of New Mexico, surrounded by ancient cliff dwellings and sun-dappled woodlands, the **Double E Ranch** offers tenderfoot cowgirls and old hands alike an invigorating authentic western experience on a working cattle ranch.

Cowgirl Camp lasts a week and includes meals, accommodations, and plenty of chances to work on your horsemanship (horsewomanship?) skills. Women who expect to be pampered in a luxurious, spa-type environment are advised to saddle up and move on out; the women at the Double E are there to participate in daily ranch activities, including cutting cattle, rounding up strays—there's even a mini-rodeo with barrel-racing and other events. Women with no horseback experience are welcome, and with a guest capacity of just 18, you'll have more one-on-one attention than at some other guest ranches. There's also a Level II camp for ladies with a bit more riding experience. The price for the camp is reasonable, running about $1,500 a week in 2009.

It's not all hard work, however. In addition to plush comforters, air-conditioning, coffee service, and thick towels in guest quarters, meals feature hearty ranch fare and fresh-baked desserts. And there are plenty of chances for hiking, nature rides, bird-watching, exploring the ancient Native American culture of the region, or just curling up with a good book.

Cowgirl Camp is just one of the activities scheduled at the Double E. At various times throughout the year, the ranch also hosts mounted shooting clinics, horsemanship clinics, rides to Native American ruins—even college-credit courses.

The Double E ranch is adjacent to the **Gila Wilderness** and **Gila National Forest** (www.fs.usda.gov/gila)—some of the most awe-inspiring scenery in North America. Other area attractions include the historic silver-rush town of **Silver City** (www.silvercity.org), the hot springs of **Truth or Consequences** (www.truthor consequencesnm.net), the surreal geology of **City of Rocks State Park** (www.emnrd.state.nm.us/PRD/cityrocks.htm), and the ghost town of Chloride, N.M. —*ML*

ⓘ **Double E Ranch** (✆ **866/242-3500;** www.doubleeranch.com).

WHEN TO GO: Cowgirl Camps are offered throughout the year; check website for schedule.

✈ Silver City, N.M. (28 miles/45km).

299

Doug Foley's Drag Racing School
Start Your Engines!
Cities throughout the U.S.A.

The green flag waves, and you're off! Smoke from squealing tires fills your nostrils as your big-block Chevy engine roars, and within seconds you've reached blue-lipped speeds of over 130 mph (209kmph). This experience was once limited to experienced racers like Mario Andretti and Doug Foley, but the thrill of drag racing can now be enjoyed by anyone—even teenagers—at Doug Foley's Drag Racing School.

The schools, which started in 1997 in Atco, New Jersey, are now located throughout the U.S. There are a range of courses available to speedsters, including half-day Dragster Experience, 2-day Super Comp, and —for those who'd rather leave the driving to others—a Dragster Ride-Along in a specially built two-seat dragster. No granny-mobile, the two-seater still packs 800 horsepower and a couple of g-forces. And if your need for speed is unquenchable, the schools also offer a competition license for students who have completed the three-run Dragster Experience. After time trials, racers compete in three rounds of elimination racing to determine who will win the championship and the winner's commemorative plaque (champagne not included). Prices vary per course, ranging from about $150 for a ride-along to a couple thousand dollars for multi-day courses.

There are advanced driver training programs available, but most courses assume that all attendees are drag racing novices. With safe driving in mind, courses begin with a complete safety and procedural orientation taught by Doug Foley himself, and each driver is issued state-of-the-art safety equipment. The Junior Dragster Racing School is a 2-day course that involves both students and their parents; racers go through exhaustive training and prep work before taking a dragster out onto the track.

For corporate and personal gifts, client entertaining, employee incentives, and private parties, Doug Foley's Drag Racing School can provide an unforgettable event (did someone say *bachelor party?*). Perks can include full catered food and beverage set-ups, track-side photography, custom-made video, T-shirts, and custom company branding campaigns that include banner placement, promotional literature—and a lifetime of memories. —*ML*

ⓘ **Doug Foley's Drag Racing School** (✆ **866/DRAGSTER** [37247837] or 856/753-8000; www.dougfoley.com).

WHEN TO GO: Courses are scheduled throughout the year nationwide; check the website for details and schedule.

300

Congo Camp
Feel the Beat
Maui, Hawaii, and Pike, California, U.S.A.

Whether you're a drummer, a dancer, or just excited about joining a group of people who are, Congo Camp is your chance to live out your fantasy. Imagine a community of hundreds of people dedicated to one thing: drumming, and the dancing that accompanies it. Whether you're an expert Congolese drummer, or a newcomer looking to share in the fun of dancing to the ancient rhythms of Africa, Congo Camp is a great chance to hone your skills in a friendly, supportive atmosphere. And the thrill of playing side by side with others who share your passion only makes the experience that much more exhilarating.

There are two camps each year; a summer camp is held in July in the forested mountain community of Pike, California, midway between Sacramento and Reno, Nevada. Winter camp is held in March at Camp Keanae on the Hawaiian island of Maui. Each camp lasts about 10 days, but those who show up for a day or who want to attend classes on a drop-in basis are also welcome. Work-study opportunities are also available. Classes in singing and dancing as well as drumming are held several times each day, and there are

more informal sessions held at special events like the Hawaiian beach party.

Congolese drumming involves much more than the sound from a musical instrument—it's described as an all-encompassing, empowering communal experience, and the camp reflects that tradition. Food is served three times a day, and children are welcomed to participate in supervised arts and crafts, dance and musical activities. Indoor and outdoor camping accommodations are available. There's even an African-style marketplace where vendors display handicrafts, clothing, jewelry, and more. And for folks who want to enjoy the atmosphere without attending classes, the camps welcome vacationers who simply want to relax, swim, sunbathe, and soak up the good vibrations. —*ML*

ⓘ **Congo Camp** (ⓒ **530/288-3603;** www.congolesecamp.com).

WHEN TO GO: Mar or July; check website for exact dates.

✈ Sacramento (85 miles/137km) or Maui (30 miles/48km).

301

Fire Dancing Boot Camp
Baby, Light My Fire
Major Cities across the U.S.A.

Flames are whipping around your head and body in a flash of light and heat while the speakers are thumping out a rhythmic

bass groove. A disco inferno? Not exactly—you're at fire dancing boot camp, and you're learning the ancient art of poi,

Playing with fire at the Temple of Poi fire dancing boot camp.

having a blast and getting one of the best workouts of your life. Originally practiced by the Indigenous Maori people of New Zealand, poi—which translates as "ball"—was used to enhance strength and flexibility by men and women alike. The weighted poi ball is tethered to a rope and swung in a coordinated rhythm to work out arm, shoulder, and back muscles. And once you've mastered the initial steps, the poi is set aflame and suddenly you're caught up in a brilliant dance with fire.

Novices are encouraged to take a few poi classes before attempting fire poi. (Classes are reasonably priced at around $20 per class.) In addition to poi, fire staffs, hoops, and fans can be incorporated, depending on the class level and instructor. Boot camps and lessons are offered in a number of major cities, but California has earned its reputation as a hotbed of fire dancing, and well-regarded schools such as **Fire Groove** in Los Angeles (www.firegroove.com), **Fire Arts Collective** in Oakland, and San Francisco's **Temple of Poi** (www.templeofpoi.com) offer a series of boot camps, online classes, DVDs, performances, private lessons, and respected instructors with years of experience and safety training. There are several levels of classes available, often with discounts for multi-class series.

Fire dancing has, in just a few years, gone from being a cult-like practice seen at alternative art and music festivals like **Burning Man** (www.burningman.com; see **330**) to gaining more mainstream interest. Fire dancing performers are now in demand at everything from bachelor parties to corporate retreats. And long-time practitioners have embraced fire dancing's community spirit, in some cases attesting to the spiritual dimension of the art form. But newcomers shouldn't be put off; beginners swear it's a great workout and probably the most fun you will ever have playing with fire. —ML

ⓘ **Fire Groove** (𝄇 **323/640-0191;** www. firegroove.com). **Fire Arts Collective** (www.fireartscollective.com). **Temple of Poi** (𝄇 **415/543-4911;** www.templeofpoi. com).

302

Michael Jordan Flight School
He Shoots, He Scores!
Las Vegas, Nevada, U.S.A.

You're dribbling down the line, the basketball hammering the hardwood beneath your hand, and the hoop is in sight. You're just about to take your shot when in front of you appears . . . Michael Jordan! The 6-foot, 6-inch tower of talent tries to block your shot, but you've got your game on this afternoon. Fake left, hop right, and shoot—it's in. Two points later, His Airness smiles and shakes your hand. He is, after all, your coach today.

Since 1997, Michael Jordan, the former shooting guard for the six-time NBA championship-winning Chicago Bulls, has been downloading his awe-inspiring basketball skills at Michael Jordan Flight School basketball camps. But if you think "basketball camp" means worn-out balls, ratty nets, and smelly locker rooms, think again—accommodations, equipment, and facilities at the Las Vegas Mirage Hotel and Casino are nothing like high school. But this 4-day camp isn't a relaxing poolside retreat. Attendees should be physically fit and prepared for intense, all-day practice with elite NBA and Olympic coaches and players like Larry Brown, Mike Krzyzewski, Chuck Daly, and Kareem Abdul-Jabbar, as well as some "air time" with Jordan himself. In addition to one-on-one sessions with coaches and players, there are competitive league games for all players, and campers who don't wish to play can still get involved as assistant coaches.

Despite all the hard work and sweat, there's still a little room for some downtime, and many campers cite the networking and social events as a prime benefit of Flight School camps. A cocktail reception, closing ceremonial brunch, autograph sessions, a high-stakes poker tournament—even a ladies' tea—are on the schedule. An experience like this doesn't come cheap—rates for 2009 were $17,500—but there are perks aplenty, including Jordan brand shoes and apparel, commemorative gifts, photos, videos, and, best of all, the lifetime bragging rights to saying, "Yeah, I shot hoops with Michael Jordan. He's pretty good." —*ML*

(i) **Michael Jordan Flight School** (© 503/402-8688; www.mjseniorflightschool.com).

WHEN TO GO: Michael Jordan Flight School is scheduled annually; check website for dates.

✈ Las Vegas McCarran International Airport.

🛏 $$$ **The Mirage Hotel and Casino,** 3400 S. Las Vegas Blvd. (© 702/791-7111; www.mirage.com).

Jim Gibson's Motocross Training Camp
Down & Dirty
Southern California, U.S.A.

Ripping through the dirt, floating through the air, roaring around a steeply banked curve—these are the stuff of motocross dreams. And every year, hundreds of motocross riders make these dreams come true at Jim Gibson's Motocross Training Camp. To casual spectators, motocross might look like simple dirt-biking, but it is in fact an incredibly nuanced competitive sport that requires discipline, strategy, and training, as well as considerable physical endurance and strength. Spend a little time at Jim Gibson's and soon you'll be flying like the big boys.

Jim Gibson's Motocross Training Camps take place at some of Southern California's most challenging motocross tracks. The typical camp lasts 4 or 5 days, costs around $1,000, and includes everything from dormitory-style accommodations and meals to exercise and dieting tips. Bike rentals are available depending on availability. The focus here is not on the freestyle acrobatics that are famous at events like X Games (see **339**), but rather the straight-ahead racing skills that will put riders in the winner's circle.

Gibson emphasizes skills like holeshots, where riders jockey for position early in a race. Precision braking is another key strategy, and cornering safely and successfully can make or break a rider. Physical conditioning may be more important here than in any other motorized sport, because riders are handling 200-pound (91kg) bikes moving at top speeds between 50 and 70 mph (81–113kmph), and the motocross camps give riders plenty of opportunities for weight training, running, and gymnastics.

Gibson, a former factory rider for Yamaha and Honda (big names in motocross), was a member of the gold medal-winning team at the 1982 Motocross des Nations event in Wohlen, Switzerland. He went on to win several more medals and awards in U.S. and international motocross. He's available for training sessions not only at his motocross camps, but also for group lessons and private one-on-one sessions. —*ML*

(i) **Jim Gibson's Motocross Training Camp** (© **951/698-9272;** www.jgmxl.com). **WHEN TO GO:** Year-round.

Getting dirty at Jim Gibson's Motocross Training Camp.

304

Richard Petty Driving Experience
NASCAR Nation
Locations across the U.S.A.

You're roaring down the track at 140 mph (225kmph), and up ahead is your first turn, a steep bank of asphalt that looms before you like a smooth, paved mountainside. Underneath the hood are 600 horses of pure, NASCAR-inspired power. The car soars into the curve and as you clutch the wheel with your sweaty grip, the wide, treadless tire stick to the course like black glue. Suddenly you realize this may be the most fun you've ever had.

The Richard Petty Driving Experience has been giving thrills like this to speed junkies for over 15 years. Starting at the Charlotte Motor Speedway in North Carolina, the company capitalized on its success there and has now expanded to 27 speedways from New England to Southern California. After arriving at your chosen track, you'll be issued a driving suit, attend a mechanical and safety orientation, get strapped into your car, and then hear the four words that set any racetrack renegade's heart aflutter: "Drivers, Start Your Engines!"

There are a range of driving programs offered by the RPDE, from the Rookie Experience (eight laps over one session lasting about 3 hr.) through the Talladega

Super 16 (16 laps over the super-speedway's wicked 33-degree banked curves) up to premiums like the Brickyard Experience (24 heart-pounding laps on the famed Indianapolis Motor Speedway).

The RPDE also offers a ride-along program for folks who'd like to get a taste of what 165 mph (266kmph) feels like by riding shotgun in a car driven for three laps by one of the instructors. The ride-along option is also offered to folks who aren't able to drive a four-speed manual transmission (required of all solo drivers).

After you and your fellow drivers clamber out of your stock cars, you'll be feted in a closing ceremony, and all attendees receive a graduation pack with a lap-time sheet and graduation certificate. The RPDE is also open to group events and corporate outings, and can custom-tailor a program to meet anyone's need for speed. —ML

(i) **Richard Petty Driving Experience** (© **800/BE-PETTY** [23-73889]; www.1800 bepetty.com).

WHEN TO GO: Open year-round; check website for dates and locations.

305

Rock 'n' Roll Fantasy Camp
So You Wanna Be a Rock & Roll Star?
Locations worldwide

The crowd is roaring, the spotlights are blazing in your eyes, your ears are ringing from the towering speakers, and next to

you onstage is Roger Daltrey from The Who. Behind you on drums is Alan White from Yes. And on vocals, you've got Steven

Roger Daltrey works with campers at Rock 'n' Roll Fantasy Camp.

Tyler from Aerosmith and Brian Wilson of The Beach Boys and . . . wait a minute, what is this, some kind of rock 'n' roll fantasy?

Yes, actually, it is—the kind of fantasy you can only get from Rock 'n' Roll Fantasy Camp. There are a number of other rock music camps out there, but this is the original and, many say, still the best. The camps, which last about 5 days, are held in cities like Los Angeles, New York, Las Vegas, and London. (One-day camps are also occasionally offered.) Practice and recording sessions take place at legendary sites like Abbey Road Studios in London and the Capitol Records building in Hollywood. Best of all, each camp concludes with a live performance taking place at classic rock venues like the House of Blues, Whisky-a-Go-Go, and The Cavern (where a little combo called The Beatles got their start some years ago in Liverpool, England).

The camps, which are popular as gifts and corporate retreats, are a total immersion in rock music, and everyone from novice songwriters and newbie drummers to ax-shredding, head-banging guitarists gets to participate in the fun. But there's plenty of work involved, too: In addition to the more than 10 hours of jamming each day, small group classes are led by professional musicians (imagine having Ted Nugent or Bruce Kulick of Kiss as your teacher!). Master class sessions in bass, drums, guitar, songwriting, and other skills are also offered. Campers eat meals and stay in the same hotel as celebrity musicians, so there are plenty of opportunities for one-on-one encounters with your rock idol.

After registering for Rock 'n' Roll Fantasy Camp, each camper is assigned to a band based on his or her interests and skill level. Campers practice an original song to be performed with their band at the final night's concert, known as "Campapalooza," which is open to the public and recorded on a DVD, so you can relive your rock 'n' roll dream over and over again. All this making of fantasies come true doesn't come cheap. A few days to a week at camp can run you anywhere from around $4,000 to more than $10,000. But really, you can't put a price on living the dream. —ML

ⓘ **Rock 'n' Roll Fantasy Camp** (✆ **888/ 762-2263** or 44/0845-0943256 in the U.K.; www.rockcamp.com).

WHEN TO GO: Whenever you're ready to live the dream.

306

Rock Climbing Camp
Rock On
Northern California, U.S.A.

You've seen them at the gym, those lean, muscular types intent on one thing and one thing only: the rock climbing wall. Is it the mental challenge of scaling those technically difficult, dangerous heights that keeps them so focused? Or is it the sheer physical endurance and strength that attracts men and women of all ages to the sport? Find out for yourself at a professionally run rock climbing camp located in some of the most spectacular scenery in North America: the Sierra Nevada mountains of California.

Camps sponsored by **Mountain Adventure Seminars** are available for newcomers to the sport as well as advanced rockheads who are looking for some new peaks to bag. Most last about 2 days, and are located at various places in the Sierra Nevadas. Some previous climbing experience—indoor or out—is expected, and depending on the location of the base camp, some backpacking experience and general outdoor skills may also be required (this ain't the Ritz). And if you still have some energy after a day of climbing, there are ample bouldering opportunities in many of the camping areas.

In addition to climbing instruction, you may be able to take advantage of on-site "mini-clinics" on topics like climber self-rescue or anchoring techniques. Class sizes are strictly limited, so the guide/climber ratio is ideal (on more advanced camps, there are two students per guide). Not able to make it to one of their scheduled camps? Not to worry: The team of instructors at MAS also offers private instruction and guiding for individuals and groups, including overnight adventures. And if you're looking for a great group activity for your family reunion, scout troop, office staff, or church group, look to MAS to put together a great event, whether it involves rock climbing, snow shoeing, backcountry skiing, or hiking. —*ML*

ⓘ **Mountain Adventure Seminars,** 148 Bear Valley Rd., Bear Valley, CA (✆ **209/ 753-6556;** www.mtadventure.com).

WHEN TO GO: Check website for schedule.

✈ Sacramento, CA, or Reno, NV.

307

Woodward at Copper
720s Off Big Air
Copper, Colorado, U.S.A.

The world is upside down. Now it's right side up again, but you're floundering in a pit of blue foam. Time to grab the overhead rope and haul yourself out of the pit,

so you can go back to Big Air, with its 43-degree pitch, and try another backflip. Elsewhere in the vast Barn at Woodward at Copper pro freeriders, amateurs, and

Practicing tricks at Woodward at Copper.

novices are doing somersaults on trampolines, slingshotting up the 8-foot (2.4m) wall in the Skate Bowl, and arcing into 720s off a jump.

Jazzed by the loud rock music, the action is constant at Woodward at Copper, the year-round ski and snowboard camp at Copper resort in Colorado. The 20,000-square-foot (1,858 sq. m) barn, filled with a terrain park and pipe progression, is the heart of the camp. Inside, the Gym Cross Zone contains six Flybed trampolines (three lead into foam), a Tumble Track in foam, and a Spring Floor. The Snow Skate Zone has the 35-foot-long (11m) Big Air drop covered in Snowflex (a brush-like surface that simulates snow), with three different-sized jumps that lead to a foam pit. This zone also has an 8-foot (2.4m) Cliff Drop into foam, a 5-foot (1.5m) Skatelite drop into foam, a loose foam pit,

and a SnowFlex Jib run with rails and boxes, and a quarter-pipe. The Skatelite area has a big Skate bowl, and 3- and 5-foot (1 and 1.5m) Mini Ramps.

Snowsliders who want to learn tricks and moves come here to learn gravity-defying feats in a controlled environment. The coaches are medal-winning pro snowboarders, pro freestylers, and gymnasts. They take students through a progression in this setting, where if a student blows an aerial and lands awkwardly the impact is blunted by foam instead of unforgiving snow.

Skiers and snowboarders can sample the camp in mini-sessions, pick up punch cards for drop-in sessions, or take multi-day classes. During the winter, Woodward at Copper runs day sessions; half of the day is spent in the Barn and the other half in parks and pipes on the slopes. During the summer, there are weeklong sessions for ages 8 through 18, and shorter sessions for groms (8–12).

Copper, a year-round resort 75 miles (121km) from Denver, is a small ski village at the base of the mountain offering 2,450 acres (971 hectares) of skiable terrain. The parks and pipes here have snagged awards from *Transworld SNOWboarding* magazine. Lots of mountain winter sports are offered here, from cross-country skiing and tubing to sleigh rides and dog sledding. Copper is a good location in the summer for people who want to hike, mountain bike, and play golf in the high country. —LF

ⓘ **Woodward at Copper** (℃ **888/350-1544** or 970/968-3400; www.woodwardatcoppercolorado.com).

WHEN TO GO: Year-round.

✈ Denver (75 miles/121km).

🛏 For a variety of local options, contact **Copper Mountain Resort** lodging (℃ **888/350-1544** or 888/219-2441; www.coppercolorado.com).

308

StuntWorld Action Camp
Be Your Own Stunt Double
Las Vegas, Nevada, U.S.A.

Most folks who come to Las Vegas gamble with a little cash—or a lot. But a more action-packed good time awaits those who would rather gamble on making it out of a burning building or a high-speed car chase than surviving an encounter with a one-armed bandit. If you've ever wondered if you have the right stuff to be a stuntman or stuntwoman, step right up and take a shot at **StuntWorld Action Camp,** created by stunt legend Check Borden.

The classes take place in a studio just a few minutes from the Las Vegas strip, and participants can choose half-day programs (with two stunt classes) or full-day programs (with four classes). Full days also include a catered lunch, because a day of barroom brawls and jumping out of helicopters really builds up an appetite. The cost structure favors groups of 12 or more (a full day runs about $625 for one person, but only $535 per person if you have 12 or more in your group), and the events are ideal for corporate retreats, bachelor and bachelorette parties, birthdays, and family reunions.

Borden, who has some 300 stunt credits to his name, has doubled for actors Val Kilmer, Liam Neeson, and George Clooney. He's put together a dizzying variety of classes: Fight choreography will teach you the art of giving and receiving a punch in the face. Rappelling shows you how the pros jump out of a helicopter and live to tell about it. Car hits will teach you how to take a fender to the gut. Precision driving not only offers a lesson in stunt driving, but also teaches defensive driving skills that might come in handy on your daily commute. And after a class on fire gags, being engulfed in flames will be a no-brainer. StuntWorld also has an impressive list of trainers with years of experience who act as instructors and safety experts, ensuring that what happens in Vegas stays out of the ER. —*ML*

ⓘ **StuntWorld Action Camp** (✆ **702/982-5097;** www.stuntworldactioncamp.com).

WHEN TO GO: Open year-round; check website for class schedules.

✈ Las Vegas.

🛏 $$ **Las Vegas Hilton,** 3000 Paradise Rd. (✆ **800/732-7117;** www.lvhiton.com). $$ **Luxor Las Vegas,** 3900 Las Vegas Blvd. S. (✆ **888/777-0188;** www.luxor.com).

309

Survival Skills Weekend
Stayin' Alive
Verona, New York, U.S.A.

The hiking trail you were on has disappeared in a dense woodland, and darkness is gathering around you. The only sound you can hear is the howling of a distant wolf. Quick—what's the most important tool you'll need to survive in the wilderness? Dry matches? Water? A flashlight? Actually, it's none of these things (though each is good to have on hand). The answer to survival questions like these is familiar to graduates of the Survival Skills Weekend courses, held in a 200-acre (81-hectare) private wilderness in upstate New York.

There are many wilderness survival schools, but John D. McCann's series of Survival Skills weekends (there are three levels, beginner to advanced) stands out for its hands-on, deep-woods approach and the practical experience he brings to his students. A former Marine drill instructor, McCann is also the author of *Build the Perfect Survival Kit*, the first book of its kind. The 48-hour weekend courses are limited to a maximum of 10 students and cover everything from water purification and squirrel trapping to clever ways to start a fire, like connecting the positive and negative ends of a cellphone battery with a length of steel wool—the steel wool will ignite. (Kids, don't try this at home!) Campers are asked to bring their own food, clothing, and basic camping equipment; a cookout dinner is provided for all on Saturday night.

Though it sounds like a lot of serious work—and much of it is—participants also rave about the fun and excitement involved in the survival experience, otherwise known as bushcraft. McCann also helps students avoid the pitfall of buying a lot of unnecessary or overpriced equipment they won't need. A CD, for example, is reflective enough to signal a passing plane, and an Altoids tin comes in handy as a makeshift frying pan. But the most useful piece of survival equipment, according to McCann, is the one you're least likely to forget at home—your brain. —*ML*

ⓘ **Survival Skills** (ℂ **845/471-2434;** www.bepreparedtosurvive.com).

WHEN TO GO: Courses are scheduled throughout the year; check website for dates.

✈ Albany International Airport (113 miles/182km).

Tornado Chasing
Whirlwind Tour
Great Plains, U.S.A.

The day started out clear and bright, but by noon the skies have darkened, and ominous storm clouds now block the sun. A few raindrops splatter on the windshield as you race across the prairie, following a tip from the satellite tracking system. You and your fellow adventurers scan the horizon, looking for signs of trouble, when the clouds in the western sky begin spinning around in a slow, deadly waltz. Then, like a dark sword, a funnel cloud dips toward the earth, and the race begins—you're chasing after a tornado!

Ever since *Twister* tore into movie theaters in 1995, tornado chasing has gained a new cachet, and a number of professional outfits have sprung up around the Midwest offering storm chasing tours. Prices and schedules can vary widely, but most offer van or SUV-based tours lasting a few days to a couple of weeks (prices can run close to $3,000 for a tour), usually during the peak months of May through July. The better companies offer tours led by qualified meteorologists and researchers who, backed by years of experience and a dazzling array of high-tech equipment, have a fairly good success rate of leading teams to tornadoes, supercell thunderstorms, and other extreme weather events.

The plains of Texas and Oklahoma (also known as "Tornado Alley") are ground zero for tornado chasing, though tours can travel from the Canadian Plains through the Dakotas and down toward the Mississippi Valley. Expect to spend a lot of time on the road, much of which will be spent not looking at tornadoes—extreme weather is a fickle guest, and doesn't always show up on schedule. Tornadoes also frequently occur at night or are totally obscured by rain. On slow days, some tour operators might offer visits to attractions like Mt. Rushmore (www.nps.gov/moru), Carlsbad Caverns (www.nps.gov/cave), or the world's largest ball of twine in Cawker City, Kansas (cute, but not exactly an F5 twister). It's all worth it, however, if you're able to see in person—and capture in photos or on video—one of nature's most awesome and destructive forces. —ML

TOURS: Storm Chasing Adventure Tours (✆ **303/888-8629;** www.storm chasing.com). **Silver Lining Tours** (✆ **303/ 644-4296;** www.stormchase.net).

WHEN TO GO: May–Aug.

311

Bull Riding Adventure Experience
So You Want to Be a Cowboy?
Locations across the U.S.A.

He weighs 2 tons and he's really, really angry that you're sitting on top of him. But you can handle this bull—you think. After all, you've had a few days of instruction at one of America's top ranked bull-riding clinics, and when that chute opens, you'll be ready for the ride of your life.

Lyle Sankey has been teaching rodeo skills like bull riding, team roping, and bareback bronco riding to professional competitors for years at his rodeo school in Branson, Missouri. He's now expanded his offerings to engage participants in a bull riding "Vision Quest" experience that lets novices try their hand at one of rodeo's most demanding events. Depending on the venue and schedule chosen, these camps can last from 1 to 4 days, and include classroom time, rides on the mechanical bull and, finally, the real thing: a bull whose size and temperament is matched to your age, athletic ability, and ambitions—you hope.

Participants are welcome to bring their own equipment if they have it, and instructors will evaluate and tune it up as needed; otherwise, the Sankey schools are willing to loan you their equipment. (The exception is boots—if you don't already own them, consider buying a good pair of Western boots with a relatively flat shank.) And you will also be required to have medical insurance, for reasons that are obvious; if you don't already have insurance, Sankey schools can put you in contact with providers of short-term medical insurance.

Bull riding takes a special kind of energy and ambition, but it's not limited by gender—both men and women are welcome at these schools, and female students from Sankey have excelled to the point that they have been featured as bronc riders in music videos. All ages are welcome as well; students from 7 to 70 have enrolled. And if you're just not sure you're ready to ride that bull, the "ground school" option lets you participate in everything, including the mechanical bull, until you're ready to tackle the real thing. —ML

ⓘ **Sankey Rodeo School** (✆ **417/334-2513;** www.sankeyrodeo.com).

WHEN TO GO: Open year-round; check website for dates and locations.

Holding on for dear life at the Sankey Rodeo School.

312

Wayne Gretzky Hockey Fantasy Camp
Slapshot!
Phoenix, Arizona, U.S.A.

You're skating up the ice with the puck in front of you, and the goal is in sight. An opening appears and you're lining up the shot, when WHAM! Out of nowhere, a body slam from the opposing team's Number 99 checks your dreams of hockey glory. Wait—Number 99? Yes, that was Wayne Gretzky, the Great One himself, on the ice with you.

Wayne Gretzky Hockey Fantasy Camp, an intensive retreat for hockey fanatics, takes a group of puckheads and over the course of 4 days molds them in the image of Gretzky himself—or a reasonable facsimile thereof. Held annually in the Phoenix area, the camp is limited to 72 players in order to ensure plenty of ice time, as well as one-on-one coaching from some of the best players in the history of the sport. (We're talking about legends like Theo Fleury, Larry Robinson, Gordie Howe,

Bobby Hull, Barry Melrose, Ed Mio, and Gretzky's brother Walter.) Players are divided into teams based on skill levels and experience, and all teams will play at least one game with Gretzky.

Skating with the Great One doesn't come cheaply. The camp costs $9,999 but includes plenty of perks: hotel accommodations in sunny Scottsdale, custom jerseys, sticks and gloves, a video of your game with Gretzky, and plenty of ice time for drills and games at Alltel Ice Den, home of the NHL's Phoenix Coyotes. The final evening includes watching a Coyotes game from the luxury of Gretzky's private box. Perhaps best of all, a portion of the proceeds from the camp benefits the Wayne Gretzky Foundation, which supports hockey training equipment and league play for underprivileged youth. —*ML*

ⓘ Wayne Gretzky Fantasy Camp (✆ **888/901-7529;** www.gretzky.com/ fantasycamp).

WHEN TO GO: Feb (check website for exact dates).

✈ Phoenix Sky Harbor International Airport.

🛏 $$$ **Resort Suites of Scottsdale,** 7677 E. Princess Blvd., Scottsdale, AZ (✆ **888/222-1059;** www.resortsuites.com).

313

Jazz Vermont
This One Time, at Jazz Camp . . .
Resorts throughout Vermont, U.S.A.

As the sun dips behind the lofty peaks of Vermont's Green Mountains, there's an electricity in the air that leaves you a little breathless. A crowd of people are gathered all around you on the velvety green lawn when you climb the steps to the outdoor stage. Your buddies in the band strike up the first few notes, then you lift your horn and out pour the sweetest swinging notes you've ever blown. One thrilling hour later, your set wraps up and another sound fills the air—the thunderous applause from hundreds of true jazz aficionados. This, you decide, is bliss.

Though perhaps not what you think of as a typical adrenaline adventure, Jazz Vermont has been making dreams like this come true since 1984, when an impromptu group of players realized they were having the time of their lives while vastly improving their music skills. The jazz camp moves to a different resort location each summer; past venues have included the Killington Grand Hotel in Killington, Marble Island Resort in Colchester, and Bolton Valley Resort. About 70 musicians now make the trek each year, along with a limited number of spouses and other family members. Non-musician guests are treated to a full slate of activities such as tennis, yoga,

antiquing, painting, and hiking the verdant hills of rural Vermont. The cost for participants runs in the mid-$1,000 range, plus extra for guests.

Despite the bucolic settings, this is no lazy summer jam session—folks here are serious about taking their music to new heights, and though no improvisational experience is needed, players are expected to be intermediate-level or higher and able to sight-read the music of Glenn Miller, Count Basie, Duke Ellington, and other jazz standards. Musicians should also bring their own instruments—mercifully, an exception is made for piano players.

The camaraderie that forms in the 6-day retreat is like no other; many first-time attendees are startled to find that the drummer they befriended only days ago is actually a neurosurgeon the rest of the year. And most of those first-timers feel compelled to return again—some 70 percent of Jazz Vermont musicians are repeat guests. —*ML*

ⓘ Jazz Vermont (✆ **800/242-8785;** www.jazzcamp.com).

WHEN TO GO: An annual mid-summer event.

314

Parkour
Brawn & Brains
Worldwide

In the opening chase scene of the 2006 version of the 007 film *Casino Royale,* James Bond pursues a bad guy who scrambles across rooftops, slides through a burnt-out car, climbs up the skeletal iron beams of a building under construction, then meets his prey face to face atop a tower crane. All the leaping, bounding, climbing, and jumping is not simply the work of graceful stuntmen or a good flight choreographer. The action sequence demonstrates an extreme form of *parkour,* a sport that has leaped from an underground movement into a mainstream activity in recent years.

Parkour, a made-up word, can be defined as "the art of movement, when one's body and mind are trained to overcome obstacles efficiently, with the goal of moving from one point to another as quickly and gracefully as possible." The *traceurs* (as participants are called) usually practice their sport in an urban environment. They vault over railings and drop down to a street, dive through a gap between fence posts, jump to reach the top of a wall and pull themselves over, continuing to navigate through, around, over, or under whatever obstacles are in their way.

David Belle and Sebastian Foucan (who played the evildoer in the opening *Casino Royale* scene) are credited as two of the founders of modern parkour, which started in France during the 1990s. They built upon the foundation created by George Hebert, who prior to World War I developed a Methode Naturelle technique of physical training using obstacle courses (parcours).

Today, parkour can be found all over the world. In the U.S., Denver is a hot spot, as are Washington, D.C., Chicago, and Seattle. Good international scenes are Toronto, London, and Paris. A Colorado-based group called "The Tribe" is made up of skilled traceurs who in the last few years have helped develop parkour in the U.S. by teaching classes, acting as unofficial ambassadors for the growing sport, and creating the **American Parkour** website. Check out the website to connect with others doing parkour in your area.

The best traceurs blend strength, training, and critical thinking skills, but newcomers can learn and embrace the sport at much lower levels. Training to learn such maneuvers as the cat leap, the wall run, and the roll, whether on one's own or through schooling, is vital. Today, three gyms in the North America are devoted exclusively to parkour: In Denver, Ryan Ford runs **Apex Movement.** Other training facilities are **Primal Fitness** in Washington, D.C., and **Money Vault** in Toronto. In London, there's **Parkour Generations,** and in Australia, a good resource is **Australian Parkour Association** (www.parkour.asn.au). A growing number of fitness gyms are offering parkour courses. Parkour is a blend of brains and brawn, but one that requires skill and training, because it can be dangerous. Before taking a parkour class, ask the instructor how long he or she has been doing it and whom they trained with before starting to teach. —*LF*

ⓘ **American Parkour** (www.americanparkour.com). **Apex Movement** (ℂ **720/242-9250;** www.coloradoparkour.com). **Primal Fitness** (ℂ **202/635-1941;** www.primal-fitness.com). **Money Vault** (ℂ **647/350-1111;** www.themonkeyvault.com). **Parkour Generations** (ℂ **44/7825-410134** or 44/7984-348218; www.parkourgenerations.com).

7 Races & Festivals

The Empire State Building Run Up
Upwardly Mobile
New York, New York, U.S.A.

No one needs an introduction to the Empire State Building. This 107-story skyscraper dominates the Manhattan skyline and is a giant amongst giants with 1,860 steps, 6,500 windows, 73 elevators, 2 banks, 5 entrances, 3 cafes, and 250 maintenance staff. It is undoubtedly the most famous building in the city and has drawn the multitudes to peer from its observation platform, including a rather large ape called King Kong. Built in 1931, it has been the scene of countless romantic movies as well as the final jumping off point for some 30 suicides. (One such jumper threw herself off the 86th floor in 1979, only to be blown back onto the 85th floor relatively unscathed.) The building, located on Fifth Avenue and 34th Street, has survived the Great Depression, near bankruptcy (initially it was nicknamed the "Empty State Building"), and a catastrophic plane crash when a B25 Mitchell slammed into its side in 1945. Every year it also survives one of New York's most bizarre and grueling foot races—the great Empire State Building Run Up.

Looking somewhat out of place in togs and trainers amidst such Manhattan Art Deco splendor, 250 runners gather in the building's glass and marble lobby. They are congregated for what is essentially a handrail marathon, a vertical sprint to the top through a narrow grey stairwell. They trod a mind numbing 1,576 steps to the 86th floor at 1,050 feet (315m), their ears popping from the change in altitude, to a viewing platform that is often shrouded in clouds. Women go first, dashing across the lobby and jostling up the stairwell in what is a seriously competitive race with not an animal costume in sight. Participation is by

Participants approach the finish line atop the Empire State Building.

invitation only, though anybody is free to make an initial application to the organizers who are called the New York Road Runners. Competitors are chosen by ability and background and there is a nominal registration fee of $30 if chosen. Runners come from all around the world to test their stamina on what proves to many a stairway to hell, where the sheer monotony and exertion means the climb is tough mentally as well as physically. Approximately 10% never make it to the top. Australian professional cyclist Paul Crake holds the overall record, completing this stair crazy challenge in 9 minutes, 33 seconds (that's 6,593 ft. an hour), the only runner to ever reach the observation platform in under 10 minutes. The winner receives no prize money, just a commemorative medal and a free

Previous page: A rider on the California "Death Ride" takes the rain in stride.

plane ride back to the event the following year. Thankfully, all the runners are allowed to take the elevator back down.

First held in 1978, the Empire State Building Run Up is the oldest and most prestigious event in a new urban endurance sport called tower running. Now there are similar events all over the world in cities as diverse as Sydney, Moscow, Vienna, and Detroit. One thing they all have in common is a mighty towerblock with hellish steps, some surpassing the Empire State in height and agony. Bangkok's event at the Westin Banyan Tree Hotel, for example, has 1,093 steps. Tower running is certainly for the fit and upwardly mobile and one thing is guaranteed wherever you choose to do it—if the view does not leave you breathless, the run up will. —CO'M

ⓘ **New York Road Runner's Club** (ⓒ **212/860-4455;** www.nyrr.org).

WHEN TO GO: Early Feb. Check website for details.

✈ JFK, LaGuardia, and Newark Liberty.

🛏 $$$ **The Michelangelo Hotel,** 152 West 51st St. (ⓒ **212/765-0505;** www. michaelangelohotel.com). $$ **Hilton Garden Inn,** 63 W. 35th St. (ⓒ **212/594-3310;** www.hiltongardeninn.hilton.com).

Endurance Endeavors **316**

Iditarod
Call of the Wild
Anchorage, Alaska, U.S.A.

Apparently the word "iditarod" is Alaskan Indian for a "distant place," but I'm not fooled. Those in the know realize it is a word that has no equivalent in English but can be summed up as *a grueling, relishing challenge, whipped up and freeze-dried with masochistic lunacy*. How else can you describe Alaska's most famous endurance race, an epic journey of 1,150 miles (1,852km) over desolate tundra, dense forest, frozen rivers, and gale whipped coast? Every first Saturday in March, some 90 competitors gather in Anchorage—teams of mushers (sled drivers) with their frisky bands of yapping Siberian huskies and Alaskan Malamutes. They set off for the distant town of Nome in the north through a wilderness trail that passes through tough sounding settlements such as Rohn Roadhouse, Cripple, McGrath, and Shageluk. The mushers are equipped with axes, snowshoes, and arctic parkas. God knows they'll need them as they endure a 2-week slog through temperatures that can reach 50°F (10°C) below zero, waist deep snow, howling blizzards and jet black darkness. This race is so tough even the dogs wear boots.

Such pain ahead is belied by the festival atmosphere in Anchorage as the race sets off. Thousands of well bundled spectators gather on the city streets to see the dog teams bound into action at 2-minute intervals. In fact, this is all very much ceremonial as the serious time clock does not get started until the teams depart from the town of Wasilla. Nevertheless, the atmosphere in Anchorage is electric—the locals take this dog race very seriously. Evidence of this can be seen by the city statues to race runners from the past such as Balto the Dog. Race winners become local legends and walk away with $70,000 in prize money, plus a truck. Anyone can enter—though it's mostly locals, people come from far and wide to participate in this legendary event. To enter you need to put down a $4,000 fee. The whole community turns out with many volunteering as stewards and marshals and rescue teams.

Such community spirit can be traced back to the origins of the race. In 1925 a diphtheria outbreak in Nome threatened to wipe out the local Inuit population. A town doctor sent back word to the state capital that he needed an urgent supply of the life-saving serum. Thus became the "Great Race of Mercy." Eskimos, Russians, Norwegians, and Irish formed a team of 20 dog teams that ran a rescue relay north through the remote and dangerous Yukon. They got there just in time to save the day. The famous run was re-enacted in 1973 as part of Alaska's centennial celebrations and it has been running ever since. The record for the race is 10 days and women have proved just as capable at competing with the most manly of mushers. Deaths are not unknown and doctors and veterinarians are positioned at every checkpoint to ensure the wellbeing of every competitor. As well as extreme temperatures and rugged landscape, racers must look out for that most dreaded of incidents—a collision with a moose. —CO'M

ⓘ www.iditarod.com.

TOURS: Alaska Iditarod Tours (✆ **1/604-720-0744;** www.iditarodtours.com). **Alaska Tours** (✆ **1/866-317-3325;** www.alaskatours.com).

WHEN TO GO: First Sat in Mar.

✈ Ted Stevens Anchorage International Airport.

⊨ $$$ **Anchorage Marriot Downtown,** 820 W. 7th Ave., Anchorage (✆ **1/907-279-8000;** www.marriott.com). $$$ **Hampton Inn Anchorage,** 4301 Credit Union Dr., Anchorage (✆ **1/907/550-7000;** www.hamptoninn.com).

317 Endurance Endeavors

Antarctica Ultra Race
The Loneliness of the Distance Ultra Runner
Patriot Hills, Ellsworth Mountains, Antarctica

Go where even penguins fear to tread, where the sun never sets, and a savage and beautiful landscape will break down even the hardiest stamina. Antarctica is the end of the world, the frozen continent, the coldest place on the planet, and the last place on earth you'd think of going for a run. Yet every year a contingent of 20-odd, stubborn athletes brave its wind blasted interior to jog across 100km (62 miles) of ice, rock, and snow drifts. They appear like moon walkers, wrapped up in Gore-Tex and face masks with goggles and gloves ensuring not an inch of human flesh is exposed to withering snowstorms and hurricane gales. They may sit out for days in the desolate Patriot Hills, 483km (300 miles) north of the South Pole, waiting for the bad weather to pass before they dash across the tundra in a race that usually takes

20 hours. They risk −4°F (−20°C) temperatures on a landscape 900m (3,000 ft.) high with the occasional field of bottomless ice chasms to keep the runner alert.

Antarctica is famous for monumental peacock-blue icebergs shaped in surreal formations, craggy glaciers that crash into the sea, sheer ice-encrusted walls that form magnificent canals, and jagged peaks that jut out of icy fields. On the shores, several hundred thousand penguins can be found nesting and chattering away along the coast. Humpback, orca, and minke whales are often visible, nosing out of the frigid water, as are elephant, Weddell, leopard, and crabeater seals. Birdwatchers can spend hours studying the variety of unique seabirds that reside here, including petrels and albatrosses. Yet the ultra marathon runners see none of this as the course is so far from the shore there is absolutely no life, just a pristine ice block that allows them to boast they are one of the few who have run on the seventh continent.

First run in 2004, the Antarctic Ultra Race is the ultimate conclusion in a recent phenomenon known as ultra running. No longer content with city marathons and country runs, a small but growing band of athletes is choosing to run races of between 201 and 306km (125–190 miles) in isolated parts of the world. Such events are the supreme test in endurance, motivation, and concentration with many participants describing the experience as a type of epiphany, where everything superfluous falls away, the world becomes simpler, and the pain and hardship of such gruelling marathons ultimately lead to elation and a sense of purpose. It is no accident that most ultra runners are over 40. This could be explained by the fact that

most events are expensive—the Antarctica trip costs $16,500, with the 8-day itinerary setting out from the Chilean Patagonian town of Punta Arenas. Yet a more fitting explanation is that some people are just not happy with golfing or sailing. They seek adrenaline rushes and excruciating challenges in unforgettable places, and the Antarctica ultra marathon certainly meets the criteria. —CO'M

ⓘ www.icemarathon.com.

WHEN TO GO: Dec. Check website for details.

✈ Punta Arenas, Chile.

🛏 $$ **Hotel Diego de Almagro Punta Arenas,** Av. Colón 1290 Ciudad, Punta Arenas (ℂ **56/61/208800;** www.da hoteles.com). $$ **Hotel Cabo de Hornos,** Plaza Muñoz Gamero 1039, Punta Arenas (ℂ **56/61/715-000;** www.hoteles-australis. com).

Endurance Endeavors **318**

The Great Divide Race
Blazing Saddles
Montana, Idaho, Wyoming, Colorado & New Mexico, U.S.A.

Being chased by a bull moose is just one of the challenges a bike rider encounters when undergoing the epic Great Divide Race. Crossing paths with a grizzly bear is another. If the rattlesnakes don't get you, the mosquitoes certainly will as you sleep on rocky ground in desolate forests on this solo cycle dash from the Canadian border to Mexico. Peddling against strong headwinds, struggling with a flat tire in the pouring rain, or advancing slowly up a mountain pass through biting snow is normal. Riders have been known to faint from heat exhaustion, lie 2 days in a tent with food poisoning, and shiver in pre-dawn bouts of hypothermia. Swollen feet, a blistered rear end, and chronic sunburn are the usual corporal complaints while that

all essential bike may be grounded with broken chains, splintered spokes, and bent rims. All these adrenaline-inducing ingredients add to the recipe for the Great Divide Race.

Yet perhaps the hardest aspect of this heroic American ride is its utter loneliness. There is nobody around to help with that unreadable map or massage that chronic case of tendonitis. The basic ethos of this 2,500-mile (4,025km) gauntlet through the wilderness of five Midwestern states is you must do it on your own. There must be no pre-arranged help and the entire route must be completed within 25 days. If you break down, you must walk to the nearest town and resume the journey exactly where you stopped. There are no support vehicles, and though riders can join up along the way, they must not help each other in any way, including sharing the slipstream nor bicycle parts or tools. New equipment can be sent by courier and cyclists can pull into any town along the way and stock up on essentials, eat in a diner, even sleep in a motel if they have the time, which they usually do not. Normally sleep involves four uncomfortable hours by the side of a dirt track—night cycling is essential to keep on course and on time.

The first person to attempt this transcontinental cycle ride was a Scotsman in 1892 on a bike made of wood. A battalion of black *buffalo* soldiers distinguished themselves by breaking between both borders on two wheels 5 years later. It was not until the 1990s, however, that a formal time trial was set and the first race began in 2004 when four of seven riders finished the course. Now, two dozen riders roll unceremoniously out of Roosville Moun tain in Montana at noon on the 19th of June every year. They must reach Colo rado by Day 12 and the record for the entire route is a super-human 15 days. Many riders abandon the race exhausted and take a Greyhound home. Others limp past the finishing line in Antelope Wells,

New Mexico, delirious with hunger, fatigue, and joy. Despite the hardship, they have experienced something more than a race. The Great Divide is a journey where cyclists wake up amidst herds of wild horses and free wheel down mountains during sunrise with eagles the only spectators. Every state line is a boost and to run a finger along a map of the route so far covered gives a sense of achievement more profound than 50 laps around a velodrome. The terrain is gorgeous with red isolated barns sitting on desolate plains, high alpine mountains, and old mining ghost towns all part of the itinerary. The Great Divide Basin and the Wyoming red desert unfold before each rider, and the sense of discovering new ground is enough to keep going. Curling up in that damp sleeping bag after a good day on the saddle covering 100 miles (161km) is an achievement not everybody can boast. The rider deserves his sleep. He just makes sure he has his can of bear mace within reach if needed. —CO'M

ⓘ www.tourdivide.org
WHEN TO GO: June 6
✈ Lethbridge, Alberta, Canada.

Marathon Des Sables
Dune Runners
Sahara Desert, Morocco

The Marathon of the Sands is often referred to as an ultra-marathon when in fact it is the anti-marathon. Here in the sweeping Sahara desert of Southern Morocco, there are no crowds to cheer you on like there is when you shuffle through a Manhattan street in the New York marathon. No music blares from passing bars nor are there traffic police blocking side streets. Instead you join a

long line of lonely runners snaked across high, orange dunes with the only sign of life the numbing pain in your blistered feet. Temperatures of 125°F (52°C) make it feel like you are running in a rather large hair dryer and the 30-pound rucksack on your back convinces you that somehow you have joined the French Foreign Legion by accident. This 6-day, 243km (151-mile) endurance run over sand and rock, through sand storms and freezing nights, is in fact six marathons in one. The prospect of competing in it is an adrenaline rush in and of itself. The actual competition is a fatiguing, yet gratifying exhilaration. Needless to say there is not a large woolly animal costume in sight.

Instead, competitors wrap their heads in hats, sunglasses, and scarves to protect themselves against the heatstroke that frequently downs some of the 800-plus participants. An Italian runner got lost one year and wandered this vast space south of the Atlas mountains for 9 days, surviving on boiled urine and dead bats. Runners burn up to 2,000 calories a day. They must carry food for the entire week along with clothes, a sleeping bag, and a survival kit. Organizers dispense 9 liters (over 2 gal.) of water a day for each participant, just enough to prevent dehydration and not enough to wash. The survival kit includes tropical disinfectant and an anti-venom pump to deal with bites from snakes and scorpions. There is also a distress flare and signalling mirror for those who need help.

Started in 1986 by Frenchman Patrick Bauer, the exact marathon route frequently changes. The starting line is usually a 5-hour drive from the kasbah town Ouarzazate, known as "the door to the desert." It sometimes ends in Erfoud, a sand city that is the frequent location for Hollywood sandal epics such as *The Mummy*.

You feel like a mummy after Day 2. Day 4 is an 80km (50-mile) night dash and though the route is lit up with beacons, a sandstorm can wipe out all visibility and runners must rely on their compasses to get them through. The rest camps are anything but luxurious, with thin canvas tents holding exhausted runners. There is little or no privacy, with competitors having to get used to relieving themselves in the open for all to see. Despite such discomforts and a $3,000 registration fee, this gruelling race is always oversubscribed and places are sold out within 10 minutes of their release. Over 7,000 people have participated since it started, the youngest being 16 and the oldest 78. It has a strong international feel with lots of French and British, but the king of the race is a Moroccan called Lahcen Ahansal who has won it 10 times. Most people are just happy to finish it. As for the lack of large woolly animals, I lied. There is a herd of camels that follow behind to pick up stragglers. —*CO'M*

ⓘ www.saharamarathon.co.uk.

TOURS: The Best of Morocco (✆ **44/ 1249-467-165;** www.morocco-travel.com).

WHEN TO GO: Apr 1–12.

✈ Ouarzazate.

🛏 $$$ **Le Berbere Palace,** Quartier Mansour Eddahbi, Village Berbere, B.p 165, Ouarzazate 45000, Morocco (✆ **212/ 2488-3105;** www.ouarzazate.com). $$ **Dar Karma,** Juan Antonio Munoz et Carmen Cabezas 45 Taourirt, Ouarzazate 45000, Morocco (✆ **212/5/2488-8733;** www.darkamar.com).

Endurance Endeavors **320**

California Death Ride

Ride or Die (or Both)

Alpine County, California, U.S.A.

The weather ranges from snow, freezing rain, and tennis ball–sized hailstones to 100°F (38°C) of searing heat in just a few hours. Participants climb more than 15,000 feet (4,500m). The total course is 129 miles (208km) of lung-busting, leg-burning asphalt so brutal that about a third of those entering the race don't finish it. True to its name, death is not unheard of. And otherwise rational people *choose* to do this.

It's the California Death Ride (sometimes euphemistically referred to as the Tour of the California Alps), and each year thousands of people trek to remote Alpine County in northern California to spend an entire day beating their bodies and brains to a pulp to finish one of America's most brutal endurance events. The ride leaves from Turtle Rock Park outside Markleeville and heads over five mountain passes and through two national forests (Toiyabe and Stanislaus) before it ends.

Don't expect to just show up with a bike: The ride has a limited number of entrants (recently capped at 3,500 riders), so those interested should buy tickets well in advance. Training is also required, because even experienced cyclists cramp up on the event, and the ticket lottery gives preference to athletes who have completed other long-distance, high-altitude rides.

Preparation is the key to surviving the ride. Thin mountain air is a serious consideration for an event that begins at 5,500 feet (1,650m) above sea level and goes up

from there. Even the downhill portions of the ride have their risks: At speeds exceeding 50 mph (81kmph), wheel wobble is a life-threatening risk, and there are unexpected obstacles like livestock. One cyclist in the early days of the ride was killed from injuries sustained when he and several other riders hit a cow.

But it isn't all sweat and blood. The ride passes through some of the most spectacular scenery in the world, with snow-capped peaks and fields of wildflowers throughout the course. And entrants are treated to a number of great benefits, like snacks, fruit, energy drinks, bike mechanics, and massage therapists along the route—which almost makes it seem worth it. —*ML*

(ⓘ) **California Death Ride** (ⓒ **530/694-2475**; www.deathride.com).

WHEN TO GO: July; check website for exact date.

✈ Reno, NV (67 miles/108km).

⊨ $ **Zephyr Cove,** 750 Hwy. 50, South Lake Tahoe, NV (ⓒ **800/23-TAHOE** [238-2463]; www.zephyrcove.com). $$ **Fireside Lodge,** 515 Emerald Bay Rd., South Lake Tahoe, NV (ⓒ **800/692-2246** or 530/544-5515; www.tahoefiresidelodge.com).

---

321 Endurance Endeavors

Man versus Horse Marathon
Horsepower
Llanwrtyd Wells, Wales

The sight of a man sprinting toward a finishing line with his opponents, a horse and rider, racing beside him may appear like a slightly one-sided contest. Even the most powerful sprinters would find it hard to match a four-legged gallop, especially over a 35km (22-mile) course. Yet throw in some steep hills, forest paths, streams, and fences, and the apparent mismatch evens out a little. A human athlete can run

through an oak woodland much faster than a horse, for example, and the wild moors and bogs of the Welsh countryside will test the endurance of even the strongest thoroughbred and skilled rider. This annual cross-country race attracts 500 runners and more than 50 horses. They huff and puff across a rugged and beautiful landscape and though a human has won the race only twice in its 29-year

Man and horse bound through a stream in the Man versus Horse Marathon.

history, among the runners-up there are many cases of men and women beating off the stallions and mares.

It all began with a bet. Pub landlord Gordon Green overheard two customers discussing the merits of running as opposed to galloping while enjoying a drink in his quaint country pub at the Neuadd Arms Hotel in the tiny Welsh town of Llanwrtyd Wells, 165km (65 miles) north of Cardiff. Green agreed with one bookie that a man can beat a horse in the right conditions and went about proving it. The first race took place in 1980 and since then numerous runners and riders have braved wind, rain, and scorching heat to settle the matter. Every June they all gather in the town square of this old Victorian spa town (pop. 600) with its handsome white gables and multi-colored streets.

Llanwrtyd Wells sits amongst rolling green hills, its low grey slate roofs huddled along the river Irton with an old stone bridge crossing the lively stream. This part of mid-Wales attracts its fair share of nature lovers as it has excellent hiking trails and valley walks. The sweeping Brecon Beacons mountain range is nearby and farther north you'll find a lovely collection of 12th-century castles such as the handsome red gritstone Powys Castle on the English border and the desolate and eerie Aberystwyth Castle overlooking the Irish sea.

Runners get a 15-minute head start on the horses to avoid getting trampled. The time difference is adjusted at the end so any naysayers cannot accuse the race of being fixed. Within 8 minutes, the horses catch up with the humans and for the next 2 to 3 hours a cat-and-mouse game ensues as man and horse cross paths, get stuck in mud holes, gingerly descend steep hills, and wade through waist-deep streams. Water stations are set up at intervals where men and women drink hungrily from cups and the horses from buckets. The event attracts thousands of spectators who cheer on the contestants at different vantage points throughout the course. The final sprint and gallop takes place back at the village and normally the hooves win hands down by an average margin of 5 minutes. That was until 2004, when a young Welsh soldier called Huw Lobb became the first man in history to officially beat a horse. He ran the course in 2 hours and 5 minutes, beating his nearest equine foe by 2 minutes. The winner walked away with prize money of $40,000 and bookmakers had to make handsome payouts as they had calculated that a man beating a horse was simply a daft proposal. —CO'M

(i) www.green-events.co.uk.

WHEN TO GO: June 2010.

✈ Cardiff.

🛏 $$$ **The Lake Country House Hotel & Spa,** Llangammarch Wells, Powys, LD4 4BS (✆ **44/1591/620202;** www.lake countryhouse.co.uk). $$ **The Neuadd Arms Hotel,** The Square, Llanwrtyd Wells, Powys LD5 4RB (✆ **44/1591/610236;** www.neuaddarmshotel.co.uk).

---

322 Endurance Endeavors

Race the Train
Do the Locomotive
Tywyn, Wales

Here your competitor is not like any other—a 14-ton steam train with a red hot boiler, driving wheels, and darting cylinders. It chases over 2,000 runners on a 23km (14-mile) circuit through pine forests, crop fields, and deep ravines, and very few people manage to beat it. The Talyllyn Railway steam engine does have certain advantages over mere mortals. It does not need to stop every few miles for a drink of water, for example; nor does it have to negotiate uneven ground and nettle pastures. Yet it must be said that none of the athletes who race against it have to haul four wooden carriages behind with jeering spectators.

Only 5% of runners manage to beat the Victorian coal sprinter that does the rounds of the beautiful countryside and coast near the town of Tywyn in northern Wales. Originally the railway was built to carry slate from a quarry farther up in the hills that border beautiful **Snowdonia National Park** (www.eryri-npa.gov.uk). Now it takes tourists around this picturesque corner of Wales with the sweeping Cardigan Bay looking out over the Irish sea.

The race first began in 1983 as a small charity event that has now mushroomed into one of the U.K.'s most distinctive and idiosyncratic countryside runs. It attracts serious athletes who must complete the course in less that 1 hour and 20 minutes if they have any chance of beating the train. It also attracts its fair share of Sunday runners out for some fun. The cool thing is all the family can tag along for the entire circuit as the train chugs beside each runner with spectators in its carriages. For serious runners intent on beating the machine, it is key they get out way ahead in the beginning as the course becomes more difficult on two feet and the train easily catches up.

The seaside town has a carnival atmosphere with lots of stalls and games and throngs of Welsh speaking locals in what is very much a local event. The race begins at the old bridge next to the railway line and takes a 1.6km (1-mile) run through the town before becoming a cross-country scramble. Stewards stand at field gates to guide the runners and hand out water in the sometimes blistering August heat. The train needs little guidance as it follows the 150-year-old narrow gauge tracks around gorgeous countryside that includes a set of beautiful falls known as Dolgoch falls. The route sweeps beneath the hills and

Runners rival a steam engine in the Race the Train competition.

turns toward the town with the runners crossing the finish line in the town's school yard and the train resting its pistons in the railway yard. —CO'M

ⓘ www.racethetrain.com.

WHEN TO GO: Aug.

✈ Liverpool.

🛏 $$$ **Bae Abermaw,** Panorama Rd., Barmouth, Snowdonia National Park GW42 1DQ, Wales (© **44/1341/28-0550;** www.baeabermaw.com). $$ **Ty'r Graig Castle,** Llanaber Rd., Barmouth, Snowdonia National Park LL42 1YN, Wales (© **44/1341/28-0470;** www.tyrgraig castle.co.uk).

Endurance Endeavors **323**

Primal Quest
The Super Bowl of Adventure Races
Location Changes Yearly

Nicknamed "The Super Bowl of Adventure Racing," the grueling Primal Quest is the ultimate adventure race. Sounds too dramatic? During the race through South Dakota's Badlands teams paddle, run, mountain bike, and navigate their way non-stop across more than 600 miles (966km) of rugged landscape. In the process, they climb more than 100,000 feet (30,000m) of vertical gain. Co-ed teams must survive in the open wilderness with only what they carry on their backs, and depend upon solving problems together and helping each other through the mental and physical challenges.

With a focus on being an ecologically aware wilderness Expedition Adventure Race, in this competition teams of four must make the backcountry journey using only a map, a compass, and combined skills. Winning requires selfless teamwork as much as stamina and determination. In keeping with Primal Quest's ecological mantra, teams can travel only where permitted, can't build campfires, and stick to the "pack it in, pack it out" rules.

Experienced adventure-race addicts from around the world are the ones who show up for this annual competition, but only after training for months beforehand. Cross-training is a must because the full team must take part in all six stages of each race: trekking, off-road running, and orienteering; mountain biking; caving; swimming; kayaking; and a fixed-line ropes-climbing course.

The co-ed four-member teams must travel together at all times and finish as a group to be officially ranked. If one member drops out for any reason, the team must drop out. On average, since the first race in Telluride, Colorado, in 2002, almost half the teams fail to finish. Racers are tracked with SPOT satellite messengers, small sophisticated units that show where the teams are at any time.

Primal Quest is held in a different location every year and new disciplines are added, such as whitewater swimming and canyoneering. During the first race in Telluride, 62 teams from eight countries entered and the winning team completed the course in just over 3 days. In 2003, the Primal Quest 457-mile (736km) race in the Lake Tahoe area became the first adventure race to be shown on network television.

Entering the race is costly. The fee was $11,000 per team for the Badlands race in August 2009. But, the three winning teams each get more than their entry fee in prize money, plus free entry into the next Primal Quest event. —LF

(i) **Primal Quest** (www.ecoprimalquest. com).

Endurance Endeavors

324

TransRockies Run
Rocky Mountain High
Buena Vista to Beaver Creek, Colorado, U.S.A.

The TransRockies Run through Colorado is no ordinary romp in the park: Participants climb a total of nearly 25,000 feet (7,500m) in elevation over 5 days while averaging 22 miles (35km) each day. The course takes runners through 110 miles (177km) of backcountry trails—most of the course is off-road—and runners can expect to endure the full gamut of Rocky Mountain extreme conditions, including freak snowstorms, torrential rains, thin mountain air, searing heat waves, and below-freezing nighttime temperatures, with the occasional bear, skunk, or mountain lion thrown in. The payoff? Spectacular mountain vistas, great group camaraderie, and the sense of achievement that comes from finishing one of the most well-organized and best-supported running events in the U.S.

The race has six legs, each of which ends in a campsite set up for runners so that at the end of the day they can simply kick off their dirty, well-worn shoes and relax. The route goes through a few small towns as well as through the White River and San Isabel National Forests, crossing countless streams, valleys, and ridgelines along the way. It's mostly single-track trail running with a few paved trails in between, and plenty of long downhill sections as well as some slow, grinding uphills.

The event has a well-deserved reputation for supporting runners. In addition to plenty of rest and refreshment stops, there are also catered meals, massage and physical therapists, hot showers, lots of great schwag gifts, and evening celebrations including awards ceremonies and video presentations of the day's run.

Modeled after the TransAlpine running event in Europe, the TransRockies Run has one unusual aspect that makes it a standout among races: It's a two-person team affair, so participants—who usually must endure the loneliness of the long-distance runner—get more of a group experience from a partner who's there when they need some encouragement, a swift kick in the butt, or just someone to celebrate with at the end of a grueling day.—*ML*

ⓘ **TransRockies Run** (✆ **866/373-3376;** www.transrockies.com).

WHEN TO GO: Aug or Sept; check website for exact dates.

✈ Central Colorado Regional Airport, Buena Vista.

Alcatraz Swim
The Great Escape
San Francisco Bay, California, U.S.A.

An early morning fog floats over San Francisco Bay as the 7:45am ferry leaves from Pier 33, close to Fisherman's Wharf. Destination: the famous citadel known as Alcatraz, 1.5 miles across the water. The former home of Al Capone and George "Machine Gun" Kelly is now a national park and recreation center. Yet this particular ferry is not carrying day-trippers or tourists. The hundreds of people who line the deck are planning their own unique escape. They suddenly begin to strip, pulling out yellow swimming caps and squeezing into wetsuits. As the boat pulls up close to the island prison known as "The Rock" they all begin to jump in the water, three and four at a time. A noisy gaggle splashes around in the freezing foam with gulls, cormorants, and egrets flying over ahead. The swimmers tread the water, chatting among themselves and pointing in the direction of the Golden Bridge. A starting horn blows and off they go, swimming frantically toward land.

The distance looks deceptively short. One of the reasons the island was chosen as a prison is because the tides that run around it are treacherous. The strong current pulls people west and can move a floater three miles off course in less than an hour. Swimmers are advised to swim against the tide, focus on their land destination and not on the swimmers ahead as they will end up going way off course and beneath the bridge where they will require rescuing. Stewards in kayaks shepherd the group of 700 swimmers toward Presidio Park in the shadow of the famous suspension bridge. The view is unusual and unbelievably beautiful with the majestic bridge connecting two land heads with the city skyline in the distance.

That same view must have haunted the former inmates as it seemed so close yet so far. Alcatraz boasts that it had no escapees in its 30-year history as a prison. There were 14 attempts and 2 drownings. In 1962, three men managed to reach the

Swimmers fill the San Francisco Bay during the Alcatraz Challenge.

water with the aid of a drill made from a vacuum cleaner. They were never found and presumed drowned. The island's history goes back to 1775 when it was discovered by the Spanish and christened *La Isla de los Alcatrices* after the many pelicans that nested in its rocks. It served as a lighthouse, fort, and military prison before the government decided to make it a prison for some of America's most dangerous criminals. It was eventually closed because it was too expensive and there were concerns regarding the pollution it caused in the bay. Now it is a popular tourist spot, with haunted dungeons, guard towers, and parade grounds to visit.

The swimmers do their own style of parade when they reach land on the other side. A seven-mile (11km) run across Presidio Park involves negotiating steps, a dirt trail, and brick tunnel. The runners dodge walkers, cyclists, inline skaters, joggers, and dogs as they climb 400ft (120m) in a half-mile. The race must be completed within 3 hours from ferry to finishing line if they wish to be timed. Lots of stragglers run in after the time limit, still happy to have escaped from Alcatraz. —CO'M

ⓘ www.alcatrazchallenge.us.
WHEN TO GO: Second Sun of July.
✈ San Francisco.
🛏 $$$ **Ritz Carlton,** 600 Stockton St. (✆ **415/296-7465;** www.ritzcarlton.com). $$ **Hotel Rex,** 562 Sutter St. (✆ **415/433-4434;** www.jdvhotels.com).

Adventure Races
Ready to Run, Paddle & Bike?
Texas, U.S.A.

Shall we hike around this steep slope to the other side of the hill, or try to scramble over it? Do you want to push me on a bike around these barrels stuck in the sand, or would you rather I push you? These are just two of the offbeat types of decisions you and your partner may have to make during a fast-paced adventure race. Growing in popularity, adventure races are designed to get people off couches and out into the wilderness. The key to winning is coordinating with your teammate(s) to get through the event—hopefully in first place. Sort of like a local version of the *Amazing Race.*

Although there are usually three parts to the **Terra Firma Promotions** adventure races, don't expect them to be like ordinary triathlons. During these races you'll run along a trail instead of on a street, paddle a canoe instead of swim, and ride a mountain bike, perhaps on singletrack. These adventure races have teams of two, three, or four people, depending on the type and length of the adventure race.

Terra Firma Promotions is run by a Dallas-based couple, both winning adventure races—one a former pro mountain bike racer and the other an elite athlete. Most of their events are held in areas in and around Dallas, Austin, and Houston. Their sprint series is the right choice if you want to start adventure racing, because you don't need a top athlete's skill and conditioning. These events generally last 2 to 3 hours and include a three-mile trail run, paddling a canoe for about 30 minutes, then mountain biking 8 to 12 miles. Teamwork is the key, because both you and your buddy must finish. The teams that work together, whether it is learning to paddle in unison or hooking a long bungee cord between the two people while running or biking, so the slower person goes a bit faster to keep up, are the teams that do the best.

If the shorter races hook you, build up to the 12-hour races, then progress to the 24-hour events. If you've become an adventure racing devotee, collect a team of three or four people to run one of the 7- to 10-day races. The longer races are more complex. During the *Sprint* races competitors run along clearly marked trails. In the longer races, teams are given coordinates and must use a compass (no GPS allowed), a map, and a UTM corner ruler so they can plot where they have to go in the wilderness. For example, they may have to decide to follow a riverbank through a forest or run down a ravine, rather than taking a road that is farther away and longer but flatter.

Mystery events often are tossed into the mix. For example, a cargo net may be staked to the ground. Smart racers think to take off their helmets and backpacks before slithering under the net. Others try to slide under quickly, still wearing their gear, and getting caught, slowing them down. While most of Terra Firma's 12 events are held in outdoor and wilderness areas, when an event is held in an urban setting competitors may have to rappel down a building or roller blade along streets.

Though most adventure races attract athletic types, there are no restrictions on who can enter. These races emphasize teamwork above all else. And as long as you're having fun, learning a little something about getting along, and getting your adrenaline pumping, then you're doing it right. —LF

(i) (c) **972/966-1300;** www.terrafirma promo.com.

WHEN TO GO: Races run from Feb–Oct, but the major race series is in May, June, and July.

327 Foolish Fun

Idiotarod
Manhattan Madness
New York, New York, U.S.A.

A shopping cart dressed up as jetliner is being pulled down a freezing Manhattan street by four half-naked men covered in goose feathers. Another cart has the guise of a Roman chariot driven by a gladiator in a broom brush helmet with music blaring from a boom box while centurions hand out scrolls of Roman porn. Tourists happily snap photos to show the folks back home just how crazy this city is. No, you have not taken a wrong turn and ended up at the Bronx zoo. You have tripped across (like many of the competitors) the annual New York grocery cart travesty known as the Idiotarod.

The rules are there are no rules, as long as you wear no spandex and have no motor on your shopping cart. There is not even a pre-determined route in what turns out to be the most elaborate pub crawl in the world. Grocery carts become intricate floats with names and themes such as Octopussy, Top Gun, and Couch Potatoes. Some produce their own steam and even make a pretty decent cup of coffee. Competitors are encouraged to cheat by bribing judges with whiskey and sabotaging fellow competitors by tripping and blocking. It is not unheard for a food fight to break out in front of Rockefeller Center. One year some fake judges sent half of the competitors the wrong way toward Central Park.

Idiotarod is for the hip and anarchic and is thrillingly illegal—thus the lack of a predetermined route to deter the police from stepping in. Yet this race, inspired by the endurance dog sled run in Alaska of similar name, is gaining such fame and notoriety with hundreds of entrants every year that it's only a matter of time before it becomes official and indeed a major annual event. For the moment, it is a maniacal 6-mile (10km) drunken drive across this island of skyscrapers, where competitors do what they can to cross to line—even hijack legitimate shopping carts from a grocery store when their own breaks down. In 2009 there were 15 arrests for being public nuisances, but that's what you've got to do to be an idiot. —CO'M

(i) www.cartsofbrooklyn.com.

WHEN TO GO: Last week of Jan.

✈ JFK, LaGuardia, Newark Liberty.

🛏 $$$ **Inn New York City,** 266 W. 71st St. ((c) **212/580-1900;** www.innnewyork city.com). $$$ **Sofitel New York,** 45 W. 44th St. ((c) **212/354-8844;** www.sofitel. com).

The World Wife Carrying Championship
Marital Distress
Sonkajarvi, Finland

There used to be two ways to carry your wife at the World Wife Carrying Championship in Sonkajarvi, 6 hours north of Helsinki in Finland. One was the plain, old piggy back with the betrothed jiggling on her husband's back like a distressed koala bear as he ran the 253m (830-ft.) obstacle course through mud, gravel, and sand. The other was the fireman's hold where the lucky lady was thrown over the shoulders like a sack of potatoes and transferred with muscled intent across the athletic pitch and through a pool of water to the finish line. Then the unthinkable happened. Some foreigners came and beat the Finns at their own game. Estonians from the south introduced their own method that inevitably became known as the "Estonian hold." It involves the man bending before the standing woman and thrusting his head between her legs, then lifting her up until her head hangs upside down behind, facing her rear end and her arms wrap around his abdomen to strap her legs at the front allowing the male easy freedom of movement and sight. As for the lady's view? Let's just say it is not the Northern Lights this Nordic country is famous for.

The "Estonian hold" took the sport by storm and soon these upstarts from the south were breaking all records and taking all the loot home—the main prize being the lady's weight in beer and a plasma TV. A bitter rivalry broke out between both countries that continues to this day, lightened somewhat by other international competitors who approach the sport with a little more tongue in cheek, if you'll pardon the expression.

Wife Carrying comes from the sweet, old Finnish way of courting a girl by walking straight up to her and carrying her away to your village. Somebody then had the bright idea of introducing an assault course, timing it and hey, presto! The wife carrying contest was invented. The first official championship took place in 1994 in this small town of 5,000 people in the center of Finland. Now the annual event is world famous and attracts hundreds of competitors who need only 50€ ($74) and a willing wife to enter. Thousands come to watch, most of them, I suspect, ambulance-chasing divorce lawyers.

The female rider can in fact be any female over 17 and not necessarily the wife of the male carrier. She does have to weigh more than 49kg (108 lb.) and must at all times wear a helmet. The race takes place in pairs of two, giving each heat a competitive streak. There is a penalty fine of 15 seconds for dropping the wife. The

Men carrying their wives in the "Estonian hold" at the World Wife Carrying Championship.

course involves two hurdles and a 1m-deep (3¼-ft.) water trough that has a fireman dressed as a scuba diver on constant standby in case of any marital distress. There are separate prizes for the most entertaining couple and the best dressed duo. The world record to complete the course is an amazing 56 seconds, won by, you guessed it, those pesky Estonians. —CO'M

ⓘ www.sonkajarvi.fi.

WHEN TO GO: First week of July.

✈ Kuopio.

🛏 $$$ **Sokos Hotel Puijonsarvi,** Minna Canthin katu 16, 70100 Kuopio (✆ **358/ 17/1922-000;** www.sokoshotels.fi). $$ **Scandic Kuopio,** Satamakatu 1, 70100 Kuopio (✆ **358/1719-5111;** www.scandic hotels.com).

Water Splashing Festival
Out with the Rinse

Jinghong, Yunnan Province, China

Feeling jinxed? Had a run of bad luck lately? You must make your way to the laidback southern China city of Jinghong. There they have an excellent cure for misfortune—a bucket of water in the face. Apparently, there is nothing like a good drenching to wash away the blues and this city of black and white pagodas and yellow robed Buddhist monks becomes a frenzy of water dunking every April as the locals grab buckets, basins, and bottles and soundly soak whoever crosses their path. From a distance, the city's streets and square take on the appearance of an anarchic fountain with white arcs of water stretching across the air before descending into peals of screams and laughter. Everybody is fair game, so don't go expecting to avoid a soaking. There are no wet blankets at this shower party. The good thing is you can retaliate by grabbing the nearest receptacle and throwing back.

Traditionally, friends and neighbors sprinkled each other with drops of water to wish them luck for the New Year: The 3-day festival takes place during the local Dai people's New Year party. Then somebody realized it was much more fun to saturate and be saturated in turn. Girls huddle and scream as youths attack them

with water. Even the monks join in and jump in the river or nearest fountain. Buddha himself gets wet during a ceremonial bathing in the Mekong river. While all this happens, homemade bamboo rockets scream into the air and tiny, magical hot-air balloons float through the sky before being consumed in their own flames. Candle rafts float away down the river and small bean bags known as love pouches are thrown at whomever you fancy; catch one of those in the face and you know you have an admirer.

There is lots to admire about the province of Yunnan itself. Scenic valleys and fertile hills lead to lush paddy fields and tropical jungle. Here the people are more laidback than their northern cousins and the pace of life much less frenetic than Beijing or Shanghai. The people themselves are different, made up of several minorities, the most prominent of which are the Dai people. Their fun and relaxed attitude is more in line with their Thai, Laotian, and Burmese neighbors. The area has become a popular tourist destination with lots of trekking and biking possibilities in the surrounding area. Of course many come for the New Year's celebrations which run from the 12th to the 18th of April. As well as the water party, an amazing dragon boat race takes place on the river with each craft holding 50 rowers, pilots, dancers, and drummers. An extravagant parade rolls through the town with colorful floats surrounded by traditional dancers. On the final night a massive fireworks display takes place on the riverbank opposite, distracting tired and wet revelers with an awesome display. —CO'M

WHEN TO GO: Apr.

✈ Jinghong.

🛏 $$ **New Tai Garden,** 61 Minhang Rd., Jinghong, Yunnan 666100, China (✆ **86/691/216-5199**). $$ **Yunnan Aviation Sightseeing Hotel of Xishuangbanna,** 6 Menglong Rd., Xishuangbanna, Jinghong 666100, China (✆ **86/691-214488**).

Foolish Fun **330**

Thunderdome Cage Battle
The Mel Gibson Appreciation Society
Black Rock City, Nevada, U.S.A.

A huge dome welded with steel overhangs a large sand pit. Above it hangs a neon light in the desert darkness bearing the legend *The Thunderdome*. The structure is entirely covered in people clinging to the bars and hanging from the metal gridwork that allows them to see the interior below. Many looked like they have not washed or shaved in days and have a ragged, crusty look, colored by glow sticks and fluorescent clothing and the occasional beaded dreadlock. They look eagerly into the pit below, lit from time to time by the periodic camera flash. They cheer and jeer as two gladiators below bounce from bungee harnesses, whacking each other across the head with bats while a witchlike referee with tall staff and ragged skirt officiates. All you need is a Tina Turner soundtrack and you would be forgiven for thinking you're an extra in a *Mad Max* movie.

The venue is the **Burning Man** festival, the famous gathering of New Age ravers and radical thinkers in a desolate desert spot 100 miles (161km) from Reno in Northern Nevada. Here a temporary city of 50,000 hedonistic souls gathers once a year for a week of enlightened debauchery. Massive art installations, theme camps, techno parties, and incessant drumming take place in a C-shaped city at the center of which is a 40-foot (12m) effigy, the burning man that will be torched as the festival comes to an end. Colorful mutant cars roar around the playa, throwing flames and exciting mirth with some appearing as giant motorized muffins and an eight-legged mechanical spider.

The origins of the festival come from some annual San Francisco beach bonfires in the 1980s, and it has morphed into one of the biggest counter-culture events in North America. While some criticize that it has lost its free, non-commercial ethics (ticket prices are now $300), it still bans all merchandising and the only things you can buy on-site are coffee, soda, and ice. The rest you must bring yourself and gifting is encouraged where participants exchange items in brotherly love. Take the on-site Irish bar, for example, called *Paddy Mirage*, that dispenses free beer. There is a *Sobriety Checkpoint*, where sexy female police officers check you are drunk enough, and if not will judiciously pass you a cocktail.

Yet all charity stops within the Thunderdome arena as two fighters face off to a baying crowd. Anybody can participate—

in fact, the ethos of Burning Man is you must participate in some of the many events. The rather scary Thunderdome banshee referee issues the rules to each volunteer:

"One, I am always right. Two, stop and start when told, and three, don't bitch."

"You've got it." —CO'M

WHEN TO GO: Burning Man begins on the last Mon of Aug and runs for 8 days.

✈ Reno (118 miles/190km).

⛺ There are no hotels in Black Rock City. You must bring your own tent, car, or campervan.

---

331 Foolish Fun

Bay to Breakers
Naked Ambition

San Francisco, California, U.S.A.

Three women dressed as large vaginas pound the San Francisco pavement. A row of Elvises pee along a garden fence. A troop of Dolly Partons waves to a crowd while a mobile lap dancing bar complete with sofa and dancing pool is pushed up the steep incline at Hayes Street. Fluorescent ballerinas and some rather skinny rabbits chug from beer cans and limp toward the Golden Gate. There's a red naked lady and a green naked guy. Over the years, the Bay to Breakers foot race has morphed into an athletic type of Mardi Gras with all the wildlife of San

Squirrels and an acorn commune during the Bay to Breakers race in San Francisco.

Francisco turning out every third Sunday in May to trudge the 7.5-mile (12km) route from South Beach to the Great Highway. The race is very much a free-for-all with up to 60,000 participants. It holds the record for being the largest run ever, with 110,000 people jogging across the city in 1986, a sizeable proportion of them naked or dressed as penguins. The race is a real thrill for participants and onlookers alike.

Not that the event lacks serious athletes. They kick off at 8am and finish the course within an hour. Kenyan runner Sammy Kitwara broke the record in 2009 with a time of 33 minutes, 31 seconds, limping off with a prize of $40,000. Then the rest of the day is surrendered to the boozy extroverts who turn out with shopping carts piled with beer kegs, mobile bouncy castles, and elaborate pirate boats. The "Back of the Pack Club" is a determined bunch of slackers who prefer to stroll rather than run and men dressed in togas and grass skirts add to the general hilarity. The race began in 1912 to lift the spirits of a city still recovering from the 1906 earthquake. One hundred-fifty runners competed in the first "Cross City." Women were banned until the 1970s but that did not stop one Bobbie Burke completing the course in 1940 disguised as a man. That was also the first year to see a costume—a guy dressed as Captain Kidd who unfortunately came in last.

In the 1980s the event mushroomed into the monster event it is today with many now saying it has become too much of a monster. Residents along the route complain of vandalism and binge drinking and the general unpleasantness of watching overweight men run with no clothes on or observing a rather large bear pee in your front garden. Thirty-five tons of trash are left behind on the streets and whole floats abandoned at the end of the day have to be hauled off by the city to a kind of float cemetery. In 2009 the authorities decided to step in and banned beer, nudity, and floats. It caused uproar with a 25,000-signature petition and boycott campaign to keep the race weird. City Hall relented and the ban lifted. The San Franciscan right to wear body paint and little else is thus vindicated and it looks like the wild and wacky Bay to Breakers is here to stay. —CO'M

ⓘ www.baytobreakers.com.

WHEN TO GO: Third Sun in May.

✈ San Francisco International.

🛏 $$$ **Omni San Francisco Hotel,** 500 California St. (✆ **415/677-9494;** www.omnihotels.com). $$ **The Mosser Hotel,** 54 4th St. (✆ **415/986-4400;** www.themosser.com).

Foolish Fun **332**

Bathtub Racing
A Shower of Bathtubs
Nanaimo, British Columbia, Canada

A man jets across the choppy waters of Nanaimo harbor in western Canada. His boat slices through the snarly waves, rhythmically bucking upward on the rough tides. His shiny helmet and orange suit make him appear like a NASCAR racer as he leans forward and darts across the

waters. Then you notice that despite his speed he is actually riding along in a bathtub.

Nanaimo is a modern town on the picturesque coast of Vancouver Island that has one claim to fame—the oldest and fastest bathtub race in the world. First started in 1967 by a game ex-mayor fond of dressing up as a pirate, the Nanaimo World Championship Bathtub Race is now the Formula One for flying faucet riders. Originally 200 craft took to the water and jetted 58km (36 miles) across the bay to Vancouver. Now approximately 60 souped-up tubs mounted on race boats do a fast, blustery circuit along the island, beginning and ending at Nanaimo. The race has become so serious, organizers have had to split the race into two professional and amateur categories as the latest bathtub technology was excluding ordinary folks from joining in. The serious race takes less than 2 hours to complete and the winner gets a golden plug on a chain.

Nanaimo is known as the "hub, pub, and tub city." Originally a mining town, it is now a gateway to Vancouver islands and is notable for the excellent bars located in the downtown district. Once referred to as "a mall in search of a city," it comes alive for the 4-day marine festival that precedes the bathtub race held on the last Sunday of July. A town parade on the Saturday features local beauty queens, the oldest tubber, and the biggest bathtub in the world—a 10m (34-ft.) monster that is dragged through the streets and then put on display in the local Home Depot parking lot. On Saturday night there is a fireworks display and a ceremonial "Sacrifice to the Bathtub Gods" where an old boat is burned in honor of all the famous tubbers past and present. The race itself gets going at 10am on Sunday and can be viewed from the harbor pier and rocks that line the coast. Day-trippers take the beautiful ferry ride across Horseshoe bay from Vancouver to watch the mad frantic bathtub dash across the waters. A bronze statue of the man who started it all, the pirate costumed Mayor

A bathtub flies across the water in the World Championship Bathtub Race.

Frank J. Ney, overlooks the entire event. Originally the 1967 race was meant to be a one-off event to celebrate Canada's centenary. Of the 200 craft that left the pier, only 47 reached Vancouver with most sinking before they left the bay. Men thrashed around in the water cursing their luck. They insisted there must be a repeat race next year, giving them time to improve their bathcrafts. Their efforts did not go down the drain. —CO'M

ⓘ www.bathtubbing.com.

WHEN TO GO: Last weekend of July.

✈ Vancouver.

🛏 $$ **Coast Bastion Inn,** 11 Bastion St., Nanaimo, BC (ⓒ **250/753-6601;** www.coasthotels.com). $ **Buccaneer Inn,** 1577 Stewart Ave., Nanaimo, BC (ⓒ **250/753-1246;** www.buccaneerinn.com).

World Bog Snorkeling Championships
An Eel Is Wrapped Around My Ankle
Llanwrtyd Wells, Wales

"The stench of the bog was horrendous, weeds become entangled around my legs, mask, and snorkel, and an eel wrapped itself around my ankle. Once I got to the 30-yard mark, which was just halfway to the finish line, my legs felt like lead in the cold water and the finish line suddenly seemed 2 miles away." This is how one woman described her experience in the World Bog Snorkeling Championships in Llanwrtyd Wells, Wales.

At the annual competition, contestants must fight their way through two lengths of a 55m (60-yd.) water-filled trench chopped out of a peat bog, wearing a snorkel and flippers. Competitors aren't allowed to use usual swimming strokes, so must rely on flipper power. Only for orienteering purpose can they raise their head above the swampy water filled with leeches, water scorpions, and the odd fish.

Who would do this? Those looking for a rush and an unusual way to get it! People come from as far away as Hong Kong and Australia to experience this one-of-a-kind event. Past participants have included a 14-year-old girl and a woman who took part in the competition to celebrate her 70th birthday. Many years, 150 contestants or more show up at the WBC, which are held on private farmland on the outskirts of Llanwrtyd Wells. Competitors often wear the wildest costumes. Years past have seen people dressed as sumo wrestlers, men in suits with briefcases, and even a guy with an iron and board strapped to his back! The fastest in various categories and the "fancy dress" winner all get medals and cash.

If this unusual competition was truly the brainchild of two locals while they imbibed a lot of Welsh Ale, who do you think created the **Bog Snorkeling Triathlon** and the **Mountain Bike Bog Snorkeling** championships? The triathlon includes a run, a "swim" in a peat-bog trench, and a mountain bike ride. During the mountain bike bog race, competitors cycle along the bottom of a 2m-deep (6-ft.) peat bog trench using a mask and snorkel. Competitors peddle a bike with a lead-filled frame and water-filled tires. (Scuba divers are in the trench if any problems should arise with participants.)

Llanwrtyd Wells is in the Irfon Valley in the foothills of the Cambrian Mountains. This area of mid-Wales offers more than just bog-oriented entertainment and recreation. Visitors will find plenty of hiking, mountain biking, horseback riding, and fishing. You will need a rental car to reach and explore this area. The region is especially lovely to visit through the summer and fall, but the Bog Snorkeling events are held in July and August. Visit the website for the exact dates. —*LF*

ⓘ **Bog Snorkeling Championships** (www.green-events.co.uk). **Llanwrtyd Wells Tourist Center** (✆ **01591-610666;** www.llanwrtyd.com).

WHEN TO GO: Check the website for annual schedule.

✈ Birmingham or Bristol.

🛏 $ **Lasswade Country House,** Station Rd. (✆ **44/1591-610515;** www.lasswadehotel.co.uk). $$–$$$ **Lake Country House,** Llangammarch Wells (✆ **44/1591-620202;** www.lakecountryhouse.co.uk).

334 Foolish Fun

Bottle Kicking

The Beer Brawl

Hallaton & Medbourne, Leicestershire, England

A large beefy man stands in a field and throws a 5.4kg (12-lb.) keg the size of a watermelon into the air three times. When it hits the muddy ground for the third time a 300-man mob jumps on it. They kick, they scuffle, they maul their way down the field with the "bottle" at the center of a wild and violent scrum. Punches are thrown, elbows hit faces, and fists dig into ribs in what is a rough and tumble effort to get the small receptacle of beer to one of two streams a mile apart. Tempers fray and scuffles break out as the multi-backed monster moves to and fro over ditches, hedges, and barbed wire. Clothes rip and the contestants become unrecognizable as they get covered in mud and cow manure. Men are crushed beneath the brawl, some unable to breathe until the mob moves on and rolls over some fresh contestants. Concussion is common and bones are invariably broken. A fleet of ambulances sits on standby to ferry away the wounded warriors.

The Great Bottle Kicking Festival of Hallaton and Medbourne is more like a war, with these two small Leicestershire villages battling it out to keep the keg. There are three bouts with three different bottles, with the winners the first to get to their stream two times. Just as there are no rules, there is no time limit and the riot can continue late into the evening as the fighters battle each other to near exhaustion. It is also a free-for-all where anybody can join in and the effort to get the keg is by fair means or foul. It is not for those of a delicate disposition.

The event gets going with a parade and fair in these two middle England villages 64km (40 miles) west of Peterborough. A giant hare pie is cooked and cut up and then thrown to the crowd, who scramble after the food with just as much brutal savagery as the field battle. Thirty-five hundred spectators gather for this event that has pre-Christian origins. One popular story is two old ladies in Medbourne were saved from a bull when the beast was distracted by a hare. They showed their gratitude by dishing out food and beer to the poor on Easter Monday. A more likely explanation of its origins is that it was a pagan fertility ritual. An 18th-century vicar unhappy with the festival's heretical overtones tried to ban it. He relented when an unhappy villager daubed "no pie, no parson" on the rectory wall. The muddy melee is thought to have started when one year nearby Hallaton rushed the crowd and stole the beer. Thus this annual settling of scores is thought to be an early precursor of football and rugby. One thing it proves is that an Englishman will do almost anything for a beer. —*CO'M*

WHEN TO GO: Easter Mon.

✈ Birmingham (97km/60 miles).

🛏 $$ **Kilworth House,** Lutterworth Rd., North Kilworth, Leicestershire (✆ **44/1858/880-058;** www.kilworthhouse.co.uk). $ **Dingley Lodge Hotel, Bed & Breakfast,** Market Harborough, Leicestershire (✆ **44/1858/535-365;** www.dingleylodge.com).

Bloco da Lama Mud Carnival
Primal Scream
Paraty, Brazil

A mud-covered creature stumbles toward the bank of a giant sand pit. Other creatures emerge from the mud, some stumbling as they slowly drag themselves out, muck dribbling from their limbs. All that is visible are their eyes and teeth. It could be primeval man taking his first steps onto land. Instead it is a bunch of Brazilians intent on having one big party.

The fact that festival participants at Bloco da Loma dress up as cavemen and run around shouting "hooga hooga ha ha!" only adds to the Stone Age connotations. They bang drums and chant, bearing large grisly gods made from skulls and matted hair. Filthy shamans burn colored smoke and horses drag altars befitted with wigs and puppets. All the runners are completely black—the color of the mud they rolled around in on Jabaquana beach before running through the streets of colonial Paraty, frightening tourists who look disconcertingly spic–and-span and colorful. Bloco da Lama means "block of mud" and it is part of the 6-day carnival festivals that engulf the country in early February. While Rio de Janeiro, 258km (160 miles) to the east, has the big, brash sambodome, Paraty has the down and dirty mud festival. Streams of young people run through the cobbled streets of this colorful city, some bearing ghoulish puppets and floats. Huge quantities of the local brew *cachacha* is consumed as well as lots of cool beers in the bars and kiosks that line the town's beachfront. Paraty is the home of *cachaca,* a sugarcane alcohol drink popular across the country; 1.3 billion liters of it is consumed every year, much of it during carnival.

The town has a lively arts scene with a bohemian feel. Once the second biggest city in Brazil, it thrived on gold and slave trading. Then the pirates came and the city proved vulnerable to attacks. The gold route moved north and Paraty fell into rapid decline. It was only in the 1950s that this atmospheric beachtown was rediscovered and an effort made to preserve and restore its charming architecture. Now it is a popular tourist destination in the Ilha Grande Bay with great bars and restaurants and a party atmosphere.

Its carnival celebrations are unique and have not been tainted yet by the outright commercialism that takes place elsewhere. Participation is open and free and the festival is still very much a local affair, though it is increasingly attracting foreign visitors. It can be difficult to tell locals from outsiders as they swarm across the streets. Everybody is covered in mud and they all speak the same language, which is "hooga hooga ha ha." —CO'M

WHEN TO GO: Early Feb.

✈ Rio de Janeiro (253km/157 miles).

⊨ $$ **Pousada Bromelias,** Rodovia Rio-Santos (BR-101) Km 558 Graúna, Paraty (© 55/24-3371-2791; www.pousada bromelias.com.br). $$ **Pousada do Sandi,** Largo do Rosário, 01, Paraty (© 55/11/3081-2098; www.pousadadosandi.com.br).

3 Wacky Climbing Competitions

If you're eager to shimmy your way to the top of something, but think rock climbing or ice climbing is too serious, strenuous, or stuffy, perhaps you need to go out on a limb (or a log, or a greasy pole, or a tower of buns . . .) and look for a different kind of climb. Below are three climbing competitions that aim to bring out the out-of-the-ordinary climber in you. —CL

336 Greasy Pole Competition, St. Peter's Festival, Gloucester, Massachusetts, U.S.A.: Ever since Italians began settling in the Gloucester, Massachusetts area just north of Boston, they've been coming together every June to celebrate the patron saint of fisherman, St. Peter. But what started as a day of tribute eventually turned from homage into a multiday celebration, with games, competition, and merriment. One of the most anticipated of the contests is the **Greasy Pole competition,** in which participants must make their way across a 45-foot (14m) greased telephone pole extended over the Atlantic in the (mostly futile) attempt to capture a red flag posted at the end. Oohs, Aahs, and Ouches! are constant refrains from the onlookers. Upon nabbing the flag, the contestant leaps (or more likely falls) into the water below and swims to the nearby beach, at which time he's hoisted on shoulders and paraded about town. And for what? Glory! The only reward fitting enough for such a pain-inducing and ridiculous, yet wonderfully spirited celebration. *www.st peterfiesta.org/greasypole.html.*

337 Cheung Chau Bun Climbing Festival, Cheung Chau, China: Just a short ferry ride (55 min.) from Hong Kong is the charming island of Cheung Chau, home to a small, but thriving fishing village of 25,000 people. Every late April or early May the locals host the world-famous and beloved **Bun Climbing Festival** at the Pak Tai Temple Playground. The festival features 14m-tall (46-ft.) bamboo towers of buns, which the contest participants clamber up in the hopes of clocking the shortest amount of time. Meanwhile, they're bagging as many of the edible buns, made by festival revelers, as possible. Competitors are divided into three age groups, 35 and over, 18 to 34, and under 18 (participants much be at least 1m/3⅓ ft. tall). *Islands District Leisure Services Office (© 2852-3220). Leisure and Cultural Services Department (www.lcsd.gov.hk).*

338 Tree Climb at Squamish Days Loggers Sports Festival, British Columbia: Amid a virtual thicket of logger sports—axe throwing, tree falling, and birling, to name a few—filling the hours of the **Squamish Days Logger Sports Festival,** the Tree Climb may tower above them all. In this event, tree climbers are challenged to a 24m (80-ft.) pole climb and descent. A timed event, the object is to scurry up and back down in as little time as possible, with past winners clocking in at jaw-dropping times of just 30 seconds. Intermediate and novice competitions are offered as well, in which both the heights and regulations (not timing the descent, for instance) are less strenuous. Loggers from around the world congregate in Squamish, 60km (37 miles) north of Vancouver and 65km (40 miles) south of Whistler, British Columbia, each year to participate in the contests and merriment. *www.squamishdays.ca.*

The X Games
Bike Ballet
Los Angeles, California & Aspen, Colorado, U.S.A.

A motor bike and rider soar 40 feet into the air. Mid-flight the rider detaches himself from the bike, flipping it and spinning it around his head in mid-air like a spacewalker playing with a satellite toy. He keeps the bike in play by the tip of his fingers holding the back tail light as both man and motor stretch across the air. He then effortlessly pulls the machine back toward him and resaddles and straightens up just in time as the motorbike comes down and lands on its back wheel, then front wheel and he rides away. It's a graceful display of man and machine in gravity defying unison, a trick at which any moment with the slightest mistake would see the rider painfully crash to the ground with his ride on top of him.

Yet crashes, bruises, and broken bones are all par for the course at the X Games. This jump jamboree is the Olympics of extreme sport and has its own A-list of fearless superstars such as snowboarder Danny Kass and skateboarder Shaun White, known as the Flying Tomato for his shaggy red hair and mid-air antics. They may not be household names among ordinary sports lovers but they are skatepark heroes among the youth subculture that flocks to this annual event held in different locations around the U.S., but mainly in Los Angeles and Aspen. The Colorado event is the winter version, with skiers and snowboarders thrilling the crowds with aerial acrobats. Skinny guys in baggy pants show their youth was not wasted when fooling around with a board in the local park. Organizers are constantly introducing new mutant endeavours such as Ultracross, a ski and snowboard relay race, and Snowmobile Snowcross, described as NASCAR on snow. Two hundred-fifty athletes take part, including

several dozen Olympians, and crowds of up to 130,000 spectators form 2-hour queues around the block for the 3-day events. An event village is created where an X Fest takes place, showcasing the participants to the background of live rock music and interactive video games. Though it may look as though the athletes are having all the fun, the fans, in watching all the tricks and stunts, experience their own adrenaline rush.

The first event took place in 1995 and has grown exponentially since. Some initial experiments included bungee jumping and shovel racing but it soon became apparent that it was the core sports of biking and boarding that excited the crowds and got the most from its participants. Owned, operated, and promoted by the sports channel ESPN, the X Games has proved a masterly exercise in marketing, with high octane sponsors attracted by the young, predominantly male audience and their potential spending power for accessories and video games. Such clever promotion is evident when another well known biker, Danny Way, launched himself over the Great Wall of China and it is all too obvious in the amount of video clips of X Game tricks frequently downloaded by the YouTube generation.

Initially spurned by the sporting establishment, extreme sport is losing its counterculture swagger and is slowly being accepted into the fold as a genuine sport. The success of BMX riders in the Beijing Olympics is evidence of this. Much of this approval can be put down to the X Games showcasing this new generation of G-force gymnasts and what they can do with a chopper. The BMX Superpark is one of the most popular arenas used during the summer event. The smooth, dune shaped court has domed walls, extreme curves, ramps, and pits. Riders skoot about the assault course with practiced ease, sliding along high wall edges, spinning over ramps, and flipping in the air with an audacious confidence that says the future of sport is here and it is extreme. —CO'M

ⓘ www.espn.go.com.

WHEN TO GO: Summer games Aug; winter games Jan/Feb.

✈ Los Angeles, Aspen, or Denver.

🛏 Aspen: $$$ **Limelight Lodge,** 355 S. Monarch St., Aspen, CO 81611 (✆ **1/970/925-3025;** www.limelightlodge.com). $$ **Hotel Durant,** 122 E. Durant, Aspen, CO 81611 (✆ **1/970/925-8500;** www.durant aspen.com). Los Angeles: $$$ **Omni Los Angeles at California Plaza,** 251 S. Olive St., Los Angeles, CA 90012 (✆ **1/213/617-3300;** www.omnihotels.com). $$$ **Elan Hotel Modern,** 8435 Beverly Blvd., Los Angeles, CA 90048 (✆ **1/323/658-6663;** www.elanhotel.com).

Note: The X Games are scheduled in Aspen until 2012.

---

340 Spectator Delights

Motocross Grand Prix
The Mud Gauntlet
Donington Park, Leicestershire, England

Mud caked riders roar through pits of dirt leaving rooster tails of clay in their wake. They race along a track that resembles a World War I trench, disappearing into dark hollows before emerging in full flight over a hillock and crashing down onto the snaking dirt track that veers sharply around a pond of muddy water. The distinctive sound of powerful four-stroke engines buzzes in the ears of the 130,000 spectators that line the route of this famous race track in the English midlands. They have come to see teenage riders from around the world endure a bone crushing gauntlet known as the Motocross Grand Prix. Experiencing the spectacular event is a thrill for riders and on-lookers alike.

The word *motocross* is an amalgamation of two words—motorbike and cross country. Once known as scrambling, motocross has become a phenomenally popular sport with the 17-race Grand Prix taking place in locales as diverse as Shanghai and Istanbul. The U.S. occasionally stages this spill and thrill muck adventure at Laguna Seca in California, but its spiritual home is at Donington Park, in England

where the U.K. Grand Prix is one of the biggest spectator events in the British sporting calendar.

There is no doubting the skill of these young bikers as they weave through a race course that on a wet English day can resemble a flooded construction site. Studies have shown that motocross bikers require a level of fitness greater than track athletes and football players. The intense physical demand of keeping a 91kg (200-lb.) bike under a controlled speed over a rigorous track means the riders have to be young, skilled, and exceptionally strong. Riders sustain a heart beat of 190 beats per minute as they weave and jump around the circuit that lasts on average 35 minutes.

The dangers are obvious. Frequent falls and crashes see spine snapping injuries. Riders limp off with fractured shoulders and shredded muscles. Many endure battle wounds patched up with titanium plates and broken bones knitted together with steel pins. As if the race is not dangerous enough, many riders now opt for a variation on motocross known as freestyling. Here they perform acrobatic stunts during high jumps. One is called the Superman Seat Grab where the flying rider lets the bike sail before him mid-air as he stretches out and holds the bike seat. He truly does look like Superman coming to the rescue.

Other motocross variations include vintage motocross where old bikes such as the legendary British made BSA are wheeled out and put to the test on a swampy circuit. BSA was the pioneer brand that first saw bike riders test their rides on the British countryside in 1924. The distinctive high chassis and big suspension forks of motocross bikes were all features introduced to handle the ruts and mires of scrambling and bike makers such as Suzuki first proved their worth by competing in motocross. —CO'M

WHEN TO GO: July.

✈ East Midlands.

🛏 $$$ **Cathedral Quarter Hotel,** 16 St. Mary's Gate, Derby, DE1 3JR, U.K. (© **44/ 1332/546-080;** www.cathedralquarter hotel.com). $$ **Holiday Inn Express Derby Pride Park,** Wheelwright Way, Pride Park, Derby DE24 8HX, U.K. (© **44/ 1332/388-000;** www.ichotelsgroup.com).

Spectator Delights **341**

U.S. Music Festivals
The Beat Goes On
Nationwide, U.S.A.

The crush of the crowd, the blistering guitar solos, the stage diving—each summer, thousands of revelers pack auditoriums, parks, and stadiums across the country for music festivals that feature these and other thrills. Whether you're a teenage rebel looking to bust out or an aging hippie who just can't let go of your Woodstock-era tie-dye clothing, there's a music festival somewhere near you.

Lollapalooza (www.lollapalooza.com) has proved its staying power since Perry Farrell of Jane's Addiction started the party in 1991. Held in Chicago's Grant Park, the event has featured old-school rockers like Depeche Mode and new indie acts. Chicago is also the home of the **Pitchfork Music Festival** (www.pitch forkmusicfestival.com). Founded by the music site Pitchfork.com, this party distinguishes itself by letting attendees suggest set lists for the bands performing at the concert.

All Tomorrow's Parties (www.atp festival.com), a renowned British institution, has found a stateside home in the farmlands near Monticello, New York. Another small town hosts a big event when **Bonnaroo** (www.bonnaroo.com) comes to Manchester, Tennessee. The 3-day party and camp-out has hosted renowned bands like Bruce Springsteen and the E Street Band and Elvis Costello. Like many of these events, the **All Points West Music and Arts Festival** (www.apwfestival.com)

Perry Farrell thrills the crowds at Lollapalooza.

prides itself on being a green party: This 3-day concert is accessible by numerous forms of mass transit from New York City and New Jersey, and enforces a park-wide recycling program. On the other side of the continent, **Outside Lands** (www.sfoutsidelands.com) rocks the San Francisco Bay area from the leafy glades of Golden Gate Park.

Music lovers who are looking for something other than rock and roll also have plenty to choose from. **The Essence Music Festival** in New Orleans (www.essencemusicfestival.com) presents a variety of soul, R&B, and hip-hop acts. The legendary **Newport Jazz Festival** (www.jazzfestival55.com), now over 55 years old, still brings top jazz and blues talent to its stage. And folkies still flock to Rhode Island to take in the sounds at the venerable **Newport Folk Festival** (www.folkfestival50.com). —*ML*

---

342 Spectator Delights

Turkish Oil Wrestling
Slippery Customers
Edirne, Turkey

Fez wearing drummers rumble in the background as 50 or so muscular men in leather shorts gather in a stadium field. Thousands of spectators cheer them on as they smear each other with olive oil and then pair off to lock heads, grasp hands and necks, and try to land the other one on his back. The **Kirkinpar wrestling festival** is underway, reputedly the oldest sporting event in the world, dating from 1357 and a national obsession.

Eighteen hundred wrestlers gather from all around the country to decide who is the fastest, quickest, and slickest of them all. This, also the biggest wrestling event in the world, takes place in the pretty Ottoman city of Edirne on the Bulgarian border, 230km (143 miles) west of Istanbul. They all fight it out over several days until there is literally one last man standing. He receives a gold plated belt and sizeable purse and is regarded as the best wrestler in Turkey until the festival comes around again a year later.

The contest's origins are traced back to 1347 when an Ottoman Sultan rode through town with a group of warriors. They camped out for the night and two brothers started to wrestle for fun. A deadlock ensued as they were both evenly matched and neither would back down. They fought over several days until they both dropped dead from exhaustion. The spot where they were buried became the location of the annual event and now thousands flock here to the Saraych stadium to cheer and gamble on every bout. Costumed paraders take to the streets of a historic city with gorgeous mosques cornered by towering minarets. There is an old picturesque Roman section of town with wooden houses and a chaotic bazaar.

But for 1 week in June, all the action takes place in the stadium one mile from the town center. What marks Turkish wrestling so different from other wrestling is the fact that the contestants smear themselves in oil—the event goes through two tonnes every year—and the wrestlers wear buffalo skin pants that the opponent is allowed to grab and grapple to gain some leverage. The sight of two greased up muscle men in an embrace trying to put their hands down each other's leather pants does have homoerotic undertones and the event drew attention in the year 2000 when the wrestlers reacted angrily to a gay group that advertised a tour to the event. When all is said and done this is a macho affair and definitely not gay friendly. In fact it has all the modern problems associated with tough physical sports, including a doping scandal that compelled the organizers to introduce tests for performance enhancing drugs on each competitor. The competition is closed to foreign competitors but spectators are welcome to see what must be one of the most compelling gladiator sports in the world. —CO'M

WHEN TO GO: Late June.

✈ Istanbul (239km/148 miles).

🚄 $$$ **Sirkeci Konak Hotel,** Taya Hatun Sokak No: 5, 34120 Sirkeci, Istanbul (✆ **90/212/528-4344;** www.sirkecikonak. com). $$ **Hotel Sapphire,** 14 bni Kemal Cd, Hocapaa, Istanbul 34410, Turkey (✆ **90/ 212/520-5686;** www.hotelsapphire.com).

Spectator Delights **343**

Icarus Cup
Celebrating Airborne Sports
Saint-Hilaire du Touvet, France

If it flies, you'll find it at **Saint-Hilaire du Touvet's Coupe d'Icare (Icarus Cup).** Hang-gliders and paragliders soar skyward, intrepid free-fallers in wing-suits plummet earthward from helicopters, multicolored kites dip and sway, and hot-air balloons rise gracefully into the early-morning air.

According to Greek myth, Icarus used wings constructed by his father from feathers and wax to fly from his island prison on Crete. Every summer, 8,000 modern-day aviators relive his dream of flight, launching themselves into the crystal mountain air from the breathtaking Plateau des Petites Roches to glide gracefully down to Lumbin, 600m (1,968 ft.) below.

The packed schedule is based around stunt-flying displays and aerial demonstrations, but the theme of air, wind, and flight encompasses everything from a flight-related film festival to a night-launch of thousands of illuminated miniature balloons and flight-related activities for kids. The highlight is the Masquerade Contest, with prizes for the most "innovative and poetic" flying invention. Dragons, flying cars, and giant footballs drift or plummet, to the delight of an enthusiastic crowd.

Amateur pilots who obey the event's strict safety rules can even try their luck from the plateau on Thursday and Friday before the professionals take over. Bring your own wings.

In nearby Grenoble, where you'll likely bed down, make time for a ride on the Téléphériquq-Greoble-Bastille cable cars, which take you over the Isère River and its surrounding valley. The commanding views of the surrounding mountains, city, and Fort de la Bastille, are worth the trip. —DL

ⓘ www.coupe-icare.org/GB_home/html. **Rhone Alps Tourism** (www.rhonealps-tourism.com).

WHEN TO GO: Sept.

✈ Grenoble (27km/17 miles).

🚄 Paris (3½ hr.).

🚄 $$–$$$ **Park Hotel Concorde,** 10 place Paul-Mistral, Grenoble (✆ **33/4/76-85-81-23;** www.park-hotel-grenoble.fr). $$ **Hôtel d'Angelterre Tulip Inn Grenoble,** 5 place Victor-Hugo, Grenoble (✆ **33/ 4/76-87-37-21;** www.hotel-angleterre-grenoble.com).

Touching down at the Icarus Cup.

344 **Spectator Delights**

The Winter Speed Festival
Lap Land
Lac La Biche, Alberta, Canada

To be a spectator at the annual **Winter Speed Festival** in western Canada is slightly unnerving. To watch a souped-up Chevette with a monster engine tearing around an icy lake and coming toward you compels you to step back a little in case the kamikaze motor should slip and slide your way. There is no curb to keep the lunatic driver on course and there is no viewing stand for spectators to take refuge in. What you get is quite simple—a frozen lake at the edge of a forest with over 300 motorheads with their toys ripping around the icy surface. It seems anything that burns gasoline is fair game—cars, motorbikes, quads, and snowmobiles. They roar around a frozen

lake called Lac La Biche 125km (140 miles) north of Edmonton city in the oil and mountain state of Alberta.

It is a marvel how they stay on track and the tournament has its fair share of crashes and rollovers. Most of the vehicles are fitted out with special studded tires that dig into the thick ice of this oval shaped circuit, and drivers are obliged to wear full protective gear such as padded jumpsuits and chest protectors.

The snowmobile drag race is a sight to behold. A line of bullet shaped motor sleds roar to life on the desolate causeway, revved to the maximum yet still stationary. The noise is deafening as both driver and helper keep the machines at full throttle before letting go. They tear off into the distance at a remarkable speed and the ear splitting sound disappears as these super sleds cover 198m (660 ft.) in 4 seconds, actually breaking the sound barrier.

The motorbike racing is no less exciting and inspires envy in the fearlessness of these maniacal riders. Their loud dirt bikes coast through slush and snow as they take the sharp corners at speeds that defy belief. The riders lean heavily to the side with their knees scraping the surface and the bike ripping up ground as they lap the lake without flying over the side. Occasionally the back wheel slips and there's a premonition of man and machine cartwheeling into a snowdrift. But he snaps the accelerator and the wheel takes grip and propels forward.

The Winter Speed Festival is gloriously noncommercial without a hotdog stand or sponsor's sign in sight. How long it stays this way remains to be seen, as this event is gaining more fame with some 1,200 people attending in 2009.

The small oil and logging community of La Biche is surrounded by an area that is an outdoor haven for those who love fresh air. There are 150 lakes to explore and people come here to hike, fish, sled, and swim. Alberta itself is a landlocked state the size of Texas with the Rocky Mountains skirting its eastern borders. It is a huge oil producer, which is just as well as it seems a fair share of that gas is consumed by a bunch of thrill-seekers on a solid lake once a year. —CO'M

ⓘ www.classicwheels.org.

WHEN TO GO: Feb/Mar.

✈ Edmonton (219km/136 miles).

🛏 $$$ **Hampton Inn & Suites Edmonton/West,** 18304 100 Ave., Edmonton, Alberta T5S 1A2, Canada (✆ **1/780/484-7280;** www.hamptoninn.hilton.com). $$$ **Hilton Garden Inn West Edmonton,** 17610 Stony Plain Rd., Edmonton, Alberta T5S 1A2, Canada (✆ **1/780/443-2233;** www.hiltongardeninn.hilton.com).

Spectator Delights **345**

The Palio Horse Race
The Risk Jockeys
Siena, Tuscany, Italy

One of Europe's most spectacular and chaotic horse races is held in honor of the Virgin Mary. The good lady would blush, however, if she knew of the antics that take place over this no-holds-barred rush around the medieval Piazza del Campo in the picturesque Tuscan city of Sienna. Bribery, gambling, plotting, and betrayal are all par for the course in this hugely popular event that attracts thousands of spectators and pits every city district against each other and stirs up ancient bitter rivalries.

It all begins with pomp and ceremony with a parade of armored horsemen bearing medieval flags and banners through the packed streets and into the large square that is jammed with eager spectators. This event is so popular that some tenants who live overlooking the square must sign a rental contract to vacate their premises on the day in question so their landlords can rent out the balconies for a princely sum. An ox drawn war chariot bears trumpet players and drummers while the local bishop blesses each horse and jockey. There are 10 riders in all, representing the different city wards. An explosive charge is detonated as they enter the square with locals jeering from every vantage point like charged-up soccer fans. A circuit track of yellow dirt is laid around the outer rim of the plaza while padded crash barriers are set up at the most tricky corners. The multitude of people are packed tightly in the center, everybody jostling for a view of the multicolored jockeys who ride bareback and carry whips made from stretched dried bull penises.

The starting rope is dropped and off they go in a frantic helter skelter clockwise around the tight corners of the track, using their whips liberally to egg on their own horse and hit other competitors. Conventional racing rules are forgotten as the jockeys flail and hamper their fellow riders, blocking and knocking and hindering as much as they can. The tight curves see horses slide and crash into the side walls with jockeys crashing to the ground and then fleeing for cover. They go three times around the plaza while the crowd screams for their horse. One eventually edges ahead (often jockeyless but still declared a winner) and the plaza erupts in joy, acrimony, celebration, and the occasional brawl. It is all over in 90 seconds.

Il Palio is like no other race and the passion it stirs is hinged on the intense rivalry between the city district teams that go by names such as Porcupine, Panther, and Shell. Each has its own feuds and scores to settle in a race that goes back to medieval times. Alliances are made and plots laid out. Dirty tricks are not unknown, such as horses being drugged and even jockeys kidnapped. The second horse is regarded as the real loser and the district that has not won the longest is the laughing stock of the city and must bear the shameful name of granny.

The prize is a painted banner, and it is hung with pride at the huge banquet that takes place after the race. The jockey sits in place of honor at the head of the table with his fateful steed standing behind, wrapped in garlands. —CO'M

WHEN TO GO: There are two races every year on July 2 and Aug 16.

✈ Florence (75km/47 miles).

🛏 $$$ **Borgo Grondaie,** Strada delle Grondaie, 53100 Siena, Italy (© **39/577/ 332539;** www.www.borgogrondaie.com). $$ **Hotel More Di Cuna,** Via Cassia Nord, 53014 Monteroni d'Arbia, Siena, Italy (© **39/577/385166;** www.hotelmoredi cuna.it).

Bet or Not, Horse Races Take You for a Ride

If you like to bet on horse races, your adrenaline rush comes as your horse gallops closer to the finish line, hopefully in first place. Even if you're not inclined to put money down on a horse, at these annual events there is so much activity around the races you'll be entertained from early morning when the horses exercise on the track into the wee hours when owners of the winners celebrate. —LF

346 Kentucky Derby, U.S.A.: Aristides was the first to gallop across the finish line on May 17, 1875, the day the Kentucky Derby tradition began. Today, the annual

race for 3-year-old thoroughbreds, always held the first Saturday in May, is the reason and excuse for the 2-week-long Kentucky Derby Festival in Louisville, Kentucky. If you can't afford to sit in "Millionaire's Row" at Churchill Downs, buy general admission tickets for the infield. Here you can party and watch many of the rich and well-connected. *Kentucky Derby* (www.kentuckyderby.com); *Kentucky Derby Festival* (www.kdf.org).

Racing at Churchill Downs, home of the Kentucky Derby.

347 Grand National, England: Competitors must face 16 challenging fences while riding around the course. The contenders must run almost two circuits of the course, make 30 jumps, and then there's a long run to the finish line. Reportedly some 600 million viewers watch this annual steeplechase race, which is held in early April at Aintree Racecourse near Liverpool. ℭ *0151/523-2600. www.aintree.co.uk.*

348 Preakness, U.S.A.: Poet Ogden Nash wrote, "The Derby is a race of aristocratic sleekness, for horses of birth to prove their worth to run in the Preakness." Held in Baltimore in mid-May, the Preakness is the second of the three famous races—the other two are the Kentucky Derby and the Belmont—that are called the Triple Crown series. *www.preakness.com.*

349 Emirates Melbourne Cup, Australia: The Emirates Melbourne Cup is billed as "the race that stops the nation," and Australians say it's true. This almost 2-mile race for 3-year-old thoroughbreds, which is always held the first Tuesday in November, is one of the richest in the world both in prizes and in the money passing among hands through bets. Reportedly, more than $140 million was bet on the Cup alone on tote throughout Australia. *www.melbournecup.com.*

350 The Prix de L'Arc de Triomphe, France: This annual race at **Hippodrome de Longchamp** racecourse, just minutes from Paris's Eiffel Tower, attracts entries who have won flat races in other European countries. If you're going to bet, choose a horse that has the speed and stamina for this 2,400m/2.4km (7,874 ft./1½-mile) course. Viewers from 191 countries have watched this annual race, which happens the first weekend in October. *www.prixarcdetriomphe.com/en/index.html.*

The Rat Race
Swinging Through the Urban Jungle
Edinburgh, Manchester, Newcastle & Birmingham, U.K.

Race across a freeway flyover, jog the stairwell up a 12-story high-rise, abseil down its red brick facade, cycle around a city park, then wade through a canal weir before assailing a rock wall into a derelict shipyard. Cut across the abandoned dockland and kayak along the seashore before stopping at a food stand for a compulsory gorge on a local delicacy such as jellied eels or deep fried Mars bars in batter. Then bungee jump over a motorway bridge before descending into a drainage system and emerging in a busy pedestrian street full of Saturday night shoppers and jeering drunks. The U.K. Rat Race is an adventure with a difference, foregoing the muddy paths and open fields of conventional endurance races and replacing them with all the urban obstacles that four historic cities can throw at you.

The Industrial Revolution took place in the British cities of Manchester, Birmingham, Edinburgh, and Newcastle and it is in each one that a series of 2-day rat races takes place during the frisky English summer, offering the perfect urban background of abandoned factories, meandering canals, and railway sideways to challenge the most agile of athletes. The race kicks off at 7pm on a Saturday evening when black clad runners outfitted with climbing harnesses, compasses, head torches, and whistles fan across the city for a 3km run (nearly 19 miles), passing checkpoints on the way where their electronic wristbands are passed under scanners to collect points. Extra points can be gained if competitors stop to try their hand at karaoke, boxing, or speed cycling without brakes. Organizers don't

make it any easier by pelting runners with eggs and smearing the finishing line with banana skins and butter.

Yet the Rat Race is a masterpiece of organization with the entire course meticulously planned, right down to the event village from which the race starts. It offers food stalls, outfit shops, and impromptu classes in rock climbing, kayaking, and abseiling for the uninitiated. Competitors do not have to be uber-athletes (though the event does attract its fair share of ultra marathon runners) as the race is split into three ability levels with the super elite having extra challenges to perform.

The lesser elite can just sit back and enjoy the ride, especially on the second day, which is a 60km (37-mile) cycle around the city, broken up with a round of paintball or potholing. Despite the urban backdrop, the circuit takes in everything that is beautiful about these four British cities with open parks, canal paths, and woodlands all on the itinerary. It is certainly a better way to see a city than from the back of an open top bus. Anybody can enter and entrance fees vary from 30€ to 80€ (approx. $50–$125) depending on the level you choose. Teams of two or three people complete the course and the variety of activities and their often tongue-in-cheek manner means that if the climbing, ducking, and jumping don't make you breathless, the laughter surely will.—*CO'M*

ⓘ www.ratraceadventure.com.

WHEN TO GO: Throughout the summer in different U.K. locations.

Tough Guy Race
The Macho Masochists
Perton, Wolverhampton, England

Belly crawl beneath a 12m (40-ft.) pit of barbed wire before climbing a pole to assail a netted tower woven with electrified wire charged enough to knock out a bull. Below is a field of nettles for those unfortunate enough to fall. Then run, leaping across some bales of burning hay before wading chest deep through a freezing mud pond criss-crossed with hidden telegraph poles. You must then creep through 10 dirty narrow sewage pipes, one of which is a dead end. There is not enough room to turn around so you must crawl backwards shouting to your fellow participants right behind you that the way is blocked. Then you must swim through an underground tunnel filled with pitch black muddy water that has only two small air pockets if you run out of breath. If you happen to collapse and drown, other participants must trod over you before emerging to warn a team of scuba divers that a man is down. They have 3 minutes to fish you out before your brain dies from lack of oxygen.

The **Tough Guy Race** certainly lives up to its title. This 13km (8-mile) sadistic exercise in extreme endurance will test the phobias of the most hardened Rambos. Beforehand, all participants must sign a health risk waiver reassuringly called a "death warrant." Major sponsors avoid putting their name to the event, terrified they will be liable to "blame and claim." One year, seven competitors broke their legs, and hundreds suffer regularly from hypothermia. The winner gets no prize and not even a shower at the end. Participants must bathe in filthy troughs of water before drying off and going home to nurse their wounds. Yet this event, held just outside the old industrial city of Wolverhampton, is always oversubscribed and the 4,000 places always filled. Organizers now hold a summer, autumn, and winter edition to satisfy the demand for this exercise in masochistic endurance.

The first event was held in 1987 with 103 participants running the gamut of streams, woodland, and mudhills on a 103-acre farm incongruously titled Mr Mouse Farm for Unfortunates in the townland of Perton. Mr Mouse turns out to be a loquacious ex-marathon runner called Billy Wilson. A pioneer organizer of such famous runs as the London Marathon, Mr. Wilson got bored with the monotonous slog through empty city streets and decided to set up his own off-road gauntlet inspired by World War I

One tough guy helps another at the Tough Guy Race.

trenches, Vietcong tunnels, and Russian prisoner camps. Indeed many of the participants are service men from both Britain and overseas with a fair share of SAS personnel trying their luck. Yet it is a Bristol bricklayer called Vito Graffagnino who has proved the ultimate tough guy, winning this grueling race on three occasions with a record time of 57 minutes. Only 60% of the runners pass the finish line and there is a cutoff time of 5 hours, meaning stragglers are disqualified. Women are also welcome and many have completed this grim obstacle course lovingly titled the "killing fields." The race requires a high level of teamwork and cooperation with fellow participants pushing each other on through the most terrifying of installations that include a rope bridge that is just that, a thin rope strung between two trees four stories high. Not for the fainthearted. — *CO'M*

ⓘ www.toughguy.co.uk.

WHEN TO GO: Tough Guy takes place three times a year. Check website for specific dates.

✈ Birmingham (34km/21 miles).

🛏 $$ **Travelodge Wolverhampton Central,** Bankfield House, Wolverhampton (✆ **44/871/984-6221;** www.travelodge.co.uk). $$ **Barons Court Hotel,** 142 Goldthorn Hill, Blakenhall, Wolverhampton (✆ **44/1902/34-1751;** www.baronscourt hotel.viviti.com).

---

353 The Kitchen Sink

Birdsville Races
Horses for Courses
Birdsville, Queensland, Australia

In 2002, the famous **Birdsville horse race** meeting had a problem—no horses. Equine flu had forced trainers and owners to keep their race horses away this particular year. Not that anybody noticed. Thousands still gathered in this remote desert town to party over the weekend, cook kangaroo burgers over campfires, race in wheelie bins, and wrestle steers. This quintessential Ozzie outback experience has become more important than the races themselves, with a carnival atmosphere that sees bush poetry readings, country and western singing, and stand-up comedy shows. Thousands of revellers come and camp out in this town of 100 residents at the eastern edge of the vast red stretch of sand dunes known as the Simpson Desert. Everybody is remarkably friendly, oiled somewhat by lots of liquor and beer.

Such friendliness disappears if you step into the ring at the Fred Brophy boxing tent.

Here you are challenged to fight a selection of fighters with names like Crush and White Lightening. There is a dramatic drum roll as you step into the arena and if you are tough enough to knock out your opponent you walk away with a large money purse. Such casual prize fighting is banned elsewhere, earning what happens in Birdsville the slogan "only in the Outback."

Birdsville is 1,610km (1,000 miles) from the provincial capital Brisbane, with little in between but dirt track and dunes. The race meeting here is probably the most isolated in the world and many people choose to arrive by light aeroplane. The local airfield quickly fills up with single engine Cessnas as they ferry punters to and fro. The aviation link does not stop there. The races are a major fundraiser for the Royal Flying Doctor's Service, an aerial ambulance that covers the vast interior of Australia. The Simpson Desert alone is 181,300 sq. km (70,000 sq. miles) in size with some of the longest parallel dunes in the world, some reaching 30m (98 ft.) in height. It gets only 20cm (8 in.) of rain a year and is so inhospitable that the authorities have resorted to closing large chunks of it every summer to prevent the recurrence of hapless, ill-prepared tourists getting into trouble in the mid-day sun.

There is not much to Birdsville town itself. Originally a droving toll station, the abolition of droving tolls in 1901 saw the town go into steep decline. It now comes to life the first weekend of September with this 2-day event that attracts every

outback eccentric between here and Alice Springs, with a fair share of high rollers and good timers for good measure. And now, of course, there are horses. —CO'M

WHEN TO GO: First weekend of Sept.

✈ Brisbane or the small airfield in Birdsville.

🚌 Camper vans, cars, tents. The only hotel in town is closed to the public during the races. Many people sleep out in the open.

The Kitchen Sink **354**

White Air Extreme Sports Festival
Catching Some Air
England

You love skateboarding, but hate to give up kitesurfing. High-diving is a blast, but you've always wanted to try the Brazilian martial art known as *capoeira*. A rollicking outdoor concert is just your thing, but

not if it means you can't spend all day on a jet ski. How is an intrepid adrenaline adventurer supposed to choose? At the **White Air Extreme Sports Festival,** you don't have to. The only problem

The White Air Extreme Sports Festival is as much fun for spectators as it is for participants.

you're likely to have is deciding which adventure to have first.

The 3-day festival is held each year in early autumn on the scenic shores of England's southern coast. Past festivals have taken place on the Isle of Wight and at Brighton Beach; check the website for the next festival's dates and locations.

If you're at all into outdoor sports with a guaranteed rush of excitement, you'll be in your element at White Air. Roughly 40 different activities are represented at the event. Some such as mountain biking and surfing are well known; for others, such as bocking, **parkour** (see **314**), and slackline, you might need an extreme-sports glossary. (Bocking, also known as powerbocking or powerizing, is running with large curved stilts that act as springs. Parkour involves running, jumping, and clambering across a landscape riddled with obstacles.

Slacklining is a balance sport using a thin, flat nylon web; it's similar to tightrope walking except the line stretches, allowing for bouncing and other gymnastic moves.)

As you might expect at an extreme sports event, the crowd skews young, and there's a palpable sense of carefree fun in the air. Most of the sports at White Air allow newbies to try the activity through the festival's Have a Go program; just sign up for a free lesson through the website. And don't miss out on the rest of the fun—each year, high-energy bands from the U.K. and beyond perform at the festival. *ML*

(i) **White Air Extreme Sports Festival** (www.whiteair.co.uk).

WHEN TO GO: Sept/Oct. Check website for exact dates and location.

---

355 The Kitchen Sink

The Rickshaw Run
The Three Wheel Trip
India & Nepal

The Indian Auto Rickshaw is a beautiful machine. This three-wheel urban workhorse weighs 272kg (600 lb.) and has a top speed of 55kmph (34 mph). Its 150cc, 2-stroke single cylinder engine powers a seating bench on wheels so small they would not look amiss on a wheelbarrow. It has no suspension worth noting and lacks a fuel gauge so riders know when it has run out only when it sputters to a halt. Run on a toxic mixture of oil and gas, it ferries people to and fro in the sprawling mega cities of the India subcontinent. It is the last vehicle you would choose to do a 4,830km (3,000-mile) cross-country race from India to Nepal. In the marathon adventure known as the Rickshaw Run, it is the only vehicle you can choose.

Dirt tracks, tropical jungles, and Himalayan peaks are just some of the obstacles encountered on this mad cap chase that attracts up to 60 teams for an event so popular it is now held three times a year. Perhaps more formidable are the everyday mundanities thrown up by this colorful continent, such as wandering elephants, aggressive water buffalo, and lake-size potholes. Certainly most terrifying are the mammoth buses and trucks that dwarf the rickshaws on the chaotic highways. Organizers advise participants to keep to minor roads as the main thoroughfares are rickshaw death-traps, as can be seen from the frequent crumpled wreckage along the roadside.

The route is a route in the loosest sense of the word. Riders are encouraged to take whatever way they choose with only a handful of meeting points to drop into along the way. Starting and finishing lines vary, but in general the race begins and

The Rickshaw Run raises lots of money for a variety of charities.

ends in either Goa, Southern India, or Pokhara in Nepal. In between, the rolling tea hills of Ghats and the scorching deserts of Rajhastian are just some of the multitude of landscapes riders traverse. Once undertaken, there is absolutely no support provided by the organizers and drivers are expected to use their wits and cunning to get themselves out of the many scrapes and mishaps encountered along the way. Team numbers are unlimited but in general, three to four people ride a rickshaw. An unlikely 14 is the record.

Participants can choose to sleep wherever they like and the run is usually done in 2 weeks, though digressions are encouraged with the emphasis on the fact that the Rickshaw Run is not a race but an adventure. A website keeps friends, family, and sponsors informed of each team's progress and the event begins and ends with a round of cricket and gin and tonics.

First started in 2006, the **Rickshaw Run** is put together by a Bristol-based collective called The Adventurists in the U.K. The entrance fee is $1,400 per team and this gets you a rickshaw that must be returned in working order at the end of the escapade. Participants are also compelled to donate at least $1,600 to charity, and teams often raise much more for a vast array of worthy causes. In fact, charity fundraising is one of the main motives behind the venture, as well as the desire to encourage people to get off the beaten track and throw caution to the wind. "Tropical stupidity in slightly powered tin cans" is how the Adventurists themselves describe it. Just make sure to pack a can opener. —*CO'M*

ⓘ www.rickshawrun.theadventurists.com.

WHEN TO GO: Jan, Apr, and Sept. Check website for exact dates.

The Kitchen Sink 356

The Death Race
The Pits
Pittsfield, Vermont, U.S.A.

Contestants arrive at a wet and muddy farm in the Vermont Hills at 8pm. They register and weigh in at 11pm and have little chance to sleep before the race starts at 3am. They set off with a bike frame on their backs and rucksacks filled with hatchets, shovels, handsaws, duct tape, and pruners. They will need every one of these as they negotiate an obstacle course designed to test mind, body, and spirit.

The first test is to dig up a well buried tree stump and drag it a mile upriver. Then they must push a bucket through a water-filled culvert and haul a sack of sand under a pit of barbed wire. There is a 2,000-foot (600m) climb to a mountain peak, where contestants must memorize a list of American presidents before descending and repeating the list to a steward. Then there is a pile of logs to be split before crawling through a mud tunnel, at the end of which is a Lego cube that must be noted and reconstructed again at the bottom of the trail. Fail to get the colored blocks exactly right and the runners must crawl up the mud tunnel again, all the while carrying an egg that must be cooked on a fire ignited in the rain. Then each participant must haul 20% of their body weight in rocks up another mountain. Then a wheel barrow is supplied to push cement across a sloping field. They then arrive at a river where their bicycle chains are thrown into a deep pond and must be retrieved.

Sleep deprivation, mind games, physical torture, and freezing cold are just par for the course at the Death Race in Pittsfield, 150 miles (242km) south of Burlington. The 10-mile (6.2km) race usually has 40 participants who must complete the circuit in 24 hours. Only 20% do so as they dig, dive, run, and crawl through obstacles designed by a sadist. It is the most absurd form of abuse thought up by two running veterans who grew bored with marathons. The *New York Times* described it as "Survivor meets Jackass" as the mud covered entrants pit their wits against the most devious of obstacles and often find the most mundane task such as log splitting the most difficult. The grand prize for such herculean effort is $2,000, with two Marines crossing the finish line in 2009 in tandem to share the spoils. They completed the course in a mere 12 hours, which shocked the organizers into thinking it was way too easy. Heaven knows what tricky impediments they're now devising for an annual trial that is attracting more and more pain seekers. A miner's hat is an essential part of the equipment, as are a pen and paper to tackle the Lego conundrum. Life jackets are optional, and sanity is best left at home. —*CO'M*

ⓘ www.peakraces.com.

WHEN TO GO: June.

✈ Burlington (84 miles/135km).

🛏 $$ **Hampton Inn Rutland,** 47 Farrell Road, Rutland (✆ **802/773-9066;** www.rutland.hamptoninn.com). $$ **Red Roof Inn Rutland,** 401 U.S. Rte. 7 S., Rutland (✆ **802/775-4303;** www.redroof.com).

The Banger Rally
Scrapyard Scramble
England to Gambia, Africa

It is a long way from England to Gambia; 7,245km (4,500 miles) to be precise or 3 weeks of blood, sweat, and tears if you choose to do the journey the hard way—in an old car with an engine half as powerful as your average lawnmower and absolutely no A/C. The journey involves crossing roadless deserts for 3 days with no stops for water or gas. The 90°F (32°C) temperatures are made worse by the fact that you must drive with the windows closed because of the sand storm and with the heating on to cool down the overheating engine. Lethal sand pits that would ground a powerful 4WD, never mind an old, yellow Fiat rescued from a scrapyard, are just some of the surprises along the way. High roads wind over the epic Atlas mountains and through lush valleys. You pass through deserted towns, desolate plains, and chaotic cities where gangs of impoverished children mount the hood begging for change. There is an 81km (50-mile) coastal strip in Mauritania that must be traversed except it can only be done at low tide, which lasts 3 hours every day. Get stuck, and the sea will wash you away, and there is no coast guard to pick you up. French traffic police, Spanish drivers, and monster Moroccan trucks are

You never know what challenges await you in the course of the Banger Rally.

just some of the obstacles on this epic 3-week race across Europe and Africa. And it must be all done in a car you would not trust to take you as far as the corner store.

The rules are simple in this race, formally known as the **Plymouth-Banjal Challenge,** but more popularly referred to as the Banger Rally. All participating cars must have a value of less than £100 ($170) and repairs and preparations cannot exceed £15 ($26). The race was thought up by a determined motorhead called Julian Nowill who wished to counteract the expense of entering famous off-road races such as the Dakar Rally. Multimillion-dollar cars and support teams, as well as a $10,000 entrance fee, means that this famous trans-African rally is now only open to the mega-rich. The Bangar Rally is an antidote with a philosophy of the cheaper, the better and also the crazier, the better.

Two hundred tarted up Volkswagens, Peugeots, and Mazdas tear out of Plymouth town every December and January. They take the ferry across to France and then travel south over the Pyrenees and across the Iberian peninsula to Gibraltar for the final African leg to Banjul, the capital of Gambia. Vehicles include old camper trucks and even an ice cream van that was converted into an ambulance at its final destination. Amazingly, many cars survive to be sold off as taxis in Gambia with the entire proceeds going to a local charity. Cars abandoned along the way are usually swiftly stripped by the locals. Team names include the Cone Dodgers and the Badger Racing Boys. There is zero support from the organizing body and participants are expected to negotiate their own entrance into each country and use their own initiative to get out of any sticky spots. There is no prize money to speak of, but just the achievement of finishing is enough to attract 800 applicants every year. Amazingly, most drivers manage to finish the race, with much cooperation and camaraderie along the way. They rally together, so to speak. —CO'M

ⓘ www.plymouth-banjul.co.uk.
WHEN TO GO: Dec–Jan.

The Kitchen Sink **358**

Global Scavenger Hunt
Dream Trip for Adventure Travelers
Around the World

Do you want to swim with baby elephants, lend a helping hand at a Tibetan refugee camp, witness a Himalayan sunset, and bargain in some of the world's most exotic bazaars? If you have a thirst for adventure and an Indiana Jones–style personality, the **Global Scavenger Hunt** may be the ultimate trip-of-a-lifetime for you.

"It's like *Survivor, The Amazing Race,* and the Eco-Challenge all rolled into one except," with much more cultural interaction," is how one contestant, Marvin S., of Canada, described his experience. During the whirlwind 3-week Global Scavenger Hunt, travel adventure competition racers visit 10 countries on four continents. They start the race on the U.S. West Coast, learn where they are traveling next with little or no notice, and finish the competition on the U.S. East Coast 3 weeks later. Audacity, daring, flexibility, and inventiveness are just some of the qualities required to win this race, which combines authentic cultural experiences and behind-the-scenes access to such activities as cooking with a Michelin-starred chef, finding Buddha's tooth, photographing a wild orangutan, and participating in an authentic archaeological dig. While finding the clues and participating in novel experiences, teams are tested on the difficulties of handling extended travel and on how team members deal with each other.

But what makes this global travel-a-thon, during which competitors may travel a million kilometers (620,000 miles), so special is the overall annual goal: Raise $1 million for life-changing organizations. The money has helped fund micro-loans in Third World countries; helped construct three schools in Niger, Sri Lanka, and Sierra Leone; and supported Doctors Without Borders and Partners in Health, and other organizations.

So far, people from 45 countries have applied for spots in the race, making the competition a truly international experience. The annual Global Scavenger Hunt is limited to 25 two-person teams. (Singles may apply.) Teams must pay or raise the entry fee, which is $9,900 per person. The fee covers international airfare, 23 nights in first-class hotels and about 40% of the meals. Teams who raise more can earmark the funds for specific charities. Because some of the funds go to nonprofits, part of the entry fees may be tax deductible. —*LF*

ⓘ ✆ **310/281-7809.** www.globalscavenger hunt.com.

The Global Scavenger Hunt takes you all over the world and benefits charitable causes.

10 Extreme Eating Contests

Some gastronomical experiences are all about quality—the finest wines, the freshest herbs. Then there are dining events where the accent is on quantity, and a race to consume the greatest volume of food consumed as quickly as possible. The competition is international in scope, because there really is such a thing as a professional eater, something your high school guidance counselor neglected to mention. Perhaps she didn't realize that many eating contests have purses as rich as $50,000. —ML

359 The Texas King, Amarillo, Texas, U.S.A.: Eating champion Joey "Jaws" Chestnut finished in 8 minutes, 52 seconds—but a 500-pound (228kg) Siberian tiger reportedly polished off the whole thing in 90 seconds. How long would it take you to engorge 72 ounces of steak, plus baked potato, ranch beans, shrimp cocktail, salad, and roll with

butter? At the Big Texan Steak Ranch, you've only got 1 hour to consume the whole meal, or you'll forfeit the $72 you paid in advance for the dubious honor of completing the Texas King challenge. *www.bigtexan.com.*

360 Nathan's Hot Dog Eating Contest, Coney Island, New York, U.S.A.: Each American Independence Day, tens of thousands gather at this aging seaside resort to watch one of the world's most famous eating contests. The winner walks off with $10,000 and the right to wear the Coveted Nathan's Mustard Belt. To enter this competition you must qualify by winning a regional contest that season, and the International Federation of Competitive Eating (IFOCE) strictly supervises this competition. *www.nathansfamous.com.*

Challenge yourself to finish a Texas size portion in under an hour at the Big Texan Steak Ranch.

361 Jalapeño Eating Contest, U.S.A.: Laredo, Texas, and Chicago vie for the honor of hosting this contest, which is sponsored in part by La Costeña Mexican Foods. Pat "Deep Dish" Bertoletti, a Chicago hometown hero, currently holds the world record, consuming 266 of the little green spitfires in just 15 minutes. *www.ifoce.com.*

362 The Wing Bowl, Philadelphia, Pennsylvania, U.S.A.: While eating contests aren't really known for their decorum, the Wing Bowl may take the prize for the raunchiest competition. The extreme partiers start in the parking lot, where orange traffic cones are routinely used as beer funnels, and drunken fans screaming profanities and throwing trash and food are the norm—spectators in the front rows are advised to wear rain ponchos as a result. *http://wingbowltickets.ticketwarehouse.com.*

363 A Local State Fair, U.S.A.: The contest here is between you and your arteries—which will give out first? Vendors today compete to see who can come up with the most hedonistic fare. You have three choices of serving style: Deep-fried, on-a-stick, or deep-fried *and* on-a-stick. The Wisconsin State Fair is the reigning heavyweight champion with chocolate-covered bacon—yes, on-a-stick—and peanut butter and jelly sandwiches that are dipped in pancake batter and deep-fried. The Iowa State Fair touts chocolate-covered key lime pie on-a-stick and fried pickles on-a-stick. Not to be outdone, Minnesota offers a deep-fried Norwegian banana split.

364 Krystal Square Off, Chattanooga, Tennessee, U.S.A.: The purse for eating the greatest number of little square hamburgers in eight minutes has been increased to a whopping $50,000. Contestants must participate in regional qualifiers, and they'll then have to face Joey Chestnut and Takeru "Tsunami" Kobayashi, who routinely trade first and second place titles at this battle royale. www.krystalsquareoff.com.

365 Nisei Week Festival Gyoza Eating Championship, Los Angeles, California, U.S.A.: Also called potstickers, gyozas are tiny, tasty fried dumplings that are a delicious staple of Japanese and Chinese cuisine. So it should be easy to eat, say 200, right? Just ask Sonya "The Black Widow" Thomas, a petite 99-pound (45kg) champion eater who, in 2006, downed 210 in 10 minutes, only to be shut out by Joey Chestnut, who scarfed down 212. Chestnut currently holds the world record at 231 gyozas, but Pat Bertoletti gets hungrier every year and, as the world's second-place record holder, is always nipping at Chestnut's heels. www.niseiweek.org.

366 World Grits Eating Championship, Bossier City, Louisiana, U.S.A.: Grits are the comfort food for millions of Southerners. Harrah's, the gaming industry giant, and the International Federation Of Competitive Eating (IFOCE) have joined forces to create the World Grits Eating Championship at Harrah's Louisiana Downs. This is a real heavyweight brawl: At the 2007 competition, Pat Bertoletti engulfed 21 pounds (9.5kg) of grits in only 10 minutes, the most food by weight ever consumed by anyone at an eating contest. www.harrahs.com.

367 Best in the West Nugget World Rib Eating Championship, Sparks, Nevada, U.S.A.: Ribs are the kind of food that nobody really gets enough of—sweet, succulent, meaty and oh-so-rib-sticking good. At the Best in the West Nugget Rib Cook-Off, you won't have to stop, until the buzzer sounds and time's up. The world record-holder, Joey Chestnut (yes, again) consumed 9.8 pounds of these delicious meat sticks, defeating up-and-comer Rich LeFevre, who broke his left front tooth in the rapid-paced competition. Do you think that slowed him down? No—he just swallowed the tooth and kept munching. Now *that's* the stuff of champions. www.janugget.com.

368 World Deep-Fried Asparagus Eating Championship, Stockton, California, U.S.A.: Folks gather at the Stockton Asparagus Festival each April to celebrate the green, stringy vegetable, a harbinger of spring. Here, the asparagus are deep-fried. Hungry yet? Pat Bertoletti was, when the world-class gurgitator consumed over 7 pounds (3.2kg) of the veggies to steal the championship from former record-holder Joey Chestnut. www.asparagusfest.com.

8 Urban Thrills

369

Sydney Harbour BridgeClimb
A Walk of Steel
Sydney, Australia

No other bridge in the world offers this kind of adult playground. The **Sydney Harbour Bridge** has been an icon ever since it was completed in 1932. But it didn't become an adventure destination until 1998 when the **BridgeClimb** was created for folks who couldn't get enough of the structure simply by driving, riding the train, or walking across it.

Today, there are two ways to get a closer look at the bridge's intricacies and even reach its highest point. Opt for the Discovery Climb, which offers a longer and more challenging route into the heart of the bridge rather than over it. Until 2006, only maintenance workers had access to many of the pathways that you can now walk across during this 3½-hour urban hike. As you ascend the steep staircases and ladders, winding through hatchways and girders suspended high above speeding cars and buses below, your guides will discuss the Harbour Bridge's history through radio headsets attached to the shapeless grey jumpsuit that you're forced to wear. Among other things, it includes a device that attaches you to a safety cable and provides a waterproof cover in case it rains. With these provisions and your well-trained leader, the ascent itself is perfectly safe. But it can feel completely daunting at times, especially when the wind blows and traffic races below you.

As you continue heading skyward, you'll pass the point where the arches of the bridge were originally joined in 1930. When you reach the metal mountain's peak, you can actually go between the arches that are 134m (440 ft.) above the water. As you touch the raw steel and

The Sydney Harbour Bridge affords fantastic views of the city.
Previous page: The London Eye.

strong rivets holding things together here, try not to let this awe-inspiring feat of engineering knock you off balance. Take a deep breath and look around at the panoramic views of Sydney—complete with ships in the harbor, the opera house, and skyscrapers far below your feet. If it's midday, you'll see the city buzzing with daily activities. Early risers can climb the bridge at dawn and watch the sunrise. Romantics can try it at twilight. No matter what time you're up here, it's clear that this is one of the world's most unforgettable city walks. —*JS*

ⓘ **Sydney Harbour BridgeClimb** (ⓒ 61/ 02-8274-7777; www.bridgeclimb.com).
WHEN TO GO: Anytime.
✈ Sydney airport.
▭ $$$ **Park Hyatt Sydney,** 7 Hickson Rd., The Rocks (ⓒ **61/02-9241-1234;** www. sydney.park.hyatt.com). $$-$$$ **BLUE Sydney,** 6 Cowper Wharf Rd. (ⓒ **61/02-9331-9000;** www.tajhotels.com/sydney).

370

The Running of the Bulls
Mean Streets
Pamplona, Spain

A man lies squealing on the floor in the fetal position while a 1,300-pound (590kg) bull prods him with huge terrifying horns. Another man stands behind, pulling at the bull's tail in a vain attempt to attract its attention. Another bull has a third spectator pinned against a stockade wall while people clamber over the same wall frantic to escape. Hundreds of men in white pants and red neckerchiefs mill around in a commotion of fear and excitement as a line of dark, angry beasts hoof their way through the parting crowd. The famous **Running of the Bulls** in Pamplona is underway.

The brave, the insane, and the very drunk spill out into the narrow cobbled streets of this northern Spanish city every July for an 8-day orgy of singing, dancing, goring, and trampling. They are celebrating San Fermin, patron saint of wine merchants, which is fitting considering the amount of alcohol that is consumed during the course of the festival. Thousands converge here for a festival of fireworks, processions, music, and bullfighting. The actual bull running is takes places when the animals are moved in the morning from

their corral in the outskirts of town, through the streets to the bullring for almost certain death in the afternoon. Barriers are erected and six steers (castrated males) join the six aggressive (in-tact) bulls as they run in a herd through the streets in the early morning, taking approximately 4 minutes to cover the half-mile. Generally the bulls ignore the crowds and make straight for the stadium. However, if one becomes separated from the rest, all hell breaks loose. It becomes disorientated and attacks anything that moves, often running the wrong way and tossing spectators in the air. Hundreds of people are injured every year and there are 15 recorded deaths since records began in 1924.

The festival has been running since 1591 and is not unusual in the sense that bull running (known as *encierro* to the locals) takes place all over Spain, parts of Southern France, and Latin America. Pamplona is, however, the most prestigious, made famous by Hemingway and beamed across the world for its dramatic photos and near-death experiences. It is no wonder that the casualty list every year has a strong international flavor. It's nearly impossible to get a hotel room during the festival, so hundreds sleep in the park and streets during the day. They party all night and spill out onto the streets in the early morning for the daily run at 8am. Anybody can participate but you must register before 7:30am. Viewers arrive as early as 6am to get a good spot. Utter drunkenness is prohibited and indeed there is nothing more sobering than seeing a raging tank of meat and horn bearing down on top of you. Runners are also not allowed to provoke the animals, nor run the wrong way.

The cruel nature of bullfighting has meant the running of the bulls is controversial. The animal rights organization PETA conducts a *Running of the Nudes* through the streets the week preceding the festival in a light-hearted protest at the event. Yet there is no doubting Pamplona's popularity and the fear factor that attracts thousands for this carnival of carnage. —CO'M

ⓘ www.sanfermin.com.

WHEN TO GO: July 6–July 14.

✈ Bilbao (169km/104 miles).

🛏 $$ **AH San Fermin Suites,** Avda. Villava 90 (© **34/948/136-000;** www. ahsanfermin.com). ⛺⛺ **Hotel Europa,** Espoz y Mina 11 (© **34/948/221-800;** www.hreuropa.com).

371

High-Rolling in Las Vegas
Playing with the Big Boys
Las Vegas, Nevada, U.S.A.

A hush falls across the elegant room as you slowly saunter across the Oriental carpet over to your favorite dealer. Beneath the glitter of crystal chandeliers, you slide into a comfortable leather chair that affords you a view of the other players. There's the Count, gambling away the last of his family's ancient fortune, next to the Argentine cattle baron. The waitress takes your order—top shelf liquor, of course—and you place your bet: $500 on the red. Welcome to the world of high-stakes gambling, far removed from the bling and the noise of the crowded casino floor, where fortunes are made and lost with the roll of the dice.

For obvious reasons, this sort of gambling is not for everyone. At many tables, the minimum bet starts at $100, and on big weekends—when there's a heavyweight fight in town, for example—the minimums can exceed $500. Don't expect to just stroll in wearing your flip-flops and board shorts. Dress codes for ladies and gentlemen are strictly enforced, and the dealers and waitstaff wear tuxedos and elegant dresses—this isn't Hooters, after all. Gamblers who are looking for a crazy night out with buckets of free drinks might also be disappointed, because the atmosphere in these rooms is as refined as the decor, and loud, obnoxious guests who have been "over-served" will be escorted out.

Most of the larger, more established casinos have high-limit rooms with amenities like free hors d'oeuvres and cocktails, premium audio and video installations, and private restrooms. Wynn Las Vegas has an attractive outdoor balcony overlooking their swimming pool, Caesars Palace enjoys a reputation for top-notch service, and the MGM Mansion is known for the secluded atmosphere in their high-limit area. But regardless of which casino you choose, bring your wallet—and your courage. —ML

ⓘ **Caesars Palace Las Vegas,** 3750 Las Vegas Blvd. South (ⓒ **866/227-5938;** www.caesarspalace.com). **Wynn Las Vegas,** 3131 Las Vegas Blvd. South (ⓒ **877/321-WYNN;** www.wynnlasvegas.com).

MGM Grand, 3799 Las Vegas Blvd. South (ⓒ **877/880-0880;** www.mgmgrand.com).

WHEN TO GO: Year-round.

Wild Wrestling Matches
Lucha Libre Is Truly Free Fighting
Mexico City, Mexico

Mascara Sagrada flies off the ropes and body slams El Rayo de Jalisco. The crowd goes into a frenzy. Okay. Tell the truth. How often have you visited another culture and gone to a professional wrestling match? Have you ever considered bringing a wrestling mask home as a souvenir or unique gift? For an adrenaline-pumping, raucous good time, join the 16,000 screaming fans at the Arena México or attend the lucha libre fights at the smaller Arena Coliseo where you can get closer to the action. Fans cheer for the *técnicos* (good guys) and boo against the evil *rudos*. For between $10 and $30 depending on the venue and your seat, you can drink cheap beer, cheer your brains out, and really get into it.

Lucha Libre (literally "free fight") in Mexico is as hokey as most professional wrestling. The *rudos* usually dress in black, the "rules" are ignored, luchadores are thrown from the ring—as may be the referee—fighting may continue outside the ring, and chairs or anything else at hand may come into play. On a good night you might even see several luchadores come out of the audience to mix it up. Fans scream profanities at the luchadores, who scream back at the fans; the fans scream at the referees, the wrestlers scream at the referees, and everyone gets his or her adrenaline revved up. Luchadoras (female wrestlers) make the program complete on specific evenings. The best part is the fans

in their costumes (think American football games), who even bring bicycle pumps to use with their air horns.

Supposedly, World Wrestling Entertainment (*WWE,* formerly known as the *WWF,* World Wrestling Federation) got its inspiration from the lucha libre. Remember the fearsome Masked Marvel? In Mexico many of the luchadores (wrestlers) wear masks that are traced to the Aztecs and Mayans. You can buy a copy to take home for under $15. The mask keeps the identity of the luchadore secret and is never taken off in the ring. Many of the luchadores only go out in public wearing their masks, and many continue to do so even after they've retired. It's been reported that the great luchadore, El Santo, who appeared in movies as well as the ring, was buried in his silver mask. Taking a mask off during a match can result in disqualification and having a mask ripped off by an opponent is the "ultimate" disgrace.

Mexico City is huge and crowded with almost every imaginable activity to keep the visitor occupied. Horse racing and horseback riding are close by, as are cycling, scuba diving, and snorkeling. —*LF*

ⓘ www.luchalibreaaa.com.

TOURS: Mexican Fiesta Tours (www.mxfiestatour.com).

WHEN TO GO: Tues, Fri, and Sat nights.

✈ Benito Juárez International Airport.

🛏 $$ **Presidente Intercontinental,** Campos Eliseos 218, Col. Polanco; © **800/ 424-6835** in the U.S. or 55/5327-7700; www.ichotelsgroup.com). $$ **Condesadf,** Av. Veracruz 102, Col. Condesa (© **800/ 337-4685** in the U.S. or 55/5241-2600; www.condesadf.com).

373

Coney Island Polar Bear Club
A Cool New Year's Dip
Coney Island, Brooklyn, New York, U.S.A.

I love a thrill as much as the next person. Jumping out of airplanes, swimming with sharks, skiing wild backcountry terrain— somehow these activities make sense to me. But taking off my clothes in the middle of a New York winter, stripping down to nothing but a bathing suit, and running into the Atlantic Ocean? That's another story, altogether. But that's exactly what hundreds of people do each New Year's Day at Coney Island, Brooklyn's famed beach and amusement park from days of yore, at the annual **Polar Bear Club** swim. The Cyclone roller coaster (see ❹⁹⁷), which looms large over the beach, is a fast-paced thrill ride to be sure, but jump into 35°F (2°C) waters below, and it's literally breath-taking.

For the annual New Year's Day swim, hundreds of people assemble on the boardwalk at Stillwell Avenue to take the plunge. Hundreds of others observe nearby. Ask swimmers why they do this, and the answers are varied. Some say they do it to raise money for charity. (Neither swimmers nor observers pay a fee, but a donation to the club's partner, **Camp Sunshine** [www.campsunshine.org], a get-away in Maine for sick children and their families, is encouraged). Others go for it

Daredevils and cold-water enthusiasts rush the waters off Coney Island on New Year's Day.

on a dare. Still others believe there are health benefits to a dip in frigid waters. Aficionados claim that an icy plunge helps boost the immune system to ward off a cold, the flu, or relieve the symptoms of chronic maladies such as arthritis. Whatever their reasons may be, one thing all the participants can agree on is that it's an experience they'll never forget.

The Polar Bear Club recommends that in addition to your bathing suit, swimmers bring a towel, cozy after-swim footwear, dry warm clothing, and a friend (for photos and post-swim assistance, if needed). I'd add a pre-swim discussion with your doctor and a thermos of hot liquid to this list of requirements. For first-timers it is usually suggested that you turn off your brain, take a breath, and go quickly. Be prepared for a cold-water shock that can leave you breathless. Upon surfacing in the waves, some participants splash around a while in the chilly water, though more often than not, they hightail right back to the shore. If there happens to be snow on the beach, you could always take a quick roll in it for an added adrenaline rush before dressing.

In addition to the swim on New Year's Day, the Coney Island Polar Bear Club invites potential members to join them for swims at 1:00pm any Sunday between November and April, after which they may start the official membership process. Bernard MacFadden founded the Polar Bear Club in 1903 and the Coney Island group claims to be the oldest of its type in the country. The L Street Brownies of South Boston can date their existence back to 1904, but they continue to search for earlier documentation. —*LF*

(i) **Coney Island Polar Bear Club** (© **917/ 533-3568;** www.polarbearclub.org).

WHEN TO GO: Sun, Nov–Apr and every New Year's Day.

✈ JFK (17 miles) or LaGuardia Airport (22 miles).

🛏 $$ **Excelsior Hotel,** 45 W. 81st St. (© **800/368-4575** or 212/362-9200; www. excelsiorhotelny.com). $$$ **Le Parker Meridien,** 118 W. 57th St. (© **800/543-4300** or 212/245-5000; www.parker meridien.com).

Mardi Gras & Jazz
Partying in the Streets
New Orleans, Louisiana, U.S.A.

"Throw some to me," you shriek to the costume-clad revelers on the Mardi Gras parade float passing slowly by. Batting away other outstretched hands, you manage to snag one of the bead necklaces tossed into the crowd. The thrill of Mardi Gras, the culmination of two months of Carnival celebrations, reaches its apex as the parades make their way down the streets of New Orleans. From the masquerading partiers all about town to the carousers on Bourbon Street to the all-consuming pleading for "throws," at parades, Mardi Gras is festivity from start

to finish, with plenty of opportunity for thrills over the course of the celebration.

Mary Herczog, author of *Frommer's New Orleans,* is an expert on "throws." She has both tossed throws from a float and been in the crowds—she calls the fanaticism surrounding the trinkets "bead lust." As she explains, "First you stand there passively. All around you the strands fly thick and fast. You catch a few. 'Hmm,' you think, 'they look kind of good around my neck.' You reach more aggressively as the strands fly overhead. 'Wait. That guy/ cute girl/kid got a really good strand! How come I'm not getting any like that!' Now you find yourself shrieking 'Throw me something, Mister.' You jump. You wail. You plead. You think, 'This is really stupid. It's a 5¢ piece of plastic—oh, look a really glittery strand! I want it. I want it." The enthusiasm and excitement of a Mardi Gras parade is infectious.

You may have images of the more tawdry side of these parades, perhaps of women baring their chests, so the stud on the float will throw an extra nice set of beads to them. But there are more civilized and family-friendly spots from which to watch and hopefully participate. One of these areas is along St. Charles Street, where the parades are on one side of the street, while only foot traffic is allowed on the other. Bourbon Street is the setting for a more debauched scene, where you'll see vulgar activity among the often drunken crowds.

New Orleans is also associated with musicians playing mellow jazz. During quieter days (before and after Mardi Gras), you may be able to sit on a balcony in the French Quarter and hear the sound of a saxophone wailing in the distance. If you're a jazz fan, the annual **New Orleans Jazz & Heritage Festival (Jazz Fest)** is a must. It takes place annually in late April to early May. This festival offers its own set of thrills. Every spring, the festival showcases jazz, gospel, Cajun, zydeco, blues, R&B, rock, funk, African, Latin, Caribbean, folk, and much more on a dozen stages. Since its inception in 1970, some of the world's greatest musicians, ranging from Wynton Marsalis, Fats Domino, and Harry Connick, Jr., to the Preservation Hall Jazz Band, Miles Davis, and Jimmy Buffet, have performed. Fans flock from around the world to see their beloved favorite musicians. The energy at Jazz Fest is high, even if some of the acts take it slow and easy, like the city itself. —LF

ⓘ **Now Orleans Metro and Convention Visitors Bureau** (✆ 800/672-6124; www.neworleanscvb.com). **New Orleans Jazz Fest & Heritage Festival** (✆ 504/410-4100; www.nojazzfest.com).

WHEN TO GO: Carnival season is early Jan through late Feb. Mardi Gras (always a Tues) takes place every year 47 days before Easter.

✈ New Orleans

🛏 $$ **Bourbon Orleans Hotel,** 717 Orleans St. (✆ **504/523-2222;** www.bourbonorleans.com); $$–$$$ **Loews New Orleans Hotel,** 300 Poydras St. (✆ **800/23-LOEWS** [235-6397] or 504/595-3300; www.loewshotels.com); $ **Prytania Park Hotel,** 1525 Prytania (✆ **800/862-1094** or 504/524-0427; www.prytaniapark hotel.com).

Skateboarding Millennium Park
Street Riders to Pros Play Here
Calgary, Alberta, Canada

The first time you drop in the 4.2m (14-ft.) section of the concrete clover bowl at **Shaw Millennium Park,** I hope you're ready. I also hope you're a really good skater and that you're wearing your helmet and pads—because you'll be going extremely fast and the concrete is hard. Hopefully, you'll have practiced in the 1.2m (4-ft.) and 3m (10-ft.) bowls first or, more appropriately, at the beginner (Intro) and intermediate (Central) areas of the park.

Though western Canada is renowned for extreme skiing opportunities, there's also plenty of fun to be had sans snow. At the

Shaw Millennium Park is a haven for skateboarders.

Millennium Skate Park, there's plenty of room for boarders of all skill levels—from street riders to pro-level experts such as Devin Morrison, one of the best skateboarders in Calgary, who periodically shows up. Called the world's largest skate park, when the next phase is completed it will cover more than 8,360 sq. m (90,000 sq. ft.). According to a city report, there are more than 10,000 skateboarders in Calgary. The park is open 24/7 and attracts an average of 1,000 users daily. (It's less crowded on weekdays and evenings.)

The Intro Area is set up with a pool, small rails, curbs, stairs, and ledges. This is a great place to learn drop-ins, Ollies, and get really comfortable. The Central Area is awesome with higher rails, a six-foot bowl with metal coping, stairs, ledges, pyramids, pool type wall rides, banks, larger transitions, double drop. Here you can work on those vert Ollies, Axle Stalls, catch some air, and Rock to Fakie. Then there's the oh-my-gosh Expert Park. How about a 30-foot full-pipe connected to a 15-foot halfpipe, and a clover bowl with 4-, 10-, and 14-foot sections? Rippers heaven! This is a park for observers as well as participants.

Calgary is a major Canadian city with numerous museums, world-class shopping, and great restaurants, including the Teatro and the Belvedere. **Eau Claire Market** (pedestrian only) and **Prince Island Park** are great to just relax and take it easy. The **Glenbow Museum** has a wonderful interpretation of the settlement of western Canada and the life of its Native tribes. Hiking, running, fishing, and biking are popular pursuits within the city. **Banff,** one of the truly beautiful mountain towns in the world, is only an hour and a half drive from Calgary. —*LF*

ⓘ **Shaw Millennium Skate Park,** 1220 Ninth Ave. SW (✆ **403/268-2489;** www.calgaryskateparks.ca).

WHEN TO GO: Year-round.

✈ Calgary.

🛏 $$ **Kensington Riverside Inn,** 1126 Memorial Dr. NW (✆ **877/313-3733** or 403/228-4442; www.kensingtonriverside inn.com). $$$ **Fairmont Palliser,** 133 Ninth Ave. SW (✆ **800/441-1414** or 403/262-1234; www.fairmont.com).

376

Riding the London Eye
Big Wheel, Bigger View
London, England, U.K.

The world's largest observation wheel, the **London Eye,** is like a giant Ferris wheel, but with capsules that hold up to 28 people, instead of the usual two-seater arrangement of a Ferris wheel. This is no mere amusement park ride—after all, what is there to see from the top of ordinary Ferris wheels? From the top of the Eye, you can take in a glorious view, the vast panorama of one of the world's greatest cities.

Opened in 2000, it is the fourth-tallest structure in London. How high are you? Picture stacking 64 red London phone booths atop each other and you'll get a sense. You're 135m (443 ft.) above the city when you're at the top of the Eye.

Passengers are carried in 32 air-conditioned "pods" that make a complete revolution every half-hour, hardly a breakneck pace—at the bottom, the pods keep moving, but so slowly that disembarking is no problem. The capsules are surrounded by windows, allowing riders to take in the dramatic London skyline.

From the top of the wheel, in clear weather, you can gaze in all directions for some 40km (25 miles)—as far as Windsor Castle—over this famously spread-out metropolis, easily spotting not only the Gothic spires of the Houses of Parliament and Westminster Abbey across the river, but also the British Museum, St. Paul's Cathedral, Nelson's Column in Trafalgar Square, Buckingham Palace, the Tower of London, Tower Bridge, and the green necklace of parks that runs through central London.

At 424m (1,391 ft.) in circumference, it's the world's largest observation wheel. Built out of steel by a European consortium, it was conceived and designed by London architects Julia Barfield and David Marks, who claim inspiration from the Statue of Liberty in New York and the Eiffel Tower in Paris. Some 2 million visitors are expected to ride the Eye every year.

The Eye lies close to Westminster Bridge. (You can hardly miss it). Tickets are £16 for adults, £12 for seniors and students, £7.75 for children 5 to 15. It's open October to May daily 10am to 8pm; June to September daily 10am to 9pm.—*LF*

(i) **London Eye,** Millennium Jubilee Gardens (© **0870/5000-600;** www.londoneye.com).

WHEN TO GO: Year-round.

✈ London.

$$$ **London Bridge Hotel,** 8–18 London Bridge St. 9 (© **44/20/7855-2200;** www.londonbridgehotel.com). $$ **Vicarage Private Hotel,** 10 Vicarage Gate, South Kensington (© **44/20/7229-4030;** www.londonvicaragehotel.com).

Breathtaking City Views

We've devoted many of the pages in this book to fast-paced, quick-moving adrenaline adventures. But we think that slowing down and taking the time to stand still and take in an extraordinary view can be a thrill on its own. Each of the following city views is spectacular. —LF

377 Table Mountain, Cape Town, South Africa: During the 10-minute ascent in the cable car to the top of Table Mountain, which towers over Cape Town, the view begins to stretch from urban to endless ocean. Step out of the car and there are paths to meander that lead to 360-degree views. You'll see Cape Town, Table Bay, Robben Island (the prison-turned-museum where former South Africa president Nelson Mandela was incarcerated for many years), and even the Cape Peninsula, which is nearly the southern tip of Africa. If you want to stretch your legs, take one of the hiking paths up or down this mountain, which tops out around 1,068m (3,560 ft.) above the ocean crashing against Africa's shores below. See **194** for information on abseiling down Table Mountain. *www.tablemountain.net; www.capetown.travel.*

378 Victoria Peak, Hong Kong, China: It's just an optical illusion. Those tall buildings you're passing only look like they're leaning, as you ride up Victoria Peak in the world's steepest funicular railway. After the 8-minute ride to the top, the bustling Hong Kong Harbor and its islands are laid out before you. From the viewing area on the Sky Terrace, your eyes are drawn to the intense blue of the water surrounding the islands packed with buildings. Take time to walk on some of the lush footpaths, such as the one that leads into Victoria Peak Garden. *www.thepeak.com.hk/en.*

379 CN Tower, Toronto, Ontario, Canada: The ride to the Observation Deck at the skinny CN Tower in urban Toronto takes just 58 seconds in a glass-sided elevator. When you step out you're on the Look Out Level at 341m (1,136 ft.) above sea level. From the Observation Deck, you'll find awe-inspiring 360° views. For a bigger thrill go one level below, step out on the Glass Floor, and look down. To reach the Sky Pod for a sky-high view of Toronto, you'll need to take a second elevator, which shoots up another 33 stories. You can also dine in *360,* the revolving restaurant on the Observation Deck. *www.cntower.ca.*

380 Red Rocks Amphitheatre, Morrison, Colorado, U.S.A.: Denverites love to attend concerts at Red Rocks, an open-air amphitheatre that's nestled between two towering 250 million-year-old sandstone monoliths. From the seats in the theater is a stunning view of the sprawling Denver metro area and the farmland and prairies beyond. On a clear day you'll swear you can see to the Kansas border. You don't need a concert ticket to enjoy walking around the park's trails that thread through rocks and meadows. Unless there's a concert, you can visit the amphitheatre to learn about this site's unusual geology, the famous musicians who've played here, and lunch at a window table in the Ship Rock Grill. *www.redrocksonline.com.*

381 Petrona Towers, Kuala Lumpur, Malaysia: You can see these two 88-story buildings—the tallest twin towers in the world—from almost anywhere in the city. And you can see most of the city from the glass-walled skybridge—the highest double-decker sky bridge in the world. It links the 41st and 42nd floors in the two buildings. You won't be allowed much time on the bridge, so be prepared to take photos quickly. The bridge tours are free, but it's popular so get to the Towers early. *www.petronas.com.my.*

382 Shanghai World Financial Center, Shanghai, China: The view from one of three transparent walkways on the 100th floor observation deck, the highest in the world, is dizzying. The ground is 467m (1,556 ft.) below you and the spectacular city of Shanghai envelopes you from all sides. From this vantage point you can also see the Huang Pu River. *www.swfc-observatory.com/en.*

383 Top of the Rock, New York City, New York, U.S.A.: Perhaps there's no skyline in the world as glamorous, glorious, and recognizable as that of New York City. The Top of the Rock is a new three-level observation deck on the 67th, 69th, and 70th floors of 30 Rock efeller Plaza. Two of the floors have outdoor terraces where you can look through big panes of safety glass to enjoy the view. If you want a breeze along with the view, head to the 70th floor, which has an open-air, unobstructed view of the city, the rivers that surround it, and beyond. *www.topoftherocknyc.com.*

An incomparable view of New York City from the Top of the Rock.

384 Macau Tower Convention and Entertainment Center, Macau: Take the glass-fronted elevator up to the Observation Lounge, which has vast windows and glass sections on the floor making visible the ground 220m (732 ft.) below. If you're gutsy, do the Skywalk X stroll around the outer rim, which is just 2m (6 ft.) wide and has no handrails! (You're strapped in with an overhead safety system.) If you're fearless, snag a quick view of Macau as you take the SkyJump, a 20-second flight over Macau's cityscape. This adventure is listed as the World's Highest Commercial Decelerator Descent in the *Guinness Book of World Records*. *www.macautower.com.mo.*

385 The Eiffel Tower, Paris, France: You can see most of Paris from the top of this monument built in 1889 for the Centenary of the French Revolution. If you've indulged in too much French cuisine, walk up the more than 700 steps (or take an elevator) to the second floor. The view is nice from here, but for the best views of the Parisian skyline you must take the elevator up to the top of the tower to the indoor and outdoor observation decks. From here, at 276m (905 ft.), you'll be able to pick out famous sights, from the Arc de Triomphe and the Trocadero Gardens to the Sacre Coeur and the Pantheon. *www.tour-eiffel.fr.*

386

Dinner in the Sky
Up, Up & Away
Locations Worldwide

If you feel like you can't sit through another business lunch, or the thought of attending one more quarterly sales meeting leaves you bored to tears, here's a twist that will leave you breathless: Hold your next get-together hundreds of feet off the ground. No, not in some skyscraper, but on an open platform that's suspended from a gigantic crane.

The company behind this high-flying idea, Dinner in the Sky, has evolved into an international marketing group that franchises the events in 28 countries around the world. Locations and costs vary, and the company arranges for local permits and other details. The specially designed platform can accommodate up to 22 guests, and there's room for three chefs or waiters in an aisle at the table's center. And yes, they will lower you down to Earth when it's time for a restroom break, then back up again for more bird's-eye sightseeing.

These affairs are not for those with vertigo—guests are strapped into leather seats that have no walls or railings behind them. Such safety features would, of course, block the views. And what views they are: Guests have been transported above the glittering casinos of Las Vegas, the skyscrapers of London and Toronto, the cathedrals of Amiens, France, and the minarets of Istanbul.

Meetings and dinners aren't the only uses for floating aloft. Entertainment events have included poker games and New Year's Eve parties. Some clients have included a second crane with a band to provide live entertainment (dancing is, of course, discouraged). The company has expanded their offerings to include Weddings in the Sky and a range of other custom offerings. When it comes to developing your next creative event, the sky really is the limit. —*ML*

Dinner in the Sky gives eating out a whole new meaning.

ⓘ **Dinner in the Sky** (✆ **32/02/333-3810;** www.dinnerinthesky.com).

387

Trapeze School
Channeling Cirque de Soleil
New York, New York, U.S.A.

As it turns out, flying through the air with the greatest of ease isn't so easy. But you're bound to have fun trying.

Up above the crowds of Manhattan's busy streets, the Trapeze School of New York is open all summer on the rooftop of Pier 20 alongside the Hudson River. (If you're in town during the chillier seasons, don't worry; there's also a year-round tented location in Chelsea.) When you arrive and meet your instructors, you'll go through a brief safety briefing and demonstration. Then it's time to strap on your belt, hook your carabineers onto two ropes, and begin climbing—up an extremely narrow metal ladder for 7m (23 ft.). These steps are where the panic starts to set in, and your heart starts pumping faster. When you finally reach the top, take a look at the priceless views. You'll see the city's magnificent skyline on one side, and the famous Lady Liberty standing tall in the New York harbor on the other.

Standing on the thin wooden platform getting ready to fly, remember to douse your sweaty palms in chalk and keep breathing as your instructor holds onto the back of your belt and you lean forward to grab hold of the trapeze bar. It's heavier than it looks. Once you're in position, with both hands steady and knees slightly bent, the instructor yells "Hep," and that's your cue to jump. Legs together, toes pointed, stomach in, arms strong. Suddenly, you're swinging forward in a giant arch, high above the crowded city streets, away from the noise and chaos below. People are cheering, but for a split second, all you hear is the wind and perhaps your own voice—unsure at this point if you're screaming with fear or delight (or, most likely, both). Before you know it, another instructor who's on the ground, holding

your safety rope, calls "knees up." You immediately use the momentum to bring your legs up to your chest and then over the bar in one smooth move.

As your crawl over to the dismount area, and flip yourself off the net onto solid ground, your hands feel raw and adrenaline is rushing through your body. As your classmates take their turns, stretch out and revel in what you've accomplished for a couple of minutes. Before you know it, you're climbing up again to attempt another skill, maybe even a split.

If you get the hang of things, your finale performance will be to try a catch with the professional trapeze artist swinging on a bar opposite you. The real trick here is to just relax and let go. Like the school's tagline says, "Forget fear, worry about the addiction." Even if you don't master any fancy moves during your first class, the euphoria of simply soaring through the air, high above New York City, is enough to keep your head in the clouds for at least a few days.

The trapeze school also offers lessons in Boston, Baltimore, Los Angeles, and Washington, D.C. —*JS*

Trapeze School, New York City.

(i) **Trapeze School of New York** ((C) **917/797-1872;** www.newyork.trapeze school.com).

WHEN TO GO: Year-round at the indoor location; May–Sept for the outdoor classes.

✈ JFK, LaGuardia, or Newark airports.

⊨ $$ **Excelsior Hotel,** 45 W. 81st St. ((C) **800/368-4575** or 212/362-9200; www. excelsiorhotelny.com). $$$ **Le Parker Meridien,** 118 W. 57th St. ((C) **800/543-4300** or 212/245-5000; www.parker meridien.com).

388

Marrakech Markets
Northern Africa's Bargaining Mecca
Marrakech, Morocco

Treasure hunting in the walled city of Marrakech stimulates all the senses. A daily soundtrack of five calls to prayer blasts from microphones in skyward-reaching minarets. Bright carpets hang off rooftops. Groups of veiled women in colorful robes stroll along the city's dusty alleyways, while men in *jellebas* (traditional robes) sit in cafes sipping steaming glasses of sweet mint tea. Fragrant spices waft through the breeze. Chicken tagines infused with lemons and olives, accompanied by heaping plates of couscous, provide a hearty lunch. Shopkeepers extend a pair of *babouches* (slippers), urging you to caress the smooth soft brown leather.

Marrakech has been a trading center for decades, and it continues to be one of the world's hottest shopping destinations. The city has managed to retain its centuries-old delights—Islamic palaces, comedic storytellers, and snake charmers—while also embracing tourism and giving itself a significant makeover. Behind its plain brown walls on narrow maze-like streets, you'll find a range of surprises—from the Souk des Teinturiers, where pieces of colored wool hang to dry, to a posh new riad to leatherworkers fashioning shoes with the same tools their great-grandfathers used, to unconventional modern clothing and jewelry designers.

Although Marrakech is navigable on your own, consider arranging a short tour with an official guide on your first morning. (Ask your hotel to set you up with someone reputable and knowledgeable; don't just go with one of the many unofficial guides on the street aggressively offering to show you around.)

After you've gotten your bearings, set off toward the souks. But be forewarned: Browsing and talking with local shopkeepers in Marrakech is addictive. This adventure can easily hold your attention for more than one afternoon. If you want to have a slight advantage at the bargaining table, it pays to do your research first at **Ensemble Artisans,** on Muhammed V Avenue. Here, all prices are officially set at fixed rates by the government, which means there's no bargaining. The costs are good benchmarks to keep in mind when you start trading offers in the souks.

When you enter a souk, it's customary for the shopkeeper to start a casual conversation of small talk and offer you tea. If you're not interested in purchasing anything, decline the tea politely and try not to loiter. But once you express genuine interest in something, let the bargaining begin. It's fair to counter the shopkeeper's original offer by about one-third, and go back and forth two or three times. You

The souk of Marrakech.

can always walk out if you don't like the final price, but the idea here is to enjoy the challenge as you try to negotiate a deal. As you barter, you don't know whether or not you'll get a price you're happy with. If you do, you'll come away from the souks with more than an item; you'll have the memory of a thrilling and unique experience.

Babouches (slippers), silk scarves, handmade leather bags and poufs, and *jellebas* are handsomely crafted and relatively inexpensive souvenirs for friends and family back home. Babouches shouldn't cost more than $10 per pair; scarves shouldn't cost more than $20; and poufs shouldn't cost much more than $30 or $40. But traditional carpets are significantly more expensive keepsakes. If you're interested in purchasing these beauties, make sure to study up on them before arriving in Marrakech. You'll want to be educated about the wide variety of rugs unrolled before you.

As fantastic as the souks are, the city's streets offer other thrilling attractions, just wandering around and getting lost exposes you to the sights, smells, colors, and essence of Moroccan daily life. Stop shopping long enough to spend time at the Djemaa el Fna (a daily stage for entertainment, and a UNESCO World Heritage Site), the Bahia Palace, the Musee Marrakech, the Ben Youssef Medersa, the Villa Nouvelle, and at least one of the city's stunning gardens. —*JS*

ⓘ **Moroccan Tourist Office** (② 212/ **537-67-4013** or 212/537-3918; www.visit morocco.com).

WHEN TO GO: Apr–Oct.

✈ Marrakech-Menara Airport.

🛏 $$–$$$ **Dar Les Cignones,** 108 Rue de Barima, Medina (② **212/524-382740;** www.lescigognes.com/en).

389

Overnights at Museums
Sleepovers with Dinosaurs
Museums in the U.S.A.

Have you ever fantasized about spending the night in a museum and having the whole place to yourself? You could spend time at the exhibits and displays without having to fight the crowds and really get to experience the place as though it were made only for you. Though you may not have exactly the same experience as Ben Stiller in the popular movie *Night at the Museum,* in which the exhibits come to life at night, you can still have an up-close-and-personal overnight encounter. Several museums now offer the opportunity to spend the night inside their doors. From flashlight tours in search of wild animals to

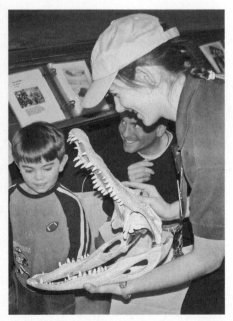

The kids will be thrilled to spend the night at a museum.

visiting with Sue the T-Rex, to sleeping in bunks on a World War II battleship, many museums are awakening people to history during the hours when much of the nation is asleep.

The scenes in *Night at the Museum* were filmed at the New York City **American Museum of Natural History,** which offers sleepovers for ages 8 to 12 (plus a parent or guardian). At the AMNH, the lights dim and everyone goes on a flashlight tour led by museum staff, visits exciting exhibits throughout the museum, and sees a current IMAX film before settling down to sleep, perhaps next to an Alaskan brown bear or a 94-ft.-long (28m) blue whale.

The **Field Museum** in Chicago has been running the "Dozin' with the Dinos" sleepovers for many years. The nocturnal adventures include family workshops, performances, exploring museum exhibits, and a sleeping spot in the Genius Hall of Dinosaurs located in the Evolving Planet exhibition. There are two packages; the higher priced one also includes a behind-the-scenes tour with a museum scientist.

You'll enter the World War II era when spending a night on the **USS *Missouri,*** the battleship that's now a memorial and museum based in Pearl Harbor in Honolulu, Hawaii. Campers experiencing the Battleship *Missouri*'s overnight encampment get a personalized dog tag, sleep in the same area where the crew slept, store their gear in lockers, and eat Navy-style chow on the ship's mess deck. The encampments are open to scouting, school, and other groups that meet insurance coverage requirements.

Adult encampments may be arranged on the **Battleship *New Jersey,*** the floating museum on the Camden, New Jersey, waterfront across from Center City Philadelphia. Whether it's a group of children or adults, the tour may include visiting the Combat Engagement Center, where you'll participate in a simulated launch of a Tomahawk missile, to climbing down the original ladders to view the Admiral's cabin and sleeping in the sailors' quarters.

This same trend is catching on in zoos. How about a zoo slumber party for your child's birthday? Families, scout troops, and school groups can take the Roar and Snore Overnights at the **Philadelphia Zoo.** Themed sleepovers, such as *Critters of the Night* or *Froggin' Frenzy* can be arranged.

The age limits for children who can attend these overnights vary from museum to museum. In general, attendees must bring their own sleeping bag. In some museums you'll sleep on carpeted floors, in others on cots, and on the battleships in the quarters actually used by the sailors. —LF

ⓘ **American Museum of Natural History** (𝒞 212/769-5000; www.amnh.org). The **Field Museum** (𝒞 312/922-9410; www.fieldmuseum.org). **USS *Missouri*** (𝒞 877/MIGHTYMO [644-4896] or 808/455-1600; www.ussmissouri.com). **Battleship *New Jersey*** (𝒞 866/877-6262 or 856/966-1652, www.battleshipnewjersey.org).

WHEN TO GO: Contact the museums or battleships directly for schedules.

Taking in a Football (Soccer) Match in Buenos Aires

The Match Box

Buenos Aires, Argentina

Boca Junior fans take up positions behind the goal. Long blue and gold banners are unfurled and spread across the crowd as fireworks crackle and fizzle in the sky above. Thousands of flags flap in the Buenos Aires breeze, red smoke from flares streams across the stadium, and a tangle of ticker tape covers the green grass of the football pitch below. The fans burst into song just as the whistle is blown and kick-off begins. They have come to cheer and jeer at the *Superclasico,* one of the fiercest and most important sporting rivalries in the world between two Argentine teams, Boca Juniors and River Plate. The venue is Boca's intimidating and claustrophobic home ground known as *La Bombonera* (the chocolate box), a 60,000 capacity stadium located in a poor, working class district south of the city center. This entire country of soccer fanatics shuts down to catch the game, and even the nearby tourist tango street known as El Caminito is shuttered up and empty as people crowd in front of TVs in cafes, bars, and restaurants. That's how important football (soccer) is here. The excitement that builds during a match is enough to keep your adrenaline rushing all day long.

Up in the stands the match seems to have little impact on the crowd. The pitch can barely be seen from under all the flags, banners, armpits, and elbows. The fans keep up a continuous song amazingly to the accompaniment of a four-piece brass band and a troupe of drummers in the middle of all this surging chaos. Suddenly Boca score and the entire crowd squashes itself into a tight space by the fence as they rush down and scream with joy. It's utter mayhem. This goal leads to an even more intense continued chant and song until River Plate score and suddenly the Boca section is very quiet. It is the turn of the opposition fans to jump and gesticulate and shout obscenities.

Shortly into the second half Boca score again and the fans, known as *Barrio Bravos,* are stage diving off the top steps and climbing the razor wire fence. The second half passes in a burr of noise and surging bodies. Then the whistle goes and the place goes absolutely berserk. The riot squad moves in on the other side of the fence to prevent a pitch invasion. Sometimes the pitch is overrun and it is not uncommon to see the manager whirled around in the air. In championship finals the players throw their clothes into the crowd and run around the pitch in their underwear. People climb all over the goal posts. The net is torn down and dissected and disappears into a thousand pockets. People are lying in prostrate star shapes on the pitch. Grown men are crying. The stadium literally bounces as the multitude

jump up and down in pure jubilation. Eventually the pitch simply can't contain all this excitement and the crowd bursts out onto the streets. The fans have taken over a bridge across a 14-lane highway. It's covered in flags and banners and human beings. A breakaway mob has stopped the cars and a tail snakes back for miles with hundreds of blaring horns and youth hanging from car windows waving flags.

Meanwhile, the opposing fans are shuffled quickly out the back, cursing bitterly and swearing revenge the next time around. —*CO'M*

(i) **Boca Juniors** (www.bocajuniors. com.ar); **River Plate** (www.cariverplate. com.ar).

WHEN TO GO: Year-round.

✈ Buenos Aires.

🛏 $$$ **Tailor Made Hotel,** Arce 385 (✆ **54/11/4774/9620;** www.tailormade hotels.com). $$ **Miravida Soho Hotel and Wine Bar,** Darregueyra 2050 (✆ **54/ 11/4774-6433;** www.miravidasoho.com).

391

Dancing Tango in Argentina
Get Up & Tango
Buenos Aires, Argentina

Men and women gather in a dimly lit salon, chatting casually at round tables before the mournful chords of an accordion echo around the room. The crowd suddenly breaks into a set of couples. They embrace and, cheek to cheek, sweep across the dance floor. Chests together, their legs twirl and invade each other's space. They pass sultry looks and caresses, accompanied by the yearnful music. The *milonga* is underway, a tango gathering where anybody can turn up and grab a partner. They just better know what they are doing. The intensity and excitement of this dance are

historied, and participants must show their respect.

Tango was born in the late 19th century in the poor barrios that fringed Buenos Aires City. Waves of immigrants, mostly Italian but also Spaniards, Jews, Arabs, French, Irish, and Poles, began arriving on Argentine shores. Though they arrived from all over the world, they had much in common. They were young, single, and working class. They harbored an immigrant's feelings of loneliness, displacement, and nostalgia. And they all, of course, had a love of music.

A new type of popular culture was born in the city's bars and bordellos. Tango became its voice, echoing stories of lost loves and sad memories. The music and dance evolved. Some men took it so seriously they practiced together for want of a partner (the girls were just too expensive). Their moves became a source of pride and perhaps a chance to improve their appeal to the opposite sex.

The new dance from the barrios was disdained by the rich establishment. It was uncouth and immoral. They banned their daughters from practicing it. Yet the sons of the aristocracy were attracted by its romance and danger. They slummed it in the *arrabales* (city fringes) and picked up some steps. Packed off to university in Europe, they brought this new erotic dance with them. It was enough to give a puritan a heart attack. Kaiser Wilhelm banned it. Prince Louis of Bavaria denounced it as absurd. (Strangely enough Pope Pius was unimpressed and called it too languid for his tastes.) All to no avail—the chattering classes took to it enthusiastically and the tango became the music and dance of European high society in the 1920s. The tango craze began.

Europe legitimized the tango. The high-class salons of London, Paris, and Rome reverberated with the music. What was born in rags, now wore a tux. Yet Buenos Aires will always be its center. It is a mecca for thousands of tango dancers around the world who visit the seductive Argentine capital to try their steps in a multitude of venues. Dancehalls vary from elaborate belle epoque theaters with gilded box seats to grungy warehouses with new age wall hangings and tattooed clientele. One of the best and most historied tango shows in the city is **El Querandí** (Perú 32; ✆ **11/4345-0331**). The style here now is sexy, with its origins as a bordello with all male dancers. (Call for showtimes and prices.) Another great tango palace is **Esquina Carlos Gardel** (Carlos Cardel 3200 at Anchorena; ✆ **11/4876-6363**).

The music is very much alive and evolving, varying from classic instrumentals to crooning divas. There is even a languid modern dance version called tango electronica. —*CO'M*

WHEN TO GO: Year-round.

✈ Buenos Aires.

⊨ $$ **Gurda Tango Boutique Hotel,** Defensa 1521, San Telmo (✆ **54/11/4307-0646;** www.gurdahotel.com). $$ **Tanguero Boutique Hotel,** Suipacha 780 (✆ **54/11/4328-7006;** www.tanguerohotel.com).

392

Game Show Contestant
Come On Down!
New York, New York, or Los Angeles, California, U.S.A.

The lights are blazing upon your sweating face, the live audience is squirming in their seats, and Alex Trebek is waiting for your answer. Tick, tick, tick. "What . . . is . . . the Bay of Fundy?" you mutter. Bing! "Correct!" he hollers as you exhale nervously, adding $200 to your score and thanking your lucky stars that you stayed awake during geography class. If you've been watching game shows like these from the comfort of your living and saying to yourself, "I can do that," then give it a go and show the world that you can be the next big winner. Whether it's a trivia show like *Jeopardy!* or a game of chance like *Wheel of Fortune,* the producers are looking for contestants like you.

Different game shows have different criteria for their contestants, and the application process for each reflects that. Most have eligibility requirements that stipulate the applicant not be related to anyone working for the parent company, and not have appeared on any version of the show before. Some shows like *Who Wants to Be a Millionaire?* choose their contestants from a group of eligible guests at a live New York City taping of the show; they have already completed a written test and an interview process. *Jeopardy!* requires a rigorous online test and a live audition at their studio in Culver City, California. Contestants for *The Price Is Right* aren't chosen at random from the hundreds of audience members at the show's Los Angeles taping, but are screened beforehand at an interview process.

Location counts: Los Angeles and New York are the best places to be, because most tapings occur in those cities. Out-of-towners visiting those places may actually have an edge, since producers like to have contestants from across the country—if you're planning a trip to either of those cities, apply ASAP. There are also occasional tapings that occur around the country; *Jeopardy!* even has a Brain Bus that tours the country looking for potential contestants.

Regardless of which show is your favorite, some basic tips apply. Make sure you watch the show regularly enough to know the rules and some winning strategies. Some experts recommend getting the board game or playing online versions of the show. Practicing public speaking is as important as practicing the game itself—producers don't want players to freeze up or panic when the cameras are rolling. Just like when applying for a job, little things count, like filling out your application properly and dressing for success. And, as in everything else in life, enthusiasm counts and may be the thing that separates you from the thousands of other people applying for the right to hear those famous words: "Johnny, tell us what she's won!" —*ML*

ⓘ **Jeopardy!** (✆ **800/482-9840;** www.jeopardy.com). **The Price Is Right** (✆ **323/575-2458;** www.etix.cbs.com). **Who Wants to Be a Millionaire?** (✆ **800/433-8321;** www.millionairetv.com). **Wheel of Fortune** (✆ **800/482-9840;** www.wheeloffortune.com).

393

Rolling the Dice in Monte Carlo
Luck, Be a Lady Tonight
Monte Carlo, Monaco

Joseph Jagger did it in 1873 while playing high-stakes roulette, taking advantage of an almost-imperceptible glitch in the roulette wheel. Charles Wells did it several times in 1891 and 1892. And who knows, with lady luck at your side, you too may break the bank at the Monte Carlo Casino. Steeped in the glamour of old-world Europe and the mystique of James Bond, the casino is one of the most popular destinations in this tiny principality on the French Riviera, known for years as a playground for the world's super-wealthy, super-tanned, and super-ostentatious.

Surrounded on three sides by France and on the fourth by the Mediterranean, Monaco can be reached by way of several rail, bus, or highway connections to other coastal cities. (The best way to arrive, of course, is on your private yacht.) There are several casinos in Monte Carlo, but the most famous and the only must-see is the opulent 1863 Beaux Arts palace designed by Charles Garnier, who also created the Paris Opera. Though the Monte Carlo Casino once enforced a strict dress code, that has relaxed considerably in recent years, and jackets are now "recommended" for gentlemen after 8:00pm in some of the gaming rooms, but not all.

Regardless of how you dress, carry a good wallet—many of the gambling salons here, such as the Salons Prives and the Supers Prive, have high limits. Others, like the Salle Blanche and the Atrium, are appropriate for folks who are happier playing a few casual hands at slot machines. And remember to bring your passport or ID card, because the casino is strictly off-limits to citizens of Monaco. Perhaps that's because it's a little like the Fort Knox of Monaco: The casino is the principality's main source of income. —*ML*

ⓘ **Direction du Tourisme et des Con-grés** (𝒞 **377/92-16-61-66;** www.monaco-tourisme.com).

TOUR: Casino de Monte-Carlo (𝒞 **377/98-06-21-21;** vip@montecarlocasinos.com).

WHEN TO GO: Year-round.

✈ Nice, France (24km/15 miles).

🛏 $$$ **Hotel Port Palace,** 7 av. John F. Kennedy (𝒞 **377/97-97-90-00;** www.port palace.com). $$ **Hotel Balmoral,** 12 av. de la Costa (𝒞 **377/93-50-62-37;** www. hotel-balmoral.mc).

9 Animal Encounters

Diving with Great White Sharks
A Close Encounter with Jaws
Dyer Island, South Africa

If you've ever been fascinated by great white sharks, but shudder at the thought of actually coming into contact with them in nature, it's time to face your fears. Over the past several years, cage diving with real-life Jaws has become one of South Africa's most popular wildlife adventures.

To experience your own meet-and-greet with these mighty predators, get up early and head to **Gansbaai,** a quaint fishing village just 2 hours by car from Cape Town. Most dive boats depart from here and explore the waters around **Dyer Island,** a breeding ground for penguins, and **Geyser Rock,** home to more than 50,000 seals. The channel between these two islands is known as "shark alley," and it's arguably the world's best viewing spot for great white sharks. Thousands of the migratory creatures move through this area during the South African winter. For more information about protecting sharks and their marine environment, check out the **South African Shark Conservancy** (www.sharkconservancy.org).

After a quick breakfast and an informative overview about what you'll soon see, it's time to set off into the Indian Ocean, where you'll be on the water for approximately 4 hours. (*Tip:* If you tend to get seasick, take precautions; the seas can get extremely rough.)

As you start out enjoying the views from your relatively safe perch on the boat's deck, your crew will search for a place to anchor. Once settled, they'll begin spooning fish-based chum—a smelly mixture of mashed up sardines, sardine oil, and tuna—into the water to begin attracting the stars of the show.

Soon, it's time to overcome your trembling knees and dive in for a closer look.

Dressed like a seal in a black hooded wetsuit, with big goggles and a mask on your face, you and four other passengers will get into a metal cage that's tethered to your boat in the water, and wait. From overhead, the crew will quickly hang ropes with live bait—probably tuna—trying to lure the sharks even closer to you. When the dive master yells "shark, on the bait," you'll drop into the cold cloudy water, with goggle-covered eyes wide open. You'll spend about 20 minutes in the cage below the surface.

If you're lucky, an open-jawed great white will swim right past you, dive for the bait as the crew swiftly takes it away, maybe knock your cage, and continue on its way. The waters can be murky, making visibility low, but even a young shark grows to almost 4m (12 ft.) and weighs nearly half a ton, so it's pretty hard to miss. Once you've got a dorsal fin in your line of sight, hold steady and, if you dare, try to catch a glimpse of its deep blue eyes before it whooshes past you. *JS*

(i) **Cape Town Tourism Information Center,** Shop 107 Clocktower, V&A Waterfront ((C) **27/21-405-4500;** www.tourismcapetown.co.za).

TOUR: Marine Dynamics Tour, Gansbaai ((C) **27/028-384-1005;** www.sharkwatchsa.com).

WHEN TO GO: July–Sept.

✈ Cape Town Airport.

🛏 $$ **The Cape Cadogan,** 5 Upper Union St., Cape Town ((C) **27/21-480-8080;** www.capecadogan.com).

Previous page: Gorilla and young in Rwanda.

Night Diving with Manta Rays
Big Wings off the Big Island
Kona, Hawaii, U.S.A.

Manta rays are huge, magical beasts. Although completely harmless, they can be awfully intimidating at first sight as they propel themselves through the water with wingspans that reach up to 5m (16 ft.), long skinny tails, and up to a ton of weight. Watching these gentle giants glide, pivot, and somersault above your head in the middle of the ocean's dark lair is one of scuba diving's biggest thrills.

There are a few places in the world where you can dive with manta rays in their natural environment (Micronesia and Mexico are two others), but the Pacific Ocean off the Big Island of Hawaii is probably the best. In fact, divers often call the clear calm water off of Kona "manta heaven." The two volcanoes here, on the western side of the island, have helped create an underwater paradise of caves, cliffs, and tunnels that attract a stunning array of marine life. Diving during the day offers a wide variety of mind-blowing sights. Yet the most unforgettable dive must be done at night.

Beneath the moonlight, as you descend 9m to 21m (30–70 ft.) into the ocean and shine your dive lights up toward the surface, millions of miniscule organisms congregate, attracted to the glow. Mantas, in turn, are attracted to the plankton you've made appear and they come quickly to feast on the dinner being served with wide open mouths. As they gracefully push through the water like cape-wearing ballerinas, you'll be amazed by how close they come to you, sometimes just an inch away.

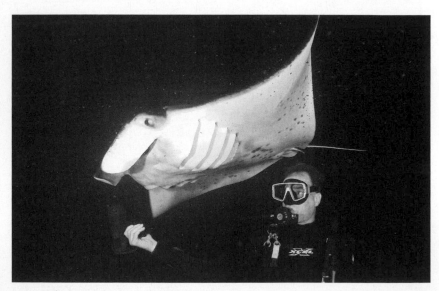

Night diving with manta rays in Hawaii.

In such close proximity to your new nimble friends, you might be tempted to pet one. Resist the urge. The rule with mantas is to look but not touch. You don't want to risk scraping off a layer of mucus and subjecting the mantas to bacterial infection. For more information on research, education, and conservation efforts, visit the **Manta Pacific Research Foundation** (www.mantapacific.org).

In the depths of the ocean, the adrenaline surges fast. As you're gazing in wonder at the manta rays, a moray eel might tickle your legs on the prowl for fish. You may also see shrimp, crabs, and some sleeping sea creatures. After 45 minutes or so (the length of a typical dive), the divers turn off their lights and start rising toward the surface for air. As their audience exits, the mantas slowly disperse.

Even if you're not scuba-certified, you can still witness the mantas' dance. Snorkelers are permitted to watch the show from the surface. While you won't get as close as divers or be in control of the food supply, you can still get a good rush from this position. —JS

ⓘ **Big Island Visitors Bureau,** 65–1158 Mamalahoa Hwy., Kamuela (☏ **800/885-1655**; www.bigisland.org).

TOUR: Jack's Diving Locker, 75–5813 Alii Dr., Kailua-Kona (☏ **800/345-4807**; www.jacksdivinglocker.com).

WHEN TO GO: Year-round, though summer and fall offer the best conditions.

✈ Kona airport.

🛏 $$ **Waianuhea,** 45-3505 Kahana Dr. (☏ **808/775-1118**; www.waianuhea.com).

---

396 Up Close & Personal

Swimming with Crocodiles
Defying Danger Down Under
Darwin, Australia

The majority of the world's saltwater crocodiles, locally known as "salties," live in Australia's Northern Territory. These predators are some of the oldest and largest living reptiles on Earth. A male crocodile can grow to almost 6m (20 ft.), with his weight reaching up to 998kg (2,200 lb.). A powerful muscular tail takes up about half of his length to propel him through the water at almost 15km (9 miles) per hour, twice the speed of an Olympic swimmer. Crocs also have the strongest bite force ever measured. Clearly, getting close to one of these creatures would be an awfully dangerous endeavor. Except in Darwin's new **Crocosaurus Cove,** where adrenaline seekers can safely come face-to-face with Choppa, a 5.5m (18-ft.), 771kg (1,700-lb.) saltwater crocodile.

A sturdy acrylic box—called the "cage of death"—separates you from Choppa's jaws (and the rest of his body), but that doesn't make this experience any less menacing. Wearing your swimsuit and goggles, you enter the "cage," an enclosed see-through structure without bars. You're then lowered into the water, where you can spend a heart-thumping 15 minutes marveling at the massive croc. Choppa might try to hug your cage, bare his giant teeth, or swim around you.

When your pulse slows down after this fear-factor stunt, spend some time exploring the city of **Darwin.** Set on the Timor Sea, this mining and tourism center is the largest and most populated city in the Northern Territory, but the least populous of Australia's capital cities. Inhabited by the Larrakia Aboriginal people for thousands of years, Darwin wasn't settled by Europeans until the 19th century. Since then, what began as a pioneer outpost and small port has developed into a modern and multicultural city, as well as an important gateway to nearby Asia. For visitors, it makes a great base for trips into other parts of the Northern Territory, including **Kakadu National Park, Litchfield National Park,** and **Katherine Gorge.** —JS

ⓘ **Darwin Visitor Centre,** 6 Bennett St., Darwin (✆ **61/8-8980-6000;** www.tourism topend.com.au).

TOUR: Crocosaurus Cove, Corner of Mitchell & Peel sts., Darwin (✆ **61/88-981-7522;** www.croccove.com).

WHEN TO GO: Apr–Sept.

✈ Darwin International Airport.

🛏 $$$ **Crown Plaza Hotel Darwin,** 32 Mitchell St. (✆ **61/88-982-0000;** www. ichotelsgroup.com). $$ **Medina Grand Darwin Waterfront,** 7 Kitchener Dr. (✆ **61/88-982-9999;** www.medina.com.au).

Up Close & Personal **397**

Snorkeling Shark Ray Alley
A Daring Dip with Sharks & Stingrays
Ambergris Caye, Belize

Belize lies alongside the second-longest barrier reef in the world, making it an obvious hot spot for all sorts of scuba diving and snorkeling. But the most spine-tingling area to explore is Shark Ray Alley, which is swarming with—you guessed it—sharks and stingrays!

Off the southern tip of Ambergris Caye, Shark Ray Alley is set within Belize's oldest marine reserve, **Hol Chan Marine Reserve,** a narrow channel cutting through a rich and well-maintained shallow coral reef. "Hol chan" literally means "little channel" in Mayan. The entire reserve covers only about 7.8 sq. km (3 sq. miles) and is divided into four zones. But there's a lot to see in this small space.

The nurse sharks and southern stingrays swimming with you in Shark Ray Alley are actually relatively harmless, but it sure doesn't feel all that way! Even experienced snorkelers get a major rush in the shallow water here. Nurse sharks can reach about 4m (14 ft.) and weigh almost 150kg (330 lb.). The good news is that their diet doesn't include humans; it primarily consists of crustaceans, mollusks, sea urchins, octopuses,

squid, and marine snails. Their relatively small mouths limit the size of their prey,

Stingrays get up close and personal in Belize.

though they can suck food into their large throat cavities.

Southern stingrays have flat, diamond-shaped bodies, which are often grey or brown with white bellies. Their tails are serrated, but not venomous. Like nurse sharks, they're suction eaters and can vacuum up a whole lot of grub. But they're generally tame and used to people floating around them. Along with the sharks and stingrays, you might also encounter barracuda, moray eels, and sea turtles, as well as plenty of fish and coral.

A couple of tips. This action-packed reef is an extremely popular snorkeling destination, and deservedly so. To avoid crowds, go in the afternoon when most cruise passengers have left and the light is ideal. Also, as tempting as it is to reach out and touch the rubbery sharks and stingrays, remember that you're not actually in a petting zoo. Some guides will allow you to gently stroke a shark or stingray, but always do so with caution and only if given a direct invitation. For more information about nurse sharks and conservation efforts in Belize, visit **The Nature Conservancy** (www.nature.org). —JS

ⓘ **Belize Tourism Board,** 64 Regent St., Belize City (ⓒ **501/227-2420;** www.travel belize.org).

WHEN TO GO: Nov–May.

✈ Philip S.W. Goldson International Airport in Belize City.

🛏$$ **Matachica Beach Resort,** 5 miles north of San Pedro, Ambergris Caye (ⓒ **501/220-5010;** www.matachica.com).

---

398 Up Close & Personal

Swimming with Manatees
Not Cuddly, But Endearing
Crystal River and Homosassa Springs, Florida, U.S.A.

Be passive and don't splash—with a little luck these sea cows may come up and nudge you as you swim, snorkel, or scuba dive with them. Some may even let you pet their cloudy-grey skin and get close enough to see the whiskers on their sagging snouts. These massive air-breathing mammals need warm water to survive, and they find it in the **Crystal River National Wildlife Refuge,** in the Kings Bay area near the town of Crystal River on Florida's west coast. During the winter, you may also be able to swim with them in the Homosassa River. Though by necessity you may be calm in the water, the excitement you'll experience when you encounter these endearing creatures will keep you exhilarated long after you've surfaced.

The manatees, who can grow up to 12 feet long (3.6m), and weigh up to 3,500 pounds (1,588kg), like the waters along Florida's west coast and head inland along spring-fed rivers during the winter to stay warm. They need an undisturbed habitat, so although once common on the rivers throughout the Sunshine State, their numbers have plummeted due to development. Many bear scars from boat collisions. Because of their tremendous size and their tendency for slowness, boats often hit them before they're able to move out of the way.

The manatees thrive in **Homosassa Springs Wildlife State Park,** where the water is only about four feet deep. Visit the **Fish Bowl,** a floating underwater observatory, and you'll have a below-the-surface view of manatees and fish. Over the course of the day, you'll have the opportunity to participate in three manatee programs, two Wildlife Encounters, and an alligator program scheduled for visitors who want to learn more about Florida's wildlife.

Several tour operators offer guided tours on the Crystal and Homosassa rivers for snorkeling and swimming with the manatees. Where you go will depend upon the time of year you visit. Some operators offer manatee tours in the Crystal River year-round, and in the Homosassa River November through April. Many tours leave early in the morning—that's often the best time to interact with the manatee. The actual time in the water is usually about 1½ hours.

During the winter, you can also see manatees at the **Lee County Manatee Park.** Here, you can rent a kayak and go out on the water, and learn more about these mammals from the volunteer naturalists onsite each day. The "manatee season" here runs November to March. On the Save The Manatees website you can learn more about manatees and find a list of other places in Florida where you can see these massive cute creatures. —LF

ⓘ **Crystal River National Wildlife Refuge** (ⓒ **352/563-2088;** www.fws.gov/crystalriver). **Homosassa Springs Wildlife State Park** (ⓒ **352/628-5343;** www.homosassasprings.org). **Lee County Parks & Recreation** (ⓒ **239-690-5030;** www.leeparks.org). **Save the Manatee** (ⓒ **407/539-0990;** www.savethemanatee.org).

TOURS: Swim With The Manatees (ⓒ **352/628-3450;** www.swimwithmanatees.com). **American Pro Diving Center** (ⓒ **800/291-3483** or 352/563-0041; www.americanprodiving.com).

WHEN TO GO: Winter.

✈ Tampa (75miles/121km).

⊨ $ **Best Western Crystal River Resort,** 614 Northwest Hwy. 19 ⓒ **800/435-4409** or 352/795-3171; www.crystalriverresort.com).

Up Close & Personal **399**

Swimming with Humpback Whales
Where the Whales Come to You
Dominican Republic

You're lying in the water in a dead man's float and you hear a sound like none other in the world. But did you hear it or did you feel it right down to the core of your being? Either way, you've just experienced the song of a humpback whale that is slowly swimming toward you, and you'll remember this moment for the rest of your life. Being in the water with a 40-ton creature is unlike any other animal encounter. You're a guest in the vast home of this magnificent animal.

In the **Sanctuary of the Marine Mammals of the Dominican Republic,** you enter the ocean as silently as possible,

remain passive and quiet, and let the whales' curiosity bring them to you. Scuba diving in the area isn't permitted and swimming after a whale while snorkeling will drive them away. So you float quietly as a 5,000-pound (2,268kg) calf comes within touching distance and checks you out. Mom rests quietly 40 to 50 feet (12–15m) below you and keeps an eye out to make sure her baby is safe.

It is almost unimaginable that humans almost drove these incredible beings to extinction. And, it's just as incredible that while they are now recovering they allow us back into their habitat. Every year

Whale-watching with a front row seat in the Dominican Republic.

between December and mid-April thousands of humpback whales migrate to the **Silver Bank**, located approximately 97km (60 miles) north of the Dominican Republic, to breed and calve. The location is ideal as the water is warm, 75° to 80°F (24°–27°C), the area is full of large, dangerous coral heads, which minimizes boat traffic; and the killer whales don't inhabit these waters. Thankfully, the Dominican Republic declared this area a whale sanctuary in 1986.

Most tours to the Silver Bank are booked for 7 days, although some 10-day tours are available. The ships usually accommodate between 20 and 30 passengers and provide ample room for relaxation along with food and beverages. Whale-watching takes place from the ship and from tenders that take you to areas where you can slip over the side and assume the floating position. From the deck, you can see whales breeching, pec slapping, skyhopping, and lobtailing. It's up to the experienced crew to determine when it's safe to enter the tenders and the water. Not all the whales you see will be

appropriate to interact with. Many of the whales are here for breeding and the males get aggressive when vying for a chance to mate.

Aside from shopping and basking on the beach in the Puerto Plata area, visitors can experience snorkeling, scuba diving, deep sea fishing, windsurfing, kiteboarding, and a limited amount of golf. —*LF*

ⓘ **Whale Routes info** (www.whaleroute. com). **Dominican Republic Tourism** (𝒞 **888/374-6361**; www.godominican republic.com).

TOURS: Aquatic Adventures (𝒞 **954/ 382-0024**; www.aquaticadventures.com/ silver_bank). **Conscious Breath Adventures** (𝒞 **305/753-1732**; www.conscious breathadventures.com).

WHEN TO GO: Mid-Jan to mid-Apr.

✈ Puerto Plata/Santiago.

🛏 $$ **Grand Oasis Marien**, Puerto Plata (𝒞 **866/863-9281** or 305/604-7880; www.grandoasismarien.com).

Diving with Sharks
Feeding Frenzy
Grand Bahama Island, The Bahamas

"Keep your hands down. We wouldn't want you to lose any fingers. If a shark gets too close, bop it on the nose with your gauges. If anyone wants to back out, now's the time to do it." These were the directions delivered during our pre-dive briefing. After hearing the warnings, everyone is given a chance to back out and get their money back. Very few do.

A shark-feeding dive is a real adrenaline rush, particularly for first-timers and those who fear sharks. But the dives, in addition to packing a daredevil-esque wallop, are also educational; they allow participants to sympathize with these wonderful creatures that are being killed at unprecedented rates.

Both **UNEXSO** and **Xanadu Undersea Adventures** provide shark-feeding dives off Grand Bahama Island. After a safety briefing, certified divers are taken on a 30- to 40-minute boat ride to Shark Alley. Once in the water, divers drop to approximately 12m (40 ft.) and kneel on the bottom with their backs to an old recompression chamber. One or two dive masters swim with hand spears to keep watch over the area. As if on cue, larger fish start to arrive and are followed by the sharks. The sharks in this area are almost all Caribbean reef sharks, but occasionally a nurse shark shows up. While not usually aggressive, 2.4 to 3m (8–9 ft.) sharks can be quite intimidating, especially because they're here for a meal.

One of the dive operators serves as the feeder. Dressed in a chain mail suit, he takes pieces of fish from a container, holds them out, and lets a shark grab the food from his hand. Divers are close enough to the feeding sharks to see the membrane over the sharks' eyes close as they nab the fish. Frequently, the sharks swim right over the heads of the kneeling divers (remember to keep you hands down!). During the dive, the feeder will "trance" one of the sharks, by putting a chain mailed hand over the shark's nose. The shark behaves as though it's been anesthetized or hypnotized and can be brought over to the kneeling divers to be touched. The entire experience, which needless to say is a fantastic photo opportunity, lasts approximately 30 minutes.

These two dive operators and several others also provide regular scuba dives around Grand Bahama to such sites as **Theo's wreck** and to **underwater caves** and **tunnels** that surround the island. It's possible to encounter sharks on any of the open water dives.

For those looking for shark-less encounters, Grand Bahama Island is a tourist center with shopping, gambling, beaches, and numerous leisure activities. Freeport/Lucaya has more hustle and bustle than the more laid-back beach locations outside of town. —*LF*

ⓘ **The Islands of the Bahamas** (www.bahamas.com/grand-bahama-island/grand-bahama-island).

TOURS: UNEXSO (✆ **800/992-3483;** www.unexso.com). **Xanadu Undersea Adventures** (✆ **242/352-3811;** www.xanadudive.com).

WHEN TO GO: High season is Dec–May.

✈ Freeport.

🛏 $$$ **Island Seas Resort,** William's Town, Freeport (✆ **800/801-6884** or 242/373-1271; www.islandseas.com). $ **Royal Palm Resort & Suites,** E. Mall at Settlers' Way, Freeport (✆ **888/790-5264** or 242/352-5759; www.royalpalmsuites.com).

Diving with Giant Squid
Facing the Red Demon
Baja, Mexico

Anti-squid armor on? Check! Blue-water diving tether properly attached? Check! It's time to meet the Red Demon squid of Mexico. You've spent several hours in "Squid School," training for your first encounter with the giant Humboldt squid, but you're still a bit nervous. You know these creatures grow up to 1.5m (5 ft.) long, weigh 32kg (70 lb.) or much more, have big suckers on their tentacles for grabbing their prey, and a parrot beak for ripping flesh. There's always the chance that a squid could wrap a tentacle around your leg and try to pull you downward. Fortunately, you're only going down to a maximum depth of 12m (40 ft.) and you're tethered to your boat at the surface, so you can be quickly pulled up should one of gangly beasts grab on.

These super predators travel in packs called shoals that range from tens to hundreds. They've come from depths around 150m (500 ft.) up toward the surface to feed. The *pangas* (local squid fisherman) have put bait in the water to attract these predators.

You're escorted down to a 12m (40-ft.) depth in the Sea of Cortez by one of the expert divers; there you start to watch the dance. Because of the underwater bioluminescence, colors flash as the giant squid swirl around. You see red, yellow, white, and even black. Watch the squid stalk prey, feed, and interact with each other—it's like nothing you've ever seen

before. If you feel relaxed enough, now's the time to start shooting underwater photos or filming.

Shark Diver has teamed with legendary giant squid expert **Scott Cassel** and **C Wolf Expeditions,** who have studied, documented, and dived with giant squid for years. There are no formal dates for squid diving expeditions. The trips, for a maximum of four divers per group, are planned when requested. Only divers who have made at least 200 dives and have current certification will be allowed on the trips.

The 5-day trip centers around 3 days of diving with the giant squid. Guests stay at the luxurious **Loreto Bay Resort,** an 3,237-hectare (8,000-acre) community neighboring the historic fishing town of Loreto in Baja Sur, Mexico. Around the dives there is time for other activities. Guests have the opportunity to play golf, go horseback riding, sailing, and deep sea fishing. —*LF*

ⓘ **Shark Diver** (ℂ **888/328-7449;** www.sharkdiver.com).

WHEN TO GO: July–Oct.

✈ Loreto International, Baja California Sur, Mexico.

🛏 $$$ **Inn at Loreto Bay Resort,** Paseo de la Mision (ℂ **877/865-6738** in the U.S. or 613/133-0010; www.explore loretobay.com).

Stingray City Scuba Dive
A Stingray Gave Me a Hickey!
Grand Cayman Island, The Cayman Islands

Stingrays are swimming around me, lazily flapping their wings. I touch the top of a tiny one swimming between my legs, and its skin is the texture of sandpaper. As another one swims over me, I gently touch its underside; it's as smooth as a cashmere sweater. I'm scuba diving in Stingray City, a wide sand channel in Grand Cayman Island's **North Sound.** Another one bumps me, going for the food I'm holding in my fist. They're like Hoover vacuum cleaners—as bottom dwellers they can sense and suck up mollusks inches under the sand. I don't release the food fast enough, so the stingray, who has obviously perfected his technique with other divers at this popular spot, does a quick side maneuver and "kisses" my wetsuit near my hand. Startled, I drop the food, the stingray snatches it,

and swims away. The hickey on my arm—a bruise that lasts for days—attracts attention at the beach bar that evening and gives me an excuse to talk about my exciting dive at Stingray City.

Several dive operators on the island offer the Stingray City dive. They leave from various points on the island, including the Seven Mile Beach and the east end of the island. During the boat ride out to the dive site, a dive master or a guide will tell you all about why the stingrays gather here. Once, this spot in the North Sound was popular with fishermen, who would dump their leftover bait and fish. The stingrays quickly realized that they could easily find food here. Since then, the fishermen have moved on because it became too easy to hook a stingray instead of their intended catch. Meanwhile, other boats began showing up, bringing divers and snorkelers. (The dive itself is easy—the sandy bottom ranges from 9–12 ft./2.7–3m deep.) Today, the number of boats allowed here at one time is limited by wildlife zone regulations developed by the island's government.

The Cayman Islands—there are three—have long been recognized for having some of the best diving spots in the world. Little Cayman's **Bloody Bay Wall** is one of the longest walls in the world, with steep cliffs descending down thousands of feet. In addition to diving, there are plenty of other adrenaline rush-inducing activities including kiteboarding, one of the Caymans' fastest growing sports, parasailing, paddleboarding, rock climbing, and hiking. Shoppers may get their own adrenaline charges buying black coral jewelry and electronics in the duty free shops in George Town. —LF

Swimming with the rays at Stingray City.

(i) **Cayman Islands** (☎ 345/549-0623; www.caymanislands.ky).

TOURS: Red Sail Divers (☎ 877/RED-SAIL [733-7245]; www.redsail.com). **Ocean Frontiers** (☎ 800/348-6096; www.oceanfrontiers.com).

WHEN TO GO: Year-round, but dives are weather dependent.

✈ Grand Cayman.

▨ $$$ **Westin Casuarina,** West Bay Rd. (☎ 800/937-8461 in the U.S. or 343/945-3800; www.westincasuarina.com). $$$ **Ritz-Carlton Grand Cayman,** Seven Mile Beach (☎ 800/542-8680 in the U.S. or 343/943-9000; www.ritzcarlton.com/grandcayman).

---

403   Up Close & Personal

Snorkeling with Sea Lions
Oceanic "Puppy Dogs"
Galápagos Islands

I am floating facedown in the water looking at white-tip reef sharks below me, when out of the corner of my eye I spy a small freight train coming straight at me. Just before it crashes into my face, it veers away. I'm relieved, but a rush of excitement comes over me. What was that?

My first encounter with a sea lion was while snorkeling in Gardner Bay off the island of Española (also called Hood Island), in the Galápagos Islands. Once the initial shock of the near miss wears off, swimming with several of these oceanic puppy dogs becomes a delight. They'll sneak up on you from behind or put their face right in your mask. At one point I decided to tumble in the water and a nearby mother and youngster copied me. It was a delight akin to scuba diving with playful dolphins.

The waters of the Galápagos are teeming with sea life, and approximately 17% of the species present are specific to this region off the coast of Ecuador. Both diving and snorkeling are fantastic, and most tours give you the opportunity to snorkel right from shore. Sea lions can usually be found at Champion Inlet off Floreana (Charles Island), the Pinnacle off Bartolome, at Puerto Egas off Santiago (James Island), as well as Gardner Bay. When snorkeling in the Galápagos you're also likely to

encounter rays, white-tip reef sharks, eels, turtles, penguins, dolphins, marine iguanas, and huge numbers of reef fish and invertebrates. If you're really lucky you may even see a Hammerhead shark. On land, you'll see sea birds, giant tortoises, reptiles, and land mammals.

The majority of visitors who come here take a multi-day boat tour, which allows them to visit several of the islands in the **Galápagos Marine Park.** There is also

Sea Lions on the Galápagos.

lodging on a few of the larger islands, but most people prefer the all-inclusive week-long boat-trip packages, where on-board guides give guest lectures and lead excursions.

If you plan to spend time in the water bring a wet skin for the hot and wet season (Dec–June) and a 3mm wet suit for the dry season (June–Nov), when temperatures hover around 66°F (19°C). These can be purchased from your local dive shop, are not very expensive, and will make your time in the water more comfortable and enjoyable. I also suggest bringing your own fins, mask, snorkel, a mesh bag for your gear, and an underwater camera or a soft housing that will protect your small digital down to at least 15 feet. Your tour company should provide a recommended packing list and luggage weight restrictions.

For most visitors, a trip to the Galápagos is a once-in-a-lifetime experience, so do what you can to see as much marine and land life as possible. And don't forget your sunscreen! —*LF*

(i) **Galápagos Online** ((©) **866/681-8687;** www.galapagosonline.com). **Visit Galápagos** ((©) **858/581-9209;** www.govisit galapagos.com).

TOURS: Ecoventura, 6404 Blue Lagoon Dr., Miami ((©) **800/644-7972;** www.eco ventura.com). **KLEIN Tours,** Av. Eloy Alfaro and Caralina Aldaz, Quito, Ecuador ((©) **888/50 KLEIN** [505-5346] in the U.S.; www.kleintours.com).

WHEN TO GO: June–Nov.

✈ San Cristobal or Baltra (near Santa Cruz Island).

⊨ $$$ **Royal Palm Hotel,** Via Baltra Km 18, Isla Santa Cruz ((©) **800/528-6069** in the U.S. or 593/5/5527-409; www.royal palmhotel.net). $$ **Finch Bay Hotel,** Pinta Estrada, Island Santa Cruz ((©) **593/5/5526-297;** www.finchbayhotel.com).

Up Close & Personal

404

Monarchs of Michoacán
A Flutter of Excitement
Near Angangueo & Ocampo, Mexico

High in the mountains of northeast Michoacán, you're hiking up a mountain, no doubt fighting for breath in this altitude. Then you arrive in a grove of fir trees—and whatever breath you had left is truly snatched away. It's as if you had stepped into a kaleidoscope, with fragments of obsidian and gold flitting randomly around you. The branches on all sides sway under the weight of *butterflies,* massed millions of **monarch butterflies,** their gossamer wings whispering softly as the wind blows through the forest. This is what you came here to see—but the vision is so much more astonishing than you expected.

The monarchs have been coming here since time immemorial; the ancient Aztecs revered these poisonous black-and-orange butterflies, which they believed were the reborn spirits of fallen warriors, dressed in battle colors. There are actually seven monarch nesting grounds in Michoacán (nesting season lasts from mid-Nov to Mar). Only two, however, are open to the public: **El Rosario** and **Chincua,** both reachable by day trip from the graceful Colonial-era city of Morelia, which is about halfway between Mexico City and Guadalajara. Save the trip for a sunny day if you can—the effect is most dazzling with the benefit of a little sunshine.

You can visit the sanctuaries on your own, but a licensed English-speaking guide is a worthwhile investment—they

Delicate monarch butterflies envelope visitors in Michoacán.

can answer the kids' scientific questions, transport you reliably over the back roads to the sanctuary, and steer you right to the nucleus of the butterfly colony, which constantly shifts around the mountain throughout the season. Guided butterfly excursions take 10 to 12 hours and usually provide lunch. While it varies, the hike through the mountain forest will probably take around an hour each way; it's often a steep walk, so wear sturdy shoes. One option at Chincua is to ride up on **horseback;** a local handler will lead the horse for you (facilities for renting are at the sanctuary gate). English-speaking guides can be contacted through a cooperative called **Mex Mich Guías** (www.mmg.com.mx). —*HH*

ⓘ **Michoacán** (www.michoacan-travel. com).

✈ Morelia.

🛏 $$ **Best Western Hotel Casino,** Portal Hidalgo 229, Morelia (ⓒ **52/443/ 3131-328;** www.hotelcasino.com.mx). $$$ **Villa Montaña,** Patzimba 201, Col. Vista Bella, Morelia (ⓒ **52/443/314-0231;** www.villamontana.com.mx).

405 Up Close & Personal

Diving in Aquariums
Giant Fish Bowls
Denver, Colorado, U.S.A.

Talk about living in a fish bowl! Here I am in the Denver Aquarium—and by "in," I mean *in* the water—scuba diving alongside pink and blue Mexican hogfish and silvery blue tang fish. As if that weren't exciting enough, I also go nose-to-nose with a 350-pound (158kg) Queensland grouper, notice through my dive mask the aquarium's 65 year-old, 200-pound (90kg) green sea turtle passing by, and catch sight of a nurse shark lurking in the distance. The most uncanny sight of all, though, is the group of people on the far side of the glass

watching *me*. Even alongside all these big fish in a little pond, *I'm* the rock star.

Scuba diving in aquariums—as visitors can do in the **Denver Aquarium's** "Under the Sea" exhibition—is very different than diving in open water. You don't have to contend with big waves rocking the boat while you're motoring out to a dive site, or a strong current pushing you along as you view underwater coral. Here, there's no real current, and you know you're going to see some 30 species of fish flowing around you—not to mention all those kids on the far side of the aquarium glass tugging on their parent's arm and pointing to you with amazement etched on their faces.

The Denver aquarium has several underwater programs for visitors. On weekends you can either go scuba diving or snorkeling through a program run by A-1 Scuba, a local dive shop, in conjunction with Landry's Restaurants, which owns the aquarium. "Dive with the Fish" puts you right in the middle of the "Under the Sea" exhibit. "Dive with the Sharks" takes place in the "Sunken Reef" exhibit, where you'll be in the company of sand tiger sharks, zebra sharks, sawfish, and barracuda. You must be certified and present your SCUBA certification and a photo ID, but the aquarium provides all equipment, from regulators to wetsuits. If you don't scuba dive, you can just "Swim with the Fish," a snorkeling adventure for visitors ages 6 and older.

The city of **Denver** is the gateway to Colorado's Rocky Mountains, so you can combine urban and outdoor activities once you leave the aquarium. Top attractions for first-time visitors include the U.S. Mint, the Museum of Nature and Science, and the Denver Art Museum. On weekends, people crowd into Lower Downtown (which locals call "Lodo"), with its variety of nightlife, restaurants, plays, musicals, and symphonies at the multi-venue Plex.

In the summer, locals galore are out walking or riding on the more than 850 miles (1,369km) of urban trails threading the Denver metropolitan area, or heading up to the high country to hike. In the winter, several major ski resorts are within a two-hour drive. Year-round, it's an easy day trip to visit **Rocky Mountain National Park** or the **U.S. Air Force Academy** and **Colorado Springs.**

A couple of other aquariums in the U.S. afford the chance to swim with the fish. At the **Adventure Aquarium** in Camden, New Jersey, you can swim with sharks and stingrays. And the **Monterey Bay Aquarium**'s "Underwater Explorers" programs allow kids to swim in the Great Tidal Pool. —*LF*

(i) **Downtown Aquarium** ((C) **303/561-4444**; www.aquariumrestaurants.com). **Visit Denver** ((C) **303/892-1112**; www.denver.org). **Adventure Aquarium,** Camden, NJ ((C) **856/365-3300**; www.adventureaquarium.com). **Monterey Bay Aquarium,** Monterey, CA ((C) **831/648-4800**; www.montereybayaquarium.com).

WHEN TO GO: Year-round in Denver.

✈ Denver International Airport.

🛏 $$$ **Hotel Teatro,** 1100 14th St. ((C) **888/727-1200** or 303/228-1100; www.hotelteatro.com). $$ **Castle Marne Bed & Breakfast,** 1572 Race St. ((C) **303/331-0621;** www.castlemarne.com).

Up Close & Personal 406

Tiger Tug-of-War
Battle with a Bengal
Tampa Bay, Florida, U.S.A.

Feeling tough? If you really want to test your strength, consider playing tug-of-war with a Bengal tiger at **Jungala,** the new 4-acre (1.6-hectare) animal park at **Busch Gardens.**

Jungala is mainly geared for kids, but its tiger tug-of-war experience certainly isn't child's play. Twice a day, up to six visitors are permitted to challenge one of the park's 11 tigers. During this fierce competition, you'll be separated from your opponent by a secure glass partition—though it doesn't do much to ease your trepidation. These powerful beasts have an awesome

Tigers at Busch Gardens in Tampa Bay, Florida.

sure to lift your spirits. If you're with the kids, check out **Jungle Flyers,** a ziplining experience for 6- to 13-year-olds. Your teenagers might like **Wild Surge,** a four-story ride that shoots 14 passengers out of a mountain crater topped with a waterfall. But when you're ready for a faster ride, head deeper into Busch Gardens and give the **SheiKra** a whirl. Named for a sub-Saharan bird of prey, this roller coaster carries you 300 feet (90m) into the air, dangles you precariously over the side, and then takes you down a 90-degree drop and stops for 4 seconds. Just when you think you can't scream any more, it plunges toward the ground at speeds of more than 70 mph (110kmph), goes around a loop, another vertical drop, then into an underground tunnel, and finally (thankfully) comes to a stop. After this wild ride, you'll have forgotten all about that tiger. —*JS*

(i) **Jungala at Busch Gardens,** Tampa ((C) 888/800-5447; www.jungala.com and www.buschgardens.com).

WHEN TO GO: Oct–Apr.

✈ Tampa International Airport (17miles/27km).

🛏 $ **Hyatt Place Tampa/Busch Gardens,** 11408 North 30th St. ((C) **813/979-1922;** www.tampabuschgardens.place. hyatt.com). $$–$$$ **Disney's Animal Kingdom Lodge,** 2901 Osceola Pkwy., Lake Buena Vista ((C) **407/939-7429;** http://disneyworld.disney.go.com/resorts/animal-kingdom-lodge).

amount of strength. So far, the park's tigers, who weigh around 300 pounds each, have a flawless record of victory, which means that your chances of winning are slim to none. One of the most energetic animals typically beats visitors in about a minute. But even if you lose while giving it your best tug, it's sure to be one pretty thrilling minute.

If you can't help lamenting your defeat, there are plenty of rides nearby that are

---

407 Up Close & Personal

Piranha Fishing
Jaws Junior
Los Llanos, Venezuela

It is not hard to find out if the fish are biting on a river in southern Venezuela. Here the fish have teeth after all. Just toss a twig on the water and watch it jiggle as the hungry critters nibble at it. I am of course talking about the infamous piranha, 8 inches of razor sharp aggression with a voracious appetite for meat and so mean they frequently fight amongst themselves and are prone to cannibalism. It is not unusual to fish one out with a missing eye, a war wound from a previous fight. To catch them is easy as they literally bite anything. You don't even need a rod, just a stick wrapped in fishing line and a small hook. Attach a piece of meat, undo the line, swing the hook, and throw it into the water. Hold the line tense until you feel it tremble, then pull sharp and you have hooked your prey as it comes flapping out of the water giving you the evil eye in the process. Just make sure you can get it on the boat without biting you. These animals are meaner than Jaws on a holiday weekend.

Piranha are also very ugly. They have a silver and gold scaled body the size of a man's hand but it is the jutting lower jaw with fearsome pointy teeth that makes plain they would come last in any aquarium beauty contests, not least because they would eat the other contestants if given half the chance. They are unique to South America and in particular the vast plains of Los Llanos, a huge marshland that stretches across southern Venezuela and parts of Colombia. Las Llanos is a wildlife treasure trove and we're not just talking of the cute furry kind: 3m (10-ft.) anacondas lie in the shallow waters, their black skin peeping above the water looking like old abandoned truck tires. Fearsome crocodile lurk along the river banks, their long jaws open like mobile animal traps. Fat families of capybara, the largest rodent in the world, play in the river while massive flocks of scarlet ibis fly overhead.

Other birds include the jabiru, scarlet macaw, and numerous species of hawk and heron. When you fish in the river you'll occasionally see the pink belly flash of a large river dolphin, while jaguars, pumas, and ocelots lurk in the foliage.

Vast distances and a poor road network mean Los Llanos is difficult to get around independently. For a true Los Llanos experience, choose a vast ranch (locally known as a *hato*) to stay in (see recommendations below). The best provide daily field trips on horseback or boat to explore this massive area and of course fish the famous piranha. You can also immerse yourself in the region's unique cowboy culture where fat men in large Stetsons sing folklore songs while strumming on giant harps. Here the locals ride bareback with an old rope for reins. The *Llaneros*, as these rugged horsemen are known, are a fiercely proud people whose bravery helped Venezuela achieve independence from the Spanish.

As you sit down for dinner in this flat badland, a huge starry sky hangs overhead and silent lightening flickers along the distant horizon. No doubt a plate of the favorite local dish will be put in front of you—piranha. —*CO'M*

WHEN TO GO: Anytime but the dry season, from Dec–June, has the best opportunity for wildlife watching.

✈ Caracas, then 9 hr. by car.

🚌 $$ **Hato El Cedral,** Mantecal, Los Llanos (☎ **58/212/781-8995;** www.elcedral. com). $$ **Hato Piñero,** El Baúl, Los Llanos (☎ **58/212/991-8935;** www.hatopinero. com).

Gorgona
Welcome to the Jungle
Colombia

It hasn't taken long for nature to regain complete control of Gorgona island. From the 1950s to the 1980s, this 26 sq. km (10-sq.-mile) landmass in the Pacific was a maximum security prison—Colombia's Alcatraz—but since the facility was closed and Gorgona declared a Parque Nacional Natural (Natural National Park) in 1985, the jail buildings are now evocatively overgrown with dense vegetation, complete with monkeys swinging from vine to vine.

Like its more remote cousin to the west, the shark-diving destination Malpelo (see **75**), Gorgona is one of those places where the natural environment is almost comically inhospitable to humans. Poisonous snakes slither along the floor of the rainforest here, and menacing sharks patrol the waters just offshore. (No doubt, this state of affairs helped with inmate detainment during the island's prison years.) Visitors who come ashore at Gorgona today are strictly supervised, limited to groups of 80 at a time, and forbidden from wandering too far away from the coastline, for fear of encountering those deadly critters. Nature is nothing if not fierce on Gorgona.

As with so many ecosystems that have been isolated from the mainland for thousands of years, Gorgona shelters a wealth of endemic plant and animal species in its rainforests, including the small (and endangered) **blue lizard** of Gorgona. It's said that a permanent cloud hangs over the top of Gorgona, as its mountain peaks are perpetually shrouded in mist. Of course, this moisture acts as a sort of steroid for the already aggressive tropical flora here.

Whales and their calves can be spotted off Gorgona from August to October.

There is only one place to spend the night on Gorgona, and only one place to eat: The handsome lodge and dining room are both run by the park service and look like something out of *Swiss Family Robinson*. With the interior of the island mostly off-limits to visitors, tours of the island are limited to its perimeter, which has plenty of well-marked **nature trails** (though going with a guide is highly recommended); there it's possible to get a good look at the unique marine birds, reptiles, and plant life that have grown up and evolved here. Snorkeling and diving among the coral reefs in the emerald waters off Gorgona are excellent (as long as sharks don't make you flinch), and **humpback whales** even pass by the island from August to October with

their calves. Gorgona also has some of the finest sandy beaches in Colombia, backed by palm trees and a thick curtain of green, letting you know that the creepy-crawly jungle is never far away on this island. —*SM*

ⓘ www.parquesnacionales.gov.co.
TOUR: Aviatur (✆ **57/1/382-1616;** www.concesionesparquesnaturales.com).
✈ Charter flights from Guapi, 30 min.
🚢 Cargo ship (8–10 hr.) or chartered speedboat (4–6 hr.) from Buenaventura.
🚤 Book through **park service** (✆ **57/1/382-1616**) or tour agency.

Up Close & Personal 409

Horseback Riding on Native Land
Galloping in Northern New Mexico
Taos Pueblo, New Mexico, U.S.A.

Besides black bears, cougars, and other assorted wildlife, few visitors may enter the Taos Pueblo Indians' private lands in New Mexico, in the foothills of the Sangre de Cristo mountains. The only way into this stunning, wild, sacred landscape is on horseback, under the guidance of the **Taos Indian Horse Ranch,** founded by Pueblo resident Stormstar (also known as Cesario Gomez).

Led by Stormstar and his Pueblo compatriots, your horse will pick its way over rocks, trundle down water-created paths, canter through thick forest, and gallop through wide open meadows, always in the presence of the magnificent Taos Mountain. Sacred to the Pueblo, it will likely draw you in and create its own presence within you too as you wander through its foothills.

Less predictable are the impromptu appearances by local birds and mammals, which may include bald eagles and moun-

tain lions. Stormstar recalls the time even he was startled when a black bear stepped out from the forest onto the path three feet in front of his favorite horse. "I had just broken this horse, and he reared back when the bear appeared out of nowhere. The bear was more scared than we were though, and he ran for the river so quickly I was the only one in the group who saw him."

Even the Taos ranch's greenest horses couldn't be more surefooted. "They grew up in these hills, and they don't want to tumble any more than you do. You just need to give them their head," says Stormstar. (Translation: Don't pull too tight on the reins; trust your horse to know the landscape far better than you.)

"We set the pace according the weakest rider," Stormstar says. After more than 35 years in the business, he and his guides can tell how you'll ride by the time you're perched in the saddle. They'll cater to your skills with easy trail rides or tougher treks up

The land around Taos, New Mexico, is beautiful, rugged horseback riding terrain.

into the Sangre de Cristo Mountains; some routes require overnight stays. They also provide covered wagon and hay wagon rides, but it's the horseback rides that draw devoted fans back year after year.

If you're not going out on an overnight riding trip and you can arrange it, book a private ride or go with a small group, so that you'll be able to tailor the ride more closely to your skill level. More importantly, you'll have the opportunity to talk with your guide rather than sitting in a nose to tail group. As the conversation deepens, you'll learn about medicinal plants as well as the history of the people and what they consider their holocaust, how they were treated by the Spanish before and after the 1680 revolt, the 1847 siege by U.S. soldiers, and how Teddy Roosevelt took their land for the Carson National Forest—and how that land was returned by President Nixon.

You shouldn't visit Taos without going to the **Pueblo**, a UNESCO World Heritage Site. The existing structures are more than 800 years old, and the land has been continuously occupied for more than a millennium. Taos Pueblo residents are conservative and private, limiting most visitors to the town plaza area and casino. Stormstar says Taos Ranch is the only authorized guide into the foothills.

Much of the tourist activity in **Taos** itself centers on the Plaza and the surrounding blocks. It's like a smaller Santa Fe without the kitsch. The range of art galleries, museums, shops, and restaurants satisfies all tastes and budgets. The **Taos Ski Valley**, about 18 miles (29km) from town, accommodates all skier levels but encompasses some of the toughest runs in the country. Nearby **Angel Fire Resort** affords skiing, golf, fishing, and, in late August and early September, a wonderful series of classical music concerts. —*LF*

ⓘ **Taos Pueblo,** Veterans Hwy. (ⓒ **575/758-1028;** www.taospueblo.com).

TOUR: Taos Indian Horse Ranch, 340 Little Deer Run Rd. (ⓒ **800/659-3210** or 505/758-3212; www.taosindianhorseranch.com).

WHEN TO GO: Year-round; best riding May–Oct.

✈ Albuquerque International Airport (135 miles/217km).

🛏 $$–$$$ **Casa de las Chimeneas,** 405 Cordoba Rd. (ⓒ **877/758-4777** or 575/758-4777; www.visittaos.com). $–$$ **Taos Hampton Inn,** 1515 Paseo del Pueblo Sur (ⓒ **800/HAMPTON** [426-7866] or 575/737-5700; www.hampton.com).

Killer Whale Safari
Orcas in the Lofoten Islands
Nordland, Norway

Imagine, if you will, a string of northerly isles where colorful fishing shacks stand against a backdrop of craggy granite cliffs, where red-cheeked children play in the shadow of rugged gray pinnacles. Beautiful and awe-inspiring, the Lofoten Islands are a Grimms' fairy tale come to life.

The Lofotens are a remote island archipelago in the north Atlantic and a district in the county of Nordland, Norway. The landscape is breathtakingly cinematic, with ice-tipped peaks fringed by deep blue seas and a rocky shoreline fronted by sandy beaches. The Lofoten islands stretch 250km (155 miles) south-southwest from the fjord of Ofoten to the outer Roest islands. Although the islands lie north of the Arctic Circle, the passing Gulf Stream keeps temperatures relatively mild. The air is fresh and clean, kissed by sea spray and Arctic breezes.

The main islands are Austvågøy, Gimsøy, Vestvågøy, Flakstadadøy, Moskenesøy, Varøy, and Røst. On the eastern coast of Austvågøy, Svolvær is the largest town in the archipelago. A Norwegian fjord, the **Vestfjorden,** separates the islands from the mainland. This body of water is the heart of the Norwegian cod fisheries. If fishing for monster cod is on your agenda, head to the old fishing camp of **Henningsvar,** with its quaint waterfront, *rorbu* cabins (www.henningsvar-rorbuer.no), and fish-drying racks—nicknamed "Lofoten's cathedrals."

In late autumn, when the herring return to the Vestfjorden for the winter, they are chased by between 500 and 700 hungry orcas, also known as killer whales. Orcas can grow up to 4 to 5 tons, live to be 60 years old, and hang out with their family their entire lives. (Well-mannered, too; they eat only one herring at a time.) You can take a "killer whale safari" to see these amazing animals up close with one of several outfitters, including **Orca Tysford** (✆ 47/75-77-53-70; http://tysfjord-turist senter.no/safari), which takes visitors out on the sea by large boat or inflatable dinghy and—if you're really crazy—lets you snorkel as a pod of killer whales passes by. **GoArctic/Orca Lofoten** (✆ 47/45-83-27-10; www.goarctic.no) offers "Nature, Seabird & Orca Excursions" from October to mid-January.

Perhaps the most dramatic experience in Lofoten is a tour over turbulent waters—the "Lofoten Maelstrom" (called the Moskestraumen by local fishermen), one of the world's strongest tidal currents in open waters. The treacherous strait separating Moskenesøy from the offshore island of Vaerøy to the south has been called "the world's most dangerous waters." Take a ride on the Maelstrom—or just go fishing—with **Moskstraumen Adventure** (✆ 47/977-56-021; www.lofoten-info.no/mosk-straumen-adventure) in the town of Å.

Dramatic scenery is not the region's only natural draw. Here, in northern Norway, the skies give the mountains and the sea a run for their money. The aurora borealis (northern lights) paint the evening skies from September to April, and in the summer the Lofotens become the light-filled Land of the Midnight Sun. —*AF*

ⓘ www.lofoten-info.no or www.visit norway.com.

✈ Bodø to Svolvær.

From Skutvik, take the 2-hour ferry to Svolvær. Ferry information and reservations: **Lofotens og Vesterålens Dampskibsselskab A/S** (also known as **DDF**; ✆ **94-89-73-34** or 81-03-00-00; www.ovds.no).

$$$ **Anker Brygge,** Lamholmen, Svolvær (✆ **76-06-64-80;** www.ankerbrygge.no). $$ **Nusfjord Rorbu,** Flakstadoy (✆ **76-09-30-20;** http://nusfjord.no).

411 Safaris

Gorilla Safaris
I Spy an Endangered Animal
Volcanoes National Park, Rwanda

Seeing mountain gorillas in the wild isn't easy, which is exactly what makes it so exciting. Unfortunately, only about 700 of these magnificent creatures still live in their natural environment—in the Virunga range of volcanic mountains on the borders of the Democratic Republic of Congo (DRC), Rwanda, and Uganda, and in the Bwindi Impenetrable National Park in Uganda. In other words, the chance to see one is slim.

But a large number of endangered mountain gorillas reside in northwest **Rwanda,** often called the land of a thousand hills, and most are found in the **Volcanoes National Park.** In recent years, the country's **tourism office** (www.rwandatourism.com) has made great strides toward protecting its population of apes, but the animals remain at risk from poaching, habitat destruction, and diseases transmitted by humans. While gorilla safaris generate the greatest amount of revenue for Rwanda's tourism industry, the country's priority is to maintain responsible travel and conservation efforts. The steep mountainous terrain and dense rainforest acts as somewhat of a deterrent for less intrepid or less active travelers. For others, the country's location near the DRC, where insurgent groups are still involved in violent conflicts, makes it undesirable. (Although there were no travel restrictions on Rwanda at the time of this writing, it is advisable to check U.S. State Department warnings before booking a trip.) To further limit visitors, permit fees remain expensive at $250 and no more than 56 tourists are allowed to enter the park each day. These obstacles make a gorilla safari one of the world's most difficult, exclusive, and exhilarating wildlife experiences.

Seeing gorillas in the wild is the thrill of a lifetime.

For those who do journey to Rwanda, the Virunga volcanoes—Karisimbi, Bisoke, Sabyniyo, Gahinga, and Muhabura—make a striking backdrop as you travel into the Volcanoes National Park. Conservationist Dian Fossey, who lived in this area for 18 years studying and protecting gorillas, described the Virungas like this: "In the heart of Central Africa, so high up that you shiver more than you sweat, are great, old volcanoes towering up almost 4,500m (15,000 ft.), and nearly covered with rich, green rainforest." To learn more about Fossey, her work with mountain gorillas, and how you can help protect the endangered species, visit www.gorillafund.org.

Rwanda's enthralling, lush green landscape is a good distraction during the beginning of what can be an arduous trek. Be prepared to hike for several hours, climbing at altitudes between 2,400 and 3,000m (8,000—10,000 ft.), in wet and muddy conditions, before glimpsing an ape. Trails are often slippery, covered with vines, leaves, and fallen branches. Along the way, you might see golden monkeys, buffalo, and a wide variety of birds. But coming across mountain gorillas is what really makes your efforts worthwhile.

Male silverback gorillas can stand taller than 1.7m (5½ ft.) (such as when beating their fists against their chests to show stature or scare off opponents), and weigh more than 181kg (400 lb.). If they feel the need to ward off danger, they can charge, scream, or bare their teeth—so tread carefully. But in general, gorillas are easygoing animals that survive on a mostly vegetarian diet of celery, nettles, bamboo, and thistles. You may see them going about their daily business during the day: eating, grooming, taking care of their young, or resting and hanging out in a group. At first sight, it's hard to remember that these huge, hairy, human-like creatures are actually gentle and social beings, something like the hippies of the animal kingdom. But after an initial adrenaline rush, it's easy to feel peaceful in their midst. —JS

ⓘ **Rwanda Tourism Board,** Boulevard de la Revolution 1 (✆ **250/576-514;** www.rwandatourism.com).

TOUR: Gamewatchers Safaris (✆ **877/710-3014;** www.porini.com/gorilla_safaris_4day.html).

WHEN TO GO: June–Sept and Dec–Feb. (Nov is also a fine time to go, but trekking can be particularly muddy and difficult due to frequent rain.)

✈ Kigali International Airport.

🛏 $$ **Mountain Gorilla's Nest** (www.rwanda-mountain-gorillas-nest.com). $$$ **Virunga Lodge,** Parc National des Volcans (✆ **866/599-2737;** www.volcanoessafaris.com/go/ecolodges/virunga-lodge).

Safaris **412**

Lion Safaris
Walk with the Pride
Victoria Falls, Zimbabwe

Picture yourself strolling with Simba and his friends through a *Lion King* incarnate. Imagine reaching out to rub the lions' arching backs and soft bellies, then watching as they stride forward with grace through the African bush, trying to hunt their prey. Sounds surreal, doesn't it? Even impossible. But that's a pretty accurate description of what you can actually experience during a lion encounter in Zimbabwe.

In the Masuwe River Concession, 10 minutes from Victoria Falls, you can walk among these golden cats as if you're a member of their pride. Because the animals are only 6 to 18 months old, the experience is deemed relatively safe, but it might take a while for your wobbly knees and racing heart to get the message.

With only a stick in your hand, you can walk toward groups of cubs as they run circles around you. You can pet them, watch them play, and stroll beside them. It's one of the most awesome wildlife experiences on Earth.

But we're not talking about a petting zoo or swimming with dolphins here. While lions may be cute, even young ones aren't completely harmless. The cubs you'll see and touch were raised to think of humans as dominant members of their pride, but they're still predatory carnivores and it's important to stay calm, even as your adrenaline flows, so you don't spook them. In fact, the main point of your walk with the lions is to help them get acclimated to the wild and develop their natural hunting skills. You might even see one of the older cubs make a kill; the lions here have successfully hunted more than 25 different species ranging from birds and rabbits to zebra and buffalo.

The unique half-day lion encounter in Zimbabwe is part of a program that aims to ethically introduce the offspring of rehabilitated captive-bred African lions into their natural environment. More than 200,000 lions used to roam the Africa continent, but recent estimates suggest that there has been an 80% to 90% decline in the population over the past 30 years. The objective of the lion rehabilitation and reintroduction project is to replenish depleted lion populations and safeguard the species' future.

To spend more time with the lions and really help facilitate their release into the wild, check out the longer volunteer trips offered by **African Impact's Lion Rehabilitation Programme** (www.africanimpact. com/volunteers/lion-conservation-zimbabwe). For 2 to 6 weeks, you can do more than walk with these cubs. You can feed and care for them, watch as they learn to stalk their prey, gather data, and conduct research on the impact of tourism on their natural environment. You'll also spend time discussing conservation efforts with the local community in schools and national parks. And don't worry; it's not all work. There's plenty of time to play, too. You can go on a safari or try one of the many other adventures offered here such as white water rafting, bungee jumping, and helicopter rides. But the biggest thrill of all is tickling and playing with young lions, knowing that one day they'll be proudly roaming the Zimbabwean wilderness. —*JS*

(i) **African Lion and Environmental Research Trust (ALERT)** (© **44/0-203-371-7835;** www.lionalert.com).

TOUR: Lion Encounter, 165 Courtney Selous Crescent (© **263/13-44386/43078;** www.lionencounter.com).

WHEN TO GO: Year-round.

✈ Victoria Falls International Airport, connecting through Harare or Johannesburg airports.

⊨ $–$$ **Zambezi Waterfront,** Victoria Falls (© **263/13-44510;** www.safpar.net/ waterfront.html). $$–$$$ **Stanley and Livingstone at Victoria Falls,** Nakavango Estate (© **27/011-658-0633;** www. stanleyandlivingstone.com).

Tiger Safaris
Visit the Jungle's Royals
Madhya Pradesh, India

Royal Bengal tigers have been literary stars for decades—just think of Rudyard Kipling's *The Jungle Book* and Yaan Martel's *Life of Pi*. But in real life, these cats are in pretty big trouble. Fewer than 5,000 currently live in the wild, and India is home to less than 1,400 of them—compared to its population of nearly 50,000 a century ago. Poaching and forest destruction have taken their toll on India's national animal. Unless protection swiftly increases and ecotourism can play a major role in helping that happen, your chances of seeing these mighty creatures outside of a zoo will continue to dwindle. Even now, it may take hours or days before you lock eyes with one, but if you do, you won't be able to move, let alone look away. Even the sound of a tiger's deep roar, which you can hear from 3km (2 miles) away, is enough to send shivers down your spine.

These huge animals can weigh up to 227kg (500 lb.) and reach speeds of 80km (50 miles) per hour. In general, they tend to be elusive, which makes this adventure a slow-moving one. You'll spend the bulk of your time in the jungle waiting and watching and waiting some more. But your patience will pay off when a tiger or tigress saunters into view.

Bandhavgarh National Park (www.bandhavgarhnationalpark.com) in the central Indian state of Madhya Pradesh is one of the best places to go looking for tigers. Set between the Vindhya and Satpura hills, an estimated 46 tigers roam the 449 sq. km (173 sq. miles) of land here, which is one of the highest densities of any park in India. This area was formerly a maharaja's personal hunting grounds, as evidenced by the ruins of a 2,000-year-old fort set high on a hilltop.

You'll explore the dramatic landscape mostly by jeep (though elephant rides are sometimes possible), staying on clear paths that run through the dense jungle and expansive grassy meadows.

While you're keeping one eye open for tigers, don't forget to pay attention to the large cast of supporting species here, including leopards, spotted deer (chital), Sambar deer, gaur, wild boar, wild dogs, jungle cats, hyenas, porcupines, jackals, and foxes. There are also numerous birds like grey-headed fishing eagles, plum-headed parakeets, and malabar pied hornbills.

Bandhagarh National Park was added to India's **Project Tiger** (www.projecttiger.nic.in) in 1993. The government began this conservation endeavor in 1973 to "ensure a viable population of tiger in India for scientific, economic, aesthetic, cultural, and ecological values," and there are now 27 tiger reserves in the country. If you want to spend more than a few days on safari, add Kanha and Pench national parks to your itinerary. If you'd rather stay in Rajasthan and not travel as far inland, Ranthambhore Tiger Reserve is a good alternative. —*JS*

ⓘ **Indian Tourism Board**; Transport Bhavan, Parliament St., New Delhi (✆ **91/011-273-11995;** www.incredibleindia.org).

TOUR: India Safaris and Tours (✆ **91/11-2680-7550;** www.indiasafaris.com).

WHEN TO GO: Oct–June.

✈ Indira Gandhi International Airport in Delhi, with a connection to Jabalpur.

🛏 $$$ **Mahua Kothi** near Bandhavgarh (✆ **866/969-1825** or 91/22-660-11825; www.tajsafaris.com/our_lodges/mahua_kothi).

414 **Safaris**

Canoe with the Hippos
What a Big Mouth You Have, My Dear!
Rivers in Africa's National Parks

As the hippo yawned, the huge pink crevasse opened up and exposed rows of sharp teeth and big tusks. Hippopotamuses are vegetarian by nature, but even so you carefully skirt around them while canoeing in one of Africa's national parks. The sight of one next to your canoe is enough to make your heart skip a few beats.

Paddling down the Zambezi River at its broadest reaches in Zimbabwe's Mana Pools National Park, you're gliding around lush islands topped by wild fig trees. On the riverbanks African buffalo are grazing, and baboons scamper up trees as the elephants move in to drink. In the distance, you can see the steep hills of the Zambian escarpment dressed in thick, scrubby brush. Canoe safaris let you view animals at their level. In addition to seeing the tremendous hippos while canoeing, you may pass elephants on the banks slurping up water with their trunks and crocodiles resembling rotting tree trunks motionless in the river.

Your guides and you watch for hippos. When a pod of them is spied all the canoeists give them time to move to deeper water before passing by in the shallows close to the riverbank. You don't want to startle a hippo—especially males who can weigh up to four tons. They submerge if they feel threatened and can pop back up to the surface anywhere, including underneath your canoe, possibly capsizing you.

Choose the month of your safari with the weather in mind. During the dry season, June to October, the wild animals tend to stay near the river and the lush vegetation along its banks. During the rainy season, when it's hot and humid, the animals gravitate toward the escarpment.

Hippos and paddlers share the river in Lower Zambezi National Park.

347

Most of the canoe trips are on portions of rivers that tend to be flat water. Where you overnight can range from rough tent camps alongside the river or on sandbars, to luxury tent camps and lodges. Ask your outfitter what kinds of accommodations they offer.

Several safari companies offer tours on the lower Zambezi River, which runs through the **Lower Zambezi National Park** in Zambia (www.zambiatourism. com/travel/nationalparks/lowerzam.htm) and the **Mana Pools National Park** in Zimbabwe (www.zambezi.com/location/ mana_pools_national_park). Mana Pools, a UNESCO World Heritage Site, encompasses a portion of the Zambezi River as it emerges from a gorge and spreads across a floodplain. In the park there are large pools that are remnants of ancient ox-bow

lake that the river carved out eons ago, where hippos and crocs congregate.

The **Zambezi Travel & Safari Company** (see below) offers a variety of canoeing tours year-round, plus combination canoe and walking safaris on the Zambezi through Mana Pools. Many of the trips are semi-participatory, although the guide does the cooking and the washing up. Chiawa (see below) offers canoeing safaris in Zambia's Lower Zambezi National Park with overnights at luxury camps. —LF

ⓘ **Zambezi Travel & Safari Company** (✆ **44/1548-830059;** www.zambezi.com). **Chiawa** (✆ **260/211-261588;** www.chiawa. com).

WHEN TO GO: June–Oct.

Whale-Watching
Dolphins, Porpoises & Whales, Oh My
Isle of Mull, Scotland

Whale-watching will teach even the most active adventurer about the virtue of patience. During a typical cruise, you'll spend a good chunk of your time waiting on the observation deck, scanning the open seas. Be prepared to grab hold of a railing if the waves get choppy, which they tend to do on breezy days. As you keep looking around and hoping to see a large whale or majestic dolphin leap out of the ocean, the anticipation mounts. When you finally spot a fin, perhaps on a minke whale, your heart skips a beat. As its vast body finally comes arching out of the water, followed by a powerful tail flapping down with a giant splash, your adrenaline starts pumping.

When it comes to seeing marine mammals in their natural habitat, Scotland's west coast offers some of the best viewing and greatest diversity in the world. Base

yourself in **Tobermory** on the Island of Mull, which is part of an island chain called the **Hebrides** in Argyll-Bute. From Glasgow, Tobermory is about 4 hours by car and ferry, and it's well worth the ride. The area is revered for its mountains, forests, and beaches—on a coastline that stretches for more than 483km (300 miles).

After you arrive in town, stop by the **Hebridean Whale and Dolphin Trust** (www.hwdt.org) on Main Street to get current information about what's been most recently spotted at sea. According to the organization, "Of the 83 species of whales, dolphins and porpoises (cetaceans) currently recognized in the world, 24 species have been recorded in the waters off the west coast of Scotland in recent years." Sightings often include harbour porpoises, bottlenose dolphins, common dolphins, Atlantic white-sided dolphins, white-beaked dolphins, killer whales, minke whales, humpback whales, and northern bottlenose whales.

To improve your chances of seeing these highly intelligent and communicative creatures in the wild, look for splashes—or waves that look like they're breaking the wrong way. Also keep an eye out for extremely flat patches of water, which could be a sign that a cetacean just dived in there. Finally, pay attention to feeding seabirds. If lots of them are diving in one particular spot, it could mean that fish have been rounded up to the surface by a larger predator such as a minke whale, making it easy for the birds to dive in and enjoy a good meal. Meanwhile, you should have plenty to feast your eyes on as you scan the waters. —*JS*

ⓘ **Scotland Tourism Organization,** 94 Ocean Dr., Edinburgh (ⓒ **084/52-255-121;** www.visitscotland.com). **Welcome to Scotland,** Station Rd., Inverness-shire (ⓒ **014/79-841-900;** www.welcometo scotland.com).

TOURS: Sea Life Surveys, Leoaig, Tobermory (ⓒ **016/88-400-223;** www.sealife surveys.com). **Silver Swift,** Raraig House, Raraeric Rd., Tobermory (ⓒ **016/88-302-390;** www.tobermoryboatcharters.co.uk).

WHEN TO GO: Apr–Sept.

✈ Glasgow Airport.

▙ $$$ **Glengorm Castle,** Tobermory (ⓒ **016/88-302-321;** www.glengorm castle.co.uk). $$ **Failte Guest House,** Main St. (ⓒ **016/88-302-495;** www.failte guesthouse.com).

---

416 From a Distance

Seal Island
A Smorgasbord for Great White Sharks
South Africa

If you've ever tuned into *Shark Week* on the Discovery Channel, chances are you've already seen Seal Island. Sixty thousand cape fur seals inhabit this rocky outcrop near Cape Town, and that constant supply of fresh red meat is a honey pot for the ocean's most fearsome predator—great white sharks. Their spectacular hunting behaviors, which involve those aerial feats so often shown on sensationalist nature programs, are not found in any other white shark habitat in the world— bad news for the seals of Seal Island.

The great whites that feed in False Bay, which surrounds Seal Island, are especially famous for their surface breaching: The sharks launch their entire bodies out of the water in order to snatch an unlucky seal from the surface. Whales normally leap all the way out of the water like this, for reasons unrelated to killing prey, but breaching takes on a whole new terrifying dimension when it's a menacing 2,000kg shark doing the deed. *Air Jaws* became the most successful shark show in history when it introduced TV audiences to the unique shark breaching off Seal Island. What's also striking is how close to shore these shark-on-seal attacks take place— almost within sight of Simonstown harbor in some cases.

For those who care to witness this extremely violent link of the food chain in person, there are plenty of charter outfits along False Bay, near Cape Town, that operate boat excursions to Seal Island— though the boats seem alarmingly small and flimsy given the size and acrobatic capabilities of the sharks touted in their marketing materials. (If surface viewing is all a bit too tame for you, very adventurous types can also find outfitters that will put you face to face, through a shark cage, with *carcharidon carcharias*.)

Within a certain distance of Seal Island in each direction, there's a sweet spot called the "Ring of Death" where the sharks wait for unsavvy seals—usually, the young, old, or infirm ones—to make a mistake. If the seals cross the Ring of Death near the murky bottom of the bay, they'll pass under the sharks unnoticed and make it to the open sea safely. But if they swim too near the surface, it's only a matter of time until a great white attacks, and that's almost always a fatal encounter.

Though you can get close enough to hear and smell the teeming seal population there, Seal Island itself cannot be visited—and you probably wouldn't want to, anyway. The attraction here is undoubtedly the wildlife interaction offshore, not any sort of natural beauty onshore. The rocks are thick with seal guano, and there's no soil or vegetation on the island,

which reaches a maximum "elevation" of just 6m (20 ft.). To lay eyes on Seal Island from the water, it doesn't look like land at all, just a heaving mass of intertwined seals that have survived another day inside the Ring of Death. —*SM*

ⓘ www.capetown.travel.

TOURS: African Shark Eco Charters, Simonstown (ⓒ **27/21/785 1947;** www.ultimate-animals.com). **Boat Company Tours,** Simonstown (ⓒ **27/83/257-7760;** www.boatcompany.co.za).

✈ Cape Town (35km/22 miles).

🚢 Transport available via tour operator (see below).

🛏 $$ **Four Rosemead,** 4 Rosmead Ave. (ⓒ **27/21/480-3810;** www.fourrosmead.com). $$$ **Mount Nelson,** 76 Orange St. (ⓒ **27/21/483-1000;** www.mountnelson.co.za).

From a Distance 417

Seeing Giant Condors
The Flight of the Condors
Colca Canyon, Peru

"There's one." "There's another." And, before your eyes are soaring some of the rarest and most magnificent creatures on Earth: Giant condors. The viewing area is almost a mile above the Colca river running through Colca Canyon in Peru, and the canyon walls make a perfect backdrop to the soaring birds.

Colca Canyon is one of the few places in the world to provide such an up-close view of the giant condors. You and the other tourists in the area (fewer than 100), have been sitting on the ledges 3,900m (13,000 ft.) above sea level, at the scenic **Cruz del Condor** in the cool morning air waiting for this moment. Then, as the sun warms the air in the deep canyon and creates the proper thermals, about two dozen giant

condors leave their nesting ledges on the steep canyon wall below you, spread their 2.7m (9-ft.) wings, and soar like gliders. You can spot the younger ones because they are still brown, while the more mature ones have developed white collars and white wing markings. After 20 to 30 minutes, they soar off in search of food and you sit there a bit awe-struck. Personally, it was one of the most memorable moments of my life.

Andean condors, the largest birds in the Western Hemisphere, are rare, but lucky travelers may see them circling overhead, or flying off nests on mountainside ledges in such places as Perum, Ecuador, and Colombia. These birds are actually vultures with a ruff of white feathers,

Giant condors soar overhead in Colca Canyon, Peru.

white patches on the wings, and a wing span that can stretch up to 10 feet. The San Diego Zoo sponsored a breeding program based in Colombia and about 70 condors have been released in that country's highlands during the past 2 decades. In the U.S., the California condors are endangered. It's estimated that about 350 are left; some are flying free while others are in a breeding program.

Colca Canyon, located in southern Peru, for years was called the world's deepest canyon. Based on recent measurements, some surveys indicate it is now ranks number two (many geologist say that Cotahuasi Canyon in southwestern Peru is deeper), but even so, it's still approximately twice as deep as the Grand Canyon. With the exception of hotels built for tourists, the area around the canyon is predominantly primitive Peru. The pre-Inca manmade terraces are farmed by hand as they were 600 years ago. The villages are much the same as they were in the mid-1500s, when they were created by the order of the Spanish Viceroy Toledo. Most of the roads are unpaved and it's not unusual for your car to move at the pace of the local woman driving her cow and calf down the road.

Aside from viewing the giant condors, Colca Canyon offers great trekking and it's possible to arrange rafting on the Colca River. It's also possible to take bike trips along the narrow, rugged roads in the canyon. Several hot springs along the river are wonderful to soak in any time.

Once known as the Lost Valley of the Incas, Colca Canyon is usually reached via Arequipa, the second largest city in Peru. Contrary to what might be implied in some local literature, this is not a day trip and a minimum of 2 or preferably 3 days is suggested. A leisurely trip from Arequipa to the Colca Valley took us almost 5 hours. The road goes through **Salinas y Aguada Blanca National Reserve,** where you can usually view vicuñas, and climb passes that are in excess of 3.2km (2 miles) above sea level. —*LF*

ⓘ **Peru Tourism Bureau** (www.visit peru.com).

TOUR: Dasatariq Tour Operators (✆511/ **5134400;** www.dasatariq.com).

WHEN TO GO: Apr–Nov (avoid the rainy season, Dec–Mar).

✈ Arequipa.

🛏 $ **Colca Lodge,** Fundo Puye-Yanque-Caylloma, Colca Valley (✆ **51/54-531191;**

www.colca-lodge.com.) $$$ **Casitas del Colca,** Parque Curiña s/n Yanque, Arequipa (✆ **51/610-8300** or 51/54-959-672-480; www.lascasitasdelcolca.com).

From a Distance 418

Wildlife Viewing on Maria Island
Tasmania's Secret Hideaway
Tasmania, Australia

For many travelers, going to Australia can feel like traveling to the end of the earth—but if you really want to explore the edge of the world, consider this scenario. First, you catch a plane or an overnight ferry from Melbourne to Australia's smallest state, the sparsely populated island of Tasmania, off the country's southern coast; then you catch another ferry that carries you from Tasmania's eastern shoreline several miles out to sea, across a strait known as the Mercury Passage, to a little figure-eight-shaped island where the only settlement is a ghost town. This is where Tasmanians themselves go to get in touch with nature.

This lovely and remote spot is Maria Island—and if you're planning to check it out, be sure to stock up on supplies and rented bikes ahead of time, because Maria Island has no vehicular traffic, no shops, no electricity, and no permanent residents other than the few Tasmania Parks & Wildlife Service employees who watch over the hilly, 19km-long (12-mile) island and its wildlife inhabitants.

During Australia's summer holidays, several hundred visitors a day take the 35-minute ferry ride to **Darlington,** the abandoned city on Maria Island's northern tip. When they arrive, they're greeted by a recreational and historical wonderland. Bike paths run the length and width of the island, allowing those with the energy and desire to sample the island's diverse flora

and fauna in full (for a bike-route map, go to the Parks & Wildlife Service website; see below). The island's native wombats and Tasmanian pedamelons (both plant-eating marsupials) were joined in the early 1970s by several species imported from the Tasmanian mainland, including the Eastern grey kangaroo, the red-necked wallaby, and the Tasmanian devil.

Maria Island is also known for its bird population—it's one of the last refuges of the endangered forty-spotted pardalote, the Cape Barren goose, and the sea eagle. **Haunted Bay,** on the island's southern end, is famous for its fairy penguins, whose mournful calls gave the bay its name.

The national marine park that extends for a kilometer off Maria Island's coast is a vibrant ecosystem of fish, seals (four species), dolphins, and birds. The island is on the whale migration route as well, with Southern Right whales, pilot whales, and humpback whales making regular appearances.

The island is also rich in history, both natural—within walking distance of Darlington you'll encounter both limestone **Fossil Cliffs** and sandstone **Painted Cliffs,** known for their stunning iron oxide patterns—and human. The island has gone through a number of settlement phases, starting as a basic camp for whalers and sealers in the early 1800s (the stench of boiling whale blubber forced the camp elsewhere) and then becoming a convict colony in the 1820s. During the island's industrial phase, work revolved around a cement factory, and visitors stayed at the truly grand **Grand Hotel,** a French chalet–style structure complete with dining and billiards rooms (it's now closed). It was built by an Italian entrepreneur who hoped to develop Maria Island as a tourist destination as well as a production center for wine and silk. The island's romantic billing as the "Riviera of Australia" never quite took hold, and by the time of the Great Depression, islanders had turned to farming and fishing. Maria Island was designated a national park in 1972. *—AF*

ⓘ **Tasmania Parks & Wildlife Service** (www.parks.tas.gov.au/index.aspx?base= 3495 and www.discovertasmania.com/us).

✈ Hobart (2 hr. away).

🚢 Triabunna (90 min. from Hobart): **Maria Island Ferry & Eco Cruises** (ⓒ 61/ **04/1974 6668;** www.mariaislandferry. com.au; 35 min.).

🛏 **Tasmania Parks & Wildlife Service** (ⓒ **61/03/6257 1420;** www.parks.tas.gov. au/index.aspx?base=3503).

---

419 From a Distance

Watching Wildlife Come to Life
Arctic Circle Refuge
Wrangel Island, Russia

Northwest of the Bering Strait, the arctic winters are long, and I mean loooooong. For 2 months, November 22 to January 22, the sun never rises at all. A lonely landmass in the Chuckchi Sea, Wrangel Island lies shrouded in snow until June, an icy wind moaning overhead.

And yet the sun returns every spring, and when it does, it's miraculous. Tens of thousands of migratory birds—blacklegged kittiwakes, pelagic cormorants, glaucous gulls—arrive to nest on the jagged cliffs. Ringed seals and bearded seals dip their snouts through holes in the ice, hungry for fish. Walruses lumber out onto narrow spits to give birth. Female polar bears emerge drowsily from their winter dens, newborn cubs snuffling in their wake. Arctic foxes scavenge the rocky beaches, where snowy owls swoop down on unsuspecting lemmings.

A few months later, in the summer, the tundra teems with life. Rivers, swelled with snowmelt, gush through the narrow val-

leys, and the last remaining Russian population of snow geese paddles around glacial lakes in the island's interior. Brilliantly colored Arctic wildflowers mantle the slopes in shades of pink and yellow. Shaggy musk oxen browse sedges and grasses of the ancient tundra, a relic of the Ice Age. The walruses bask on ice floes and rocky spits, going through their annual breeding rituals. It's a sight to see—but very few travelers ever get the chance.

Located 193km (120 miles) off the coast of Siberia, right on the 180-degree line that divides the Western and Eastern hemispheres, Wrangel Island became designated as a nature reserve (or *zapovednik*) in 1976 to protect the delicate Arctic ecosystem, in particular the snow geese and polar bear, that were being hunted to death. There are no lodgings on the island—a small research base is the only habitation—so the only way to visit is on a ship (and an icebreaker at that), with smaller craft for shore visits. Wrangel is typically one stop on a Bering Strait voyage that also includes the Kuril Islands and Kamchatka. On your way through the strait, you'll also have a good chance of sighting minke, gray, and even beluga whales. These are long, expensive, summer-only expeditions, and few companies run them—if you see one offered (there were two in July–Aug 2009), jump on it. —*HH*

ⓘ and **TOUR: Polar Cruises** (ⓒ **888/484-2244** in the U.S., or 541/330-2454; www.polarcruises.com).

From a Distance 420

Arctic National Wildlife Refuge
Eye to Eye with Polar Bears
Alaska, U.S.A.

The polar bear is standing quietly and sniffing the air, looking mean, ruthless, and directly at you! At almost eight feet tall and weighing about 850 pounds, this female polar bear is among the largest land carnivores. (The males can weigh more than 1,500 lbs.) This is a sight few will ever see unless they're in one of the most remote reaches of the United States, the **Arctic National Wildlife Refuge.** One of the most pristine remaining locations on Earth, the Arctic National Wildlife Refuge is located above the Arctic Circle in the northeastern corner of Alaska.

Fortunately or unfortunately, depending upon your viewpoint, there is an area of approximately 1.5 million acres within the reserve that is believed to be rich in oil. Whether there is enough oil for 2 years or 3 months consumption and whether there should be drilling in this section (called 1002) is an ongoing debate. Part of the debate hinges around the impact on the polar bear and caribou populations. The area is an extremely important locale for denning females who birth their cubs here, and for the porcupine caribou herds that summer on the costal plains in 1002. Currently, permission for drilling has been denied.

Because it is so remote, tourism is not big in this wildlife refuge but guided trips are available. **Warbelows Air Ventures** provides flights from Fairbanks to the Village of Katovik, an Inupiat village in the reserve. The trips, which take place in September and early October, include a night in the village, guides, and a guarantee you'll see polar bears.

Other companies such as **Alaskan Alpine Treks** and **Alaska Discovery** provide 1- to 2-week trips in June and early July that include rafting and hiking around the beautiful Brooks Range. The trip provides the opportunity to see wolves, caribou, moose, bears, arctic fox, Dall sheep, and even muskoxen. If you go in the summer, consider trying to time your trip to catch the migration of the Porcupine caribou herd, when the animals number in the thousands. You'll also experience perpetual daylight, itself an extraordinary experience. Your only concern will be dealing with mosquitoes that some locals contend are large enough to saddle and ride. The trip is a photographer's dream. If you like fishing, Arctic char and grayling are waiting for you.

You'll be flying in a bush plane from Fairbanks to reach the wildlife refuge. Before you depart, take a few days to enjoy this town. There are a number of galleries offering good Eskimo art and lots of opportunities to learn about native culture. If you're there in the winter and get to see the Northern Lights, also known as the **Aurora Borealis** (see ㉔), you come home with once-in-a-lifetime photos. Don't miss the University of Alaska Museum of the North, where you can explore more than 2,000 years of Alaskan art through ancient and modern stone and bone sculptures, paintings, and photographs. —*LF*

ⓘ **U.S. Fish & Wildlife Service** (✆ **907/ 456-0250;** www.arctic.fws.gov).

TOURS: Warbelows Air Venture Inc. (✆ **800/478-0812;** www.warbelows.com). **Alaska Discovery** (✆ **800/586-1911;**

www.alaskadiscovery.com). **Alaska Alpine Treks** (✆ **770/952-4549;** www. alaskanalpinetreks.com).

WHEN TO GO: Sept to early Oct for polar bear viewing.

✈ Fairbanks.

🛏 $$$ **The Westmark Fairbanks Hotel,** 813 Noble St. (✆ **800/544-0970** or 907/456-7722; www.westmarkhotels. com). $$ **Minnie Street Bed & Breakfast Inn,** 345 Minnie St. (✆ **888/456-1849** or 907/456-1802; www.minniestreetbandb. com).

---

421 From a Distance

Bear Watching
Are We Having Salmon Tonight?
Katmai National Park, Alaska, U.S.A.

The first time you see a Grizzly bear up close your heart moves roughly 10 inches north and lodges in your throat. These things are huge! A male can weigh well over 1,000 pounds. Get too close, and you could be dinner. But keep your distance, and in observing the bears roam and fish in their natural habitat, you'll have an experience like no other.

One fabulous opportunity for viewing takes place in **Katmai National Park and Preserve,** on the Alaska Peninsula, just across from Kodiak Island. The bears are abundant here as are their readily available food sources, making finding and watching them a fairly easy challenge. Watching a group of bears go after salmon can be amusing and fascinating. Just as fishermen may disagree as to the best fly, lure, or bait to use, there is no universal bear fishing procedure, and their different methods often result in an entertaining array of antics. Some go deep, some splash around, and others sit and wait for the food to come to them. You'll find the bears fishing, arguing and squabbling in many rivers in this

area, including the Naknek River and the Brooks River, plus on many lakes.

There are three basic types of tours to Katmai. Because there are no roads that go there, all three options rely on a seaplane for transport. The first type of trip is a day trip beginning with a seaplane flight from a town such as Homer. The flight over glaciers, between mountain peaks, and over the shoreline is almost as awe-inspiring as the bears. The plane lands on a beach near the park and you walk in with your guide to view the bears.

A multi-day trip option starts with a seaplane trip to a small ship anchored off-shore in a quiet bay. Skiffs then take pas-sengers in for bear watching. The boat, which serves as a floating lodge for visi-tors, moves daily giving the passengers the opportunity to view different bears in a variety of areas. Meals are provided and you'll have the opportunity to learn from a naturalist on board as well as share experi-ences with other passengers.

Finally, travelers can stay within the park at lodges and campgrounds (you get

Grizzlies fish for their dinner in Katmai National Park.

there by seaplane usually from King Salmon) including **Katmai Wilderness Lodge** and **Brooks Camp Lodge.** Many guests have had wonderful lodge stays, but keep in mind these are lodges and not the Ritz. Guest experience often depends on individual accommodations, so it's recommended that you request a written confirmation of rates and specific rooms or cabins, and early arrival.

How safe is bear watching? Guides explain proper people behavior to their guests. (No, you don't send your 6-year-old to stand next to a bear so you can take a photo.) Although the bears are wild animals, they are generally non-confrontational. They have plenty of food and are comfortable as long as they don't perceive you as a threat. Some may think that invading a natural habitat is unethical behavior. But creation of the remote park and its bear watching programs has resulted in many of these magnificent bears winding up in photos on a wall rather than as a rug on a floor.

In addition to the magnificent bears, the park is home to a wide variety of birds, including eagles and puffins, and other animals including moose, red fox, beaver, and seals. Katmai is one of the best sports fishing grounds in the world and a great place for canoeing and kayaking as well. A trip to the **Valley of 10,000 Smokes,** site of one of the most destructive volcanic

blasts in modern times, is a good day trip. Homer is a great location for halibut fishing charters. Contact **Homer Ocean Charters** (ⓒ **800/426-6212;** www.homer ocean.com) or **DeepStrike Sport Fishing** (ⓒ **866-535-6094;** www.deepstrikeak. com) for more information. You can even arrange for your fillets to be flash frozen and shipped to your home for scheduled arrival. —*LF*

ⓘ **Katmai National Park** (www.nps.gov/ katm); **Coastal Bears of Katmai National Park** (www.katmaibears.com).

TOURS: K Bay Bear Viewing (day trip from Homer; ⓒ **877-522-9247;** www.katmai alaskabearviewing.com). **Katmai Costal Bear Tours** (live aboard; ⓒ **800-532-8338;** www.katmaibears.com).

WHEN TO GO: June–Sept (Generally mating is mid- to late July, and you'll see cubs in Aug when the large males leave.)

✈ King Salmon and Homer with seaplane to the Park.

🛏 $$$ **Lands End Resort,** 4786 Homer Spit Rd., Homer (ⓒ **800/478-0400;** www. lands-end-resort.com). $$$$ **Katmai Wilderness Lodge** (ⓒ **800/488-8767** or 907/ 486-8767; www.katmai-wilderness.com). $$$$ **Brooks Camp Lodge** (ⓒ **800/544-0551** or 907/243-0649; www.katmailand. com).

Tracking Wolves
Hearing Haunting Wolf Howls
Yellowstone National Park, Wyoming, U.S.A.

I couldn't move the high-powered spotting scope fast enough to track the two wolf pups trotting to keep up with their mother. They were in a wolf pack that was racing across the frozen landscape, as if the alpha male was following the scent of one of the elk grazing in Yellowstone National Park. Lined up on the roadside, everyone in our group was grinning ear to ear, thrilled that we got to see the pups playing with each other before eerie sounding howls from wolves hidden in the woods triggered a mass exodus.

We had started the day before sunrise at a lookout point in the Lamar Valley. Steam from our coffee matched the mist in the air, as the sun crept above the horizon and lit up the hillsides. When the birds started chirping, it was time to move on and look for the wolves. At Yellowstone, the wolf viewing tours start early in the morning because this is often the best time for sightings.

The wolves in Yellowstone were hunted almost to extinction in the early 1900s but are now protected and monitored. At the end of 2008, there were at least 124 wolves in 12 packs living in the park, according to the Forest Service. You can go scouting for wolves yourself, but the chances of actually seeing them are much better during one of the guided wolf tours. In addition to improving your chances of actually seeing wolves, most tours are led by naturalists who give insights into the lives of wolves, other animals in the park from elk to bison, and teach you about Yellowstone's ecology.

Several times a year, **Wolf Discovery** and **Wolf and Elk Discovery Lodging and Learning** programs are offered. Guests stay at the Mammoth Hot Springs lodge in the park and go out daily to see wolves' habitats and learn more about their behavior and the Park's conservation efforts. The hikes or drives, depending upon the season, are led by a Yellowstone Institute naturalist.

People who desire a more intensive introduction should take one of the Yellowstone Organization's field seminars that offer a comprehensive overview of wolf evolution, behavior, and communication. Guests stay in cabins at Lamar Buffalo Ranch (see below), while learning about Yellowstone wolf restoration, how wolves relate to prey species, scavengers, and other animals. Participants go out in the field to observe wolves and visit the carcass of an animal killed by wolves. —*LF*

ⓘ **Yellowstone National Park** (✆ **307/ 344-7381**; www.nps.gov/yell).

TOUR: Wolf Lodging and Learning programs and Field Seminars at **Yellowstone Association Institute** (✆ **307/344-2293**; www.yellowstoneassociation.org).

WHEN TO GO: Spring, fall, or winter.

✈ Jackson Hole, WY (56 miles/90km), or Bozeman, MT (87 miles/140km).

🛏 The lodging and learning programs and the field seminars include lodging at park properties.

Dog-Sledding in No-Man's Land
Icy Nomad of the North Atlantic
Greenland

Among those ostensibly no-man's-land-masses that transatlantic flights pass over between North America and Europe, Greenland seems the most unlikely travel destination in and of itself. Iceland, maybe. But Greenland? It's the world's largest island that isn't a continent in its own right (about a quarter of the size of Australia), with a coastline as long as the equator. The bulk of the island lies above the Arctic Circle, and for all those terrific statistics and surface area, only 57,000 people live here, almost all of them Inuit, and concentrated on the marginally hospitable west coast. Eighty-one percent of Greenland is covered by an ice sheet, and if it were to melt, sea level worldwide would rise by 7m (23 ft.).

Greenland's greatest natural attraction is the **Ilulissat Ice Fjord,** a UNESCO World Heritage Site on the west coast, where the **Sermeq Kujalleq** glacier meets the sea in often-spectacular fashion. Sermeq Kujalleq is one of the fastest and most active glaciers in the world, calving over 70 cubic km (17 cubic miles) of ice annually, a rate that has sped up significantly in the past decade due to climate change in the Arctic. For now, however, Greenland is still connected to the North Pole by ice, which makes it—you guessed it—the **home island of Santa Claus.** (Read more at www.santa.gl.)

Besides the sublime quiet and majesty of nature here, perhaps the most quintessential Greenlandic experience is going for a **dog sled trip.** In the east and north of Greenland, some 29,000 sled dogs (one for every two residents of the whole island) are a vital, if pungent, form of transport in the winter; dog sleds always have the right of way. A number of tour outfitters, including Greenland Holiday (see below) also go on rip-roaring journeys over the ice and snow. Greenland sled dogs, which usually work in teams of 12 to 15 dogs per sled, are a unique breed descended from wolves and cannot bark; they howl instead.

Getting into the local way of life in Greenland represents some challenges; first and foremost of course are the harsh territory and weather. Then there's the Inuit food: The national dish of Greenland is boiled seal meat with rice and onions *(suaassat),* while a local gourmet deli item is *mattak* (raw whale skin with a thin layer of blubber).

So why is it called "Greenland" when it's mostly covered by white? The etymology of the island's name is a matter of debate: Some chalk it up to the Viking explorer Erik the Red, who might have given it this name as a sort of tongue-in-cheek way of attracting settlers from Iceland. More likely, Greenland is a corruption of *Hronland,* which meant "Land of the Whales" in ancient Norse. —*SM*

ⓘ www.greenland.com.

TOUR: Greenland Explored (✆ **44/2921/ 251515;** www.greenlandholiday.com).

✈ Kangerlussuaq, flights from Reykjavik, Iceland, and Copenhagen, Denmark.

🛏 Where you stay will depend on where your dog-sled tour takes you.

Camel Trekking in Mongolia
One Hump or Two?
Mongolia

Genghis Khan had it all wrong. Thundering across the steppes of Mongolia on horseback makes for an impressive Hollywood spectacle, but camel riding is traveling in style. With their loping gait and comfortable, furry humps, camels are to horses what a new Lexus is to a hand-cranked Model T. And camel trekking is the best way to see the farthest, most isolated reaches of Mongolia, a mysterious kingdom that was closed to Westerners from the 1920s until the fall of the Soviet Union.

Adventures to this landlocked nation begin and end in Ulaanbaatar, the capital and largest city. From there, you'll be in the capable hands of your tour guide, who will introduce you to the nuances of world-famous Mongolian hospitality: No stranger, according to tradition, can ever be turned away, and charging for a meal or a visit is unthinkable. Most camel treks use a combination of trucks and camels to get visitors around this dry, rugged land, twice the size of Texas with a tiny fraction of its population.

You'll be traveling in the footsteps of famed American archaeologist Roy Chapman Andrews, allegedly the inspiration for Indiana Jones, who uncovered a treasure trove of prehistoric dinosaur fossils in the arid sands around the Flaming Cliffs, one of Mongolia's most renowned attractions. It's not unusual for even casual hikers to find fossilized remains of dinosaur eggs and bones scattered on the ground. For a thrill from more recent times, check out the Bronze-age cave paintings at Mount Ikh Bayan. In the heart of the Gobi Desert lies Gobi Gurvan Saikhan National Park and the famous Three Beauties, towering peaks that mark the eastern edge of the Altai Mountains.

When it comes to trekking Mongolia, camels are the beast of burden of choice.

Throughout your trip, you can expect to stay in *gers*, round tentlike structures that are similar to the yurts of Siberia. You may fall asleep to the ethereal sounds of throat singing, the Mongolian warbling that has captured the imagination of music lovers worldwide. And throughout it all you'll be surrounded by the serene beauty of the Gobi Desert and the incomparable hospitality of the Mongolian people. —*ML*

TOURS: **Black Ibex Expeditions** (✆ **976/ 11-318-848;** www.discovermongolia.mn). **Muir's Tours** (✆ **44/0118-950-2281;**

www.nkf-mt.org.uk). **Nomadic Expeditions** (✆ **800/998-6634** or 609/860-9008; www.nomadicexpeditions.com).

WHEN TO GO: June or Sept.

✈ Ulaanbaatar.

🛏 $$ **Ulaanbaatar Hotel,** 14, Sukhbaatar Square, Ulaanbaatar (✆ **976/70-116-688;** www.ubhotel.mn). $$ **Narantuul Hotel,** 2 khoroo, Baruun Durvun zam, Ulaanbaatar (✆ **976/11-330-565;** www.narantuul hotel.com).

Along for the Ride 425

Emperor Penguins Cruises
Hobnob with Royalty
Antarctica

Would you like to hobnob with royalty on a cold-weather cruise to Antarctica? You can on an Antarctic cruise to see the emperor penguins on **Snow Hill Island,** a snow-covered ice shelf in the ice-choked waters of the Wendell Sea. During these cruises, an icebreaker ship crosses the Drake Passage to the Weddell Sea and stops near Snow Island, close to the tip of the Antarctic Peninsula. Weather permitting, you'll take helicopter flights from the ship to a rookery for a few days. There, you'll watch the adult penguins, the deepest diving birds on the planet, caring for their young chicks. To observe this amazing cycle of life in this other-worldly place is an unparalleled experience.

The first sound you'll hear upon reaching the rookery is the shrill whistling of chicks begging their parents for food. Eventually, you'll see hundreds of penguins milling about on the snow. The adults look regal, dressed in tuxedos. Tucked amongst them are the small chicks, with their fuzzy white fur. At times, adults toboggan their bodies across the

snow and slide into the open water to find food for their young.

The cruises to Snow Island are usually only once or twice a year in the fall, when the Emperor penguin chicks are young and the adults still very protective. The largest of all penguins, the emperor penguins live and breed on the fast ice in the coldest climate on earth. After a female lays an egg she gives it to the male, who keeps it warm through the winter (often by huddling together with other males). The female then heads out to the open sea to feed. She returns in time for the young to hatch and cares for them while the males trek to the open ocean in search of food. When the males return, together the adults care for the chicks until they are old enough—about 6 months—to enter the open sea on their own.

After departing Snow Hill Island, you'll sail down Iceberg Alley, past the translucent icebergs, and visit rookeries of Chinstrap and Gentoo penguins just arriving to breed and raise their young during the austral summer. Passage for most outfitters is on the *Khlebnikov*, a Russian icebreaker that was retrofitted as a cruise ship in the early 1990s and in 1997 was the first ship to navigate the Antarctic with passengers. With its 45mm-thick icebreaker hull, it can ram through ice-locked surfaces opening up watery passages. The *Khlebnikov* has 56 cabins (space is limited for these cruises), with comfortable but not luxurious accommodations aboard. During the expeditions naturalists and lecturers are on hand to educate you on the emperor and other penguins in rookeries around the Antarctic, in addition to offering much more information about the White Continent itself. —*LF*

TOURS: Quark Expeditions (✆ **866/961-2961** or 203/803-2888; www.quark expeditions.com). **Travel Wild Expeditions** (✆ **800/368-0077** or 206-463-5362; www.travelwild.com). **Polar Cruises** ✆ **888/484-2244** or 541/330-2454; www. polarcruises.com).

WHEN TO GO: Fall. Only one or two cruises are offered per year.

✈ Ushuaia, Argentina

---

426 Along for the Ride

Kayaking with Orcas
Killer Whales All Around
Inside Passage, BC, Canada

You're sitting in camp with a cup of coffee watching the fog burn off the water, your mind in a peaceful state of repose. Someone yells, "Orcas!" It is amazing how fast a dozen people can shift to high gear, stop what they are doing, get into their sea kayaks, and start paddling. Their single-minded goal is to be in the vicinity of the Orcas as they breach, spyhop, blow, or cruise by. What a rush to be inches from the surface and see half a dozen black fins cutting through the water and listen to their conversation over the hydrophone that's been lowered into the water by a guide. You will not be able to go to sleep without turning the pages of your mental scrapbook filled with Orca photographs.

The killer whales (actually members of the dolphin family) are also called blackfish or sea wolves. They stay together in a matrilineal group of varying size. They probably got their nickname because many of them eat seals, minke whales, sea lions, and walruses, and they hunt in packs like wolves. The Orcas in this area are here to feed, mostly on the salmon.

The **Inside Passage** runs between the eastern side of Vancouver Island and mainland British Columbia. The protected waters of such sections as Johnstone Strait are ideal for sea kayaking and with a little instruction beginners are soon moving easily through the water. The kayak vacations are camping trips that generally last between 4 and 7 days. You'll pack your gear in waterproof bags and carry it with you. Depending upon the outfitter, you'll either paddle to your initial campsite or be ferried by a motorboat. Your guides will assist you and provide your meals, but they are not your Sherpas and you'll be expected to pitch in as if you were camping with a group of friends. Much of your time will be spent on the water, and in addition to the Orcas you'll have chances to see a large variety of wildlife including bears, sea lions, dolphins, bald eagles, otters, and salmon. With luck, you'll even see a humpback whale. You'll also do some hiking and be able to totally chill until you are incredibly relaxed.

For a change of scenery after chasing Orcas for a few days, be sure to visit

Vancouver Island. It's almost 483km (300 miles) long and 81km (50 miles) wide, so it takes several days to explore. The west coast is more rugged than the east coast, with its Golden Hinde Mountain (named after Sir Frances Drake's ship) that tops out above 2,100m (7,000 ft.). The waves crashing on the shore at Tofino are enough in themselves to attract visitors. Most of the towns are small and fun to visit. —LF

ⓘ **Tourism British Columbia** (✆ **800/ 435-5622;** www.hellobc.com).

TOURS: Northern Lights Expeditions (✆ **800/754-7402** or 360/734-6334; www. seakayaking.com). **Out For Adventure**

Tours, 685 Heriot Bay Rd. (✆ **866-344-5292** or 250/285-3600; www.outfor adventure.com).

WHEN TO GO: June to mid-Sept.

✈ Port Hardy Airport (general aviation) or Victoria International Airport.

🛏 $ **Haida-Way Inn,** 1817 Campbell Way, Port McNeill. (✆ **800/956-3373** or 250/956-3373; www.pmhotels.com). $$ **Hidden Cove Lodge,** Port McNeill/ Telegraph Cove (✆ **250/956-3916;** www. bcbbonly.com/1263.php).

Along for the Ride 427

Ostrich Racing
Winner by a Neck
Oudtshoorn, South Africa

Ostriches aren't nice. They have an ornery attitude, a mean peck, and their claws are sharp enough to rip open a lion's face. They aren't pretty, and they don't like to cuddle, either, so they rarely elicit the "ooohs" that greet many African animals. What, then, is an enterprising adventurer to do when encountering one of these 300-pound, nine-feet-tall birds? Why, jump on their backs and race them, of course.

Ostrich riding and racing is the unofficial town sport of Oudtshoorn, a small hamlet in the Little Karoo region of South Africa located a few hours' drive northeast of Cape Town, where most flights into this region will land. There are a number of ostrich farms in the area, and many sponsor organized ostrich encounters, where visitors can learn about these flightless birds' natural history before commencing the racing. By most accounts, ostriches don't take kindly to having someone sitting on their backs, so they run as fast as possible in hopes of getting rid of you.

There are a few ground rules you'll need to know before you hop on an ostrich. Riders must weigh less than 80kg (176 lb.), and will need to be strong enough to be able to hang onto the moving animal by holding its wings and steering by grabbing its neck— no easy task when you're loping along at 32km (20 miles) per hour. (Grace is not one of the features of this sport.) An ostrich race is an impromptu affair, and depends on the number of willing volunteers in your party, though there are ostrich derbies organized by civic clubs throughout South Africa.

The semi-arid region of Little Karoo is ideal for raising ostriches, and the town of Oudtshoorn was once the undisputed heart of the world's ostrich plume trade; the town's rows of "feather palaces," homes of multi-millionaire ostrich farmers, attest to its former glory as the center of this international trade. Ostriches have staged an impressive comeback since their 19th century heyday, having less to do with their plumage than with their eggs—one of which will feed 20 men—and their meat, a low-fat alternative to beef that is darker and tastier than chicken. Their leather, too, is soft and durable and is used for fashion accessories such as boots and wallets. All these items and more can be found in the retail shops of the Ostrich Capital of the World. —*ML*

TOURS: Pathfinders (✆ **04/702-814;** www.pathfindersafrica.com). **African Overland** (✆ **021/853-7952;** www. africanoverland.co.za).

WHEN TO GO: Year-round.

✈ Oudtdshoorn or Cape Town (418km/ 260 miles).

⊨ In Cape Town: $$$ **Kensington Place,** 38 Kensington Crescent, Cape Town (✆ **021/424-4744;** www.kensington place.co.za). $$ **De Waterkant Village,** 1 Loader St, Cape Town (✆ **021/409-2500;** www.dewaterkant.com). In Oudts-horrn: $ **Rosenhof Country House,** 264 Baron van Reede St. (✆ **27/44/272-2232;** www.rosenhof.co.za). $$ **Retreat Groen-fontein,** follow signs from R62 btw. Oudt-shoorn and Calitzdorp (✆**27/44/213-3880;** www.groenfontein.com).

---

428 Along for the Ride

Camel Racing
Loose Camel
Alice Springs, Australia

When it comes to speed in the animal world one naturally thinks of sleek race horses or majestic leopards. You never think of a 2m (7-ft.) gangly creature with knobby knees, old teddy bear fur, and a rather large hump on its back. It's hard to believe that the towering awkwardness of the desert camel can, with a little encour-agement, turn into an 1,800-pound bullet traveling at 64kmph (40 mph) through dust and mayhem with a human clinging to its hump like a surrogate foal. This is exactly what happens in Alice Springs, Australia every July, where the "ships of the desert" transform themselves into "speedboats of the Outback."

The Camel Cup originally began with two bored Australians in the 1970s racing their dromedaries along the dry river bank that cuts through this legendary town in the dead red center of the Australian out-back. The race has since morphed into a serious 400m (1,312-ft.) race around an oval track at a venue known as Blather-skite Park. The event is organized by the

Lion's Club and has limited numbers of rider places. Camels are privately owned and usually used to ferry tourists around the rest of the year. Four thousand specta-tors turn up to cheer and jeer, including the Afghan ambassador, resplendent in robe and fez and looking almost as incon-gruous as the four-legged, long-necked bulls amidst the festival atmosphere of suntanned Australians intent on having a good time.

Camels are not usually associated with the land down under. Yet Australia has a sizeable herd of even-toed ungulates as they were once the main mode of transport to get around this desolate spot and were introduced by the British from their ex-col-ony in Pakistan. They have thrived so much there is now talk of an annual culling to keep their numbers down. Usually used to lumber tourists around the nearby McDon-nell ranges or through Finke Gorge National Park, the camels have their moment of glory every second Saturday in July when they show their real mettle and ungulate for real. So famed is the Camel Cup, a statue of the beast of burden greets passengers off the train from Adelaide or Darwin after the 1,500km (930-mile) journey.

Alice Springs is a small modern town of 26,000 people. Known as Mparntwe amongst the local aborigines, it has become a center of indigenous art with galleries such as those situated in the Todd Mall retracing the area's 50,000-year history and reliving the aborigine legends that the dry red dirt was carved by caterpillars and wild dogs. Less poetic were the shepherds, gold miners, and telegraph workers who soon turned the settlement into a sizeable collection of Australians with English, Irish, and Scottish roots. They turn out in force to watch the race with comical sideshows, busy food stalls, and busier beer tents keeping the crowds occupied between races. The races themselves often get off to a discouraging start. All the animals must be lined up and seated before the race sets off. Often the camels have different ideas, facing the wrong way, refusing to sit, and then refusing to move. Many dart off with the jockey clinging for his or her life as they round the dusty bends at breakneck speeds. The riders often lose their grip and fall with the camel sprinting off into the distance, prompting the legendary cries from the stands: "Loose camel!" —CO'M

___

ⓘ **Camel Cup** (ⓒ **61/8/8952-6796;** www.camelcup.com.au).

WHEN TO GO: Second Sat in July.

✈ Alice Springs.

🛏 $$$ **Bond Springs Outback Retreat,** North Stuart Hwy. (ⓒ **61/8/8952-9888;** www.outbackretreat.com). $$ **Comfort Inn Alice Springs,** 46 Stephens Rd. (ⓒ **61/8/8952-6100;** www.comfortinn.com).

10 Offbeat Adventures

429

The Gloucestershire Cheese Rolling Race
The Cheese Chasers
Brockworth, Gloucestershire, England

You'd think rolling a piece of cheese down a hill and chasing after it would be a piece of cake, or cheese for that matter. This is what the locals have been doing in the south western English county of Gloucestershire since medieval times, or since Roman times as some will tell you. Yet when you see Cooper's hill and its ridiculously steep incline, you realize that this annual event is not the walk in the park it seems. The spectacle of 20 adults bouncing and tumbling down a precipitous field of long, wet grass after a hurtling roll of hard cheese is enough to crack your ribs, and their ankles. Competitors cartwheel and flop like rag dolls as they pursue the elusive cheddar. Ambulances line up at the bottom to conveniently ferry the injured off to a nearby hospital. Back injuries are not uncommon and all the runners suffer some sort of bloody graze or twisted ligament. The 2009 winner was taken away smiling on a stretcher clutching his 3.6kg (8 lb.) prize of solid curd to his chest. Health and Safety concerns have closed down the event three times in the past decade, and there is a special search and rescue team on standby for those who do not naturally roll to the bottom. As if this was not enough of a headache for organizers, who have the Orwellian title of "the Cheese Roll Committee," local vegan groups are calling the race unethical and demanding that the cheese should be replaced by a non-dairy alternative.

Four thousand spectators turn up to a race that is now beamed across the world and in recent years was viewed live in Brazil. There are actually five races in total, one of which is for women only. They take place at midday in the green rolling hills of Brockworth, an hour west of London, in an area more famous for its nature trails through the Cotswolds or the traditional horse racing meeting in nearby Cheltenham. Once a year, on the May bank holiday Monday, cozy English country pubs in the area such as The Cheese Rollers pack with locals before and after the race, plotting tactics, gaining some Dutch courage, and afterward watching video highlights and nursing their wounds.

The race's origins are a complete mystery with written records going back only 200 years. Many claim it has pagan origins, that it is a fertility rite, or a spring celebration. Some say that it was introduced to anticipate a good harvest or initiate new age healing. Such theories are not hard to believe in an area that has a magical heritage and has served as the backdrop to many a *Harry Potter* movie. The truth however is probably something very simple. Somebody just realized that chasing a roll of cheese down a hill is very good fun. —*CO'M*

ⓘ www.cheese-rolling.co.uk.

WHEN TO GO: Last Mon in May.

✈ Bristol (63km/39 miles).

🛏 $$$ **Plush Hotel,** Bristol Airport, Redhill, North Somerset, Bristol (ⓒ **44/1934-862410;** www.bristol-airport-hotels-plush-hotel.com). $$ **Hotel 24/7,** 15 Acramans Rd., Bristol (ⓒ **44/7711-626662;** www.hotel24seven.com).

Previous page: Exercise your inner 6-year-old boy at Dig This.

430

The Tomato Food Fight
Pulp Friction
Buñol, Spain

Imagine tomato goo running down your face, tomato seed creeping up your nose, and tomato pulp lacquering down your hair. This is exactly what will happen to you if you find yourself in a little village called Buñol in eastern Spain on the last Wednesday of August. You have just walked into the infamous **La Tomatina.**

The biggest food fight in the world starts with competitors scrambling up a greasy pole to dislodge a smoked leg of ham which is skewered at the top. After this feat of athleticism has been achieved old trucks trundle up the cobbled streets and dump 136,078kg (300,000 lb.) of over-ripe tomatoes onto a crowd of 40,000 tomato-pelting revelers. And so the fight ensues as skimpily clad women and bare-chested men hurl squashed tomatoes in any and every direction in what is a large communal effort at making a very large Bloody Mary. The red juices run down their arms and legs and stain the streets. For an hour there's a haze of slush, sludge, slime, slop, and swill. Finally, a water gun fires to signal the end of the festivities. The bedraggled fighters are left to stagger to the riverside where make-shift showers are set up to wash away the fresh ketchup and the authorities begin to hose down the streets of this little town as if nothing remarkable had come to pass.

Unlike many festivals in Europe, La Tomatina has absolutely no historical significance and has nothing to do with the fact that the tomato, a universally popular item on every menu, is a South American fruit that was first introduced to Europe by a Spaniard in the 15th century. The festival's origins only began in 1945 during a small carnival in this town 48km (30 miles) west of Valencia on the Mediterranean coast. Some rowdy audience members made use of a nearby grocer's cart to pelt a poorly performing comic. The next year, students from Valencia decided to reenact the event, but the police quickly broke it up. The seed was sown, so to speak, and every year the locals chose to finish the carnival with an ever growing vegetable showdown. Gradually it became an annual event, with the authorities eventually giving in and recognizing it in 1959. It has since become an international event with people flocking from all over the world to take part in the pelting and pulping.

For Buñol it is a big event (well, probably the only event) in village life. The week building up to the party is full of eating, drinking, and dancing with parades and fireworks adding to the general excitement. A giant paella cooking contest is held as Valencia is also the home of this famous simmering rice dish. Giant cauldrons bubble along the town's streets dominated by a medieval clock tower. Valencia itself has some fascinating architecture with a famous 14th-century gothic mansion called Llota de la Seda and a brand spanking new sci-fi riverside complex known as the City of Arts and Sciences. The port city is also famous for its vibrant nightlife and excellent restaurant scene. However, for 1 day of the year the focus shifts to the tiny village west. Young and old, fit and flabby gather in the main square of Buñol to throw over 150,000 ripe tomatoes at each other in a type of Ragu rave that is televised live around the country. —CO'M

ⓘ www.tomatina.es.

WHEN TO GO: Last Wed in Aug.

✈ Valencia (48km/30 miles).

🛏 $$$ **Hotel Las Arenas Balneario Resort,** Eugenia Vines 22–24, Valencia (www.valencialasarenashotel.com). $$ **Sorolla Palace,** Avda Cortes Valencianas 58, Valencia (✆ **34/961/868-700;** www.hotelsorollapalace.com).

431

Panning for Gold in Australia
The Genuine Article
Sovereign Hills, Ballarat, Victoria, Australia

There is nothing like a nugget of gold to get the heart racing. Especially if you have just fished it out of a muddy stream that offers more such nuggets and there is a bank up the road that will exchange it for hard cash. If greed gets the better of you there's an underground mine nearby that has surrendered pure gold boulders the size of adolescents. Then you can drop into the local foundry and watch $50,000 worth of molten gold poured into a bullion bar. Sovereign Hills offers this and much more.

To walk around this genuine 19th-century mining town 115km (71 miles) west of the state capital Melbourne is like waking up and finding yourself in an episode of *Deadwood*. Costumed locals go about their business in 19th-century garb and atop horse carriages. Stores and workshops line the thoroughfare with a blacksmith hammering out horseshoes and a candle maker displaying his waxy goods. Aproned grocers operate Wild West versions of a 7-11 convenience store and jewellers sell everything from the genuine article (you guessed it—gold) to tourist trinkets. There's a tavern bar that offers old time bowling and a museum displaying rocks and coins from the era. You can take a stage coach tour of the surroundings and in the mine you can see a replica of the second biggest nugget in the world, a 69kg (152-lb.) monster known as "the Welcome Nugget." If it all gets too much you can lie down in the local hotel and literally sleep on a goldmine.

It was gold that made the south eastern state of Victoria. The early convict settlers at the turn of the 19th century were literally tripping across the stuff in what must have been a supreme and bitter irony as they discovered their open jail was literally paved with gold. The real rush began in 1851 and it saw the biggest migration of fortune seekers in modern times. The population increased by half a million over 10 years as Scots, Irish, Cornish, and Chinese all got wind that there was something in those hills and it shines. Soon the region produced 20 million ounces of gold, one third of the global output. Melbourne took off as a centre of trade and commerce and Australia in general began to stand on its own two feet. The mines are also credited with establishing the country as an independent political entity. An uprising by disgruntled miners in 1854 known as the Eureka Rebellion was brutally repressed by the British colonialists but it lead the way to a fairer system of civil rights and one man one vote.

On the river it is one man and his pan as lines of visitors fish for some glinting rock. Children especially love Sovereign Hills and history buffs are in their element. It just so happens that element is gold. —CO'M

ⓘ www.sovereignhill.com.au.

TOURS: Melbourne Hosted Tours (✆ **61/3/9755-6085;** www.melbourne hostedtours.com). **Melbourne's Best Day Tours** (✆ **61/3/9397-4911;** www. melbournetours.com).

WHEN TO GO: Year-round.

✈ Melbourne (115km/71 miles).

🛏 $$$ **Crown Promenade Hotel,** 8 Whiteman St., Southbank, Melbourne (✆ **61/3/9292-6688;** www.crown promenade.com.au). $$ **Alto Hotel on Bourke**, 636 Bourke St., Melbourne (✆ **61/3/8608-5500;** www.altohotel.com. au).

432

The Haro Wine Battle
Wine Not War
Haro, La Rioja, Spain

Try not to arrive in La Rioja's medieval capital Haro on June 29. On that day, as soon as you step on the street complete strangers will douse you in buckets of wine and cackle with glee. You have inadvertently walked into the town's famous Wine Battle, an annual orgy of wine throwing that would make Bacchus run for cover. Thousands gather on the city's streets armed with buckets, basins, dustbins, giant water pistols, and even backmounted crop sprayers with the intention of drowning each other in wine. They apparently go through 49,210 liters (13,000 gal.) every year. Everybody is dressed in white but they don't stay that way for long. Soon the teeming, screaming mass is covered head to toe in purple, with sticky hair and stinging eyes. More savvy veterans cover their cars seats with plastic, their cameras with plastic wrap and some even wear goggles. All the antics are accompanied by brass bands and tractor drawn floats and culminate in a night fiesta on the town plaza with fireworks and more wine ducking.

Haro is 100km (62 miles) south of Bilbao and the center of the country's wine making tradition. La Rioja is Spain's most prodigious wine region with many historical and prestigious wineries surrounding Haro. Such was the region's wine making importance; some of the wineries even had their own train platforms to dispatch wine to all corners of the country and farther afield to the Spanish Empire. La Rioja's wineries are famous for aging rich and fruity wines that are literally a shame to throw away. The historical city of Bilbao is farther to the north on the Atlantic coast. It is the capital of the Basque region and home to the famous futuristic Guggenheim Museum designed by Frank Gehry.

The Haro wine battle is becoming just as famous, with people coming from all over Europe for this annual wine wipe-out. Its origins date back to a 10th century land dispute between Haro and a neighboring town called Miranda De Ebro over a mountain called Montes Obarenes. Every June 29 (St. Peter's Day), the Mayor of Haro ceremoniously passes through the town on horseback and then up the mountain to a small chapel. Everyone follows him on the 6.4km (4-mile) route, many of them holding some kind of receptacle with wine in it. After mass, the entire congregation solemnly bless themselves and then rush outside to begin a fervent purple hued battle in what is a reenactment of the medieval confrontation except the only thing that is spilled is wine. The melee eventually moves back down the hillside to the city bullring, where the festivities continue. If only all wars could be solved this way. —CO'M

ⓘ **Haro region** (www.haro.org). Website is Spanish only.

WHEN TO GO: June 29.

✈ Logroño (60km/37 miles).

🛏 $$ **Casa de Legarda,** Briñas (✆ **34/ 941/312-134;** www.casadelegarda.com). $$ **El Hotel Rural Villa de Abalos,** Plaza Fermín Gurbindo, No. 2, Abalos (✆ **34/ 941/334-302;** www.hotelvilladeabalos. com).

433

Air Guitar World Championship
The Riff Raffers
Oulu, Finland

The rock star struts across the stage, flicking back his long hair and pouting to the cheering audience. A roadie runs up to him and gingerly hands him a guitar. The rock star straps it on and gives a poised stroke of the wrist. He strums into a song while a group of adoring groupies screams from the sidelines. As the tempo rises his fingers become a blur on the fret board and his facial expressions vary from fury to exhilaration to complete concentration, punctuated by the occasional pelvic thrust and consummated by a dramatic high arm salute as he ends his epic 1-minute solo. By now the crowd has worked itself into a frenzy and one of the groupies has fainted. This could be any rock concert, except it is not. There is no guitar and this is no rock star.

The **Air Guitar World Championship** started as a joke in 1996, a frivolous sideshow to a music festival in the northern town of Oulu in Finland. Organizers did not realize however that they had accidentally struck a chord, so to speak, with every rock fan's fantasy to play like Hendrix. Soon the joke became the main event and now national air guitar champions from 17 countries gather at this Baltic sea port 500 miles north of Helsinki to pick, twang, lip synch, and gyrate. They smash imaginary guitars and burn pretend Fenders in re-enactments of every famous rock moment imaginable. These would-be rock gods "surrender to the music" as the American Champion Hott Lixx Hulahan proved one

Virtual shredding at the Air Guitar World Championship.

year by breaking his thumb and heroically carrying on. He obviously did not want to disappoint his fans.

As can be expected in a Scandinavian country, the silliness has a serious side and rules are strict. Under no circumstance must contestants play another imaginary instrument, such as drums or piano. Other band members are not allowed on stage but roadies and groupies are permitted as kind of props to enhance that all important rock star allure. Each rock fantasist must play two 1-minute rounds. The first a tune of their own choosing and the second a last-minute request by the four-person jury to test the air guitarist's skill in improvisation. A six-point score system much like figure ice skating is used to sort the wheat from the chaff. There are three criteria. Technical merit takes into account how close to the real deal the performer is simulating. They watch his or her fingers for fretwork, chord playing, and technical moves. The second criteria are stage presence. Does the participant have the aura of a rock star or should he return to playing solo in front of his bedroom mirror? Is there rock star

charisma in those moves or has stage fright made him forget his notes? And finally there is what they call "airness"—the overall artfulness of the contestant. Does this performance move beyond mere simulation and into an intangible realm of epic head banging greatness?

Participation is free and winners walk away with that rare thing, a real guitar which is actually a local handmade instrument called a Flying Finn. However, to reach the championships you must pass the regional heats that take place in an ever increasing number of countries. Look out for the poster. Air Guitar is coming to a town near you. —CO'M

ⓘ www.airguitarworldchampionships.com.
WHEN TO GO: Aug. Check website for exact dates.
✈ Oulu.
🛏 $$ **Scandic Oulu,** Saaristonkatu 490100 Oulu (ⓒ **358/8/543-1000;** www.scandichotels.com). $$ **Holiday Inn Oulu,** Kirkkokatu 3 90100 Oulu (ⓒ **358/8/883-9111;** www.restel.ti).

Baby Jumping Festival
Jump, Jump, Baby
Castrillo de Murcia, Spain

Six toddlers lie swaddled on a mattress in the open air. Another cluster of babies lie wrapped in blankets a few feet away while a little farther down the village street there are more infants looking up at the sky while eyed by a crowd of serious looking spectators who occasionally step forward to tuck in a child and stop him or her from rolling over onto the hard pavement. Two men emerge from the church in front. They look like court jesters, dressed as they are in medieval outfits of yellow and orange. They run down the steps and

across the small plaza not slowing down as they approach the baby obstacles. Instead they gather speed and leap across the oblivious infants and repeat the jump over each mattress laid before them, turning to jump the mattresses again while the crowd sings and church bells ring out.

Welcome to the infamous baby jumping festival in Northern Spain where Catholic child abuse gets a whole new meaning. It is the culmination of 4 days of self-imposed exorcism, when the town of Castrillo de Murcia near Burgos spills out onto its narrow streets and takes on the devil in all his forms. The yellow suited men are known as *colachos* and they spend the weekend terrorizing the locals with whips and sticks. They run through the crowded streets, dispersing jeering groups of onlookers and chasing bystanders. A sinister group of men in dark capes and top hats look on in the distance, banging a huge drum. These are the *atabaleros*, another form of the devil that must be banished from the town by the following Sunday. *El Fiesta del Colacho* takes place during the boisterous Corpus Christi celebrations that engulf the entire country with parades and singing. It happens 60 days after Easter and is a celebration of the Catholic Eucharist when the body of Christ becomes bread and wine.

Officially the Catholic church frowns upon grown men jumping over vulnerable infants on public thoroughfares. However, the locals are fanatical followers of a tradition that goes back centuries. On the final Sunday, the devils are banished to the church and every child born the preceding year is laid out on the mattresses in the streets in front. *El Colacho* is unmasked within the church and forced to flee into the small plaza where he long jumps the short people. This Lucifer leaping of the babies is regarded as a symbolic act that purges all evil and reputedly brings good luck to the children who seem to emerge unperturbed. —*CO'M*

WHEN TO GO: Late May/June.

✈ Burgos (44km/27 miles).

🚃 $$ **NH Palacio de la Merced,** Calle de la Merced 13, Burgos (✆ **34/94/747-9900;** www.nh-hotels.com). $$ **Hotel Silken Gran Teatro,** Avda de Arlanzon 8-b, Burgos (✆ **34/947/253-900;** www. hoteles-silken.com).

435

Dig This
Play in an Adult Sandbox
Steamboat, Colorado, U.S.A.

Did you play in a sandbox when you were a kid? At **Dig This,** you'll get to play in an adult sandbox, the nation's first and only recreational heavy equipment, dirt-moving compound. Feel the adrenaline rush as you take control of a Caterpillar 315 CL hydraulic excavator and start moving one-ton rocks around with subtle hand movements on the machine's gears. Want to dig ditches or build a rock pile? It's easy to do, even if you are a 120-pound (54kg) female. Just learn how the gears work and start carrying massive rocks around your playground. If you'd rather build a road or a runway to land a plane, which guys seem to like best, just choose to play with a D5G track-type dozer. The fellas start grinning from the moment they get in a bulldozer and begin building their own road to nowhere. Afterward, they shoot photos to their friends, who jealously e-mail back, "Wish I could do it." You can!

Before you're allowed to handle the real equipment, there's an introductory session, during which Dig This's New Zealander owner, Ed Mumm, or one of his staff, tells you about the machines and demonstrates how they work in a miniature sandbox. Then, a staffer sets you up in your machine of choice, demonstrates how the gears work, and goes over the safety procedures. Finally, it's your turn. You operate the machine cautiously at first, perhaps dropping a five-foot-wide boulder you're lifting while digging a ditch. But, after awhile, the feeling of pure power takes hold and you start digging up dirt or building a road more aggressively.

Participants get to operate an excavator, bulldozer, or skid steer loader at individual work sites, constructing roads, building dams, digging trenches, or creating whatever their mind envisions. Dig This offers a "First Tracks" 2-hour session for clients with limited time. It includes orientation, safety instruction, and about an hour of either bulldozer or excavator operating time. During the half-day session, participants get more than 2 hours of operating time on one of the machines. During the full-day session, participants get more than 4 hours of operating time and can split it between two machines.

Playing in the sand and rocks at Dig This is one of the most popular activities for vacationers who come to Steamboat to ski in the winter, or explore the mountains during the summer. Companies bring executives here for team-building exercises, and locals show up for birthday parties and anniversary outings.

Steamboat Springs is prettiest in the summer, fall, and winter. (Spring is mud season here and locals disappear.) In the winter, skiers and snowboarders flock to the slopes at Steamboat Resort, which coined the term "Champagne Power," because the snow is so light. In the summer, visitors hike or mountain bike on trails threading the mountainsides, or play golf. —*LF*

ⓘ **Dig This,** 1169 Hilltop Pkwy. (ⓒ **888/ DIG-THIS** [344-8447] or 970/367-4402; www.digthis.info).

WHEN TO GO: Year-round.

✈ Yampa Valley Regional Airport in Hayden (26 miles/42km).

⌷ $$–$$$ **Sheraton Steamboat Springs,** 2200 Village Inn Court (ⓒ **800/ 325-3535** or 970/879-2220; www.sheraton. com/steamboat). $–$$ **Hotel Bristol,** 917 Lincoln Ave. (ⓒ **800/851-0872** or 970/879-3083; www.steamboathotelbristol.com).

Frozen Dead Guy Days Festival
Party with Frozen Grandpa Bredo
Nederland, Colorado, U.S.A.

Yes. There really is a dead guy on ice in a shed in Nederland, Colorado! And, Grandpa Bredo is the perfect excuse for the annual **Frozen Dead Guy Days Festival** packed with partying and fun events. Birthed as a mining town, some now claim Nederland to be one of the remaining bastions of hippydom, so a festival of this nature isn't out of character.

The winters in Nederland (a community of approx. 1,400, located 17 miles [27km] west of Boulder, CO) are long, and cabin fever is severe. But, as the daylight hours increase, spring is about to arrive, and locals prep for the craziness accompanying

ski season's end, everyone is ripe for the Frozen Dead Guy events.

Grandpa Bredo died in Norway, was packed in ice, and shipped to a cryonics facility in California, where he resided in liquid nitrogen for 3 years. He was then transported to Nederland, where his daughter, Aud, and grandson Trygve, were planning to build their own cryonics facility. Grandpa was kept on ice in a shed awaiting a cure for death, but Trygve was deported for visa expiration and Aud was forced to move from her house because there was no plumbing or electricity. After much bickering and publicity, Bredo was

Contestants compete in the coffin race at the Frozen Dead Guy Days Festival.

"grandfathered" into a town ordinance forbidding the keeping of dead bodies and body parts. Trygve secured the services of a local environmental company, which packs 1,600 pounds (726kg) of ice around Grandpa every month. And a new festival was born.

The 2½-day festival, held the first weekend in March, includes lots of wacky events. The Ice Blue Ball on Friday evening includes a Grandpa Bredo look-alike contest followed by a midnight champagne tour that includes spending an hour with the Frozen Dead Guy. Saturday features a slow parade, an obstacle course, coffin race (six pallbearers carrying a coffin with a rider, all in costume), the adrenaline-filled Polar Plunge, a frozen dough ball toss, a pack your pants with snow contest, a frozen T-shirt contest, and a late night Pub Crawl. Sunday's events include the Sundance Salmon Toss, a Beach Volleyball Contest, and a Blue Ball (Rocky Mountain oysters) Eating Contest. Entry forms for these events can be obtained through the Nederland Chamber of Commerce.

Nederland is easy to reach by car and local bus service from Boulder. During early March there is still skiing at nearby Eldora Ski Resort and several major ski resorts, including Vail, Copper, Keystone, and Winter Park, all within a 2-hour drive. Central City, an old mining-turned-gambling town a dozen miles (19km) away, is home of the famous Face on the Barroom Floor. A visit to the old cemetery at the far end of town is interesting and worthwhile. And Boulder, home to the University of Colorado, is a great place to spend a day or two. —LF

ⓘ **Nederland Chamber** (© **303/258-3936;** www.nederlandchamber.org). **Visitor Guide to Boulder** (www.norman koren.com/Boulder.html).

WHEN TO GO: First weekend in Mar.

✈ Denver International Airport (59 miles/95km).

🛏 $–$$ **Mountain View Chalet Cabin Rental** (© **303/258-9219;** www.mtnview chalet.com). $ **Best Western Lodge At Nederland,** 55 Lakeview Dr. (© **800/279-9463** or 303/258-9463; www.best westerncolorado.com/hotels/best-western-lodge-at-nederland).

437

The Ivrea Orange Battle
Blood & Orange Juice
Ivrea, Italy

What would you do if some dark knight rode into town and tried to steal your fiancée's virginity? Pelt him with an orange is what. In fact, several hundred thousand if you feel like it. This is what happens in the northwestern Italian town of Ivrea every February. The normally sedate village 40 minutes north of Turin becomes a seething mass of fruit hurling maniacs, intent on whacking opposing teams with oranges that end up mulched and stomped into the ground, leaving the town looking like it has been hit by a monsoon of vitamin C. The citrus carnage has a medieval appearance as tall box carts dressed up like castles trundle through the city streets and plazas. Inside are a line of men dressed up like a juicy version of the Praetorian guard with sinister black helmets and padded suits. They are deluged by volleys of oranges from the thoroughfares packed with slinging participants, themselves dressed like aggressive court jesters with checkered scarves, grey tights, and scorpion adorned shirts. Spectators, buildings, and windows are protected by large net canopies and those wearing red scarves are deemed neutral and thus protected against a hard whack of sunny delight—in theory. In fact, everybody is at risk of getting a bruising—including the insanely unprotected riders and the unfortunate horses.

There are actually several versions of the festival's origins, one including a tale of a girl on a balcony trying to attract a boy's attention by smacking him with an orange. It is unrecorded if this come-on worked. The most compelling story comes from Medieval times when the local tyrant Count Ranieri of Biandrate used to insist on bedding every local maiden on the eve of her wedding. One such girl stood up to him however and cut his head off, hanging it from his castle battlements which was then promptly stormed by a baying crowd and burned to the ground. The veracity of this story is as shaky as the story behind the Turin Shroud on display in the nearby Turin cathedral, but it does not stop the locals and whoever else from pouring onto the streets to reenact the battle of good over evil for 3 days before Fat Tuesday, the day before Lent begins. There are nine competing teams and up to 3,000 spectators. Fifty horse carts are pulled through five flag bedecked districts that become major battlegrounds as the locals come out to defend their turf. The spectacle is open to all but you must join a team if you wish to become a true blue orange slinger. Team names include the Scorpions, the Chessmen, and the Ace of Clubs. Participants get a free meal of beans before the skirmishes commence and prizes are handed out at the end to the most valiant and accurate. Fired up on mulled wine, the participants turn an orange into a lethal projectile and injuries are not uncommon with blood and orange juice streaming down more than one head. —CO'M

ⓘ **Carnival of Ivrea** (www.carnevale diivrea.it).

WHEN TO GO: Feb.

✈ Turin (53km/33 miles).

🛏 $$$ **Grand Hotel Sitea,** Via Carlo Alberto, 35 (ⓒ **39/11/517-0171;** www.thi-hotels.com). $$ **Hotel Master,** Corso Grosseto 366/7 (ⓒ **39/11/455-5482;** www.masterhoteltorino.it).

438

The Candle Race
Totem Gesture
Gubbio, Umbria, Italy

The crowds pack the narrow streets of this medieval town. They are all waiting in anticipation and look up the steep street bordered on either side by tall medieval, gothic, and renaissance buildings from which hang banners and flags. Many people are dressed up in brightly colored silk shirts of blue, yellow, and black. They wear scarves around their necks and white pants. Drummers and trumpet players add to the sense of old world pageantry and the bells of the local church peal above the roof tops. All eyes are on the top street corner and people shout expectantly. Suddenly, the huge throng parts like the Red Sea and a train of men come rushing through carrying tall fat wooden pillars with religious figurines on top. There are three such massive masts and they sail through the crowd with remarkable speed, taking on a life of their own like some sort of animated standing stones that have just escaped from Easter Island. Around the corner they jauntily go, trailing a blaze of color as the troop of carriers sport red scarves, fez hats, and sashes. The speeding totem poles disappear and the crowd erupts into joyous clapping and screaming. Women weep and babies wail. To an outsider it might appear slightly ridiculous. Be careful to not smirk, however. The locals take the *Festa de Ceri* very seriously.

The title *Candle Race* is a complete misnomer. There are no candles and there is no race. The big sticks are made from wood not wax and the rush around town is ceremonious in nature, the teams judged by their skill in carrying these unwieldy columns rather than who crosses the finishing line first. Each pole represents a patron Saint who in turn represents a faction of the community—thus the passion, loyalty, and rivalry. St. Ubaldo is the union representative of the masons. St. Anthony is shop steward for the farmers, and St. George, chief negotiator for traders and artisans. Traditionally families are tied to a particular saint and their pride and honor is at stake to ensure their holy man conducts himself well in this annual mill around town.

The town is Gubbio, tucked in the Apennine mountains, on the slopes of Mount Ingino in central Italy, 200km (124 miles) north of Rome. Its cobbled streets and grey limestone buildings exude history and just outside the town is one of the country's best preserved Roman amphitheaters, a temple to Jupiter that is still used for shows and events. The village holds a famous medieval archery competition each year and its history goes back even before the Romans, to an ancient Umbrian race evident in bronze tablets carved in an extinct language. Known as the Gubbio Tables, they can be seen in the castle-like Palazzo dei Consoli.

It is in this mammoth, fortresslike building that the Candle Race kicks off with a swordsman dashing up and down the steps in a ceremony heavy with heritage if short on logic. Eventually the bulky, octagonal pillars emerge from the building like giant coffins. They have been there for a week, pulled from the local basilica where they must now return. But not before being hoisted into a vertical position and propelled around the town. Jugs of water are thrown over the crowd and crockery broken. Banners unfurl, trumpets blare, and the town surrenders to abandoned revelry laced with fierce pride. The candles are loose. —CO'M

---

① **Bella Umbria** (www.bellaumbria.net/ Gubbio).

WHEN TO GO: May 15.

✈ Perugia (42km/26 miles).

⊨ $$$ **Park Hotel Ai Cappuccini,** Via Tifernate (© **39/75/9234;** www.parkhotel aicappuccini.it). $$ **Relais Ducale Hotel,** Via Galleotti 19 (© **39/75/922-0157;** www. RelaisDucale-Gubbio.com).

The Holi Festival of Color
Hue & Dye
New Delhi, India

Find yourself in India's capital at a certain time of year and you'll be in for a rude surprise. New Delhi may be the subcontinent's most ordered metropolis—a planned city of wide, tree-lined boulevards and arterial roads, yet such cosmopolitan tidiness is subverted somewhat in the month of March. You'll notice it in the blue dogs that wander the Chandni Chowk market place and the pink hair of the older folks sitting in front of the modernist Lotus Temple. You'll certainly notice it when a total stranger approaches you outside the beautiful Red Fort and pours a bucket of bright orange gloop over your head.

The **Hindu Festival of Color,** known as *Holi,* is a riot of paint throwing and water splashing. Paintballs, squirt guns, and buckets are all used as neighbor turns on neighbor in a violent explosion of color letting. Mounds of vibrant powder sit in front of market stalls as vendors take advantage of the population's 2-week obsession with paint and pigment. Musicians bang on drums while dancers take to the streets in what is an exuberant celebration of the coming of spring. Gangs of youths high on traditional marijuana flavored milkshakes wander the streets with armories of dubious colorants looking for a victim. Foreigners are not immune to their attentions, so do what the locals do and don some old clothes. Many of the

dyes are permanent so it is also a good idea to cover your hair and face. Harmless dried flowers were the traditional source of color for centuries, used with flour and water. However, rampant urbanization in the region means there are fewer flowers, so poorer people are using synthetic dyes of dubious origin with serious concerns regarding toxicology. One year it was discovered some villagers were dousing each other in asbestos powder and other dyes used reputedly induced asthma, blindness, even cancer.

Holi is celebrated throughout India, Nepal, and Bangladesh, and the Hindu diaspora around the world. It is especially intense in the northern region of Braj, where different villages and towns have their own traditions, usually associated with the myths and legends of the Hindu god Lord Vishnu as the area was reputedly his youthful hunting ground. One such ritual is the *Lath Marholi* in the town of Barsama. There, thousands gather to reenact a piece of mythical domestic violence. Women beat men around the head with large sticks while the males respond with lewd and provocative songs. Not all of it is play acting. The entire countryside lights up with thousands of bonfires to celebrate the triumph of good over evil. In the town of Vrindavan, revelers gather at the tall, red, bullet-shaped temples to

Krishna to throw orange petal water and sing the Hindu folk songs known as *hori*. From here you can make a 1-day trip to the Taj Mahal, that monument to love amidst this celebration of color. —CO'M

 New Delhi.

🛏 $$$ **Taj Mahal Hotel,** 1, Mansingh Rd. (© **91/11/23026162;** www.tajhotels. com). $$ **Shanti Home,** A-1/300 Janakpuri (© **91/11/4157-3366;** www.shantihome. com).

ⓘ www.holifestival.org.

WHEN TO GO: Feb to early Mar.

440

Devon Barrel Burning
Great Barrels of Fire
Ottery St. Mary, Devonshire, England

The Devonshire town of Ottery St. Mary is a fire fighter's nightmare every 5th of November. All of Britain indulges in a week of pyromaniacal lunacy for the week preceding with giant bonfires and fireworks celebrating Guy Fawkes. Yet this small village in the south west of England throws gas on the fire (so to speak) by encouraging the locals to run through the crowded streets with flaming barrels of tar on their backs. Teenagers, women, and men all indulge in this quaint practice that sometimes results in scorched scalps and burned shoulders. The huge crowd that turns up to see the event means everybody is at risk from the burning barrels. Shopfronts are often damaged in the crush as people scream and flee the melee.

Its beginning in the afternoon is low key and gives little hint of the madness ahead. The town has a holiday atmosphere and a fairground is set up along the river Otter and a 11m (35 ft.) bonfire waits to be lit. However, there are plenty of signs posted on walls that say "You are here at your own risk" and when the locals start popping off homemade cannons made from plumbing pipe stuffed with gunpowder you know you are in for something different.

Seventeen barrels are lit and hauled through the street. Enthusiastic youths cover themselves in wet clothing and wear gloves before they put a burning barrel on their backs and run through the streets. As the evening proceeds the barrels get bigger and bigger, culminating in a 50kg (110-lb.) monster known as the Midnight Barrel. Runners must have lived in the village for at least 6 years and many guard their right to barrel burn with fierce pride. The idea is to run as long as possible with the barrel on top before the heat becomes unbearable. Experienced barrel runners skillfully spin the barrel on their backs to lessen the heat. Then the barrel is passed to another family member who continues to rush through the screaming crowd like a stuntman whose stunt has gone awry.

Nobody knows why Ottery St. Mary indulges in burning barrels. Some say it is an old pagan ritual to ward off evil, others say it comes from the medieval practice of fumigating cottages. Still others say it's a centuries-old celebration of defeating the Spanish Armada. Whatever its origins, the barrel burning now coincides with the British tradition of burning effigies of Guy Fawkes, an 18th-century catholic who tried to blow up the protestant parliament in what became known as the Gunpowder Plot. People gather around giant bonfires and it is no understatment to say alcohol is imbibed. In fact every one of the 17 barrels that flames through Ottery St. Mary is sponsored by a local pub from which it is successfully launched with much bravado. —CO'M

ⓘ www.tarbarrels.co.uk.

WHEN TO GO: Nov 5.

✈ Exeter (21km/13 miles).

🛏 $$$ **Combe House Devon,** Gittisham, Honiton, Exeter (✆ **44/1404/540-400;** www.thishotel.com). $$$ **Larkbeare Grange,** Larkbeare, Talaton, Exeter (✆ **44/1404/822-069;** www.larkbeare.net).

Bull Running in Ecuador
Horn of Plenty
Otavalo, Imbabura, Ecuador

There is plenty to thrill you in Ecuador and this beautiful country has no shortage of unforgettable sights. Tucked in the northwest of South America, it's crossed by Andean peaks that have earned the local Pan-American Highway the sobriquet "the Avenue of Volcanoes." Ice-capped, cone-shaped peaks billow smoke on either side as you take the road to the high altitude capital Quito, itself a visitor's delight with an old quarter crammed with colonial churches and cobbled streets. To the east lie lush jungles and cascading waterfalls and to the west sweeping beaches and ideal waves for surfing. Farther out in the Pacific are the famous Galápagos Islands, with their astounding wildlife (see ⓐ) that will make any photographer snap happy. Yet of all these arresting visions, there is none more unforgettable than the sight of one ton of raging black muscle storming toward you on a village square while a jeering crowd bay for your blood.

The locals say that a *fiesta patronal* is not a success unless at least two ambulances cart off some hapless victims to the local hospital. The green rolling hills and volcanoes of Imbabura province north of the capital hide a heap of indigenous villages where the locals love to gather once a year and get gouged by an angry bull. Each town has its own patron saint party on a certain weekend where brass bands take to streets playing jaunty military

tunes and kids light bonfires on the corners, burning effigies and parading in costumes. Otavala, 95km (59 miles) north of Quito and just across the equator, is one such place. This famous artisan market town has proud Indian routes where the men wear long straight black hair in distinctive ponytails and women wear multi-stranded bead necklaces, their short round bodies wrapped up in ponchos and petticoats and topped with a slanted bowler hat.

For the festival, a rickety wooden stand is built around the central plaza and a set of stockades set up around a newly laid sand pit. A tall greasy pole is raised at its center and crowned with a sack full of goodies. Inebriated men jump from their seats and race across to the pole, which they hopelessly attempt to climb while a bull storms into the arena. Mayhem breaks loose as the bull makes a bull's-eye of the man's hind quarters and charges for it. Other members of the public rush from their seats to distract the animal and are subsequently chased to the surrounding walls where they leap the fence just as the animal's fiercesome horns crash into the woodwork. Just as proceedings are getting a little chaotic, another raging male cow is released into the arena for good measure and general pandemonium breaks loose; inevitably one of the public slips and is tossed in the air like a rag doll.

Blood streams from his forehead as he rushes to the stockade with his hand held forward. People try to help him jump but no, he does not want out, he just wants a sip of their beer.

Ecuadoreans love a good party and are some of the most committed drinkers on the planet, frequently fired up by $1 bottles of industrial alcohol. No doubt such beverages have an influential role on who is brave enough to leave the stands and take a chance across the arena. The great thing about bull running here is that nobody gets hurt, at least those who don't deserve to. That includes the bull who survives to gouge another day in another nearby village. —CO'M

ⓘ **Exploring Ecuador** (www.exploring ecuador.com).

WHEN TO GO: June. Check local listings for exact dates.

✈ Quito (95km/59 miles).

🛏 $$$ **Hacienda Cusin,** San Pablo del Lago, Otavalo (✆ 593/6/2918-013; www. haciendacusin.com). $$ **Hacienda Pinsaqui,** Pan-American Hwy. Km 5, Otavalo (✆ **593/6/2946-116;** www.hacienda pinsaqui.com).

442

The Great Knaresborough Bed Race
Bed Fellows
Knaresborough, North Yorkshire, England

A team of six men push a double-decker London bus up a river. Take a closer look and you'll see the bus is actually a cleverly disguised bed with a woman on it. The men struggle through the water and up a muddy bank. They must hurry. Santa Claus and his six reindeers are in hot pursuit despite nearly capsizing in the water.

The Great Knaresborough Bed Race is exactly what it sounds like, a bed race through the North Yorkshire market town of Knaresborough. Six runners take a bed and make it road worthy. They then put a member of the opposite sex on it and race up steep hills, across a park, and down a river. Beforehand there is a parade of the 80-odd quilted roadsters that come disguised as trains, planes, and automobiles, even the occasional house. The fact that they must travel 30m (98 ft.) up a deep river gives a whole new meaning to parade float. Thousands turn out to see this colorful spectacle with much cheering and jeering as the different teams struggle over the 3km (nearly 2-mile) run. Some take the race very seriously and complete it in less than 13 minutes. Others take as long as they like to complete this four-poster caper.

The race first started in 1965 as a bit of fun between teams from the British Army, Navy, and U.S. Marines. It has since morphed into one of the major annual events that takes place in the beautiful and rugged North Yorkshire region. With 40% of this Northern England county covered in national parks, there is plenty to see and explore, including the Yorkshire Dales and North York Moors. However, for one crazy day in June the whole area turns out to watch this town parade and race. Pipe bands and vintage cars roll through the picturesque village while the quaint country pubs do a brisk trade. The race begins at Conyngham Hall and climbs up a hill overlooked by the town's castle ruins. Then it proceeds down to the River Nidd, where crowds watch as the teams struggle with their customized beds and some disintegrate in the water with cardboard and papier-mâché floating away downriver. Then they scramble up a muddy bank and race for the finishing line.

The event raises thousands of British pounds each year for different charities and is actually oversubscribed with more than 100 bed teams eager to participate. Competitors come from as far as Germany to try their luck in a race that turns out to be pure bedlam. —CO'M

ⓘ www.knaresborough.co.uk/bedrace.

WHEN TO GO: June.

✈ Leeds (29km/18 miles).

🛏 $$$ **Residence 6,** The Old Post Office, 3 Infirmary St., Leeds (ⓒ **44/113/285-6250;** www.residencesix.com). $$ **Roomzzz Central,** 2 Burley Rd. (ⓒ **44/113/233-0400;** www.roomzzz.co.uk).

443

Roller Girls Running of the Bulls
Southern Discomfort
New Orleans, Louisiana, U.S.A.

The gun is fired and they are off. A pack of brave runners dressed in white shirts hurtle through the French Quarter of New Orleans with big beefy girls on roller skates tearing after them. The bruising females chase and whack their prey with whiffle ball bats and are dressed with massive horns for added menace. There is no doubt that they are a fearsome sight as they bear down on a limping runner and beat and pummel the hapless athlete. Even more outrageous are the spectators who look on, chomping their beignets (large French doughnuts) and jeering when some slow poke is caught and gored with a bat.

Here in this Deep South city famous both for Mardi Gras and Creole, the roller girls provide a modern twist on the Pamplona Bull Run (see **370**). A wine merchant called Mickey Hanning started the event in 2007. He loved the adrenaline rush involved in the Spanish version and decided that New Orleans should host a bull run of its own. However, bulls are in short supply in Louisiana (or maybe insurance men are in good supply), so Mickey had a few words with a team of roller racers called the Big Easy Roller Girls, hoping that some tough American broads could stand in as the bulls. Their captain, a

The menacing "bulls" on roller skates in New Orleans.

woman who goes by the name of Archbishop Pummel, sent Mickey a reply, "I've got a bunch of bad ass chicks on wheels who probably wouldn't mind beating up a bunch of guys." And so the Running of the Bulls went stateside.

It takes place in July with over 30 roller girls forming teams with names like Confederacy of Punches and Crescent Wenches. The chase gets underway at the Three Legged Dog, one of the French

Quarters pretty Creole houses and over 600 runners are pursued down Bourbon Street toward the Mississippi River. For comic effect (as if things were not hilarious enough) the Roller girls are themselves harried by the Rolling Elvis, a group of Elvis impersonators on sputtering scooters. The anarchic run comes to a climax amid much pounding and pummeling at the Gazebo on the river bank. The finishing line then turns into a block party with dirty rice, jambalaya, and pecan pie washed down with beer and bourbon.

The Roller Girls Running of the Bulls is open to everybody. You just need to turn up in white clothes and a red scarf and be prepared to be terrified and humiliated. —*CO'M*

(i) www.bigeasyrollergirls.com.

WHEN TO GO: July.

✈ New Orleans.

🛏 $$$ **Le Pavillon Hotel,** 833 Poydras St. (© **504/581-3111;** www.lepavillon. com). $$ **Quality Inn & Suites,** 210 O'Keefe Ave. (© **504/525-6800;** www. qualityinn.com).

444

Irish Road Bowling
Country Roads
Ireland, West Virginia, U.S.A.

The neighbors have lost their marbles, or more likely their cannon balls. Pick any summer weekend in bucolic West Virginia and you are likely to find the locals wandering the picturesque laneways, thrashing through shrubland, shuffling in the woods, and rifling through the long grass. A large sign sits by the road asking motorists to slow down as the ancient art of Irish road bowling is under way. Men, women, and children sprint along the tarmac and with an underswing that would put the Big Lebowski to shame, fling a 28-ounce metal ball along the road to their team members up ahead. They shout "bowling" to warn the innocent that a heavy metal projectile is in motion. The idea is to throw the ball as far as possible with the least amount of strokes over a course that varies between 1 and 2 miles in length. Each team member picks up where the previous thrower landed the ball and any stray must be hunted down in the thickets, hedges and rolling pastures this rural state is famous for.

When John Denver sang of West Virginia's pastoral rural highways, he probably

Irish road bowling is taken seriously in Ireland, West Virginia.

never imagined those same roadways loitered with ball hurlers. In fact, road bowling goes way back before the 1970's radio hit. Back to the civil war, in fact, when a union troop of Irish soldiers called Mulligan's Brigade fought the many battles that took place in this southern state that is not quite southern. Between skirmishes they picked up any spare cannonballs that lay around and took some R & R by indulging in some road bowling. The rolling green hills of West Virginia must have struck them as very similar to their own country where road bowling can be traced back to the 17th century.

One townland looks so much like Ireland it was called after it, and now Ireland, West Virginia, is the nucleus of a sport that is gaining in popularity and has events in places as far off as Chicago and New York. This small rural village is 90 miles (145km) north east of the state capital Charleston and home to the West Virginia Irish Road Bowling Association.

As one aficionado put it, "All you need is a $5 ball, a piece of chalk, and a road." It is this ease and accessibility that makes the sport popular with all ages. Three generations of family members jog the roads,

chasing balls and marking landing spots. In fact, it is not much different from an energetic country walk on a lazy afternoon with the occasional burst of energy and a keen sense of competitiveness. It's enough to bowl you over. —*CO'M*

(i) **West Virginia Irish Road Bowling Association** (✆ **202/387-1680;** www.wvirishroadbowling.com).

WHEN TO GO: Spring and summer weekends.

✈ Charleston (90 miles/145km).

🛏 $$ **Embassy Suites Hotel Charleston,** 337 Meeting St., Charleston (✆ **843/723-6900;** www.embassysuites.com). $$ **Hampton Inn Buckhannon,** 1 Commerce Blvd., Buckhannon, WV (✆ **304/473-0900;** www.hamptoninn.com).

Wasserschlacts Street Food Fight
Apocalypse Chow
Berlin, Germany

It is not often you see a super hero wearing rubber gloves, a gas mask, and carrying a bin liner full of half eaten burgers. He passes the uneaten whoppers to his accomplice, who operates a giant catapult that will "whopper" the said burgers over a teeming crowd of food fighting warriors. They bear helmets, goggles, and rubber sticks and all are smeared in rotten food that varies from mushy tomatoes to soggy gherkins. The crowd faces off in the middle of a city bridge in Berlin and chants and screams before unleashing every type of wet and slicky substance imaginable, including rotten fish and dirty diapers. Gunk and slime cover everything and soon it looks like a medieval battle in a landfill site with everybody whacking each other with foam sticks and shields fashioned

from garbage can lids and hubcaps. Is it any wonder the event known as the Wasserschlacts is sponsored by a waste disposal company?

The event is all the more bizarre for its setting. The ornate Oberbaumbrucke bridge is a city landmark designed in a German gothic style with red brick arches, two pointy towers, and cross vaults. It is more used to genteel tourists strolling its two-deck structure than a thousand food anarchists clashing on the ramparts. Indeed as the food fight descends into a chaos of airborne liquid, spray, and screaming maniacs, tourists float down the river Spree below on day cruisers, taking photos of the carnage above and perhaps getting hit by the occasional stray water balloon.

The bridge is a shining symbol of unity, which is all the more ironic as the street fight is a grubby emblem of disunity. It connects the two districts of Friedrichshain and Kreuzberg, which were separated for half a century by the Cold War. When the Berlin Wall came down in 1989, the authorities thought it prudent and right that both districts should be joined. However, they never discussed it with the residents, who resented assimilation with the other. In 1998 the first crowds gathered on the bridge to taunt and challenge the other side. The idea was to conquer, not unite, and people from Kreuzberg referred to Friedrichshain mockingly as East Kreuzberg and in turn Kreuzberg was referred to its opponents as Lower Friedrichshain. What began as a simple water and flour fight evolved into an elaborate free for all, with some years seeing near riots with cars set alight and buildings damaged. Police frequently step in to stop the event and it was cancelled in 2006 and 2007. In 2003 an angry mob turned on the intervening police and pelted them with stockpiled fruit and eggs.

The whole chaotic event has a leftwing, punkish, anarchic air with more than a few participants sporting mohawks and tattoos. Gangs are formed with names such as the Cynical Offensive Brigade and they gather shopping carts, homemade water cannon, and scaffold attack towers. The only rule is that no fresh food can be used and the event is open to anybody brave enough to face the fray. If you do decide to go to battle, join the Kreuzberg crew. They have never won a battle yet as they are heavily outnumbered by much larger Friedrichshain. They desperately need your help and all your rubbish. —CO'M

WHEN TO GO: July.

✈ Berlin.

🛏 $$ **Adina Apartment Hotel Checkpoint Charlie,** Krausenstrasse 35–36 (✆ 49/30/2007670; www.adina.eu). $$ **Mercure Hotel Checkpoint Charlie,** Schützenstrasse 11(✆ 49/30 206320; www.accorhotels.com).

446

Civil War Reenactment
War Fair
Gettysburg, Pennsylvania, U.S.A.

The glow of campfires and flickering candles behind white canvas tents fades out as the sun rises over the rolling hills of Gettysburg, Pennsylvania. At 5am the bugle call of *reveille* prods the bearded soldiers from their sleep and they gather around the remaining embers of the campfire to drink oily coffee. Some dig out salt pork and hard tack from crumpled waxed paper for breakfast before battle, while others put on hand-knit wool socks and wrap up their blanket rolls. This is as authentic a civil war scene as you'll get, until someone admires a fellow soldier's Otis Baker braces and the wearer describes enthusiastically how he got them for a bargain on Craig's List.

Another shows a companion how he got his once shiny buttons to tarnish nicely with a little nail polish remover. Still, the thrill of being on-site at this, one of the most historied battlefields in the world, is timeless.

Every weekend thousands of men and some women gather at a civil war battle site somewhere along the Mason Dixon line to reenact a bloody episode from the momentous conflict. While the real war was split between north and south, federals and confederates, modern day reenactors are split between lightweights known as *farbs* and hardcore authentics known as *stitch Nazis* for their obsession with hand stitching every item of clothing down to their underwear. Some take their task so seriously they will sleep in ditches and march miles weighed down with rifles, bayonets, and knapsacks.

The most famous of these simulated battles is Gettysburg. The key battle of the civil war, where Robert E. Lee was forced to abandon his invasion of the north, is now an annual get-together for history buffs, tourists, and hardcore reenactors. Based around the July 4th holidays, the 3-day event sees five major battle reconstructions, live mortar fire demonstrations, and a living history village with costumed locals partaking in blacksmithing and period medical demonstrations. The real battle itself was one of the bloodiest in this tumultuous period in American history with 51,000 casualties, including 8,000 dead. For 3 days General Lee directed a confederate onslaught against the union defenses on ridge lines south of the town. The federals were lead by General George Meade, who eventually forced his southern opponent to retreat back to Virginia. Gettysburg was then the site of Lincoln's famous speech that rallied the unionist cause.

The actual battle site is now a national cemetery and military park. The Gettysburg reenactment takes place several miles away on some sweeping hills along Pumping Station road. Thirteen thousand reenactors gather to relive certain key moments, and visitors can drop in and see reconstructions of critical moments such as General Lee having a staff meeting to plot out his strategy and the important battle for Culp's Hill. A 50-cannon salute starts the event and visitors pay a $24 entrance fee to witness talks and demonstrations with themes such as the *Medical Horrors of the Battle* and *Spies of the Civil War*. However, the true excitement lies in actually joining the fight and reliving the battles that include 500-horse mounted cavalry maneuvers and big gun artillery movements. Volunteers just need to turn up at the registration post every morning and pay a $20 fee to join the fight. You need to bring your own uniform and equipment and there is a thriving trade in period props to make every participant look the part. —CO'M

ⓘ **Gettysburg National Military Park** (✆ 717/334-1124; www.nps.gov/GETT).

WHEN TO GO: Weekend closest to July 4th.

✈ Harrisburg (38 miles/61km).

🛏 $$$ **Wyndham Gettysburg,** 95 Presidential Circle (✆ 717/339-0020; www.wyndham.com). $$ **Brickhouse Inn Bed & Breakfast,** 452 Baltimore St. (✆ 717/338-9337; www.brickhouseinn.com).

Exotic Eating

The waiters are laughing among themselves and pointing at you—they know you're not from around here, but you somehow stumbled into their little eatery and you're going to consume something you've never eaten before. Perhaps it was alive only minutes before, crawling up a tree, or maybe it was a pet you cherished as a child. No matter. You're hungry, you're tired, you don't speak the language and besides, how bad can it be? Plus, eating as the locals do gives you a sense of pride and exhilaration—no matter what's on the menu. Your waiter approaches, a sly smile on his face, carrying a steaming hot plate of . . . something. *Bon appétit!* —ML

447 Fugu in Japan: Hundreds of people are killed each year by eating this delicacy when it's prepared with less-than-flawless precision—but why should that stop you? Fugu (commonly known as pufferfish) contains a lethal poison, deadlier than cyanide, that's concentrated in its liver and sex organs. Chefs are required to get a special license to prepare fugu, and any chef whose customer dies from his preparation is honor-bound to kill himself by seppuku. But if the fish doesn't kill you, the bill might: One fugu dinner usually costs about $400.

448 Hakarl in Iceland: Eaten fresh, this meat of the basking shark is quite toxic, owing to the amount of uric acid in its body. After careful preparation, which involves burying the shark in gravel until it rots, it's not much better—some have compared the strong ammonia taste to eating solid urine. Vomiting is a frequent response for newcomers to this delicacy, but drinking a shot of Brennivin, the local booze charmingly known as "Black Death," makes it go down easier.

449 Pulque in Mexico: This milky, alcoholic drink was once the exclusive domain of Aztec chieftains and nobles. To extract this nectar from a mature agave plant, farmers must tap the heart of the plant with a fat wooden tube and then suck out the sap, which is known as *aquamiel,* or "honey water," for its sweet taste. After fermenting, the drink takes on a sour flavor that can be cut with spices, fruit or other flavoring.

450 Fried Spider in Cambodia: Crunchy on the outside, soft and chewy on the inside. Sounds like a perfect snack, right? It is for Cambodians, who flock to the town of Skuon (north of Phnom Penh) to dine on spiders—specifically, Thai zebra tarantulas—that are tossed in a mix of garlic and salt, then skillet-fried to perfection. They're only about 3 inches long, but the cost of about 8¢ (1¢ per leg?) makes them an affordable meal. Market vendors swear that when mulled in a rice wine cocktail, spiders are great for those with backaches or breathing problems.

451 Durian in Malaysia: The noxious smell of this spiky, 2.3kg (5 lb.) fruit has been compared to everything from dirty diapers to turpentine, with top notes of sweaty gym socks and a stale, vomit-like finish. No wonder it's banned from most hotels, airports, and public transportation in Southeast Asia. Even taxi drivers—not known for their delicate olfactory sensitivities—won't allow it in their cabs. So what's the allure? Cracking open the fruit, which releases even more of its stench, reveals the pulpy, cream-colored flesh that has a smooth, gelatinous consistency and a flavor like almond custard. It's an acquired taste.

452 Bull Penis in China: Yes, of course it's an aphrodisiac, one of many favored by Chinese gourmands. Bull penis is usually sliced lengthwise, then filleted in such a way that when it's served in soup—the usual presentation—it curls up and takes the shape of a pale, fleshy flower. The flavor and consistency are similar to calamari. If you're afraid you can't handle this, maybe your waiter could bring you something more palatable, like goat penis, chicken feet, donkey vulva, or dog penis. Naturally, you'll want to wash down whatever you're having with a refreshing slug of deer-penis juice.

453 Rats in Thailand: How could anyone resist these furry critters, especially when they're freshly roasted and served piping hot? The rats are trapped in rice paddies (where they fatten up on rice plants), drowned, skinned, then cooked in a wok with oil and spicy chili paste. Most first-timers are surprised at how pleasantly flavored rat meat is; not gamey at all, it's sometimes compared to rabbit. And the burgeoning market in rats helps to control the rodent population. Now, would someone please forward that info to the New York City subway authority?

454 Sago Worms in Papua New Guinea: The Asmat cannibals of Papua New Guinea would often eat the brains of their enemies, right out of the skull, mixed with a handful of sago worms. If you're more of a sago worm purist, however, you may want to forgo the brains and dine on these plump little slugs the modern way, roasted on a spit, or simply smoked. The larvae of the sago palm weevil, sago worms are about an inch or two long and are full of protein and other nutrients. Fans of the worms, who usually grab them by their hard little heads and tear off the body with their teeth, then throw the head away, describe the flavor as sweet and nutty.

455 Cuy (Guinea Pig) in Peru: You eat regular pig, so why not try guinea pig? Be aware, however, that unlike other delicacies that are disguised in soups and sauces, cuy are served whole, with the head and all limbs firmly attached. You'll find this dish on menus in Lima, Cuzco, and other large cities, where it's subject to a significant mark-up (tourist rip-off, perhaps?). In smaller towns like Arequipa, however, it's much more affordable. Depending on preparation, the skin can be crispy (again, like pork) and the meat is rich and flavorful.

456 Tacos de Sesos in Mexico: A mind is a terrible thing to waste, yet thousands of cow brains are tossed aside annually, without a thought to how delicious they could be cooked and stuffed into a soft, warm taco. Sad, isn't it? A favorite in Mexico for centuries, sesos have a pillowy texture and not much flavor of their own, so they're generally spiced up with some kind of hot salsa picante, a sprinkle of fresh cilantro, or a squeeze of lime. Though once banned in the U.S. due to fears of mad cow disease, tacos de sesos have staged a comeback and can sometimes be found at discriminating taquerias north of the border.

Auld Reekie Terror Tour
Gloom & Doom All Around
Edinburgh, Scotland

If you're among those who prefer their history served with a tinge of terror and a dash of the macabre, the Auld Reekie Terror Tour is just the thing for you. The city of Edinburgh is famous for its underground vaults, corridors, and buildings, and this tour highlights the places where torture, witchcraft, and crimes most foul were the norm.

Edinburgh, the capital of Scotland once known as Auld Reekie (the name translates as "old smoky" and referred to the smoke billowing out of coal chimneys), is rich with history going back to the prehistoric Stone Age settlements on the craggy hills that loom over the town. Not all of Edinburgh's history, however, has been a tale of fair maidens and gallant knights. This is the home of Major Weir, who with his sister was executed for witchcraft in 1670. It's also the town that inspired Robert Louis Stevenson's famous novel *The Strange Case of Dr. Jekyll and Mr. Hyde*, based on the actual life of local socialite criminal Deacon Brodie.

There are a number of tours available, including the **Ghost and Torture Tour,** which takes visitors to a reputed witchcraft temple still in use today. Tours last about 75 minutes and are available during the day and into the night. Guides on the **Terror Tour** regale visitors with stories from the Black Plague, which swept across Scotland in the 14th century and caused many of Edinburgh's citizens to be quarantined in horrific squalor. The tour, which is lit primarily by candles to heighten the effect, leads visitors through rooms and corridors where ghostly paranormal activity is reportedly high. If that doesn't scare you, the grisly **Torture Museum** might; it features implements used to extract confessions from witches, warlocks, prisoners, and other undesirables.

The tour might not be for everyone—some visitors have referred to it as crowded and campy, with a none-too-frightening spook tacked on to the end, and the pub at the tour's end is generally considered a tourist trap. But touristy or not, after reliving the tales of plague victims, witches, and murderers, you may need a drink. —*MI*

ⓘ **Auld Reekie Terror Tour,** 45 Niddry St. (✆ **44/131/557-4700;** www.auldreekietours.com).

WHEN TO GO: Year round.

✈ Edinburgh.

🛏 $$ **Malmaison,** 1 Tower Place (✆ **44/131/68-5000;** www.malmaison.com). $$$ **The Witchery by the Castle,** The Royal Mile (✆ **44/131/225-5613;** www.thewitchery.com).

Previous page: The Vild-Svinet roller coaster in Denmark.

Dracula Tours of Transylvania
Count Me In
Romania

The long, dark shadow of history casts a gloomy air across the Carpathian Mountains of Romania. In a country where the tyranny of Nicolae Ceauşescu is still a recent memory, an even more ominous legend has taken hold of the imagination—a legend that, like its namesake, refuses to die. Vlad III the Impaler, who inspired the legend of Count Dracula, was a murderous ruler famed for his bloody torture and executions; impaling his victims and displaying their bodies in public was his favorite method of planting terror in the minds of his numerous political enemies. The sites where Vlad was born, lived, and was buried are now open for visits.

Most tours of this ruggedly beautiful country begin and end in the capital city of Bucharest. Dracula tours to Transylvania (a region in west-central Romania) will usually include sites such as the citadel of Sighisoara, where Vlad was born, and the Snagov Monastery, where Vlad was buried after his assassination. Though some tours include stops at Bran Castle, an impressive medieval fortress, Dracula purists know that the ruins of the castle at Poienari are more likely to have been Vlad's redoubt.

Separating historical fact from Hollywood-style vampire stories can be difficult, and some commercial tours seem to highlight the kitschier aspects of the Dracula

Dracula's castle in Romania.

legend. Vampire-themed hotel rooms with velvet-lined coffins, dinners with blood-wine drinks, and costumed entertainers driving stakes through an actor's heart, however amusing, might not be suited to every visitor's tastes. (You may have to forgive your waiter if his plastic vampire teeth fall into your goulash.)

None of this silliness, however, should detract from the dramatic beauty and cultural charms of a region that seems rooted in the past. Quaint villages, grand cathedrals, and vibrant cities are yours to enjoy,

as long as you avoid the man in the black cape with the bad teeth. —*ML*

ⓘ **Romanian National Tourist Office** (✆ **212/545-8484;** www.romaniatourism. com).

TOURS: Adventure Transylvania (✆ **40/727/394-727;** www.adventure transylvania.com). **Dracula Tour** (✆ **203/ 795-4373;** www.dractour.com).

WHEN TO GO: May–Oct.

✈ Bucharest.

459 Spooks & Scares

Eastern State Penitentiary
The Silent Treatment
Philadelphia, Pennsylvania, U.S.A.

Eastern State Penitentiary, which opened in Philadelphia in 1829 (and closed in 1971), was designed to be an enlightened institution that would reform, not punish, the prisoners interred there. But the experiment went horribly wrong. Strict solitary confinement in tiny cells, it was believed, would allow prisoners to reflect on their crimes, become penitent and mend their ways; the word "penitentiary," in fact, originated at Eastern State. In practice, however, the severe deprivation of all human contact drove more than one prisoner mad. Author Charles Dickens visited the hulking neo-Gothic structure and was appalled: "I hold the slow and daily tampering with the mysteries of the brain to be immeasurably worse than any torture of the body," he declared.

Located just a few blocks from Philadelphia's renowned **Museum of Art** (www. philamuseum.org) and **Fairmount Park** (www.fairmountpark.org), Eastern State Penitentiary now gives visitors the chance to experience the same degree of shock and disgust that Dickens felt by taking a tour of the 11-acre site. In addition to regular daytime tours, limited groups are

Scare yourself stiff at a tour of Eastern State Penitentiary.

allowed to visit ESP during twilight hours and on specially scheduled winter tours. For the truly brave at heart, Eastern State is also the home of **Terror Behind the Walls,** widely recognized as one of the best—and most realistic—haunted "houses" in the country. Actors portraying inmates and guards reenact the horror experienced inside ESP for guests during Terror Behind the Wall's seven-week run each fall.

When it was opened, Eastern State was the largest building in North America and reportedly the most costly. Its revolutionary approach to crime and punishment is reflected in the building's design; eight spokes radiate out from a central tower, giving prison guards unprecedented access and visibility. Prisoners' cells had only the most spartan furnishings and a small skylight known as "the eye of God." Entrance to the cells is gained through a small pair of doors, intended to ensure absolute quiet for the prisoners' reflection. Strict silence was so essential to the atmosphere at ESP that guards wore socks over their shoes to muffle their footsteps.

It wasn't just the environment that was severe at Eastern State. Prisoners could leave their cells only with hoods over their heads, and punishments for violating rules on silence and other transgressions bordered on the medieval. Some prisoners were forced to stand outside in freezing weather, stripped to the waist, while water was sprayed on them. One particularly gruesome punishment involved an iron clamp on the tongue that would cut deeper into the inmate's mouth if he moved. Were these sadistic punishments and the macabre atmosphere the cause of the numerous paranormal sightings in the prison? Possibly—but nobody's talking. —ML

(i) **Eastern State Penitentiary,** 22nd and Fairmount Ave., Philadelphia, PA (C) **215/236-3300;** www.easternstate. org).

WHEN TO GO: Year-round.

✈ Philadelphia International Airport (13 miles/21km).

🛏 $$$ **Hotel Windsor,** 1700 Benjamin Franklin Pkwy., City Center (C) **215/981-5600;** www.hotelwindsor.com). $$ **Alexander Inn,** 301 S. 12th St. (C) **215/923-3535;** www.alexanderinn.com).

Spooks & Scares **460**

Museo de las Momias
Where's My Mummy?
Guanajuato, Mexico

The dead rest in peace—you hope. But Mexico is a country famous for its friendly relationship with the deceased, and in one of that country's most beautiful colonial cities, the dead have come back and are receiving visitors by the thousands. Room after room of mummified corpses in near-perfect states of preservation are on view at el Museo de las Momias (the Museum of the Mummies) in Guanajuato. For a tingle down your spine and a quickened pulse, pay a visit here.

The one-of-a-kind museum is located in a hillside underneath a cemetery in this picturesque mining town, located in a mountainous region of central Mexico roughly 350km (220 miles) northwest of Mexico City. The town itself is a tangle of old colonial pathways, staircases, and charming plazas. If you're looking for the museum (or any other specific place), expect to spend at least a few minutes getting directions or getting lost. There is a city bus marked "Las Momias" that might make the trip a little easier; the bus doesn't go directly to the museum, but just ask the driver to point out the street that leads uphill to the museum.

The mummies were exhumed from the local cemetery because of a grave tax the city once levied on the families of the dead. Beginning in the 1860s, families who either moved away or were unable to pay the tax had their deceased taken out of the cemetery to make way for the newly departed. Due to the arid conditions in the region, and possibly the influence of some gases and minerals in the gravesites' soil, the bodies were remarkably well-preserved. Many are wearing all the clothes in which they were buried; some have only shoes or socks remaining. Infants and the elderly alike are represented in the glass-cased exhibits. And according to local legend, not all the dead were dearly departed—one woman is said to have been buried alive. The position of her arms and the scratch marks on her face give credence to this story.

After you return to the land of the living, don't miss out on Guanajuato's other sights. The city was once a wealthy mining town, supplying much of Spain's silver during its colonial heyday, and its fortunes are well-represented in the city's many 18th-century villas, churches, plazas, and ranching haciendas. A visit to the boyhood home of artist Diego Rivera (Calle Positos 47) and the Museo del Pueblo de Guanajuato (Calle Positos 7) round out a visit to this quaint city. —ML

ⓘ **Museo de las Momias,** Esplanada del Panteón (✆ **52/473/732-0639**). **State Tourism Office,** Plaza de la Paz 14 (✆ **52/473/732-1574**).

WHEN TO GO: Year-round.

✈ Leon/Guanajuato, Mexico.

🛏 $$ **Hotel Posada Santa Fé,** Jardín Unión 12 (✆ **473/732-0084;** www.posada santafe.com). $$$ **Hotel Antiguo Vapor,** Galarza 5 (✆ **473/732-3211;** www.hotel avapor.com).

461 Spooks & Scares

International Museum of Surgical Science
A Monument to the Macabre
Chicago, Illinois, U.S.A.

The **International Museum of Surgical Science** is an unintentionally macabre shrine to medicine, with some utterly bizarre exhibitions. This museum is both educational and fascinating, but don't come here expecting state-of-the-art interactive computer displays. This place has more the look and feel of a Victorian curio cabinet, and is a type of monument to the macabre.

Not for the faint of stomach, it occupies a historic 1917 mansion in Chicago's renowned Gold Coast designed by the noted architect Howard Van Doren Shaw, who modeled it after Le Petit Trianon at Versailles. Displayed throughout its four

floors are surgical instruments, paintings, and sculptures depicting the history of surgery and healing practices in Eastern and Western civilizations. (It's run by the International College of Surgeons.) The exhibits are old-fashioned (no interactive computer displays here), but that's part of the museum's odd appeal.

You'll look at your doctor in a whole new way after viewing the trepanned skulls excavated from an ancient tomb in Peru. The accompanying tools bored holes in patients' skulls, a horrific practice thought to release the evil spirits causing their illness. (Some skulls show signs of new bone growth, meaning that some

Skulls & Bones & Catacombs

If your taste in adventure runs toward the dark side, few places will satisfy your macabre impulses more than a visit to an old catacomb, tomb, or ossuary. Some go back to ancient times, while others were in operation as recently as the 1970s. Because these are often underground tours through miles of human remains, they're not recommended for the claustrophobic, the squeamish, or for anyone—kids or adults—who may have nightmares as a result. Don't say we didn't warn you. —*ML*

462 Les Catacombes de Paris, France: After many generations, the graveyards of Paris were filled to overflowing—literally. By the late 1700s, bodies spilling out of many graveyards had become a public health menace, so city officials decided to move the remains into the city's vast underground network of tunneled quarries. For decades, the city's graveyards were emptied and the bones were interred in these tunnels, which have been open to the public since 1810. The entrance to the Catacombs is near the Denfert-Rochereau Metro stop in the Montparnasse area. After walking through a simple museum, you're free to wander through stacks and stacks of dried bones and artfully arranged skulls. *www.catacombes-de-paris.fr.*

463 The Catacombs of the Capuchins, Palermo, Italy: A mysterious preservative found here acts as a natural mummifier, maintaining human remains in a startlingly lifelike way. The Sicilians found here are well-attired and smartly coiffed, as if expecting visitors. Rosalia Lombaro, who was buried when she was just 2 years old, is one resident visitors never forget. She still has all her hair tied back in a faded ribbon and is so well preserved that she appears to be napping, giving her the nickname "Sleeping Beauty." *Azienda Autonoma Turismo (© 39/91-6058111).*

464 The Skull Tower, Nis, Serbia: In 1809, Serbian rebels fighting the Turkish Ottomans advanced toward Nis, only to be thwarted on Cegar Hill by the much stronger Turkish forces. Rather than surrender, Serbian troop leader Stevan Sindelic fired at his own gunpowder supplies; the resulting fireball killed Sindelic, his troops, and the Turks. As a warning to other Serb rebels, the Turkish commander had the rebels' bodies decapitated and their skulls built into the walls of a tower, with Sindelic's skull at the top. In 1892, after the tower deteriorated from exposure to the elements, a chapel was constructed to enclose the tower. It remains a moving monument to the sacrifices of war. *www.ni.rs.*

465 The Catacombs, Rome, Italy: There are dozens of catacombs in and around Rome, but most are closed to the public. Those that allow tours are usually operated by religious orders and have limited operating hours. The **Catacombs of St. Domitilla** stand out; after entering through a sunken 4th-century church, you'll see the actual bones of the deceased and an impressive 2nd-century fresco of the Last Supper. In the **Catacombs of St. Sebastian,** highlights include early Christian mosaics and graffiti. The biggest, most popular, and most crowded site, the **Catacombs of St. Callixtus,** has a vast network of galleries that house the crypts of 16 popes, as well as early Christian statues and paintings. *www.catacombsociety.org.*

466 Veliki Tabor, Zagorje, Croatia: Sometimes there's a terrible price to be paid for beauty. Just ask Veronika of Desinic, a lovely 15th-century maiden who captured the heart of Frederich, son of Count Herman II of Celje, who resided in the castle known as Veliki Tabor. The star-crossed lovers eloped and were married against the wishes of the evil Count. He had Veronika tried as a witch; the judges, however, took pity on the beautiful woman and set her free. Not one to be easily dismissed, the furious Count had her drowned and her body bricked up inside Veliki Tabor's pentagonal tower. During a 1982 renovation of the castle, a woman's skull was supposedly discovered; it now resides in a place of honor in the castle's chapel. Some say the ghost of Veronika can still be heard. *www.visitcroatia.net.*

467 Choeung Ek, Cambodia: Choeung Ek is one of the sites known as the Killing Fields, where the Khmer Rouge regime slaughtered some 17,000 people between 1975 and 1979. Over 8,800 bodies have been discovered at Choeung Ek; many of the dead were inmates in the nearby Tuol Sleng prison, where tours are also available. Open pits where mass graves were found are scattered around the site; the bones of those killed here still litter the area. A tall monument, now a Buddhist stupa (or reliquary), contains skulls carefully arranged by age and gender—it's 17 stories high, to remind visitors of the April 17, 1975, date the Khmer Rouge seized power.

468 The Catacombs of St. John, Syracuse, Italy: The catacombs of St. John, accessed through the ruins of the Chiesa di San Giovanni, were originally developed by the ancient Greeks as an underground aqueduct. Early Christians used it to bury their dead because they were forbidden by the Romans from using city graveyards. The site now contains roughly 20,000 tombs, housed in long tunnels that are honeycombed with coffins; they're now empty, having been looted by grave robbers long ago of any artifacts or remains. *Turismo, Via San Sebastiano 43 (✆ 39/931-481232).*

469 Kostnice "Bone Church," Kutna Hora, Czech Republic: For sheer creativity, it's hard to match the interior design of this Gothic church. A widely used graveyard since the Black Plague, the church cemetery had plenty of skeletal remains at hand, and what better material to decorate the inside of the church? Apparently Frantisek Rint, the fellow hired in 1870 to put the countless heaps of bones in order, thought they were the perfect decorative touch to liven up his plain little church. Rint used human bones and skulls to create, among other charms, a chandelier of bones, necklace-like strands of skulls draped from the ceiling, a coat-of-arms—even the artist's signature was written in bone. *www.kostnice.cz.*

470 St. Michan's Church, Dublin, Ireland: The limestone walls of this church's burial vault act as a preservative, so the bodies buried here are remarkably well mummified. Visitors can see the remains inside four of the vault's opened coffins; sharp-eyed viewers will note that two of the bodies were cut into pieces before they were put in their caskets. Rumor has it that Bram Stoker visited the site as a child, inspiring him to write Dracula some years later. *www.visitdublin.com.*

lucky headache-sufferers actually survived the low-tech surgery.) There are also primitive battlefield amputation kits, a working iron-lung machine in the polio exhibit, and oddities such as a stethoscope designed to be transported inside a top hat. Other attractions include an apothecary shop and dentist's office (ca. 1900) re-created in a historic street exhibit, and the hyperbolically titled *Hall of Immortals,* a sculpture gallery depicting 12 historic figures in medicine from Hippocrates to Madame Curie. —*ML*

ⓘ **International Museum of Surgical Science,** 1524 N. Lake Shore Dr. (ⓒ **312/ 642-6502;** www.imss.org).

WHEN TO GO: Year-round.

✈ O'Hare International (15 miles/24km).

🛏 $$ **Hotel Allegro,** 171 N. Randolph St. (ⓒ **800/643-1500;** www.allegro chicago.com).

Plenty of spine-tingling relics are on display at the International Museum of Surgical Science in Chicago.

Spooks & Scares **471**

Winchester Mystery House
An Unsolved Mystery
San Jose, California, U.S.A.

Staircases that lead directly up to a ceiling and stop. Doors that open onto solid walls. A séance room with a floorless closet and a secret passageway. A window with a spider web design featuring 13 colored stones, to match the 13 palm trees in the driveway, and the 13 bathrooms, and the 13 coat hooks in the closets, and the chandeliers with 13 lights. Even if you don't believe in the supernatural aura that surrounds the **Winchester Mystery House,** you can't deny that there is something

utterly bewildering and spine-tingling about this immense, ornate Victorian mansion.

According to legend, Sarah Winchester was devastated by the deaths of her daughter and her husband William. As president of the Winchester Repeating Arms Company, Mr. Winchester was renowned as the man whose rifles tamed the American West—at a cost of thousands of lives. When his grieving widow sought the advice of a spiritualist following his death, she was told that the ghosts of

The Winchester Mystery House.

those killed by his rifles would haunt her unless she built them a home. So she built, and built, and built, employing carpenters and craftsmen working 24 hours a day for 38 years until she created a seven-story monstrosity that confounds all explanation. When she died in 1922, work immediately stopped, so quickly that in many cases nails were left half pounded into place.

The house was built around an existing farmhouse, parts of which can still be seen inside the rambling structure. Because there were no blueprints, the house was added onto in an irregular pattern until it spread out over most of the current 4½-acre (1.2-hectare) site. Some claim that the confusing pattern of hallways, staircases, and rooms were designed by Mrs. Winchester to confuse the spirits who might still haunt the mansion. Repeated sightings of spirits, and of voices that haunt the employees who work there, have only added to the creepy atmosphere of this uniquely bizarre landmark.

The Winchester Mystery House is located in the heart of San Jose, surrounded by the high-tech industries of Silicon Valley. Tours lasting about 65 minutes are offered year-round except for Christmas Day, and there are a number of options, including a behind-the-scenes tour and—for the brave at heart—special flashlight tours offered only during the Halloween season and every Friday the 13th. Because of the design of the house, not all tours are open to children or the physically handicapped. —ML

ⓘ **Winchester Mystery House,** 525 S. Winchester Blvd. (ⓒ **408/247-2101;** www. winchestermysteryhouse.com).

WHEN TO GO: Year-round.

✈ San Jose.

🛏 $$$$ **The Fairmont San Jose,** 170 S. Market St. (ⓒ **866/540-4493** or 408/998-1900; www.fairmont.com). $$ **Moorpark Hotel,** 4241 Moorpark Blvd. (ⓒ **408/864-0300;** www.jdvhotels.com).

Ypres Battlefields
In Flanders Fields, the Poppies Blow
Ypres, Belgium

In the early days of World War I, with the German army advancing through Belgium toward France and England, just one city stood in their way: Ypres, an ancient city in West Flanders that was heavily fortified with ramparts during its reign as a medieval trading capital. Surrounding the city on three sides, the Germans bombarded it relentlessly until the beleaguered city finally fell to the invading army. But after Ypres was captured by the Germans, the Allied response was swift and strong. Troops from France, England, New Zealand, America, Australia, Canada, Senegal, and Algeria rallied to rout the Germans from the city's walls. After many bloody battles, the Allied forces eventually succeeded, but at a horrific cost: About half a million men lost their lives to gain just a few miles of territory—in just one battle. It was the single deadliest military campaign of World War I.

Ypres (pronounced *ee*-pruh) is situated in the softly rolling hills of the West Flanders Heuvelland, or Hill Country. Because of its out-of-the-way location, visitors often combine a trip to the city with a visit to Bruges or other coastal destinations. Trains from Bruges depart hourly and are recommended over the local buses; look for the Dutch name of the city, Leper, on local signage.

Tour guides are able to bring to life many of the features of the area's battlefields and of the city itself. Because Ypres was reduced to rubble following the bombardments of World War I, many of the buildings were entirely rebuilt after the war. Perhaps the most famous of these is the Cloth Hall (Lakenhalle), an opulent reminder of the city's wealth when it was a center of the textile trade. Surrounding it are many of the town's guild houses and mansions, which now hold cafes, hotels, and restaurants.

Ypres isn't all faded glory, however; the city hosts a carefree carnival known as Kattestoet, or Festival of the Cats. The event, taking place every 3 years in May, celebrates the role that cats played in ridding the Cloth Hall of mice. When the cats themselves became a nuisance, hundreds were tossed from the hall's belfry (today, stuffed feline toys substitute for the real thing). Bellewaerde Park (www.bellewaerde.be) is an area amusement park with terror-inducing rides like the Screaming Eagle, as well as a wildlife reserve. —*ML*

TOURS: Visit Ypres (✆ **32/57/20-43-42;** www.visit-ypres.be). **Over the Top Tours** (✆ **32/57/42-43-20;** www.overthetop tours.be).

WHEN TO GO: Year-round.

✈ Brussels (124km/77miles).

🛏 $ **Old Tom,** Grote Markt 8 (✆ **32/ 57/20-15-413;** www.oldtom.be). $$ **Regina,** Koning Albert I 45 (✆ **32/57/21-88-88;** www.hotelregina.com).

Charleville Castle
Ireland's Haunted Fortress
Tullamore, County Offaly, Ireland

Even in a land steeped in mystery and superstition, **Charleville Castle** stands out as one of the most haunting places in all of Ireland. Paranormal teams from around the world, including television crews from *Scariest Places on Earth* and *Most Haunted*, have investigated the goings-on at the castle and come away with reports that the place is indeed visited by denizens of the spirit world. Perhaps they saw the ghost of Harriet Bury, the 8-year-old girl who fell to her death while sliding down the banister of the castle's ornate stairwell. Or maybe it was the glowing orbs of light that many local residents claim to have seen in the castle and

on the grounds. Whatever the circumstances, Charleville Castle remains an eerily beautiful place and a must-see for visitors interested in things that go bump in the night.

Built in 1798 by Charles William Bury, Earl of Charleville, the Gothic-style castle is located about 97km (60 miles) west of Dublin in one of the oldest forests left in the British Isles, filled with the immense oaks revered by ancient druid priests. The castle, in fact, is reportedly built on the site of a prehistoric druid ceremonial circle, which may explain some of the supernatural energy that surrounds the place. One of the oldest and most massive oak

Spirits haunt the halls of Charleville Castle.

trees on the property, the King Oak, has an ominous legend attached to it: When one of its branches falls, a resident of the castle will die. Foolish superstition? In 1963, the tree was struck by lightning and a large branch broke off. Two weeks later, Colonel Charles Bury, the last of the Bury family to own the castle, suddenly died.

Even without its otherworldly reputation, Charleville Castle would be well worth a visit. Its exquisite limestone exterior is marked by lofty, crenellated towers and battlements. Hand-carved stairways, stunning plasterwork, and a dining room designed by William Morris, a founder of the Arts and Crafts movement, are among the highlights of the guided tour. And, of course, what haunted castle would be complete without a dungeon? Charleville Castle has that, too, along with all the flickering chandeliers and secret passageways your fluttering heart could desire. —*ML*

ⓘ **Charleville Castle** (ⓒ **0506/41581;** www.charlevillecastle.com).

WHEN TO GO: Most travelers prefer to visit Ireland between Apr and Oct; expect more crowds and higher prices in July and Aug.

✈ Dublin (97km/60 miles).

⊨ $$$ **Bridge House Hotel and Leisure Club,** Tullamore (ⓒ **57/325600;** www.bridgehouse.com). $$ **Days Hotel Tullamore,** Main St., Tullamore (ⓒ **63/91136;** www.dayshoteltullamore.com).

Spooks & Scares 474

Haunted New Orleans
Boo, Y'all!
New Orleans, Louisiana, U.S.A.

If any city can lay claim to being America's most haunted city, New Orleans would have to be the one, where the dead are buried aboveground and moss hangs heavy in the live oak trees. Two Civil War soldiers appear in a mansion's upstairs window, singing an old drinking tune. Heavy footsteps echo in the hallway from a man who was buried alive in the courtyard of his crumbling villa. The sound of a piano plays from a room where there is no piano. A young girl appears in a mirror of a hotel room—but she's not in the room. Visitors to this fabled city can see the sites of these and other supernatural occurrences on tours of haunted New Orleans.

There are a number of tour operators in the Crescent City; some tours specialize in haunted hotels and bars, other tours focus on cemeteries, while still others traverse the gloomy mansions and villas of the French Quarter and the Garden District.

Tours can last from 1 hour to an entire day, and group tours for wedding parties, conventions, and school events can be arranged. Most of the ghost and vampire tours operate in the evening; cemetery and voodoo tours are more likely to occur during the day (cemeteries are usually closed at night—to the living). Reservations are often required, and it's recommended to call ahead to ask about schedules, group sizes, and other specifics. While some tour operators offer great storytelling and historical information, others emphasize the campier, more theatrical side of ghouls and ghosts.

With almost 300 years of colorful history, New Orleans is one of America's most unique cities, though much of her history has been dark, turbulent, and bloody. It was a wealthy port for most of its early years, and much of that wealth was derived from the slave trade. It was also the site of numerous deadly epidemics and several devastating hurricanes and floods. All of these contribute to the town's rich store of macabre tales. From voodoo queens and mansion murder scenes to haunted cemeteries and slave quarters, New Orleans and her ghosts are ready to meet you. —ML

(i) **New Orleans Metropolitan Convention and Visitors Bureau** (© **800/672-6124** or 504/566-5011; www.neworleans cvb.com).

TOURS: Magic Tours, LLC, 714 N. Rampart (© **504/588-9693;** www.magictours nola.com). **Haunted History Tours,** 97 Fontainebleau Dr. (© **888/6-GHOSTS** [446787] or 504/861-2727; www.haunted historytours.com).

WHEN TO GO: Year-round.

✈ New Orleans.

🛏 $$$ **Hotel Monteleone,** 214 Royal St. (© **800/535-9595** or 504/523-3341; www.hotelmonteleone.com). $$ **Le Pavillon Hotel,** 833 Poydras St. (© **800/535-9095** or 504/581-3111; www.lepavillon.com).

---

475 Rides

Star Flyer at Tivoli Gardens
Make Me a Star
Copenhagen, Denmark

In the middle of Copenhagen's charming (if schmaltzy) Tivoli Gardens is a ride that has thrill-seekers clamoring for more: The Star Flyer sends riders streaking through the air at speeds up to 72kmph (45 mph) while dangling 78m (260 ft.) above the ground. It's guaranteed to get the adrenaline pumping in even the most jaded amusement park tourist.

Tivoli Gardens is located in the center of Copenhagen and is among its most cherished institutions. Since opening in 1843, millions of visitors have embraced the park's artfully manicured flower gardens, Chinese tower, and musicians. When electricity became available, Tivoli Gardens outfitted itself with millions of light bulbs, making it an enchanting nighttime attraction. The wooden roller coaster—still in operation—debuted in 1914, and The Daemonen, the biggest roller coaster in Denmark, joined it in 2004. The newest ride in Tivoli Gardens is Vertigo, a flight simulator that launches passengers through the air at 97kmph (60 mph).

The Star Flyer is sure to please even the most jaded amusement park tourist.

The Star Flyer is the world's tallest carousel tower; riders board one of 12 passenger seats that are attached to a central star-shaped car. As the car ascends, it rotates on its axis, causing the 12 seats to lift into the air and spin around

10 Haunted Houses of the American South

Perhaps no other region of America conjures up visions of ghostly apparitions like the South. Stately old antebellum mansions, often abandoned to the ravages of time, loom from behind moss-draped trees. The specter of Confederate soldiers, still fighting a lost cause, adds to the gothic atmosphere. Many of these houses are now hotels or B&Bs, making your visit easier—but no less chilling. —*ML*

476 LaLaurie Mansion, New Orleans, Louisiana: Dark goings-on at this French Quarter mansion have been a part of New Orleans legend for years. Delphine LaLaurie, the wealthy socialite behind these stories, was reputedly a sadist who mercilessly beat and tortured her slaves. During a dinner party in 1834, a fire started in the kitchen, reportedly by the slaves who were chained to the stove. That night, after guests witnessed the sight of chained and beaten slaves, the LaLauries fled the city in disgrace. The discovery of graves, reportedly hidden in the foundation of the home, has done nothing to dispel the grim reputation of this most haunted house. *www.hauntedamericatours.com.*

477 Menger Hotel, San Antonio, Texas: Teddy Roosevelt, who recruited cowboys fresh off the Chisholm Trail to join his Rough Riders, reportedly still frequents the bar at this ornate 1859 palace, looking for new recruits. Located next to the Alamo, some of the soldiers who died in that famous battle still come by, wearing their buckskins and boots. Most famously, a hotel chambermaid named Sallie White, who was murdered by her husband at the hotel, still performs occasional duties, delivering fresh towels to hotel guests. Now *that's* service. *www.mengerhotel.com.*

478 Magnolia Manor, Bolivar, Tennessee: This elegant manor home from 1849, owned by the same family until the 1970s, is now a B&B. Guests have reported seeing the same apparitions. An elderly woman sits in a rocking chair in the corner, quietly humming a tune. She also walks the hallways, carrying a lit candle. Whitey, a white cat owned by a previous resident, slinks along hallways at night. Doors open and close on their own, and lights switch on and off. *www.magnoliamanorbolivartn.com.*

479 Hammock House, Beaufort, North Carolina: The infamous pirate Black Beard (also known as Edward Teach) supposedly kept a young woman against her will in this 18th-century house, whom he hung from an oak tree in the backyard—her screams still haunt the night air. Other incidents have darkened the reputation of this old house. Richard Russell, who owned the home in the 1740s, tried to punish one of his slaves, but the slave pushed him down the stairs, breaking Russell's neck. He occasionally returns, looking for the rebellious slave. When the Union Army occupied Beaufort during the Civil War, three officers visiting the home disappeared, though they can be heard stomping around the hallways. Their bones were discovered near the back porch in 1915. *www.beaufort-nc.com.*

480 Kehoe House, Savannah, Georgia: It's the twins that most visitors to this charming hotel tell of seeing. The two children were playing in the chimney when they were accidentally killed. Guests staying in Rooms 201 and 203 report hearing children's laughter and the patter of small feet running. Other guests and employees of this 1892 inn, listed on the National Register of Historic Places, have had to contend with doors opening and closing on their own, and the vision of a woman dressed in white. *www.kehoehouse.com.*

481 **The St. James Hotel, Selma, Alabama:** There are no pets allowed in this elegantly restored hotel, but guests keep hearing the sound of a barking dog in the interior courtyard. Some say he's the pet of Jesse James, the outlaw who frequented the hotel in the 1800s, and is sometimes seen—especially in Rooms 214, 314, and 315, or at his favorite corner table. Maybe Jesse comes back looking for his other pet, the beautiful, raven-haired Lucinda, who can still be seen strolling the hallways, the scent of her lavender perfume wafting after her. *1222 Water Ave.* ✆ ***334/872-7055.***

482 **Peavey Melody Music, Meridian, Mississippi:** This nondescript building was the original home of Peavey Electronics. Shortly after it was built in 1906, a tornado struck Meridian, killing scores of people; the victims' bodies were stacked on the second floor of this building, which was a funeral parlor at the time. Many of the injured were children who died here while waiting for medical assistance. Employees have heard running and the laughter of children on the second floor late in the evening. *www.visitmeridian.com.*

483 **Cedar Grove Inn, Vicksburg, Mississippi:** The wealthy Southern gentleman John Klein gave this stately Greek Revival mansion to his bride Elizabeth as a wedding gift in 1840. Guests to the inn describe smelling the smoke from his pipe at odd intervals. After several family graves were moved in 1919, visitors started seeing a young girl whose grave was among those moved. *www.cedargroveinn.com.*

The charming Eliza Thompson House hosts a variety of ghosts.

484 **Eliza Thompson House, Savannah, Georgia:** If you're a light sleeper, avoid Room 132 in this lovingly restored B&B. Guests there report hearing the gleeful laughter of children all night long—sometimes even being pushed out of bed to join in the play. Eliza's son James, a confederate soldier, was killed by a horse right in front of the property, and his visage is sometimes seen looking out the window. *www.elizathompsonhouse.com.*

485 **Sturdivant Hall, Selma, Alabama:** Wealthy banker John Parkman, president of the First National Bank of Selma, owned this elegant home during the Reconstruction period until he was arrested for cotton speculation. While trying to escape from prison, he was killed. He still wanders the grounds of his former home, opening doors with strong breezes on otherwise windless days, and leaving imprints on freshly made beds. *www.sturdivanthall.com.*

the tower. Not only is this a thrilling ride, but it's also a great way to sight-see as the city of Copenhagen reveals itself below. There's more to see on the ground, too: Live concerts featuring world-class musicians such as Sting, the Pet Shop Boys, and Smashing Pumpkins occur during summer months. The amusement park's Concert Hall and Pantomime Theater also host performances, plays, and classical concerts, and there are dozens of places to eat, drink, and relax after all your thrill rides are over. —ML

(i) **Tivoli Gardens** (© **33/75-03-38;** www.tivoli.dk).

WHEN TO GO: May–Sept.

✈ Copenhagen.

🛏 $$$ **First Hotel Vesterbro,** Vesterbrogade 23–29 (© **33/78-80-00;** www. firsthotels.com). $$ **Hotel Fox,** Jarmer Plads 3 (© **33/13-30-00;** www.hotelfox.dk).

Rides 486

Zero Gravity Thrill Amusement Park
One-Stop Adrenaline Shopping
Dallas, Texas, U.S.A.

If you're looking for one-stop adrenaline shopping that's kid friendly, the **Zero Gravity Thrill Amusement Park** in Dallas is the place for you. This adventure playland promises fun for the whole family—assuming, of course, you have a pretty daring family.

Start off by **bungee jumping** from the park's seven-story Air Boingo tower. Next, try the Skycoaster, which simulates hang gliding 110 feet (34m) above the ground and reaches speeds up to 60 mph (96kmph). When you're all strapped in and ready to fly, you can pull your own ripcord and off you go. If you'd rather not go alone, that's fine too. Thanks to ultra-strong steel cables and professional hang-gliding harnesses, up to three people can fly together at a time.

After you come down from these heights, check out the **Texas Blastoff,** which rockets you and a friend (or family member) up into the air for 150 feet (46m). Using four strong bungee cords attached to two steel towers, this ride launches you in a seat-like harness made from racing seats. With your whole body, including your feet, strapped in, you'll race up toward the sky, going from zero to 70 mph (112kmph) in 1.2 seconds! Expect to flip, twist, and turn along the way.

With adrenaline coursing through your veins, you should feel free to call it a day. But if you're ready for one more thrill ride, it's time to attempt a freefall from **Nothin' but Net.** You're lifted almost 16 stories high, just below the top of the tower, and then dropped 100 feet (30m) into two safety nets below. There's no bungee cord, no parachute, no harness—it's just you soaring through the air. A patented release system ensures that you'll fall straight on your back, even if you try to twist or turn, guaranteeing a smooth landing—a welcome end to your fast-moving day. —JS

(i) **Zero Gravity Thrill Amusement Park,** 11131 Malibu Dr. (© **972/484-8359;** www.gojump.com).

WHEN TO GO: Sept–May.

✈ Dallas Fort Worth International Airport (15 miles/24km).

🛏 $$–$$$ **Hotel Palomar Dallas,** 5300 E. Mockingbird Lane (© **888/253-9030;** www.hotelpalomar-dallas.com). $$ **Omni Dallas Hotel at Park West,** 1590 LBJ Fwy. (© **972/869-4300;** www.omnihotels. com).

Interactive Flight Simulators
Fly to the Space Station
Washington, D.C., U.S.A.

Would you rather test your skills at air-to-air combat in an F-4 Phantom II jet fighter, or launch into space on a shuttle? Lucky you—you don't have to choose. You can do both at the **Smithsonian National Air and Space Museum** on the National Mall in Washington, D.C. The simulation rides are designed to fool your senses, and they do without subjecting you to g-forces. These rides grew out of simulations for military applications.

If you want to fly a jet with a pal, choose the two-person **F-18 Super Hornet Experience.** After a fast training session, the "pilot" takes off from an aircraft carrier using a throttle to control the speed and a joy stick to control whether the plane goes up, down, or does 360° barrel roles. (Empty change from your pockets before taking this ride!) The second person on the flight is the gunner, who releases virtual radar-guided and heat-seeking missiles at approaching targets.

If you'd rather be a passenger, choose the **Space Walk** or **Wings.** On the Space Walk you'll be sitting in an astronaut's chair inside a shuttle during the launch. You'll get the sensation of floating gravity-free as you fly through space until you reach the Space Station. Once there, you'll get a personal tour of the inside of the station, then suit up for an outside stroll. Watching Wings, you'll sit in the pilot's seat for a fast-paced tour of the history of aviation by flying various planes ranging from the Sopwith Camel of World War I, to early bi-planes all the way through to the F-5 Tiger jet.

If after the flight and space-flight simulators you're still in need of more excitement, there are roller coaster rides, like the **Cosmic Coaster,** which takes you on a white-knuckle journey through the cosmos. Be prepared to rock and roll, and even scream as you "fly" through a futuristic image of space.

Entry to the museum is free, but there is a charge (under $10) for the simulator rides, which are located in the West Wing Gallery 103. After paying, you enter a queue for the ride you've chosen. Most of the rides take about 5 to 6 minutes.

You can also take these simulator rides at the Smithsonian National Air and Space Museum satellite at the **Steven F. Udvar-Hazy Center.** This companion facility near Washington Dulles International Airport houses the space shuttle **Enterprise,** the **Lockheed SR-71 Blackbird,** and other large planes. At this facility, you can also see the **Space Walk in 3D** (using 3D glasses), which increases the sense of being out in space. —LF

ⓘ **Smithsonian National Air and Space Museum,** National Mall Building, Independence Ave. at Sixth St SW (✆ **202/633-1000;** www.nasm.si.edu/museum). **Steven F. Udvar-Hazy Center,** 14390 Air and Space Museum Pkwy., Chantilly, VA (www.nasm.si.edu/UdvarHazy).

WHEN TO GO: Year-round. Closed Christmas Day.

✈ Ronald Reagan Washington National (5 miles/8km). Dulles International (26 miles/42km). Baltimore-Washington International (30 miles/48km).

🛏 $$ **Embassy Suites Hotel Downtown,** 1250 22nd St. NW (✆ **800/ EMBASSY** [362-2779] or 202/857-3388; www.embassysuitesdcmetro.com). $$$ **Hilton Washington,** 1919 Connecticut Ave. NW (✆ **800/HILTONS** [445-8667] or 202/483-3000; www.washinton.hilton.com).

Rides 488

Gilley's Dallas
Riding El Toro
Dallas, Texas, U.S.A.

Rockin' and rollin' takes on new meaning as you desperately try to hang on to the mechanical bull that is jerking forward and backward, and side to side. It looked like fun when you and your friends dared each other to try it, but now that you're being shaken around you're not so sure. Whoa! You fly off on to the blow-up mat designed to cushion your fall. Tip from one rider: Never try it as a twosome.

Bull riders traditionally train on mechanical bulls, but riding these critters in bars became a craze after the 1980 movie hit *Urban Cowboy*. The original Gilley's was a honky-tonk bar opened by country singer Michael Gilley and Sherwood Cryer in Pasadena, Texas, in 1971. People flocked to Gilley's to ride the mechanical bull and

hang around this Texas-size western bar, with its tin ceiling, just like characters did in this movie's tale of young love.

The original bar closed in the 1980s, but in 2003 Gilley's Dallas opened just south of downtown. Today, brown and white Titian, a mechanical bull with massive horns, awaits riders who have come to Gilley's Showroom for the country music performances on Friday and Saturday evenings. Come before the shows start on a Saturday and you may be able to get free country dance lessons. While there's no food in the Showroom, the Studio Bar and Grill is just a few steps away.

Gilley's Dallas is a large entertainment complex near the convention center, with a variety of rooms and entertainment

Try your luck on the mechanical bull at the famed Gilley's honky-tonk bar.

areas designed for parties and corporate events. During private events your guests can ride a mechanical horse and rope a mechanical calf, participate in an armadillo race, or ride Titian.

You'll be on the bull for only a few minutes (or perhaps just seconds), but Dallas has plenty of attractions to keep visitors busy, including a few adrenaline-inducing ones. See **326** and **486**. In addition, history junkies will likely get a thrill from the Sixth Floor Museum in Dealey Plaza, which focuses on the life, death, and legacy of President John F. Kennedy. If you've got children with you, visit the **Dallas World Aquarium and Zoo** (www.dwazoo.com)

or the **Speed Zone** (www.speedzone. com/dallas), where racing go-carts, dragsters, and more offer hair-raising excitement. —*LF*

ⓘ **Gilley's Dallas,** 1135 S. Lamar St. (𝄐 **214/421-2021;** www.gilleysdallas.com).

WHEN TO GO: Year-round.

✈ Dallas Fort Worth International Airport (21miles/34km).

🛏 $$–$$$ **Magnolia Hotel,** 1401 Commerce St. (𝄐 **214/915-6500;** www. magnoliahoteldallas.com). $$–$$$ **Sheraton Dallas,** 400 N. Olive St. (𝄐 **214/742-5678;** www.sheratondallashotel.com).

489 Rides

The Slingshot at Ratanga Junction
Now I'm Free, Freefallin'
Cape Town, South Africa

It even looks scary: A few slender steel supports that rise hundreds of feet high are the only things holding you up. You're then strapped into a body harness that keeps you in a prone position while being hoisted 10 stories above the ground. If you're still with us, you then pull on a rip cord and plunge 30m (100 ft.) toward the ground at speeds exceeding a mile a minute and then—oh yes, there's more—you begin your high-speed ascent to the clear blue skies above. And then you begin your descent at the same breakneck speed.

The Slingshot is getting rave reviews as one of the scariest rides at **Ratanga Junction**—or anywhere. It's one of the latest additions to the full panoply of white-knuckle rides at this theme park. Located in the Century City area of Cape Town, the park is located just a few minutes from downtown. Visitors should be aware that the Slingshot is the only ride that isn't included in the theme park entry tickets—an extra fee is charged.

The Slingshot at Ratanga Junction.

11 Roller Coasters

The first roller coaster must have been invented by an adrenaline junkie—who else would design a machine that straps you into a metal cage and throws you off the equivalent of a tall building at speeds that turn your lips blue? —*ML*

490 Steel Dragon 2000, Nagashima Spa Land Amusement Park, Mie Prefecture, Japan: Costing over $50 million and with the longest track length of any coaster in the world at over 2,440m (8,133 ft.), the Steel Dragon enters the elite class of roller coasters known as "gigacoasters." It's also the tallest chain-lift roller coaster, towering over the Spa Land Amusement Park at 95m (318 ft.), and its top speed is an ear-bleeding 153kmph (95 mph). *www.nagashima-onsen.co.jp.*

491 Kingda Ka, Six Flags Great Adventure & Wild Safari, Jackson, New Jersey, U.S.A.: At 456 feet (137m) above the ground and a top speed of 128 mph (206kmph), Kingda Ka is a double world-record holder—for height as well as speed—and a force to be reckoned with. The acceleration on this beast is from zero to 128 mph (206kmph) in just 3.5 seconds. The duration of this ride, however, at only 50 seconds, may leave some visitors feeling short-changed. *www.sixflags.com.*

492 Dueling Dragons, Universal Studios, Orlando, Florida, U.S.A.: This unique ride features two competing coasters, one themed Fire, the other Ice. At three points during the ride, passengers come within inches of each other. Don't plan on staying right-side up, either. Fire, for example, has five inversions, including two corkscrews, a vertical loop, and a couple of white-knuckle Immelmanns (a half-loop followed by a half-twist). *www.universalorlando.com.*

493 Extremis: Drop Ride to Doom!, London, England, U.K.: You have been tried, sentenced, and must now face the consequences for your crimes. A hangman in a black hood awaits to administer your final punishment at this theme ride. A noose drops in front of you, the trap door opens, and suddenly you're freefalling 4.5m (15 ft.) in the dark. *www.thedungeons.com.*

494 The Roller Coaster at New York-New York Casino, Las Vegas, Nevada, U.S.A.: This roller coaster takes riders (in fiberglass imitations of New York yellow cabs) in and among the casino's now-familiar replicas of New York City. With a drop of 144 feet (43m) and a top speed of 67 mph (107kmph), it's not breaking any records— except perhaps for ticket prices ($14 per rider). Some folks have complained that the restraints are poorly designed and cause neck pain—something you might not want to gamble on. *New York–New York Hotel & Casino*, 3400 Las Vegas Blvd. S. (© **702/740-6969**; *www.nynyhotelcasino.com).*

495 Vild-Svinet, BonBon-Land, Denmark: The Vild-Svinet (which translates as "wild boar") takes passengers on a freaky 97-degree ascent up, then tosses them down to the ground with a steeply banked curve, a loop, a helix, and a hump that lets riders experience zero gravity. The ride is about 1 minute long. *www.bonbonland.dk.*

496 **Balder, Liseberg, Gothenburg, Sweden:** This is a prefabricated wooden coaster, which runs as silky-smooth as a steel coaster. It's not an especially tall or fast ride, clocking in with a respectable top speed of 90kmph (56 mph) and an altitude of 35m (118 ft.). Nonetheless, fans rave about this 2-minute ride for its impressive zero-gravity feature; riders experience the thrill of catching air 10 times during the 1,053m-long (3,510-ft.) ride. As a result, it has twice been voted Best Wooden Tracked Roller Coaster in the World. *www.liseberg.com.*

497 **The Cyclone, Coney Island, New York, U.S.A.:** This is the classic old woodie that makes true roller coaster fans get misty-eyed. Debuting in 1927 to much fanfare, it's been delighting riders ever since; it's even listed as a National Historic Landmark. With a top speed of 60 mph (97kmph) and a height of 85 feet (26m), it's a terrific ride. It's a bit aggressive, and is not afraid to knock heads during hairpin 180-degree turns. It's also a long, 2,640 feet (792m) of track, giving riders enough time to experience every bit of its uneven, rough-and-tumble wooden ride. *www.coneyislandcyclone.com.*

498 **Millennium Force, Cedar Point, Sandusky, Ohio, U.S.A.:** This Midwestern monster takes no prisoners, and broke 10 international roller coaster records when it opened in 2000. Millennium Force takes riders up a 310-foot (93m) hill, then drops them at speeds of up to 92 mph (148kmph). There's airtime galore, and at 6,595 feet (1,979m), it's a sweet, long ride. The ride was also the first to use a magnetic braking system, and first in the U.S. with a cable lift system. *www.cedarpoint.com.*

499 **Katun, Mirabilandia, Ravenna, Italy:** This 49m-tall (164-ft.) inverted steel roller coaster thrills riders with a vertical loop, a cobra roll, a zero-gravity roll, and a pair of corkscrews. Six inversions total mean you're upside down almost as long as right-side up; add to that a ride of almost 1,200m (4,000 ft.), and you'll know the reasons the Mayan-themed Katun is considered one of Europe's best rides. *www.mirabilandia.it.*

500 **The Legend, Holiday World, Santa Claus, Indiana, U.S.A.:** This record-breaking wood-and-steel hybrid roller coaster has won several awards. It has the most air-time of any wooden coaster (a total of 24.2 secs.) and, with three wicked 90-degree turns, it's a chiropractor's dream. It has eight dives into dark, cool underground tunnels (another world record), making this dark-light-dark-light experience a thrill for everyone. Its impressive track length (6,422 ft./1,927m) and a top speed of 67 mph (109kmph) keep speed junkies coming back for more. The park is open from early May to mid–October. *www.holidayworld.com.*

The Legend is a rough ride, but wooden-coaster enthusiasts swear by it.

If you're a hard-core adrenaline junkie and need more, the park has plenty to offer. Some visitors say the Cobra is even more terrifying than the Slingshot: It's a roller coaster that drops you at four times the force of gravity. The Tarantula has two giant arms that lift riders almost five stories high before dropping them in a downward spiral to the ground. For your cool-down rides, you might want to chill out on watery Monkey Falls, an immense log flume ride, or Crocodile Gorge, where just about everyone is guaranteed to get soaked. Add to this the park's numerous restaurants and live entertainment, and you have a full day of fun. —ML

(i) **Ratanga Junction** ((C) **0861/200-300;** www.ratanga.co.za).

WHEN TO GO: Check website for park schedule.

✈ Cape Town.

🏨 $$$ **Kensington Place,** 38 Kensington Crescent, Cape Town ((C) **021/424-4744;** www.kensingtonplace.co.za). $$ **De Waterkant Village,** 1 Loader St., Cape Town ((C) **021/409-2500;** www.dewaterkant.com).

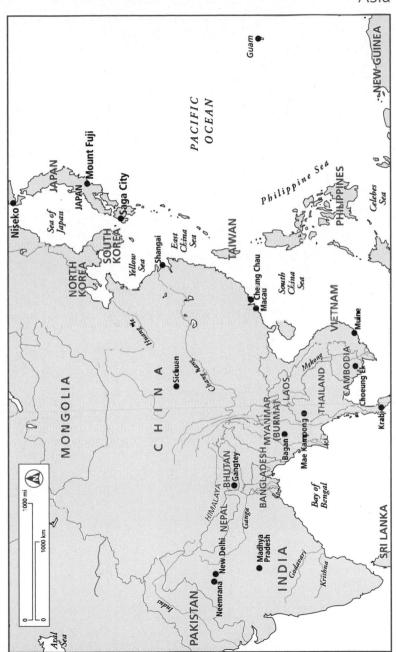

The United States

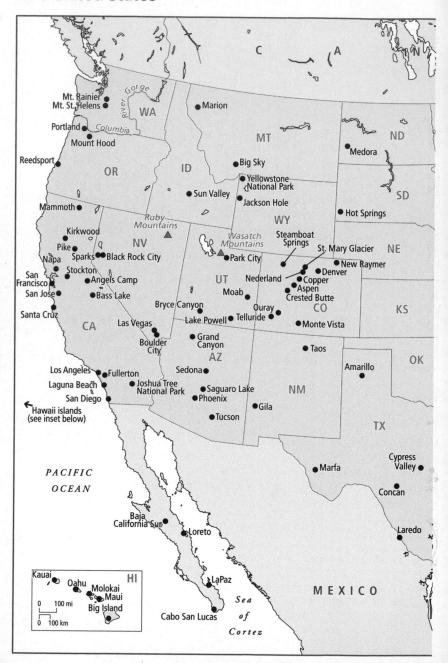

Europe

Africa

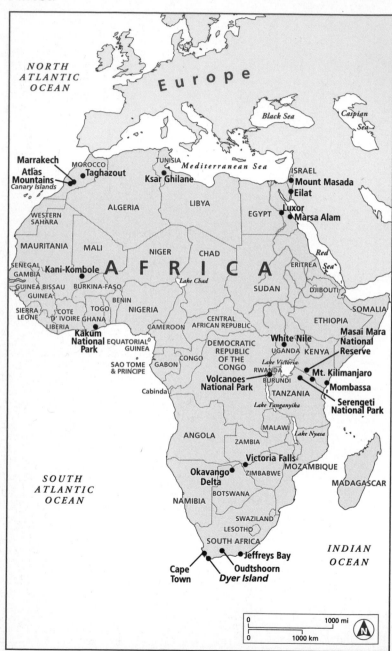

NORTH ATLANTIC OCEAN

Europe

Black Sea

Caspian Sea

Marrakech
Atlas Mountains
Canary Islands
MOROCCO
Taghazout
TUNISIA
Mediterranean Sea
Ksar Ghilane
ISRAEL
Mount Masada
Eilat
Luxor
Marsa Alam
ALGERIA
LIBYA
EGYPT
WESTERN SAHARA
MAURITANIA
MALI
NIGER
CHAD
Red Sea
ERITREA
SENEGAL
GAMBIA
Kani-Kombole
AFRICA
Lake Chad
SUDAN
DJIBOUTI
GUINEA BISSAU
GUINEA
BURKINA-FASO
BENIN
SOMALIA
SIERRA LEONE
TOGO
NIGERIA
ETHIOPIA
COTE D'IVOIRE GHANA
CAMEROON
CENTRAL AFRICAN REPUBLIC
Masai Mara National Reserve
LIBERIA
Kakum National Park
EQUATORIAL GUINEA
DEMOCRATIC REPUBLIC OF THE CONGO
White Nile
KENYA
UGANDA
SAO TOME & PRINCIPE
GABON
CONGO
Lake Victoria
RWANDA
Mt. Kilimanjaro
Mombassa
Cabinda
Volcanoes National Park
BURUNDI
TANZANIA
Serengeti National Park
Lake Tanganyika
MALAWI
Lake Nyasa
ANGOLA
ZAMBIA
Victoria Falls
MOZAMBIQUE
Okavango Delta
ZIMBABWE
MADAGASCAR
NAMIBIA
BOTSWANA
SOUTH ATLANTIC OCEAN
SWAZILAND
LESOTHO
SOUTH AFRICA
INDIAN OCEAN
Jeffreys Bay
Cape Town
Oudtshoorn
Dyer Island

0   1000 mi
0   1000 km
N

Australia & New Zealand

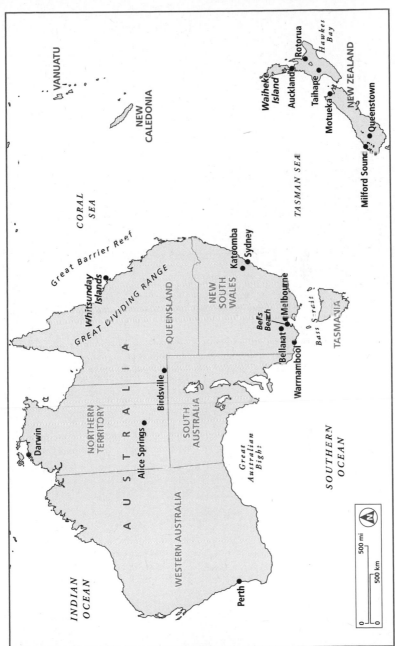

South America

UNITED STATES
OF AMERICA

· Bermuda

*Bahama
Islands*

*Gulf
of Mexico*

*Turks &
Caicos Islands*

ATLANTIC
OCEAN

MEXICO

Guanajuato
Mexico City

CUBA

*Cayman
Islands*

DOMINICAN
REPUBLIC

*Virgin
Islands*

HAITI

Acapulco

GUATEMALA

BELIZE
HONDURAS

JAMAICA

PUERTO
RICO

Caribbean Sea

EL SALVADOR

NICARAGUA

Léon

**Panama
City**

Bonaire Is.

TRINIDAD
& TOBAGO

**Monteverde
Cloud Forest**

COSTA
RICA

San José

PANAMA

VENEZUELA

FRENCH
GUIANA

Malpelo Is.

COLOMBIA

GUYANA

SURINAM

Galapagos Is.

Otavalo

ECUADOR

Iquitos

Ceará

PACIFIC
OCEAN

PERU

Cuzco

BRAZIL

LaPaz

BOLIVIA

·**Easter Is.**

CHILE

PARAGUAY

**Rio de
Janeiro**

Atacama Desert

Paraty

Mendoza
Portillo

40

ARGENTINA

URUGUAY
Buenos Aires

40

Santa Cruz

*FALKLAND/MALVINAS
ISLANDS*

SOUTH GEORGIA

Isla Navarino

*Scotia
Sea*

0   1000 mi

0   1000 km

N

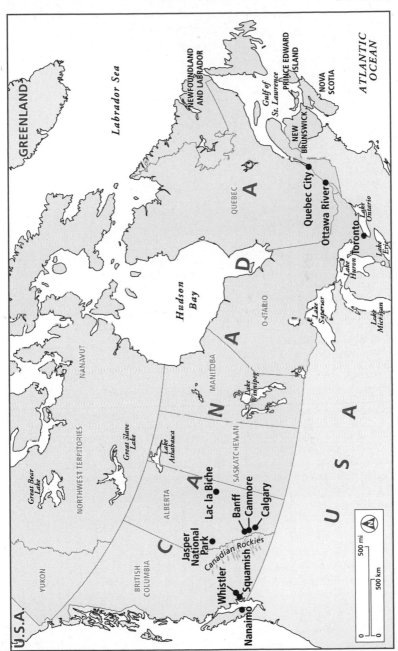

Indexes

Geographical Index

Alphabetical Index

Photo Credits

p ii, top: Courtesy Cypress Valley Canopy Tours; p ii, 2nd from top: Courtesy Echo Canyon River Expeditions; p ii, 3rd from top: Courtesy of CMH Heli-Hiking; p ii, bottom: Courtesy of Yosemite Bicycle and Sport, in California, Photo by Rick Garner; p iii, top: Courtesy Vietnam Motorbike Tours; p iii, 2nd from top: Courtesy of Woodward at Copper Mountain, Photo by Dave Lehl; p iii, 3rd from top: Courtesy of West World Images; p iii, bottom: The London Eye Company Limited; p 1: Courtesy Cypress Valley Canopy Tours; p 2: Courtesy Incredible Adventures; p 6: Courtesy of SkyThrills!; p 7: Courtesy of Black Tomato; p 10: National Park Service; p 12: Courtesy of Zero Gravity Corporation; p 15: Courtesy of Balloons Over Bagan; p 17: Courtesy of Shotover Canyon Swing; p 23: Courtesy of Incredible Adventures; p 24: Courtesy The Last Resort, photo by David Allerdice; p 25: Courtesy of Skywalk; p 30: Courtesy Kitty Hawk Kites; p 33: Courtesy of Just Fly Rio, photo by Paulo Celani; p 37: Courtesy Echo Canyon River Expeditions; p 39: Courtesy of Lady Elliot Island Eco Resort; p 42: Courtesy Jean-Michel Cousteau Fiji Islands Resort, Photo by Chris McLennan; p 45: Courtesy Stuart Cove's Dive Bahamas, Photo by William Cline; p 46: Courtesy Papua New Guinea Tourism Promotion Authority, Photo by Franco Banfi; p 52: Aviatur – Fundacion Malpelo; p 53: Courtesy Hidden Worlds Cenotes Park; p 57: Courtesy of Sea Kayak Adventures, Photo by Terry Prichard; p 58: Courtesy Paddlers Kayak Shop; p 59: Courtesy of Adventure Cat Sailing Charters, Photo by Charlie Bergstedt; p 64: Courtesy of Sea Canoe Thailand; p 67: Maine Department of Tourism; p 68: Rachel Falk; p 70: www.photo.is; p 73: Courtesy Hawaiian Sailing Canoe Adventures, Photo by Bob Raimo; p 76: Courtesy Tourism Whitsundays; p 78: Courtesy Shotover Jet; p 81: Courtesy Whirlpool Jet Boat Tours; p 83: Courtesy of Eventos Douro / Portuguese National Tourist Office; p 86: Courtesy of Tourism Newquay; p 88: Courtesy of Israel Ministry of Tourism; p 90: Courtesy TYF Adventure; p 104: Courtesy Ohau Visitor Bureau, Photo by Jan Cook; p 106: Courtesy of The Surf Sanctuary; p 108: Courtesy of CMH Heli-Hiking; p 110: JNTO; p 111: Courtesy of Crystal Mountain Treks, Photo by Jenny Gurung; p 113: Hawaii Tourism Authority (HTA) / Tor Johnson; p 114: National Park Service; p 116: National Park Service; p 120: Courtesy of Israel Ministry of Tourism; p 122: Mike Spring; p 126: Courtesy of CMH Heli-Hiking; p 127: Courtesy Oregon Peak Adventures, Photo by Joe Whittington; p 129: White Mountain National Forest/Ken Allen; p 130: Courtesy Black Feather Adventures; p 131: Park City Mountain Resort; p 136: Courtesy Appalachian Mountain Club; p 140: Courtesy Snowkite Soldier; p 142: Courtesy Utah Olympic Park; p 143: Courtesy Hawksnest Ski Resort; p 148: Courtesy Abseil Africa; p 149: Todd Burleson / Alpine Ascents International; p 152: Courtesy Ouray Chalet Inn, Photo by Lora Slawitschka; p 156: Yamnuska Mountain Adventures, Photo by Bryce Jardine; p 159: Eva Lesiak; p 160: Courtesy Uprising Adventure Guides, Inc.; p 162: Courtesy Excursions Of Escalante, photo by Lisa Jennica Sara; p 163: Courtesy of Costa Rica Canyoning; p 168: Courtesy Hill Country Adventures, photos by LeAnn Sharp; p 171: Courtesy Raccoon Mountain Caverns, photo by Jerry Wallace; p 172: Courtesy of Yosemite Bicycle and Sport, in California, Photo by Rick Garner; p 173: Courtesy Vertigo Biking Bolivia, Photo by Jules Guerin; p 175: Jeremy Wade Shockley/Fedora Photo; p 176: Courtesy of Bike Hawaii; p 178: Courtesy of Blazing Saddles; p 181: Courtesy Phat Tire Ventures; p 183: Jack Brink; p 184: Courtesy of The Mammoth Site; p 186: Photo by Richard Rader; p 187: © Michael McLaughlin; p 192: Courtesy Colorado Cattle Company & Guest Ranch; p 193: Kennedy Space Center; p 195: Courtesy of Surfin Dirt Mountain Boarding, Photo by Garry Harper; p 205: Courtesy of Bluegreen Communities; p 206: Courtesy Vietnam Motorbike Tours; p 207: Courtesy Kasbah Du Toubkal, photo by Alan Keohane; p 211: Courtesy of Artisans of Leisure, Photo by Marc Lesser; p 214: Erlendur Þór Magnússon for Arctic Adventures; p 215: Courtesy Amazon Explorama Lodges; p 217: Courtesy Earthwatch, Photo by Laurie Marker; p 225: Tourism Australia; p 226: Jack Brink; p 234: Syzygy Productions; p 235: Courtesy Double E Ranch; p 241: Courtesy of Temple of Poi, Photo by David Yu; p 243: Courtesy of Jim Gibson